COALITION

The Inside Story of the Conservative–Liberal
Democrat Coalition Government

DAVID LAWS

Biteback Publishing

First published in Great Britain in 2016 by
Biteback Publishing Ltd
Westminster Tower
3 Albert Embankment
London SE1 7SP
Copyright © David Laws 2016

ISBN 978-1-84954-966-0

10 9 8 7 6 5 4 3 2 1

A CIP catalogue record for this book is available from the British Library.

Set in Sabon by Adrian McLaughlin

Printed and bound in Great Britain by
CPI Group (UK) Ltd, Croydon CR0 4YY

MIX
Paper from
responsible sources
FSC® C020471

For James

'The Prince who walks away from power walks away from the power to do good.'

—Niccolò Machiavelli

CONTENTS

ACKNOWLEDGEMENTS

I am extremely grateful to all those who have assisted me in writing this book over the nine months since the May 2015 general election.

I would particularly like to thank Nick Clegg, who kindly allowed me to access some of his own private papers and records to check facts. Thanks, too, to Phil Reilly, whose hard work made these records more accessible and easier to navigate.

I would also like to thank others who gave their time and advice, including Danny Alexander, Tim Colbourne, Ed Davey, Will de Peyer, Lynne Featherstone, Olly Grender, Stephen Lotinga, James McGrory, Christian Moon, Jonny Oates, Matt Sanders, Chris Saunders and Katie Waring. Of course, all errors, omissions and opinions are my responsibility alone.

I would like to record my sincere thanks to the brilliant Claire Margetts, whose hard work over the past four years has helped me to keep my own detailed accounts of the period of coalition government. It would have been very difficult to write this account without drawing on those records.

The extraordinary opportunity I had in government to observe and to participate in the events which are described in this book would not have been possible without the support of many people in my constituency and beyond. I will always be grateful to the kind, generous and supportive people of Yeovil constituency, who returned me as their Member of Parliament from 2001 to 2015. Being MP for the Yeovil constituency was the greatest privilege of my life, and I look back only with pride and pleasure on my time in that role.

I am extremely grateful to my superb Yeovil office staff of Sue Weeks, Claire Margetts, Sarah Frapple, Sadye McLean and all our loyal volunteers.

Thanks also to Alec Newton and to all those who worked so hard in my office in London over the past fourteen years. I am grateful to Theo Whitaker, Graham Westrop, Khloe Obazee, and all those who gave their time during the 2015 general election campaign. Cathy Bakewell and Sam Crabb were my election agents during four general elections in Yeovil; their patience, dedication and wisdom are much appreciated and were critical to our success.

The early part of the 2010 parliament was a very difficult time for me personally, and I would not have remained an MP or returned to government without the marvellous and unconditional support of Olly Grender, Cathy Bakewell, Joan Raikes, Paddy and Jane Ashdown, Nick Clegg, Sam Crabb, the late and wonderful Pauline Booth, Jo and Martin Roundell Greene, John Dyke and – of course – James and my mother. To these few people, and to the many others not named here, I will always be particularly grateful.

Working in the coalition government was a fantastic opportunity to put principles into practice. I was supported impressively by my civil service private office teams, whose dedication and professionalism made me conscious of how much we should appreciate our civil service and its fine traditions of political impartiality and high standards. I enjoyed working with Sir Jeremy Heywood and his team in the Cabinet Office, as well as the Permanent Secretary at the Department for Education, Chris Wormald, and his colleagues.

In the Cabinet Office, I had the pleasure to work with Jonathan Crisp, Nick Donlevy, Katie Harrison, Suzanne Kochanowski and Natalie Perera, who staffed my private office for varying periods. In the Department for Education, my excellent and utterly dedicated team was variously composed of Wilhelmina Blankson, Lydia Bradley, Philip Cattle, Samuel Cook, Laura De Silva, Tom Dyer, Becci Fagan, Camilla Frappell, Samuel Kelly, the formidable Georgina Manley and Ursula Ritz (who both brilliantly managed my packed diary by frightening me and many others into keeping to time) and Daniel Sellman. My four irreplaceable policy advisers were Tim Leunig, Chris Paterson, Matt Sanders and Julian Astle. They contributed hugely to all we achieved and prevented me from making many errors.

I am also grateful to the dedicated policy team based in the Deputy Prime Minister's Office, who gave both Nick and me high-quality and rigorous advice.

In this book, I describe in detail my working relationships with senior colleagues in the coalition government. All relationships have their good and bad patches. In fact, the moments of tension and difficulty were relatively rare, and it was a great pleasure and honour to work with most of those referred to in these pages.

If there are few real 'villains' in my account, it is because in my experience most politicians in all of the political parties are decent, hard-working people. So, my particular thanks to those in both coalition parties whom I worked most closely with: Danny Alexander, Vince Cable, Nick Clegg, Nick Gibb, Michael Gove, Jonathan Hill, Jeremy Hunt, Norman Lamb, Oliver Letwin, Nicky Morgan, John Nash, George Osborne and Liz Truss. And my apologies for anything you find in here which you would rather had stayed secret!

Finally, I am grateful to the team at Biteback Publishing for their work on this volume, and in particular to the patient and extremely efficient Olivia Beattie, and the irrepressible Iain Dale, who encouraged me to tell the tale that follows.

DAVID LAWS
Kennington
January 2016

INTRODUCTION

This is the inside story of the Liberal Democrat–Conservative coalition government of 2010–15. It is the first detailed and extensive account by one of those who served in this government.

I was one of a small number of MPs and advisers who helped negotiate the coalition between the Liberal Democrats and Conservatives in May 2010. I attended the first Cabinet meeting, on Thursday 13 May 2010, and I was there at the last Cabinet meeting, at 9.45 a.m. on Tuesday 24 March 2015. Only fifteen other ministers were present on both occasions.

In writing this account, I have drawn on my own records of my time in government. I have also been able to access some of the records and recollections of my close colleagues. This has allowed me to produce a detailed account of the government and its work.

Where I put conversations in quotation marks, it is generally because I was present to hear exactly what was said. Where I was not present, I have usually sought to summarise the reported conversations, unless I have highly reliable accounts of particular exchanges to draw on. Of course, in both cases it is impossible to vouch for every word spoken, but I am confident that I have provided a fair and accurate account.

In telling the story of the coalition, I have sought to be as open and revealing as possible. But I have obviously had to respect the rules about the privacy of certain government information, not least where national security is concerned. I have also had to weigh carefully where revealing sensitive information about individuals, or repeating conversations held in the expectation of privacy, might be considered unreasonable or dis- courteous. I have held back much from my account which might fall into these categories – but generally only where these details are not fundamentally important to the story I am telling.

I do not, however, pretend that this account is exhaustive or that it allocates to each area of the government's work a fair, measured and proportionate amount of space. Inevitably, this book reflects my own sense of what was important in the government's work and the areas that I was involved in. However, the roles I held in government – Chief Secretary to the Treasury, Minister of State in the Cabinet Office, and Minister of State for Schools – gave me a very good vantage point to assess the most important areas of the coalition's work.

It must also be understood that as a Liberal Democrat member of the government, I was in a better place to view the internal workings of the Liberal Democrat side of the coalition, and my account draws very much on this particular perspective.

I decided to write this book now for three reasons. Firstly, I think it is important that historic narratives of periods such as this should be written, and in this era of intensive media coverage and freedom of information it seems unnecessary to wait for twenty or thirty years before the true story can be told.

Secondly, I think there are some important lessons for my own party and others to consider following the period of coalition. This account seeks to be honest and self-critical in order that the right conclusions can be drawn for the future. And many of the issues described in this book are still relevant to the major political challenges that we face today, so that I hope my story may assist people in understanding these challenges and drawing the right conclusions.

Finally, I am very proud of what the Liberal Democrats achieved in the coalition. I want this book to stand as a record of some of the great progress I believe we secured, as well an honest account of our mistakes.

Having written this account, and reviewed the story I had to tell, two risks were evident to me which I should draw to the reader's attention. Firstly, when looking back over a five-year period of government in which so many different challenges and issues arose, it is inevitable that what catches the eye of any author are the dramas, conflicts and controversies. I record many of these in the pages which follow. The inevitable risk is that the reader may conclude that coalition was one long process of dispute and strife – whereas, in fact, the 2010–15 government was, on the majority of issues, very much united, and successfully pursued an ambitious programme of social and economic reform. There were few issues on which the coalition parties divided in the House of Commons, and there were similarly few issues on which the coalition was defeated – as least in the elected chamber. What this account seeks to do, however, is to pull back the curtain behind this generally united front, to show how decisions were made and why.

The second cautionary note is about individuals, and the impression of them which may be formed by references and quotations from particular events over a five-year period in government. It is possible to perfectly accurately record what someone has said at any point in time, while simultaneously creating an overall impression of the individual which may prove partial or inaccurate. We all at times say things which, taken out of context, can create a distorted impression of who we are and what we stand for. For this reason I have taken the opportunity towards the end of the book to offer a more rounded evaluation of a few of the most important characters in this narrative. In politics, as in life, individuals are rarely always right or always wrong, and their characters can be far more complex than much one-dimensional reporting allows for. I hope that the portraits I have created are fair to politicians in both coalition parties.

I have sought to write an account that is balanced, rounded and fair. But, of course, I do not claim to be a neutral and impartial observer of events. I helped to create the coalition and was a strong supporter of this government and of my party leader and friend Nick Clegg for five years. On 7 May 2015, the Liberal Democrats received a brutal judgement from the electorate on our period in office, losing all but eight of our fifty-six seats in the House of Commons. I have never believed in questioning or second guessing the decision of the referee. But I hope that in a small way this book will help to contribute to a fair evaluation of the service of my party, the Liberal Democrats, to the people of our country.

An Exit Poll

MAY 2015

On the evening of Wednesday 6 May 2015, Nick Clegg had completed the final leg of his election campaign tour. The Liberal Democrat leader's final sweep through the UK had started at sunrise in the far south-west of England, at Lands's End, on the previous day and it had now finished in the far north of Scotland, at John O' Groats.

Now, on Wednesday night, Nick Clegg was travelling back to his constituency in Sheffield, in a tiny plane, accompanied only by his senior press spokesman – the laddish, sharp-tongued cheeky chappy James McGrory.

The small plane was making its way south through a ferocious storm, and was being pitched around in the black sky. 'Don't worry,' said the pilot, 'this plane is thirty years old, and it hasn't come down yet!' Nick Clegg didn't feel particularly reassured. James McGrory dropped off to sleep.

Sitting in his seat, and reflecting back on the exhausting six-week election campaign, the Liberal Democrat leader felt that it had gone as well as could be expected. His performance in the election debates had been well received, and he felt that the campaign was much better managed and organised than in 2010.

By late evening, the Deputy Prime Minister was safely home in Sheffield with his wife, Miriam, preparing for the final day of the election.

Much further to the south, in my house in the village of South Petherton, just a few miles from Yeovil in Somerset, I was making my preparations for the last day of our local campaign. I was also looking through for the last time the briefing papers that our Liberal Democrat team had prepared in the event that there was a hung parliament.

I was one of a small team of four MPs and one peer who had been selected a year earlier by Nick Clegg to form our negotiating team for any potential co-alition talks. While Danny Alexander was the chair of this group, he was widely expected to lose his seat. And on Sunday 3 May, Nick, Danny and I had met in south London and we had agreed that I would take over the leadership of our negotiating committee in the event that Danny was no longer an MP on 8 May.

Preparations complete, I was in bed by midnight and fell instantly to sleep.

Next morning, my alarm woke me at 4.30 a.m. and by 5.30 I was meeting a group of young Liberal Democrat activists in the streets of south Yeovil. We were gathering early so we could put out a final election-morning leaflet in this key part of the constituency.

For any candidate, the last day of an election is simultaneously nerve-racking and quite soothing. All the hard work is done and you know that the end is finally in sight. But you also know that just a few votes could be critically important, so you have to work right to close of polls at 10 p.m.

The Liberal Democrats held fifty-six seats in the House of Commons. My own private calculations showed that on a bad night we could be left with as few as twenty, and on a good night it could be as high as thirty. So twenty-five parliamentary seats for the Liberal Democrats was my central prediction – and I fully expected my own constituency of Yeovil to be one of those we held, albeit with a very much reduced majority.

The morning was cloudy, with very light rain. We had finished putting out our leaflets by around 7 a.m. and we passed one of our local councillors, Bridget Dollard, heading off to man the local polling station.

Throughout the day, as always on election days, we called our voters to encourage them to cast their votes. The reception we received was generally positive, but there was one early sign that caused me concern. My superb and experienced election agent, Sam Crabb, reported that in one part of Yeovil – the parish of Brympton – the turnout was unusually high. Indeed, he said that there were queues at the polling stations before 9 a.m. – unheard of in this part of Yeovil. Brympton was a key Lib Dem/Conservative battleground, where a lot of floating voters lived. What was galvanising voters to turn out in such areas so early, I wondered. That night we would find out the answer.

My day started in Rowan Way, with hard-working activists such as Emma

Dunn and Kris Castle. It ended in Westland Road – a 'heartland' Liberal Democrat area, just outside the gates of the famous helicopter factory, where our vote seemed to me to be as strong as ever. Knowing that the next twenty-four hours were likely to be very busy, and almost certainly without opportunities to sleep, I finished my 'knocking up' of Lib Dem voters at 8.30 p.m., and I was back home in South Petherton by 9 p.m. – just one hour before polls closed in one of the closest general elections in fifty years.

In Sheffield, Nick Clegg had also spent the day out door-knocking, in the more affluent parts of his seat, seeking to win over former Conservative voters in what was now a Lib Dem/Labour marginal seat. He was home in the early evening and made his final preparations for what was bound to be a whirlwind forty-eight hours.

In South Petherton, I packed my bags into my car, with all the material that I would need in the event of hung parliament negotiations. The national election result still seemed highly uncertain, but a hung parliament was regarded as a high probability and I expected to go straight from my count in Yeovil to Whitehall – possibly using as a first base my ministerial office in the Cabinet Office, at 70 Whitehall.

But before 70 Whitehall, it so happened that I was off to 4 Whitehall. 4 Whitehall, South Petherton, was the home of the unassuming, hard-working, mild-mannered, but formidable Joan Raikes, the chairman of my local constituency party and a loyal and long-standing supporter of mine and of Paddy Ashdown, my predecessor as Yeovil MP.

By tradition, Joan hosted a dinner for the Lib Dem parliamentary candidate on general election night – to keep our minds off the count taking place just a few miles away. I arrived at Joan's at around 9.50 p.m. – just in time to settle down to dinner before the BBC exit poll was released. Joan switched the television to BBC1 and served up dinner – lamb casserole. The countdown to 10 p.m. began, and at that moment Joan got up from the table to get some drinks from the kitchen.

And then it was 10 p.m. The BBC election night music played, sending tingles down my spine. And suddenly there was David Dimbleby with the BBC exit poll result. I held my breath and leaned forward:

> We are saying the Conservatives are the largest party. Here are the figures which we have. Quite remarkable this exit poll. The

Conservatives on 316, that's up 9 since the last election in 2010.
Ed Miliband, for Labour, 77 behind him at 239, down 19. If that
is the story, it is quite a sensational story.

It might be sensational, but my focus was no longer on the balance between
the Conservative and Labour results. What on the earth was the Liberal
Democrat projected seats total? I rose to my feet and squinted at the television
screen, over on the other side of the room. My heart sank. Alongside the
forecast number of Conservative and Labour seats was the Liberal Democrat
figure: ten. If that was true, there would be no coalition. And, more seriously,
most of our parliamentary party had just been wiped out.

The projected seats total was spectacularly lower than almost anyone
had previously forecast.

Of course, it was 'only an exit poll', and on television Paddy Ashdown
was saying that he would eat his hat if the number was proved right. But
we had been through all this in 2010, when the exit poll had projected far
fewer seats than we had expected. We had thought the exit poll must be
wrong in 2010, but it turned out to be almost exactly right.

I was immediately convinced that the figure of ten Liberal Democrat seats
was going to be about right. Not only was this a disaster for my party, but it
also meant I could not even take for granted my own constituency in Yeovil.
Indeed, I immediately recalled a recent conversation with Ryan Coetzee, our
chief election strategist, in our London HQ when I asked for their analysis
of the canvassing and polling figures for Yeovil. 'They look all right,' I was
told. 'But to be honest, we are not focusing much on your seat. If we don't
win Yeovil, we'd only have about ten seats left anyway.'

I texted Sam Crabb, who was already at the count in Yeovil. 'You seem to
be ahead on the postal votes,' he texted back, 'but it is close. Maybe 43 per
cent to 37 per cent.' I was temporarily cheered – this was about the margin
of victory overall that I had expected.

Over the previous few days, I had pressed Nick Clegg to fix a telephone
conference call for soon after the exit poll results, so that we could talk about the
implications of the likely result. The conference call was due shortly. Meanwhile,
Joan and I ate large bowls of chocolate ice cream for temporary cheer.

I dialled in to our conference call at 10.30 p.m. We could no longer
rely on 'Switch', the 10 Downing Street switchboard, which fixed up these

conference calls in government, since we were now in political mode, not government mode. On the call when I joined it were Jonny Oates, Nick's chief of staff; Danny Alexander; Stephen Lotinga, Nick's press chief; and Ryan Coetzee, chief election strategist. Paddy Ashdown, the general election chairman, was still on the BBC, trying his best to play down the exit poll.

While we waited for Nick to come on the call, Ryan said, 'This poll has just got to be wrong, hasn't it?' He asked me how things were going in Yeovil, and whether we thought we had lost. I cautiously reported back the early, positive, signs from the count. Then, at around 10.35, Nick joined the call.

'Look,' he said. 'This exit poll is pretty shocking, but I just don't know if we can take it seriously. Apparently there is some other exit poll out which is much better for us. We could talk for ages now about what we might do, but until we know if this exit poll is right, I just don't see that we can have an intelligent conversation. Anyway, if this poll is right, then frankly we are totally stuffed, and there isn't much for us to talk about or decide.'

It was therefore agreed that we would end the call and talk again at around 2 a.m., when the results would be much more certain. I had been very clear with my agent that I wanted no communication from him until the result could be reliably gauged. Even when I am winning easily, I cannot stand having a running commentary on my re-election chances.

But on this occasion I was simply too nervous to wait. I texted Sam again and asked what the result was looking like.

'I'm afraid it's not good,' was the reply. 'The ballots that have been cast on the day are just massively against us. There seems to have been a big swing to the Tories since the postal votes.'

'Am I going to lose?' I asked.

'Yes, I am afraid so,' was the reply.

'You're sure?'

'Yes,' he said.

I told Joan. Then I rang my mother to warn her.

Then I phoned Nick Clegg. 'Nick, I am sorry to tell you, but I have lost Yeovil. This must confirm that the overall result is going to look just as the exit poll has forecast.'

There was a pause at the other end of the phone. Then Nick's voice. 'God. Awful. First Danny. And Vince. And Ed. Now you. We are being totally wiped out.'

'How are things in Sheffield?' I asked.

'Well,' he sighed. 'It looks OK. I think we are a few thousand on the right side of the line. But I cannot feel remotely happy about it. Going back to Parliament with ten MPs and without any of you is going to be so tough. And it is just such a massive setback for the party.'

We ended the call and I decided to go to our constituency office in Yeovil, to be ready to travel to my election count when the result was imminent.

I said goodbye to Joan and asked her to call my mother again, who I knew would be bitterly upset. I left 4 Whitehall, knowing that this would now be the only Whitehall address I would need to visit for a very long time.

My result was supposed to come in around 2 a.m. but it was endlessly delayed. I sat alone in my office in Yeovil as Lib Dem MP after Lib Dem MP fell. Simon Hughes, in London, looked close to tears – he had lost after thirty-three years as MP. A shell-shocked Vince Cable had also lost, astonishingly, in Twickenham. Ed Davey, who had won Kingston and Surbiton against all odds in 1997, was also gone, along with the brilliant Pensions Minister and local campaigner Steve Webb in Thornbury and Yate. The only recompense to me was that it didn't feel personal – the Liberal Democrats were simply being swept away in an electoral tsunami.

Then, finally, at around 5 a.m., I headed for my own count to accept my defeat. Our Lib Dem counting agents looked shattered – including many of my brilliant constituency office staff, who knew their own jobs were now gone too.

The result was declared, and I left by a side door, dodging the press.

On the edge of Yeovil, I stopped the car in a lay-by and replied to a whole series of sympathetic text messages coming through from political friends and foes alike. And then, with the public show of the count behind me, and in the privacy of my car, it was no longer possible to hold back all the emotion.

It was no longer necessary to drive straight for London, as I had planned, so with the sun of a new day rising in the sky, I headed elsewhere, to rest and recuperate.

After pulling in to a service station for petrol, I had a call from Danny Alexander.

'Hi, it's Danny here. I am sorry about your result.'

'Likewise,' I said. 'Are you OK?'

'Yes,' replied Danny. 'We fought a very strong campaign, but I always knew it was going to be tough.'

'Well, one silver lining is that we won't have to spend the next five days locked away with Labour or the Tories talking about coalitions,' I said.

'Yes,' laughed Danny. 'I don't think we need today's planned meeting of the coalition negotiating committee any more either!'

'That's probably a good thing,' I said, 'because not a single one of our team was re-elected. Steve Webb has also lost, as has Lynne Featherstone. In fact, we need to tell Nick that he did a pretty bloody awful job of choosing the negotiating committee!'

'I'm sure Nick would appreciate hearing that!' joked Danny.

This painful day might have been over for Danny and for me, and we might even be able to engage in a little gallows humour. But it was not over for Nick Clegg.

He had known, of course, immediately, that this was the end of his leadership, and that the scale of defeat was so serious that an announcement could not be delayed.

But the emotional pressure was immense, not just because of his personal circumstances but because of his feeling of horror as he saw one MP after another lose their seats.

He chain smoked all night. On an early morning conference call, he revealed to his closest staff that he would travel back to London after the Sheffield count and announce that he was standing down as leader.

Nick's speech writer and press adviser, Phil Reilly, went round to Nick's home in Sheffield and together they wrote out his resignation speech.

Then the Liberal Democrat leader was off to his Sheffield count, trying to keep his composure in the face of jeering Labour supporters and the endless drip-drip-drip of bad news from constituency counts across the country.

Only after the count did Nick allow his emotions to get the better of him in his car, travelling to the airport.

At the airport, he and his team met up with one of his closest political advisers, Matthew Hanney, who looked exhausted and shell-shocked. On the plane down to London, Nick practised his resignation speech – and he was determined to get through it all without breaking down.

Nick Clegg's team, led by his trusted chief of staff Jonny Oates, had prepared for every possible eventuality. They had hired a central London venue, knowing that this was where Nick would deliver one of two speeches: either his response to a hung parliament, with possible terms for entering a second coalition, or his resignation speech. It was now to be the latter.

The speech was well received, and Nick got through it – just about – while holding his emotions together.

By some awful coincidence, there was then a Victory in Europe Day commemoration to attend in Whitehall, with David Cameron and Ed Miliband.

The three party leaders met in a room in the Foreign Office, where an over-zealous army officer insisted on taking them in great detail through the arrangements for the event. Other Conservative ministers present looked uncomfortable, and avoided looking the former Deputy Prime Minister in the face.

The Prime Minister also seemed uncomfortable and ill at ease. Later, after the ceremony, he spoke briefly to Nick, telling him that he had been reading the Liberal Democrat manifesto just a few days before and that he thought some of its policies were 'really quite good'. David Cameron admitted that just the day before he had also been drafting his own possible resignation statement. The Prime Minister was also clearly surprised by some of the seats his party had won, admitting that he had only visited seats such as Twickenham to 'tweak our tail'.

'I'd say just this,' replied Nick Clegg. 'Build on what we achieved together – don't squander it.'

From George Osborne, there was a heartfelt and generous message, by text, as is the way in modern government, as well as in modern life: 'You didn't deserve it. I have admired you and what we did together in government.'

And then, for Nick Clegg, there was the most difficult part of all: returning home to his family, including his three young boys, who had been hearing all day on the news of their father's humiliation, and now his resignation.

On Saturday morning, Nick Clegg woke early, feeling very low. He dragged himself out of bed and said to his son Antonio that they should go to the shops together and buy a mobile phone. In the world beyond government, Nick Clegg would now need a new telephone to replace the security-protected devices he had been required to use since 2010.

Nick was nervous about the possible public reaction to him out in Putney High Street, near to his house. He worried that people would be confrontational or rude, but in fact the response was universally warm and almost overwhelming. Person after person came up to commiserate with him.

One woman hugged him, saying that she was very sad at the result and that the Liberal Democrats had done a brilliant job in government. 'Thanks so much for your support,' said Nick.

'Oh,' the lady replied. 'It's a bit embarrassing. I actually voted Green!'

Another woman came up to say to say that Nick and his party did not deserve the results which they had received. 'You did the right thing going into government. You made some mistakes, definitely, but you did a lot of good things too. We are worried that the Lib Dems aren't there any more to moderate the others. You are going to be missed.'

The warm reaction – in excess even of the public reaction after 'Cleggmania' in 2010 – made an impact on Nick, and he could see that it did on his son, too. On the previous evening it had seemed that the only story was about Liberal Democrat failure and electoral humiliation. But there was another story, too – the story of a small party of MPs who went into government at a time of national crisis, and of that party's five years of work in government to bring the economy back from the brink and make Britain a fairer and more liberal country.

It is a story of some errors, and of many achievements.

And that is the story which this book will tell.

2010

A HUNG PARLIAMENT

MAY 2010

General Election Day 2010 – at last, the long wait was over. And, at last, there was some room in my kitchen again. When Gordon Brown seemed likely to call an election back in 2007, I had ordered the printing of our first general election leaflet. When Mr Brown changed his mind, my local party considered that it was too expensive to reprint this leaflet again, so I had been obliged to store 45,000 A3 'Election Flying Start' leaflets in the kitchen of my constituency home – for two and a half years. Now they were all gone.

I did the usual things for a general election day: got up at around 5 a.m., delivered 'Good Morning' leaflets to voters in Freedom Avenue and Springfield Road in Yeovil, then visited some polling stations, and afterwards knocked on doors to remind Liberal Democrat supporters to vote.

I finished in East Yeovil at around 8.30 p.m., and now, just as on election night 2015, I was at 4 Whitehall, South Petherton, about to have dinner with local party activist Joan Raikes while waiting for the first exit polls.

For the first and only time in my political career, I was not that worried about the result in my own constituency. The Liberal Democrat campaign had been successful both locally and nationally – boosted by Nick Clegg's very strong performances in the televised election debates.

I was expecting a majority of over 10,000 in Yeovil, and the latest intelligence from those at the top of the national party suggested that we could expect to win over eighty seats across the UK – well up on our present total of sixty-three seats.

At 10 p.m., as Joan and I were about to start eating, the BBC election programme began, with its stirring and distinctive election night music. I was optimistic and excited. Eighty seats would be the party's best performance since well before the Second World War, and it would also guarantee a hung parliament, and herald a possible Liberal Democrat role in government.

But as the first forecasts flashed onto television screens across the country, I received a huge shock. The projected vote share and seat number were well below both our party's and the media's expectations. Instead of the large numbers of gains we expected, we saw predicted losses. I was inclined to dismiss the projections as a rogue poll, particularly as I heard the positive news coming in from my election count and from other Somerset constituencies.

Eventually, the call came through from my election agent, Sam: 'You need to come to the count. You've won comfortably – the majority will be over 11,000.'

By the time I had reached the Westland Centre in the heart of Yeovil, the counting had finished. I was home and dry with a majority of 13,036, the largest in the constituency's history.

The returning officer called the candidates and election agents together and went through the spoilt ballot papers. All the candidates agreed solemnly that the ballot paper on which was written 'They're all useless bastards' couldn't be considered as a vote for any of us.

I made my acceptance speech and then got in my car to drive back to London.

Most winning candidates on election night either join their supporters for some drinks and celebrations or head straight to bed.

But I could do neither – a year before, Nick Clegg had asked me to be one of four MPs who would constitute the Liberal Democrat negotiating team in the event of a hung parliament, just as he would do five years later, ahead of the 2015 campaign. The plan was for the four of us – Danny Alexander, Chris Huhne, Andrew Stunell and me – to head back to London as soon as our election results were confirmed, so that we could start our planning.

As I drove back to London, listening to the election coverage on the radio, I realised that our excellent Liberal Democrat results in Somerset were the exception. Nationally, we had lost a number of seats we'd expected to hold, and we had missed securing almost all our target seats. After the ecstasy of Cleggmania, it was a massive disappointment.

I was the first MP back into our party headquarters in Cowley Street in

London, where the mood was sombre. But however disappointing the results were, it was impossible to ignore one salient fact: the UK was heading for a hung parliament in which the Liberal Democrats would be a powerful player. Indeed, it was possible that our party was on the threshold of entering government for the first time since the Second World War.

The final polling projections had the Conservatives on 306 seats, Labour on 258, and the Liberal Democrats with 57. The smaller parties had around 30 seats combined.

Nick Clegg had made clear throughout the general election campaign that in the event of a hung parliament we would talk first to the party with the greatest electoral mandate to form a government – 'the largest number of seats and votes', as we put it. This did not mean that we would only contemplate going into government with the largest party, but we thought it would look very odd to talk first to the losing party. The party with the largest number of seats and votes was the Conservative Party.

Nick arrived back in London from his own count in Sheffield later than expected, at around 10.40 a.m. He did his best to look positive, but he was shattered by the disappointment of losing seats, after what had seemed such a successful campaign. On the steps outside our 4 Cowley Street headquarters, he announced to the waiting media that he would stick to his pledge: the party with the largest number of seats and votes would have the first opportunity to form a government.

Once inside party headquarters, Nick made a speech from the top of the main staircase to Liberal Democrat staff and volunteers, thanking them for their hard work. When he finished speaking there was warm applause, but he turned quickly away and entered the small first-floor conference room, choking back tears of emotion and disappointment.

This small conference room that Nick now entered was hardly a fitting assembly point for our first power-sharing discussions. It had been used for the last twenty years or so as the preparation room for Liberal Democrat press conferences, which were held next door in a larger, oak-panelled, conference room. In this small room, the party leader, a researcher and one or two press officers would regularly prepare to launch the latest little-noticed Liberal Democrat policy paper. Amongst the small audience of people seated next door awaiting the press conference would be Liberal Democrat researchers and staff, to make up the numbers. If we were lucky, there would also be a junior reporter from the *Financial Times*, someone from the BBC and a stray regional reporter who found himself without anything better to do.

But now this little conference room was bursting full of senior MPs and party staff. We were there to consider the formation of the next government of the United Kingdom. There was not much time for wondering what had gone wrong.

In considering how to react next, we were not starting from a blank piece of paper. For six months, Danny Alexander, Chris Huhne, Andrew Stunell and I had been meeting to consider what our strategy would be should we find ourselves facing a hung parliament.

We had produced for Nick Clegg, in early March, a confidential paper entitled 'Post-Election Strategy: Recommendations'. Its principal conclusions had been accepted by Nick, in spite of the fact that Chris Huhne had tabled a last-minute 'Minority Report'. Chris had made clear that he believed the only viable strategy for the Liberal Democrats in a hung parliament was to go into a full coalition. The rest of us considered that in some circumstances it would be better for us to remain outside government – possibly in a 'confidence and supply' arrangement, where, in exchange for various policy agreements, we would support a minority government in key votes.

Our post-election strategy paper had anticipated that the Conservatives would be the largest party. Our conclusion was:

> In the event of the Conservative Party failing to secure a majority but having the strongest mandate, we can expect an immediate, very warm, and very public approach from David Cameron. It would be important to respond positively to such an invitation, by entering into discussions in which all options are on the table.

However, the strategy paper concluded – against Chris Huhne's wishes – that a full coalition was 'extremely unlikely', because we did not expect the Conservatives to concede on key Liberal Democrat demands such as electoral reform. We also assumed that any policy deal might not be strong enough to persuade Liberal Democrat members to support a coalition.

Now, in the late morning of Friday 7 May 2010, we prepared for this 'immediate, very warm' offer. And every way we looked at the numbers, it seemed unlikely that a coalition with Labour could be a success – even together, the two parties would not be able to command a majority in Parliament. Nor were we remotely attracted by the idea of putting the unpopular Gordon Brown back into Downing Street.

But a coalition with Labour was not completely impossible, if minor parties supported it, and in any case it would strengthen our negotiating position if we had two large parties to talk to rather than one.

As Chris Huhne now pointed out: 'It is absolutely vital to strengthen our bargaining position by making a rainbow coalition a real possibility. If we can do this, we might even persuade David Cameron to accept a referendum on voting reform.'

So, we decided that although we would talk to the Conservatives first, we should not rule out talks with Labour. Gordon Brown had already been in contact with Vince Cable and was desperately trying to fix an early call with Nick Clegg.

Nick was already forming a clear view of what he thought should happen next. As he put it to our meeting on Friday morning: 'I have to say that based on the existing arithmetic in the Commons, I am incredibly dubious that a rainbow coalition can deliver. I also think the markets would go nuts. It would be really difficult to take tough action to tackle the deficit, and that could mean higher interest rates and the UK being targeted by the markets in the same way as Greece, Portugal and the other high-debt countries. I am seriously worried about that prospect.

'And as for Gordon Brown, I have to tell you that I believe he would be incapable of leading a coalition government, and that he would be unacceptable to the country. But let's be absolutely clear, a minority Conservative administration would lead quickly to a second general election. This would be bad for the economy, bad for the country, and a big political risk for us. I think it will be tough to negotiate what we want from either the Conservatives or Labour. But failure would condemn us and the country to a second general election.'

Later in the day, David Cameron made his 'big, open and comprehensive' offer to the Liberal Democrats from St Stephen's Club in Queen Anne's Gate. And in the afternoon, he spoke to Nick Clegg and pressed for early talks with the Liberal Democrat negotiating team; these were fixed for 7.30 that evening in the Cabinet Office in Whitehall.

Our team met for half an hour at the National Liberal Club beforehand – although we had some difficulty in persuading a sceptical doorkeeper to let us in.

Meanwhile, Gordon Brown had also made a strong pitch by phone to Nick Clegg, asking for parallel talks with the Labour Party. Nick made clear that such talks could not yet start: he had promised to talk first to the largest party in Parliament, and he was determined to honour that pledge.

These first talks with the Conservative side that evening went well. David Cameron had assembled his negotiating team from his most trusted allies: William Hague, George Osborne, Oliver Letwin, and his chief of staff, Ed Llewellyn. Both sides found the discussions to be warmer, more relaxed and more open than might otherwise have been expected. The Conservative team seemed to be interested in serious talks about how a joint policy programme could be drawn up that would deliver as many of our key priorities as possible.

In preparing for the possibility of coalition talks, and in drawing up the Liberal Democrat manifesto, we had already settled on what our main policy priorities would be. These were highlighted on the first pages of our manifesto and clearly communicated during the election campaign. The four main priorities were: clearing up the economic mess left by Labour and building a 'green' economy; raising the tax-free personal allowance to £10,000 per year; introducing a £2.5 billion 'pupil premium' to target more support at children from disadvantaged backgrounds in the schools system; and delivering an ambitious programme of political reform – including proportional representation.

We briefly discussed all four issues with the Conservatives in our Sunday-evening meeting. As we expected, the issue of proportional representation was going to prove the most difficult to negotiate. David Cameron had already proposed some kind of 'review' about voting systems, but I made clear in this first meeting that this would be regarded by my party as an unacceptable solution, designed to kick the issue into the long grass. William Hague responded: 'This is a very difficult issue for the Conservatives.'

George Osborne suggested that a confidence and supply agreement might be acceptable to the Conservative team although 'David Cameron's strong view is that he would prefer the stability of a full coalition.'

On Saturday 8 May, Nick Clegg spent most of the morning meeting with the Liberal Democrat 'shadow Cabinet' and with our new parliamentary party. The agreement of our parliamentary party and of the 'Federal Executive' of the Liberal Democrat Party would be necessary to approve any coalition agreement. Even after this, the party constitution required a further vote of approval by a special conference of party members. This 'triple lock' meant that there was no question of going into coalition without the strong support of a majority of the party.

Nick Clegg, Danny Alexander and I had expected many of our MPs to be unenthusiastic about the prospect of doing deals with the other two parties, and particularly with the Conservatives – our 'traditional' enemy at Westminster. In fact, at these first two meetings, most of our MPs spoke out strongly in favour of some kind of stable agreement being reached. Chris Huhne warned that without an agreement, we might rapidly face a second general election – which he predicted could cost us twenty of our fifty-seven seats. None of our MPs relished the prospect of a second general election, and there was a concern that we might be blamed by the electorate if we were not seen to be acting in the national interest.

Most MPs highlighted how unpopular it would be to go into coalition with a Gordon Brown-led Labour Party. Many stressed what our negotiating team had already decided: even if we could not extract a pledge on proportional representation, we should press for a referendum on the Alternative Vote. The Alternative Vote was a far more modest form of electoral reform, in which candidates were ranked in preference order by voters. The votes of the bottom candidates were then redistributed until one candidate had at least 50 per cent of the vote.

On Saturday afternoon, we held a first, brief, and secret meeting with the team that Gordon Brown had decided would negotiate for Labour: Peter Mandelson, Andrew Adonis, Ed Balls, Harriet Harman and Ed Miliband. This took place in a conference room in Portcullis House, where many MPs had their Westminster offices, rather than in the Cabinet Office itself. Chris Huhne undiplomatically took it on himself to try to raise the issue of Gordon Brown's leadership and whether he should be stepping down as Labour leader to clear the way for a coalition deal. This irritated the chair of our negotiating team, Danny Alexander, because it had already been decided that this issue should be addressed in private by Nick Clegg. 'No, Chris, that is not a matter we are discussing,' Danny interrupted.

On Sunday, our first substantive talks began with the Conservatives. We were back in the Cabinet Office, in a huge room up on the third floor that had once been used by Michael Heseltine when he was Deputy Prime Minister. It was probably the largest office I had ever seen, and it was to be taken over in due course by the Conservative minister Francis Maude.

On the commencement of the talks, we declined an offer from Gus O'Donnell, the head of the civil service, to have civil servants in the room 'facilitating' the meeting. It was a good decision: it allowed us to deal with each other in a direct, open and straightforward way.

William Hague and George Osborne suggested that we might want to meet the Governor of the Bank of England and the Permanent Secretary to the Treasury later in the day. We rejected that offer too – concerned that this might simply be a subtle trap, designed to manoeuvre us into supporting Conservative economic policy. This was undoubtedly the right decision and avoided the Bank of England and the Treasury becoming entangled in the politics of forming a coalition.

We decided to tackle the toughest issues on this first day: political reform in the morning session and economic policy in the afternoon.

Some of the political reform agenda was easy to agree on. The Conservatives speedily signed up to our proposal to move to fixed-term parliaments. We had suggested four years. George Osborne intervened to suggest five years – 'in case the economy takes a bit longer than expected to fix', he said. It turned out to be a very important decision.

On House of Lords reform, there was also a joint agreement to move to a predominantly elected House, though William Hague warned that 'the leadership of our party is fine on this. But our backbenchers are rather more anti.'

We Liberal Democrats had already signalled in the first talks on Saturday night that electoral reform would be the potential deal-breaker for us. But we did not wish the talks to be seen to fail solely on a matter of political reform. So we agreed that if we had to reject the coalition option, the main reasons we would give would relate to economic and social policy.

We now decided to see if we could break the log jam on electoral reform, using a proposal that I had advocated in our preparations for coalition talks over the past few months.

Danny Alexander now put forward this proposal: a referendum on the Alternative Vote, in exchange for our support for Conservative proposals to redraw the parliamentary boundaries, to reduce the number of MPs and make constituencies more equal in terms of voter numbers. This was designed to be just one part of a radical package to transform Britain's outdated political system. For Nick Clegg, deficit reduction and political reform were to be the two main pillars of the coalition policy agenda.

We tried to 'sell' the Alternative Vote to the Conservatives as a reform of the first past the post system, but it did not take long for George Osborne to see what we were getting at. 'This would be really difficult for the Conservative Party,' added William Hague.

'But surely you could just impose this on your backbenchers,' said Chris Huhne. 'Everyone knows that while the Liberal Democrats are a democratic party, the Conservatives are more like an absolute monarchy.'

'Chris,' interrupted William Hague. 'You are right. The Conservative Party is like an absolute monarchy – but an absolute monarchy that is qualified by regicide. If we took this deal back to our colleagues in the Conservative parliamentary party, we would no longer be their leaders. They would instantly get rid of us.'

George Osborne said that he also considered that a whipped vote of Conservative MPs on an AV referendum would be 'impossible'.

'Look, in that case this is all very difficult,' I said. 'We have problems too. We cannot sell a coalition deal to our MPs and to our party members without a referendum on voting reform. And this is already the weakest acceptable type of voting reform. You have to realise that if we go into coalition with you, it is inevitable that our vote share will decline. Without the prospect of voting reform, a coalition would just be too dangerous for us.'

George Osborne made one last attempt at agreement: 'We could give you a guaranteed free vote on AV in the Commons before the end of this year. It would probably get through, because it is Labour policy as well. But we cannot go further.'

We had made good progress on a range of issues, but we seemed to have hit a brick wall. Neither side would concede further. 'OK,' said Danny Alexander, 'I think we need a time-out, to take stock.'

In the afternoon, we turned to economic policy. We discussed deficit reduction and agreed to consider some small in-year cuts in public spending in 2010. Our own election manifesto had suggested that substantive spending cuts should probably start in 2011, to allow the economy to recover before fiscal tightening began. But since our manifesto had been written, our own economy had strengthened, while the international and financial market situation had become much more risky. We considered that a modest and symbolic cut in public spending in 2010 would send out a strong signal to the financial markets, help bring economic stability and reduce any pressure on the UK bond markets – and hence on interest rates.

On taxation, we made clear that we were not willing to budge on our manifesto pledge of delivering a £10,000 personal allowance before the end of the parliament.

George Osborne was concerned about whether a £10,000 allowance was affordable. 'The advice from the Treasury is that deficit reduction needs higher taxes as well as spending cuts,' he said. 'Fine,' we argued. 'Raise taxes on those on very high incomes.' We insisted that this was a bottom-line issue for us: 'It is good for those on low incomes, will help improve work incentives and will create a fairer tax system,' argued Danny Alexander.

I also insisted that we would accept nothing less than a £2.5 billion pupil premium, which had to be additional money and not just 'smoke and mirrors'. George Osborne tried to avoid being pinned down on the numbers – 'I'm not against it, but it will be very tough to fund' – but I was determined not to give an inch. My Liberal Democrat colleagues watched our tussle with amusement – I had fought similarly hard for the pledge to be included in our own manifesto.

By the end of the afternoon, we had made a lot of progress but we could not reach an agreement on electoral reform. We returned to Nick Clegg's office in the House of Commons. Nick had spoken to Gordon Brown earlier in the day and he told us that the Labour leader was 'desperate for a deal. He is saying he will step down, to clear the way for a Liberal Democrat–Labour coalition. He is also promising a referendum on AV.'

Some senior Liberal Democrats still thought that a coalition with Labour would be politically toxic. Others wanted to explore the possibility further – if only to strengthen our bargaining position.

Nick was worried. 'If we go with the Tories, we have a coalition with political legitimacy, but we cannot take this risk without major political reform. But if we go in with Labour, it will be very unpopular, and the government could collapse a few months later, because the numbers for a coalition with Labour just don't stack up. We are between a rock and a hard place.'

Andrew Stunell cautioned against us rushing into any decisions: 'We are all very tired. We need to take a deep breath and get this right. And we need to realise that from a public and media perspective there is a real, real difficulty legitimising Labour after they have lost the election so badly.'

Monday 10 May was undoubtedly the most dramatic day of the coalition talks. We met the Conservative team again in the morning. They weren't prepared to budge on the AV referendum; instead they tabled a draft confidence and supply agreement. This would have allowed the Conservatives to form a minority administration, while the Liberal Democrats would have stayed on the opposition benches. The Liberal Democrats would have been obliged to vote with the Conservatives on confidence votes and on the Budget. In addition, we would have had to sign up to support a programme based on 'the bulk of the Conservative manifesto.'

In exchange, we would secure policies including: membership of a new Financial Stability Council, which would be 'consulted' on Budget issues; a 'priority' for raising income tax thresholds over the parliament; a free vote in the House of Commons on an AV referendum; and a 'significant' pupil premium funded by cuts elsewhere. It was hardly exciting. When the talks broke up in the late morning, we agreed to report back to our parliamentary party. We promised that Nick Clegg would then phone David Cameron back with our decision before the Conservative shadow Cabinet was due to meet at 4 p.m.

When we left the Cabinet Office, we already knew what the Conservative team did not – that if we decided to give the Labour Party a serious chance to form a coalition government, Gordon Brown was willing to announce his resignation as Labour leader later that afternoon to clear the way for talks.

It was now almost time to bring this other option into play.

At 1.40 p.m. our negotiating team met with the entire Liberal Democrat parliamentary party in the debating chamber off Westminster Hall. There was a distinct sense of excitement in the room when we arrived, ten minutes late. MPs and senior peers were waiting to find out the latest news from our talks. Neither negotiating team had been leaking our talks to the media, so most people had little idea what was going on.

We reported back on our discussions. Almost no one in the room was enthusiastic about the idea of a confidence and supply agreement. The general view was that such an agreement offered us responsibility without power. And most people expected that any such arrangement would fold within a few months – forcing a second general election. It was feared that we would then be blamed by many voters for creating economic uncertainty and by others for supporting the Conservatives in government for any period of time.

On the day after the general election, Paddy Ashdown had reminded me of the famous Sherlock Holmes quotation from Arthur Conan Doyle's *The Sign of Four*: 'Once you eliminate the impossible, whatever remains, no matter how improbable, must be the truth.'

The parliamentary party had now rejected two strategic choices – standing on one side and allowing a minority administration, and signing up to a confidence and supply agreement. There was now only one strategic choice available: full-blown coalition. The question was with which party.

At 4 p.m., Nick Clegg telephoned a disappointed David Cameron to inform him that we were rejecting a confidence and supply agreement. It was coalition or nothing. David Cameron was in no doubt about the seriousness of his predicament when just an hour later Gordon Brown stepped into Downing Street to announce formal talks on a coalition with the Liberal Democrats. The Prime Minister also announced his intention to step down as Labour leader to facilitate a Liberal Democrat–Labour government, sending shock waves through Westminster.

A panicked David Cameron was now able to persuade his Conservative parliamentary colleagues to sign up to offering an AV referendum. But he could not be sure that we would reject a Labour coalition. And if Labour were in power, the odds were that Mr Cameron would not just be out of office, he would be out of the leadership of his party. When he went home to his wife and family that evening, he thought that the Conservatives might already be shut out of power.

While David Cameron was trying to rescue the Conservative hopes of government, the Liberal Democrat negotiating team were waiting in Room 391 of Portcullis House for the first major negotiating meeting with the Labour team, which was due to start at 7.30 p.m. We knew the parliamentary arithmetic made a coalition with Labour almost impossible to achieve, but we were willing to give the talks a real chance. As we waited for the Labour team to arrive, the first rumours swept Westminster that the Conservatives were about to make their own offer of an AV referendum.

7.30 p.m. came and went, as did 7.45 p.m. We were all tired, though excited, and we were a little baffled that the Labour team were now late for a rather important meeting.

Eventually, at around 8 p.m., the door swung open and in came Peter Mandelson, Andrew Adonis, Ed Balls, Ed Miliband and Harriet Harman. Peter Mandelson apologised for their team being late. He explained that there had just been a Cabinet meeting, in which Gordon Brown had announced his resignation. Cabinet ministers, he said, had wanted to pay tribute to the outgoing Prime Minister and Labour leader.

We then got down to the negotiations. They were not easy. Hovering over the talks on both sides were doubts over whether the parliamentary arithmetic would allow a Liberal Democrat–Labour coalition to govern effectively. We would need a confidence and supply agreement with the Democratic Unionists, said Peter Mandelson, and we would need to hope that the Scottish Nationalists and others would support the new minority coalition on key votes.

There was a long discussion about constitutional reform and the Alternative Vote. Ed Balls interrupted to make clear that the Labour parliamentary party could not necessarily be relied upon to support an AV referendum, given the views of a significant minority of their MPs. This was perhaps true and certainly worrying – not least because a referendum was actually a Labour Party manifesto commitment.

Peter Mandelson sought to counter these concerns by suggesting that the Tory Party might not deliver on an AV referendum either. I reminded him that Labour had also failed to deliver after the Jenkins Review of voting systems in 1998. He took the point while warning: 'Watch out for News International. They will work hard to defeat any referendum on this.'

We failed to make solid progress with Labour in other areas, too. There was no acceptance of other key Liberal Democrat policies on the tax-free allowance, the pupil premium, civil liberties and the environment. Labour had been in power for thirteen years and all the policies we now wanted to alter were their policies. They were, quite simply, much more resistant to changes than our other potential coalition partner, who had also been out of power for thirteen years. There simply wasn't the sense of cooperation and constructive engagement that there had been in the Conservative talks. The Labour Party was arrogant, exhausted, divided and almost certainly incapable of running a minority government. Many Labour MPs thought the party should accept defeat and rebuild in opposition. 'It would be like being shackled to a rotting corpse,' I concluded, when we returned to brief Nick Clegg in his office at the end of the night.

All four members of the negotiating team felt the same way after the talks – we were all now recommending a full coalition with the Conservatives, provided we could secure an AV referendum as well as all our other main priorities.

Nick Clegg was clearly surprised by the strength of our opinion. He had just been lobbied by three former Liberal Democrat leaders – Paddy Ashdown, Sir Menzies Campbell and Charles Kennedy – all of whom wanted to go into coalition with Labour. Nick insisted that we hold one more round of talks with Labour the next day, to test whether an agreement might still be possible. This meeting took place, but it did not change our decision – indeed, it was clear that we were still nowhere near consensus on key issues on which we already had agreement with the Conservatives.

By the time we met with the Conservatives again, at 2 p.m. on Tuesday 11 May, only one outcome was likely, namely a full Liberal Democrat–Conservative coalition. Meanwhile, Gordon Brown waited in 10 Downing Street to hear our final decision.

We had a lot of ground to cover in talks with the Conservatives and not much time. We went through a draft coalition agreement, inserting some bullet points and amending others. The commitments on the tax threshold and the pupil premium were toughened up to meet our requirements.

The new wording on the AV referendum was included, and the Conservatives clarified what they were and were not promising. 'We will make sure this Bill goes through Parliament. We will deliver the referendum, exactly as promised. And then we will beat the hell out of you in the vote!' laughed Oliver Letwin.

The section on House of Lords reform was swiftly agreed. Nobody paid much attention to George Osborne's off-the-cuff comment: 'The four of us in the Conservative negotiating team all agree on this, but we are rather atypical for our party!'

We finished on the issue of Europe, with some wording that had been agreed between David Cameron and Nick Clegg. The two leaders had discussed their attitudes to Europe in some detail and had mutually agreed that they would not let the coalition be 'hijacked' by this issue.

By now it was getting late in the day. The Cabinet Secretary, Gus O'Donnell, was becoming increasingly nervous. During one break in the talks, he came up to me and whispered, 'How much longer is all this going to take? I have got a very unhappy Prime Minister in 10 Downing Street who is desperate to resign. I really don't think I can hold on to him much longer, but I don't want him going until I know I have an alternative government.'

We were putting the final touches to the agreement when the door of our negotiating room opened and one of our political advisers shouted, 'Gordon Brown is coming out to do a press conference.' While some of our advisers bashed away on their computers to complete the final draft, Gordon Brown stepped out into Downing Street at 7.15 p.m. to announce his resignation and that of his government.

We switched a television on in the corner of our large negotiating room, and I stood in front of it to watch Brown's statement, along with William Hague, George Osborne and Oliver Letwin. We watched in silence, with only the sound of a helicopter overhead, which was filming the scene below and waiting to track the outgoing Prime Minister's car on its way to Buckingham Palace.

I had never found Gordon Brown to be a sympathetic character, but there was a lump in my throat as he finished his speech and guided his rarely seen children to the waiting car.

Next to me, George Osborne knew he was now on the verge of becoming Chancellor of the Exchequer – at the age of just thirty-eight. He turned to me, smiled and slapped me on the back, in celebration and to mark our new alliance. I smiled weakly back. For some reason, this suddenly seemed more like a moment to reflect, rather than to celebrate.

As Gordon Brown's car set off on its way to the palace, our two teams of negotiators finished our work. We agreed that we would leave the Cabinet Office separately, making short statements and then reporting back to our party leaders.

Our Liberal Democrat team left the building first, at 7.30 p.m. After a brief statement on the Cabinet Office steps, we made our way back to Parliament, chased down Whitehall by camera crews and photographers.

Three minutes later, the Conservative team left the Cabinet Office, and barely ten minutes later – at 7.43 p.m. – Gordon Brown and his wife, Sarah, left Buckingham Palace, the Labour leader having resigned as Prime Minister. It looked perfectly choreographed, but it was a close-run thing. Gordon Brown was determined not to leave Downing Street in the dark. Had he resigned while the talks were ongoing, the United Kingdom would have been left in limbo for the arrival of its next government.

The Liberal Democrat Party still had to meet later to approve the final co-alition agreement. But already David Cameron had been asked to Buckingham Palace to see the Queen, to be invited to form a new government. For three hours or more he could not be certain that he had a coalition partner.

Meeting in Local Government House in Smith Square at 10 p.m., the mood amongst Liberal Democrat MPs was, however, jubilant. As MPs read through the draft coalition agreement, it was clear that they were delighted by just how much of our manifesto we had managed to negotiate into the document.

Nick Clegg was asked by one MP what his role would be in the coalition. When he replied, with a mixture of modesty, pride and shock, it was to say: 'If this all goes ahead, I will be the Deputy Prime Minister.' There was a huge cheer in the room. It wasn't something that Liberal Democrat MPs had ever heard their party leader say.

At the end of a long debate, the parliamentary party approved the co-alition deal by fifty votes to nil, and our peers also later voted thirty-one to nil in favour. It was striking that no parliamentarian had voted against the agreement, though some – such as Charles Kennedy – had abstained.

It was a night of celebration and delight, and eventually we were able to inform the waiting media that the Liberal Democrats were forming a stable coalition with the Conservative Party.

Not every MP was delighted, however. Sir Menzies Campbell, the former party leader, did not vote against the coalition, but – viewing the scenes of celebration – he muttered within my earshot the words of Robert Walpole: 'They now ring their bells, but they will soon wring their hands.' I understood very clearly the massive risks that he was alluding to. What we had been through may have been testing, but it was just the easy part. Now we had to form a government, ensure that the government delivered, and protect our party from the backlash that was sure to come.

But all that was for later. As we left Local Government House at close to midnight on a warm spring evening, I reflected on a historic day and some of us now looked forward to what role we might be asked to play in the new government.

Forming a Coalition

MAY 2010

On the evening of Tuesday 11 May 2010, after David Cameron had returned from Buckingham Palace, the work of forming the first UK coalition government for sixty-five years had begun.

In spite of our inexperience, the process was swift and efficient. It had taken Belgium eighteen months to negotiate a stable coalition after their elections in 2010. It had taken only five days for the UK coalition to be agreed and now the formation of the government proceeded smoothly too.

While the Liberal Democrats were still securing internal agreement to the coalition programme, David Cameron announced that William Hague was to be Foreign Secretary and George Osborne was to be Chancellor.

During the coalition talks, the two negotiating teams had not discussed ministerial appointments. This was left for direct discussions between David Cameron and Nick Clegg. The two party leaders had already agreed that the Liberal Democrats would have four places in the Cabinet, based roughly on the ratio between the numbers of Liberal Democrat and Conservative MPs.

Nick Clegg was to be Deputy Prime Minister, with cross-government responsibility, including chairmanship of the powerful Home Affairs Committee. Nick had also agreed with the new Prime Minister that he would be in charge of the political reform agenda – a central part of the coalition agreement, and a high priority for the Liberal Democrats. Nick Clegg was aware that he could have asked for and secured a role such as Home Secretary or even Foreign Secretary. But he did not want to spend all his time abroad, and he was also concerned that running a large department would divert him from the essential task of ensuring that the Liberal Democrats delivered across government as a whole.

Vince Cable was the second most senior Liberal Democrat MP, as the party's deputy leader and Treasury spokesman. Vince's expertise was clearly in economic policy. But George Osborne had been appointed Chancellor, and neither he nor Vince Cable wished to be working together.

It was therefore agreed that Vince Cable would be the new Business Secretary, an appointment confirmed by Nick Clegg with Vince Cable before the coalition agreement was signed off by Liberal Democrat MPs.

Chris Huhne was the third most senior Liberal Democrat MP. In 2007 he had finished just a few hundred votes behind Nick Clegg in the leadership election. The next day Nick had a very difficult telephone call with his rival, who was clearly upset at having lost the leadership battle. Nick had then offered Chris the party Foreign Affairs portfolio – a senior position, but one that Chris regarded as marginal to the main domestic policy debate. The call ended angrily, with Chris having rejected the role.

Later on, the row was patched up. Nick agreed instead to give Chris the Home Affairs portfolio, shifting Ed Davey to Foreign Affairs. During the telephone call, Chris set another condition for his support for the new party leader: he wanted a guarantee that if the Liberal Democrats went into a coalition government after the 2010 general election, he would have one of the Lib Dem Cabinet posts.

'Of course,' replied Nick, thinking that such a scenario was unlikely, and that Chris would in any case have a good claim in such circumstances.

Given the importance of environment and climate change to the Liberal Democrats, this now seemed an obvious department for us to occupy. It was also a complex area of policy, where having an economically literate Secretary of State would be important. The role was offered to Chris Huhne, who enthusiastically accepted it.

The original intention was that Danny Alexander, Nick Clegg's trusted chief of staff, would not be a full Cabinet member. He had been earmarked for a role in the Cabinet Office, in the centre of government, working with Oliver Letwin to help make the coalition operate effectively. But it was soon realised that with only one Conservative MP for Scotland, the Liberal Democrats had a strong claim to occupy the post of Secretary of State for Scotland. David

Cameron therefore agreed to combine Danny's responsibilities in the centre of government with the Scotland Office role. As a consequence, the Liberal Democrats would now hold five full Cabinet positions.

Nick Clegg had decided to allocate the final Cabinet post to me. He tried to reach me by mobile phone late on the Tuesday night, but my phone had run out of battery. By the time I received his message, after midnight, Nick had sensibly gone to bed.

When I called him back the following morning, Wednesday 12 May, I was crossing Parliament Square on the way back from completing a morning round of interviews at the Millbank media centre.

'Thanks for calling back, David,' said Nick. 'Cameron and I are pulling the government together. I have to decide what departments we are in. Obviously I want to find a role for you. I think there is a strong case for us securing the areas that our party has a strong identity in, which is why I wanted Climate Change. So I was also thinking about something like Transport for you.'

I had no desire to be Transport Secretary, nor did I think it would be remotely sensible to have no Liberal Democrat in the engine room of government – the Treasury. This was where much of the focus of government would be, and this was where we had to have Liberal Democrat clout if we were to secure the funding for our own policy priorities.

'Well,' I said. 'I don't want to be presumptuous, but we really need someone in the Treasury. I think we should seriously consider the role of Chief Secretary, which is an area I already know well. The fact is that this parliament is going to be about the economy, and we have to have someone there. And if we want to protect our priority areas and promote our own manifesto priorities, we just cannot entrust that to the Tories.'

'OK,' said Nick. 'That is useful. I will be talking to Cameron soon. I will bear that in mind. But I have to go – I'm at home, and I am supposed to be getting the children to school.'

I went back to my office and waited for the call that almost all MPs hope will one day come.

Eventually, my mobile rang. It was the operator from 'Switch'. 'If you could make your way to Downing Street, the Prime Minister would like to see you in about half an hour.'

I left my office and walked the short way from my 1 Parliament Street office to the gates of Downing Street. I was quickly ushered through, for once being able to avoid going through the security scanner. I did my best to look calm and nonchalant as I took the famous walk along Downing Street that so many hopeful politicians had completed before me.

To my relief, the famous door of No. 10 opened just before I arrived at it, and I was ushered through into the lobby of the famous house. It was only the second or third time that I had been there since becoming an MP in 2001. It was an opportunity that Liberals and Liberal Democrats were not in the habit of enjoying.

As if to make that point, as the doorman closed the black door behind me, I saw that someone had cellotaped to the inside window of Downing Street a cutting from that day's *Sun* newspaper. Under the uninspiring headline 'Britain's Leading Lib Dums' were photos of Vince Cable, Danny Alexander, Chris Huhne and me. The doorman was clearly using the cutting to help identify us as we turned up to join the government. Clearly not everyone in Whitehall had been expecting us.

After a short wait in a side room ('The Prime Minister is just speaking to the President of France'), I was eventually invited to make the short walk along the central corridor of No. 10, to the lobby just outside the Cabinet Room. 'Please go in,' said the smart young lady accompanying me. 'The Prime Minister is waiting.'

David Cameron was sitting in his place at the Cabinet table, with his jacket off, wearing a white shirt and a blue tie. He invited me to sit opposite him. A photographer then popped in to capture the great moment. 'David, as you may know from Nick, I want you to join the government as Chief Secretary to the Treasury. You'll be working with George, who I think you know, and who is looking forward to working with you. The economic challenge is obviously the big thing for us, so it's going to be terribly important to get it right. I suggest after this you go straight to the Treasury, where George will be waiting for you. Good luck.'

I had got the job I wanted, and the job I believed was essential if the Liberal Democrats were going to make the coalition a success. The meeting in the Cabinet Room was all over in a couple of minutes, and then I was back in the lobby outside. Before leaving, I was asked to go upstairs to meet with Nick Clegg. I walked up the grand Downing Street staircase, with all the pictures of former Prime Ministers. It reinforced the sense that this was history in the making.

Nick Clegg and Danny Alexander were 'squatting' in one of the grand reception rooms on the first floor. No one seemed to have thought to provide the Deputy Prime Minister with a proper office yet.

Nick was going through the junior ministerial positions with Danny. He showed me who he proposed to appoint as ministers of state, and I gave my views. Norman Lamb was initially earmarked for Minister of State at Health, but this was changed to Parliamentary Under Secretary at the Department for International Development, and Paul Burstow was substituted instead. Tim Farron and Jo Swinson were also being considered as Parliamentary Under Secretaries, at the Department for Environment, Food and Rural Affairs and the Department for Culture, Media and Sport respectively. It later turned out that the two party leaders had rather misjudged the numbers of junior ministers each party had. Nick Clegg thought he had enough for one Lib Dem MP in each department, but this was not the case. Reluctantly, he had to drop Norman Lamb, Tim Farron and Jo Swinson from his first ministerial team.

I chatted very briefly with Nick, and we agreed that we should speak again soon. I was now expected in the Treasury, where a £160 billion Budget deficit was awaiting me.

'There Is No Money'

MAY 2010

'There is a car outside to take you to the Treasury.' One of the posh young ladies who had come into Downing Street with the new Conservative team was waiting for me when I came back down to the lobby. 'There'll be photographers opposite when the door opens,' she said. 'So make sure you cover up any important papers, or they will "snap" them with long lenses. The car is the black Jaguar, just outside.'

'Oh, I can walk,' I said. 'I don't think so,' was the reply. 'There will be media all over you. You will get in the car and it will take you round to the main entrance to the Treasury, just opposite St James's Park. When you get there, the Chancellor will be waiting for you at the entrance, just at the top of some steps. Shake hands with him, then the two of you will face the cameras. He will say something nice. Hopefully, you will too. Then you go into the Treasury together. No questions from the media.'

The No. 10 door opened, and I walked out to the large, black Jaguar that was waiting just outside. I didn't think it appropriate to look too happy, given that I had just been charged with the job of making huge cuts to public spending, so I did my best to look serious. But I had not bargained for the shrewdness of the waiting photographers. As I climbed into the back of the car, one of them shouted out, 'For God's sake, smile, you miserable bastard.' He then caught me with a broad grin on my face as I glanced back to see who had shouted such an unexpected request.

The gates of Downing Street opened and the police officers held back groups of tourists and pedestrians who were gathered on the pavement outside. The Jaguar headed down Whitehall as I thought about what I would say when we reached the Treasury, and before long we had parked just outside the main entrance

George Osborne was waiting for me, looking relaxed and confident. We each said a few words about the big job we were undertaking together, in front of a cluster of journalists and a few camera crews, and then we turned around and disappeared into the Treasury building.

Once up on the second floor, we shook hands again and George turned right towards his large office. I was shown left, and headed down a long, wide corridor towards the 'Outer Office' of the Chief Secretary, where all of the private secretaries and other advisers worked. The Chief Secretary had his own dedicated staff of seven, who all seemed very friendly and welcoming.

My private secretary, Chris, then led me through into my own office – large, traditional and high ceilinged, with impressive views over St James's Park. I noted a general air of solidity and stuffiness. The pictures on the walls were of nineteenth-century sail boats. They looked like they might have been the only items left in the government art collection when someone went to select some items to adorn the walls.

The only sign of modernity in the room was a stand with a white flip chart, near the door. I was later told that it had been brought in by my Labour predecessor, Liam Byrne, and was regarded by the civil service with disapproval, as a sign of new-fangled management consultancy. It was with relish that my private secretary removed it a few days later.

I was now the twenty-eighth Chief Secretary to the Treasury since that post was created in 1961, and the first ever Liberal or Liberal Democrat to hold the position. The role was created in order to reduce some of the burdens on the Chancellor of the Exchequer, and the Chief Secretary's job was to focus on the control and management of public spending, which now accounted for over 40 per cent of the economy.

In theory, the role was one of the most junior in the Cabinet, as deputy to the Chancellor. But, in reality, the position could be quite powerful, as the office holder had his or her hands on the finances of the government, and would not only play a key role in fixing the budgets of each department but also had to approve major new items of spending. And because the Treasury had to maintain its power over the rest of Whitehall, there was a protocol which meant that however senior the Cabinet minister, anyone who wanted to deal with the Chief Secretary had to come to the Treasury to meet him. The Treasury travelled out of its building to see no one, other than the Prime Minister and – in this coalition government – the Deputy Prime Minister. The former Prime Minister, John Major, sent me a kind note soon after my appointment, telling me that the Chief Secretary position was the job he had most enjoyed in government.

Of course, what was yet to be established was how powerful the Chief Secretary's job would be in practice in a coalition government. Quite simply, there were no precedents. And what the Treasury was very used to from recent experience were Chief Secretaries who had almost no influence.

Tony Blair, when Prime Minister, used the Chief Secretary's post primarily to spy on Gordon Brown. Quite simply, his Chancellor often refused to tell even the Prime Minister what policy options he was considering.

In just thirteen years of Labour government, between 1997 and 2010, there were ten different Chief Secretaries in the Treasury. They were usually bright, upcoming ministers – which was why they soon moved on to higher things. But no doubt it did not help their engagement or longevity that those who served during Gordon Brown's time as Chancellor were often regarded with ill-disguised suspicion by their Treasury boss, and were often also kept in the dark about key decisions.

My successor, Danny Alexander, was once being briefed by a senior Treasury official on the contents of a Budget Statement, and in the privacy of his office he was being talked through the detail of the Treasury Budget 'scorecard'. These highly secret documents were prepared before each Budget to cost each policy that Treasury ministers were considering, along with its potential impact on the public finances. 'The last time I was asked to brief the Chief Secretary on the Budget scorecard, I had to give him the wrong figures, Chief Secretary,' the Treasury official revealed.

'What!' said Danny Alexander. 'That's outrageous! Why?'

'Well, Chief Secretary,' was the reply, 'Gordon Brown was very clear that we should not give away the Budget contents to the Chief Secretary. He was worried that it would get back to No. 10. So we had to talk the then Chief Secretary through a bogus scorecard. It was all most embarrassing.'

It was clear that the Chancellor and I would soon need to make some major decisions on public spending and on the whole long-term tax, spending and borrowing strategy of the government. We had inherited a Budget deficit of almost £160 billion – a massive 11 per cent of national output. Some people had argued that this deficit had arisen only because of the severe recession and the associated short-term collapse in tax revenues. In fact, Labour had been running a deficit of around 3 per cent of national income when the economic shock first hit in 2007 – in spite of the fact that the economy had been growing for the longest continuous period for centuries.

The UK had entered recession with one of the largest structural budget deficits in the developed world. Labour had sharply increased public spending as a share of gross domestic product, in the belief that this would be paid for by a rise in tax receipts as a share of the economy, and by ever-increasing economic growth. But receipts had underperformed in the run-up to the crash, leaving the Budget deficit higher than planned.

At the end of my first day in the Treasury, I was handed a secret note on options for reducing the Budget deficit over the period of the parliament. I sat late into the evening reading the paper, feeling ever gloomier as I did.

The Treasury paper had been prepared for the incoming government. It set out three possible strategies to reduce the enormous gap between tax revenues and public spending.

Option A involved moderate tax rises, modest cuts to public spending, and a gently declining deficit. It was clear from the accompanying analysis that Treasury officials were not recommending this option. Indeed, it seemed to be little more than a straw man to knock down.

Option C involved such dramatic cuts in spending and such vast increases in taxation that any government seeking to implement it would be out of office before Christmas. The Treasury note treated it more favourably than Option A, but it was also clear to me that it was designed as a frightening, extreme option that we were not expected to sign up to. I wrote various rude comments on this section of the paper, and in general crossed and ticked sections of the paper energetically as I went through it.

That left Option B – the middle way, which Treasury officials were clearly inviting us to sign up to. Even this involved eye-wateringly large spending cuts and tax rises. I indicated on my paper that I favoured something slightly less draconian than the proposals in this paper – a sort of Option 'B Minus'. The strategy I preferred, with my changes, was almost exactly what the government was later to announce in its June Budget.

I decided that I wanted to read through the long and detailed paper again the next day, to reflect upon its contents. So I popped the paper into the top drawer of my desk and, at around midnight that night, I walked home, deep in thought about the challenges and difficult choices that lay ahead. I had already made clear to my officials that I would not be using the chauffeur-driven Jaguar that had been allocated to me – I did not see how I could be the person charged with tackling wasteful government spending while being driven around in a luxury car. The Permanent Secretary was apparently delighted; the government car service less so. It took about two weeks before they finally gave up trying to talk me round.

The next day, Thursday 13 May, I was back into the Treasury early, at 7 a.m. I opened the drawer of my desk to recover the top secret paper on government fiscal options. It was gone. I searched every drawer, but could find it nowhere.

I was becoming a little worried that my first action as a government minister might have been to lose a top secret Treasury briefing, and imagined that even now one of the department's contract cleaners might be flicking through a detailed paper on fiscal options, which could soon be on its way to the front page of the *Daily Mirror*.

I asked my private secretary if he had seen the paper. 'Of course, Chief Secretary,' he said. 'Seen it, summarised your views and circulated your paper with your helpful annotations to the Chancellor, the Permanent Secretary and senior officials.'

I desperately tried to remember quite how rude I had been about Option C and how many expletives had covered the paper. It was an early lesson in how the civil service works.

Anyway, my views needed communicating to colleagues, even if I might have appreciated a little more time to consider precisely what I wanted to say.

As I was planning my work programme for the weeks ahead, my private secretary then came into my office with an off-white envelope, on which was scrawled in blue ink the words 'Chief Secretary to the Treasury'.

'Minister, it's from your predecessor as Chief Secretary, Liam Byrne.'

I tore it open and pulled out the note. It was on 'Chief Secretary to the Treasury' notepaper, with a blue embossed crest. Dated 6 April 2010, it read simply: 'Dear Chief Secretary, I'm afraid there is no money. Kind regards – and good luck! Liam'.

My first reaction was to laugh. My second was to think it was a slightly insensitive thing to say, as it appeared to be making light of the mess in the public finances.

'Oh well,' I thought, 'I'll keep it. It will make a good diary story. Or maybe I'll use it as a talking point for the *Financial Times* interview I've agreed to.'

I had long forgotten that there was a precedent for outgoing ministers leaving their successors such notes. They were often kept private but not always so. Famously, in 1964, the outgoing Conservative Chancellor of the Exchequer Reginald Maudling had left his successor, James Callaghan, a note that said: 'Good luck, old cock ... sorry to leave it in such a mess.' This had been made public and caused the Conservatives considerable embarrassment.

But I was too busy and probably too tired to understand just how politically explosive the note would be. Five years later it would even take centre stage in the next general election campaign. I folded the letter back into an envelope and put it in my desk drawer.

That morning, the coalition government held its first Cabinet meeting, in the Cabinet Room that has been the meeting place for UK governments ever since 1796, when Pitt the Younger arranged for two separate rooms to be knocked together as one.

I took my seat around the boat-shaped table, which dates from 1959, and which Harold Macmillan commissioned to allow people to be seen properly wherever they are located.

It was the first coalition Cabinet for sixty-five years, and the mood was positive and upbeat. Even Vince Cable had entered into the spirit of things. 'Our coalition may not have been brought about by mutual love,' he said, 'but my Indian relatives once told me that arranged marriages are often much more successful than the conventional kind.' There was a wave of laughter around the Cabinet table. Vince wasn't always to be so cheery in Cabinet over the next five years.

We quickly agreed the only substantial agenda item – to cut ministerial pay by 5 per cent and then freeze it for the rest of the parliament. And then we were all ushered out into the Downing Street garden for the first Cabinet photograph. Twenty-nine ministers and one Cabinet Secretary were in the photograph. Sixteen of these thirty individuals would survive the five years and sit together around the table at the final Cabinet meeting.

Later that day, the full Cabinet gathered at Buckingham Palace for our formal swearing-in as members of Her Majesty's Privy Council, and so that Secretaries of State could receive their formal seals of office. It was undoubtedly exciting to sweep in through the gates of Buckingham Palace, past camera-clicking tourists, as the first coalition government assembled.

The whole ceremony lasted over an hour, with all of us standing, including the Queen. Each minister had to 'kiss hands' with Her Majesty, while kneeling on a stool with one knee – it was certainly easier for some ministers than others.

We all had to swear the ancient oath of a Privy Counsellor, including that 'you will not know or understand of any manner of thing to be attempted, done or spoken against Her Majesty's Person, Honour, Crown or Dignity Royal, but you will let and withstand the same to the uttermost of your power...'

With these early formalities complete, it was now down to work.

The coalition agreement had specified that 'the parties agree that modest cuts of £6 billion to non-frontline services can be made within the financial year 2010/11'. I was now responsible for delivering these savings.

Six billion pounds was a small amount in the context of overall public spending and the economy: around 0.5 per cent of GDP. Cuts on this scale would have little adverse impact on economic growth. But though small economically, this was a big decision symbolically and politically. All over Europe, governments with large budget deficits were seeing their interest rates on debt soar. In the UK, we had to demonstrate to the financial markets and to the public that even though we had a government of two different parties, it was a government that could deliver on its economic agenda and get the public finances back under control. Delivering the £6 billion of cuts swiftly and efficiently was therefore crucial. I now started work on this in earnest.

Treasury civil servants had already completed background work on the cuts that were needed in each area. They had followed the existing political 'steer' that the NHS, overseas aid and defence were to be exempt from the reductions. But they had pencilled in large cuts to the education budget, of well over £1 billion. I made clear that education was a priority for the Liberal Democrats and that I was not prepared to tolerate any cuts to early years education, schools or 16–19 education. George Osborne accepted my decision, which meant that officials had to redo the numbers to find slightly larger cuts elsewhere.

I then met the Treasury spending team. I was about to find out the Treasury secrets of how to carry out a successful Spending Review. It turned out to be rather simpler than I had expected.

'Chief Secretary,' said the lead official. 'Based upon your steers, we have created the following table of cuts for each department. This is based on the efficiency and other savings which we believe each department can make. Once you agree these figures, we will send them out to each Secretary of State. We will ask them to agree the numbers by 24 May, when we are due to unveil the cuts. We will ask each department for more money than we actually need, so that you can negotiate a lower amount without endangering the £6 billion target. All our cuts add up to about £8 billion, so provided you settle for at least 75 per cent of what we have asked each department for, we will be OK. But if you agree less with any department than 75 per cent, then we will need more than 75 per cent from another. If any department won't agree, you should point out that they are playing a dangerous game, because if it is a difficult spending round and they are the last to settle, they may have to make up all the savings still required. It is one way to try to persuade your colleagues to get on and settle quickly. Where possible, departments may just agree their figures with officials. But departments which do not accept their figures will be required to have their Secretary of State talk to you on the phone or meet you. If they want to meet you, they will have to come to your office. The Treasury doesn't do "home visits".'

'OK,' I said. 'But I am not leaving this to the very last minute. You can tell departments that I will not settle with anyone later than midnight on the Friday before the Monday of the announcement. This has got to be done well, and not all glued together in a rush.'

On Monday 17 May, George Osborne held a press conference in the Treasury to make his first policy announcement: that he was setting up a new 'Office for Budget Responsibility', so that the economic assumptions used by the Treasury were in future independently audited rather than being open to political interference. It was a good and positive announcement, with little that was controversial. I joined the Chancellor in one of the large downstairs rooms in the Treasury. The media all looked a little bored, given that it all seemed rather sensible and dull.

Towards the end of the press conference, the Chancellor called upon me to speak, and to lighten the mood a bit I decided to mention the Liam Byrne note that I had received a few days before. I had not mentioned the letter to George Osborne, and nor did I have a copy with me. I paraphrased the Byrne note as 'I'm afraid there is no money left', inadvertently adding the word 'left' to the end of the sentence.

I could tell that a few of the journalists had perked up a bit after my story, but I did not realise what a touchpaper I had lit until I got back to my office upstairs.

Within minutes, the Chancellor's head of press had dashed into my office. 'Where is this letter?' he asked. 'The media are going nuts about it. It's going to be a huge story. *The Sun* want to put it on their front page tomorrow. They all love it.'

I showed our press team the note, but refused to hand it over. I was told later that the No. 10 head of press, Andy Coulson, had sent out an 'instruction' telling me to hand over the letter. Feeling now a little guilty about what I had done, I refused the request. George Osborne supported my decision. He might have been a little upset that his own announcement was being completely eclipsed. But by now it all hardly mattered – the media were busy mocking up their own letters for the next day's papers.

The rest of the week was spent securing the £6 billion savings from Cabinet colleagues. I managed to persuade Ken Clarke, the Justice Secretary, to settle first, to encourage the others. I spoke to him over the phone and he sounded as nonchalant and relaxed as if he were settling a small bill for monthly garden maintenance: 'Yes, I agree your figure of 320, David,' he said. 'I think it was actually 325,' I replied. From the other end of the line there was a rustling of paper. 'OK. Fine by me,' was the reply. I had secured my first contribution to our savings target: £325 million from the Justice Department. My officials seemed relieved, and looked on with benign approval. They had a Chief Secretary who could be trusted to do the job.

In my outer office, where the private secretaries worked, a large piece of white paper was stuck to the wall. Down the side was a list of departments. Next to each was the savings target for the department. The next column was the amount that I had agreed with the relevant Secretary of State. Of course, Treasury officials were listening in to each call.

Most ministers proved easy to deal with. Chris Huhne at Energy and Climate Change, Philip Hammond at Transport, Michael Gove at Education,

Eric Pickles at Local Government and Iain Duncan Smith at Work and Pensions were all amongst the 'good boys'.

The awkward squad were Home Secretary Theresa May, Business Secretary Vince Cable and Culture Secretary Jeremy Hunt.

Jeremy Hunt had clearly already received the full Department for Culture, Media and Sport indoctrination in how to deal with the threat of the Treasury axe. I spoke to him on the phone. He made three points. Firstly, that he was of course entirely signed up in principle to making the savings needed across government. Secondly, that however desirable this was across the government as a whole, the arts lobby were terribly influential and would create a most awful political stink if we forced the requested scale of cuts onto them. And thirdly, that his department and its budget were so small that their cuts would in any case make little difference to overall public spending – the tiny savings weren't, in other words, worth the political risk. This latter excuse was, I discovered, used by all smaller departments and particularly by the Foreign Office.

Jeremy Hunt then offered to 'meet me' way below the minimum amount I was prepared to settle for. I said this was too little. Jeremy then said that if he could not get a good settlement from me, he would be willing to appeal to the Chancellor. I wasn't impressed with this attempt to bully me, and was confident that George Osborne would feel obliged to support me. After all, the demand for these cuts had originated from the Conservative Party. However, we were quibbling about £10 million or £20 million, and we were already well on track to deliver our overall savings. I decided to agree a final figure that was lower than the minimum amount I wanted, but on the strict condition that Jeremy Hunt would have to deliver the full cuts in the next, far more serious, spending round that was to come.

Vince Cable was also surprisingly difficult. He had been our Treasury spokesman until May 2010, and at that time he had been very 'gung-ho' for cuts. He had even been advocating the complete closure of the Business Department, which he had now taken over. But by the time he came to see me at the Treasury, he seemed to have gone native overnight.

The Business Department was too large to claim that it was too small for its cuts to matter. So Vince had clearly been briefed with another line by his department. Vince claimed that all the possible savings in the Business Department had already been made, under the outgoing Labour government, and that he couldn't possibly deliver anything like the scale of savings needed.

I didn't buy the argument and pointed out where I thought cuts could be made without creating problems. There was a stand-off and I refused to give way.

Eventually, the Business Department offered up a small number of cuts, including a proposal to terminate a grant made by the last government to a Sheffield business called Forgemasters. I was rather surprised by the specificity of the cut, and was suspicious that by proposing a cut in the backyard of the Sheffield constituency of the Liberal Democrat leader, the Business Department was trying to offer up cuts that it felt could not be politically accepted.

I rejected the Forgemasters cut as an item for the £6 billion of savings, and said it needed to be swept up into a wider review of projects approved and grants made at the end of the last period of Labour government. I also hoped that this would give a chance for a sensible discussion about both the economics and the politics of this proposed cut.

Eventually, and rather grumpily, Vince Cable settled with me at a figure above my minimum level. In return, I agreed that some £500 million of the £6.25 billion of savings that we eventually made could be used to fund priorities such as business rates relief, new investment in further education colleges, extra apprenticeships and more investment in social housing – much of which benefited Vince's own department.

That left only the Home Secretary to settle with. To my surprise, Theresa May insisted on coming to see me in my department. We fenced over the figures. Eventually, the Home Office was forced to accept my minimum offer at 11 p.m. on Friday 21 May – one hour before my midnight deadline.

The Chancellor and I were delighted. We had exceeded the £6 billion cuts target by £250 million, and had settled with colleagues over two days before the date we had fixed for the announcement.

The announcement of these first steps towards returning the UK budget to balance was made jointly by George Osborne and me in the Treasury courtyard on a beautiful, sunny spring day. The UK and indeed world media were seated in front of us, and Treasury officials leaned out of windows around the court-yard to watch the spectacle. Two rostrums had been erected against the wall of one side of the courtyard, and the Chancellor and I spoke from these.

George Osborne made some opening comments and I then set out the details of the cuts. I made clear that we could not go on as a government increasing borrowing at the rate of £3 billion per week, and we were taking the first steps to restore order to the public finances.

It was a decisive display of unity by the new government and helped to boost confidence in the financial markets that the coalition would deliver.

But I also made clear that the new coalition government would 'cut with care'. The Liberal Democrat presence in the government would ensure that areas such as education would not face the axe, while low-paid public sector workers were to be exempt from the civil service pay freeze. It was a crucial part of the Liberal Democrat role, to ensure that the burdens of austerity did not fall on those in society with the lowest incomes. That was a crucial issue for me and for our party. I saw myself as the Liberal Democrat representative to the Treasury, not the Treasury's representative to my party.

I was also able to announce the money for 40,000 more apprenticeship starts, more social housing starts and an investment pot for the run-down colleges' estate.

The financial markets were content. The Liberal Democrats were content. And our coalition colleagues were happy too. It was a good start. Two days later, I was called to the House of Commons to set out the results of the Spending Review. Our case was an easy one to make, while Labour MPs found it difficult to pick holes in our strategy or to claim that the cuts were in any way regressive.

I had then earmarked the rest of the week to start preparing for the Emergency Budget, which had now been announced for 22 June. The Emergency Budget would set out plans for government spending, taxation and borrowing from 2011 right through to the end of the parliament. I had decided to complete my own fast-track assessment of the spending plans of all departments ahead of this.

I wanted to make sure that the Liberal Democrat side of the coalition would not have to agree to a total envelope for public spending until we had established whether or not this could be delivered within the constraints of the overall commitments both parties had made. I was particularly keen to ensure that there would be adequate funding for important pledges such as the £2.5 billion pupil premium, the guarantee on NHS funding, and the target of meeting the UN objective of spending 0.7 per cent of gross national product on overseas aid.

So I set about holding detailed meetings with all the spending teams in the Treasury to seek to establish what savings could be made at acceptable political, economic and social cost.

Separately, I met in 11 Downing Street on Thursday 27 May with George Osborne and his senior advisers and Treasury civil servants to sketch out the broad parameters of the forthcoming Budget. We discussed for the first time the possibility of raising value added tax from 17.5 per cent to 20 per cent. George Osborne also revealed that he had just held a private dinner with Ruth Kelly, the former Labour minister. She had suggested that the respected Labour peer and leading Blairite John Hutton might be willing to chair a commission to reform public sector pensions. That certainly appealed to George Osborne's sense of political mischief.

I promised to complete over the upcoming bank holiday weekend a report to the Chancellor on possible public spending savings, for him to take away and read on his forthcoming visit to the Far East.

But the next day, Friday 28 May, was to be a day in my Yeovil constituency. I finished work late on Thursday evening in the Treasury and said good night to my private secretary. I was already loving my job and looking forward to spending Sunday and Monday preparing my Spending Review paper.

I shut the door of my Treasury Office on Thursday night to head for home. I did not know that the next time I would return to this office, it would be to practise my resignation statement.

RESIGNATION

MAY 2010

O n Friday 28 May, I drove back down from London to my Yeovil constituency. I had a day full of engagements, as well as two scheduled
advice centres for constituents.

On the way down to Somerset, my mind was buzzing with thoughts about
how to handle my upcoming review of departmental budgets.

I was due to see the editor and chief reporter of one of the local newspapers, the *Western Gazette*, in my constituency office, at around 11 a.m.

About fifteen minutes before this meeting, I was contacted by the Treasury
press office. They said that they had been approached by the *Daily Telegraph*
with a story about my private life and my parliamentary expenses. They were
forwarding it to me, they said, and would need a response.

For all my life, I had chosen to keep my sexuality private, from my family,
friends and colleagues. But I was in a relationship, with another man, and
I had chosen to keep this secret. Given the way the parliamentary allowances
system operated, it would have been hugely in my financial interest to be
open about this relationship, but I had never wanted to reveal this aspect
of my life. There seemed no good moment to come out, and there seemed
many good reasons to put off difficult and uncomfortable conversations.

In trying to keep my relationship a secret, I put myself in a position where
I could be seen to be in breach of a recent rule which meant that MPs could
no longer pay rent to family or 'partners'; a rule that had not existed when
I first entered the Commons. But I had not considered us to be 'partners',

and as the effect of my actions was to reduce my claims upon the taxpayer, I did not consider it at the time to be wrong.

But now I was faced with either denying that I was in a relationship, which would not be true, or admitting that I was, in which case I might be under huge pressure to resign.

Not only did I have these considerations to deal with, but I realised that within twenty-four hours I would have to tell all my family, my friends and my close colleagues something of huge sensitivity about myself that I had chosen to hide for forty-five years.

I knew that I could just about deal with revelations about my private life, and I could account for my decisions about my parliamentary allowances. What I could not cope with was dealing with both issues in one go. And as I was now the person charged with making potentially painful cuts in public spending, I knew that I could not have the authority to do this while awaiting the results of an inquiry by the parliamentary ombudsman, to whom I would refer myself, which usually lasted many months.

Two minutes after I'd absorbed this news, the editor and chief reporter of the *Western Gazette* turned up to interview me in my offices about my 'exciting and challenging new job in the heart of government'. For forty-five minutes, I did my best to retain my composure and answer the questions. I knew that by the time the interview came to be printed in this weekly publication, most of the contents of the discussion would be out of date and irrelevant. The story about me would be a very different one.

After that was a horrible thirty-six hours – breaking the news to James, my mother, my family, and my closest friends; endless phone calls with Paddy Ashdown and Nick Clegg, both of whom were magnificently supportive; discussions with my local constituency staff and constituency chairman; and, finally, taking the very personal decision to resign from the job that I cherished.

Jane Ashdown was kind enough to look after me at the Ashdowns' house in Norton sub Hamdon – my car tucked around the side of the houses, out of press view.

Nick Clegg, Paddy Ashdown, and the Prime Minister were all very supportive and tried to persuade me to stay. But you expect that from friends and colleagues. When you are a politician in this type of circumstance, you owe it to everyone else to accept the responsibility to determine, yourself, whether to stay or go.

I was sure that it was in my personal and family interest for me to resign, and I never doubted that this was in the government's best interest too.

By the end of Friday, I was determined on resignation. On Saturday, Nick Clegg and Paddy Ashdown made further attempts to change my mind, but my view was now settled. Poor Nick and Miriam Clegg were supposed to be enjoying a relaxing weekend in Paris with their family – their first break for many months. Nick had to get back on the train and come back to London.

It was decided that my resignation should be on camera, and not just be a statement to the press.

On Saturday afternoon, 29 May, I left Somerset in my car. My constituency chairman, the formidable and loyal Cathy Bakewell, drove. Nick Clegg's then press chief, Jonny Oates, joined us to field media calls.

As we made the three-hour car journey to London, I received many kind text messages from colleagues, urging me to continue. I was particularly touched to receive messages from Conservatives such as my next-door MP, the Cabinet Office minister Oliver Letwin.

Halfway to London, we suddenly realised that if I was going to resign, I had to let the Prime Minister know, and not only Nick Clegg.

We pulled in to a service station off the A303, just after Stonehenge, and from there I made the call. David Cameron was at Chequers. It was a short conversation and I made clear that my decision was not reversible. I had joined the government in the Cabinet Room of No. 10. I left it on a mobile phone outside a petrol station in Wiltshire.

We stopped in Kennington, near Paddy Ashdown's house. There we were met by a car and driver from the government car service. As Chief Secretary, I had just signed off on a deeply unpopular (with the drivers!) cut of one third in the budget for this service. I had also rejected the chauffeur-driven Jaguar used by my predecessors as Chief Secretary. I must have been rather unpopular with the drivers, who relied on this spending for their livelihoods, but if my driver this day felt any sense of pleasure, he didn't show it.

Jonny Oates and I were driven across the river towards Westminster. As we entered the Treasury courtyard, we were met by a private secretary from my office and Sean Kemp, a Liberal Democrat press officer, who was hugely supportive and perhaps a little emotional.

As it was a Saturday, the Treasury was empty. We went up to my office on the second floor, and I was left for ten minutes to practise my resignation statement, which I had written by hand on two sheets of A4 paper.

Jonny insisted on me reading through the resignation statement in front of him, to test my resilience. Then Sean came in: 'They're ready for you now.'

On my desk, I left a short note of good wishes for my Liberal Democrat successor. I also left a gift given to me by my local constituency party just after the general election, when I had taken on the role of Chief Secretary. It was a knife, with a gold Liberal Democrat election rosette on it. 'It is a reminder that when you are cutting, you must cut with care and while remembering what principles our party stands for,' I was told when it was presented to me.

I read out my resignation statement in a large, modern, characterless room on the ground floor of the Treasury. There was only a television camera, with a crew of two people hovering behind it. We said nothing to each other, and we did it in one take. It did not take long to read the few paragraphs, and I completed it without stumbling, but while looking exhausted and emotionally drained.

Then I was led back to the Treasury courtyard, where I thanked Jonny Oates and Sean Kemp for their support. The private secretary who was with us gave me a brief hug, and whispered, 'Don't worry, you'll be back.'

The black government car service vehicle I had arrived in thirty minutes before was no longer in the Treasury courtyard. Instead, a taxi was waiting for me. There could hardly be a clearer signal that my resignation had now taken effect. I got into the back of the cab and we drove out of the Treasury. I had been in government for just eighteen days. Now the coalition I had helped form would continue without me.

A New
Chief Secretary

It was autumn of 2010, and I was sitting in Michael Gove's office in the Department for Education – out of office, but still 'in the loop'.

Michael Gove leaned back in his seat: 'I must say that Danny Alexander is doing an absolutely brilliant job as Chief Secretary isn't he? I think he is carrying the Laws flame aloft in the Treasury. I think of him as Luke Skywalker to your Obi-Wan Kenobi.'

I smiled and nodded, not sure whether this was all a good thing or not. In life, one doesn't always welcome hearing what a brilliant job your successor is doing, and in any case I couldn't remember who Obi-Wan Kenobi was, and had rather mixed the Jedi master up with the small astromech droid, R2-D2. As a consequence, I was struggling to see the relevance of the Education Secretary's comparison.

But in the few months since my resignation, the new Chief Secretary had certainly settled in well.

During the car journey to London on 29 May to make my resignation statement, Nick Clegg had called through for a final discussion before my announcement. 'I have been thinking who might replace me,' I said. 'I think Vince should probably stay at Business, and I guess he would want to. But both Ed Davey and Chris Huhne are very economically literate. Either of them would do a great job as Chief Secretary.'

There was a pause. Then Nick Clegg said, 'They would be good. But I have already thought about it, and I am going to switch Danny Alexander to the Treasury and put Mike Moore in as Scottish Secretary.'

I was surprised, for a moment, by this decision. Danny Alexander was very young and had limited experience of economic policy. I had not considered him to be the most obvious choice to be Chief Secretary. But I could immediately see the reasons why Nick had made this decision. Danny was Nick's chief of staff. He was highly trusted, extremely hard working, competent and reliable. He had written our manifesto. He had led our coalition talks. He was already at the centre of government. He knew and got on well with George Osborne.

And Danny was very easy to underestimate. He had come in as a new MP in 2005 and in my mind at the time he was likely to be a middle-rank member of our shadow team. His CV – as a national parks press officer and campaigner for entry into the euro – did not seem as strong as that of many of the new generation of 'Orange Book Liberals'.

But I soon realised that Danny was very, very ambitious; very, very, bright; and capable of robust, independent thought. There was nothing mediocre about him at all. And within a year of being elected, he told me that one day he intended to be leader. I could see that he was deadly serious.

Danny was in fact the obvious choice as Chief Secretary because of his own abilities and his character. It would also have been very difficult for coalition working if the new Chief Secretary had been either Vince Cable, the 'sage of Twickenham', who might easily overshadow George Osborne, or Chris Huhne, the sharp-elbowed Energy Secretary and former economic journalist, who was not overburdened by modesty and who would also undoubtedly be a challenging colleague to deal with.

I did my best to brief Danny Alexander over the phone on the work I had been doing. In his first days he had to deal with media questions about his tax affairs, and with cynical journalists who questioned whether this young, tall, ginger-haired, slightly geeky young man could really hold down one of the toughest jobs in politics.

Danny knew that he had to prove himself quickly. He immersed himself in the work of the Treasury and soon showed his officials that he would be a highly effective replacement. He worked the longest hours that he had ever worked in his life – on many occasions from 6 a.m. to 1 a.m.

The Emergency Budget was scheduled for late June, and the new Chief Secretary had to work on it with the Chancellor. As Danny Alexander was not only Chief Secretary but the sole Liberal Democrat in the Treasury, he had to be consulted not just on spending issues but on the whole tax, spending and borrowing strategy. However, most of the June Emergency Budget decisions had in fact already been taken in the first couple of weeks in government, when I was in the Treasury. These included decisions to raise more money from capital gains tax, and to increase value added tax from 17.5 per cent to 20 per cent.

Danny Alexander also had to oversee the review of grant decisions made by the previous Labour government at the end of its term in office, including a decision to axe a grant to Sheffield Forgemasters, the heavy engineering firm located just outside Nick Clegg's own constituency. It was not, of course, the job of the Treasury to reject cuts offered by departments. Neither Danny nor Nick wanted to be seen to interfere in a budget decision for political reasons. So when the Business Department recommended termination, the axe came down on the Forgemasters grant. In retrospect, it seems naive to have cut funding to such a major business on the doorstep of the Deputy Prime Minister, in the heart of a Labour-controlled city, within weeks of the coalition being formed.

It helped that Danny Alexander and George Osborne got on so well. They liked and respected each other and had a similar sense of humour. When the time came to agree the June Budget, it seemed obvious for the Conservative Prime Minister and Chancellor to meet with the Liberal Democrat Deputy Prime Minister and Chief Secretary to approve the package of measures. The civil service were used to labelling meetings between two senior ministers 'bilaterals'. With four senior ministers present, the Budget meeting was noted in the diary as a 'Quadrilateral'. And so was born the 'Quad' of four top coalition Cabinet colleagues, who met effectively as an inner Cabinet on a regular basis for the rest of the parliament, and who took many of the key decisions on the work of the government.

Lower-profile, but perhaps even more important, were the regular weekly bilateral meetings between Nick Clegg and David Cameron, which took place in the Prime Minister's small Downing Street office. These new, semi-formal mechanisms completely displaced the need for any formal 'coalition committee', as either the Quad or the bilaterals resolved all matters of dispute that could not be sorted out at a lower level, for example between Oliver Letwin and me in the last three years of government.

After the Chancellor's Emergency Budget in June, which set the borrowing, spending and tax framework for the next three years, Danny Alexander now had to carry out the first full-scale, multi-year Spending Review. This was the moment I had been starting to prepare for just before I left the government.

Our decision to occupy the Chief Secretary's post now came into its own. Danny was not only able to veto the proposed Conservative cuts that we did not support, but he was able to ensure that Liberal Democrat priorities such as the pupil premium were fully funded. To my delight, Nick Clegg and Danny Alexander ensured that there would be a pupil premium introduced in 2011, which would rise from £625 million in this first year to the promised £2.5 billion by the end of the parliament. This would not be carved out of general schools funding, but would be on top of a guarantee to protect spending for each pupil in cash terms.

Had the Liberal Democrats not been in government, it is unlikely that there would have been a pupil premium of any significance, and the Conservatives would have cut real schools spending by around 10–15 per cent over the parliament, which we were able to reject. Instead of a cash freeze in the schools budget under the Conservatives, there was now modest real growth under the coalition.

Nick Clegg played a key role in insisting that the schools budget should be protected in real terms and that the pupil premium should amount to the full £2.5 billion that had been promised in the Liberal Democrat manifesto as one of our four flagship pledges. Indeed, it was Nick Clegg who telephoned Michael Gove, the Education Secretary, to give him the good news about his budget settlement – at a time when the Deputy Prime Minister and Michael were still working well together.

Nick Clegg played one other crucial role in this first Spending Review – insisting on a proper, long-term, funding settlement for the BBC. Senior Conservatives were considering putting the BBC on a short leash, with one- or two-year budget settlements and deep cuts in areas such as the World Service. After the Liberal Democrat leader's personal intervention, the BBC was granted a healthy and long-term budget settlement.

Of course, most of the Spending Review negotiations involved tough decisions, not extra spending. Danny Alexander agreed large cuts to the Local Government Department and to the Department for the Environment, Food and Rural Affairs. William Hague, at the Foreign Office, was able to strike a deal directly with George Osborne – the only Cabinet minister given this privilege as of right. As a consequence, Treasury officials felt that the Foreign Office got off rather lightly – a fact confirmed by their subsequent opening of a swathe of new embassies and consulates. The Foreign Office would have fared rather worse if its budget had been left to the decisions of a Liberal Democrat Chief Secretary.

Ken Clarke, the Justice Secretary, who had been the first to agree the in-year cuts to his department with me, now took a tougher line. He warned of prison riots if he was required to deliver the cuts requested by the Treasury, and insisted on taking his appeal to the Prime Minister and Chancellor. Ken eventually settled with George Osborne, but as it was all completed rather informally, the record of what had been agreed was a little vague. The Chief Secretary's office had to argue the settlement out with the Ministry of Justice for months to come.

The generals and admirals at the Ministry of Defence fought hard for their budget and tried to threaten and bully the Chancellor and Prime Minister into making concessions. Ultimately, the Ministry of Defence settlement was probably one that both sides were pleased with – it involved a much smaller cut than requested by the Treasury, but delivered material savings all the same.

Jeremy Hunt at Culture, Media and Sport, in spite of the undertakings made to me in May, rolled out the usual arguments about small savings leading to a large amount of political noise. 'Cultural' figures were mobilised to make a fuss, but eventually the Treasury took a large slice out of the budget anyway. It probably should have been more.

At the Department of Energy and Climate Change, Chris Huhne was rather difficult. At the best of times, he was a person who would cross the political street for a good row. He eventually settled, and secured a good deal for his department – not least because green issues were a Liberal Democrat priority.

Theresa May, the Home Secretary, was a tough negotiator and fought her own corner with some determination. But she was a straightforward person to deal with, and Danny Alexander came to like and respect her: 'She is tough, but she will listen and respond,' was the Chief Secretary's view.

Vince Cable, in the Business Department, was now becoming the toughest, and from a Treasury perspective, most awkward, Cabinet minister in government. He was conscious that the Treasury considered his science budget to be important for economic growth, as did he. So it was clear that science could yield only modest savings. The Business Secretary was also a passionate advocate of vocational education and adult education, in the face of Conservative indifference and Treasury scepticism about value for money. Vince saw himself as the guardian of this budget line against the 'barbarism and snobbery' of the Treasury and the Conservatives.

But once these areas of the business budget were relatively well protected, there was only one budget line left that could possibly yield the massive savings required to meet the Treasury's demands for cuts. That budget line was for higher education. And with the Browne Review into higher education finance now about to report, that was to put the issue of university tuition fees right into the political spotlight. It was not a happy tale.

Tuition Fees: A Tale of Two Errors

2010

It was 5.45 p.m. on 9 December 2010. The division lobbies of the House of Commons had finally been cleared of MPs.

The Commons Chamber was now packed, and after a heated five-hour debate, MPs and journalists were awaiting the results of the vote on the co-alition government's proposals to raise tuition fees to up to £9,000 per year.

Outside, in Parliament Square, students and other protestors chanted loudly and angrily, and a large police presence stood guard in front of the locked gates of the Palace of Westminster.

The four tellers who had counted the votes now lined up in a row in front of the Speaker, and MPs could immediately see that the government had won, because the tellers from the winning side take their position on the right as they face the Speaker.

There was a hush, and then the results of the vote were read out by the clerks, to subdued cheers from the government benches and cries of 'shame' from the opposition side.

The clerks passed the slip with the voting numbers on to the Speaker, who waited for silence and then read them out once more: 'The Ayes to the right – three hundred and twenty-three. The Noes to the left – three hundred and two. I think the Ayes have it, the Ayes have it. Unlock.'

There was a second vote, with a similarly thin government majority.

Meanwhile, journalists rushed to get the detailed breakdown of the voting figures. A handful of Conservative MPs had voted against the fees rise, but the real news was the division in the Liberal Democrat ranks. Only twenty-seven (twenty-eight, counting one Lib Dem 'teller') of the fifty-seven Lib Dem MPs had supported the coalition plan. Eight had abstained or been absent. But fully twenty-one had voted against their own party. In other words, the Lib Dems were split down the middle.

Many of the Liberal Democrat rebels were junior backbenchers – but not all of them. Two former party leaders, Sir Menzies Campbell and Charles Kennedy, voted against their own party. And Liberal Democrat president Simon Hughes had abstained. It was a serious split, and it made it almost impossible for the Lib Dems to present their actions on the key issue of tuition fees in an effective way to the public. If half of Lib Dem MPs could not support their party leadership, why should the country?

It was the biggest Liberal Democrat split of the parliament by far, and no other issue would be so often cited by voters and commentators throughout the parliament as evidence of how the Liberal Democrats had 'sold out' or broken trust. For Nick Clegg – a party leader who had promised 'no more broken political promises' – it proved to be a political disaster and an albatross forever hanging around his neck. No issue caused greater damage to the Liberal Democrats in the coalition government than university tuition fees. It was not only that we failed to deliver on two separate pledges – one to phase out tuition fees and another to prevent any further increases in fees. Worse still, the issue of tuition fees – badly managed by the party in and out of government – came to be seen as the 'proof' of betrayal by voters who were already unhappy to see the Liberal Democrats in coalition with the Conservatives on any terms. It became both an issue of 'trust', and a symbol of the 'betrayal' of coalition.

Had there not been the U-turn on tuition fees, many of the voters who cited this as a reason for no longer voting Liberal Democrat would still have found some other 'betrayal' to point to, in order to justify withdrawing their support. But because of the mismanagement of the tuition fees issue, the Liberal Democrats handed to our opponents and to our sceptics an enormous ready-made stick to beat us with. And they did.

It did not matter that the policy ultimately proved successful – protecting university budgets and enabling student numbers, including those from disadvantaged backgrounds, to rise.

How on earth, then, did the Liberal Democrats manage to get the substance so right, but the politics so disastrously wrong?

To understand what went wrong, we have to go back to the first introduction of fees for higher education. When governments introduce unpopular measures, this often seems to create wonderful political opportunities for opposition parties. Campaigns can be started. Petitions can be initiated. And votes can be won. But what can look like great political opportunities at the time can end up being political disasters in the long run.

Tuition fees were first introduced by the Blair government in 1998, at the rate of £1,000 per year. They were opposed at the time by both the Conservatives and the Liberal Democrats. Both parties promised to abolish the fees in their 2001 manifestos.

Liberal Democrats, not least in university constituencies, began to campaign on this issue to win votes. Many felt that education should always be free at the point of access and feared that tuition fees might deter students from poorer backgrounds.

In 2003, Labour under Tony Blair again broke a promise on tuition fees and voted through 'top-up fees' of around £3,000 per year. These had been explicitly ruled out by Labour in its 2001 general election manifesto.

At the time, Tony Blair was being advised by Andrew Adonis, a former Liberal Democrat, whom I knew well and who I had worked with when the issue of tuition fees was being considered by the first Scottish coalition government in 1999. Before a parliamentary debate and vote on tuition fees in 2003, Adonis sent me a copy of a speech he had written for the Prime Minister, justifying the higher level of fees. On the front page of the speech he wrote, 'After you have read this, and no doubt after the Commons vote, do let me know what aspects of this speech you actually disagree with.'

It was hardly surprising that tuition fees were unpopular with students. Costs that were previously socialised and paid by the taxpayer were now being borne by the students themselves.

But Tony Blair's speech had made a powerful – and, what is more, a progressive – case for tuition fees, not least as these were not now to be paid upfront, but only after graduation, as a 'tax' on income above a certain threshold.

Free tuition had been a huge public subsidy to the minority of students who were going to university, who were disproportionately from more affluent backgrounds. Free tuition was largely an irrelevance in terms of improving access to university, for two reasons. Firstly, all the data showed that it was a pupil's performance in the school system that determined who went on to university – and too many poor children were just not getting the qualifications in school to access higher education.

Secondly, since fees would now only be paid after graduation, and after a graduate's income passed a certain level, there was no reason to believe that poorer students should not be able to access university.

Tony Blair, Andrew Adonis, and many Labour ministers made a powerful case that if you wanted to create more social mobility, and improve access for lower-income students, you had to invest where it made a real difference – in school and indeed in the 'early years' of education.

Gordon Brown, then Chancellor, had seen the introduction of the unpopular top-up tuition fees as yet another way of destabilising Tony Blair. He and his close advisers maintained for a while that a 'graduate tax' would be fairer than tuition fees. However, when they looked at the operational difficulties of introducing such a tax, they decided that these were too intractable to overcome.

The Liberal Democrats, now under Charles Kennedy's leadership, went on opposing tuition fees. The further rise to £3,000, and the breach of Labour's manifesto pledges, made this a highly resonant political issue for many voters. The Liberal Democrat campaign for abolishing tuition fees may have helped us to win certain seats from Labour, particularly in university towns, though Labour's unpopularity over the Iraq invasion probably had a greater impact.

The Lib Dems again put the abolition of tuition fees into their 2005 manifesto. Meanwhile, the Conservatives dropped their opportunistic opposition to fees – indeed, most Conservative MPs privately saw fees as inevitable in a system where many more students were going on to university.

But by 2006/07 some Liberal Democrats were also questioning whether abolishing tuition fees should be our top expenditure commitment any more. It was already hugely expensive and was becoming more so. While some on the left of the party regarded 'free education' as an article of faith, others wondered whether this increasingly expensive and badly targeted policy could any longer be justified.

When Charles Kennedy stood down as leader in January 2006 over his problems with alcohol, the new leader, Sir Menzies Campbell, decided that we needed to consider extricating ourselves from the fees policy. He asked me to take over as the party's spokesman on Children, Schools and Families, where I began to develop in more detail the idea of introducing a pupil premium of up to £2.5 billion per year. This was designed to tackle the real cause of inequality in Britain – the massive educational gap between the outcomes for children from poor backgrounds and other children. The extra £2.5 billion would allow us to target more resources on the poorest 25 per cent of children, to give schools the resources they really needed to help these young people. By helping poor children to secure good qualifications at GCSE and A-level, we would then improve their access to higher education. This was undoubtedly the real route to social mobility.

Sir Ming also then asked the able young MP Stephen Williams to take over as universities spokesman. Stephen had himself grown up in a poor family, and at school he had been on free school meals. He was passionate about social mobility, and like me he knew that the key to this was in schools and the early years, not in free tuition for children from middle-class families.

Stephen had been elected in the university seat of Bristol West, and a more risk-averse MP in such a position would have stayed well clear of the poisoned chalice of having to get our party off its tuition fees hook. But, in spite of this, Stephen determined to take on the challenge. It was a very brave thing to do, but Stephen considered that it was both right and electorally possible. In his own constituency, he judged that the party's policy on Iraq was of far more importance to his success in 2005 than our policy on tuition fees.

When Nick Clegg took over as leader, he also gave his backing to Stephen to change our policy on fees. But then the problems began. To change our stance, we needed to get a party policy working group to agree to it. We then had to get the policy through the elected Federal Policy Committee, and then through party conference, where it would be voted on.

The policy working group wasn't united on the issue, but Stephen was confident that he could deliver a majority for dropping the pledge. In place of this, Stephen wanted extra help for student maintenance and a much fairer deal for part-time students. That made good sense to me.

Meanwhile, the forces of opposition began to mobilise. The so-called left in the party had decided that free tuition should be a rallying point for those who feared that the Lib Dems might be moving too much to the liberal right. Bizarrely, in my view, these people somehow considered subsidies for generally more affluent students to be more important than, for example, investing in the early years and in schools. In 2008, a number of party members stood for the Federal Policy Committee on a 'keep our fees policy' ticket. And they were elected. Joining this group were some MPs in university towns, who had been elected on this platform and who feared the electoral consequence of a change. One such MP even threatened to resign and cause a by-election if our policy changed. And, of course, our campaigns department liked the nice, simple 'free tuition' position, and also argued that this should be retained.

Nick Clegg could see the need to change the fees policy, not least as the UK and world economy hit the buffers in 2007/08 and public borrowing soared. But he was already fighting on a number of fronts to secure sensible policy positions for our 2010 manifesto – ensuring that tax policy focused on increasing the tax-free allowance, and making sure the party confronted the need for public spending cuts.

Nick Clegg sought to get other senior colleagues on side to change the tuition fees policy, but many were ambiguous at best about change. Vince Cable, our Treasury spokesman, wanted to retain free tuition, but only for students with excellent A-level grades. I regarded this policy as eccentric at best, since it would focus student subsidies overwhelmingly on children from the most affluent backgrounds.

Chris Huhne and Ed Davey were also consulted. Both could see the need for change in the party position, but both judged that it might prove politically impossible. The majority view at the top was that trying to change the tuition fees policy would anger many MPs and voters, and quite possibly cause a huge row at party conference, where it was judged that the vote would be lost. Chris Huhne and others argued that it might be better to maintain the existing policy until the government review set up under Lord Browne in 2010 had reported, after the election. This review was widely expected to push for higher fees – something which, it was argued, would make our current position unaffordable, and which would therefore make it easier to seek a change in policy.

Nick Clegg eventually considered the issue carefully with his key advisers, including those whose role was to take the temperature amongst the party activists who attend conference. 'This cannot be won,' he was told. 'The opposition is just too great. We will end up with a massive row, just a year or so before the general election, and the party conference will then insist on keeping a policy that the leadership has tried but failed to dump. It will be a disaster. And the problem is that Stephen Williams has come up with a very rational policy alternative on part-time students and maintenance, but this is not a position that is simple to communicate, and it isn't winning the waverers over.'

The upshot was that Stephen eventually put to the Federal Policy Committee something of a policy fudge. The final Liberal Democrat policy working group paper argued for an eventual goal of abolishing fees, but it also drew attention to the costs of this objective. It proposed a mildly watered-down version of abolishing tuition fees, in which there would be a means-tested fee bursary system for both full-time and part-time students. Students from the most well-off families would still – for the time being – be obliged to pay full fees.

Being a complex compromise, it satisfied no one. The Federal Policy Committee discussed this draft paper in December 2008, and they struck out four whole sections – maintaining, therefore, the free fees policy. This policy was then endorsed by the spring party conference in 2009. It was the first, massive, error on tuition fees. But it was not the last.

Stephen Williams had worked hard for two years for a better solution than this, and he was massively disappointed. He considered resigning as universities spokesman. Had he done so, I had decided that I would also resign, because at the time I was the Liberal Democrat team leader for all the public services departments, and I had strongly supported his approach.

Stephen was persuaded to stay in post, not least to secure some of the other excellent and progressive policies contained within his paper. But we were not in a good position. Our MPs and leadership team were deeply split on whether the tuition fees policy was either sensible or affordable.

Before the general election in May 2010, Nick Clegg, Danny Alexander and Vince Cable decided to make one further attempt to ensure that the party line was more realistic. They went to meetings of the Federal Policy Committee and managed to persuade the committee that instead of committing to abolish fees in one parliament, these should be phased out over two parliaments – over six years.

The committee eventually accepted that there was a huge fiscal hole and that there was a need for some spending discipline. They therefore agreed this change.

So, this was the position that it was agreed to put into our manifesto – phasing out tuition fees over six years. It was better than promising the complete, immediate, abolition of tuition fees. But it was nonetheless a big mistake. The policy may have been popular with students, but it was not sensible or sustainable – and it had precious little to do with social justice.

Meanwhile, the National Union of Students created a further potential headache for our party. Knowing that the Labour government had established the Browne Review of higher education, in order to make the case for even higher tuition fees after the general election, they approached Liberal Democrat MPs and parliamentary candidates, asking us to sign a petition that called for a softer version of our policy – not scrapping fees, but voting against any increase.

The petition asked candidates to pledge not to vote for any rise in fees, and instead to commit themselves to looking for a 'fairer alternative'.

In no time at all, our MPs were merrily signing this petition. Unenthusiastic about the policy, I ignored three requests to my office to sign it, over a three-month period. I had also decided that no mention of tuition fees should appear in my own local election literature.

Eventually, it was pointed out to me by the NUS that I was the only Liberal Democrat MP not to sign the petition. As education spokesman, I was asked how I could explain this. Frustrated by my colleagues, but also keen that this should not become an embarrassing pre-election story, I decided that I had to sign the petition.

When our manifesto had been put together by Danny Alexander and his team, I had argued strongly that investment in the £2.5 billion pupil premium should be our number one education investment. I was convinced that this was the policy most likely to extend real opportunities to young people from disadvantaged backgrounds.

Nick Clegg and Danny both saw the logic of this position. Vince Cable, then our Treasury spokesman, was more difficult about the pupil premium pledge – he saw it as too expensive and he did not like the idea of guaranteeing that this would be extra money, as opposed to being recycled from the rest of the education budget. I insisted that the education budget should be fully protected from inflation, so that the pupil premium really could make a difference. In late 2009 and early 2010 there was something of a stand-off, and eventually I made clear that I was not prepared to remain as schools spokesman unless I got my way. Nick Clegg gave me full backing, and the manifesto was now changed to give me the cast-iron pledge I wanted.

Our manifesto was now drawn up to set out four key pledges that we would commit to deliver if we had influence in the next parliament. Those four pledges included a higher tax-free personal allowance of £10,000; a £2.5 billion pupil premium; sorting out the economic mess and investing in a green economy (really two policy points, glued into one); and political reform (including a fairer voting system).

That these were our priorities was no secret. They were set out on the front page of our manifesto and heavily briefed to the media.

By now Nick Clegg had also established the group of four MPs to consider our negotiating position in the event of a hung parliament – Danny Alexander, Chris Huhne, Andrew Stunell and me.

Our final report was produced in March 2010 and presented to Nick Clegg. This report confirmed our four key policy priorities. Tuition fees weren't listed as a priority; however, the issue was covered in a more detailed section of the paper on education. The pledge to scrap fees over two parliaments was referenced, and there was the following commentary:

> Tuition Fees: We are ideologically isolated on this issue, so unlikely to be able to secure an agreement. The sole exception is on the position for part-time students, where parity of treatment is a fair principle whatever the system of student finance you adopt … On tuition fees we should seek agreement on part-time students and leave the rest. We will have clear yellow water with others on raising the tuition fee cap, so let us not cause ourselves more headaches.

In other words, the coalition negotiation team concluded that we should not prioritise the policy of phasing out tuition fees in the election campaign or in coalition negotiations – because we were unlikely to be able to achieve this. But the underlying assumption was still that we would resist raising the tuition fee cap. We maintained our position on our four key pledges throughout the election campaign.

During the coalition talks in early May 2010, the issue of tuition fees came up, as it was bound to do. The Conservatives were pledged to await the Browne Review conclusions, due in a few months' time.

It was clear that no position in the coalition agreement could easily reconcile our different views, and so we decided to 'park' the issue until the Browne Review had reported. We set out in the coalition agreement six principles against which to judge Lord Browne's proposals, including their impact on the participation rate of disadvantaged students, and on student debt. The six principles offered us plenty of 'wiggle room'. We then provided for a specific opt-out for Lib Dem MPs: 'If the response of the government to Lord Browne's report is one that Liberal Democrats cannot accept, then arrangements will be made to enable Liberal Democrat MPs to abstain in any vote.'

This wording was agreed before it had been decided that the Business Secretary, who would lead on this policy area, would be our own Vince Cable.

Some people have questioned whether the negotiating team were tough enough in the wording that we secured. This misses the point. We actually conceded nothing. 'The response of the government to Lord Browne' did not mean the response of the Conservatives. By entering a coalition, we were becoming the government ourselves, and no government policy could be fixed without Liberal Democrat agreement. This was even more the case once Vince Cable became the Secretary of State in charge of the policy.

There was nothing wrong with the lines negotiated into the coalition agreement. It was our next steps that were deeply flawed.

In May 2010, the Browne Committee was close to having completed its report. There were soon leaks of its expected proposals to put up tuition fees – possibly to remove the cap on them altogether.

Vince Cable was under a great deal of pressure from the Treasury to find savings for the Spending Review that was taking place. He was strongly committed to protecting the further education and training budgets, and was worried that for the Conservatives these were considered low priority and 'not the things our supporters rely on'. Vince Cable and George Osborne were also both keen to protect the science budget. These decisions effectively meant that big savings needed to be found in higher education. Either universities had to slash student numbers and cut their research budgets, or students would have to pay more.

Danny Alexander was by now Chief Secretary, and his major focus was on delivering the cuts to public spending. Vince was already proving to be a difficult proposition for the Treasury in delivering the required cuts, so they felt they needed to keep up the pressure on him to deliver.

Nick Clegg was, of course, immersed in a multiplicity of issues across government, including handling the economic strategy, the emerging and controversial NHS Bill, and the beginning of the campaign for the Alternative Vote referendum. In the early summer, Nick and Danny were planning on the basis that Vince Cable would devise a graduate tax-type policy, which would involve abolishing the existing tuition fees, while raising more money from students after they had graduated.

Other senior ministers such as Chris Huhne were now immersed in the details of their own departments. Early in the coalition, the general mindset was one of finding the best solutions in the national interest, rather than promoting each party's own interests. Both the Liberal Democrats and the Conservatives had already, as a consequence of going into coalition, had to change their policies in a number of areas. The Conservatives, for example, had dumped their high-profile pledge to slash inheritance tax for the rich. The Lib Dems had accepted the need to make modest in-year public spending cuts in 2015. In neither case had a public narrative of 'betrayal' secured much traction. This lulled the Liberal Democrat leadership into a false sense of security.

However, after going into coalition, the Liberal Democrat poll ratings had plunged. Many Lib Dems were horrified to find their party in government with their most prominent political opponents. Other voters, who had supported the Liberal Democrats as some sort of 'protest' vote, suddenly found that they were supporting a party of hard choices in government.

Vince Cable's initial thought was that he should avoid a rise in tuition fees but accept a graduate tax instead. He floated this idea in a speech to the South Bank University in July 2010 and his speech was welcomed by the National Union of Students. A graduate tax was more popular with the public than the alternative of increasing tuition fees – though it had never been Liberal Democrat policy.

The assumption in Nick Clegg's office, and the view of Danny Alexander, was that the Business Department would now come forward with a 'graduate tax' that raised more money for higher education while moving away from anything which looked like the existing tuition fees system. This would, arguably, help to get us off a very big political hook.

The problem was that Vince Cable had trailed the idea of a graduate tax without properly working through the detail. By the time he did, he realised that the graduate tax had many potential weaknesses. What if UK students went abroad after graduation? Would they then escape paying? How would money be recouped from foreign students, who were coming to the UK in growing numbers? Would the money raised from a graduate tax really be passed on to universities, or would it be top-sliced by the voracious Treasury? How would a graduate tax differentiate between very expensive courses at top universities, and shorter, cheaper courses at less prestigious universities? Vince Cable's officials in the Business Department and universities minister David Willetts pushed back strongly against the graduate tax proposal, as did Lord Browne.

By October, Vince was having to execute an untidy U-turn, and he now publicly ruled out a graduate tax. It was all beginning to get very messy politically, and our own MPs were concerned. Former leaders such as Charles Kennedy and Sir Menzies Campbell were threatening to vote against any rise in fees.

With the benefit of hindsight, it is clear that this was the moment when Vince Cable, Danny Alexander, Nick Clegg, Chris Huhne, senior advisers and I should have met and thrashed out both the economics and the politics of the issue.

With a divided party and plunging poll ratings, this was the moment to decide to veto any rise in fees. There would still, as a consequence, be clear yellow water with the other parties, even though we would not be able to force the abolition of fees.

The problem, however, was in part that the policy Lord Browne had devised was far better than our existing policy. It had been designed to be more progressive than the existing tuition fee system, to require lower upfront contributions from graduates (by raising the repayment threshold), to wipe out the fees after a period of time for lower earners, and to protect university finances. It was very good policy. It was just very rotten politics for a party that had pledged both to phase out fees and to prevent them from rising.

But the conclusion of the Spending Review was now bearing down fast. Vince Cable had to deliver his cuts. Danny Alexander had to deliver the overall public spending discipline. Nick Clegg felt that we had designed a policy to meet precisely the principles set out in the coalition agreement. The assumption at the top of the party in government was that we were going to have to accept some alternative to continuing with the existing system – an alternative that raised more money. So, while the alternative options for raising money were considered in great detail, along with the challenge of party and media management, there was little or no serious discussion over whether to veto altogether a plan to extract more money from students.

In the inner circle, only a few spoke out. Nick Clegg's press secretary, James McGrory, questioned on a couple of occasions whether it was politically sensible to allow any rise in fees. 'Look,' he said, 'isn't this going to be impossible to sell, however much better the new policy is, given what we said in opposition?'

I was concerned, meanwhile, about the huge scale of the fee rise being considered. Vince Cable had rejected completely uncapping tuition fees, but there was now a proposal to allow them to rise to as high as £9,000 in some 'elite' institutions. I considered that a rise to £6,000 would already be quite high enough, and I favoured a new cap at this level. But no Lib Dem Cabinet minister made a case for sticking with the existing £3,000 fee level.

The closer we got to the vote, the more politically chaotic things became. Many Liberal Democrat MPs were threatening to vote down their Secretary of State's own package. Vince Cable's private view was that as Secretary of State he would look ludicrous if he were to abstain on his own policy package. He made clear to Nick Clegg that he believed he needed to vote for it in the House of Commons. But the Business Secretary also publicly floated the notion that he might abstain on his own proposals if other Liberal Democrat MPs would abstain too. The parliamentary party began to split down the middle. Many doubters were determined to vote against the fee increase. Some were willing to abstain. Others wanted to support the new system. 'I've never abstained on anything in my life. I'm not starting now. I support Vince 100 per cent. It's a good system he's proposing,' said Gordon Birtwhistle, the straight-talking Burnley MP, at one of the last meetings of our parliamentary party before the key votes.

A number of junior Liberal Democrat MPs were now considering resigning from their unpaid posts as parliamentary private secretaries. On 6 December, days before the vote in Parliament, the *World at One* radio programme excitedly proclaimed that they had an exclusive interview with Edinburgh West Liberal Democrat MP Mike Crockart, who was said to be considering resigning as a PPS. 'Mr Crockart, are you going to resign?' the breathless interviewer asked. On a rather poor mobile phone line, viewers heard

'Mr Crockart' confirm that 'yes', he was indeed thinking of resigning. 'I will be voting 100 per cent against,' he said.

It later turned out that this was not, in fact, Liberal Democrat MP Mike Crockart at all. In fact, the BBC had the wrong mobile phone number for Mr Crockart and kept phoning another individual – a random member of the public – and asking him his views on tuition fees. Eventually this individual just got fed up and decided to play along. Political turbulence was turning to farce. Two days later, the real Mike Crockart voted against the tuition fee plan and resigned anyway.

As the day of the vote got closer, the protests increased and Liberal Democrat MPs came under greater pressure from constituents. On the night of the vote, riot police were called to deal with protestors at the Treasury, and later that evening, after the vote, the Prince of Wales's car was surrounded in Regent Street by a mob, one of whom landed kicks on the doors.

The legislation was passed, with the votes of twenty-seven Liberal Democrat MPs. But the party had been deeply split – wrecking the chance of presenting the public with a coherent narrative to explain our actions. Our support amongst students, which had been as high as 42 per cent at the general election, plunged to 11 per cent.

Now 'broken promises', 'tuition fees', 'Liberal Democrats' and 'Nick Clegg' would be closely tied together in the public mind. Having made the first big error before the general election in keeping our tuition fees policy, we had now made our second big mistake, allowing fees to rise. If we had vetoed the rise, some extra money for universities would have had to have been found by the Treasury, and it seems likely that university budgets would also have faced a significantly bigger squeeze. Bluntly, it would have been a worse solution in policy terms, but the damage to the Liberal Democrats would have been hugely reduced.

Tuition fees was by far the biggest Liberal Democrat mistake of the parliament.

Ironically, however, the new policy itself was eventually and by any fair judgement a huge success. It helped protect universities from what would otherwise have been massive cuts. After a temporary and small dip, it allowed a big rise in student numbers. And because the new system was both highly progressive and required no upfront contributions, the number of children from disadvantaged backgrounds attending university started to increase too.

In contrast, in Scotland, where tuition was nominally 'free', the universities struggled with budget cuts and student numbers started to decline.

But while the policy might have been a success, the politics were not. Smaller coalition parties often get accused of 'selling out' and compromising on too much. We had now handed our political opponents a massive stick to beat us with, and we had crafted a striking and simple totem of 'betrayal' for all those voters who never wanted us to go into coalition with the Conservatives at any price.

It was a costly mistake – a tale of two errors.

Settling In

2010

It was a Sunday in late 2012, and I was at home, ploughing through a red box a foot deep in paperwork, sent to me from my offices in the Education Department and Cabinet Office.

At the bottom of the box, I found a note from one of my private secretaries to a senior official in the Education Department. It had obviously arrived in my box by accident, having become wrongly attached to another note.

It was marked 'Urgent' and it said:

> Dear Susan,
> You kindly agreed to draft a policy note for the Minister of State, on School Accountability. He has had a meeting cancelled at short notice for Monday, and I fear that he now intends to use the time to think about this himself! I know you are incredibly busy, but is there anything that you could have ready on this by 1 p.m. tomorrow, even if in outline?

In truth, we have an excellent civil service which is more than happy – on the whole – with ministers who 'think for themselves'. But there is no doubt than on arrival into government for the first time there is a tendency for new ministers to think, 'What do I do now, then?' and there is a risk of being folded into the comforting blanket of civil service support and direction.

When the Liberal Democrats came into government in May 2010, it was the party's first taste of real power at a UK level since the Second World War coalition government under Winston Churchill. And not only was this a very long time back in history, but a wartime coalition offered little real equivalence to being in government now.

At first, it took some time for Whitehall to adapt to two-party government. It was true that Nick Clegg was given the title of Deputy Prime Minister and had been appointed chair of the powerful Home Affairs Committee of Cabinet. It was true, in addition, that he was allocated a huge room in the Cabinet Office to operate from.

But the civil service staffing resources initially granted to the Deputy Prime Minister were modest at best, leaving him and his small political team badly overstretched during his first year in government.

Liberal Democrat Cabinet ministers and junior ministers now disappeared into their departments – left to sink or swim, with little advice on what to do and how to do it.

The four other Liberal Democrat Cabinet ministers were each allowed to appoint two special advisers, but junior Liberal Democrat ministers had little or no special adviser support and found themselves struggling to compete in Conservative-controlled departments.

In the centre of government, relations were generally good. Nick Clegg's press team got on well with Andy Coulson, David Cameron's head of government communications, admiring his professionalism and focus.

The Liberal Democrat team found Steve Hilton – the Prime Minister's chief 'strategist' – to be a little more baffling. They regarded his policy thinking as distinctly off the wall, not least when he came up with madcap ideas that seemed completely undeliverable. In one meeting, in early 2011, Steve Hilton suggested that one of the UK's biggest problems was too much cloudy weather – 'Why can't we fly planes over the eastern Atlantic', he suggested, 'to drop chemicals on the clouds and force them to break up, and get rid of their rain before they get to our shores?' Civil servants seemed dumbstruck, while Liberal Democrat advisers tried to suppress laughter – and watched as the relationship between hardnosed Andy Coulson and head-in-the-clouds Steve Hilton slowly deteriorated. 'This is taking blue-sky thinking to extremes,' muttered one Liberal Democrat adviser as he left the meeting.

The relations at the top of the government itself, meanwhile, were remarkably good.

Nick Clegg and David Cameron stuck to their regular bilateral meetings to agree policy changes and resolve any potential differences. Where necessary, they would frequently speak informally with each other during the week and at weekends, and would also be in touch through text messages and emails. Civil servants, used to the endless wars between Tony Blair and Gordon Brown, found coalition government to be a lot more grown-up and cooperative.

The relationship between Danny Alexander and George Osborne was so close that some Liberal Democrat advisers began to worry that the Chief Secretary had gone native. And one Conservative suggested to the journalist Matthew d'Ancona that 'Danny is like the first special forces guy sent up the river to assassinate Colonel Kurtz in the film *Apocalypse Now* – the one who becomes totally devoted to his original target. Danny was soon wearing warpaint and was very much Colonel George's man.'

'Native' or not, Danny Alexander was certainly highly regarded by the Treasury spending team, who appreciated having a minister to work with who had a voracious appetite for the job, and who ensured additional power for the Treasury through his membership of the Quad.

When I had left the government in late May 2010, Danny Alexander had not just taken over as Chief Secretary, but he had retained his informal responsibilities at the centre of government, liaising with Oliver Letwin to iron out any differences between the coalition partners. With his membership of the National Security Council, almost every Cabinet committee, and the Quad, this made Danny indisputably the fourth most powerful member of the coalition government.

By now, the Quad had become the real inner Cabinet of the coalition, where many of the most difficult issues would be resolved. The Quad also became the main mechanism through which the market-sensitive Autumn Statements and Budgets were agreed between both coalition parties – often over four or five meetings over the course of the eight-week run-ins to these major political and economic events.

The meetings of the Quad took place in the Cabinet Room, but they were usually quite informal, with no civil service minutes being kept. Indeed, there could be occasions when, after a Quad, one or more of the conclusions were disputed by the two parties.

The meetings were attended by a select number of staff – this usually included Cabinet Secretary Jeremy Heywood, chiefs of staff Jonny Oates (for Nick Clegg) and Ed Llewellyn (for David Cameron), and a small group of civil servants and special advisers from the participants' offices.

Later in the parliament, the Quads would occasionally be joined by Oliver Letwin and by me when there were major initiatives or programmes on which we had both been working.

By late 2010, good progress was beginning to be made on much of the policy programme that had made up our 2010 general election manifesto – including on the four key pledges that been highlighted on the front page.

In the July 2010 Budget, we had made the first move to increase the tax-free personal allowance, with a long-term ambition of raising this to £10,000 per year and taking millions of low earners out of income tax altogether.

We had helped pay for this change with measures such as a banking levy and a higher top rate of capital gains tax, both of which were also proposed in our election manifesto.

On education, the new £2.5 billion pupil premium had been announced in the October Spending Review, with the introduction of the premium due to take place in schools in April 2011. Nick Clegg had also gone beyond the Lib Dem manifesto pledge to announce a new 'fairness premium', which would give more support to those from disadvantaged backgrounds from age two to age twenty-one. As part of this, there would be a new fifteen-hour entitlement to early years education for two-year-olds from the poorest households.

On the economy, both parties were honouring their pledges to put in place a serious plan to reduce the government's Budget deficit, and action was being taken on the big banks to ensure that they would no longer be a future threat to macroeconomic stability. On the green economy, Chris Huhne was setting out ambitious plans to boost investment in renewable sources of energy, and a 'Green Deal' was planned, to improve incentives for home energy insulation.

On political reform, too, there was progress – legislation to deliver fixed-term parliaments and a referendum on a new Alternative Vote system for Westminster elections. Meanwhile, we were introducing a new Freedoms Bill, and scrapping Labour's plans to introduce identity cards.

Beyond these four key Liberal Democrat pledges, other major progress on our manifesto promises was being made, too. Steve Webb, the new Pensions Minister, was embarking on a major overhaul of our pensions system. We had also announced, in spite of the overall squeeze on public spending, that we would set out plans to meet the UN target of spending 0.7 per cent of gross national product on overseas development assistance. There was, in conclusion, much for Liberal Democrats to be proud of, though much of this had been overshadowed by the rows over higher tuition fees.

At the very end of 2010, there was a further brief squall in government over the issue of the NewsCorp bid to purchase BSkyB. This sensitive issue was ultimately to be decided by the Business Secretary, Vince Cable, who was required to act in a quasi-judicial capacity.

There was huge press and political interest in the issue, and senior Conservatives were concerned not to upset the Murdoch media empire, which they very much wanted to keep on side.

On 21 December, on a cold and icy evening, I was driving back down to Yeovil from London when I heard that Vince Cable had been secretly taped saying that he had 'declared war on Murdoch'. The statements, while privately made, were clearly inappropriate and entirely inconsistent with the Business Secretary's quasi-judicial role. For a few brief hours, Nick Clegg and David Cameron considered whether their Business Secretary would need to resign. Instead, the decision was taken to remove all responsibility for competition and media policy issues from the Business Department and transfer it to the Culture Department, under the leadership of Jeremy Hunt. I later phoned a depressed-sounding Vince at his Twickenham home and urged him to stay in his post. Fortunately, we were now entering the Christmas parliamentary recess, which allowed the row to die down. Vince went away skiing over the New Year and came back having decided to stay on.

Politicians in both coalition parties were looking forward to a well-earned break after an extraordinary and historic eight months of coalition government.

For the Liberal Democrats, in particular, it had been a tough year, with support for the party plunging after the coalition was formed, and with the furious row over tuition fees having seriously split the party and angered many supporters.

For the Conservatives, it had been a much more satisfactory year. In spite of failing to secure an overall majority, they had negotiated a strong and stable coalition deal, which gave them a healthy majority in Parliament.

Both coalition parties had been criticised by Labour for cutting spending too rapidly and for seeking to balance the books too quickly. But Labour's poor recent economic record meant that it was no longer able to speak with credibility, and recent economic growth data seemed to show that the economy was now recovering well.

As for the National Health Service, that Achilles heel issue for former Conservative governments, the coalition leaders thought that they had quietly dealt with that potential problem, with twin promises to protect the NHS Budget in real terms and avoid more top-down and destabilising reorganisations of the health service.

But inside the Health Department, the new Secretary of State was rapidly planning a reform plan which would do exactly that.

NHS Reform: The Self-Inflicted Wound

2010–11

It was Thursday 27 May 2010 – a day before, little did I know it, the *Daily Telegraph* would run their story on me – and I was tidying up the papers on my desk in the Treasury, and preparing to head home.

My private secretary knocked lightly on the door of my office and crossed the room, holding in his hand a ten-page ministerial submission for me to read. 'You'll want to have a detailed look at this, Chief Secretary,' he said. 'What is it?' I asked. 'It's from the Department of Health – their plan to reorganise the whole NHS. Pretty astonishing stuff in my view.'

Civil servants aren't in the habit of expressing views of their own on policy issues, so I was immediately alerted to the fact that this was something worth paying attention to.

I put down the papers I was looking at and skimmed quickly through the Department of Health paper. To my amazement, it seemed to be proposing a fundamental reorganisation of the whole NHS in England. This was in stark contrast to the detailed coalition agreement, which asserted that the government would resist any further top-down reorganisation of the system.

My own strong view was that the NHS needed a period of organisational stability, so that it could focus on securing the efficiency savings that would be needed to allow it to live within a frozen real NHS budget, without a serious deterioration in the standards of care and access.

The coalition had already promised to protect the NHS from cuts, but this still meant that the NHS budget would be flat in real terms over the entire parliament, in contrast to its average real growth rate of around 3 per cent over the past few decades.

The NHS tended to need more money just to 'stand still' because of the aging population and the higher costs from medical advances, real pay growth, new technology and more widespread use of expensive drugs.

In the coalition negotiations, from 7 to 11 May, we had barely discussed the NHS. We had merely agreed to protect the health budget in real terms. Indeed, when we concluded our talks and were running through the final draft of our coalition agreement, I noticed that the NHS was not even mentioned specifically in the document. Feeling that this was a political own goal, I said to the Conservative team: 'Do you realise that at present the coalition agreement doesn't even mention the three letters "NHS", even though the Prime Minister has claimed that this is his top political priority? We have sections on education, pensions and banking reform. Nothing on the NHS.'

There was an embarrassed silence. 'OK,' said Oliver Letwin. 'We agree that is an issue. Let's mention the NHS in the Spending Review section. We could even put it in the title of this section?'

And so it was that Section 2 of the coalition agreement changed from being entitled 'Spending Review' to 'Spending Review – NHS, Schools and a Fairer Society'. It wasn't much of a change.

There was still not a jot about detailed policy on the NHS or on health-care in the first coalition agreement. The assumption in both parties was that the NHS needed a period of policy stability after extensive and regular changes under Labour.

This assumption was made more explicit in the detailed coalition 'Programme for Government', which was published soon afterwards. This document included the pledge that 'we will stop top-down reorganisations of the NHS that have got in the way of patient care'.

But it now turned out that within the Department of Health there was one individual who did not share this commitment to policy and organisational stability – the new Conservative Secretary of State, Andrew Lansley. And within two weeks of the coalition agreement being signed off, the new Secretary of State was developing and circulating his plan for change.

In the days when Gordon Brown ruled the Treasury, this type of major public service initiative from a mere Secretary of State would have been subject to huge political and policy scrutiny, including from the then Chancellor himself.

But George Osborne had problems of his own to focus on – the state of the UK economy and the need to cut spending, raise taxes and sort out the deficit in the public finances. George certainly saw himself as a powerful force across the government. But at this stage he did not regard his job as that of second guessing every initiative presented by those charged by the Prime Minister with running the big departments of state. And the Department of Health presented this plan to the Treasury as part of their solution to make efficiency savings, which was the Chancellor's major preoccupation.

In 10 Downing Street, the Prime Minister was also finding his feet, establishing himself in government, being briefed on his role in maintaining and controlling the UK's nuclear deterrent, and generally focusing on the broad economic challenges.

David Cameron, who had once worked for Andrew Lansley at Conservative Party headquarters, had never really been a man for policy detail. He and the Chancellor took their eye off the ball, and so it was that a government that had pledged to 'stop top-down reorganisations of the NHS' began to embark on a reorganisation that was 'so big you can see it from space', as the chief executive of the NHS was later to admit.

One other Cabinet minister might have been able to stop the reform juggernaut from lurching forward – the Chief Secretary to the Treasury, responsible for public spending. But one day after briefly reading the first paper on the Lansley plan, I had resigned from the government. In my place was a new Chief Secretary, Danny Alexander, with his hands full with a multi-year Spending Review. So it was that both No. 10 and HM Treasury dropped the ball.

Had I stayed in the Treasury, it is possible that the NHS proposals would have been halted or seriously amended. From first glance, I thought the proposals from Andrew Lansley made neither policy nor political sense.

My worries were not about the parts of the Bill that dealt with the private sector. The claims that this was all part of a 'privatisation agenda' were wildly overblown, and very hypocritical from former Labour ministers who had themselves been quite content to use the private sector to improve NHS funded services.

What I thought completely daft were the massive changes to the NHS commissioning function. This was designed to radically alter the organisation of the NHS across the whole country. It was immediately clear that it would distract top NHS managers from their main job of finding efficiency savings, while the reorganisation rolled on over two or three years. Many experienced NHS managers would now leave, some to be immediately re-employed after receiving massive redundancy payments.

Worse still, the reorganisation would shift the budget control from NHS managers, charged with serving the interests of patients, to general practitioners. It might seem logical to place GPs in charge of healthcare commissioning, but it was highly risky too – the equivalent of asking teachers to commission education services. There were bound to be conflicts of interest.

Not all GPs wanted to take on the new roles. Many who did were not well qualified for them. For some GPs, a big financial decision in the past might be whether to renew the practice photocopier contract. They were now getting responsibility for budgets of up to £0.5 billion.

In the wholesale reorganisation that followed, many excellent and experienced NHS managers were given huge pay-offs to leave their posts. Sometimes they were then expensively re-hired in some other corner of the NHS. They were frequently, in practice, replaced by more junior staff without the same level of ability.

The political row over the NHS changes grew – in Westminster, in the media and out in the country. The NHS was supposed to be a low-key area of coalition policy. My view and that of George Osborne and David Cameron was that a good political outcome on the NHS was that it remained out of the news and out of the political debate. Now that could hardly be further from the reality.

Oliver Letwin and Danny Alexander were asked to scrutinise the NHS plans, and decided that on balance they should continue. An agitated Andrew Lansley made clear that he resented the high-level scrutiny. He considered that the changes he was making were necessary to reduce management costs and improve NHS services by putting practitioners in the driving seat. He had thought that he had the Prime Minister's support and understanding for his changes.

Both coalition parties were now feeling the heat politically on this issue, but after the political shambles of tuition fee policy, the pressure was arguably greater on Nick Clegg and the Liberal Democrats.

In 2011, the level of political controversy rose and Nick Clegg was tempted to withdraw Liberal Democrat support for the Bill. A critical debate and vote at the Liberal Democrat spring conference was the trigger for a 'pause' to consider how the Bill might be amended.

What was difficult by this stage was that in much of the country the reforms were already taking effect. Senior executives in Primary Care Trusts were already leaving their posts and in much of the country the reforms were already becoming a fact on the ground. It had become difficult, perhaps even impossible, to turn the clock back.

It was now therefore arguable that the proposals were best amended rather than being sunk altogether. After much very careful consideration, that was the course that Nick Clegg decided upon. Instead of sinking the Bill completely, he used the 'pause' to consider the defects of the Bill, and then insisted on a series of changes and safeguards.

By 2012, looking back, the Liberal Democrat leader regretted not going further. 'I should have pulled the rug out from under the NHS reforms and just killed them dead in 2010,' he told friends. 'I was trying too hard to work in a cooperative way with the Tories in that first six months of the coalition, but in retrospect it was a mistake not to just stop it.'

And in spite of the changes to the Bill, the organisational damage was already done, and could not be reversed. The reform programme was a huge distraction, and also made it more difficult to advance other, more valuable, reforms to the often outdated NHS system.

David Cameron was furious. In late 2011, he suggested privately to Nick Clegg that Andrew Lansley would soon need to be moved from his job as Health Secretary. The Prime Minister even suggested moving Vince Cable from Business and making him Secretary of State for Health. Nick Clegg rejected what he now regarded as a poisoned chalice.

By the end of the parliament, the long-term impacts of the NHS reforms were clearer still.

In late 2014, we had to grapple with declining service standards in the NHS as the real budget freeze gradually began to bite. Steering the NHS was now more difficult, as the Lansley reforms had deliberately broken off many of the levers that could previously be pulled to manage and control the service.

It was all a case study in how not to deliver major policy change early in a new government. It was an error by Andrew Lansley but also a complete failure of oversight from David Cameron and George Osborne in particular.

For the public, the NHS reforms were generally unpopular, though not much understood. And because they were all about the organisation of the management of the NHS, the changes were actually not very visible to patients and to voters. The long-term political impact of the NHS row was therefore much more limited than seemed likely at the time.

What clearly was going to be noticed by voters was the state of the economy. The first six months had gone well, with respectable growth and swift and decisive action on tax, spending and borrowing.

As 2010 now slipped away in icy winter weather, both coalition parties needed the economy to keep on growing in order validate their new economic plans – the bedrock on which the coalition had been formed.

But what neither David Cameron nor Nick Clegg could know, as they toasted the New Year in, was that instead of continuing to grow, the British economy was now shrinking.

2011

STORM CLOUDS: THE ECONOMY AND THE BUDGET

2011

The leaders of both coalition parties knew that ultimately the coalition would be judged on its ability to restore growth and return the government's budget to balance, or close to balance.

When the coalition was established in May 2010, growth had finally resumed. The first nine months of the year saw quarterly growth posting an average of gain of around 0.8 per cent – more than enough, if sustained, to reduce unemployment, increase tax revenues and reduce borrowing.

The Treasury therefore judged that the economy was strong enough for the government to tighten its 'fiscal policy' – in other words, squeeze public spending and increase taxes. This would clearly have some impact on growth, but the Treasury thought that the impact would be very modest. Tighter fiscal policy would also allow the Bank of England to maintain ultra-low interest rates. The official benchmark UK interest rate was now a mere 0.5 per cent, and it was expected to remain low for some time. So, economic policy was explicitly designed to combine tighter fiscal policy with very easy monetary policy.

But as 2010 progressed, it soon became clear that there were two big threats to the government's plan. One risk related to the state of the Eurozone economy, which was mired in slow growth. The financial markets were now questioning whether some of the weaker southern European states would be able to stay as members of the Eurozone, given their high public debts, low rates of growth and soaring unemployment.

The doubts about these countries' economic futures were causing the interest rates on their bonds to rise to dangerous levels: this made their debt sustainability worse, and further undermined their growth prospects. It was a vicious circle of high interest rates leading to low growth, leading to higher public borrowing and hence to even higher interest rates.

The miserable state of the Eurozone economies was badly affecting UK exports into Europe – our biggest export market. Questions about the very future of the single currency were also blighting the investment plans of major UK companies. And UK consumer confidence was further hit by the endless media coverage of the European economic crisis, and the bleak assessments of its potential impact on the UK.

Each day, people arrived home from work to watch news programmes dominated by bleak economic news and forecasts of financial calamity – no wonder they did not feel optimistic about the economy or their own financial prospects.

Unsurprisingly, by the beginning of 2011 UK consumer confidence had plunged and the savings rate leapt. The rise in VAT in January 2011, from 17.5 per cent to 20 per cent, was a further blow to household finances, and came on top of other pressures on family budgets.

It was not only the state of the Eurozone and the impact of public sector austerity that were affecting sentiment and spending. Inflation was now also much higher than expected, due to a global surge in food and energy prices.

The weak state of the developed world economies would normally subdue price rises. But rapid growth in developing countries, such as China and India, along with some specific commodity price pressures, was pushing up global inflation – and further squeezing people's living standards.

UK inflation was supposed to be kept by the Bank of England at 2 per cent or less, but by January 2011 it had risen to 4 per cent, and throughout 2011 it went on rising, to reach a peak of 5.2 per cent in September. Meanwhile, average wage rises had fallen below 2 per cent, with many public sector workers having their pay frozen.

With inflation soaring well above pay rises, most workers were now seeing a dramatic decline in their real take-home pay. Only pensioners were protected from these developments, as the government had introduced its 'triple lock', ensuring that pensions rose by whichever was highest: wages, prices or 2.5 per cent.

Towards the end of 2010, economists still expected healthy growth in the last quarter of the year – growth of around 0.5 per cent in the quarter, or an annual rate of a modest but acceptable 2 per cent.

But if all this wasn't enough, there was now a period of icy weather and heavy snowfall across the UK. Economists began to scale back their estimates of growth as they revised downwards their projections for the weather-affected construction sector.

When the figures for growth in the last three months of 2010 were finally announced on 25 January 2011, they shocked the City, Westminster and the Chancellor. Instead of growing modestly, by 0.5 per cent, the economy actually contracted by 0.5 per cent. George Osborne was ridiculed for blaming the decline on the weather; even taking this into account, the economy had failed to grow.

In the coalition 'script', 2011 and 2012 were supposed to be years of recovery and declining borrowing. The Chancellor and the Treasury hoped that the growth setback would be short, but they were to be disappointed.

Instead of growing, the economy now embarked on an eighteen-month period of flat-lining, when the UK seemed constantly to be flirting with recession. High inflation, a Eurozone in crisis, declining real incomes and rock-bottom consumer confidence – this was the poisonous economic cocktail the coalition had to survive on for a year and a half.

Every piece of economic news was carefully and nervously scrutinised by ministers and by the Treasury, in the hope of finding some of the famous 'green shoots' of recovery. But green shoots were in short supply.

In the run-up to the March 2011 Budget, George Osborne pressed Nick Clegg to consider a cut in the new top rate of tax, which applied on incomes over £150,000. The existing 50 per cent rate had been introduced by the outgoing Labour government, as a political trap for the Conservative Party. The Conservatives had steered around the trap before the election, but now wanted to act.

A 50 per cent top tax rate was one of the highest marginal income tax rates in the world – higher even than in communist China. George Osborne was concerned that such a high rate was bad for the UK and would deter businesses from setting up in the country.

Nick Clegg, however, made very clear that he could not accept any light-ening of the tax burden on those on the top incomes while the government was making difficult decisions that increased the burden on those on low pay. But the Deputy Prime Minister did agree to the Treasury commissioning a report to establish what revenue the 50 per cent rate was generating – which would report before the 2012 Budget.

Meanwhile, George Osborne worked on a plan to cut the UK corpora-tion tax to the lowest level in the developed world, to help make the UK more competitive.

In the Budget Quads, Nick Clegg and Danny Alexander pressed for a second, big, rise in the personal income tax allowance, and they were once again successful. On Budget Day, 23 March 2011, it was confirmed that the income tax allowance would rise by another £630, to £8,105 in April 2012. During the election, David Cameron had said that a £10,000 tax allowance was unaffordable. But now the Liberal Democrats were delivering another of their big, front-page policy pledges and freeing hundreds of thousands of low-paid workers from paying income tax.

Otherwise, the Budget was a subdued affair, with the Chancellor having to announce a downgrading of economic growth forecasts. With little money to spend, George Osborne was able to announce only a small amount of good news – including a modest 1p cut in fuel duties. This was a small cut, but welcome relief at a time of soaring petrol and diesel prices.

To counteract any anti-green message from the fuel duty cut, Nick Clegg was able to secure the announcement of a new 'green investment bank', to be launched in 2012, with over £2 billion of spending capacity and future powers to borrow to invest in green technologies.

It was not a bad Budget, all things considered. And once again the two coalition parties had worked closely and cooperatively, in spite of the tough economic climate. But with the economy on its back, it was hardly surprising that there was no political dividend from it.

The latest polling figures, in March 2011, showed Labour in the lead on 42 per cent, up 12 per cent since the general election. The Conservatives were still on 35 per cent, just 2 per cent down on their general election vote share. But the Liberal Democrats were languishing on just 9 per cent – fully 15 per cent down on their May 2010 polling.

Coalition had not been kind to the Liberal Democrats. Nick Clegg realised that it was now more important than ever that the party should win the forthcoming, crucial, referendum on electoral reform. Without a change in the voting system, the Liberal Democrats could face a massive loss of seats at the next general election. We knew that this was a crucial test.

Political Reform:
Progress and Pot-Holes

2011

It was 3 March 1998. Paddy Ashdown, then Leader of the Liberal Democrats, was at home in south London, preparing for an important and secret dinner with Labour Prime Minister Tony Blair, which was due to take place the next day. The two leaders were intent on discussing their joint plan to change the face of British politics by establishing a coalition government, with Liberal Democrat MPs in the Cabinet. This was planned to happen at around the same time as Roy Jenkins produced his government-commissioned report on changing the voting system for Westminster to include some element of proportional representation. A referendum on the Jenkins plan was pencilled in for early 1999.

In the upper echelons of the Liberal Democrats, this prospect of a coalition with Labour was controversial. There were, in particular, concerns about what it would mean for the party's identity and its future electoral prospects.

Before Paddy Ashdown went to bed on the evening of 3 March, he received an email from the influential Liberal Democrat campaign director, Chris Rennard. Chris was aware of the Ashdown–Blair plan, and he was worried about one key part of it. Essentially, he thought that going into coalition without ensuring that some form of proportional representation was delivered was very risky.

On the third page of his confidential note, Chris set out the heart of his concerns:

Coalition may be our end game (I agree with you that it is), but there is the question of when?

A coalition would inevitably reduce our share of support (this will be acceptable at some point) in return for a permanent share in power.

But the loss of our independence and acceptance of collective responsibility will hit us hard in the polls. We will lose significant support back to the Tories and some to Labour. This is as much a fact in my political judgement as Newton's laws of physics.

You asked me to study the effects of coalition/PR elections abroad. The situation is messy – few of our sister parties handle it well – but in every case the junior coalition partner loses support (the Progressive Democrats are now down to 2 per cent).

My conclusion must be that the loss of support may be acceptable in return for PR and with it permanent influence. But it is suicidal without PR ... And my prediction (I haven't let you down on this very often and I have usually been cautious) is that with The Full Monty [Ashdown's code for a coalition] 10 per cent would be our likely vote share ... If we fought in a coalition under AV, we would lose vote share, but the change in system would make up for this.

Without [PR] the prospect of The Full Monty means that much is to be lost in unity, nothing to be gained electorally and our ten years of success may end in the wilderness which befell our party in the 1920s.

It was a stark warning.

In fact, Chris Rennard's memorandum did not just argue for the Alternative Vote system of ranking candidates and re-allocating voting preferences until one candidate has over 50 per cent. It pressed for a proportionate voting system of some kind – perhaps some combination of the Alternative Vote and proportionality, as was eventually recommended by the Jenkins Commission.

But the big point of the Rennard memorandum was that a coalition would dilute party identity and lose party support – so that going into coalition would be highly dangerous without a prospect or promise of voting reform.

The plan for a coalition between the Liberal Democrats and Labour eventually came to nothing, and Labour kicked the Jenkins plan for voting reform into the very long grass.

But the concern about the electoral risks of any future coalition without voting reform remained a salient consideration for all those at the top of the Liberal Democrat Party. Indeed, this was the primary reason why the Liberal Democrats decided in 2010 to make a referendum on voting reform a pre-condition of going into coalition. If the Conservatives had refused to make this referendum offer, the outcome in 2010 would almost certainly have been some sort of loose confidence and supply arrangement.

Had Gordon Brown and the Labour Party resigned immediately after the May 2010 general election instead of holding talks with the Liberal Democrats, we might never have had the leverage to extract this referendum concession from the Conservatives. Instead, the Conservatives would have had to govern in some sort of minority administration – with or without a confidence and supply agreement. What political outcome would eventually have resulted from this is one of the big unknowns of modern UK politics.

Of course, the Liberal Democrat support for fairer voting was not just a tactical consideration. We believed that the percentage of votes for each party should be represented properly in Parliament – that seemed to us a fundamental part of a fair democracy. But no other major UK political party was willing to support such a change, because the current system gave them more seats than their vote shares justified.

And the reason that voting reform was such a high priority for us – essentially a deal-breaker – was precisely because we knew that if we went into coalition with either other major party, we could lose up to half of our vote. We had to protect against that by reforming the voting system so that we secured fairer representation for each vote gained.

Of course, there were other political reforms that the two coalition parties agreed to in May 2010 – notably, elections for the House of Lords, and the reform of party political funding.

But the early coalition priorities for political reform were an AV referendum, the redrawing of parliamentary boundaries, and legislation for five-year fixed-term parliaments.

The Fixed Term Parliaments Act was eventually successfully passed into law by Parliament in September 2011. This would take away from the Prime Minister the right to call an election at a time of his or her choice, within a five-year term limit. The fixed-term parliament had always seemed justified as a way of delivering stability and avoiding political manipulation, but it was now doubly important as a way of giving greater assurance and certainty to coalition parties.

However, it was always going to be much harder to secure a majority for any change in the voting system for Westminster. The truth was that neither the Conservative Party nor the majority of the Labour Party were much interested in changing the current system. Both parties felt that the current system suited them, giving them regular opportunities to hold power without having to share it with other smaller parties.

The Conservatives were particularly resistant to change. An AV referendum was at the outer extremity of what they were willing to consider, and they only granted us this because they thought that there was a serious risk of us otherwise going into coalition with the Labour Party. But even during the coalition talks, the Conservatives had made no secret of their opposition to an AV system.

However, with the coalition off to a close and cooperative start, and given the 'hit' the Liberal Democrats were taking in the polls both before and after the vote on tuition fees, the prospect of the Conservative leadership taking a more neutral line on the AV referendum rose. Michael Gove was believed to be 'sympathetic' to AV, and the Prime Minister seemed likely to stand back from involvement in the 'No to AV' campaign.

The referendum was fixed for 5 May 2011, just one year into government. This date was chosen because it was felt that there was a better chance of winning a referendum earlier in a parliament, rather than when economic austerity had reduced public support in the middle or later part of the parliament. Nick Clegg and his team also wanted the AV referendum on the same day as the local elections, in order to maximise turnout. Both decisions seemed sensible to most of the Liberal Democrats involved.

In the autumn of 2010, Nick Clegg discussed the AV referendum privately with David Cameron. The Liberal Democrat leader explained that AV was only a modest change, and how in any case it might not damage the Conservatives. The point with AV was that its impact depended on precisely whom voters gave their second preferences to. Nick Clegg explained that after being in power with the Liberal Democrats, the Conservatives might see more Lib Dem voters giving them their second-preference votes in seats that were close between Labour and the Conservatives. So AV, the argument went, might actually be helpful to both coalition parties.

David Cameron listened sympathetically to the case put to him. He told the Deputy Prime Minister that he didn't have strong views on the issue and he suggested that both party leaders should 'stand back' from detailed involvement in the referendum battle. The Prime Minister also implied that he was content for the public to make up their minds on the issue, and he mentioned that some Conservative Cabinet ministers might actually come out in support of the Alternative Vote.

Neutralising the Conservatives was important, because Labour had now decided to take no party position on an AV referendum, in spite of supporting one in their own 2010 general election manifesto. As Andrew Adonis of Labour had privately warned me before the 2010 general election, there were between seventy and eighty Labour MPs who were bitter opponents of any voting reform – even a modest measure such as AV.

The prospects of winning the AV referendum seemed reasonable for much of 2010, and even in early 2011 many of the opinion polls forecast a win for the Yes camp, which seemed for a while to be both better funded and better organised.

But as the prospects of change rose, the resistance in the Conservative Party rose with it. Under pressure from Conservative MPs, David Cameron now shifted his position and started to campaign actively against any change to the voting system.

Instead of remaining neutral, the Conservative leadership helped persuade Tory donors to give money to the anti-AV movement and an increasingly hysterical battle was waged, which even targeted Nick Clegg on a personal basis, blaming him for coalition compromises such as that on tuition fees. The No campaign had decided that their trump cards were 'the three Cs' – cost, complexity and Clegg.

Eventually, in April 2011, David Cameron himself entered the fray, publicly describing AV as 'undemocratic, obscure, unfair, crazy'. Whatever this was, it certainly wasn't neutrality.

Nick Clegg was angered by the Conservative change in gear and frustrated by the Yes campaign's failure to step up its own performance.

The main problem with promoting AV with the public was that it was a compromise system designed to maximise the chance of winning over waverers in the Labour Party and elsewhere who opposed full proportional representation. But it was not in any way a 'real' proportional system, and under some circumstances it could even exaggerate the normal first past the post swing, for example when one of the main parties was particularly unpopular with voters of the other parties. Nick Clegg had even referred to AV as a 'grubby little compromise' when questioned about his attitude to electoral reform prior to the 2010 election.

While the public could easily understand the case for full PR, and while they generally understood the existing first past the post system, the AV compromise was more difficult to justify and sell.

The No campaign not only produced ludicrous estimates of potential costs of change (£250 million, they claimed), but they also focused on the likelihood that some candidates who had secured the most votes in their seats would not actually be elected, where such candidates had not achieved more than half the votes and where the voters for the other parties united against them on second preferences. AV was described as a system where the losers could suddenly become winners. Many members of the public found that very hard to understand.

As these negative messages were put across, reinforced by a press who generally opposed change, the polls began to move away from the reformers. In May 2010, only a third of voters supported first past the post. By spring 2011, the figure was above 50 per cent. And the voters who were undecided in the polls taken during 2010 now suddenly started to make up their minds – and they were opting for continuity, against change.

On 3 May, just two days before the referendum and the local elections, the Cabinet held its regular Tuesday morning meeting. Chris Huhne, without warning Nick Clegg, decided to create a row over AV. This seemed designed not only to highlight the misleading nature of Conservative propaganda but also to promote Chris Huhne himself as the person 'speaking up for the Lib Dems'.

Sitting just a few places away from the Prime Minister, Chris Huhne angrily challenged David Cameron over the methods of the No campaign. David Cameron was taken aback by the directness and strength of the attack, and he refused to answer the questions put to him. Coalition relations were deteriorating rapidly, over an issue that went to the essential interests of both parties.

Meanwhile, the Yes campaign tried, rather unsuccessfully, to get across a populist message that they thought might appeal to an anti-political public.

Under the slogan 'Make Your MP Work Harder', they tried to persuade a sceptical public that AV would force incumbent MPs to reach out beyond their core supporters, in order to be sure to attract second-preference votes.

This was not necessarily an easy message to communicate, and it fared particularly badly in seats with incumbent Liberal Democrat MPs. A week before polling day, I was campaigning for both the local elections and the AV referendum in the village of Mudford, just outside Yeovil. We were canvassing the social housing properties stretched out along the main road into Yeovil – usually a strong source of Liberal Democrat support.

My constituency agent came back from canvassing at the door of a passionate supporter, who our records showed had voted for us in every one of the last five sets of elections.

'Is she still backing us?' I said. 'Well,' said my agent, 'she's fine in the local elections, but she won't support us in the AV referendum.'

'Why the hell not?' I asked, in desperation. 'Surely she realises this is *good* for the Lib Dems and I am supporting it.'

'Well, the problem', my agent replied, 'is that she said, "I am really angry with the Yes campaign. They are telling me that if I vote Yes, my local MP will have to work harder. Well, I already think David Laws works very hard, and I don't want to see him worked any harder. So I'm voting against the change. I think Mr Laws deserves a bit of time off occasionally, like the rest of us."'

I sighed deeply. If this was what we were facing, how could we win? That was the moment I felt the referendum was lost. People just could not grasp what the change was all about. And with Labour standing on the sidelines, the forces of conservatism were just too strong.

On 5 May, when the polls closed and the first exit polls were available, it was clear that the AV proposal had been heavily rejected. The eventual figures were 68 per cent against and just 32 per cent in favour. It was a crushing blow to hopes of electoral reform, and the scale of the defeat would make returning to the issue extremely difficult.

What I did not find out until beyond the end of the 2010–15 parliament was that Oliver Letwin had commissioned private Conservative Party polling on the popularity of the AV electoral system before the May 2010 election. This had initially appeared to show that electoral reform was popular with the public and that any referendum was likely to produce a 60/40 result in favour of change.

However, the Conservatives had then re-run the poll after exposing the public to the arguments against AV – including that the second-place candidate in an election could emerge as the 'winner'. At that point the public position reversed – 40 per cent of voters then favoured change, with around 60 per cent against.

Before the May 2010 election the Liberal Democrats had invested a lot of time thinking about how we could secure a referendum on voting reform. We hadn't spent enough time thinking about whether and how a referendum could be won.

The loss of the AV referendum was not the only disappointment that Nick Clegg faced on 5 May 2011. In the first major set of local government elections since the coalition was formed, the Liberal Democrats lost a staggering 750 seats out of the 1,850 we were defending. These were the worst results since the founding of the Liberal Democrat Party.

We were now crystallising the costs of going into coalition. It was no longer all about polls – these were real votes in real ballot boxes, and real candidates and real councillors who were being defeated.

The electoral costs of coalition were arguably even higher than they normally would be for a smaller party, because of the tough decisions needed on the economy and the disastrous handling of tuition fees.

We now had to face this swelling electoral tsunami with no prospect of any compensating change in the Westminster electoral system. The loss of the AV referendum punctured our coalition life raft. It remained to be seen how we could now stay afloat.

MEN ON A MISSION

2010–15

'And I should also flag up that tomorrow we are going to see the publication of the new Welfare Reform White Paper by Iain Duncan Smith and Steve Webb.' Nick Clegg was briefing Liberal Democrat MPs at our weekly parliamentary party meeting in autumn 2010.

I glanced up from my place, sitting towards the back of Committee Room 11, in the House of Commons, where I was signing a large pile of letters to my constituents. 'My God, coalition is an amazing thing,' I thought. 'That is perhaps the most astonishing, counter-intuitive and unexpected political sentence that I can ever recall hearing. Steve Webb and IDS publishing their *joint welfare* plan!'

When the former Conservative leader and right-winger, Iain Duncan Smith, was placed in the Department for Work and Pensions with left-wing Liberal Democrat boffin Steve Webb, it seemed like a marriage made in hell. It remained one of the unlikeliest pairings in the coalition government, yet it was also one of the most successful. Indeed, IDS and Steve Webb worked together as Secretary of State and Pensions Minister, respectively, for the whole parliament – one of the longest-lasting coalition pairings. (Only Nick Clegg and David Cameron lasted out the whole parliament together, and they were not in the same 'department'.)

Steve Webb was regarded by most self-respecting 'Orange Book Liberals' as an old lefty who needed watching closely. In opposition, when Liberal Democrat shadow ministers were asked by their Treasury team to come forward with ideas for spending cuts, Steve Webb could always be relied upon to return with bold ideas for revenue-raising that, on closer inspection, invariably turned out to be poorly disguised tax increases on middle- and upper-income groups.

Steve was never particularly close to Nick Clegg and, in an embarrassing incident in 2009, a journalist on a plane going up to Scotland, who was sitting behind Nick and Danny Alexander, claimed to have heard the Lib Dem leader speculating about an upcoming reshuffle of his team in which he described his colleague as a 'problem' and a potential 'pain in the arse'. The story was partially denied, but not very convincingly.

Yet when the coalition was formed in May 2010, Steve Webb's name was one of the first on Nick's list to be a minister of state – the level below Cabinet. Steve might not have been a natural 'Orange Book' Clegg supporter, but a person of such talent and intellect simply could not be ignored. And by the end of the parliament this former 'pain in the arse' was one of the ministers Nick Clegg most respected.

Steve Webb was one of the few MPs to have worked at the respected Institute for Fiscal Studies, and he had an impressive understanding of the Work and Pensions portfolio. He was a natural for pensions policy, which was a high-priority area in our manifesto.

But how on the earth did right-wing, plain-spoken IDS get on with left-wing, rather academic, Professor Webb?

Firstly, because there were some surprising aspects of their characters in common – both held strong, Christian, views which affected their outlooks. Both ministers were 'men on a mission'.

Secondly, because each man proved to be rather less one-dimensional than might have been expected. Iain Duncan Smith was not a mere 'slash-and-burn Tory'. He had founded the Centre for Social Justice and had a genuine interest in helping people out of poverty and welfare dependency. And Steve Webb proved in government to be far more pragmatic about the need to find savings than anyone could have expected. He spent billions with his reforms, but also presided over changes to the pension age and taxation that saved the Treasury – and indeed businesses – tens of billions of pounds. In short, Steve Webb accepted the disciplines of government, largely left Nick Clegg to fight the bigger battles with the Treasury on welfare cuts, and concentrated on his own passion: transforming the UK pensions system.

Finally, the Department for Work and Pensions was one of the only departments where the major policy areas were carved out and left almost entirely to either one party or the other. Steve Webb ran the government's pensions policy, while IDS led in other areas – with a particularly focus on his major ambition of introducing a new, streamlined 'Universal Credit', which was designed both to be much simpler than existing benefits and to improve work incentives.

So, a matching that could have been a nightmare soon became a very happy marriage.

But while the Department for Work and Pensions might have been a surprising hub of coalition cooperation, the general area of welfare policy became a major political battleground.

There were not, in fact, just two people in the welfare 'marriage', there were four – and that made this marriage, in practice, rather a crowded one.

The two other big players in welfare policy were George Osborne and Nick Clegg, and as the parliament progressed they fought out the big welfare battles across the coalition, and often behind the backs of DWP ministers.

Steve Webb wanted to be left alone to reform pensions. For decades, the basic state pension had been allowed to shrink in relation to average incomes, because it only rose by inflation each year. So as society became wealthier, many pensioners became relatively poorer.

Governments therefore introduced more means-testing into the pensions system to 'top-up' the incomes of the poorest pensioners. However, these means-tested benefits turned into a powerful disincentive to save, as for many people their savings income would simply be deducted from their means-tested benefits. Hence, not only were the poorest pensioners in danger of becoming relatively poorer, but they were in danger of becoming entirely reliant on the government – never a great place to be.

The Liberal Democrat vision for pensions was of a higher 'universal' pension paid to almost all citizens, which would be a protection against poverty and which would rise in value each year and would at least keep pace with the incomes of the rest of the population.

The Liberal Democrats also wanted to encourage people to save money on top of this universal state pension, through personal or occupational pensions. To overcome the well-known inertia about saving for retirement, the coalition committed to press ahead with the plans proposed by Lord

(Adair) Turner, under the previous Labour government, to automatically enrol all employees in a pension – which they could opt out from if they wished.

To help pay for these changes, the state pension age would need to rise, not least to help fund the consequences of the increasing life expectancy of the population.

Iain Duncan Smith largely supported the Liberal Democrat strategy on pensions, but his personal priority lay elsewhere. IDS's major objective was to make work pay and to help tackle dependency. That did not mean that he was opposed to welfare reforms and savings – far from it. But IDS's aim was not cuts for cuts sake, but wider social reform and social recovery.

Although the British economy had unemployment levels that were quite low by the standards of many other European nations, we still had a significant problem with 'worklessness'. Two million or more citizens of working age were classed as unemployed. This was bad enough, but the UK also had almost two and a half million people on incapacity and other sickness benefits – these were people not in work because of illness, disability, mental health problems, drug addictions and other issues. Since the Conservative government of the 1980s, the tendency had been to remove these people from the unemployment figures and then basically write them off.

There was almost no serious support for people with illness and disability to get back into work, and the benefits system was rigid and was not designed to help people who could only, for example, work part time.

Worse still, the benefits system paid people a lot more if they were classified as sick than if they were unemployed. So there was a strong incentive for non-working people to be on sickness benefits rather than unemployed – and once they were on these benefits, their chances of getting back into work were slight.

These were not the only problems with the system. Work incentives for many people were almost entirely absent: many low-paid jobs paid little more than you got on benefits, and people were often given 'benefit check-ups', which highlighted if it was not worth their while working.

Other parts of the benefits system incentivised part-time hours, often no more than sixteen hours per week – in other words, the system acted to discourage some people from taking full-time jobs.

Finally, the rules around single parents were ludicrously designed, to allow people to avoid employment for decades if they wanted to. Until relatively recently, lone parents weren't obliged to work until their youngest child turned sixteen. A parent who had a few children might have no work obligation for a quarter of a century. This child age threshold was brought down very significantly, but there still needed to be more support and obligation to work.

Taking all of these groups of people together, there were perhaps five million people who were fit to work but were either unable to find suitable jobs, or else capable of doing longer hours than they were currently working.

There were also aspects of the benefits system open to abuse – for example, many people who gained disability benefits were then not regularly re-tested, so that their condition might have improved but they still received support.

Iain Duncan Smith's vision, which I very much shared, was to create a benefits system that strongly supported work, where bad incentives and the scope for abuse were removed. The vision was about giving people opportunities to work, in order to gain purpose in their lives and an adequate level of income. It was not a vision merely driven by a desire to slash budgets or stigmatise claimants.

George Osborne had a rather different perspective. As Chancellor, bluntly, he wanted the financial savings that welfare cuts could bring. He saw the DWP budget as a cash cow to be milked, and he was sceptical of Iain Duncan Smith's 'big idea' of Universal Credit, partly because he was not an admirer of IDS, and partly because he feared that the complex and ambitious UC plan would turn into an administrative nightmare. He was not the only Cabinet minister who thought this way – one described Universal Credit to me as 'Iain's lunatic plan, which will end in disaster'. Indeed, in the 2012 reshuffle, the Chancellor sought to have Iain Duncan Smith removed from the Work and Pensions Department to be Justice Secretary. IDS made clear he would rather resign than leave the job he was passionate about.

The Chancellor was also sceptical of the power of welfare reform to boost employment, and he was more inclined to think that making life less comfortable for people who were dependent on welfare would push them into work.

George Osborne saw 'welfare' as a big political dividing line. He wanted Labour to be seen as the party of 'welfare scroungers', and he hoped that the Conservatives could position themselves as the party of the 'strivers'.

Relations between the Treasury and the Department for Work and Pensions were therefore often bad and sometimes awful. On some occasions, IDS also refused the No. 10 policy team the statistics and analysis they requested. In return, the Chancellor often declined even to notify the Work and Pensions Secretary of major announcements in his own policy area. When, towards the end of the parliament, the Conservatives re-committed themselves to the pensions triple lock – a major and expensive decision – Iain Duncan Smith was only notified after the press had already been briefed.

George Osborne knew that he could be tough on IDS because the Prime Minister was not the Welfare Secretary's biggest fan either. 'Unless it's got the letters "UC" in it, Iain's just not interested,' David Cameron once complained, in front of fellow Quad members.

Ironically, therefore, Iain Duncan Smith often had to rely on the fourth of the big welfare players – Nick Clegg – to protect his budget from dramatic cuts.

Nick Clegg was a pragmatist on welfare. He understood that cuts in all areas of government were needed, and that by cutting welfare it was possible to more effectively protect areas such as education and the NHS. He also understood that the welfare system that we had inherited from Gordon Brown was in many areas both bloated and badly designed, with far too many people on higher incomes receiving means-tested benefits.

But Nick was also deeply sceptical about the scale of cuts George Osborne wanted to extract from welfare, and he regarded it as indefensible for the government to target those on the lowest incomes rather than those with the greatest wealth.

The Lib Dem leader thought that a major weakness of both David Cameron and George Osborne was that they had little sympathy with or understanding of people on very low incomes, and were inclined to write them off politically as 'not our voters'.

Throughout the parliament, Nick Clegg and his advisers, including his chief economic adviser Chris Saunders, carefully scrutinised every welfare cut proposed by the Chancellor. As the parliament went on, Nick became increasingly concerned about the enthusiasm of David Cameron and George Osborne for cutting the incomes of some of the most vulnerable in society, while they resolutely protected the rich. 'If Osborne wants to balance the books on the backs of the poor then for me that is a red line,' the Liberal Democrat leader told his chief of staff in late 2012. 'I would end the coalition over this.' Increasingly, every Budget, Autumn Statement and party conference became a moment when the Conservative leadership seemed to want to take from the poor, while the Liberal Democrat priority was to ensure that austerity 'started from the top', so that the richest made the greatest contribution.

In the early stages of the parliament, though, the divisions were generally less stark. Both coalition parties cooperated closely to make large-scale welfare savings, generally targeting the options for reform that seemed most palatable and defensible. A lot of these options involved removing benefits from those who were not poor.

In the first spending cuts in May 2010, child trust funds – paid to all children regardless of family income – were abolished. They seemed like a luxury in an era of austerity.

The June 2010 Budget saw a much greater scale of savings than this: tax credits withdrawn from those on higher incomes, a three-year freeze on non-means-tested child benefit, the capping of housing allowances, a switch from using the retail price index of inflation to the consumer price index for annual uprating (saving billions of pounds), changes to disability living allowance rules, and what would later become the so-called bedroom tax.

In the Spending Review, in October 2010, the huge welfare budget was once again targeted for cuts – with a controversial plan to taper away child benefit for higher earners, which many Conservative MPs hated; a one-year cap on contributory claims for employment and support allowance; more cuts to working tax credits and child tax credits; and savings from disability benefits, the savings credit and housing benefit. There was also a new, highly popular, household benefit cap. In short, every benefit was now put under the microscope.

But one area that the coalition was not going to cut was pensions and pensioner benefits.

The 2010 Liberal Democrat manifesto had promised to reconstruct Britain's pensions system, with a higher basic state pension so that pensioners no longer needed to rely on means-tested benefits. These reforms were also designed to restore the incentives to save for retirement – incentives which had been undermined as an increasingly measly basic state pension was 'topped up' for poorer pensioners with initiatives such as 'pensions credit', a means-tested benefit which was withdrawn as people saved more.

Establishing a higher, universal, state pension meant doing two things: firstly, finding the money to establish this new, higher, level; and, secondly, making sure that over time the state pension did not go on shrinking in relation to the incomes of the rest of the population.

So, the Liberal Democrat 2010 manifesto promised to introduce a new triple lock for pensions increases – this would guarantee a very generous annual state pension rise, which would be at whichever was the highest: price increases, wage increases or 2.5 per cent.

George Osborne was nervous about signing up to this Liberal Democrat policy in the coalition negotiations in 2010. He was eventually persuaded by three arguments: that the immediate costs were likely to be low, given the level of wage rises and inflation; that this was part of a move to reduce mass means-testing and restore the incentives to save; and that he didn't want to be seen to be blocking extra money for pensioners. The Conservatives had long regarded the older population, with its high propensity to vote, as a key electoral target.

In June 2010, the introduction of the triple lock was confirmed, and this took effect from April 2011.

Steve Webb then set out to answer a second question: how to introduce a new, higher, universal pension – the 'single-tier pension' – in an era of austerity. It seemed a most unpromising prospect, but by seeking to make savings from future spending on other parts of the pensions system, Steve soon devised a long-term plan to gradually achieve this outcome.

Other members of the government looked on at Steve's work with admiration. 'I have rarely spent a more rewarding half-hour in politics than when I was listening to Steve Webb explaining the government's pension reforms in the House of Commons last week', the Leader of the House of Commons, Andrew Lansley, told the Cabinet in January 2013, after the single-tier pension was finally announced.

This did not mean that pensioner benefits were completely uncontroversial in coalition. In each Budget and Autumn Statement for the full five-year period of coalition government, Nick Clegg and Danny Alexander pressed the Conservatives to make savings in areas such as the winter fuel payments and free TV licences for older pensioners.

These pensioner 'bungs' were highly popular, and much needed by some older people. But they were paid out regardless of income. Indeed, older

Cabinet ministers such as Vince Cable and Ken Clarke were entitled to help with their winter fuel costs, even as they received the £135,000 salary of a Cabinet minister. The system was clearly a nonsense, and ripe for reform.

George Osborne could see the case for making savings, but David Cameron wouldn't budge.

In the 2010 general election, the Labour Party had run a scare story, suggesting that the Conservatives were planning to cut the winter heating allowance, free bus passes and free TV licences. To 'close down' the issue, David Cameron made a cast-iron pledge to leave these benefits untouched. Every time the issue was raised, usually in the Quad, the Prime Minister would step in to halt any serious discussion: 'Look, we have been over this ten times before,' he said in the Quad in 2013. 'I'm not doing this. I made the pledge in 2010, and I'm just not having the TV people do one of those "split-screen moments" on me, where they show what I said in 2010 and contrast it with what I am saying now.'

Eventually, George Osborne himself raised the possibility of cutting the winter heating allowance, in a 2013 letter to the Prime Minister that looked at options for funding the Dilnot proposals on social care costs. But still David Cameron blocked change. Ken Clarke, Vince Cable and millionaire retirees would continue to receive an annual welfare cheque to help them to pay their gas and electricity bills.

Towards the end of the parliament, David Cameron once privately indicated that he would avoid repeating his pledge to protect pensioner benefits in the 2015 general election campaign. But he changed his mind when he discovered that the cuts would only save around £100 million if the pensioner benefits were only withdrawn from the richest pensioners. 'It's not worth the political hassle for that kind of money,' the Prime Minister said in 2014. Rich pensioners were safe under the Conservative Party, even as the incomes of some of the poorest people in the country were reduced.

As the Autumn Statement loomed towards the end of 2011, the issue of benefit savings came back onto the agenda. The surge in food and energy prices had now driven inflation way above its target rate of 2 per cent. Indeed, it was expected to peak in around September 2011 – the very month that by convention was used to fix the increase in benefits for the year ahead.

By September, with inflation reaching 5.2 per cent, the Treasury was taking fright at the big increase in the benefits bill that would now be triggered.

And at the Department for Work and Pensions, Iain Duncan Smith was also worried about allowing benefits to rise by 5.2 per cent at a time when wages were only rising by around 2 per cent.

I soon became aware of a Treasury proposal to freeze all benefits in cash terms for the 2012 year. This change would save the government a large amount of money, but it would result in a 5 per cent fall in the real incomes of most of the poorest people in the country.

I could not see how cutting the real incomes of the poorest people by 5 per cent could possibly be reconciled with the coalition pledge to 'protect those on low incomes from the effect … of spending constraints'. It was also very clear that such a change would lead to a big increase in relative poverty.

Iain Duncan Smith argued that the amounts at stake were small – 5 per cent of a small weekly benefit is a seemingly small amount of cash. But that missed the whole point that for the poorest people, even small amounts of cash are a large proportion of disposable incomes. If you are living on the breadline, £5 a week is a lot.

It seemed incomprehensible to me that at precisely the time that this 5 per cent real cut in benefit levels was being considered, the Conservatives were actively planning to bring down the top rate of income tax, from 50 per cent to 40 per cent.

The government-commissioned review on the 50 per cent rate was close to completion, and given the views of the Chancellor it seemed inevitable to me that the review's conclusions would give a green or at least an amber light to cutting this highly visible tax rate.

At a lunch in October 2011 with Matthew Hancock – George's Osborne's former chief of staff, who was still very close to the Chancellor – I made the case that the top rate should remain at 50 per cent until April 2014, when it should be reduced to 40 per cent. I suggested that it would be politically foolish to cut the 50 per cent rate until we had delivered on the coalition's tax priority – raising the personal tax allowance to £10,000 per year.

Matt Hancock disagreed. To my surprise, he argued that the 50 per cent rate had to be reduced as soon as possible. 'We have to get the issue well out of the way before the next general election,' he said. I suspected that this was also the Chancellor's view. It seemed to me to be profoundly unwise.

In late October I fixed to see Nick Clegg to talk about the Autumn Statement. With the economy growing much more slowly than expected, it was clear that the Autumn Statement was going to be rather grim. Nick confirmed this: 'The growth forecasts are coming in lower for next year, and George and Danny are going to have to announce higher borrowing figures than planned. It will be rather uncomfortable, and there isn't much money to do anything nice. We are going to have to extend the period of public sector pay control, by moving from a complete freeze to a 1 per cent cap. Danny and George have scraped up a few billion to spend on infrastructure, but it's not massive.'

I made a few points: 'Firstly, I am very concerned about this Treasury pressure to freeze benefits. That will cut the real incomes of the poorest people in society by 5 per cent. That just isn't consistent with the pledges we have made to protect the poor from austerity. Secondly, we need to stop all this Tory talk of cutting the 50 per cent tax rate now – that would be politically disastrous. The increase in the allowance should be the priority, and we should only cut the top tax rate when the £10,000 has been delivered. Thirdly, I just think we need to go further and faster on increasing the tax allowance. A lot of next year's planned allowance rise is needed just to uprate for inflation. We should be going for a really big leap in the allowance – either now or in next year's budget. And, finally, with the economy on its back, we need to look at different things we can do to incentivise both private and public investment.'

Nick and I agreed on most of the points. 'But I'm finding Danny a bit difficult on the benefits issue,' he said. 'With the borrowing figures going up, Danny is under huge pressure to do more to cut spending, and he and George are very worried about a 5 per cent uprating. But I agree with you on this, and I am going to veto a cut. It would be outrageous to hit the poor in this way while we are spending vast amounts of money on things like reducing corporation tax.'

So, the 5.2 per cent benefits rise went ahead, despite the opposition of the Prime Minister, the Treasury and the Work and Pensions Secretary. At least the poorest people in the country received some protection from the massive rise in food and energy prices, and relative poverty fell slightly instead of rising. But the Treasury was not amused.

A year and a half later, in April 2013, Nick Clegg and I were sitting in the Cabinet, listening to an economic update from the Chancellor. 'And some other good news is that real household income was up last year, at the fastest rate for seven years,' said George Osborne, looking rather pleased with himself.

Nick and I frowned at each other across the Cabinet Room – neither of us could understand how this great boast could be true, given wage increases were still so moderate.

Encouraged by my similar doubts, Nick interrupted George Osborne: 'How can household incomes have risen so rapidly last year?' he asked.

'Ah,' replied George, looking a little embarrassed. 'Well, that's because we raised benefits and pensions by the full 5.2 per cent inflation rate.' Nick and I couldn't help grinning widely.

'Oh, I see,' replied Nick, trying not particularly hard to avoid revealing his pleasure at the Chancellor's sudden discomfort. 'Thanks, George, that's very useful.'

But if anyone thought George Osborne was a convert to protecting welfare spending, they were to be proved wrong.

Equal Marriage and
the Power of One

2010–13

It was Monday 15 April 2013. Parliament was back for its first day after the Easter recess. The past week had been dominated by the news of the death of Lady Thatcher.

In the evening, the Quad of David Cameron, Nick Clegg, George Osborne and Danny Alexander met for dinner in 10 Downing Street to discuss the state of the coalition and to seek to resolve a number of policy differences.

At dinner there was a subdued mood. It was a difficult time for the coalition, and for once it was not just the Liberal Democrats who were under pressure.

Over food and wine in the 10 Downing Street flat, the Prime Minister told Nick Clegg and the other Quad members: 'Gay marriage has been an absolute disaster. It has totally split my party. It has been as bad for me as tuition fees were for you, Nick.' The Prime Minister said that he now realised that it had been a big mistake to upset the 'Tory base' in the country. He pointed out that in his view this was a key reason why the Conservatives were losing support to UKIP.

In a week's time, the latest growth numbers might show the UK back in a triple-dip recession. The Conservative Party's poll ratings were being undermined by the rise of UKIP, and Conservative MPs were in a belligerent mood over Europe.

The Conservative Party was also, as the Prime Minister acknowledged, nursing its wounds after a massive split on the issue of same-sex marriage. On 5 February 2013, equal marriage legislation was passed in the House of Commons by a huge majority – 400 MPs in favour and 175 against. It was a big leap forward for equality. However, embarrassingly for the Prime Minister, the majority of Conservative MPs had voted against the liberalising measure or abstained – only 127 Conservative MPs voted Aye, while 136 voted No and another 40 were missing or abstained.

Equal marriage was not in the coalition agreement, and nor did it appear in any of the three main party general election manifestos of May 2010.

That it was delivered at all was due to the passion, commitment and courage of one rather junior Liberal Democrat minister.

During the Lib Dem leadership election in 2007, Lynne Featherstone had been a strong supporter of Chris Huhne when he and Nick Clegg fought hard for the leadership. Indeed, after Nick Clegg won, Lynne was only appointed to the new shadow Cabinet on the insistence of the defeated leadership candidate.

Lynne Featherstone was definitely not regarded as one of the new 'Orange Book Tendency', which was in the ascendancy in the parliamentary party after Nick Clegg became leader. Indeed, she seemed to many colleagues to represent the 'radical left' in the party, and her warm and relaxed approach could easily be mistaken for a lack of focus and edge. By 2015 this had all changed, and the MP for Hornsey and Wood Green had become one of Nick Clegg's most trusted and respected allies.

In May 2010, Nick Clegg asked Lynne to represent the Liberal Democrats in the Home Office. She was appointed as the lowest rank of minister – a Parliamentary Under Secretary. Ministers of this tier are parliamentary workhorses – covering low-level debates and mopping up other work that the more senior ministers don't want to do or don't have time for. Lynne could easily have disappeared without trace.

But, early in government, she attended a seminar for new ministers at the Institute for Government. Two experienced former ministers – Lord Heseltine and Lord Adonis – gave some good advice. They warned that a junior minister should decide on one or two things that he or she really wanted to do, and pursue those priorities ruthlessly. Otherwise, there was a real risk that after one or two years in the job they would find that all they had done was process the paperwork generated by their over-active departments.

Lynne quickly took this advice to heart. She had always been a passionate advocate of equality, and was now the Equalities Minister. She decided to pursue the controversial issue of legalising same-sex marriage.

The Labour government of 1997–2010, with the active support of the Liberal Democrats, had made major steps forward in attitudes and policy towards homosexuality. Through public leadership and legislative change, the cause of equality had been decisively advanced.

In 2006, David Cameron, the new Conservative leader, had made what sounded very much like a case for same-sex marriage at his party conference. This was a significant change in attitude for a party that had once actively promoted inequality through the hated Section 28.

Later, in February 2010, before the general election that year, Nick Clegg became the first UK party leader to give clear public support to the principle of same-sex marriage, when a direct question on the subject was put to him in an interview. But the other two party leaders, David Cameron and Ed Miliband, were not prepared to match this support for equal marriage at that time.

Over the two and a half years that followed the 2010 election, Lynne Featherstone maintained a single-minded focus on securing the support to make her vision a reality.

She first obtained the backing of Nick Clegg, which he gave instantly and enthusiastically. 'This is a great, liberal, cause – I will do everything to support you,' he said.

Then, carefully and gradually, Lynne began to work on Conservative ministers and advisers, too. A key issue was to get the support of Theresa May, the Home Secretary and Lynne's boss. It would be difficult, on the face of it, to imagine two more different political figures. Theresa May often came across as dry, stern, unsympathetic and traditional. And in the past, she had often been on the 'wrong side' of debates on gay rights. Lynne Featherstone, by contrast, was warm, liberal, tolerant and highly progressive.

But in spite of these apparent differences, Lynne and Theresa had struck up an unlikely but very positive political partnership. The unlikely duo was as surprising as that of Steve Webb and Iain Duncan Smith at the Work and Pensions Department.

Theresa May had changed her mind about same-sex issues, and said so on *Question Time* early in the period of coalition government. Other ministers might have regarded such a volte-face with begrudging suspicion, but Lynne Featherstone was delighted, and seized the opportunity to secure the Home Secretary's support – which never wavered.

The next hurdle was to ensure the backing of the Prime Minister, and this was achieved with the assistance of fellow ministers such as Nick Herbert. David Cameron was genuinely part of a new generation of Conservatives who had gay friends or relatives, and who were more liberal in matters of personal behaviour and sexual inclination.

Extraordinarily, the greatest early opposition came from some of those in the Labour Party and in the gay rights movement, who claimed to regard same-sex marriage as 'unnecessary', or who were simply too tribal to be able to accept that this massive step forward could be taken by a government which was not of their own political colour. So it was that the early opponents of same-sex marriage included Labour MPs, such as Chris Bryant, and even a senior and influential executive at the gay rights charity Stonewall.

By September of 2011, Lynne had secured the coalition of support that she needed. She and Nick now planned to launch a public consultation on same-sex marriage at the Liberal Democrat autumn conference. However, it turned out that the Conservatives in 10 Downing Street did not want a Liberal Democrat minister to get the credit for this bold move, and before the Liberal Democrat conference, the Tories leaked the news of the consultation and sought to claim all the credit for David Cameron – ironically, given his later regrets about the issue.

Same-sex marriage was supported by a clear majority of the public at this time, but it was not supported by the Conservative Party or most of its members. Nevertheless, the Prime Minister used his own 2011 conference speech to declare: 'I don't support gay marriage despite being a Conservative. I support gay marriage because I am a Conservative.' Sitting at home watching the speech, Lynne Featherstone first felt rather irritated by seeing her work expropriated by another politician. But she soon realised that the Prime Minister's backing was now so strong that he could not walk away – the success of the legislation could only be a matter of time.

Of course, this was to underestimate the strength of the opposition to the new proposals. Most of the churches were up in arms – often displaying precious little of the 'brotherly love' they claimed to expound. Letters and emails rolled in to the Home Office and to MPs' offices complaining of the 'downgrading' of marriage, and warning of the direst developments if the new proposals were allowed to become law.

And out in the country beyond Westminster and Notting Hill, the Conservative Party of the shires began to chunter and grumble. In October 2012, a poll of Conservative Party constituency chairmen showed that 71 per cent opposed same-sex marriage. Many Conservative MPs were under pressure from their supporters to block the measure. And some of the more right-wing Conservative Cabinet ministers began to let their opposition be known.

In mid-October 2012, I met officials and political advisers, in my Cabinet Office capacity, to check progress on the Bill. By then, Lynne Featherstone had moved from the Home Office to the Department for International Development in the September 2012 reshuffle. She was confident that she had put in place all of the support and detail necessary for her proposals to pass into law. The legislation on same-sex marriage was now the responsibility of the Department for Culture, Media and Sport and its Secretary of State, Maria Miller.

'Minister,' the lead official said to me, 'you will be interested to know that we have received 228,000 responses to the government consultation – the largest ever response to a government consultation.'

We agreed a plan that there would be a discussion of the proposals in Cabinet before there was any request for agreement from the members of the Home Affairs Committee. One of the political advisers told me: 'We need to get the PM and DPM to agree this at Cabinet, so that the "rebels" are deterred from making a big thing of it.'

'Who is going to be awkward?' I asked.

'Philip Hammond [the Defence Secretary] and Owen Paterson at Environment are the worst,' was the reply. 'But Iain Duncan Smith could be a problem too.'

The issue came to Cabinet in mid-December. There was a brief discussion of the Bill, with most people being supportive. Then, from the far end of the Cabinet table, Owen Paterson signalled that he wanted to speak.

'Prime Minister, I just wanted to check this will be a free vote for the Conservative Party.'

'Of course it will. I've made that clear a long time ago,' said a visibly irritated David Cameron. 'By the way,' he added, turning to his Chief Whip, 'we really need to get this through Parliament as quickly as possible. I don't want this going on and on for ever. It needs to all be done before the summer.' He didn't say 'before the Conservative Party conference', but people knew what he meant.

The crunch vote on the Equal Marriage Bill came the following February, and split the Conservative Party down the middle. The Bill went through with a huge majority of 225 MPs, but only on the votes of Liberal Democrat and Labour Members. The majority of Conservative MPs voted against the Bill or abstained – to the shock and concern of the Prime Minister and his leading lieutenants.

A few days after the vote, Nick Clegg found himself talking to a shell-shocked Prime Minister. 'I don't think Cameron had any idea what he was letting himself in for,' he told me later. 'The whole equal marriage policy was a sort of accidental revolution, which was driven by the quiet determination of Lynne Featherstone, the active support of the Liberal Democrats, and the benign but passive backing of Cameron and Theresa May. Cameron and Osborne agreed to the policy before they really understood how controversial it would be with their own supporters, and the next thing they knew the whole issue had blown through the roof!'

The revolt in the Conservative Party rumbled on, and even in May 2013 – three months after the clear and powerful Commons majority – senior Cabinet ministers such as Philip Hammond were still actively and publicly opposing the policy.

In the same month, Conservative ministers tried to secure government support for an amendment that would have allowed teachers to express their opposition to homosexuality – something that was totally unnecessary, as reasonable rights of free speech were already embedded in regulations relating to sex education. Both Nick Clegg and I quickly made clear we would not accept such an amendment, and it was dropped.

By July 2013, the legislation had passed its final hurdles, again with another huge Conservative revolt. David Cameron met his summer recess deadline for getting the changes accepted, and on 29 March 2014 the first same-sex marriages took place under the new law.

The new law was a notable step forward in the fight for equality: to some people it meant something practical, but to many others it was more symbolic, marking a clear acceptance of the right of homosexual people to equal treatment. Some opponents claimed it was only ever 'a signal'. Maybe. But signals can matter a lot – and this one did.

The passing of the law on equal marriage was a striking success for a coalition in which the majority of the MPs of the larger party were opposed. And it was a piece of significant social progress at a time when so much of the government's energy was absorbed by the economic crisis and its aftermath.

There can be no doubt that both Nick Clegg and David Cameron deserve considerable credit for this achievement; both leaders played a crucial role.

David Cameron deserves particular credit for taking such a brave and principled stand while leading a deeply divided and conservative party. The Prime Minister may have come to regret his decision, but he never wavered and he gave the legislation his unconditional support.

But the equal marriage law would not have been carried forward without the initiative and persistence of one junior Liberal Democrat minister – Lynne Featherstone. It was she who took the decision to progress a controversial policy that appeared in no party manifesto and was absent from the coalition agreement.

Equal marriage was one of the most important achievements of the coalition and of the Liberal Democrats in particular. And Lynne Featherstone's success demonstrates the 'power of one' – the impact that one purposeful and courageous minister can have in government.

2012

THE EASTBOURNE BUZZ

FEBRUARY 2012

One of the great joys of being a Liberal Democrat MP was getting to go away, roughly every six months, to a 'strategy meeting' of MPs and top campaigners, in carefully selected hotels across the country – usually on the outskirts of London. When I say 'carefully selected', I mean on the basis of cheapness – and my goodness we stayed in some horrible places over the years. On one visit to a particularly ghastly motel, just outside the M25 north of London, I even heard Nick Clegg's Metropolitan Police protection squad complain about being obliged to stay in such a 'dump'. 'We do have standards,' one of them remarked, only half-jokingly.

These two-day meetings – always obligatory, 'three-line whip' affairs – were billed by the party leadership as an attempt to include even the most junior MP in setting the party's strategy and priorities for the year ahead. In reality, the events were an opportunity for a social gathering and team-building event, combined with some tips on raising more money for local parties and delivering more local leaflets. I hated them.

On the first evening, there was always a rather drunken dinner, which finished with the 'Foster Awards', where Don Foster (the MP for Bath) presented awards to MPs for achievements such as being 'Clegg's Pet of the Year' or 'Tweeter of the Year'. To encourage closer cooperation between 'colleagues', the MPs were mixed up across the tables, so that each table contained a number of both 'big wigs' and more junior MPs. The Whips' Office staff also took great pleasure in seating MPs at dinner next to colleagues they didn't get on with, or who they had totally contrasting political views to. I was invariably seated next to the most left-wing member of what counted as that year's 'awkward squad'.

Given these questionable attractions, I always managed to find some matter of the utmost urgency to delay my arrival from Westminster, as well as some pressing constituency engagement that required my departure very early the next morning.

Thursday 2 February 2012 was fixed as the first of these great 'away-day' events of the year. For once, we were meeting in a hotel near the sea – in the newly won Liberal Democrat constituency of Eastbourne. By the usual standards of the hotels that were selected, this wasn't too bad, though in fairness these things are all relative.

It turned out that yet again there was some urgent parliamentary matter that delayed my arrival at the hotel, so by the time I arrived, on the Thursday afternoon, most Liberal Democrat MPs were gathered in a conference room on the ground floor, listening to a dull presentation on campaign priorities.

I came in quietly at the back of the room and noticed a free space on a table at which Ed Davey, the MP for Kingston and junior Business Minister, was sitting. I sat down next to Ed, who was concentrating hard on something on his computer screen. Leaning over, I noticed that Ed was flicking through the contents of the website for the Department of Energy and Climate Change, making notes as he went along.

He glanced over at me, and said, 'We find out tomorrow. Best to be prepared.'

A few months before, in the autumn of 2011, I had met up with Nick Clegg and talked about what we should do if Chris Huhne, our Secretary of State for Climate Change, was prosecuted by the police for a conspiracy to pervert the cause of justice – something bound to prompt his immediate resignation.

Ten years earlier, while he was returning from the European Parliament during his time as an MEP, Chris's car had been 'flashed' by a speed camera, doing 69 mph in a 50 mph zone. Chris already had nine points on his licence, and three points would mean a complete driving ban. But when the speeding declaration was returned to the police, it was his then wife, Vicky Pryce, who was declared as the driver. So, Vicky took the points and Chris kept driving.

Now, following the acrimonious break-up of their marriage, his wife was alleged to have suggested that it was Chris who had been driving. Perverting the cause of justice was and is a serious offence, and the Energy Secretary was insistent that it wasn't true. Anything else would have immediately cost him both his Cabinet job and his political career.

Now, after a long police investigation, a final decision was expected the next day from the Crown Prosecution Service on whether they were planning to prosecute him.

When Nick and I had discussed the matter back in 2011, I had made clear that if Chris lost his Cabinet position, I would not want to replace him. Firstly, the optics of a Liberal Democrat MP who had resigned from government replacing another who had just resigned were not good. And secondly, I did not have any ambition to be Energy Secretary – I was much more interested in economic policy, education or a role at the centre of government, in the Cabinet Office.

I suggested to Nick that Ed Davey – bright, hard-working, energetic and economically literate as he was – would be the perfect person to take over. Ed was only a junior minister at the Business Department, but he had impressed everyone with his work to privatise Royal Mail and to prepare the way for shared parental leave. Nick agreed with my assessment. And, so, with the Crown Prosecution Service decision imminent, Ed was being lined up so that in the event of Chris stepping down, he would be invited to join the Cabinet.

Chris, unflappable as ever, had initially turned up to the beginning of the away day in Eastbourne. However, given the press interest in the CPS decision the next day, the senior press advisers, such as Olly Grender, persuaded him to return immediately to London.

On the morning of Friday 3 February, Lib Dem MPs finished their breakfasts and made their way to the hotel's conference room for another four hours of briefings and discussion. We were all supposed to be concentrating on the campaigns session, which was – ironically – all about our environmental policies. But, in reality, everyone from Nick Clegg downwards was looking at their watches and BlackBerries for the news from London and the CPS.

In the late morning, I saw Steve Webb, the MP for Thornbury and Yate, look down at his BlackBerry. He then turned around, gloomily, and made a thumbs-down gesture to one of our other MPs. Rather oddly, the presentation continued for another fifteen minutes, but no one was concentrating.

Then Nick Clegg came in and made a short and sombre announcement of the news. The CPS had decided to prosecute Chris Huhne, who would now step down as a minister and fight to clear his name. Nick then slipped out at the back of the room with his press advisers, along with Ed Davey and Norman Lamb – who was to take over from Ed as the new Parliamentary Under Secretary of State at the Business Department. In politics, one person's disaster is always someone else's great opportunity.

Our campaign presentations then ended and people were about to depart. The mood was, of course, very subdued. But at that moment, the recently elected Liberal Democrat MP for Eastbourne, the excellent Stephen Lloyd, came in at the back of the room and shouted out: 'Can I introduce you all to the Eastbourne Buzz! Here to promote the greatest town on the south coast!' Walking in behind Stephen was a very tall man, dressed up in a very large 'fluffy bee' outfit. The bee had a smiley face and two large antennae with springs on, which bounced around on his head.

'This is the new mascot to promote our town!' declared Stephen, and in the middle of what was a reasonably serious political crisis for our party, we were suddenly all urged to get in line for a photo with the bee. It was rather surreal.

I avoided the tall bee, slipped outside, packed my bags and took a back route to the hotel car park to avoid the waiting television cameras. I drove back to Somerset with Nick Clegg's strategist, Julian Astle. We listened to the one o'clock news on Radio 4. The coverage of the Huhne resignation was extensive and unremittingly awful. 'God,' said Julian, 'imagine if Chris had won the leadership in 2007? He was only a few hundred votes behind Nick. We would now face a situation where our leader and the country's Deputy Prime Minister was facing a jail sentence. It is too awful to contemplate.'

'Yes,' I said. 'It would certainly have been sub-optimal.'

As it was, it was bad enough. We had lost an able Cabinet minister. We now faced months of bad publicity, followed by a by-election. Of course, it removed from the scene one of the few MPs with the ego and ambition to challenge Nick Clegg for the leadership. Over recent months, rather than being cowed by the prospect of a court case as any normal person would be, Chris Huhne had been flexing his political muscles and putting markers down of his intent to challenge again for the party leadership if and when there was an opportunity.

With the economy flat-lining at best, the Climate Change Secretary had been grumbling privately about the government's economic strategy and signalling the need for a new and more radical approach.

I had recently been reading a biography of Abraham Lincoln by Doris Kearns Goodwin. In this masterful book, Lincoln is quoted as saying of one of his senior colleagues and rivals for power, Salmon P. Chase, 'I suppose he will, like the bluebottle fly, lay his eggs in every rotten spot he can find.' Now there would be no more laying eggs in rotten places.

But losing one of our five Cabinet ministers was a very high price to pay for greater party unity and leadership security, and it was of course a ghastly personal tragedy for Chris Huhne and his family. And the government still had its major challenge – the economic downturn – to grapple with. And it was not a fight that was presently being won.

THE OMNISHAMBLES
BUDGET

MARCH 2012

It was Tuesday 20 March 2012 – Budget Day. Danny Alexander's economics adviser, Will de Peyer, met the Lib Dem press team in the morning to help them to prepare their press lines for both the popular and the more controversial policies that were due to be announced in the Budget.

While Will spoke, the press team carefully noted down his comments and expert analysis: 'Now, there's one issue that could be particularly controversial – it's the VAT treatment of hot take-away rotisserie chicken. We really need to look out for that one,' he said. The press team laughed. 'I'm serious, actually,' responded the Chief Secretary's adviser.

In just a few hours' time, after his Budget Statement was over, Chancellor George Osborne would have been delighted to only be fielding questions about the VAT treatment of rotisserie chicken.

Instead, he had just delivered a Budget that divided the coalition parties, totally undermined the coalition's 'all in it together' narrative by prematurely cutting the top rate of income tax, upset pensioners, caused a huge row with charities and wealthy charitable donors, and led to a controversy about pasties that made the Chancellor and his party look out of touch and isolated.

The Budget was, in fact, such a political disaster that it quickly became known as the 'Omnishambles Budget'. That is now for ever how history will remember it.

For George Osborne, normally such a politically sure-footed Chancellor, the Budget's reception was a huge setback, which even caused speculation that he might be reshuffled out of his job. This was highly unlikely. But the Budget did burst the Conservative poll bubble, and was particularly dangerous for the Chancellor, the Conservative Party and the coalition (in that order), because it occurred at a time when the economy was already looking weak and threatening to go back into recession.

Though the 'Omnishambles Budget' was largely a Conservative-inspired mess, it also caused soul searching and some division within the Liberal Democrats. Indeed, it was arguably the only major occasion in government where Nick Clegg and his senior lieutenant, Danny Alexander, fell out. It took a few months for their relationship to return completely to its normal, very close, state.

There were two major causes that earned the Omnishambles Budget its name. The first was the ill-judged Conservative decision to reduce the 50 per cent rate of tax on incomes over £150,000. The second was George Osborne's refusal to fund a Liberal Democrat demand for a big increase in the personal income tax allowance with tax rises that would fall on the rich.

The Conservatives first began to consider cutting the top rate of income tax in 2011. I was amazed when, at a meeting in spring 2011, at Chevening, the Deputy Prime Minister's grand country residence, I first heard that George Osborne was considering this change.

I have never been in favour of marginal rates of tax as high as 50 per cent, because I consider them to be both illiberal and economically inefficient. Very high rates of tax usually raise little money, as the super-rich always find it easy to use the tax avoidance loopholes that successive Chancellors seem determined to open up. So George Osborne had a case for saying that the 50p rate was just a political symbol introduced by the outgoing Labour government, and one that gave Britain one of the highest marginal rates of income tax in the world.

But 2012 was still a time of considerable austerity, with earnings growth falling well behind inflation; tax credits and other benefits being cut back; and some painful cuts in the services which the poor and vulnerable relied upon. To most people it seemed inconceivable that any government would cut highly visible taxes for the very richest at a time such as this.

I wrote a note to Nick Clegg to this effect in October 2011, warning that we should not support a cut in the 50 per cent rate until later in the parliament. I said it was essential that our pledge to deliver the higher personal allowance of £10,000 should be fully delivered before any cut in the 50 per cent rate. This, in my mind, meant keeping the top rate at 50 per cent until April 2013 or probably April 2014, and then reducing it to its old level of 40 per cent.

I suspected that for the Conservatives, cutting the 50 per cent rate was not just about 'creating the right incentives': this was also in part about impressing big business, and pleasing their wealthy donors and the right wing of the Conservative Party.

Nevertheless, I felt pretty confident that Nick Clegg would hold the line against any rushed cut in the top tax rate. Nick replied to my note, saying that he agreed with me on the 50p issue.

In January 2012, we had the first Liberal Democrat advanced planning meeting on the Budget. Present were Nick Clegg, Danny Alexander, me and Nick's top advisers.

I had pressed for some months for a bigger rise in the personal tax allowance than was already planned by the Treasury for the year ahead. I again pressed this case very hard. Raising the starting point for paying income tax was the best-known and most popular Liberal Democrat policy by far. And I also argued that this tax cut would help those on low incomes, incentivise work, boost the economy at a difficult time, and that it could also provide a much-needed boost to support for the Liberal Democrats if people could see that this was something we had secured.

Most of Nick's other advisers and press people strongly supported my proposal – not least after a grim year for the Lib Dems in 2011 and given the state of the economy. I argued that we should raise the allowance by double the level that the Treasury was planning. This would mean a big rise of £1,260, rather than the Treasury plan for slow, incremental, steady rises of £630 each year. I also argued that we could afford this tax cut, by raising the tax burden on those on top incomes – largely by closing tax loopholes and tightening up on avoidance.

I wanted a big tax cut and I wanted us to make the case for it publicly, so that we would get some political credit. The problem with the coalition was that even where we were having a positive impact on policies, no one knew about it – because our gains were usually secured in the privacy of the Quad.

Worse still, these achievements were then often presented in public by Conservative ministers, such as the Chancellor. How on the earth could voters know what the Liberal Democrats were achieving?

Danny Alexander was much less enthusiastic about a big rise in the allowance, and he was also reticent about pushing for any big rise publicly. The Chief Secretary questioned whether a big allowance rise could be afforded – which is, of course, part of the job description.

Nick Clegg inclined to my side of the argument and, somewhat to Danny's irritation, he asked me to write a paper on the tax options for funding a bigger than expected rise in the allowance. He wanted to some extent to challenge the Treasury monopoly on information flows.

By mid-January, and with the economy still weak, Nick had decided firmly on backing my plan for a larger rise in the allowance. His political strategist, Richard Reeves, wanted him to go public about the fact that we would be pressing for this in the Budget Quads, which would decide on Budget policies over the next few weeks.

Richard Reeves suggested that we should bring forward the next stage of our coalition strategy. We should move from the close cooperation and seamless unity of the early coalition period to a new phase of 'differentiation' from the Conservatives. He saw the higher tax allowance as a great issue to 'differentiate' on.

On 26 January, Nick Clegg made a major speech to the Resolution Foundation, in which he set out clearly the Liberal Democrat Budget demand to go 'further and faster on the tax allowance, as the pressure on household budgets reaches boiling point'.

The Treasury bit its lip on the issue, but it was clear that George Osborne was privately rather irritated that we were doing our negotiating in public, and that we were not only pushing for a big tax cut for working households but wanting to be credited with it too. The Chancellor's irritation only suggested to me that we were doing the right thing. Of course he wanted to take all the credit for good-news announcements himself. Who wouldn't?

By mid-February, the Treasury was still trying to quietly pare back the scale of any increase in the personal allowance, but by now it was also clear that George was pressing Danny Alexander hard for a cut in the top tax rate, from 50p to 40p. This was doubly dangerous – first, it might use up precious money needed to cut taxes for low- and middle-income earners, and secondly, it would be hugely politically inflammatory – not least for Liberal Democrat supporters.

Danny could, of course, see the potential toxicity of cutting the 50 per cent rate, but he was hopeful that he could strike a deal with Osborne where, in exchange for agreeing a top-rate cut, the Conservatives would introduce some sort of mansion tax. 'George is sympathetic. I think I can get him over the line,' he said.

I was both dubious about the politics of this, which seemed to me too clever by half, and also very sceptical that David Cameron would ever accept a wealth tax – a tax that is anathema to many Conservative supporters, and in particular to their very richest donors. I was also worried that because the Conservatives would not contemplate raising taxes on those on high incomes, they were now starting to scratch around for other tax rises to pay for the planned increase in the personal allowance. In my view, the bigger allowance rise should be paid for by the rich, and not by those on ordinary earnings.

Nick Clegg shared this view, and he had to veto a number of politically eccentric Treasury proposals to extend VAT, including extra tax on sandwiches and lunchtime snacks. 'The Treasury are completely crazy over this stuff,' Nick said. 'They keep on talking about fixing VAT anomalies, when any idiot can see the political damage the changes would do. I have stopped George from doing a number of politically stupid things.'

On 27 February, I was at a meeting in my office on the fifth floor of 1 Parliament Street with staff from the Association of Colleges. I received a call from Nick's secretary, asking if I could come over to Nick's office at 70 Whitehall for an urgent meeting. I left quickly, as I knew it must be important – Nick and Danny had just left a Budget Quad with the Prime Minister and the Chancellor.

When I got to Nick's office, there were only two people present – Nick himself and his chief of staff, Jonny Oates. There was no sign of Danny Alexander.

The Liberal Democrat leader looked agitated and irritated. 'Thanks for coming over, David. I need your advice. I am really fuming. At the Quad, George Osborne made a case for reducing the 50 per cent top tax rate. Both Cameron and I have been pretty dubious about this, but Osborne now seems to have squared Cameron, who didn't have much to say. I spelled out that I thought this was a thoroughly bad idea and that at this time any cut in the top rate would be hugely damaging to both parties, and to the whole coalition narrative about a fair spreading of the burden of austerity.'

'But what then totally wrong-footed me was that Danny then came out and supported Osborne, putting me in a minority of one. Danny is still saying we can fund the cost of cutting the 50p rate with other taxes on the wealthy, but I think the politics are awful. Osborne is now, of course, saying that if we don't support his cut for the rich, he cannot support our tax cut for those on low and middle incomes. It's quite absurd. I'm either going to have to veto the whole damn Budget, or I may need to concede a package on the 50 per cent rate to secure the real prize – a massive tax cut for working people. I feel very strongly that this raising the allowance is really needed given the pressure on household budgets and the state of the economy. So what do we do next?'

I said that I agreed with Nick that we should 'never have let the 50 per cent cat out of the bag'. But now this was done, it was very difficult to turn things round. Nick was spitting blood and so was I.

Over the next few weeks, the feverish discussions about this increasingly political Budget went on behind the scenes. Every one of Nick's advisers, other than Danny Alexander, thought that the 50 per cent cut was terrible politics. Some wanted to block the cut, even if it meant giving up on a big allowance rise. But having publicly backed a major increase in the allowance, most of us now wanted to see this delivered. Meanwhile, George Osborne kept rejecting our proposals to find extra money from wealthy taxpayers, and David Cameron finally vetoed a mansion tax.

This meant that to pay for the big rise in the tax allowance, the Treasury assembled a motley collection of tax rises that may have seemed rational in each individual case, but which were almost all politically toxic – higher rates of VAT on certain items, frozen tax allowances for pensioners, and restrictions on charitable tax reliefs.

By Budget week, the most the Conservatives would agree to on taxes for the rich was higher stamp duty on the most expensive properties.

Until the very last moment, Nick Clegg considered vetoing the whole Budget, but ultimately he did not believe that it would be right to lose a big tax cut for working people.

Eventually, he – and not David Cameron – insisted on a compromise. The 50 per cent rate would fall not to 40 per cent, but only to 45 per cent. And measures would be introduced to seek to fully 'claw back' the lost tax from wealthy taxpayers. The rich would, indeed, pay more extra tax than they gained in the 50p rate cut. But would anyone see this?

Nick Clegg agreed the cut to 45 per cent on the basis that this would still be a higher upper rate of tax than the 40 per cent rate that had existed for all Labour's recent years in office. But he was still very concerned by the likely public and party reaction to cutting the top rate. He did not give his final approval until very late in the process.

To set the scene for this highly risky political announcement, it was agreed internally that party president, Tim Farron, and I would write a joint article for *The Guardian* just before the Budget. This would set out the case for a big rise in the allowance, and make the argument that what matters is not the 'flagship' top tax rate, but how much the rich pay in total.

The Guardian delivered the article as promised. Unfortunately, the very same edition of the paper, on Friday 16 March, 'splashed' with a story that the top tax rate would fall – to 40 per cent. This had nothing to do with me or Tim Farron. But some people close to Nick Clegg had felt that there was no way this year's big surprise on Budget Day could be a cut in the top rate of tax. It might suit some right-wing Conservatives, but it would be a disaster for the Liberal Democrats for this to be the big Budget Day splash.

One person in particular was not amused that first the rise in the tax allowance, and now the top-rate tax cut, had leaked out. After seeing the *Guardian* splash, George Osborne, who was returning from a visit to the USA, was furious: 'What the hell is going on? Who leaked my whole bloody Budget?' he asked.

That morning I was visiting East Coker, near Yeovil, in my constituency. I received an urgent text message to call Nick Clegg. I pulled in to the side of a narrow lane and called Nick on my mobile.

'Look, I thought I should tell you that I have just had George Osborne on the line, and I have never heard him so angry. He is furious about the 50p leak and is blaming us – in fact he's blaming you personally. He is absolutely incandescent and is threatening all sorts of revenge. I've told him it wasn't you, and your *Guardian* article with Tim was necessary for our party and designed to be helpful. But you can see why he has put two and two together and made five. You might want to give him a call, because you two have always had cordial relations and it would be a pity to lose that.'

I texted the Chancellor to make clear the leak was nothing to do with me. He sounded pretty grumpy but suggested we meet privately to chat after Budget Day.

By Monday morning, yet more details about the Budget had leaked out – more of the small number of good-news announcements. And by the morning of Budget Day itself, the press were reporting that the Liberal Democrats had secured a huge rise in the tax-free allowance of over £1,000 – from £8,100 to £9,205. This was the biggest ever rise in the allowance in one year.

In the Commons Chamber, Liberal Democrat MPs were under strict instructions to wave our order papers in glee when the Chancellor announced the allowance rise, in order to be seen to 'bank the credit'. But Tory MPs had received the same instruction, so there was a manic display of order-paper waving as both coalition parties sought to claim the credit for the tax cut that Nick Clegg had in fact secured.

Unfortunately, by the time the Chancellor came to deliver his Budget, every conceivable bit of good news in it had already been briefed out either by someone in the Chancellor's office or by someone on the Lib Dem side.

All the media had to get their teeth into was a rag-bag of tax policies put together by politically naive Treasury boffins to raise money for the good things we had announced. If the Conservatives had been willing to tax the rich, these options could have been dropped. But they weren't.

Before long, the stories running in the media were all about a secret tax hit on pensioners – we had decided to freeze their allowance for a year to save money, and to bring all the tax thresholds into line. The next grim story was all about extra VAT on dear old caravans. Then it was a 'hidden' tax hike on the precious pasty. Then journalists spotted a tax hit on charities, and next it was churches. All this was on top of the Labour Party and the left crying foul over the cut in the very highest rate of tax. It was now a doddle for Labour to claim that 'we are not all in this together'.

On the day after the Budget, the media coverage was bad. No, not bad, but truly, universally, shockingly, ghastly. It was the worst Budget reception I could remember for years. There were already campaigns running against the 'Granny Tax', and the 'Pasty Tax', and even Nick Clegg's proposal for a 'Tycoon Tax' was being damaged by the related hit on tax relief for charitable giving.

A few days later, Nick reflected privately on the Budget to friends:

'It has completely blown up in our faces – particularly George's. Of course, it is partly a collective failure, because of coalition dynamics – we wanted the big allowance rise and the Conservatives wanted the 50p cut. But George has made a huge strategic blunder over the 50p rate, just to please business and a few Tory supporters. Cameron and Osborne are now just so desperate to think of ways to stay in power. This is a big blow to them both. It will be interesting to see what their next move will be.'

It was indeed interesting – and unexpected.

A Coupon Election –
Conservatives on the Back Foot

'There is no doubt in my mind that this has been the worst month yet for this government,' said Nick Clegg as he talked with me and close advisers in his rooms in the Cabinet Office at the end of March 2012. 'The economy is weakening. The Budget has been a disaster. But at least, for once, it's the Tories who are taking it on the chin, not us.

'I saw Cameron and Osborne last night and they are in a blind panic – they are looking hollow eyed and frightened. George, in particular, is suddenly like a wounded animal. They've never been through something like this before, and I don't think they know what to do. It's all a massive blow to George's self-confidence, but he has only himself to blame. Osborne and Cameron have shown an extraordinarily tin ear to their greatest vulnerability – that they only care for the rich and not for everybody else.'

A Conservative MP, Nadine Dorries, put it more bluntly in an interview she gave just weeks after the Budget: 'I think that not only are Cameron and Osborne two posh boys who don't know the price of milk, but they are two arrogant posh boys who show no remorse, no contrition and no passion to want to understand the lives of others – that is their real crime.' Her biting observation – 'two posh boys who don't know the price of milk' – was widely quoted and was politically damaging, because it captured in vivid terms a perception of the Prime Minister and his Chancellor at a time when the economy was slipping back into recession and when living standards were being squeezed by surging energy and food prices and microscopically small increases in pay.

At the end of 2011, the Conservative Party's poll ratings had surged after David Cameron unexpectedly exercised his veto at a European Union summit. But after the Omnishambles Budget, and with the economic optimism indices plunging, the Labour Party was as much as ten percentage points ahead of the Tories in some opinion polls. And the Prime Minister's personal poll ratings had plunged too.

The Budget had clearly done huge damage to the Conservatives and to George Osborne's reputation in particular. It had also damaged coalition relations, as Osborne blamed the Liberal Democrats for many of the pre-Budget leaks.

The Chancellor had, for a while, blamed me personally for the leak of his plan to cut the top tax rate from 50 to 45 per cent. But after the Budget, George Osborne was in a bridge-building mood, and he contacted me and suggested that we should have lunch, repair relations and talk about what the government might do next. I expected to be back in the government later in the year, after a reshuffle, and so welcomed the chance to restore our previously good relations.

Lunch was fixed for 12.30 p.m. on Thursday 29 March at the Treasury. I received a warm greeting from one of the Treasury doormen, whom I knew from my time as Chief Secretary, and then I was shown upstairs to the Chancellor's large suite of rooms on the second floor. We ate by ourselves in the Chancellor's grand office, which has a fine view over St James's Park.

George Osborne was friendly as always, but I could see that he was pretty knocked back by the awful public and media reaction to his Budget, as well as by the bleak economic news. He was distinctly less 'bubbly' and light-hearted than usual. Indeed, he looked strained and tired.

I started our meeting by addressing head-on the 50p tax issue. 'Look, I want to make it quite clear that I did not leak this announcement to the media. I also want to be very clear that I think you were crazy to put this policy in this Budget, when ordinary people's incomes are being squeezed so badly. You should have saved this cut until later in the parliament – at least until the £10,000 allowance had been delivered. And it really doesn't help that we are raising other money from rich people to pay for the 50p cut –

the optics of cutting tax for the richest few per cent of people are just awful.'
George listened without saying much.

I continued by spelling out how difficult the policy was for our party at this time: 'You really need to understand that this was an incredibly controversial policy for Nick Clegg and the Lib Dems. Indeed, Nick asked every one of his advisers what they thought on the 50p cut, and they were all opposed to it. He was under a lot of pressure to veto it, and while I certainly did not leak the policy I am going to say to you bluntly that if you think we would allow this announcement to be your great Budget "white rabbit out of the hat" you must be crazy. It would have been even more damaging if this had been the big surprise on Budget Day. And we needed to be able to "sell" to our supporters the fact that we would only allow the top-rate cut in exchange for other taxes on the rich.'

George nodded, weakly. 'Look,' he said, 'I accept that the politics have been bad. But I think the economics are good. The 50p rate doesn't raise serious money and it's one of the highest top tax rates in the world. There just isn't any good time to do this. Would it really be easier closer to the next general election? I just wanted to get it over as quickly as possible. Maybe I got the timing wrong. I accept that the media and public reaction isn't exactly adoration of me. I don't know...'

I replied that I thought that the issue was all about the timing and that this was very bad. I said I thought the announcement should have been made at least a year further on, with a cut all the way from 50 per cent to 40 per cent, and with a very clear message that it was only being delivered when the £10,000 allowance was in place. I pointed out that we now had a 45p rate, which we might well get stuck with since it would be very difficult to make another reduction in this parliament. George accepted that, and I said I was pretty sure that Nick would now veto returning to the issue before 2015.

George then said he wanted to open the discussion up a bit beyond the Budget. He said: 'Look, we're having a tough time on the economy now, but that will pass. Or at least if it doesn't we're all finished anyway! I happen to believe that this coalition is doing a good job for our country, and I am guessing that you and Nick and Danny and others prefer delivering things in government than putting out press releases in opposition? For myself, I have to say bluntly that David and I have "done" opposition. It was fun while it lasted, but I don't intend ever going back there again. I want to be in power for the rest of my political career, and I want to be able to DO things. The main priority for me now is how we get back into government again in 2015. It's going to be tough, even with Ed Miliband as Labour leader.'

George then leaned forward and came to what I took to be the central purpose of our lunch: 'We both want to be in power in 2015, but what sense does it make to be fighting each other in every single seat at the next election? Instead of battling over places like Taunton, we should be able to focus our fire on Labour. Surely we should be thinking of some sort of deal in 2015 where we don't fight each other in our key seats? It would be a sort of "coupon election", where certain coalition candidates in our key seats would get a free run against Labour. So, for example, we wouldn't stand candidates in places like Taunton and Wells, and you wouldn't stand in some of our marginal-held seats – where the main battle is with Labour. Surely that would work?'

I sighed, and smiled. I knew it was a tempting offer, and potentially a lifeline for a party like the Liberal Democrats, whose polling support had dropped by well over half from the 2010 general election level. I could tell that George intended his proposal as a serious offer and not as a trap. But taking the bait would nonetheless have massive consequences – many of them negative.

'That's a nice idea,' I said, 'but I am not sure that it would work for us. Let's assume you could impose it on your own party, and that your local Tory associations would play ball. For you, it would be a pragmatic issue of not fielding candidates in thirty or forty seats. You would still be a big, national party with a clear brand. But for us it would be a different order of decision. We would be aligning ourselves clearly and for the foreseeable future with just one of the two biggest parties. We would arguably be cutting adrift our candidates and our MPs in many seats where Labour is the challenger. And we would be destroying both our perceived independence and our ability to attract voters whose basic instincts are leftish or centre-leftish. It might – might – help us to hold more seats in 2015, though at present we are confident of seeing you lot off in our constituencies anyway, but for the longer term it would be hugely damaging. For the sake of protecting thirty or forty seats we would be saying to voters in 600 constituencies, "Don't bother voting Lib Dem here. They cannot win. They are Conservative lap-dogs. The only choice nationally is between Labour and Conservatives."'

George sighed and winced. I added: 'And if that weren't enough, I very much doubt our party would play ball. Our MPs and members have bought into this coalition because they could not see a better, feasible, alternative for us or the country. But the idea of getting hitched up long-term to you lot would create something close to a riot at our conference. I am confident Nick couldn't carry this even if he wanted to.'

George said that my response was disappointing. 'Just think about it,' he said. 'I don't believe you and Nick want to be back on the opposition benches any more than David and I do. I've done that. I am never doing it again.'

George then tried another tack: 'I know that Nick now has you leading on the reform of party funding. Surely we could do something on this issue which would undermine Labour, and would stop the trade unions from drowning Liberal Democrat and Conservative seats in union funding, as they did in May 2010? It would also really put Ed Miliband on the spot. There is nothing more that I would like to see every day from now until the general election than Ed Miliband on the TV news having to defend Labour's link with the trade unions. At the moment, that would certainly be better for the coalition parties than coverage of my Budget Statements!'

I said that we had a common interest in stopping massive political spending by 'third parties', such as the unions. But I added: 'This has to be part of a deal on party funding, including capping big donations and improving state funding of parties.'

'Ah,' said George, 'you mean giving more money to the Lib Dems, do you?' and he laughed.

'That might be a regrettable side-effect,' I said. 'But, seriously, if any proposals which we put forward just look partisan, they'll come a cropper in the House of Lords anyway, and just get nowhere.'

Our lunch continued for almost two hours, and before I left we discussed the reshuffle.

'I understand that Nick is thinking of bringing you back in some central role?' said George. 'In the Cabinet Office?'

'Yes, that seems to be the idea. Of course, I would love to come back here to the Treasury one day but Danny is doing a fantastic job...' – at this, George allowed a smile to play briefly over his face and I tried, unsuccessfully, to read his mind – '...and Nick needs more support in the centre and this would be a low-key way to come back to government.'

'Well, needless to say, some of the media will be awful,' said George. 'But it will be good to have you back in.'

The meeting was vintage George. He was amusing, self-deprecating, strategic, focusing on the long term and not just the short-term challenges, and – of course – brutally political. He is a man who understands in great detail his political opponents – their strengths and their weaknesses. All politicians follow to some extent what goes on in other parties, but in this intimate knowledge of others and this strategic sweep, George was always in a league of his own.

The Chancellor was and is a person who could be highly tactical, but it should also be understood that he has clear and generally consistent ideological bearings, and a focus on the far political horizons and not just on tomorrow's headlines.

George is liberal on issues of personal choice and morality. He is liberal in his economic outlook, even when that confronts sensitive issues such as immigration. He is metropolitan in approach, and an internationalist, not a Little Englander.

But nobody can mistake George Osborne for a political liberal – his interest is in exercising power and not in redistributing it or holding it to account. And nor is he what I would describe as a social liberal – he believes in opportunity, but he is naturally cautious about using the power and certainly the financial clout of government to extend opportunity, particularly when richer people are asked to pick up the bill.

I liked George, even when I profoundly disagreed with him. We agreed, in fact, on much. But we were in different parties because we did not seem to share the same ambition to extend opportunities to every single member of society. I believed in a more powerful role for the state in delivering opportunity and challenging the inequalities generated by a free market system. George seemed to me more comfortable with the status quo – which is why, I suppose, he is a Conservative.

After our meeting, I made sure I spoke to Nick Clegg, to update him on the 'coupon election' proposal. We met later that day in Nick's cavernous office in 70 Whitehall, with its extensive views of Horse Guards Parade. As we spoke, music from one of the practising guards' bands drifted through the windows, occasionally rising in volume as some of the more martial music was being played.

'Interesting,' said Nick. 'George has actually proposed something like that to me before. I rejected it, for the reasons you give. God, he and Cameron really are desperate for power, aren't they? They would sell their mothers to stay in Downing Street. They are also petrified of Boris Johnson coming along and challenging them for the leadership. Boris is going to win the London Mayoralty again, and will then be on serious manoeuvres.

'I've been watching George and Cameron closely now. They are alike but also different. George loves power even more than Cameron. But he is more reckless with his popularity than Cameron is. George also has a strange maturity about the limits of his own personal appeal to the electorate. He understands they don't love him and probably never will. George is quite thoughtful about Europe, and tolerant and metropolitan in his outlook, but he is clearly very, very anti-welfare spending. Cameron is a traditional shire Tory, and he can be rather cavalier. I like him and can do business with him, and he has many strengths. But he worries too much about what the press are saying about him – he sees absolutely everything through this prism. I have to say that I find Osborne easier to deal with. And the more I deal with him, the more I respect him. He is so totally blunt and transactional. George always thinks and understands what each side wants, and he is always saying, "Can't we cut a deal?"'

A few weeks later, after the latest economic statistics showed that the economy had moved into a double-dip recession, George Osborne got a small taster of the reaction of the British public to him, when he attended the Olympic Games. He was invited to present an award, and when he was introduced to the crowd, he was roundly booed. There was extensive coverage of the Chancellor's embarrassment on the UK media.

What was fortunately rather less well known was that another senior British politician was also booed while attending the Olympics. Nick Clegg was attending the Games in a low-key, private capacity on 9 August. He was with his family watching a hockey game – England versus the Netherlands – when he was invited by the organisers to go onto the pitch to be interviewed about the match. He didn't really want to go, but felt he couldn't decline. As he took the microphone and started to speak, there was an outbreak of low but audible booing. The Deputy Prime Minister, a master of many European languages, quickly started to speak in fluent Dutch to the visiting foreign fans, who then, in amazement at hearing an Englishman speak a foreign language competently, started to cheer and clap, drowning out the British boos. A relieved Nick Clegg made his way quickly back to his seat, vowing never to speak again at any sporting event.

Unfortunately, Dutch hockey fans are not able to vote in UK elections. And there were elections in the UK in spring 2012. And the prospects weren't good for either the Liberal Democrats or their battered leader.

From Cleggmania
to Cleggzilla

2012

It was autumn 2010. Nick and Miriam Clegg were driving back to their house in Nick's Sheffield constituency, accompanied by their three young boys, Miguel, Antonio and Alberto.

The Liberal Democrat leader did his best to avoid the route that took the family past enormous posters that had recently been plastered up across some of the biggest billboards in the city.

Under the huge black letters 'Cleggzilla – Bringing Havoc to a City Near You!' was a massive poster showing a monster-sized Nick Clegg in black shirt and gold tie, trampling the city of Sheffield underfoot, while a decaying Forgemasters factory occupied the bottom right-hand corner of the mammoth display.

It turned out that Nick Clegg's children were rather unmoved by these displays, but if his family was too young to take offence from such attacks, for the Liberal Democrat leader himself the period from autumn 2010 to spring 2012 had actually been very tough.

Being Deputy Prime Minister was, of course, exciting, an honour and a huge opportunity. Many of the main Liberal Democrat general election manifesto policies, such as the increased tax allowance and the £2.5 billion pupil premium, were now being delivered.

But after the ecstasy of Cleggmania in 2010, the events of the past eighteen months had been difficult to take. Liberal Democrat poll ratings plunged rapidly after going into coalition. The public row and party split over tuition fees had then made matters even worse. And after this came the spending cuts; and then the unpopular NHS Bill; and then the lost AV referendum. In May 2011, 750 Liberal Democrat council seats had been wiped out in a single night. And now, following the awful Omnishambles Budget, the country faced the prospect of a double-dip recession.

Peter Kellner, the polling guru, was forecasting that the Liberal Democrats might have as few as ten MPs left after the 2015 general election.

All these national challenges were hard enough. But it got personal, too. Excrement was pushed through the letterbox of the constituency office in Sheffield. Meanwhile, the family home in Putney in west London was under close and visible police watch. Nick Clegg's own poll ratings had plunged – including on the key issue of trust. Within six months, the Liberal Democrat leader had gone from being one of the most popular ever British politicians to being one of the most distrusted. And now Nick was beginning to doubt his ability to reconnect with the public.

In May 2012, the Deputy Prime Minister and his wife travelled to Buckingham Palace for a celebration of the Queen's Jubilee. As they got out of their car outside the palace, there was a half-hearted cheer from the crowd, followed by some loud boos. For the great, popular hero of Cleggmania, this fall from grace was difficult to take.

After the Budget was out of the way that spring, Nick asked me to have dinner with him one evening. We drove the short distance from Parliament to the Quirinale restaurant just off Millbank. The two ever-watchful Special Branch security men, who followed Nick Clegg everywhere now, sat down at a table near us, looking hopelessly conspicuous.

'Look,' said Nick. 'I wanted to discuss two things with you: the reshuffle, and my position as leader.

'First, let's do the reshuffle. Cameron keeps delaying it, but I guess it will be July or September. I want you back in – as a minister in both the Cabinet Office and the Department for Education. I want someone in the centre to help me and to take some of the pressure off Danny. Basically, you would become Oliver Letwin's opposite number, as Minister for Government Policy. But I also want you in Education because I want a stronger presence there, and someone who makes sure there is a strong Liberal Democrat imprint on education.

'More widely, I am going to return Nick Harvey, Jeremy Browne, Paul Burstow and Sarah Teather to the back benches. They've all done OK, but I just want to give some other good people a chance. And frankly, I can cover the Foreign Office and Defence issues myself, by being on the National Security Council. What we need is a bigger presence in areas where there are no Liberal Democrat ministers, such as the Environment Department. I am going to promote Norman Lamb, David Heath and Jo Swinson.'

I made a strong case for keeping my friend Jeremy Browne in the government – possibly moving him to the Home Office. Nick said that he would think about it. Then he raised his own position. It was the first time I had ever heard him consider standing down as leader.

'I need to think about whether I should fight the next election as leader. It's been a tough two years and I have to do what is right for the party. If I was going to be a liability in 2015 and reduce our support, I just would not want to stay.'

I said that I thought he should stay as leader. 'Coalition was always going to be tough. In 2015, you cannot again be the "fresh-faced boy" that you were in 2010, with all the optimism and "outsider" advantage. But if people don't love you, they can still respect you and the party. And they will be able to see that we have turned the economy around and delivered much of our manifesto. Anyway, if not you, who else? Vince Cable isn't much more popular – and he oversaw the tuition fees disaster. And I think we can agree that Chris Huhne isn't well placed either. That's it. No one else could do this job.'

Nick seemed somewhat reassured, but I could tell that he was still seriously considering his future. And the awful local election results in May, with another net loss of 336 Liberal Democrat councillors, gave him further cause for concern.

A few weeks later, on the evening of Sunday 20 May 2012, I received a call from Jonny Oates, Nick's trusted chief of staff. 'Look, this is private. Nick is feeling pretty battered and bruised at the moment. He wants to gather a few allies together later on this week to have a bit of a chat. Are you free this Wednesday? I would rather you didn't tell people about this, because it's going to be quite a small group – just Nick, Miriam, you, me, Richard Reeves and Lena [Pietsch, Nick's former press secretary, who was off on maternity leave].'

I drove over to Nick's house in Putney for 8.30 p.m. on 23 May. There was only one police officer on duty outside the house – a welcome change from my last visit, which had occurred in the aftermath of the vote on tuition fees.

Nick's eldest son, Antonio, offered us wine and nibbles and we chatted politely in the living room. Then the children went up to bed, and the six of us went through to the back of the house and sat down around the dining room table.

Nick opened the conversation:

'Thanks for coming. It's been very tough recently, for all of us, and I wanted to pull together some of those I know and trust, to talk about the party's future and indeed about my future. It seems to me that a lot of what we planned for a year ago just hasn't worked out. We expected an economic recovery, but because of the mess in the Eurozone, the economy is flat at best. All our hopes of finishing the parliament with a balanced budget, more spending and some tax cuts now look totally unrealistic. Tuition fees have been a real mess, and my reputation in particular has been seriously undermined as a consequence. We have also lost the AV referendum, which is a very big setback.

'I also have to say that I am finding Cameron hugely disappointing to work with – more cautious, less radical, less the genuine compassionate Conservative. I can see the real risk that I carry on for three more years and simply lead the party to electoral disaster in 2015. I love my job, and I feel a deep sense of responsibility to the party. But because of that, I also want to do what is right for the party, and put the party first. The absolute last thing I want to do is to overstay my time as leader, or be forced out in humiliation. I am also feeling increasingly isolated and cut off from the public, in this job.'

When Nick had finished speaking, he invited us to give our views. Richard Reeves plunged in first: 'The very worst thing now would be if the Liberal Democrats bailed out of the coalition. This would just confirm all the negative stereotypes that people have about our party. I also think Nick, quite bluntly, that you need to stay. Yes, your ratings are very negative. But I believe that any leader of our party, under these circumstances, would have negative ratings. You are still capable of being a huge asset. But we do need to do more to cut through with the public. And you, Nick, need to do something big so that people see you again in a different light. We need, for example, for you to really take on Cameron over something big that you really care about. And you need to win. After fees, we have to change the public narrative.'

Jonny Oates spoke next: 'Yes, it's been bloody tough. We can see in government that the Tories are truly awful people and they have been a disgrace over 50p and over AV. But you cannot get into a negative rut about this. You are a huge asset, and you are great at your job. You have done more in two years as a Liberal Democrat leader to advance Liberal Democrat policies on the tax allowance, the pupil premium, equal marriage, early years education, the green agenda and fixed-term parliaments than the last ten leaders put together. We need you. But we also need a clearer strategy to distinguish ourselves from the Conservatives. And I agree with Richard – we need to work on your own brand, and give people a new narrative about you. And we have to get you out of the Westminster bubble.'

'That's clear,' said Nick. 'Lena?'

'Nick, now that I am not so close to things, I think I actually have a clearer perspective,' said Lena. 'We are not doing enough in the public's eyes to make a real difference. We are moderating the Tories. But we need to do much better than that. We need our own positive narrative. But you should definitely stay. You can bounce back, Nick, I know you can. In 2015, people may not love you like they did in 2010. But they can still respect you. That is what we need to aim at.'

I was the last to speak. 'Firstly, coalition was always going to be tough, and it was always going to cost us in the opinion polls and the ballot box. We knew that. What has been worse than expected has been the state of the economy and the debacle over tuition fees. The key now is to focus relentlessly on the growth agenda and help to turn the economy around – and that means challenging the natural conservatism of both the Treasury and the Bank of England.

'But I don't accept that we are not making a difference in government. The tax allowance. The pupil premium. Ensuring benefits have been properly protected against inflation. And resisting extreme Tory policies such as the 'fire at will' employment proposals. These are all real achievements and we need to communicate them more effectively. Finally, there's you, Nick. I agree with Lena that you are a real asset to the party, and you can be an asset again in 2015. And with Chris Huhne out of the running, there is no serious alternative leader and most of your colleagues support you. I still think that the moment of maximum danger to your leadership will come at the autumn 2013 Liberal Democrat Party conference. By then, the excitement of coalition will have worn off, and people will be making calculations about who they want to lead us into 2015. Beyond that, the leadership issue will be settled because it will be too close to an election for change.'

Towards the end of the meal, Nick raised the issue of whether he should take on a big portfolio, as well as being Deputy Prime Minister, in the forthcoming government reshuffle. 'The problem is', said Nick, 'that nobody knows what a Deputy Prime Minister actually does. Perhaps I could take over the Business Department or even Education?'

Richard Reeves raised Danny Alexander's role: 'Danny is incredibly impressive, but I think he has gone a bit native at the Treasury. He has become the Treasury representative to the Liberal Democrats, when it was supposed to be the other way round. I think he is also just too powerful and doing too much. He brokers all the cross-government stuff with Oliver Letwin outside the Treasury. And he's in the Quad. It's too much.'

After the dinner, I offered to give Richard a lift back to Waterloo Station. We walked down the road to my car, parked a short distance away.

'It's bloody tough for Nick,' said Richard. 'He's a great guy, and what we are doing in some areas of government is fantastic. But I have been looking at the polling figures recently and they are truly awful. In particular, Nick's own brand has been terribly undermined by tuition fees. Trust is the key. I will always back Nick 100 per cent. But if I am honest, I don't really know for certain if Nick can win that trust back. If you just look at the polling figures, it could be getting close to irrecoverable.'

A few days later, Nick said to me: 'I have decided to go on. I have thought about it a lot – about what is best for all of us. I think that continuing in post is right for the party. But for me, the local elections in May 2013 are now key. If I cannot turn things around by then, maybe I should think again. We really need to show that we can deliver over the months ahead.'

But on both the economy and political reform, the immediate outlook was not good.

POLITICAL REFORM:
'KITTY GETS IT'

2012

Nick Clegg, as Lord President of the (Privy) Council, was once again at
Buckingham Palace for one of his regular audiences with Her Majesty
the Queen. The two of them got on well, and the Deputy Prime Minister was
one of a long line of British politicians who were immediately charmed by
the Queen's mixture of diplomacy, great experience and wisdom, discretion
and a distinctly dry sense of humour.

'What is happening in Parliament at the moment?' asked the Queen.

Nick Clegg shifted uncomfortably.

'Well, Ma'am,' he said, 'I am not sure that you are going to approve.
We are just legislating to change the rules on the royal succession. For the
first time ever in the history of the British monarchy, a first-born girl will
succeed to the throne before a later-born boy.'

The Queen was quiet, starring off into the middle distance. 'I hope this
change does not cause difficulties, Ma'am?' added the Deputy Prime Minister,
to break the silence.

'Good grief, Mr Clegg,' the Queen said, turning her face back again. 'By
then, I'll be dead!'

This small reform was one of a number of pieces of political modern-
isation on which the coalition was making progress, along with the more
substantive issue of moving to fixed-term parliaments.

But the problem was that while the small political reforms were making progress, the larger reforms – such as the Alternative Vote – were not.

After the failure of the AV referendum, Nick Clegg had decided to focus on House of Lords reform. He wanted to deliver an elected second chamber – just over 100 years since this proposal had first become Liberal policy. Nick felt strongly that legislators should be chosen by election, rather than on the basis of patronage or family history.

While Lords reform was a priority for the Liberal Democrats, the Conservatives were prioritising legislation to reduce the number of MPs and redraw the constituency boundaries. They were convinced that both changes would tilt the electoral system for the House of Commons back in their favour and help them to win the general election in 2015.

Both issues – Lords and boundaries – were crucial to the political interests of the parties. Now, within weeks of the Omnishambles Budget, the two parties and their leaders would clash over this agenda in a furious row that came as close as any to threatening the survival of the coalition. Indeed, the summer row over constitutional reform was probably the most difficult period of the parliament for coalition relationships.

Nick Clegg's view was that both parties should honour the coalition agreement in full. The Liberal Democrats should therefore vote for boundary reform, even though this threatened to reduce the party's number of seats. And the Conservatives should vote for an elected House of Lords – which was, after all, supposed to be their own party's policy.

On the back benches of both parties, however, the views were rather different. Many Conservative MPs were strongly opposed to an elected House of Lords. They didn't like the proposed voting system – proportional representation – and they feared that an elected Lords would be able to challenge the mandate of an elected Commons.

Many Liberal Democrat MPs didn't like the proposed boundary reforms, either. At a meeting of our parliamentary party on Tuesday 22 May 2012, Tim Farron, the party president, asked: 'Do we really care that much about Lords reform? Yes, it would be nice to do. But I am far more worried about the damage that the boundary reform will do. I've seen estimates that if the boundary changes go through, and given our poor opinion poll ratings, there might only be ten or twenty Liberal Democrat MPs left after the next election. If it's that bad, we ought to be grateful that the Tory backbenchers are thinking of voting against Lords reform – it will give us a great excuse to hit back and withdraw our support on boundaries.'

Tim's seemingly gloomy forecast was slapped down by Paddy Ashdown. But it was an important issue to consider. Our campaign department had privately calculated that boundary reform could cost us between eight and twelve seats – a large proportion of our total of just fifty-seven MPs.

I had my own concerns about whether the Conservatives were really willing to deliver anything substantive on the political reform agenda. Nick had asked me to lead cross-party talks on the reform of party political funding. But these were getting nowhere, due to Conservative foot-dragging – and in spite of a clear manifesto commitment. Eventually, the Conservatives told us bluntly that they were not willing to give up their big donations – they were not even willing to implement their own proposal for a £50,000 donation cap.

I was getting fed up with the Conservatives' wilful back-sliding on constitutional reform, and I was worried about the ambiguous signals that David Cameron was sending out to his backbenchers. When the Prime Minister was questioned on the issue of Lords reform in the House of Commons in early May 2012, his response was underwhelming. The Prime Minister seemed to me, deliberately or inadvertently, to be giving a green light to Tory backbench obstructionism.

And now, indeed, there were rumours that a Conservative backbencher would move an amendment to the House of Lords Reform Bill, insisting on a referendum before elections took place. That clearly risked both a delay and a defeat. We did not consider a referendum necessary on Lords reform, as it was contained in the manifestos of all of the main parties in 2010.

My own real fear was that we might loyally back boundary reform for the Commons, while the Conservatives pretended to support Lords reform but then quietly allowed it to be drowned, either in the swamps of resistance in the Commons and in the existing (unelected) Lords, or by allowing a referendum.

I thought we had two serious options. Firstly, we could just agree to take 'Lords and boundaries' off the agenda, and focus on the economy. Or we could see the boundaries reform through, but only if we were guaranteed Lords reform, without a referendum.

On Wednesday 9 May, Nick convened a meeting of his closest advisers to discuss the handling of Lords reform. We met before Prime Minister's

Questions in Committee Room 391 of Portcullis House – the room we had used for the failed coalition negotiations with the Labour Party in May 2010. The only MPs there were Nick Clegg, Danny Alexander and me. But all Nick's closest policy, press and political advisers were present.

Julian Astle made the case for junking the whole constitutional reform agenda and simply focusing on the economy and public service reform. Nick said he really didn't want to just give up on this agenda, and in his view it was of crucial long-term importance to the party and the country. He said that both sides had made promises in the coalition agreement and that we should keep them. 'We have waited 100 years for Lords reform. We have got to try to deliver it. I am just not willing to use Lords reform to junk boundaries.'

I said, 'Look, Nick, you know I am not really someone who gets terribly excited about the political reform agenda, but I do understand its importance. If you want to go 100 per cent for Lords, then we should do that. But this is going to be very tough for the Tories and I think the only way we can remotely get them to deliver is if they understand that we are not budging on Lords, and that if the Lords legislation doesn't pass, we will torpedo boundaries.

'I am also really worried that Tory backbenchers will attach a referendum condition to the Lords Bill, so that we could end up with boundary reform but then lose Lords reform as we lost AV. A public vote on this is very unpredictable, given that it will seem a big distraction right now.'

No final decisions on tactics were made at this meeting, but Nick was clear that he wanted to deliver his election pledge.

Over the next two months, there were endless discussions within the Liberal Democrats, and between the Conservatives and Liberal Democrats, to try to deliver Lords reform.

Lord Rennard suggested an ingenious compromise in which the remaining hereditary peers would leave Parliament in 2015, to be replaced by the first 100 elected peers. There would then be a referendum in 2017, before any future elections. In exchange for this and a comprehensive deal on party political funding, we would allow the boundary changes to the House of Commons to go through. I was a little worried about conceding at all the principle of a referendum. But in any case, when Nick Clegg put the suggestion to David Cameron on 16 May, the Prime Minister's response was that it was 'too clever by half', and that Tory backbenchers wouldn't buy it.

As time went on, I could see the real risk that all of the proposed political reforms – Lords, party funding and boundaries – were going to end up in the ditch. I was absolutely determined that if the Conservatives could not deliver Lords reform without a referendum, then we should immediately sink their boundary reforms. It would be fatal to our party's interests, and indeed to Nick Clegg's leadership, if we risked losing seats in the House of Commons without getting anything else in return.

I was convinced that the Conservatives would only make a serious attempt to deliver on Lords reform if they knew that we were not bluffing on the boundary changes. The Conservatives were arguing that the boundary review had been agreed in 2010 in exchange for an AV referendum. So their position was that we 'had to' deliver boundary reform as part of the 'deal' that had been done.

While it was true that in May 2010 boundary reform and an AV referendum had been part of one policy 'trade', my view was that we had no responsibility to deliver on boundary changes for the Commons if the Conservatives dumped other key parts of the coalition agreement, such as Lords reform or party funding reform. The coalition agreement had to be observed in full by both parties – it was not a menu to be selected from.

So that there was no scope for any confusion, I decided to talk directly to George Osborne, to make sure he absolutely understood our position. With Nick Clegg's agreement, I fixed a call with the Chancellor for Tuesday 29 May.

I was down in my Yeovil constituency, and about to visit a school in the village of Merriott. I pulled my car in to the side of the road, near the village church. At noon, my mobile phone rang, and it was 'Switch', the operator on the 10 Downing Street switchboard. 'Is that David Laws? I have the Chancellor of the Exchequer for you. Please hold.'

George Osborne came on the line. 'Hi, David. How are you? What can I do?'

I started by saying: 'I am worried about where things are getting to on political reform. Bluntly, I can see a major coalition bust-up, in which both sides will lose out. Maybe that is unavoidable, but I wanted to spell out very clearly where the Liberal Democrats are on this, to see if things are recoverable.

'After losing the AV referendum, delivery on House of Lords reform is now essential for Nick and for our party. We have been carefully considering this over the last few weeks and I want you to know what we have decided. Unless we get at least some peers elected by 2015, the party and Nick will insist on delaying the Commons boundary review until after 2015.'

There was a brief silence at the other end of the line, and then George said: 'If you do that, it could potentially bring down the whole coalition. You were in those negotiations in May 2010, as was I. You know that the Lib Dems agreed to support the boundary changes, in exchange for the AV referendum. Well, you've had your referendum. Now we are entitled to our boundary changes. It would be very, very serious if the Lib Dems tried to go back on that.'

I replied: 'You are correct that in our talks the issues of the AV referendum and boundaries were tied together – indeed, that was my own idea. But we are entitled to expect the Conservative Party to stick to its other pledges on an elected Lords and on party political funding. If the Conservative Party doesn't honour these other commitments, then you cannot expect us to naively deliver on boundaries. It's just not going to happen. Both sides must stick to all of the coalition agreement. Failing to deliver has a price. And even if Nick wanted to deliver boundary reform without Lords reform – which he does not – our party wouldn't go along with it. So you and the Prime Minister are going to need to do a better job in getting your MPs on board for Lords reform.'

George Osborne sighed and said: 'Well, I don't think we can get Lords reform through Parliament without a referendum. Even Liberal Democrat peers like Lords Steel and Ashdown seem to be saying that now.'

I said: 'A referendum before 2015 could well be lost, and isn't needed. And a referendum in 2015 on general election day 2015 isn't remotely enough for Nick Clegg to justify putting at risk one in five of our own seats. Let's be realistic about this.'

'Look,' said George, 'I know what this is all about. Nick is just looking for excuses to torpedo boundary reform, because he is worried about losing MPs in 2015. This stuff about the House of Lords is just a smokescreen.'

'No. You're wrong,' I said. 'Nick will deliver on your boundary changes, provided the Conservatives deliver on your pledge on an elected Lords. But without Lords, you are not getting boundaries.'

'OK,' said the Chancellor. 'Maybe there is some deal to be cut where you get 100 peers elected in 2015, with further votes being required in Parliament in 2015 or 2016 before any further elections? And we ought to have some type of regional list system, so that there is still some party patronage involved and so that elected peers are not in competition with individual constituency MPs.'

I said that we were very pragmatic and that we were open to compromises of that kind.

We also discussed party political funding, where George was his usual brutalist self: 'On party funding, I'll tell you what I am up for. We should pass tough regulations, restricting union donations to Labour and requiring individual donations by union members. We could do some deal on 'short money' that would help the Liberal Democrats a bit. But the Conservative Party is not going to sign up to caps on donations. We are getting millions of pounds from our big donors, and David and I are not going to put that at risk for ever. Why should we? But I really think we should do something on third-party donations for the unions and others that would screw Labour and force Ed Miliband into defending Labour's union links.'

I said that I would think about this further, but that any deal that looked hopelessly partisan would be likely to be killed off in the House of Lords.

We both promised to consider all the issues in more detail, and I then ended the call.

On 1 June, there was a rare meeting of the Coalition Committee, set up to deal with serious disputes, to discuss House of Lords reform. The committee had met on just one other occasion – to discuss the NHS Bill.

On this occasion, the meeting was distinctly bad tempered. George Osborne apparently came in to the meeting looking fed up and confrontational. Before the meeting started he spoke briefly to Nick Clegg: 'I got your message from David Laws. Do you actually want Lords reform, or is this really just about killing boundaries? As far as I am concerned, we had an agreement on boundaries, and I expect the Liberal Democrats to honour it.'

Nick replied bluntly that he considered that there were also agreements on Lords reform and party funding in the coalition agreement. Those should also be delivered. 'If they are not, then don't expect me to troop my MPs into the lobby to support you over boundaries. It's as simple as that.' It was all getting rather fractious.

On 27 June, Nick set out the government's plans for House of Lords reform. On the same day, at Prime Minister's Questions, David Cameron fielded more questions on the issue from sceptical Conservative MPs. The Prime Minister's answers remained distinctly lukewarm, and he seemed to be setting himself up to blame the Labour Party for any defeats on the proposed legislation. By now, the Labour Party could see that there was a real chance to cause mischief. Why should Labour support Lords reform, if the party could stand back and watch boundary reform – and even the coalition itself – fall apart?

I discussed the whole issue privately with Conservative MP and Osborne ally Matt Hancock. Matt said that he thought that as many as 100 Conservative MPs were ready to rebel on the Lords issue. On 28 June, I spoke to Jonny Oates, Nick's chief of staff, to say that I thought we ought to be making detailed preparations for the failure of Lords reform.

I was particularly worried that the Commons would vote for the principle of Lords reform but that there would then be a massive defeat on the programme motion that allocates parliamentary time. That could then signal prolonged parliamentary warfare and delay – and the prospect of a referendum amendment being carried. I put the view as strongly as I could to Nick that if we lost the vote on the programme motion we should immediately 'pull stumps' and announce that boundary reform was dead too.

I spoke to Nick's political adviser, Julian Astle, who held the same view as me. Julian still thought that the Tories did not understand just how serious we were, and how much Lords and boundaries were connected. Julian said to me: 'What we really need is a simple message – a "Kitty gets it" strategy – which leaves absolutely no room for doubt about what we are saying. What we say to Cameron is: "Here is Kitty. Kitty is the Commons boundary changes. Here is a revolver. If the Lords programme motion doesn't pass, then the revolver and Kitty are going to experience a coming together which will not be wholly to Kitty's advantage."' I laughed. Nick also liked the analogy.

And on 2 July, the Deputy Prime Minister sent a private letter to David Cameron, bluntly spelling out that the boundary changes were dead unless Lords reform went through. Meanwhile our press office prepared a 'Kitty gets it' press strategy.

On Wednesday 4 July, I walked down to Prime Minister's Questions with Nick. 'This Lords stuff is going to get really messy,' he said. 'Cameron has got my letter and has gone absolutely ballistic – totally crazy. He is saying that we promised boundary reform in exchange for the AV referendum. He is saying that the whole coalition could fall over this. He thinks if he loses the boundary changes, he will lose the next election. And if he does that, he will have to stand down as Tory leader. If we go back on boundaries, the whole Tory press will pour shit on us and shout "Betrayal", and coalition relations will be awful. Am I doing the right thing? Is what we are doing both honourable and legitimate?'

'I am certain we are right on this,' I replied. 'This is the only thing the Tories understand – clear threats and the exercise of power. This is exactly the way Cameron and Osborne behave when their interests are at stake. We cannot be soft and "Lib Demmy" about this. It doesn't matter that AV and boundaries were tied together. They were all part of one agreement, with Lords and party funding reform. All of this stands and falls together. The Conservatives agreed Lords reform very clearly during the coalition talks – they have to deliver, not just create a vague impression of trying to.'

'You're right,' said Nick. But I could see that he did not relish yet another big row.

Later, Julian Astle told me that he had spoken to Ed Llewellyn, the Prime Minister's chief of staff.

'They are in complete panic mode,' said Julian. 'Ed says that the PM doesn't accept any link between Lords and boundary reform. He is apparently saying that if any Lib Dem minister votes against the boundary reform, he or she would be instantly sacked.'

'What a ridiculous bluff,' I said. 'That would be the end of the coalition. Does Cameron want to govern alone? Or perhaps he wants a general election, even though the Tories are behind in the polls? They have nothing to threaten us with.'

On 6 July, as I was about to leave for France for the weekend, I had an urgent telephone call from Julian Astle. Julian said that he had earlier been in a meeting in Nick Clegg's office where the Lords and boundaries issues were being discussed. He said that certain Lib Dems were going very 'wobbly', and saying that perhaps if the first programme motion was lost, we should say nothing on boundaries, but try another vote when the House of Commons was back in September or October.

'Oh God, no, no, no!' I shouted. 'We cannot let this thing enter the parliamentary swamp. The time to kill boundaries is as soon as any Lords vote is lost. Waiting risks just looking weak, and those people around Nick who do not want to be tough over boundaries will just get the upper hand.'

Julian then said that in his view our House of Commons Whips' Office was particularly 'wobbly'. And that evening I saw some emails suggesting that Danny Alexander was also pressing for giving the Conservatives more time.

On Sunday 8 July, I was coming back from France, and Jonny Oates asked me to join a conference call with Nick and other senior advisers at 7.30 p.m. London time. By then, I was in Nice Airport, and I left the main airport restaurant to take the call on a high-level walkway in the airport building, with glorious views as the sun went down on a beautiful Mediterranean day.

'Switch' connected up the conference call, and as usual brought people in on the basis of seniority – with the most senior, Nick Clegg, being brought in last. Present were Jonny Oates, Neil Sherlock, Olly Grender, Jo Swinson, Danny Alexander, Alistair Carmichael, Ed Davey, Nick Clegg and me.

Nick said: 'I was at Wimbledon today and bumped into David Cameron. He said that the Lords vote was looking "very difficult", and then just shrugged his shoulders. He was also absolutely furious about James McGrory briefing in to the Sunday papers that Lords reform is a test of Cameron's leadership!'

The issue at hand was what to do if we lost the programme motion by either a modest or a large margin. Danny, Alistair and Jo all said that we should play for time and try to bring back a second motion later in the year. They were worried in particular about coalition relations if we just 'blew up' boundary reform, without giving the Conservatives a second chance. I strongly disagreed – more strongly than anyone else.

I said: 'If there is a massive Tory rebellion – which I think there will be – that is the best possible time to blow up boundary reform, particularly as it would then be absolutely clear that we are just not able to deliver on Lords. If we delay pulling the plug, we might end up having to exercise a veto after a referendum amendment has been tabled and won – and this would make it look like we were simply against consulting the public. The Tories are not in a position to end the coalition and they have nothing to rely on other than threats and tantrums. If this has to end in a car crash, then let's end it now, before the summer, so we can make a fresh coalition start in the autumn.'

Nick Clegg seemed to be on my side of the debate, but his summing up was a bit ambiguous, and the following day I sent him a strong email message, again making the case for torpedoing boundaries unless the Lords reform proposals were voted through. I said that if we lost the programme motion with a Tory revolt of more than forty of their MPs, we should pull stumps immediately.

I also telephoned Richard Reeves, Nick's former political strategist, who had left the previous week to go and work in the USA. Richard was very much of my view. He said he would contact Nick to put the case strongly. He said: 'I'm not surprised by the wobbling. This tends to happen before every big decision. Nick always gets lots of advice to keep everything low-key. There is a risk we keep trimming by 5 per cent, 5 per cent, 5 per cent. And suddenly we have moved our position entirely. Alistair and Danny are the worst offenders, and they then undermine Nick's position. I've seen this over the NHS Bill and tuition fees.'

Nick emailed me back later and said: 'Look, I pretty much agree with your view. But I am seriously worried that the whole coalition could just unravel over this. Cameron is presently weak in his party, and this whole thing could get messy.'

Later in the day, the key advisers to Nick seemed to be splitting into two camps. Danny Alexander, Alistair Carmichael, Jo Swinson and Neil Sherlock wanted to give the Tories more time if we lost the programme motion.

Julian Astle, Richard Reeves, Matthew Hanney and I were for instantly killing both boundary reform and Lords. Matthew Hanney was warning Nick that if he failed to act quickly, he might lose the support of the wider party on the issue.

However, Paddy Ashdown also phoned to say that Lords reform was so important that we should allow boundary changes to go through in exchange only for a referendum on Lords reform in May 2015. I said that I thought this would be completely crazy.

It was all getting very heated and very controversial, both within the Liberal Democrat team and between us and the Conservatives.

Tuesday 10 July was 'D-Day' for Lords Reform. Nick Clegg asked for one last meeting with advisers, but unfortunately I was at the Farnborough Air Show with senior executives from the helicopter manufacturer AgustaWestland – the biggest employer in my Yeovil constituency.

On the way down to Farnborough, I had a telephone call from Jonny Oates, saying that Nick was going to talk to the Prime Minister about Lords reform directly after the Cabinet, at 10.45 a.m. He then wanted a full adviser meeting after that. I promised to join by conference call from Farnborough.

The conference call was eventually fixed for 11.45 a.m. I was the only one on the spider phone – the rest were gathered in Nick's office in London. After the Cabinet meeting, Nick Clegg and David Cameron, accompanied by Jonny Oates and Ed Llewellyn, went next door to the Prime Minister's small office, which adjoins the Cabinet Room.

The Prime Minister said that he simply could not carry his party on Lords reform. He said that if the programme motion was put to a vote that day, then it would be lost. He claimed that he needed more time to get his party in the right place – and that he wanted to use the summer months to try to win over wavering Tory MPs. David Cameron also repeated that he did not accept that the Liberal Democrats had a right to 'kill' boundary reforms if the Lords vote was lost: 'This was a deal – AV for boundaries. I expect you to hold to that. If you don't, it could have very serious implications for this government and its future.'

But Nick Clegg was in no mood to back down. He was equally blunt with David Cameron, and told the Prime Minister that both Lords reform and party funding reform were also in the coalition agreement, and that he expected the Conservatives to honour both pledges: 'I have over-delivered in coalition. The NHS Bill. Tuition Fees. Remember? It's called a deal. If one party doesn't deliver, then you cannot expect the other to just go out and commit hara-kiri. You must understand that this coalition needs to be a fair and balanced deal. But if coalition means self-immolation, then I'm afraid I am just not up for it.'

'It got quite heated,' Nick told me later. 'Cameron said: "Look, Nick, I don't accept the link that you are making. But I accept that you are making it. Will you give me more time? If we lose boundaries, I will lose the next election and Labour will be back in. Boundaries after 2015 is of no value to me."'

Nick Clegg told the Prime Minister that he would have to consider the issue carefully, and that he would let the Conservatives have an answer within an hour.

Nick returned to his office and started the conference call by summarising his meeting with the Prime Minister: 'He thinks we will lose the programme motion vote. I explained that if that happens, I am going to withdraw my support for the boundaries legislation. He was very angry, but I said that the Liberal Democrats have followed the coalition agreement to the letter so far, but we will not be bound to it if the Conservatives fail to keep their promises. Cameron has asked for a bit more time to get his party in the right place if we lose today. Now, I know that David Laws and Julian Astle won't like that. And there are dangers. But I must say that if it is only a few more weeks then I would find it difficult not to give Cameron that time. But weeks, not months. I am inclined to delay the programme motion vote until September, to give the Tories more time.'

Danny Alexander was the first to reply, and I was pleased that his position seemed to have toughened up since the Sunday night conference call. He even said that perhaps if we were going to torpedo boundaries it would be better to do it now, so that coalition relations could recover over the summer period.

I was struggling to hear the call properly, because every time someone was about to say something important, either a helicopter would fly overhead or one of the RAF's new Eurofighters would take off and completely drown out the conversations from London.

But eventually I was able to speak. I said I didn't like the idea of more time, but could understand that if the Prime Minister was asking for just a few weeks, it was difficult not to concede that. But I said that it should be no longer than a few weeks and that we should try to avoid a programme motion vote that day.

Later in the day, the Lords reform debate took place, with Nick Clegg leading for us in the Commons. It was a bad-tempered and unpleasant occasion, and Labour did little to disguise their pleasure at the prospect of a coalition split.

The government won the Second Reading vote by 462 to 124 – a government majority of 338. But there was a massive Conservative rebellion, with ninety-one Tory MPs voting against and an estimated fifty abstaining. With Labour opposing the programme motion, that meant that a defeat was assured. Two Tory MPs resigned over their opposition to the measure.

It was clear to me that both Lords and boundaries were dead.

But the Conservatives asked for more time over the summer to win back their backbenchers. And there was some suggestion that Cameron and Osborne hoped to buy us off with a 'bribe' on party funding too.

Oliver Letwin was charged with trying to win round Tory rebels, but by early August he had to admit that he was having no success. David Cameron asked to see Nick Clegg to discuss the matter. It was their most acrimonious meeting to date.

Nick Clegg told the Prime Minister that he was about to make a public statement that neither Lords reform nor boundaries would now proceed.

'Cameron was very, very difficult,' Nick Clegg told me later. 'He went on and on about how we had a deal. He had the nerve to say that he had a lower percentage of his MPs rebelling on Lords than we did on tuition fees. I pointed out that I and half my party voted for tuition fees. We were only obliged to abstain in the coalition agreement.'

The two leaders had a blunt discussion. David Cameron claimed that he had done his best over Lords reform and he appealed to Nick Clegg to let the boundary changes go ahead – saying that he would be savaged by the *Daily Mail* and the *Telegraph* if he lost boundary reform and that 'the coalition will look like a shambles'. David Cameron also fretted that 'the only person this will help is Boris Johnson, who is clearly after my job'.

'I think he hoped we would change our minds,' said the Deputy Prime Minister, 'but I just made clear I was not budging.'

Nick Clegg's statement pulling the plug on boundary reform was welcomed by both the party and his own team.

The Conservatives were furious, and many in Whitehall and Westminster now thought that the coalition was bound to collapse.

A day after the Lords reform vote in the Commons, I bumped into the Labour peer Lord Adonis outside Parliament. He told me that he had recently met two Permanent Secretaries who were privately predicting that the coalition would be over in months and that the parliament would not run its full term. But I suspected otherwise.

And the day after Nick announced that he would not allow boundary reform to proceed, a disappointed Prime Minister emerged from the No. 10 flat to tell his closest advisers:

'I've slept on it. OK, it's pretty bad news, but it's not a catastrophe. Nick Clegg and I put this coalition together, and we need to make it work again. I want to pull the government back to the centre and not concede more to our right-wingers. I was the architect of this coalition. I will stand or fall by its success.'

It was not a happy outcome, but Nick Clegg had showed that the Liberal Democrats were not a pushover.

And the show was still on the road – just.

FIGHTING ON ALL FRONTS: IRAN, LEVESON AND O-LEVELS

2012

It is inevitable that when political history is written, it is usually written as a narrative where the reader can easily follow the twists and turns of a particular story over a week, a month, a year or sometimes longer. This might give the impression that political leaders are able to focus on one or two issues at a time and apply all their attention and skill to resolving them.

But for those in government, and particularly at the head of government, the daily events and challenges do not fall neatly into little chapters that can be carefully managed and resolved. Political leaders do not fight single battles – they have to fight on many fronts.

At any one point in time, a political leader may be juggling multiple issues and problems. There may be anywhere between five and ten really big challenges to be tackled, where significant decisions need making. There may be ten or twenty other, lesser, issues, to be tracked – each of which could blow up at any moment into a major storm.

There will also be meetings to chair, papers to respond to, speeches to give, red boxes to clear, fundraising events to attend, egos to massage, people to inspire, personnel crises requiring attention, political parties to manage, constituency demands to satisfy, family responsibilities to observe, and the voracious media to feed, field and defend against.

For David Cameron and Nick Clegg, their jobs were 17-hour-a-day commitments, dropping perhaps to a mere eight hours per day at the weekends.

And so it was that while the coalition tensions over the economy and political reform rumbled on throughout 2012, there were many other issues to deal with too.

In mid-2012, fears grew that the Israelis were planning a secret military strike on alleged nuclear weapons facilities in Iran. The Israelis had apparently concluded that the Iranians would have the necessary capability to build a nuclear device by the middle of 2013. Once this was achieved, they considered that it would take only six months to build a nuclear weapon. The Israelis were said to believe that this was the last chance to prevent the Iranians from acquiring this deadly capability. Nick Clegg met Nick Harvey, our Defence Minister, and Jim Wallace, the Liberal Democrat Advocate General, to discuss the matter. Liberal Democrat ministers also discussed the issue in a private meeting in November 2012.

Some Conservatives wanted to back possible joint US–UK military action in support of Israel in the event of major Iranian retaliation following an Israeli strike. 'I can't believe how gung-ho and neo-con Osborne is on some of this stuff,' the Deputy Prime Minister told colleagues. But Nick Clegg made clear that he would not support military action, and the Obama administration also warned the Israelis off taking offensive operations.

What looked like it could be a major international incident, with huge consequences both for security and for the world economy, through the possible impact on oil prices, was avoided. A conflict could also have been highly damaging for coalition relations, as the UK could have come under pressure to use its military assets, including mine clearance vessels, for example if the Straits of Hormuz had been closed, which seemed highly likely.

President Obama's strong opposition to military action may have helped secure world peace and economic growth, and certainly had the welcome by-product of a more stable coalition government.

One of the other big issues in 2012, which proved a running sore for the Prime Minister, in particular, was the Leveson Inquiry into press standards. Having established the inquiry, the Prime Minister was now in something of a panic about it. The inquiry threatened to shine a spotlight on the delicate issue of David Cameron's judgement in recruiting former *News of the World* editor Andy Coulson. The inquiry would also highlight the relationship between the Conservative Party and key parts of the media. The Prime Minister was deeply worried that some newspapers would not forgive him for unleashing the inquiry on them, and he was worried that this might damage his party's traditionally cosy relationship with important newspapers such as *The Sun* and the *Daily Mail*.

In the middle of 2012, as David Cameron prepared to give evidence to the Leveson Inquiry, Nick Clegg found the Prime Minister to be preoccupied with that issue above all else. Returning from a bilateral meeting with the PM in May 2012, Nick told me: 'Cameron seems to be completely traumatised by the Leveson Inquiry – he's in a total panic. Frankly, he seems to be incapable of thinking of anything else at the current time.'

The media were blaming the Prime Minister for putting in place a judge-led inquiry and he was receiving a huge amount of bad publicity in *The Sun*, the *Mail* and elsewhere.

Nick Clegg told me that Cameron's strategy was to try to 'survive' Leveson and then to try to quickly rebuild his relationship with the press, shelving any significant proposals from Leveson so as not to upset the media any further.

The Leveson Inquiry and the events surrounding it also caused a significant rupture in coalition relations. Jeremy Hunt, then Culture Secretary, was being accused of colluding with the Murdoch media empire to allow NewsCorp to take over BSkyB. For weeks on end, the Culture Secretary's political future seemed to dangle by a thread. There were suggestions that Hunt had broken the ministerial code by misleading Parliament about various aspects of the row.

David Cameron unilaterally announced that in his view there was no breach of the ministerial code and that he would not therefore be referring Jeremy Hunt for an inquiry into the matter. Nick Clegg was angry about this – the whole matter was very sensitive politically, and Vince Cable had previously had some of his ministerial responsibilities removed for having been seen to be biased in dealing with the case.

Nick got on well with Jeremy Hunt, but he had a long and difficult conversation with the Culture Secretary over the phone from Spain. He advised Hunt to refer himself in relation to the ministerial code issue, but Hunt wasn't keen to do so.

The Labour Party then tabled a House of Commons motion, proposing that Hunt should be referred to an independent review on whether he had broken the code.

Some Liberal Democrats thought that as a matter of coalition solidarity, our MPs should vote with the Conservatives against the Labour motion. Paddy Ashdown, Alistair Carmichael – the Deputy Chief Whip – Danny Alexander and I all held this view.

But many of our MPs and members held the opposite view, and they wanted to see a robust Lib Dem line. All of this was taking place during the tense row over boundaries and House of Lords reform. Some Liberal Democrats thought that this was a reason to be tough, while others thought that the party should keep its powder dry for these bigger political issues.

A few days before the crucial vote, Nick Clegg and David Cameron met privately and ended up having a major row.

The PM pointed out to Nick Clegg that he had been supportive of Vince Cable, Chris Huhne and me over our various difficulties. He now indicated that he wanted Liberal Democrat support, in return, for Jeremy Hunt.

But Nick Clegg wasn't budging. He later told me: 'I explained to Cameron that this isn't a personal issue, it is a political issue. I was quite candid with him. I said: "One of the things that I have learned to appreciate and admire about you, David, is your ruthless protection of your own party's interests. I have put the coalition interest ahead of the party interest too much. You made this decision not to refer Hunt over a possible breach of the ministerial code without even bothering to consult me. I am learning from you. Look at it that way."'

Nick stuck with his decision over the Hunt vote, and the Lib Dems abstained. A marker was put down, but the coalition stayed together.

Soon, other issues were causing coalition tensions in this stormy period from the Omnishambles Budget to the August recess.

On 21 June, I woke up to massive media coverage of a rumoured plan by Michael Gove to scrap GCSE exams and to go back to the days of two separate exams – O-levels for the brighter students and third-rate CSEs for the less able. Patronisingly, Conservative advisers had briefed that the CSE exam would at least allow 'slower' students to be able to read a railway timetable! This seemed to me to be entirely the wrong approach – we ought to be raising standards and aspirations for all students, rather than going back to the old two-tier philosophy. I felt particularly strongly about this, as I would be returning as Schools Minister in the forthcoming reshuffle. I wanted nothing to do with this plan.

I contacted Nick Clegg, who was at the time attending an environmental summit in Brazil. He emailed me back at 6.30 a.m. Brazil time to say that the plan was 'a complete bounce – and totally unacceptable'.

Nick asked his staff in London to talk to the Prime Minister's office to find out what they knew. They claimed to know absolutely nothing. By midday, we were briefing very heavily against the plan, and Nick filmed a clip for the TV news from Rio, sharply criticising the proposals – which were now running as the top story on the news broadcasts.

Nick made clear that as chairman of the Home Affairs Committee, any proposals in this area would need his approval. He also made clear that the Liberal Democrats would not contemplate a return to the old O-level/CSE divide. Nick later spoke to David Cameron, who claimed to know nothing about the plan. 'I think Michael is being outrageous just floating this. He just wants to be the darling of the Tory right,' said the Prime Minister. But he later admitted that Michael Gove had 'briefly mentioned the issue' to him.

It was clear that there was now going to be a major clash over this issue, which would further sour the already rather poor relations between Michael Gove and Nick Clegg.

The Liberal Democrat leader was also angered when, over the summer months, Michael Gove abolished a requirement for all academies and free schools to employ only teachers with 'Qualified Teacher Status'. This was not agreed across the coalition.

'I find Michael Gove both attractive and infuriating in equal measure,' Nick told his advisers. 'I am looking forward to getting David into the department, because hopefully he will both be able to improve relations between us and stop Michael from thinking he can get away with doing anything.'

Lords. Boundaries. Leveson. Jeremy Hunt. O-levels. It had indeed been a fractious summer. But the biggest challenge of all was not these issues that divided the two parties but the one that had brought us together in the first place: the economy. Two years into the government, our economic strategy was not delivering.

Hurting but Not Working

2012

It was an Education Reform summit at Lancaster House in London – in the final year of the parliament.

Michael Gove was the host, but there was no doubt who the real star of the show was: Boris Johnson, the Conservative Mayor of London.

He turned up, fashionably late, and made quite an entrance. I was standing near the door leading into the grand reception room, talking to the Spanish Education Minister, a rather glamorous, youngish lady.

As Boris Johnson approached, she spotted him immediately: 'Hello, Mr Mayor, I am the Spanish Education Minister.'

'Marvellous, marvellous,' replied the Mayor. 'Brussels is one of my very favourite places.'

'Spanish!' insisted the minister.

'Yes, I love that delicious Brussels food,' Boris Johnson continued. 'The architecture is fantastic too.'

'Spain. Spain, Mr Mayor. What's Brussels got to do with Spain? Have you never been to Spain?' was the baffled reply.

Anyone else would have been embarrassed. Not Boris. 'Ah, Spain? Spain?' he replied, ruffling his hair and looking thoughtful, as if someone had mentioned the name of an obscure hamlet in the Outer Hebrides.

And then he seemed to have remembered something: 'Ah, Spain! I must have been there! Hot, isn't it? Yes, very, very hot!' and he turned away to have a selfie taken with a swooning female teacher.

When the Mayor spoke to the assembled gathering later, he outshone everyone. Me, of course. And the amusing but uncharismatic Labour chap – that wasn't too difficult either. More surprisingly, Michael Gove too.

And which other mayor could get away with systematically insulting most of the population of his home city in just a ten-minute speech? 'I was in dear Walthamstow the other day,' he began. 'Walthamstow, who can ever forget it? What a marvellous place it is. What architectural wonders, redolent perhaps of Ancient Rome at its finest. I take in all these things as I travel – rapidly, mark you – through this magnificent place ... and on, on to Bromley, Bromley, how the very name conjures up such rich and varied images. Bromley ... the people there are fascinating, intriguing and challenging ... indeed every time I meet these fine people, they cause me to challenge the very validity of the whole theory of evolution...'

After insulting various other groups, and making a case for the return of grammar schools, he was gone.

With the amusing and charismatic Boris hovering in the background as the Conservative leader in waiting, fresh from his triumph at the Olympic Games, and with the economy in the doldrums, no wonder that David Cameron and George Osborne were still feeling so insecure as leaders of their party in late 2012. They were not only worried about whether they could win a general election in May 2015; they were also concerned that Conservative MPs might try to replace them with the popular London Mayor and quiz-show king well before then. Indeed, there were already rumours that the Richmond MP, Zac Goldsmith, might stand down in order to create a parliamentary vacancy for Boris.

Throughout 2012 there was a continuing drip-drip-drip of bad news on economic growth and government borrowing. This was a coalition government established to 'clean up the economic mess', but by the summer our strategy seemed to be running aground.

When the coalition was formed in 2010, the worst of the UK recession appeared to be over. It seemed a sensible judgement to tighten fiscal policy to cut borrowing, while maintaining a super-easy monetary policy in which interest rates were close to zero.

What we didn't expect were two developments that significantly retarded UK economic growth. The first was a massive crisis in the euro area, with sky-high interest rates and the expectation of the break-up of the single currency. The second big negative factor was soaring fuel and food prices, which drove inflation above 5 per cent and caused a massive and unexpected fall in people's real incomes.

These developments provoked calls for a rethink on UK economic strategy. The government was accused by Labour of having tightened fiscal policy too much. The more relevant question was whether the government needed to respond to the new threats to growth. By spring 2012, even the conventionally minded IMF was calling for more pro-growth policies. The UK's recovery from the recession of 2008 was now its slowest recovery from a recession in living memory.

On 25 July 2012, Parliament was in recess and I was back in South Somerset and out on my villages advice centre – touring the fifty villages of Yeovil constituency. The weather was beautiful – clear blue skies, and temperatures touching 30 degrees centigrade.

The news on the economic front was, however, considerably gloomier than the weather. At 9.30 a.m., the Office for National Statistics released its first estimate of economic growth in the second quarter of the year. This showed a bigger than expected decline of 0.7 per cent of gross domestic product – the third successive quarterly decline.

It was not only Labour who were critical of the coalition's economic strategy. Vince Cable had also been making more noise about the case for a change in approach, and on this day his friend and political ally Lord Oakeshott went fully and publicly on the attack.

Matthew Oakeshott described George Osborne as the 'work experience Chancellor' and said that he should be sacked and replaced by Vince Cable. He added to the provocation by saying that we now needed an economic 'A-team' – including me and Chris Huhne – to replace David Cameron and Danny Alexander. The Oakeshott attacks were hitting home not just in the media, but in 10 Downing Street. David Cameron stopped one of our press officers a couple of days later to say: 'God, that Oakeshott man is poisonous. The problem with him is that he's not just a pain in the backside, but he has quite a way with words, and his sound bites really hit the spot. "Work experience Chancellor! Ouch!"' George Osborne and Danny Alexander were somewhat less amused.

The stand-off in government between the Treasury on the one hand and

Vince Cable on the other was one of the worst-kept secrets in Whitehall – and it had been for some time.

But while I was supportive of the general economic approach of the coalition government, I was also concerned that the UK authorities – the Bank of England and the Treasury – could be doing more to support growth. Indeed, the debate over economic strategy was now not simply on old left/right lines. The economists at the IMF and many commentators in the City of London also wanted so see more done to combat the economic headwinds that were driving the UK back into recession. The coalition government was in danger of looking inflexible and dogmatic at a time when highly unconventional economic policy solutions were now required.

The key for me was to identify policy changes that could boost growth while allowing the government to continue pursuing its deficit reduction strategy. I knew that the Chancellor and the Treasury, and indeed the whole government, would be against anything that looked like a U-turn, and in any case stopping our debt from spiralling higher was clearly very important.

As far back as the Autumn Statement 2011, I had begun to look at what more could be done to support growth while meeting our fiscal targets. At first, I discussed with Nick Clegg an 'ease and squeeze' strategy, where we would add to capital spending immediately, matched by spending cuts in the later years of the parliament. This would provide an immediate economic boost but actually support the delivery of our targets to reduce borrowing.

Concern about the economic outlook was also one of the reasons I pushed for a bigger rise than planned in the personal tax allowance in the 2012 Budget.

At the end of April and the beginning of May that year, there were further discussions between Nick Clegg, Danny Alexander, me and our economic advisers. These meetings followed the grim news of a contraction in the UK economy in the first quarter of 2012 – which put the UK back into what economists define as a recession, i.e. two quarters of consecutive negative economic growth.

I argued that we needed to think more radically about measures to support growth, and Nick agreed that the political risk was now that we were looking 'robotic, unthinking and inflexible'.

In a private note to Nick at the beginning of May, I argued that we should be encouraging the Bank of England to massively expand the size of its quantitative easing programme, in which the Bank essentially printed more money and bought government bonds. I also proposed that its scope should be extended to include non-government bonds – as they had done for some time in the USA. I also argued that we should ensure that the next Governor of the Bank of England was more 'innovative and pro-growth' than the very cautious Mervyn King. And I said that the Treasury should be looking at ways to boost investment spending, using both on- and off-balance-sheet policies.

Nick was sympathetic to the case I was making and agreed that 'pretending our plan is perfectly designed for the new circumstances we face isn't credible'.

On 9 May, we held a meeting of Lib Dem Cabinet ministers to discuss our options on growth. Danny Alexander and Vince Cable were supposed to have produced a joint paper, but there were already policy tensions between these two leading Liberal Democrats, and no joint paper had been produced. Instead, there were two separate papers and Danny was rather irritated that Vince tabled his first.

In general, the meeting was quite constructive and we agreed that while we wanted to stick to the government's borrowing objectives and broad parameters on public spending, we would also look at other options, including: more quantitative easing, more credit easing, more action to support bank lending, possibly re-profiling capital spending, more industrial support and more action on youth unemployment. We also discussed whether the Bank of England should be given a new, more pro-growth, mandate.

However, to make progress on these issues, we would need to convince both the Conservatives and, in some cases, the Bank of England. Neither would be easy.

The Conservatives were also, of course, getting nervous about the growth outlook, not least because government borrowing was much higher than we had forecast and indeed it was now threatening to move from a gently declining trend to a trend of rising borrowing. That would be bad for the country and bad for the coalition, but particularly bad for the Conservatives and the Chancellor.

On 26 June, I walked home from Westminster to Kennington with Oliver Letwin, the senior Conservative minister who also lives nearby. Oliver said: 'I am just incredibly worried about the economic growth outlook. Maybe we will get stuck in a slow growth environment for a whole decade. If so, we might need to revisit the public spending plans from 2014 onwards, and make some bigger cuts to spending. We could use some of this for tax cuts, too.'

The rows over Lords and Leveson took up much of the government's time in June and July, but I continued to think about what more we could do to support economic growth without tearing up our deficit reduction strategy.

In July, I was having lunch with Paul Campbell, an old friend from Cambridge University, whom I had also worked with at JP Morgan, in the City of London. While asking Paul what more we could do on monetary policy, he mentioned that in the USA they were being much more radical than we were. For example, the Federal Reserve (their equivalent of our Bank of England) was regularly transferring to the US Treasury the net interest income ('funding profit') on the bonds that had been purchased under their quantitative easing programme. This could then be used by the US Treasury to spend or to reduce borrowing. The amount in question would run to billions of pounds, £10–20 billion in all likelihood, even in the UK, where the bond-buying operation was smaller than in the United States.

I thought that this could be the economic 'silver bullet' we were looking for. Could we persuade the Bank of England to transfer the billions of pounds of 'funding profits' to the Treasury (leaving the Bank with the capital gains profit that was arising through an increase in bond prices)? If so, we had a huge pot of money that could be used as a one-off boost to investment spending without increasing borrowing. I was excited about the possibility, and put the idea to Nick Clegg and Danny Alexander, and to Matt Hancock, the Chancellor's former chief of staff.

The public and private debate about economic policy intensified in late July, with the release of the latest – awful – growth figures. I sent a private note to Nick, again pressing for more radical action on both fiscal and monetary policy.

Meanwhile, Nick Clegg's office was getting increasingly nervous that Vince Cable was 'on manoeuvres' – raising more criticisms about the government's economic strategy and failing to quash rumours about his own ambitions. In an interview for the *Financial Times* on 26 July, he wouldn't rule himself out as the next Lib Dem leader, and on the *Today* programme he refused to rule himself out as the next Chancellor of the Exchequer. 'I suppose tomorrow he's going to refuse to rule himself out as the next Pope,' said Nick to his advisers, with a mixture of amusement and some irritation.

In early August, before heading off on holiday, I wrote another paper on economic policy for Nick Clegg and Danny Alexander. I warned about the grim economic news that would face us in the autumn – with massive upward revisions to government borrowing projections and downward revisions to growth. 'People will be able to say that it's hurting but it's not working,' I said. I suggested that we would have to accept a slower pace of decline in government borrowing, and that we might need to delay the date by which we forecast that debt would be falling as a share of the economy.

I suggested to Nick that he should make a major push to persuade David Cameron and George Osborne to be more radical on boosting growth. On 6 August, I met Danny Alexander to discuss the options. Danny said that Vince was pushing for an increase in borrowing to fund extra investment spending, but without any future policy tightening. That was bound to be a non-runner with the Tories. Danny also said that George was very nervous about the government borrowing numbers for this year, and he wanted to show that this year's borrowing was lower than last year's – even if this meant getting departments to shift the timing of their spending. Danny said: 'If borrowing goes up this year without any real plan to reduce it in the future, that would really strike at George's credibility.'

However, Danny did say that he had raised my idea of spending the quantitative easing profits with George Osborne, who was asking Treasury officials to look into it. Danny also seemed sympathetic to my suggestion of easing policy now and tightening later – though I suspected that the Treasury would be rather unenthusiastic about the notion.

Before I went away, Nick Clegg's office sent me a huge pack of papers on future options to cut welfare spending. The papers had been prepared by the Department for Work and Pensions. Some of the measures were politically unacceptable, including mass means-testing of child benefit, cutting payments to the poorest pensioners, removing housing benefit for the under-24s, and a three-year working-age benefits freeze.

Nick came back to me and said that he broadly agreed with my proposals to support economic growth and that he and Danny would discuss the issue with David Cameron and George Osborne in their last Quad dinner before the summer recess.

Nick said: 'We need to persuade George to be more flexible, but we also need to persuade Vince that we cannot just permanently loosen fiscal policy without both frightening the markets and wrecking our entire economic and political narrative as a government. There has to be a third way between Osborne's ultra-austerity and Vince's unqualified policy loosening.'

On Friday 10 August, I was sitting out in the sun in a beautiful village in the south of France when I received an urgent email from Nick Clegg, asking me to comment on a paper he and Danny Alexander had drawn up to inform their critically important discussion on the economy with Cameron and Osborne. The email drew a lot on our earlier discussions and it proposed reformulating the government's 'second fiscal target' – cutting debt as a share of GDP – and putting in place an economic package to boost the economy by £10 billion per year for two years. This would be paid for without extra borrowing – by using the accumulated QE profits sitting in the Bank of England. The £10,000 tax-free personal allowance would be delivered a year earlier than originally planned, and there would be a capital allowance break for plant and machinery, an infrastructure package, direct capital investment in housing for two years and a variety of other pro-growth measures. Set against this boost, Danny was proposing to make bigger efficiency savings in government spending from 2014 to 2017.

Overall, it looked like a good package and I was pleasantly surprised that we were going to propose something that would make a real difference.

That night, while I was having another pleasant meal in the south of France, Nick Clegg and Danny Alexander were having dinner in 10 Downing Street with David Cameron and George Osborne. Nick Clegg briefed me on the discussions the next day. Danny led off the discussions by pointing out that the international and domestic growth outlook was much weaker than previously expected. He explained that he and Nick wanted to look at what more could be done to support growth, while also seeking to improve the chances of meeting the government's fiscal targets.

David Cameron acknowledged that the government needed to show more flexibility on its economic strategy. He also agreed that 'we can't just allow big increases in borrowing – the sort of Vince Cable thing. If we do that, we're basically finished.' At this point, the Prime Minister drew a finger slowly across his throat.

David Cameron said that in his view, small amounts of extra spending probably wouldn't make much difference to growth anyway: 'We would get a massive political negative and very little economic positive.'

He made clear that he wouldn't want to raise government borrowing even in the short term, and even if this was offset by making bigger cuts in a few years' time.

George Osborne then interrupted to say that he liked our idea about transferring the quantitative easing profits from the Bank of England: 'Maybe we could use these to support the economy without borrowing more.' The Chancellor said that he would get Treasury officials to talk to Mervyn King about the idea.

Nick Clegg then explained that he was also very worried about the prospects of keeping to the coalition's second fiscal rule. 'To meet the existing timescale, we would need to find tens of billions more of cuts. That would be incredibly damaging to the economy and to public services.'

The Chancellor said he was prepared to look at moving the timescale for meeting this rule backwards. He also said that he would look at what more could be done to boost housing investment.

When Nick phoned me the following day to tell me how the key talks had gone, he said: 'It's all now dependent on the Bank of England passing the QE profits over, if we are to do something big. Cameron is also saying that now that we have blocked boundaries reform, he is not willing to do any more on party funding reform.' Frankly, that was no surprise. 'But he and Osborne are still obsessed by having some sort of anti-union Bill, with a higher voting threshold for strikes etc. It's all about playing to their right wing and putting Labour on the spot.'

Nick said that in exchange for an anti-union Bill, George Osborne was offering to shelve the issue of regional pay, in which public sector workers would be paid less if they in lower-wage parts of the country. 'That wouldn't be much of a trade,' I observed. 'They are saying they will concede one Tory policy for another? Very generous.' Nick laughed: 'That's what I said. Absurd.'

'Oh, by the way,' added the Deputy Prime Minister, 'we also discussed the reshuffle, including your future. We agreed that you will come back in as Minister of State in the Cabinet Office and Minister of State for Schools. It will be a lot of work. The reshuffle is on for next month. So this will be your last chance to relax for some time.' Nick was certainly right.

He and Danny had made some useful progress in getting the Conservatives to consider new, pro-growth, policies. But would this amount to anything? And would it be enough to stimulate the economy and satisfy the many critics of coalition policy – not all of whom were on the opposition benches?

A Passage to India?

2012

Before I had gone away on holiday in August, I had met up with Jonny Oates, Nick Clegg's highly influential and trusted chief of staff, to have a discussion about the reshuffle.

'It's much as Nick has told you already,' said Jonny. 'You're coming back in and there are some changes in the middle and lower ranks. To be honest, before the end of the parliament we probably need one more big reshuffle. At some stage Nick wants to give Danny a chance to run a big department himself, maybe Business. Danny is definitely pushing for that too. And that would create an opening for you to go back as Chief Secretary.'

'I'd like that, of course,' I said. 'For me, all that is unfinished business. But aren't we forgetting someone? Where would Vince go?'

Jonny said, 'Who knows if Vince will want to serve out five years? He doesn't seem to much enjoy being in coalition with the Tories. Mind you, neither do I, half the time!'

'But he isn't just going to retire, is he?' I said. 'Well,' said Jonny, 'some people think he would consider a post such as being our High Commissioner for India.'

'What!' I said. 'Surely he wouldn't leave the Cabinet for that?'

'Who knows?' shrugged Jonny. 'He loves India and I just don't know if he'll want to stick this for three more years. He found the whole row over the Murdoch issue very difficult and he isn't getting any younger.'

It was certainly true that Vince didn't seem very happy with the coalition's economic strategy. He had, of course, been our party's Treasury spokesman until the coalition began, and it was logical to give him his own economic department, rather than having him as George Osborne's deputy.

But Vince had quickly discovered that while there may be a number of Cabinet ministers with economic responsibilities, in UK governments the Chancellor reigns supreme. And now the Chancellor's deputy was the even younger Lib Dem Danny Alexander, whom Vince was obliged to negotiate with and defer to on many issues. Vince and the leading HM Treasury ministers rarely saw eye to eye on the big economic issues, and so he found it doubly uncomfortable to deal with his Treasury colleagues.

Since Chris Huhne's political career had ended in early 2012, with the CPS decision to bring charges against him, it was regarded as inevitable that if Nick Clegg was to face a leadership challenge during the parliament it would be from Vince Cable, or at least from Vince's allies. The Business Secretary offered an alternative economic strategy – slower fiscal tightening and more capital investment – as well as a sharp contrast to the impression of gilded youth and a distinctly less 'rose garden' approach to coalition relations. It was also regarded as highly likely that if Nick chose to resign before May 2015, Vince would succeed him as leader. This was certainly Nick's own assumption, though others might have stood.

Some of those who advised the DPM feared that at some stage Vince would mount a leadership coup. And on a number of occasions there were economic issues over which it was possible to imagine him resigning. But I never saw a Cable coup or even resignation as particularly likely.

I had known Vince Cable since 1997, when he was first elected as an MP and I was economic adviser to the parliamentary party. He was a member of the best intake of new Liberal Democrat MPs since the war, including people like Steve Webb and Ed Davey. He was an economic heavyweight who had been chief economist at Shell, and it was no surprise when he eventually became the party's Treasury spokesman.

Treasury spokesman was what most people initially thought was Vince Cable's limit. Yes, he was formidably bright, decent, thoughtful and clearly mature and knowledgeable. But he also seemed, dare I say it, a little dull, and fairly shy. No one remotely thought of him as a potential leader in those early days.

Vince's big moment came in 2007, when Sir Menzies Campbell decided to stand down as leader. Vince wanted to stand, but he made his ambitions known rather late, and by that time most MPs had decided to back the young, able, impressive and confident former MEP Nick Clegg – who had only been in Parliament for two years.

MPs assumed that Vince was not cut out to be a leader, and in any case they judged that we needed a younger person to take over, after all the uncharitable focus on Menzies Campbell's age.

Ironically, it was during the leadership election, which he did not stand in, that Vince really flowered.

As acting leader, he now stood in weekly for the party at Prime Minister's Questions, where he observed cuttingly that Gordon Brown had evolved 'from Stalin to Mr Bean'. Suddenly the serious but slightly dull economist became an overnight media star. And when the economic crisis emerged in 2007, there was a ready-made backdrop for a man with his economic knowledge and maturity – and he soon put everyone else in Parliament in the shade, including shadow Chancellor George Osborne.

In truth, Vince – now deputy leader – also rather eclipsed his new boss, Nick Clegg, for some months, until the new Liberal Democrat leader started to chalk up some early victories on issues such as allowing former Gurkha soldiers to settle in the UK.

I think that Vince regretted not standing for the leadership in 2007. He may have felt that he had been unfairly passed over because of his age. He had not quite given up, therefore, on the idea of one day becoming leader.

My view was that Vince would happily take on the leadership of the Liberal Democrats if Nick Clegg was 'hit by a bus'. But I doubted that Vince would ever be the driver of that bus or even the man on the pavement who shoved his leader into the centre of the road.

Vince certainly didn't lack ambition, talent or self-confidence. But he was not a natural schemer or plotter, and at heart there was something both cautious and collegiate about him. He was also shy and retiring with colleagues – he didn't gather a court of MPs around him, and he would never be found in the tea room plotting or sharing gossip. He was, in truth, something of a loner. Vince also enjoyed being in government, and I could not imagine him returning to the back benches of his own accord.

When we had regional cabinets in different parts of the country and a railway carriage was reserved for Cabinet ministers to travel in, he could always be found sitting by himself, as if both shy and averse to liaising too closely with 'the enemy'. He was like the bright, unpopular boy travelling in the front on the school bus on the way to a rugby game, while the in crowd occupied the back seats.

Back in No. 10, whereas other ministers would gather for coffee and a chat together in the lobby outside the Cabinet Room, I often noticed that Vince had entered the room first and was sitting at the long Cabinet table by himself, silent and waiting for the meeting to start.

In a coalition in which almost all ministers from both parties got on well, a visitor from Mars who was invited to Cabinet and asked to guess who its Lib Dem members were would perhaps first have identified the uncomfortable, slightly grumpy, figure of the Business Secretary, sitting just a few places to David Cameron's right. And after that, it would have got much more difficult.

Nick Clegg liked and respected Vince and saw him as a real asset to the party. He admired his work in opposition during the economic crisis, and in government he was impressed with Vince's work to protect further education from Conservative indifference, boost the number of apprenticeships, put in place a new economic strategy based on backing the successful sectors of the future, and privatise Royal Mail. In government, Nick repeatedly rejected suggestions from some of his own advisers and others to move Vince from his position in the Business Department.

Nick Clegg saw the importance of keeping the party united in government and he knew that meant keeping Vince on side. But while the two men respected each other, they were hardly friends. And the Liberal Democrat leader was frustrated by what he saw as his colleague's semi-detached attitude to the government and his tendency to publicly question the coalition's economic strategy. This became a particular source of frustration when the economy eventually recovered – Nick Clegg and Danny Alexander were determined that the Liberal Democrats should get some political credit for the recovery, but they felt that this was impossible while Vince Cable continued to loudly question its underpinnings and worry publicly about a return to an unsustainable housing boom.

If Vince Cable was reticent to promote himself, there were others who saw him as a vehicle to change the leadership, the government's economic strategy and indeed the future direction of the party. Prominent amongst these was Lord Oakeshott. Matthew Oakeshott had started his career in the Labour Party, as an adviser to Roy Jenkins. He had aspired to be Chancellor one day, and for a peer he was highly political, bright, sharp-elbowed and media friendly. He had for many years been a friend of Vince Cable, and he was now a close ally. He had a pass to allow him to visit Vince in the Business Department, and they spoke frequently on political, media and economic matters. Matthew was regarded as something of a Rasputin figure.

Over the last week of August 2012, there were the first rumblings of an attempt to remove Nick Clegg as leader. A number of very junior Lib Dem MPs were starting to press for a 'Plan B' on the economy; this could hardly be less helpful or productive, given that 'Plan B' was code for the Labour critique of coalition economic policy.

Then, on 30 August, Lord Oakeshott gave an interview to the *Today* programme in which he put Nick Clegg on notice and implied that Vince Cable should take over. This was concerning, as what Matthew was saying at any point in time might well be what Vince was thinking, magnified by about 400 per cent.

Paddy Ashdown decided to write an article in *The Guardian* in Nick's defence. This was in some ways helpful, but it served to highlight the leadership issue.

Paddy said that the only people seeking Nick's resignation were 'madmen and minnows' – a typically wonderful and provocative Ashdown sound bite. But none of this served to raise Nick Clegg's morale as he faced the new parliamentary year. The opinion polls were universally dreadful. And the rumblings around Vince Cable didn't help.

At the end of August, the Liberal Democrat leader had a private conversation with Paddy: 'Look, I need your advice. Should I just stand down? I have to put the party first and do what is right for our long-term future. I cannot just "cling on" if it isn't the best thing.' Paddy argued strongly that Nick should stay in post.

In early September, there was a minor panic when the Lib Dem press office phoned Nick Clegg at Chevening to say that they had just heard that Vince had agreed to do a Sunday TV round, but that he wouldn't say what it was about. Could he be announcing some sort of leadership challenge? The Sunday papers were full of 'Clegg leadership crisis' stories, but the names quoted were all pretty low grade. When Vince eventually appeared on BBC radio, he was mildly helpful to Nick, but perhaps not helpful enough to bury the rumours of his ambitions for good.

Of course, the irony here is that Nick had privately given some thought in 2011 and early 2012 to the potential scenario of handing over to Vince at the end of the parliament, if he judged that to be in the party's best interests in maximising support at the general election. But in public, leaders cannot be anything other than 100 per cent committed to their jobs for ever – the merest scintilla of doubt is generally taken as an opportunity to whip up a leadership 'crisis'.

Anyway, by early September Nick's mood seemed better. And at Westminster, the focus was turning to the long-expected government reshuffle. I already knew what he was intending to do, but not what David Cameron was planning.

With almost 100 government jobs to fill, reshuffles are complex organisational challenges and Prime Ministers need input from advisers, senior colleagues and, of course, the Whips' Office.

I was seated on the front bench in the House of Commons one day, waiting to respond to a debate, when I received my first insight into how the Whips' Office feed their views about individual MPs back in to those at the top of government. Sitting next to me was a junior Conservative whip with a large book on his lap, onto which he would occasionally record some brief comments.

'What are you up to?' I asked naively. 'Oh, this is the Whips' Office book,' was the reply. 'We listen to every debate and question, and write brief comments next to individual MPs' names, to record what they are saying and whether they are loyal or disloyal, helpful or hopeless, effective or dull. That sort of thing. It all goes to the Chief Whip and sometimes the PM will want to see it – particularly before reshuffles. But you have to be diplomatic. There was one notorious occasion where a very junior whip actually wrote comments on John Major's performance in the House of Commons when Major was PM. Apparently he wrote something like: "Another uninspiring contribution from this rather dull and ineffective man."' Sadly, no one spotted it, and a few weeks later John Major himself read it when he was flicking through the book. The whip lost his job in the reshuffle, and was never heard of again.'

BACK ON
THE BRIDGE

SEPTEMBER 2012

It was 11 p.m. on Monday 3 September 2012, and the night before the expected Cabinet reshuffle.

Nick Clegg's mobile phone rang just as he was going to bed.

It was Baroness Warsi, the chairman of the Conservative Party.

The next day, Nick Clegg told me about the extraordinary conversation.

'Nick, you will know it's the reshuffle tomorrow. I am going to quit the government. We've always got on well, and I thought you should know,' Baroness Warsi said.

Nick could tell that it was quite an emotional moment for her. Lady Warsi explained that she was 'furious' with the Prime Minister. She said he had been in touch with her earlier in the day, and explained that she was going to be dropped as Conservative Party chairman. She was being offered a junior ministerial post in the Foreign Office and felt patronised by the assumption that her background made her an obvious choice for this role and department.

The Conservative chairman explained to the Liberal Democrat Deputy Prime Minister that she was inclined to just resign and leave the government.

Nick liked Baroness Warsi, but it was unclear what he was supposed to do to help.

'Look,' he replied, 'I understand why you are so upset. You are a talented person and this all sounds so ham-fisted. But you are the chairman of the

Conservative Party. I am the Leader of the Liberal Democrats. There is really only so much advice I can give you. It is crucial that you make up your own mind. You should sleep on it overnight.'

Tuesday 4 September was the day of the reshuffle.

By Monday night, the first speculation was being carried by the media. And on Tuesday morning, the first major appointments were announced. Patrick McLoughlin was moving from Chief Whip to be Transport Secretary. Justine Greening was being moved from Transport to International Development – not least because of her opposition to Heathrow expansion. Andrew Mitchell, formerly the International Development Secretary, was taking over as Chief Whip. Ken Clarke was being demoted, moving from the Justice Department to be Minister without Portfolio. Nick Clegg had told me a few months before that David Cameron was set on sacking Ken completely, so this was at least a better outcome from a Liberal Democrat perspective. But the arrival of the bone-dry Chris Grayling as Justice Secretary was less welcome. Baroness Warsi, as she had warned Nick, was also demoted from Conservative chairman, and given a rather odd, negotiated, title of 'Senior Minister of State at the Foreign and Commonwealth Office'.

The biggest surprise of the reshuffle was the promotion of the embattled Jeremy Hunt to take over as Secretary of State for Health. A few months before, in the middle of the row over NewsCorp and the BSkyB bid, it had looked as if Jeremy might be returning to the back benches. He was now taking over a politically crucial department and one of the biggest Cabinet posts. I texted him to congratulate him – Jeremy is a decent person, and he had also been supportive of me at difficult moments.

Andrew Lansley was demoted from Health to Leader of the House of Commons – a punishment for 'retoxifying' the NHS as an issue for the Conservatives with his widely unpopular NHS Bill. David Cameron tried to move Iain Duncan Smith from Work and Pensions to the Justice Department, but the former Tory leader refused to budge.

Other changes were less high-profile. The unheard-of Conservative MP David Jones became the new Welsh Secretary. So low-profile was he that at the first meeting of the new Cabinet, David Cameron's deputy chief of staff, the super-posh Kate Fall, turned to Lib Dem director of communications Olly Grender and said, rather too loudly, 'Olly! Olly! Who IS that new person over there on the end of the Cabinet table? I've never seen him before! I assume he must be one of your Liberal people?'

Given Kate Fall's role in coordinating the Conservative part of the reshuffle, a somewhat bemused Olly Grender, rather relishing the moment, whispered back, 'He is one of yours, Kate, a Conservative! He's the new Secretary of State for Wales – David Jones. Your boss just promoted him.' Kate Fall looked distinctly embarrassed. 'Olly! How awful that I didn't know,' she said.

On the whole, the Conservative reshuffle looked like a move to the right.

Nick Clegg carried out his own reshuffle, but without changing his Cabinet members. He confirmed that he wanted to give up our ministerial posts at the Foreign Office and Defence. It seemed to some people odd to vacate these important departments, but Nick's view was that he and Danny Alexander would be intimately involved in any big foreign or defence issues through their senior positions in government and membership of the National Security Council. Instead, we secured new ministerial berths in the Department for Environment and Rural Affairs, and in International Development. Jeremy Browne was moved into a senior role in the Home Office, as Minister of State – my lobbying had saved him from being dropped.

A number of Liberal Democrat ministers were asked to leave the government altogether, and this was a particular blow to effective and dedicated colleagues such as Paul Burstow, Sarah Teather and Nick Harvey.

After addressing the bad news, Nick Clegg had to deal with the promotions – including mine.

At 1.15 p.m., I was instructed to leave my office in 1 Parliament Street, and – for media management purposes – I was given a ludicrous and elongated route to meet Nick Clegg outside the Cabinet Office. I cut through Portcullis House, walked along the river and past the massive Ministry of Defence building, and then turned left and came back down Whitehall – crossing the road and meeting Nick and a gaggle of journalists and cameras outside 70 Whitehall. This was where we had first started our route into government in May 2010, when we had entered these doors to take part in talks with the Conservative Party. After my resignation in 2010, and two years on the back benches, I was now at last back on the bridge.

Nick and I paused for a few seconds to shake hands in front of the cameras, and then we were inside the building and on the way to Nick's grand first-floor office. The two of us sat down together briefly.

'Look, it's great to have you back. You're going to be hugely helpful to me and can hopefully take some of the weight off both Danny and me. As you know, I have agreed with Cameron that you will have two roles: Minister of State here in the Cabinet Office and Schools Minister in the Department for Education.

'In the Cabinet Office, I want you to be Oliver Letwin's opposite number, and I want you to lead on the mid-term review. I want you to try to sort out issues of contention with Oliver and the Tories in most areas of domestic policy. Of course, Danny will continue to lead on all the economy stuff, and you don't need to get involved in defence and foreign issues. But health, education, Home Office, justice, local government, welfare, the environment, immigration – I want you to keep an eye on all that lot for me, working with our ministers in all those departments, and sorting out problems where they arise. On education, I want to make sure that the Lib Dem voice is properly heard and that we drive our agenda, and ensure that the DfE is not only about what Michael Gove wants. And I hope that you can improve relations between my office and Gove's, so there are fewer disputes between us. Oh, and see if you can sort out his mad idea about bringing back the old O-level/CSE divide! That's all!'

I got back to my old office in 1 Parliament Street, which as a minister I would now be vacating. My researcher then popped into my office and said he had the No. 10 switchboard on the line for me. Could I speak to the Prime Minister? It felt like a replay of May 2010, except on this occasion I did not need to do the 'walk' down Downing Street, as I was not being brought back as a full Cabinet minister.

Half an hour after I was supposed to be speaking to David Cameron, the call finally came through.

'It's David Cameron here. I think you've seen Nick already, so you'll know we both want you back in with two hats on – Schools Minister and Minister of State at the Cabinet Office. Education under Michael Gove has been one of the best and most radical areas of the government, and I hope that this reform project can continue, with you and Michael working together. As for the Cabinet Office, well, it's been a somewhat difficult time for the coalition, and we need a period where both parties can now work together in the interests of the country. I hope you can facilitate that – working with Oliver Letwin and others.'

I replied briefly: 'I am looking forward to both jobs. I am grateful to you and Nick for your support over the last couple of tough years for me, and for bringing me back into the government.'

'Look,' the Prime Minister replied, 'I think you have been in the wilderness long enough now. Of course you'll get some flak from some people, but it's the right time to have you back. If I were you, I'd check in with Michael at the Education Department as soon as you can.' And that was it. He was off to make the next twenty or thirty calls to those on the way up and the way down alike.

I took the Prime Minister's advice, and fixed to arrive at the Department for Education at 4.30 p.m. There, in the best traditions of the civil service, waiting to greet me in the lobby, were the Permanent Secretary at the DfE, Chris Wormald, and Michael Gove's able young private secretary, Pamela Dow. They looked like a bride and her father waiting patiently for the groom. For me, it was a very welcome 'reception committee', because I knew both of these excellent civil servants. Chris Wormald had run Nick Clegg's Deputy Prime Minister's Office with considerable skill and energy in the first couple of years of coalition. And Pamela Dow happened to be a personal friend of mine, as well as being a dedicated and top-class civil servant.

I was shown up to my office on the seventh floor and introduced to my private office staff, who until an hour or so before had been serving the highly able Conservative minister Nick Gibb, who had now effectively been sacked.

There was an odd atmosphere of palpable expectation and instability.

Chris Wormald said, 'Congratulations, Minister! You are now the second-longest-serving current minister in the Department for Education.'

'I can't be,' I said, 'I've only been here for seven minutes.'

'I'm afraid so,' Chris replied. 'All the others have gone in the reshuffle. The department is a bit shell-shocked. We've lost all our ministers, you see. Michael Gove is the only former minister still here.'

Sure enough, not only had Nick Gibb and my Liberal Democrat predecessor, Sarah Teather, been axed, but John Hayes had been removed and so had Tim Loughton. 'We understand Lord Hill also wants to leave,' said Chris. I was sad about that, because I both knew and liked the mild-mannered, moderate and thoughtful Schools Minister and former adviser to John Major.

Later I met Lord Hill, whose glass office was adjacent to mine. 'I am really sorry to hear you are going,' I said.

'Yes,' he said. 'Look, I have enjoyed it. But it is a bit of a nightmare being the only Lords minister in a department of this size. I have to field every single education question or piece of legislation in the Lords, while you have five ministers in the Commons. And as well as that, I have had a massive range of responsibilities – leading on academies, free schools, the whole of capital funding and so on. I never get to see my wife these days, and after rather enjoying that for a while, she's getting a bit fed up. I think the PM wants me to stay, but I have taken a final decision to resign. I'm not going to change my mind. The wife would kill me!'

To my surprise, the next day Lord Hill was still in the department. 'The PM hasn't been able to find the time to see me yet. But I am not changing my mind. I expect to be free tomorrow,' the reluctant minister said, shrugging his shoulders.

The following Monday, I came in feeling sure that Lord Hill would be long gone. He wasn't. 'Jonathan, have you decided to stay, after all?' I asked, sticking my head around his office door.

'Hmmmm,' he said. 'It's a bit embarrassing really, and the wife isn't amused.'

'What happened?' I said. 'Would he not see you?'

'Worse,' he said. 'I went to see him at the end of the week to resign, and I assumed someone had told him what I was there for. But he just said: "Look, I'm terribly busy. I've got to see the French Ambassador. I think you are doing a great job. I'm delighted you're staying." And then he was off. I seemed to have failed to resign, and I think I just missed the moment. Embarrassing, really! I will have to wait for the next reshuffle.'

'Jonathan,' I said. 'What a shambles!' And we both laughed. Actually, I was very pleased that he was staying on.

Michael Gove was not around that afternoon, so we fixed to meet the next day.

In the evening, I received a friendly text from George Osborne: 'Welcome back. Good to have you back at the centre. I know you will enjoy working with Michael at the DfE.'

That evening, with the reshuffle over, Nick Clegg and David Cameron met to review the changes.

'God, it's painful work, isn't it?' said Nick Clegg, explaining that some of his colleagues had taken the news much harder than he had expected. 'Not something we want to do more often than necessary.'

David Cameron agreed that he also found reshuffles a nightmare. 'And most of them change nothing,' he observed.

'Apparently Cameron got a pretty hard time from some people,' Nick Clegg told me the next day. 'He said that Warsi and Greening were pretty difficult and rude about being moved.'

'I'm worried about this Tory reshuffle,' he continued. 'The moderates like Ken and Baroness Warsi have been demoted. The hardmen like Grayling are in, and right-wingers like Owen Paterson – a very bone-headed man, in my opinion. It's all the very worst of Cameron – tactical stuff to buy off the Tory right. I wonder if Cameron still believes in all that 'compassionate Conservative' stuff. It feels like the Conservative Party that we entered the co-alition with is turning into something much more right-wing and traditionalist. Can we work with these people for another three years? I just don't know.'

BACK ON TRACK

2012

Wednesday 5 September was my first full day back in government. In the morning, Nick Clegg and I travelled to the brilliant Mulberry School in Tower Hamlets, for a visit designed to highlight my new role in the Education Department as well as the Liberal Democrats' strong commitment to the opportunity agenda.

Afterwards, I met with Nick Clegg and his advisers and we discussed the aftermath of the reshuffle. There was a problem with Jeremy Browne's new role at the Home Office. Basically, his detailed brief hadn't been agreed with the Conservatives first. Theresa May had now given her Tory junior ministers the 'big stuff' like immigration and policing, leaving Jeremy with the less important issues to handle.

In addition, somewhat incomprehensibly, someone had forgotten about the Women and Equalities brief, which Lynne Featherstone used to lead on at the Home Office. Following Lynne's move to the Development Department, nobody seemed to know where this was now located.

To make matters worse, the Cabinet was now expanding, with new Tory ministers, as the demoted Baroness Warsi and Ken Clarke were still allowed to attend Cabinet. Nick Clegg and Jonny Oates were inclined to press David Cameron for a matching increase in Lib Dem Cabinet membership.

At 1.30 p.m. I went back over to the Department for Education, where I had my first formal meeting with Michael Gove. Michael was very welcoming and we had a good first conversation. I set out the policy areas I wanted to lead on and – in contrast to Jeremy's situation at the Home Office – Michael said he was sure these would all be fine and he would come back to me to confirm it the next day.

I also said that I hoped that I could improve relations between Michael's office and Nick Clegg's.

After about half an hour, his private secretary opened the door of his office and said:

'Secretary of State, you are going to need to leave now for Cabinet. By the way, Minister Laws, you are apparently now attending too. Here are your papers.' And with that, I was presented with a file of papers for that afternoon's Cabinet meeting.

I had mixed feelings. I had wanted a low-key return to government, and this wasn't quite it. But on the other hand, what politician doesn't relish the opportunity to be back at the top table?

Michael and I rushed downstairs and got in the back of his chauffeur-driven black Jaguar, which took us the quarter of a mile or so to Downing Street. We chatted as the big security gates were unlocked, and the car then headed up Downing Street, past machine gun-wielding police. It stopped just outside the famous door of No. 10. I got swiftly out of the car, hoping to avoid the cameras on the other side of the road. But Michael Gove stopped me and said, 'I think this is a bit of a coalition moment, David.' So we paused for a few moments, standing side by side, while the photographers clicked away. And then the famous black door opened, and I was inside the lobby of Downing Street again for the first time in two years.

From the reception lobby, we walked together down the red-carpeted corridor that leads to another lobby area, outside the Cabinet Room. Cabinet ministers were already milling around, drinking tea or coffee. There was a sense of 'new school year' excitement, not least amongst the new members of the Cabinet. I spoke briefly to William Hague, who said he was disappointed to lose Liberal Democrats from his Foreign Office team. 'Jeremy was an excellent colleague. I shall miss him,' he said. 'I am a bit surprised you lot are giving up Foreign Affairs and Defence.'

I was located at the far end of the Cabinet Room, looking right down the famous oval table, near to Oliver Letwin and David Willetts. It was hardly a prime slot, but it did have the undoubted virtue of giving a very clear view of all Cabinet members, and it was a spot from which it was easy to catch the attention of the Prime Minister. From some seats, on the same side of the table as the PM, it is very tough to catch his eye to speak – particularly if he isn't desperate to bring the minister in question into the debate. I once saw Theresa Villiers, the Northern Ireland Secretary, who was usually seated in the black spot on the PM's side of the table but on his extreme left, signalling to catch David Cameron's eye for thirty minutes before she was finally allowed to speak.

The first agenda item was on the economy. George Osborne said that he had good news to report: 'Growth in the last quarter has now been upgraded. It was minus 0.7 per cent. It is now minus 0.5 per cent.' I saw Nick Clegg smile at this notion of a growth upgrade. We were thinking the same thing and exchanged amused glances.

It was good to be back in the government again. I may not have hidden my pleasure very effectively. 'David clearly loves being back – he's like a pig in shit,' said Nick Clegg to a friend that evening.

It was interesting to see how the Cabinet now operated, since I was last there, and to assess how the various key figures interacted. David Cameron was clearly a businesslike, and slightly impatient, leader of his team. He was eloquent, a very good chair of discussions, and always very well briefed. He was rarely if ever wrong-footed, and there was never any question that he was in charge. But if there was a number two in Cabinet it was clearly Nick Clegg, and not George Osborne, Theresa May or William Hague.

Nick sat directly opposite the Prime Minister, who treated him respectfully as a joint leader of the coalition and brought him into major discussions as the first speaker. The Deputy Prime Minister spoke often, but economically and effectively. He was also well briefed, thoughtful and insightful.

George Osborne saved most of his interventions for the discussions of economic policy, when he spoke carefully, forensically and usually with the odd joke thrown in. He listened carefully to other contributors, but there was never much doubt about what he thought about the varying quality of his colleagues – and his quick wit was often used to good effect.

Vince Cable was listened to closely. David Cameron and George Osborne were careful to treat the Business Secretary with respect, even when he was decidedly 'off message', which wasn't infrequently. William Hague spoke rarely, and usually only on his Foreign Affairs responsibilities. Theresa May, the Home Secretary, also tended to stick to her own brief.

Michael Gove crackled and sparkled in Cabinet as almost no other minister could – he was incapable of making any points without being amusing or provocative or both, though sometimes the flamboyant style submerged the serious points which he was making. And if he ever spoke without making a joke, you knew that he really was deadly serious about the subject in hand – often foreign affairs or extremism matters.

Finally, Ken Clarke sat there in the centre of the Cabinet, on Nick Clegg's left, a true representation of coalition values in action. He had, of course, been sitting around the Cabinet table for some decades and there was definitely a sense that he had seen it all before. He was invariably brimming over with common-sense reflections, which he willingly dispensed in his genial and blunt manner. In summary, and at least at the higher levels, this was a good team.

The past few months had been quite tough for the coalition government. The economy was contracting. The Budget was a mess. We had fallen out over O-levels, Lords reform, party funding, the boundary review and Jeremy Hunt. David Cameron had been hugely distracted by Leveson.

Many in Westminster wondered if the coalition could survive almost three more years, but both party leaders had now firmly decided that they wanted to see their work through.

So our attention now turned to how to best get the show back on the road.

David Cameron suggested that we have a small political meeting on Monday 17 September. It would essentially be the Quad of David Cameron, Nick Clegg, George Osborne and Danny Alexander, as well as me, Oliver Letwin and a few senior advisers. The aim would be to set a course for the year ahead, including a discussion of the planned mid-term review.

David Cameron's original plan was that we should all gather at Chequers, out in the glorious Buckinghamshire countryside, on the Sunday night. We would then have a relaxed dinner together and get down to the serious business on Monday morning. 'I think that would be an awful idea,' said Jonny Oates. 'A Lib Dem–Tory sleepover at Chequers! God, that's the last thing we need right now.' So, it was agreed instead that the Conservative team would gather at Chequers on the Sunday night and we would join them first thing on Monday morning.

Instead, Nick Clegg suggested that our team should meet at his Putney home on the Sunday evening, to plan out what we were going to propose.

On my way over to Nick's house, I had an urgent call from Vince Cable. He was worried that we might agree to a large package of anti-trade union measures that David Cameron and George Osborne were pushing hard on. Vince said he thought this was only on the agenda because the PM and Chancellor were worried about Boris Johnson, who was very much 'on manoeuvres', and was himself campaigning hard for tough measures on the unions. Indeed, in that day's *Mail on Sunday*, there was an article entitled '"I'll crush the strikers": Boris Johnson steals Cameron's thunder with plan to beat union militants'. I reassured Vince that I would resist anything that didn't have a very solid and convincing policy rationale.

I arrived at Nick's house in Putney at around 7 p.m. Miriam was out and the only people present were Nick, Danny Alexander, Jonny Oates and Julian Astle, one of our senior policy advisers.

Nick was doing all the cooking – lamb and some rather unimpressive couscous, washed down with water. I reflected that the Conservatives were probably having a better time and better food at Chequers, but I decided to keep my thoughts to myself.

Earlier that day, Danny had sent us all an email with some of his thoughts on the mid-term review. He argued that it should focus on the delivery of big and bold policies for both coalition partners, rather than going for lowest common denominator stuff.

He also said that we needed to develop a plan that kept to our economic course but moved to 'add pluses to the Plan A'. It was clear that Danny was going cold on doing anything to give a more radical stimulus to growth, though by now he seemed to be fully signed up to my proposal to use the profits from quantitative easing to boost capital spending without adding to government borrowing.

Danny also warned about putting too many new ideas into the mid-term review. He said that on the Lib Dem side this would just lead to more calls for a special conference to debate a second coalition agreement.

Danny then listed the six bold and forward-looking policies that he wanted us to promote. These were: a further rise in the tax-free personal allowance to £12,500; introducing a mansion tax, even if this was time-limited and removed when borrowing had met its targets; a policy to boost education or childcare; a big programme of green, renewable, investment; a 25-year infrastructure plan; and a further dose of 'localism'.

Over dinner, we discussed Danny's note and we then all threw in our own ideas. Both Nick and I were dubious about moving all the way to a £12,500 target on the allowance. We felt that this was too expensive and best left to our next election manifesto. But we did agree that once we had reached the £10,000 level we should at least press for further small increases – if only to keep up with inflation.

We then moved on to a long discussion on wealth taxes. I said that I saw two problems here. Firstly, I thought David Cameron was simply never going to agree to a mansion tax. I also said that if we kept banging on about higher taxes on the wealthy, it looked like we thought it was an end in itself. I said I thought the only reason to back higher taxes on the wealthy was to tackle the deficit without putting an unfair burden on the poor. So I argued for insisting on taxes on the rich to reduce the need for unfair spending cuts that would hit the poor. I also said that I thought that the Tories would be willing to consider higher council tax bands on very expensive properties, because it built on the existing system rather than being something new, and therefore more frightening, to some of their supporters. I argued for saving money on the expensive tax reliefs on pensions, which overwhelmingly favour the rich.

We agreed to look closely at whether there was more we could do on early years education, and I suggested a package to invest more in education and training for 18–21-year-olds, possibly linked to removing unemployment benefits for this group. I wanted 18–21-year-olds to have a more generous work, education and training offer, removing the need for any of them to be on the dole.

We then discussed green issues, and there was a general feeling that we were simply failing to find green policies that cut through with the public. All of us were very frustrated with the 'Green Deal', designed to provide free upfront household energy-saving investment, which would be paid for over time through energy bills, and by the failure of the Climate Change Department to make this policy a practical success.

Finally, we agreed that we had no incentive to hand the Conservatives a big anti-union Bill, not least now that they were refusing to make any serious moves forward on party funding.

The next day, I was up at 5 a.m. As well as the Chequers summit, we were today announcing the coalition's decision on how to proceed with the reform of GCSEs.

Danny Alexander came to my house just after seven, and he, Julian Astle and I drove to Chequers. It was my first visit to Chequers, and having already visited

Chevening – the impressive country house now being shared by Nick Clegg and William Hague – I was expecting something rather inspiring and grand.

We approached the house by a relatively inconspicuous driveway, stopped briefly at a security checkpoint and then drove around and through some large stone walls into a gated courtyard. In contrast to the striking entrance to Chevening, with its extensive flight of steps up to the front door, the entrance to Chequers was much less grand.

Chevening has the air of a grand country house of the eighteenth century. Chequers feels distinctly nineteenth century, and has the more intimate feel of a property that might feature in an Agatha Christie film, where most of the guests would be murdered and Miss Marple would be called upon to solve the mystery.

The three of us were shown through into a large reception room, where coffee awaited us. In another room, not far down the corridor, we could hear laughter and muffled discussion amongst the Conservative team, who had arrived the night before. There was a newspaper rack, but all that day's newspapers were missing, with the exception of the *Daily Mirror* and *The Independent*, which looked distinctly unread.

Eventually, David Cameron, George Osborne and Oliver Letwin came in, and we had a brief discussion while sipping coffee. The Conservatives had brought along some of their top advisers: the impressive and suave Rupert Harrison, George Osborne's confident and effective economic adviser; a slightly over-eager-to-please Patrick Rock, who apparently ran the Downing Street Policy Unit; and Ed Llewellyn, the PM's trusted chief of staff.

We had to wait a little while for Nick Clegg, who was launching the new qualification reform plans with Michael Gove at a school in west London. When Nick arrived, we all went upstairs to a large room, dominated by a huge table similar in scale and shape to the Cabinet table. Through the extensive windows, we could see beautiful views out across the gardens and fields around the house.

The PM sat in the middle of the table, with his back to the wall, and looking out over the fields. It was all a mirror image of the Cabinet Room in Downing Street. Opposite David Cameron was Nick Clegg, with George Osborne to his right. I sat next to George.

We started on the Autumn Statement. George Osborne explained that the borrowing numbers were getting worse, because growth was slower than expected.

To my great surprise, David Cameron said: 'Can't we just cut NHS funding and save some money that way? We could freeze NHS spending in cash terms, instead of sticking with the real-terms protection. That would save a lot.'

I immediately interrupted to say: 'I think that is not a good idea. Even with a real-terms protection, the NHS is going to be under a lot of pressure by the end of the parliament. We pledged – actually, you did in your manifesto – to protect the NHS in real terms. If we back off, that is not only a broken promise, but it could leave the NHS in a real mess just before the general election. My view is that by the end of the parliament we may actually need to consider putting in more money.'

George Osborne then raised the possibility of delaying the delivery of our commitment to achieving 0.7 per cent of national income on development assistance. 'That would save billions of pounds in a few years' time,' he said.

David Cameron looked highly dubious: 'Is it really worth all the political hassle of being seen to go back on a very clear pledge?' he said. 'I'm not keen – the NGOs would be really angry and they would mount a huge campaign against us.'

Nick Clegg and Danny Alexander raised the issue of winter fuel payments, which were still being given to some quite affluent pensioners.

'Look,' said David Cameron, 'we've been through this before. I am not interested in re-opening this discussion. I made a promise on this during the election campaign and I am not having one of those "split-screen moments" where they play back what I said then and what I am saying now.'

George Osborne made the case for big welfare cuts, including cancelling all uprating of benefits. Both Nick Clegg and I pushed back on this. 'Why would we want to cut the real incomes of the poorest people in society?' I said. 'The coalition agreement is clear that we are supposed to protect the poorest people from cuts.'

Nick then said: 'It is totally unacceptable to me if the next stage of austerity is all about cuts to welfare, with nothing from the rich. Let me be clear: I am not agreeing to that. We are going to have to look at tax rises on the rich.'

I saw George Osborne roll his eyes. 'Nick, tax rises on the rich aren't that easy. And there are only so many Russian oligarchs in London that we can raise money from.'

I mentioned tax relief on pensions, and then Nick said: 'What we need is a wealth tax. Preferably something like our mansion tax.'

'Nick, you must be joking,' said Cameron. 'I see that Ed Balls has now committed Labour to this great Vince Cable idea, too! This means all of my dreams have come true at once! With Ed Balls and Vince Cable banging on about mansion taxes every day, the Conservative election coffers are going to be filled by our affluent donors in no time at all. They really, really, really hate this. This policy, combined with Vince Cable and Ed Balls, is the biggest money-making machine the Conservative Party has ever had. And I am not giving that one up!'

It was exactly as I had predicted. Here was an idea that was going nowhere, even if Danny Alexander thought that George Osborne was more sympathetic.

We didn't seem to be making much progress. Oliver Letwin then said that he had thought up a wonderful idea for the Autumn Statement. It sounded utterly bizarre to me.

'It's called "Shares for Rights",' said Oliver. 'How it would work is that people who are self-employed would be able to get tax-incentivised shares in their own business. In exchange for these shares, they would lose all their employment rights. No more needless bureaucracy. And the key then is that the manager of the business could then sack any of these employee sharehold-ers he or she wanted to, without any conditions and with no notice at all.'

There was silence around the table. I frowned. Nick Clegg looked com-pletely baffled. David Cameron said: 'OK, Oliver. Very radical. I think we should look at that a bit more.'

We then moved on to discuss possible policy announcements at our annual party conferences.

David Cameron said: 'Look, the big thing for me is we want this Bill to sort out the trade unions.'

The Cabinet Secretary, Jeremy Heywood, had previously been asked to draw up a detailed policy note for both the PM and the DPM, setting out of all the options for reform. He must have known that it risked being a highly divisive issue, and also that some of the reform arguments were quite weak. He had produced an elegant and helpful paper, with a masterly conclu-sion in the best traditions of Sir Humphrey Appleby of Yes Minister fame: 'The arguments for and against moving ahead with the reforms immediately are finely poised and could be used to support action or the status quo.'

Nick Clegg said: 'We have some concerns about that. And in any case, we cannot move on some of this trade union stuff without sorting out party political funding, which is already in the coalition agreement. This trade union stuff is completely new.'

David Cameron began to get rather irritated and impatient, which I noticed was his response rather quickly if he didn't get his own way: 'Look, I have no idea what the connection is here. This is a completely new Lib Dem notion, which you are bringing up today for the first time.'

I said: 'That's not actually true. I've discussed it with Lord Feldman. He said he had sent some proposals on this to you, including caps on donations.'

'No. No,' said Cameron. 'I've seen nothing. Frankly, this is a bit frustrating. I'll need to speak to Andrew.' He flushed rather red and said: 'I thought we'd agreed this union stuff. Didn't Danny and George do a joint paper on possible reforms? Anyway, if you take the view you do, I'll have to look at where we are on party funding. But it's rather annoying that it's all being dealt with in this way.'

I regarded this as bluster from a Tory leader who wanted to bury an existing agreement on party funding reform while expecting us to sign up to a right-wing attack on the trade unions.

We then had a long discussion on the mid-term review. Nick Clegg pushed hard for implementation of the Dilnot Report on social care costs, which was designed to cap social care charges for elderly people whose poor health required them to go into expensive care homes. Somewhat unhelpfully, Danny Alexander said that he wouldn't say much as he didn't support the Dilnot findings.

David Cameron then said that the Tories had a radical idea for the mid-term review, which he was personally very keen on. This turned out to be giving social tenants the right to sell their properties and receive all the money from the sale. In exchange, they would agree never to claim any more housing benefit. 'It's our big idea,' he said. 'Setting the people free.'

A number of us expressed scepticism. I asked why people in social housing deserved such a huge giveaway, in comparison to people in private rented accommodation. I also suggested that if people chose to blow their windfall, say on a Caribbean holiday, it would in reality be impossible to refuse to rehouse them, not least if they had children. The whole idea seemed to me to be half-baked and unserious.

We went through six or seven other policies that could be included in the mid-term review, and then we stopped for lunch. We reassembled downstairs, in a pleasant but modestly sized dining room that led out onto the gardens.

Before lunch, Nick Clegg and David Cameron went for a brief walk in the Chequers rose garden. Nick told me later that the Prime Minister pressed hard for new measures to curb union powers: 'Boris is really making the running on it, and I think he's got some good points.'

Nick made clear that he wasn't going to agree any trade union reform, not least on how the unions funded the Labour Party, while the Conservatives were blocking the reform of political party funding, which had been written into the coalition agreement. 'Cameron is panicking about his right-wing MPs and wants to keep them on side. He told me he thinks his right wingers are "completely mad", but he wants to keep them on board,' said Nick later.

Over lunch, we discussed the Leveson Inquiry and press regulation, and the upcoming European summit on the EU budget.

On Leveson, it was clear that David Cameron didn't want to do anything to upset the press. Nick Clegg spelled out that while, as a liberal, he was of course determined to defend press freedoms, his basic view was that Lord Justice Leveson's recommendations should be implemented unless they were quite clearly disproportionate. Nick said: 'People simply won't understand the government setting up this inquiry and doing nothing about it.'

We also had a brief discussion about Labour under the leadership of Ed Miliband. One of David Cameron's advisers, Oliver Dowden, said: 'Ed Miliband won't cut it as a potential Prime Minister. The voters can see that. We must do everything we can to keep him in his place.' David Cameron replied: 'If that is our strategy, it is obviously working rather well, given our own opinion poll ratings at this time!' The most recent polls had the Conservatives as much as seven or eight points behind Labour.

We then moved on to the issue of Europe. Both leaders agreed on taking a very tough line on the European Union budget. It would be more difficult to find a common coalition position on the wider issue of the reform of the EU.

After a pleasant lunch of chicken and a glass of rather good wine, the coalition summit came to an end.

We had achieved very little agreement on the Autumn Statement, but a bit more progress on the mid-term review, and we had settled a clear common position on the EU budget.

It was certainly no love-in, but after a rocky few months, the coalition was definitely getting back on track.

Party Games

I was meeting with Oliver Letwin in the small restaurant tucked away in the basement of 10 Downing Street. There were only four tables here, and it certainly wasn't a place for discreet conversations.

I cannot remember what we were discussing, but I quietly suggested that a good solution would be a minor reorganisation of government.

'My dear boy,' said Oliver Letwin, chuckling. 'It is simply impossible. Impossible.'

'Why on the earth should it be?' I replied. 'If the Prime Minister wants it…'

'Oh David, how charmingly naive you are,' was the reply. 'The Prime Minister doesn't decide these things! When I was first in government, I assumed, like you, that if the Prime Minister wanted something, it just happened. Then I realised it wasn't that simple. I realised that power lies elsewhere. I went looking for it. I assumed the Cabinet Secretary must be the real source of power. I soon established that I was wrong there too. Then I suspected that the person of real influence must be the head of the Home Civil Service – but I was yet again wrong.'

Now shaking uncontrollably with laughter, and struggling to avoid spraying half-drunk coffee across the table in front of us, Oliver only just managed to blurt out: 'It took me precisely two years before I finally realised who it is that runs Britain. Our great United Kingdom is actually entirely run by a lady called Sue Gray, who is the Head of Ethics or something in the Cabinet Office. Unless she agrees things, they just don't happen. Cabinet reshuffles, departmental reorganisations, the whole lot – it's all down to Sue Gray. Nothing moves in Whitehall unless Sue says so. And even when we ministers resign, she gets to censor our memoirs too! Our poor, deluded voters think the Prime Minister holds the reins of power. Wrong! David, the truth is that our real leader, Sue Gray, sits at a small desk in the Cabinet Office. If only the Chinese and Russians knew! They have probably been bugging all the wrong phones for years.' And then he descended into a fit of giggles.

My regular weekly 7.30 a.m. breakfasts with Oliver Letwin, the Conservative Minister for Government Policy, and my Cabinet Office counterpart, were some of my favourite moments in government. We got on well, trusted each other and sorted out a lot of coalition problems that might otherwise have gone unresolved. Oliver also had an infectious chuckle – the 'Letwin giggle', which, once started, could not be stopped. At times, the coalition parties needed a sense of humour. Oliver often supplied it. One time when patience and a sense of humour were in great demand was the period of weeks running up to the autumn party conferences.

It was Wednesday 19 September 2012, in the middle of the afternoon. Nick Clegg, Danny Alexander and I were meeting in Nick Clegg's office, which looked across Horse Guards Parade towards St James's Park. The following week was the beginning of the annual party conference season, where for four or five days each week the main political parties would meet to showcase their policies and in some cases debate them.

Each year during the coalition, we would discuss for some weeks the policy announcements that each party wanted to make at its conference – which had to be agreed across the government as a whole. Some of the announcements would amount to small tweaks to existing policies, while others would be much more significant in scale.

Each party would draw up its list of policy priorities in private, a month or two before conference season, and we would then compare lists and see if agreements could be made.

Oliver Letwin and I had swapped lists soon after the Cabinet reshuffle, and we had exchanged views on which policies would be more or less acceptable. Today, the two lists would go to a political Quad in order to seek agreement.

Having agreed our strategy, Nick Clegg, Danny Alexander and I made our way from Nick's office down the connecting corridors to the large and echoing lobby that connects the Cabinet Office to 10 Downing Street. At this point between the two buildings is a glass security double door. Civil servants can key in a number to get the two glass doors to slide open. Politicians can press a buzzer and be let through by the security staff in Downing Street.

As the second glass door closes behind you, it is possible to turn around and see a large notice pinned onto the glass door: 'No Cats Beyond This Point'. This is apparently an attempt to discourage people from allowing the Chancellor's cat to roam from 11 Downing Street to 10 Downing Street to the Cabinet Office – and from there to freedom.

After passing into 10 Downing Street, you notice that you are now walking on rather smart red carpet. The corridor dog-legs, and in a matter of seconds you have come to a second door – usually open. A small flight of steps connects through to the main part of 10 Downing Street. A further short walk takes you to the grand Downing Street staircase on your left, and then you are into the lobby outside the Cabinet Room – which is immediately on your right. So, from the Deputy Prime Minister's Office to the Cabinet Room is only about a minute's brisk walk.

On this occasion, we arrived in the Cabinet Room before the Conservative team – but we didn't have long to wait. After a couple of minutes, the full cast was assembled. David Cameron was in his normal seat, with Nick Clegg directly opposite. George Osborne sat on Nick's Clegg's right, between me and the Deputy Prime Minister. Danny Alexander sat to the Prime Minister's left, with Oliver Letwin to the other side of the PM.

The mood was very relaxed and convivial – to an extent sufficient to make any watching left-wing Liberal Democrat or right-wing Conservative rather nervous. Of course, no left-wing Liberal Democrats or right-wing Conservatives were ever let anywhere near the Quad. But if the atmosphere was friendly and even 'chummy', the conversations were, as ever, business-like and blunt.

In front of us were papers setting out the policies proposed by each party, highlighting the agreed policies and those that were more controversial.

The Conservatives were still pushing hard on a deal on trade union legislation. In exchange, George Osborne said he was willing to make the 'massive' concession to us of a 'call for evidence' on a decarbonisation strategy.

I said: 'I'm not quite sure that works for us. You are suggesting, George, that we should give you a massive policy concession which will run on the front page of every newspaper when you announce it. In exchange, you propose to give us a tiddly announcement of a consultation which would probably get page 48 of the *Financial Times* and page 15 of *Green Energy Weekly*. Do you seriously expect us to accept that?'

George laughed. Clearly he was trying it on. Nick Clegg said: 'Look, the only way I will touch legislation on trade unions is if it is part of a package on party funding reform. If not, I'm just not interested.'

The Conservatives were clearly not interested in party funding reform.

George Osborne and his adviser, Rupert Harrison, then pressed the case for a 'trade', where Vince Cable would get his 'Business Bank' with up to £1 billion in equity – but, in exchange, the Chancellor wanted us to approve the somewhat dotty 'Shares for Rights' idea that Oliver Letwin had proposed at Chequers.

Nick Clegg said: 'This really seems to me to be a totally wacky idea. You give people a shareholding in the business they work for, and in exchange they lose their employment rights? It is really weird, and surely nobody is actually ever going to want to do it.'

George Osborne said: 'Look, Nick, if nobody takes it up you've got nothing to fear, have you? Anyway, it's very helpful to me – a bit of red meat to throw to our activists at party conference. In exchange, you get the Business Bank and you get to shut Vince Cable up! I have to say that I'm not actually sure that the Business Bank is going to deliver either!'

Nick said he was rather worried about the notion that both sides were prepared to agree to policies on the basis that they weren't going to work. But he made clear that he thought that the Business Bank had a much better chance of delivering than 'Shares for Rights', and on that basis he was willing to agree the deal.

We then went through a list of about twenty other policy proposals, including a proposal from the Justice Secretary, Chris Grayling, to allow householders to act 'disproportionately' against burglars – more crowd-pleasing stuff for the Tory faithful. I groaned audibly when we came to this item. 'Don't worry,' whispered George Osborne, 'we've announced this same policy at every Conservative conference for the last ten years, and this latest proposal won't make much difference.'

Oliver Letwin assured us that the policy would be very sensible and that it would still be designed to stop householders from beating burglars to a pulp on their doormats. 'Of course,' joked David Cameron, 'if you tried to burgle Oliver's house you would probably be invited in for coffee and breakfast!'

At the end of the meeting, David Cameron, flicked over the papers in front of him and suddenly said: 'Oh, one last thing, Nick. You guys have got some proposal to remove the word "insulting" from Section 5 of the Public Order Act. I think this is a free speech thing, isn't it? Look, I'm not violently against this, but my briefing says that the Home Office have now got cold feet – because doing this would allow members of the public to insult police office without recourse to action. So I'm pretty sceptical of this and I just think we should leave it out for now. Would you be OK with that?'

Nick Clegg agreed to put the issue on hold, which was fortunate really because just twenty-four hours hours later the government's Chief Whip, Andrew Mitchell, was accused of insulting a police officer at the gates of Downing Street – barely 100 metres from the Cabinet Room in which we were all sitting. It all led to a massive row and to the Chief Whip's resignation. Announcing a change of the law at this time might have been challenging to say the least.

The meeting was all over within around an hour. Most of the policies were agreed or clearly rejected, leaving just a few loose ends to tie up. But I felt that overall it was a rather uninspiring policy list.

The Liberal Democrat conference was, as ever, the first of the season – and it was due to begin on Saturday 22 September.

Nick Clegg and his advisers had decided some time ago to make a long-overdue formal apology for our U-turn on tuition fees, in the form of a video. The aim was, as far as possible, to draw a line under the issue and to make a very clear apology well before the general election.

The apology was recorded in mid-September and was to be broadcast on a televised party political broadcast. The whole sensitive issue was briefed out by Nick Clegg's media team on the Thursday before the conference. Vince Cable was 'put up' on *Newsnight* to explain the apology and to defend Nick and the party.

The agreed message was that we should have changed the policy before the election because it was becoming more expensive and difficult to afford, and because we could not guarantee to deliver the policy given the views of the other two parties.

But instead of sticking to the line, Vince appeared to suggest that he personally had always been rather sceptical of the policy before the election, whether or not the Lib Dems were able to govern alone. The press office and Nick's advisers were rather upset, and felt that the Business Secretary was protecting his own reputation rather than sticking to the agreed line. 'Vince pretty dreadful on *Newsnight*. We will need to clear up after him,' was the text from the press office.

The beginning of the Liberal Democrat conference was dominated by a lot of leadership speculation and polls purporting to show that Nick Clegg had the worst ratings of any political leader since Michael Foot. However, the polls didn't suggest that any other leader would make much difference to the party's prospects – indeed, one poll suggested that the Liberal Democrats would add just 2 per cent to their ratings if Vince Cable took over from Nick. And that would be before the media got its teeth into any new leader.

The weather in Brighton was pretty miserable all week, but the conference was far from disastrous, and we saw off a half-baked motion on economic policy from the left-wing fringe. It was fortunate for the leadership that our party opponents were so incompetent, because a better motion on the economy might have won majority support for a change in the government's economic strategy.

However, I wasn't pleased with the main messages from the conference, which were all about taxing the rich rather than reducing the pressure on those on low and middle incomes. There seemed to me a real risk that we were defining ourselves by policies such as Europe, environmental taxes and immigration, when people wanted to hear about bread-and-butter policies that would help them on issues such as education, taxes and the cost of living.

The conference ended as usual with the leader's speech. It was solid and unshowy – billed as 'a serious speech for serious times'. There certainly weren't many jokes in it, and the loudest applause was when Nick Clegg announced that former leader Paddy Ashdown would be returning to chair our general election campaign. I was sitting on the front row for the speech, in the area reserved for ministers. Halfway through, during a particularly 'worthy' passage on the environment, Danny Alexander, seated a few places to my right, suddenly turned to me and shouted that I urgently needed to dig

Simon Hughes in the ribs – sure enough, he was drifting off to sleep next to me and was just being spotted by the TV cameras. We got to him just in time.

At the Labour Party conference, Ed Miliband made a well-received speech, without notes, claiming the 'One Nation' mantle for his party. Nick Clegg was dubious about the adulatory press coverage secured by the Labour leader. He told me: 'I was abroad and the news filtered through from London that Ed Miliband had made some "great" speech. It was all made to sound as if he was the new Martin Luther King. But I'm sceptical. I suspect that this is one of those speeches which cuts through more in the Westminster bubble than it does in the wider country. Either way, I am not convinced that Miliband is really up to being PM. I think he is a clever policy wonk, but not a real political leader.'

EDUCATION:
A 'COALICIOUS' START

2012–13

I was once again sitting on the front bench of the House of Commons.
It was Monday 17 September, and Michael Gove had just finished
delivering a statement setting out the coalition's planned reforms to GCSEs.

We were listening to the response from the Labour Party spokesman,
Stephen Twigg.

Suddenly, Michael Gove glanced down at his BlackBerry and burst out
laughing.

'What is it?' I whispered to him.

He passed me his BlackBerry and pointed to an email he had just received.
It said:

> Dear Mr Gove, I hope you will not mind me contacting you. You
> may remember that we spoke briefly at the Conservative Party
> conference seven years ago, although I do recall that you were in a
> hurry when we met. I read in the newspapers this week that Lord
> Hill, your Education Minister, was hoping to retire but hasn't been
> able to. I am an experienced local councillor with a keen interest
> in education. I would be happy to take over as Education Minis-
> ter, if that would help. I would also be willing to join the House of
> Lords if needed. Yours etc.

I had a feeling that being in the Education team was going to be fun, and – outside the Treasury – it was the policy area that I most cared about and was most inspired to be part of.

When I arrived at the Education Department, the relations between the two coalition parties in this policy area weren't particularly good. Michael Gove and Nick Clegg should have been able to get on well together ideologically, but in practical terms they did not – in spite of Nick personally securing an excellent settlement for Education in the 2010 Spending Review.

Nick cared greatly about education, and he had established his own Social Mobility Cabinet Committee to coordinate action across government to spread opportunity to young people from all social backgrounds. But under Michael Gove, the Department for Education had become something of a Whitehall bunker: the Prime Minister and Chancellor largely allowed their Education Secretary to do what he wanted, and neither Michael nor his closest advisers wanted the Deputy Prime Minister to have much more influence than this.

Just before my arrival, there had been two large policy disputes: the greater was on qualification reform, where Michael Gove's advisers seemed to have floated the idea of abolishing GCSEs and returning to the old system of the brightest children studying O-levels, with others taking the dumbed-down option, CSEs. If this was the ambition, it was one that both Nick Clegg and I were completely opposed to.

Over the summer recess, Michael Gove had also used discretionary powers, granted to him under legislation introduced by the previous Labour government, to abolish the requirement for teachers in academy schools to have 'Qualified Teacher Status'. Nick Clegg had not been consulted about this, he did not agree with it, and he was angry both about the change and about the way it had been implemented.

I was confident that I could both improve relations and deliver more Liberal Democrat policy influence. Michael and I appeared to agree on much policy detail, and we were also on very friendly terms. We had each been Education spokesman for our respective parties while in opposition.

Both Michael and I were passionate about improving the educational outcomes and life chances of children from disadvantaged backgrounds. We believed that many more pupils could and should achieve high standards before leaving school and college, and we saw nothing inevitable about the fact that almost two thirds of young people from poor backgrounds failed to secure even the modest benchmark standard of five GCSEs (including English and Maths) at grade C or higher.

We both had bold plans to raise the educational bar and close the educational gaps that were closely related to social background. We both had a low tolerance for educational mediocrity and for underperforming schools or local authorities. We both wanted rigorous and challenging school inspection. We both supported a growing academies programme, to replace the leadership of the weakest schools, and a free school programme to allow new, high-quality, non-selective, state-funded schools to emerge. I was a supporter of Michael's plan to remove the many low-grade educational qualifications that were of little value to young people but which had been allowed to balloon under the previous Labour government. Michael was a supporter of the Liberal Democrat plan to introduce a £2.5 billion pupil premium to narrow the disadvantage gap by giving schools significant extra funding for children from poor backgrounds.

Michael and I also got on well. We had at times cooperated in opposition, and Michael had dealt with Liberal Democrat colleagues with courtesy and respect – which could not always be said for senior Conservatives. The Education Secretary had also given me robust support – both publicly and privately – after I had resigned from the government in 2010. We were both supporters of the coalition. Michael was at the economically and socially liberal end of the Conservative Party, and I was at the economically literate and liberal end of the Liberal Democrat Party. So we trusted each other. Michael agreed that I should run most aspects of schools policy – certainly, all of those that I asked to have responsibility for. He also allowed me to bring into the department a ferociously bright economist called Tim Leunig, who also happened to be a Liberal Democrat. That did not matter to Michael: we both admired Tim's rigorous intellect and willingness to challenge ministers directly and test the quality of their proposals. Tim Leunig provided policy advice, while Nick Clegg's excellent special adviser, Matt Sanders, provided both policy advice and a close sensitivity to party political concerns.

It wasn't just that Michael and I agreed on much and trusted each other. I also greatly liked him. He was amusing, intellectually impressive, thoughtful and never, ever, dull. Our ministerial meetings were always entertaining, and when he spoke at Cabinet he always communicated his points in an engaging way. In 2013, when we both warned the Cabinet against any attempt to water down the protections around the schools budget, I was earnest and technical. Michael Gove simply cited Voltaire: 'Is the Cabinet not aware of the story about Voltaire? On his deathbed, the old man called for a priest to help absolve him of his sins. "Do you repudiate the devil and all his disciples?" the priest asked. "My dear boy," replied Voltaire, "this is no time to be making new enemies." Prime Minister, this is no time in the parliament to be breaking pledges that we have kept for the last three years.'

Michael Gove was also an Education Secretary who genuinely loved learning for its own sake and who thought deeply about it. He wasn't, if truth be told, terribly good with numbers, and he always struggled a bit when we came to Spending Reviews or complex mathematical manipulation. But he thought he knew what a good education was. And he wanted this for every child. He was also not afraid to be challenged and he liked to engage in debate.

In late 2012, my new policy adviser, Tim Leunig, took it into his own hands to email a long note to Michael, criticising the proposed new, highly traditional, history curriculum. Michael had been intimately involved in creating this new curriculum – perhaps too intimately. The email was long and thoughtful, but also rather blunt. It rubbished almost the entirety of the new curriculum, and concluded with the sort of line that was most definitely not normally addressed to a Secretary of State by a relatively junior civil servant: 'You will, personally, be mocked if you release these syllabuses for consultation, and rightly so. I urge you not to do so.'

The email was sent the day after Boxing Day, at just after 1 a.m. Michael Gove and his family were on holiday in America at the time. Any normal Secretary of State would have one of two reactions. The first might be to ignore the missive, as too impertinent to deserve a direct response. The other might be to send a brief reply, noting the comments and suggesting a discussion some time in the New Year.

Instead, within thirty-six hours the Secretary of State had sent back a response that was simultaneously courteous, amusing and thoughtful:

> Dear Tim,
> I am out of the UK right now – trying to broaden my horizons but in fact only expanding my waistline. Thank you so much for being

so detailed and candid. The two things I value most in advice – and advisers – are evidence and honesty. It probably won't surprise you to know that drawing up the history curriculum has been the most difficult exercise of all the subjects … it is the subject most susceptible to being viewed through a political prism. There may be different Conservative and Liberal perspectives on physics, for all I know – perhaps liberals as instinctive believers in greater pluralism and the virtues of coalition may be more inclined to believe that two different objects can occupy the same space at the same time…

The note then continued for four further detailed A4 pages, in which were covered subjects including: the history of Nazi Germany; whether the 1688 revolution could be considered glorious; the Sonderweg; gay rights; Viscount Sidmouth; the utility of curriculum aims; the rivalry of Bolingbroke and Harvey; the impact of the work of Defoe, Swift and Pope; the Greeks; the Romans; the Aztecs; the Victorians; and the Tudors.

How many Secretaries of State would send a reply like that to a junior adviser from a different political party over the Christmas break? It was possible to disagree with Michael Gove. It was impossible to dislike him.

But some people most certainly did. While Michael Gove could be the politest of all men, and could charm opponents when he wanted to, he could also be a political street fighter who relished argument and saw himself as a great slayer of vested interests. One Conservative ally commented privately that 'Michael is like a cross between Jeeves and Che Guevara'.[1] The Education Secretary was disliked by a large proportion of the teaching profession, who saw him as excessively confrontational and stuck in an out-of-date vision of education. Few teachers and educationalists really understood the Education Secretary, or felt that he shared their own ambitions to improve the life chances of all children.

And while there were large areas of policy agreement between Michael Gove and me, there were differences too. Michael believed that making schools more autonomous, not least from local authority oversight, was highly likely to improve their performance. So his aim was to make as many schools as possible academies, as quickly as possible. 'Academisation' was for Michael Gove both his main vehicle for school improvement and his ultimate

---

1   Quoted in *In It Together*, Matthew d'Ancona (Viking, 2013)

ambition for all schools. I considered that academisation was important as a way of replacing the leadership and governance of weak schools, and as a liberal I was also strongly in favour of devolving power to schools – all schools. But I considered that most schools already had a large degree of autonomy, and that for many schools, the conversion to academy status was unlikely to have a huge impact on their performance. I thought some local authorities were very bad at overseeing their schools, but the evidence was that others seemed to be doing quite well. The same could be said of academy chains. I did not think that it was sensible for 24,000 schools all to come under oversight from Whitehall. Instead I wanted a 'contestable' middle tier of local authorities and academy chains, with the weakest providers being replaced.

I also placed a much higher priority on the pupil premium and on gap narrowing than the Conservatives, and wanted to see more investment in high-quality early years education, particularly for children from low-income backgrounds.

Michael Gove was less interested in early years education. He also had a strong scepticism about many policy areas that the Liberal Democrats and others were inclined to think important. Careers advice and guidance was one of his great hatreds. I sometimes thought he might have experienced some traumatic event in earlier life at the hands of a careers adviser, so instinctive was his gut dislike for the field. He also saw the subject as a distraction. 'I have met Andreas Schleicher [the Organisation for Economic Co-operation and Development's head of education] many times. He has never told me that the real problem of English education is that we have too few careers advisers,' he commented when the subject was under intense debate in 2013.

Nor did the Secretary of State care to strengthen subjects such as sex and relationship education, in spite of attempts by the Home Secretary, Theresa May, to get him to engage in the subject.

And that leads to something else Michael Gove despised – cross-departmental working. He regarded anything cross-departmental as an unproductive waste of time. The Education Secretary would rarely attend meetings with other departments, and would sometimes discourage his junior ministers from attending, too. At Cabinet in 2013, he cited the actor Greta Garbo, one of whose famous 'lines' was 'I just want to be left alone', as a model of how focused government should work. He didn't leave it at that, either.

'People often criticise "silos" and "Balkanisation",' he told baffled Cabinet colleagues, 'but why? Silos are surely a good thing. They protect important things like our nuclear deterrent. We need silos. And what's wrong with "Balkanisation"? Balkanisation was actually an extremely good thing. It meant respecting the integrity of small nation states and avoiding artificial constructs which just don't work. I think that "Balkanisation" has had a bad press for far too long.'

The Education Secretary was a vocal critic of the distinctively cross-departmental 'Troubled Families Initiative', even though it was one of the Prime Minister's great policy passions. When he did attend meetings on this issue, he would launch strong attacks on Louise Casey, the Troubled Families unit boss.

Michael was instinctively suspicious of government attempts to micro-manage, and in one Cabinet committee meeting when a proposal to legislate for a new fuel poverty target was being made by Energy Secretary Ed Davey, he mischievously suggested that we might introduce a new 'book poverty target' too. 'We could send in government inspectors to people's homes to count the number of qualifying family books and measure the "book poverty rate". We could then identify the number of households under a particular book number threshold, pass an Act of Parliament to guarantee a minimum number of books per household, and then the government could bus extra books around the country in order to reduce the book poverty rate,' he suggested, with a semi-straight face. Ken Clarke roared with laughter. Ed Davey looked less amused.

It wasn't only other Cabinet ministers whom Michael Gove wanted to hear little from. The involvement of the Prime Minister and Deputy Prime Minister wasn't welcomed either.

Mostly, David Cameron and George Osborne trusted Michael and left him alone to pursue his radical agenda. And when the Prime Minister did try to intervene, he wasn't always successful. In 2013, David Cameron pushed for a Schools Bill to be contained in the next Queen's Speech. Like other Cabinet ministers, Michael Gove was required to go along to the Parliamentary Legislation Committee to try to persuade senior ministers that his legislation deserved time in a crowded parliamentary schedule. The Home Office, as usual, had a list of seven or eight Bills it wanted. Theresa May fought for each one. Michael Gove, by contrast, baffled his colleagues on the committee by telling them he actually didn't really want another Education Bill, even though it was the Prime Minister's idea. It was quietly dropped.

When No. 10 or the Deputy Prime Minister was insistent on intervening, things could get more heated.

Michael Gove had brought with him into government some excellent and thoughtful policy advisers, such as the respected Sam Freedman. He had also brought with him a Grade-A political Rottweiler called Dominic Cummings, who was regarded as so divisive that his entry into government service had been vetoed by Andy Coulson and David Cameron in May 2010. But when Andy Coulson left the government in 2011, Mr Cummings was allowed in.

Dominic Cummings was bright, serious, very close to Michael Gove, and highly influential in the Department for Education. He was one of those rare advisers who is immersed in both policy and politics. And he had a restless desire to challenge, reform and shake things up. In this, he was very much a Goveite. When he spoke to me once of a change he and Michael Gove wanted to make to the school accountability system, he described it as 'Michael's terrorist demand'. That is how he saw politics.

As well as being bright, Dom Cummings was also blunt, rude, impatient and tactless, and had a low opinion of most civil servants, most ministers, and most certainly the Prime Minister and his deputy. He once came to see me to complain about Nick Clegg's involvement in some policy issue. 'This isn't personal or political,' he said, slouched in a seat in my office, dressed in slightly scruffy casual clothes. 'I don't like Clegg, but I think Cameron and No. 10 are complete muppets as well. They have no idea what they are doing. Cameron hasn't a clue about Education. He just wakes up one morning and says, "I need a headline. Give me a headline." And he screws things up for us. We have to keep these people well away. Our policy is to tell No. 10 absolutely nothing about what we are doing. If we tell them, they always fuck it up – leaking it out in a half-baked way and getting most of it wrong.' The feeling was mutual – Dom Cummings was disliked and distrusted both in 10 Downing Street and in Nick Clegg's office. His intelligence was respected, but he was regarded as a destructive personality who risked veering out of control.

The Education Department under Michael Gove sought to be a semi-autonomous arm of government. The Prime Minister was blocked or ignored. Best attempts were made to bypass policy approval from the powerful Home

Affairs Committee of Cabinet, chaired by Nick Clegg. Statistics on free schools sent to the Treasury and the Deputy Prime Minister's office were shamelessly inconsistent – the Treasury had to be persuaded that more capital money was needed and that new free schools were not reducing 'basic need', while the DPM's office needed to hear the opposite. They did.

Michael Gove and Dom Cummings liked to get their way on everything, without compromise. That was sowing the seeds of future conflict, though this was hardly visible in the 'Coalicious' days of September 2012. On my arrival in the department, only a small article in the *Times* newspaper hinted at problems. It suggested, contrary to assumed opinion, that Michael Gove did not welcome my arrival in the department. The suggestion was that a powerful Liberal Democrat, close to Nick Clegg, could only mean arguments ahead.

Michael Gove was a glittering star of the government, feted by the media, who liked to have his way. I was happy to be a deputy to Michael, and was firmly focused on policy delivery – I had no desire to compete with him for column inches in the newspapers. I was coalition minded, and instinctively willing to compromise. But I was ultimately unbending about the issues that I thought important, and I was insistent that the Liberal Democrat view in government was to be respected. When challenged on issues I considered vital, I had clear bottom lines – and on these I was willing to be stubborn. Very stubborn. And because of my position in the Cabinet Office and at the centre of government as one of two key ministerial advisers to Nick Clegg, I had excellent access to the Deputy Prime Minister and to the Chief Secretary, Danny Alexander.

This meant that while Michael Gove could overrule me in the Education Department, I could challenge his decisions outside the department. Dom Cummings referred to this unusual situation as 'top trumps', telling another adviser: 'Michael can top trump Laws. But Laws can top trump Michael, by deploying the Clegg card and the Alexander card.' With education being one of the areas that both parties in the coalition considered a high priority in both policy and political terms, this threatened clashes ahead.

But for now, in September 2012, it was mostly sweetness and light – though I soon realised that my proposal for a 'contestable tier' of academy chains and local authorities was going nowhere. Neither Michael Gove nor Dom Cummings liked the idea; local authorities competed with careers advisers, sex education experts and cross-departmental committees on Michael's 'most hated' list. However, I eventually agreed with a suggestion from Lord Nash (who took over from Lord Hill) and Tom Shinner (an able young policy adviser brought into the Education Department by Michael Gove) that we would establish regional school commissioners as a partial answer to the problem of the 'middle tier' – the need for some organisation that sat between the Education Department and individual schools, to ensure they could be properly held to account when performance was weak. This at least meant that the growing number of academies would be overseen at a more local level, rather than from a few offices in Whitehall.

We made more progress on qualification reform. Initially, we compromised to agree on the development of a new and more challenging qualification, to be taken at age sixteen. This would replace the GCSE but not return us to the old O-level/CSE divide. There would also be only one national examination board, to avoid competitive 'dumbing-down' of standards. As a liberal, this was not a proposal I particularly liked. But with Michael Gove and Nick Clegg in agreement, I decided not to make a fuss about it. As part of agreeing this more stretching qualification at age sixteen, Nick Clegg insisted on introducing a new 'catch-up premium' of £500 per child, which would be given to secondary schools for each pupil they took on who had not already mastered the basics of maths and English at the end of primary school.

We spent almost more time trying to think up a name for the new qualification than on agreeing the policy. In a meeting that felt like something out of a political comedy sketch, we ran through a list of around fifteen different names.

I rejected 'World Class Qualification', as something with the letters 'WC' seemed too open to parody. The normally sensible Julian Astle suggested 'Developed Certificate of Secondary Education', but I considered 'DCSE' was likely to prompt media references to 'Dumb'.

'Well, Minister,' said the senior civil servant in my meeting in early September 2012, 'we have other names here: School Certificate?' 'Too dull,' I replied.

'School Diploma?' 'Yawn.'

'Standard Certificate of Education?' 'Waffley.'

'Standard Certificate of Secondary Education?' 'Ditto.'

'General Certificate of Education – Standard Level?' 'Too long.'

'International Certificate of Education?' 'Too foreign.'

'Baccalaureate?' 'Much too foreign!'

'General Baccalaureate?' 'Waffley and foreign.'

'International Certificate of Secondary Education?' 'Too complex.'

'General Certificate of Skills and Knowledge?' 'God no, it would make Michael vomit.'

Another civil servant also chipped in. 'Yes, Minister. Some of us also feel that "GCSK" sounds like a drugs company.'

'I agree,' I said, wondering privately how many people's time had been spent compiling this awful list. 'What else have we got?' I asked.

'Well, Minister, we have "Higher Certificate of Education".'

'Hmmmmmmm,' I said. 'Not sure.'

'I should also say, Minister,' the official chipped in, 'that this name might annoy the Scots a bit – it's very similar to the name of their qualification.'

'Yes,' said another official. 'It also raises the question: "Higher than exactly what?"' There was a lot of sage nodding.

'Well,' I said in conclusion. 'This isn't great. We are supposed to be launching a brand-new qualification in a few weeks' time for millions of young people, which may be used in our education system for the next forty years, and we can't think of a bloody name.'

After some mulling over the weekend, I decided on a new name: Standard Level.

But when I saw Michael Gove the following week, he had done much better.

'David, I don't know what you would think of the following,' said Michael Gove, in his DfE office, where pictures of Lenin, Margaret Thatcher and Malcolm X decorated the walls.

I was sure I wasn't going to like it. 'It's not "O-level", is it?' I said, smiling.

'Certainly not,' said Michael. 'How about "English Baccalaureate Certificate"?'

'Perfect,' I said. 'Simple. Liberal Democrats love anything with the word "Baccalaureate" in. But it's also got "English", so will please the Conservative Party.'

'Yes,' said Michael Gove. 'It also fits with the English Baccalaureate measure which I introduced recently, to incentivise children to study a solid core of subjects. I can therefore present this new qualification as a wonderful development of policy, as if I had planned the whole thing as part of some great strategy many years ago – instead of actually having to glue together a coalition compromise.'

It seemed a reasonable compromise, and was launched by Michael and Nick Clegg later that month: a new, more stretching, qualification of world-class standards, but accessible to the overwhelming majority of pupils without high-level special needs. After the new English Baccalaureate Certificate was launched, I was amused to see some paperwork from an official in 10 Downing Street commenting on the Prime Minister's view of the proposal: 'He's a bit frustrated that once again he hasn't had a proper chance to comment on issues of substance before an Education announcement.' Clearly, the Cummings strategy of keeping the PM out of the loop was working well.

But over the next few months the carefully stitched-together compromise began to steadily unravel.

Ofqual – the exams regulator – was both publicly and privately very critical of the plans, arguing that they were rushed and unclear. Ofqual also felt that a move to a single exam board would be risky.

It soon became obvious that there were differences of opinion within the coalition on what we had actually agreed. Michael Gove and his advisers thought that they had only agreed to convert a small number of existing GCSEs into the new EBCs. I was entirely opposed to this proposition. I felt that if we were going to replace some GCSEs then we really needed to do this in all subject areas and introduce EBCs in place of all the widely taken GCSEs. This would make the scale of required reform even larger.

After Michael and his advisers had originally floated the re-introduction of O-levels and CSEs, in July 2012, Nick Clegg had sent the Education Secretary a lengthy and carefully argued letter, suggesting that the right solution for the coalition was simply to reform and strengthen the existing GCSE brand.

I now wondered whether we should be pressing to return to this solution. It would clearly be irresponsible to press ahead with the abolition of existing GCSEs if there was no robust system ready to put in its place – we would effectively be gambling with the education of millions of children. My advisers in the Education Department, Tim Leunig, a civil service policy expert, and Matt Sanders, a special adviser, both agreed. They wondered if we could get Michael Gove to change his mind. Michael's former policy adviser, Sam Freedman, who had now left the department, was in favour of a U-turn. But Michael's existing senior advisers, Dom Cummings and press adviser Henry de Zoete, were opposed to a change. They both felt that 'Michael will be trashed by the *Daily Mail* if he goes back on this'.

I knew that it would not be easy to persuade Michael to alter course, and that a fully fledged Liberal Democrat 'assault' was likely to be counter-productive. I reported back to Michael Gove a particularly worrying meeting I had had with Glenys Stacey, the head of Ofqual, where she signalled her view that the new EBC proposals involved far too many risks. I then let Tim Leunig and Ofqual take the lead in changing Michael's mind, but offered Michael options for changing course – including scrapping EBCs entirely, and opting simply to reform GCSES.

Before Christmas, we were meeting one day in Michael's office when he said: 'We've all had a very good year in this department, and we are getting great reviews from the media and from within government. This is probably the time to correct any mistakes that we've made, while we are on a high. It's better to do these things when you are very strong than when you are weak. We have political capital in the bank. Perhaps now is the time to use some of it? Let's think about this over the Christmas break.' Most of us knew what he was referring to.

Before we departed for Christmas, Tim Leunig sent a powerful email to Michael Gove, copied to me, making the case for dropping EBCs and the single exam board model, and for reforming GCSEs instead. Michael was an admirer of Tim, and knew that the views he expressed were wholly without political motivation. I hoped that this would help to turn things around.

In mid-January, Michael indicated to me that he did not want to drop the EBC, but at a dinner with him in the Churchill Room of the House of Commons, on the 21st, he finally seemed to have changed his mind.

The final 'deal' on the future of GCSEs was struck a few days later between Dom Cummings and me at an 8 a.m. breakfast meeting at the Cinammon Club, a minute's walk from the Education Department.

We agreed to reform GCSEs and drop the EBCs altogether. We also agreed to move away from the old, Labour Party-led accountability target of all pupils seeking to secure five C-grade GCSEs, including English and Maths. Instead I proposed, and Dom Cummings agreed, that we would move to a new measure focusing on eight GCSES, rather than five, of which at least five had to be 'E-Bacc' subjects – the core academic subjects that Michael Gove was particularly keen to promote. This was a good agreement, with big implications for the future education of millions of children. It would avoid an excessive focus on pupils on the C/D grade borderline, it would encourage more subjects to be studied and it would powerfully incentivise the study of a core of valuable academic subjects. On 7 February, Michael Gove and I announced the U-turn – which was widely welcomed and did us no political damage at all.

'I think it is peace in our time,' I said to Dom Cummings.

'Maybe more like the Molotov–Ribbentrop pact,' was the slightly grumpy reply.

The Economy: A Lesson Learned

2012

It was October 2012. The Deputy Prime Minister was supposed to be enjoying a short break in Spain during the half-term holiday. It was decided, unusually, to send out a dedicated police protection officer to keep an eye on Nick and his family, at this time of international tension. The police officer concerned was supposed to turn up in a low-key way, a day or two before the Cleggs arrived, in the small village where Miriam's family lived.

But 'low-key' in a small Spanish village turned out to be a little challenging. Within an hour of the policeman's arrival in the village, Miriam had received a text message from a Spanish relative, asking if the 'British secret policeman' had been sent out as an advanced guard to look after the family. Nick Clegg asked how people could possibly have identified the man as a British policeman.

'Oh,' was the reply. 'I don't think it's much of a secret anymore. There is a very tall, very ruddy-faced Englishman who has just checked in to the only hotel in our village. He speaks no Spanish and stands out like a sore thumb. He is the talk of the village. Everyone is gossiping about it.' Someone even asked if they should offer to cook him a meal.

If the undercover police protection was less undercover than desired, it was at least the source of much family mirth.

It was now six weeks later – 9.45 a.m. on Tuesday 18 December, to be precise. The whole Cabinet was gathering in the Terracotta Room, upstairs in 10 Downing Street, and there was a distinct sense of anticipation and excitement in the air. Her Majesty the Queen was making a rare visit to

Downing Street, and for the first time in her reign, she was going to sit in on a Cabinet meeting. It was all part of the celebrations of the Queen's Golden Jubilee, and it was an historic occasion – the first visit to Cabinet by a serving monarch since 1781, under the Lord North administration.

The Queen may be an unflamboyant, even low-key, personality, but when it comes to star quality, she is in a league of her own. Here were gathered all of the most senior figures in the government, from the Prime Minister downwards. Some, such as Ken Clarke, had served in government for decades. But everyone was excited, and perhaps even a little nervous.

Eventually, and on time of course, the Queen arrived, and in a hushed room she walked down the two rows of ministers – facing each other – gently shaking our hands. Only when she came to George Osborne did she stop briefly. 'Ma'am,' said David Cameron, 'you will know the Chancellor of the Exchequer – our "money man".'

'Oh yes,' said the Queen, 'I think the last time we met we were looking at all those gold bars in the vaults of the Bank of England? Such a pity that so few of them are still ours.'

We were then all escorted next door for a photograph before the Cabinet meeting took place.

We were told where to sit or stand, and naturally the Queen was herself seated right in the middle of the front row, between David Cameron and Nick Clegg. The photographers clicked away, as everybody stood nervously in position, nobody saying a word.

It must have been a rather serious and dull shot, and the photographers looked a little disappointed.

Then, just as we were all about to stand up, the Queen suddenly said: 'You can all smile, you know.' The tension was instantly released, and the whole Cabinet roared with laughter. The next day all the newspapers carried a photograph of 'the laughing Cabinet'. It was an unconventional formal photograph, with some ministers turning their heads to the Queen.

But in the centre of the photograph one person is still absolutely focused, looking directly down the lens of the camera, serious – though with perhaps just a hint of a smile playing around her lips: our ever-professional, much loved, long-serving Queen.

'You can all smile.' It was a prompt for a more interesting Cabinet photograph, but it might also have served as encouragement for a government that had not been able to do much collective smiling for the previous twelve months. 2012 was a year most members of the government wanted to forget.

Of all our problems, the greatest was the state of the economy. We needed to show that government borrowing was on a firm downward track. We needed some economic growth to buoy tax revenues. And if we were to win back public support, we also needed real incomes to rise.

Instead of growth strengthening during 2012, it was actually weakening. Two further quarters of negative growth in the first half of the year had pushed Britain back into a technical recession, and by July the economy had been shrinking for nine months in a row.

The lack of growth was, of course, a gift to the Labour Party, which argued that the downturn was being caused by excessive fiscal tightening – cuts to public spending and increases in taxation. Ed Balls, the shadow Chancellor, argued for a slower pace of deficit reduction, and even some right-wing commentators started to argue for additional action to stimulate growth.

Within the government, there were some voices arguing for calm. In September, while other ministers talked of pressing the 'growth buttons', Ken Clarke – always with the air of someone who had seen it all before – gave some wonderfully laid-back advice to his colleagues: 'I've seen a number of recessions in my time in government. Some of them when Margaret [Thatcher] was here were actually far more painful than this one. Everyone is saying that they are shocked that we are flat-lining. I'm not shocked. I'd expected this all along. People have borrowed too much. It will take time to work all that off. And look at our export markets and the mess the Europeans are making of it all. Flat-lining in this environment is to be expected. We should be grateful to be flat-lining. It will take a few more years to recover. "Bouncing along the bottom" for a while may be the best we can hope for.'

Not everyone was as relaxed. The Conservatives in particular were in a panic that government borrowing would fail to decline, or might even rise. That would destroy the coalition's whole economic and political narrative.

Nick Clegg, Danny Alexander and I were looking for other ways of supporting growth, and were determined to resist Conservative inclinations to cut public spending further in order to chase the borrowing targets. We feared that this could exacerbate the growth problem.

I was particularly keen that we thought more radically – for example, by using the profits from quantitative easing to invest in more capital spending without raising government borrowing.

Vince Cable, by contrast, was more inclined to challenge head-on the whole government economic strategy. He was arguing for something that looked much more like the Ed Balls plan – a slower pace of fiscal tightening, and more borrowing to invest.

Nick Clegg and those close to him were worried not just about the economy, but about the potential for a massive party split. Would Vince, Nick worried, even consider walking out of government before the recovery finally emerged?

All these issues about policy choices had been considered at the informal Quad dinner at the beginning of August 2012. George Osborne had promised to go back to the Treasury and look at ideas such as using the QE profits to boost capital spending.

At the end of October, the government received a small nugget of good news when the growth figures for the third quarter of the year were reported. These showed quarterly growth of 1 per cent – strong, but much of it an artificial rebound from earlier economic weaknesses, combined with a one-off 'Olympic Games boost'. George Osborne spoke to ministers more optimistically, but Vince Cable was sceptical. 'Some people may be inclined to see in these numbers the light at the end of the tunnel,' he said. 'But my fear is that this is more likely to be the light of a train coming at us very fast from the opposite direction.'

The Treasury still seemed to me to be failing to come forward with creative proposals to support growth, and the Bank of England – under Governor Mervyn King – was sitting on its hands too.

At the end of October, the Heseltine Report was published, urging the government to devolve more economic powers from the centre to the regions. George Osborne didn't seem very impressed. At a meeting, he described the Heseltine Report as a 'very personal' report, and a 'bid to steal every department's capital budget'.

David Cameron joked that the whole thing sounded like a 'fourth-term priority'. The ever-sharp George Osborne added: 'Yes, a fourth-term priority – but for a different government!'

The Prime Minister urged that we should be diplomatic in responding to the Heseltine Report as 'Michael is a very big beast in the political jungle. Upsetting him over this would be as risky as interrupting a silverback while he's mating.' It was an interesting and vivid image.

Later in the parliament, George Osborne was to become a belated supporter of more localism. For now, he certainly seemed rather sceptical. Even in early 2013, when the Chancellor first started to advocate the devolving of money from central government to local areas, one seasoned government adviser told me: 'George's view is that the money will either be wasted by central government or by local government. He thinks the only advantage of devolution is that you can slice 10 per cent off the money as you devolve it, so that the Treasury pays out less.'

Given the conservatism of the Treasury and the need to reduce government borrowing, I began to place a greater emphasis on getting the Bank of England to support growth, directly or indirectly.

Unfortunately, I was told in early October that while the Treasury had secured agreement to hand over the massive profits from quantitative easing, now totalling over £30 billion, the Bank of England had allegedly vetoed this being used for anything other than deficit reduction purposes. I regarded this with scepticism, and suspected a conspiracy of inactivity between the Bank of England and the Treasury. But this was impossible to prove.

I pressed Nick Clegg on the issue, and he promised to raise it with Sir Mervyn King. Nick and the Governor were due to play tennis on the morning of 1 November, and Nick arrived slightly late for a meeting with his team that morning as a consequence.

'How did it all go?' I asked. 'Well, I won the tennis,' said Nick. 'That was the easy bit. Though the Governor, in fairness, is a little older and heavier than me!'

We then moved on to the even weightier issue of monetary policy. 'We discussed this after the tennis,' said Nick. 'Actually, it was rather odd. We had a long and detailed discussion about monetary policy and quantitative easing in the changing room. I discovered that it's really quite difficult to engage seriously in the details of monetary policy and quantitative easing with someone, when you are both dressed only in your underpants.' Someone suggested that this was more detail than we needed.

Anyway, the upshot of their great 'underpants summit' was that the Governor hadn't budged on the issue of QE profits, but it was agreed to have a further meeting on monetary policy in the more stately surroundings of the Bank of England.

On 9 November, the Treasury and the Bank of England made a joint announcement of a transfer of £35 billion of QE profits from the Bank to the Treasury. None was to be allocated to boosting investment. For me, it was a massive missed opportunity, and I worried that if we were now heading for a triple-dip recession, we had closed down one of the best options we had to avoid it.

Nick, Danny and I travelled to the Bank to meet the Governor on Tuesday 15 November. We met in his rather grand reception room, and then – after some pleasantries about cricket and tennis – we went through into a rather more modest room, with a few sofas around the walls.

The Governor was gloomy about growth and he said that he thought the UK economy was likely to grow only very slowly over the next couple of years. 'The only upside is if the world economy grows more rapidly, which I don't expect, or if our exchange rate devalues.'

I pressed the Governor on what more we could do to support growth, including being more radical on monetary policy – for example, extending the scope of quantitative easing beyond government bonds.

'We could do more,' said the Governor. 'But I'm rather worried by inflation. We have been above the 2 per cent target now for some time. Increases in things like tuition fees haven't helped on the inflation front, of course.'

Nick Clegg pointed out that underlying inflation and pay growth were actually quite modest. 'Surely we shouldn't be keeping monetary policy tighter than needed because of increases in managed prices like tuition fees?' he said. 'Most inflation has been from higher food and energy prices, which we can do little or nothing about.'

'Yes,' said the Governor, 'that's true. But people have to know we are serious about inflation. We cannot lose our credibility.'

I said that I didn't think the Bank's credibility was in question, and I asked who he was worried about in relation to possible criticism. 'Oh, there was a critical piece in *The Spectator* recently,' the Governor said. It was hardly convincing, or comforting.

I left the Bank feeling that the Governor had no Plan B of any kind, and that he was simply reconciled to the economy flat-lining for the foreseeable future.

With Mervyn King due to retire, Nick, Danny, Vince and I discussed what we could do to secure more radical leadership at the Bank. I had already met a few weeks earlier with Adair Turner, who made very clear his interest in the post. But later in the year, George Osborne made an even bolder choice, by securing the services of the impressive Canadian Mark Carney, who also seemed to be more willing to take radical action.

Meanwhile, we spent most of October and November focused on the contents of the Autumn Statement. This was a tough time for Nick. He faced pressure from Vince for a major economic U-turn, with £20 billion more borrowing to fund an increase in capital spending. I also wanted to see more done to boost growth, and with monetary policy and QE profits ruled out, I turned my attention to actions that would immediately boost investment and cut taxes, while helping to meet our fiscal rules by identifying fully offsetting cuts to public spending towards the end of the parliament.

The Treasury's agenda was to stick as close as possible to current plans, while seeking to identify savings to deliver the spending plans that had been set out for 2015/16. And the Conservatives wanted the biggest possible cuts in welfare spending. Nick was determined to ensure that any welfare cuts were defensible and he wanted the scale of such cuts to be reduced, by securing a large contribution to austerity from those on high incomes.

During the lengthy negotiations on the Autumn Statement, Nick had to square his own team as well as reaching an agreement with the Conservatives.

In mid-October, we found out that Vince had written a letter to the Chancellor that was highly critical of the government's economic strategy. It suggested essentially moving to a Plan B that sounded very similar to Labour's economic strategy.

With some difficulty, we managed to persuade Vince not to send the letter or, as importantly, to leak its contents. Towards the end of October, Vince also became very concerned about the possibility of having to deliver further cuts to his Business budget. In a highly unusual move, he ordered his departmental officials not to cooperate with or give any information to officials in the Treasury – prompting a bit of a stand-off between the Business Secretary and Danny Alexander. Vince Cable then wrote to Danny, copied to all other senior members of the government, calling for an 'alternative path of fiscal consolidation' and saying that pending this, his officials would not cooperate in delivering any further cuts.

But if there were pressures in the Lib Dems to Nick's left, there were also some tensions on his right. Danny Alexander, as the Chief Secretary responsible for meeting the government's spending plans, wanted to consider large cuts to welfare spending in both 2015/16 and 2016/17. Danny had some good reasons for wanting to secure this scale of cuts: it would help to reduce the pressure on departmental budgets, and it would assist in funding a planned freeze in the deeply unpopular fuel duty, as well as paying for further increases in the personal tax allowance.

Nonetheless, the scale of Danny's ambition surprised us all. On the evening of Wednesday 10 October I travelled to the Chief Secretary's house in Balham for a private discussion on the Autumn Statement. Danny's wife was out, and we met in a somewhat untidy lounge, after carting away large quantities of children's toys. Over a curry and some wine, Danny shared with me his early thoughts over the Autumn Statement.

Most striking was a plan to cut just over £10 billion from welfare in 2015/16 and some £11.6 billion in 2016/17. These were even larger figures than George Osborne had said publicly that he wanted to deliver. Osborne had floated a figure of £10 billion of welfare cuts in 2015/16 in his speech to the Conservative Party conference just a few days before. Nick Clegg had immediately and publicly rejected this scale of cuts.

I was blunt with Danny that I just did not believe that his proposed cuts to welfare were deliverable or politically acceptable. We went through his list item by item. I considered that welfare cuts of around £3 billion in 2015/16 and £6 billion in 2016/17 were more realistic and acceptable.

To try to counter-balance Danny's hawkishness, Nick asked me to lead my own review of savings that we could find on welfare – and I reported back to both Nick and Danny on what I thought would be a more achievable package. Nick was getting increasingly agitated about the issue, because he was determined not to end up in the same position as in Budget 2012, when both Treasury members of the Quad had agreed a position on the 50 per cent rate of tax that left the Deputy Prime Minister in a minority of one.

The issue came to a head the next day, when the three of us met in Nick's grand room in the Cabinet Office. Danny carefully set out his plans, and circulated a paper with the options. I expressed my concerns and identified the proposals I was most worried by. Danny then started to respond, but he was cut off by a visibly irritated Deputy Prime Minister. 'Look, let's be absolutely clear about this. I'm not accepting £10 billion of welfare savings. I have already made that clear. Publicly. I'm fed up with the Treasury always trying to bounce me into these things. I want us to start by looking for contributions from those on higher incomes, not those on the lowest incomes. We need to put the Tories on the spot over a mansion tax or at the very least more council tax bands on the biggest properties. And regardless of what the Treasury wants to do, I'm not accepting £10 billion of welfare cuts. The Treasury just needs to accept that. In March this year I accepted the cut in the top rate of tax, in part because I worried that otherwise we might have no Budget at all. Now I have learned my lesson. This time it's different.'

There was silence around the table. Nick had made his point.

We drew up a list of Lib Dem proposals of tax rises for those on higher incomes, modest welfare cuts, and other changes we wanted to see – such as a further rise in the tax-free personal allowance.

Given the poor growth outlook and massive upward revisions expected on government borrowing, the Treasury also wanted to look at other options – such as delaying the target of spending 0.7 per cent of GNP on overseas development assistance. The view of both George Osborne and Danny Alexander was that there was a strong economic case for postponing the target until 2018, which would produce huge savings. But both Nick Clegg and David Cameron took the view that they had made a pledge on the overseas aid target and that they both wanted to keep to it.

Having settled our own Liberal Democrat position, we now had to engage with the Conservatives. Nick first had a number of meetings with Iain Duncan Smith, the Secretary of State for Work and Pensions. Nick was amused to find that IDS wanted the Liberal Democrat leader to fight his battles with the Chancellor; he admitted that George Osborne was asking for more savings from his departmental budget than he was comfortable with.

One problem to be resolved in the Quad was the fraught issue of energy prices, following Ed Miliband's commitment to an energy price freeze. This one policy announcement had thrown David Cameron and George Osborne into a complete panic, and they were thrashing around to find some way of cutting energy prices, regardless of the green impact. This was causing a major row with Ed Davey, the Lib Dem Secretary of State for Climate Change.

In the middle of November, there were Quads on the questions of welfare savings and possible tax changes. Nick Clegg also met George Osborne separately on a number of occasions to try to resolve the key issues. 'I find George easier to deal with these days,' Nick told a friend during the negotiations. 'You can do business with George. You may not agree with him, but he is rational and calm and mature.'

Matters came to a head at the Quads on 19 and 20 November. Nick Clegg pressed hard for either a mansion tax or more council tax bands for the most expensive properties.

George Osborne seemed pragmatic, but the Prime Minister certainly wasn't. He again made clear that he would veto any increase in tax on expensive properties: 'My party donors would hate it.'

By now, Nick Clegg was getting distinctly fed up. When he returned from the Quad that day, he told me: 'I had to spell it out clearly to Cameron and Osborne. I told them I wasn't accepting £10 billion of welfare cuts and that I would veto the Autumn Statement completely rather than tolerating that. We would simply cancel the Autumn Statement.'

At this suggestion, David Cameron had looked shocked. The eyes of the Cabinet Secretary, Jeremy Heywood, had bulged visibly. The meeting ended without a conclusion.

I made clear that I agreed with Nick's strategy: 'The Tories need a substantive Autumn Statement more than we do. Anyway, there would still have to be an Autumn Statement. It's just that there wouldn't be anything in it. After the Omnishambles Budget, George Osborne desperately needs to have a good, solid Autumn Statement. And he will know that he needs a credible agreement with us – without this, the odds of us losing our triple-A credit rating will increase and there will be more talk of a "Downgraded Chancellor". So we are in a very strong place.'

'I guess so,' said Nick. 'But I just find these endless squabbles so tedious. What is wrong with Cameron right now? The Tories are so blinkered and frustrating. They don't want the rich to pay more – it's always "our donors wouldn't like it". And Cameron seems to be in such a funny place at present. He is incandescent about us vetoing boundary reform and working with Labour in the Lords to torpedo this. He is all over the place on Leveson and press regulation. He is in a huge flap about his party and the issue of Europe. I guess he and Osborne are just panicking that they will lose in 2015 and their careers will be over. Anyway, I'm not accepting £10 billion of cuts that will fall hardest on the poor. If they want that then I'm not agreeing the Autumn Statement.'

Nick's Clegg's strong stand eventually forced George Osborne to back down. The final agreement on the Autumn Statement was secured between Nick and George at Nick's house in Putney on Sunday 25 November.

The agreed package included extra taxes on those on high incomes through restricting pension tax relief, freezing higher-rate tax thresholds and tackling various tax avoidance schemes. Welfare cuts in 2015/16 could therefore be scaled back to around £3.5 billion. Fuel duty was frozen, the personal allowance increased again and corporation tax was cut by 1 per cent.

By massaging the figures aggressively and shifting some spending into the next financial year, George Osborne was forecasting that borrowing would go on falling – by a vanishingly small amount.

It wasn't the most exciting Autumn Statement but, as Liam Byrne might have said, 'there was no money left'. About the most eye-catching announcement was the new and bizarrely named 'Office of Unconventional Gases' – something that might have been borrowed from television satire.

The upward revisions to borrowing were pretty dreadful, but Labour struggled to set out a convincing alternative strategy.

The Chancellor was beginning to feel that his own position was strengthening after the disaster of the Omnishambles Budget. I saw George in his 11 Downing Street office in the middle of November. He was his old, mischievous, politically wily, confident self: 'Labour still don't have any economic credibility – they just cannot explain how borrowing more is the answer to a borrowing problem.'

Then, as ever with the Chancellor, we came to the brutal, transactional, bit: 'Look, I am still very keen to do something to hit the trade unions. We could do something on party funding that would help the Lib Dems, but we are just not interested in capping donations – it would lose us money from our big donors.

'I also want to return to this issue of the 2015 elections. I am definitely one of those Conservatives who favours some sort of pact in 2015 between the Conservatives and the Liberal Democrats. Maybe we could still have some type of coupon election, where we each don't put up candidates against the "coalition" candidate? I still think that the Conservatives can get to the 42 per cent or 43 per cent that we need to form our own majority, but it will be tough. I don't want to go back into the wilderness of opposition, and I want to keep the Conservative Party in power. I assume anyway that Nick Clegg, David Laws and Danny Alexander want to see the current coalition continue beyond 2015? You lot wouldn't have much of a future if your party is in coalition with Labour, would you? I can't imagine you having nice chats like this if Ed Balls was Chancellor!'

I patiently explained to George what I had told him earlier in the year – that however tempting a coupon election might seem to both parties, it was unlikely to be acceptable to my party: 'It would be tantamount to becoming a small, bungalow annexe to the Tory mansion.'

'It's a real, real pity,' said George. 'Think about it.'

Then the Chancellor moved on to a final sensitive matter.

'The one issue I am getting a bit worried about is Europe and our back-benchers. They are becoming unmanageable on this issue. The problem for pragmatic people in the Conservative Party like me, people who are sceptic-ally pro-European, is that we used to be able to argue that Europe was just a big distraction and didn't matter very much. But we cannot easily make that case any more. The public are more sceptical, so we could lose votes to UKIP. And with the state of the European economy and its impact on the UK, we can hardly argue that it's all a sideshow.'

The coalition agreement was supposed to 'park' Britain's policy on Europe for the parliament. But Conservative policy on Europe was now very much on the move.

2013

Europe: The
Iceberg Resurfaces

2012–13

Nick Clegg was speaking to David Cameron in November 2012. 'I said very clearly to him,' he told me later: '"David, if your strategy on Europe is to stay in the EU but to unilaterally renegotiate the British position and then change all the rules and then put that to a referendum – well, I just think that is hugely risky and could easily backfire."

'He just shrugged at me and said: "You may be right. But what else can I do? My backbenchers are unbelievably Eurosceptic and UKIP are breathing down my neck."'

'That's the problem with Cameron,' Nick Clegg said. 'He is very bright, but very tactical. He's so busy wondering how to get through the next few weeks that he could endanger Britain's international position for the next few decades. It is all very, very risky.'

The issue of Britain's role in Europe had divided the Conservative Party and Britain's voters for at least three decades.

When David Cameron became Conservative leader in 2006, he had attempted to bury the issue in order to focus on areas that were of higher priority to voters, not least swing voters.

But many Conservative activists, voters and MPs were fundamentally opposed to the UK being a member of the EU, and they wanted to fight this battle to the end, regardless of other considerations.

When the coalition was negotiated, Europe was such a sensitive issue that it was not even touched on by the two party negotiating teams – it was left for direct discussion between David Cameron and Nick Clegg.

The two coalition leaders essentially decided that policy on Europe should be put in the deep freeze. The UK would move neither significantly towards nor significantly away from the rest of the European Union. But it was agreed that while there would not be an immediate referendum on Britain's relationship with the EU, there would be important legislation for a new 'referendum lock', whereby the approval of the British people would be required before any significant future change in Britain's relationship with the EU. No such change was expected until after 2015.

In the first two years of the coalition, the issue of the EU remained rather low-key politically. Most of the focus was on the increasing crisis in the Eurozone. The naturally Eurosceptic British Treasury and the Bank of England both expected in 2011 and early 2012 that the euro would not be able to sustain the scale of speculation that was threatening the Eurozone. They felt that either the euro would collapse or a number of the weaker countries would be forced out.

Indeed, in May 2012 the then Bank of England Governor, Sir Mervyn King, told Nick Clegg that he thought the southern European countries could not adhere to the constraints of a single currency. He privately predicted that Greece, Cyprus, Spain and Portugal would all end up having to leave the EU – perhaps for as long as fifteen years.

Yet again, the British establishment, like the City of London, underestimated not only the political commitment of European countries to the single currency and the principles of the EU, but also the ultimate willingness of the European Central Bank to demonstrate greater flexibility over monetary policy.

Towards the end of 2011, the iceberg of European Union politics once again fleetingly broke the surface of British politics. In December 2011, David Cameron unexpectedly used his veto at an EU heads of government meeting, to block a proposed new EU treaty. The UK ended up in a minority of one, against all twenty-six other EU member nations. Since this action did not have Nick Clegg's explicit agreement, it led to a brief but serious coalition row.

However, the use of the veto was very popular, not just with Conservative

MPs but with the public. Mr Cameron and his party even enjoyed a brief bounce in the opinion polls.

If the Prime Minister was now feeling in any way that he could ride the European tiger to his political advantage, he was soon disabused of the notion. It became increasingly clear from the mid-point of the parliament onwards that the Conservatives had no chance at all of meeting the unrealistic targets for net migration that they had set themselves in opposition. These targets never properly took into account that with the EU policy of open borders within the union in place, the government lacked the instruments to deliver on such targets. With high unemployment in many parts of Europe, and much lower wage rates, particularly in Eastern Europe, large numbers of EU citizens came to the UK to work.

But with the UK's own economy still struggling, there was a ready political market for a party willing to blame many of the nation's ills on the European Union, and from 2013 onwards support for the UK Independence Party rose rapidly. Indeed, from late 2012 onwards, UKIP were consistently polling ahead of the Liberal Democrats.

UKIP support was also eating into the Conservative vote share, increasing the pressure for Cameron to adopt a much more Eurosceptic position.

These pressures on the Prime Minister to toughen up his position on the EU led to a return to a more hectoring UK tone over Europe. But many in the Foreign Office and elsewhere worried about whether this was more likely to be counterproductive in securing the gains Britain needed to make.

Vince Cable and Ed Davey, Liberal Democrat ministers in the Business Department, often found that there were natural allies of Britain in other EU countries, not least in Eastern Europe. But these countries were often politically nervous about being seen to align with the UK. One EU foreign minister told his UK opposite number: 'We have so much in common with the UK agenda. But we cannot be seen to be working with the UK – it's like being caught playing with the bad boy in the playground. And the really big boys – Germany and France – wouldn't be happy with us. The UK needs to grandstand less and influence more.'

It was a message put directly to Mr Cameron at a dinner in May 2012 in his Downing Street flat. Nick Clegg and a somewhat reluctant Miriam González Durántez, Nick's wife, had agreed to attend a dinner with David and Samantha Cameron.

Nick later told me that, having been quite subdued for the first part of the meal, Miriam suddenly became very vocal over the issue of Conservative policy on the European Union – she took on David Cameron directly and 'gave it to him with both barrels'. The Deputy Prime Minister's wife didn't hold back, blasting the Prime Minister for just lecturing other European countries without actually winning them over. She told the PM that it was a disastrous strategy, warning that it might play well with British voters but it would achieve nothing – delivering less UK influence, rather than more.

For once, Nick Clegg was able to sit back, as his wife fenced with David Cameron across the dining room table. Neither would concede an inch.

A few days after the dinner, Nick predicted: 'The calls for an in/out referendum are just going to grow and grow. There is now a real likelihood that in the next parliament there will be a referendum, whoever is in power. And if that happens there is a serious risk that Britain could leave. It could be a complete disaster for both Britain and the EU. We are living through a time of nationalism and extremism. It is incredibly worrying.'

In early July 2012, the first signs emerged that Conservative Party policy on Europe and the referendum might be on the move, in response to political pressure.

On the afternoon of Saturday 30 June, David Cameron telephoned Nick Clegg. He rather nervously informed his coalition partner that he was writing a newspaper article on the European Union. He explained that he was going to say that he could see circumstances where the UK would need to have a referendum on the EU. He underlined, of course, that this would be a Conservative policy for the next parliament.

Nick was surprised and concerned. He told the Prime Minister that he thought the policy change was unnecessary and would end in tears. He pointed out that the coalition had already legislated for a referendum when there was next a proposal for a major transfer of powers to Brussels. 'When we passed that legislation, you and William Hague were very clear that just picking a random date and having a referendum made no sense. Why change the position?'

'I warned him that he cannot hope to buy off his EU critics,' the Liberal Democrat leader told his advisers. 'I said whatever you promise to deliver, they will want more. And by shifting position you are just going to look weak. If you are planning to say that you want changes from other EU members before a referendum, how do you know that other EU nations will be willing to help us? Frankly, at the moment other European nations are far more worried about their currency falling to pieces than the internal political niceties of the UK. I told him I think this is all just crazy.'

David Cameron's reply wasn't very convincing. He admitted that the EU issue was very tricky and claimed that he needed to correct what he felt was misreporting of comments which he had made in Brussels, which had made him seem too pro-EU: 'I have to do this. It is a party management issue. I am under a lot of pressure on this. I need to re-calibrate.'

From July 2012, the situation in the Eurozone began to slowly stabilise. The new President of the European Central Bank, Mario Draghi, had gone on the record in late July stating that he would do anything necessary to protect the euro. 'I didn't quite intend to go that far,' admitted Mr Draghi when he met Nick Clegg. But whatever the intention, it did the trick. Markets stabilised. Confidence in the euro grew. Interest rates started to decline from lofty levels in many EU states.

But nothing was combatting the steadily more Eurosceptic drift of Conservative Party policy, and now even Britain's closest allies outside Europe were beginning to notice and express concerns.

In August 2012, Nick met the US Ambassador, who expressed concern over Mr Cameron's rightward shift on Europe. The ambassador told the Deputy Prime Minister that the US administration was worried that 'you guys may soon not count in Europe any more'. In particular, he expressed US concerns that David Cameron was no longer being listened to in Europe.

Nick Clegg said that he agreed, but suggested that this message needed to go directly from the US President to the British Prime Minister. 'I told him that the US probably needs to speak out publicly on this.'

In late 2012, there was a brief moment of coalition convergence when David Cameron and Nick Clegg united to fight for a sensible settlement on the EU budget. Together, they succeeded and forced other EU members to sign up to a real cut in the budget – necessary to demonstrate that the European Union could accept the need to make at least some savings at a time of great austerity.

However, by now Downing Street had let it be known that in the New Year the Prime Minister would make a major speech on the European Union, which would set out a new Conservative position for the post-coalition era. It was increasingly expected that this would include a UK renegotiation of key elements of our relationship with Europe, combined with a referendum after the renegotiation. This was clearly going to be a very important political moment.

In early 2013, Nick called a political meeting in his Dover House office to discuss the Liberal Democrats' own position on Europe.

Paddy Ashdown surprised everyone by making a case for pre-empting the Conservatives on Europe: 'Nick, let's be frank. A referendum would be popular with the public. It would demonstrate our confidence as pro-Europeans. It would pre-empt Cameron. Bluntly, there will eventually have to be a referendum on this. We are best if we are first out of the traps.'

I made the counter-case: 'Look, I guess this would be very popular in places like the south-west. But we are kidding ourselves if we think we can win any votes out of this. People who want a referendum generally want to vote "No". We cannot win those people over while we remain a clearly pro-European party. We have ballsed this up before for tactical reasons and we should not repeat that mistake. And what happens if we end up in coalition with Labour after the next election? Are we then going to hold the referendum? We would have to, because we cannot afford another tuition fees-type reversal of position. And in my view we and Labour could never win a referendum on Europe. So, Nick, do you want to be the person who offers this and then conspires to lead the UK out of the EU?'

That was the clear majority view. 'OK,' said Nick. 'Let's hold our position on this. We let the Tories talk about Europe, Europe, Europe. Meanwhile, we must stick with jobs, the economy and helping with household budgets. These are the things people really care about. And anyway I strongly believe in the position we took in 2010. A referendum is probably eventually inevitable. But the right time to hold it is when there are major treaty changes being proposed – that way people know what they are voting on and we get the chance to advocate real changes.'

UKIP continued to surge in the polls, in spite of hints of a more Euro-sceptic Conservative position.

Senior Conservatives were privately clear to me: 'We need to come out for an EU referendum, or we will be destroyed by UKIP in the 2014 European elections, and maybe lose a lot of votes in 2015 too.'

Over Christmas and New Year, we had to make the final tweaks to the draft mid-term review document. Danny Alexander emailed me one amendment – a bland addition to the Europe section: 'The government is strongly committed to full membership of the European Union, as a central pillar of our future prosperity and security.'

I was amused to see what the Conservatives would make of this. A nervous Oliver Letwin, on a New Year's Day conference call, said in response: 'Ah! I'll need to check this one with the Prime Minister.'

Two days later the reply came back: 'The Chief Secretary's proposed wording is not acceptable to the Prime Minister. We would prefer to revert to: "The government is committed to membership of the European Union."' We had had our fun, anyway.

In early January, another political leader was getting nervous about Europe: Ed Miliband.

The Labour leader secretly met Nick Clegg and said: 'Look, this is all very difficult. I am considering whether I should go for a referendum on Europe. What do you think? What are you going to do?'

Nick Clegg explained: 'We are going to stick to our position. I'm not going to shift on this. And I am happy to make common cause with you on it.'

'That's reassuring,' said Ed Miliband. It was clear that he was himself under pressure from Ed Balls and other senior Labour figures to advocate a referendum.

A few days later, the Labour leader came out clearly against the referendum option.

The Prime Minister also asked to see Nick Clegg. This time, it was just the two coalition leaders, over a drink.

It was a relaxed, open and civilised conversation, which started with a brief discussion of old problems: boundary reform and the Lords. The Conservative leader also mentioned his nervousness over the rise of UKIP.

Cameron also revealed that he was thinking of a reshuffle in September. He asked whether Nick Clegg would consider moving Vince Cable, as he was 'driving George nuts' with his public criticism of the government's economic strategy.

'No,' said Nick. 'Of course, I find him very difficult too at times, but I am not going to split my party.'

Nick Clegg then moved the conversation on to the future. He said that it was important to keep open all options for after the next election – 'but I don't know how I can do that if your party is just going to veer off to the right'.

David Cameron said that his 'hunch' was that the next election would have almost exactly the same outcome as the last one, and that he wanted to keep open the possibility of a second coalition.

Nick Clegg said that he could probably persuade his party, but that he doubted David Cameron could persuade his. 'I think I could, actually,' said the PM, 'but I would need to do more of what you did last time, and have more collective agreement in the party.'

David Cameron's big speech on Europe was initially billed for mid-January 2013, to be delivered either in Bruges or somewhere in the Netherlands.

Downing Street was already getting worried about the possible reaction. On 7 January, Ed Llewellyn, David Cameron's chief of staff, had told his Liberal Democrat counterpart, Jonny Oates: 'Expectations for the speech are now way too high. There's no way we can now win on this.'

Other Conservatives also seemed to be nervous about the speech. To my surprise, Michael Gove decided to use part of the weekly ministers' meeting at the Education Department to discuss the PM's forthcoming speech. 'Who thinks this speech, now, is a good idea?' he asked. 'Surely it's completely barmy to do this speech now? It can only stir up the Europe issue without bringing it to a conclusion. In any case, why are we proposing to speculate now about what might happen in Europe in a couple of years' time, after a negotiation of indefinite length, which might then lead to a referendum, the nature of which is poorly understood? Surely we should not be giving this speech at all?' The other Conservative ministers looked distinctly uncomfortable. I said little.

On Thursday 17 January, there was a striking intervention from the USA into the European debate. It was made known that President Obama had called David Cameron directly to warn him about the negative impact of increasing the UK's distance from the rest of the European Union.

Following this and terrorist attacks in Algeria, the Prime Minister's speech was moved back from 18 January, and relocated to the UK. The big speech was finally scheduled for Wednesday 23 January. Ed Llewellyn, whom David Cameron and his team often referred to privately as 'Mini Metternich' after the scheming Austrian diplomat, visited Nick Clegg the night before with a copy of the final text.

As expected, the speech proposed a renegotiation of the UK's relationship with the EU within two years of the next general election. It then proposed that this should be put to a referendum of the British people, with the UK government supporting a Yes vote to stay in, provided negotiating objectives had been met.

Nick was particularly concerned by the suggestion that enabling legislation for the referendum should be passed in the present parliament.

The speech seemed to be well received by the media, but Nick Clegg was less convinced. 'It's all triumph and euphoria for the Tories and the right-wing media now. But this has almost certainly sown the seeds of permanent division in the Conservative Party. People like Liam Fox are never going to vote to stay in, no matter what David Cameron comes back with. And this makes it very difficult to go into coalition with the Conservatives in 2015. We would have to go in with a party that wanted to spend its first two years in government flying around Europe on an endless renegotiation.'

'Once again,' Nick told me, 'Cameron is always thinking about the immediate problem, and not what happens next. This is all about getting through the next few months. Cameron is going to love tomorrow's headlines. And he will then hope something will turn up to salvage his renegotiations. He really is an optimist. He thinks there is always going to be something that will turn up and bail him out.'

And in the short term, it was the Prime Minister's major opponent who was now on the back foot. Ed Miliband raised the EU referendum at Prime Minister's Questions. But under questioning from the Prime Minister, the Labour leader went further than he had intended to go, ruling out a referendum completely. He met up with Nick in a room behind the Speaker's Chair after Prime Minister's Questions. Looking rather shell-shocked, he said to Nick: 'You do think I have done the right thing, don't you? You do realise the position we are both taking is rather brave? I think the Parliamentary Labour Party will be OK with me, even after today, because last week's PMQs went pretty well for me.'

Nick suggested that the two leaders should let the flaws in the Prime Minister's position play out. He pointed out there if there had to be a referendum on Europe, it could probably only be won if the case was made by a Eurosceptic party.

Another, former, Labour leader was directly critical of the Conservative approach: 'David Cameron's strategy is a bit like the guy in *Blazing Saddles* who says, "Put your hands up or I'll blow my brains out!"' said Tony Blair.

A few days later, the Prime Minister still struggled to explain his negotiating strategy to Nick Clegg. As Nick told me later: 'I told Cameron that I just didn't understand his strategy. I said either your renegotiation is just going to be symbolic and insubstantial, like Harold Wilson. In which case, what's the point? Or you are going to have to go for a full renegotiation, which you may never achieve with other countries on this timescale. Cameron looked pretty sheepish, and just said: "I know, Nick. That's why I won't be spelling out for some time what I am going to negotiate on."'

Nick was distinctly unimpressed: 'If I had given such a hollow speech, the media would have killed me,' he said. 'There is a serious risk that Cameron will fail on this. It makes a second coalition with the Conservatives not impossible, but very undesirable.'

Later in the parliament, in spring 2014, Nick Clegg met the German Chancellor, Angela Merkel, when she visited London. They discussed the prospects of winning a referendum if the Conservatives were in government beyond the 2015 general election. 'I am willing to help David and the UK a bit in renegotiating your position in the European Union,' Europe's most powerful political leader said. But Merkel made clear that she could only help 'on the margins', noting: 'It isn't possible to make big changes without a whole new treaty – which is out of the question.'

The Deputy Prime Minister said he was not sure that marginal renegotiation would be enough for the Prime Minister or his party to win a referendum. Angela Merkel just shrugged: 'What do they expect me to do about that?' she said. Mr Cameron had got himself out of a short-term fix, but at the price of massive long-term risk.

MID-TERM
MOMENTS

JANUARY 2013

It was a cold January evening in 2013, and Nick Clegg was standing in the street in St James's, London. There was a small crowd around him, and one or two frozen-looking journalists.

The Liberal Democrat leader had been asked to unveil a new green plaque, marking the location of the building in which the Liberal Party had been founded over 150 years earlier.

After a short speech by the Deputy Leader of Westminster Council, Nick Clegg began: 'Congratulations to the Liberal Democrat History Group, who have done so much to raise funds for this memorial...'

To his side, a party press officer muttered, '"Plaque", not "memorial"!'

'... Not memorial,' the Deputy Prime Minister corrected himself, 'this ... sign of our party's rich history.'

The small crowd chuckled at the slip-up, which Nick laughed off in his usual self-effacing style. But it was not an auspicious sign as the New Year got underway.

Nick Clegg had spent his Christmas holiday giving careful reflection to the state of the coalition, and the Liberal Democrats. He was not the only one. Chris Huhne, who hoped to return to the Cabinet soon, was clearly already thinking a number of steps ahead.

Early in the New Year, he said to one of Nick Clegg's advisers: 'If

Nick's ratings don't improve soon, he may have to consider stepping down.'

Irritated by Huhne's ill-disguised ambition, Nick asked to see him in mid-January.

'Chris, one thing you need to know: I'm here to stay,' he said.

'Nick,' replied Chris Huhne, 'I don't know who has been talking to you, but I have been misquoted. I really didn't say that.'

'You have to laugh,' Nick said to friends later. 'Chris will always be Chris. The man's sheer chutzpah is something to behold! Anyway, he tells me that he expects to be acquitted soon. I guess he will want to be back in the Cabinet. He'll just have to wait a bit.'

This Christmas, Nick was feeling positive about the Liberal Democrat achievements in government, and strong in relation to his position in the party.

But as he told me early in the New Year, he was still worried about why the party's poll ratings were so low and what could be done to move the dial: 'I don't think we've put a foot wrong since September, but there is absolutely no sign of it making any difference with the public. I am enjoying myself much more now, and we're delivering so many things, but there is no sign yet of breaking through. Anyway, the government's mid-term review is important for us. We need to show people that the coalition is both persisting and delivering.'

I had spent a good deal of my time on the mid-term review since I had returned to government. There were different views about what type of event this should be. At one stage, it was considered that the review might be a big political moment – essentially almost a second coalition agreement, and an occasion for a renewal of coalition vows. That idea had quickly faded – neither coalition leader wanted another 'rose garden moment' – and more to the point, neither did their parties.

George Osborne and the Treasury would probably have been happy to drop the mid-term review altogether. The Chancellor saw it as a potential fiscal risk; there was a chance the two party leaders could end up agreeing expensive new policies.

But both David Cameron and Nick Clegg could see that there was value in working together on the government's agenda for its last couple of years, and they both hoped that the mid-term review could provide an opportunity for some new policy thinking.

The work on the review resumed in earnest after the party conference season in mid-October. I led the work on the Liberal Democrat side, and Oliver Letwin led for the Conservatives.

There could not have been anyone on the Conservative side easier to work with than Oliver. He was ferociously bright, trusted by the Prime Minister and Chancellor, and far more influential than his Minister of State rank suggested. Yet he was also modest, funny, charming, courteous, decent, thoughtful, honest and constructive. In short, here was someone whose work – if observed closely – would restore the confidence of the most deeply cynical critic of politicians.

If a terrible virus threatened to wipe out most of the politicians in Parliament, and you could save only five or ten people to establish a new government, then Oliver Letwin would have been high on my shortlist for an early shot of protective anti-virus.

Here was a person who was fun to work with and who clearly relished the important role he had been given. He worked behind the scenes, not for the greater glory of himself or to achieve prominence in the media, but in the interests of a better-governed and more liberal country. He had an infectious chuckle that would often continue for a prolonged period of time. And on the rare occasions when he was being very serious, and perhaps having to defend some extreme right-wing Conservative position that he was uncomfortable with personally, he at least had the decency to look embarrassed about it. In short, he was a wonderful colleague to work with, and my private secretaries and I used to look forward to our every meeting with him.

We enjoyed his anecdotes too.

At one breakfast meeting in early 2013, the sight of a bowl of porridge sparked off a wonderful story from his time at Eton. 'I was invited one weekend to the very, very grand country house of school friend of mine. I had never seen anything like it – all incredibly posh. The breakfast wasn't served to you – you had to get it yourself from a very long table, weighed down with extraordinarily nice food, at one end of the room. I was invited to go up first. I didn't really know what I was doing, and I was incredibly nervous. I didn't realise that I was going the wrong way down the breakfast table. I piled my plate with eggs, bacon, mushrooms and tomatoes and then at the end of the table I came to a huge bowl which contained a lumpy brown substance. I had no idea what it was, but assumed it was a very sophisticated and upmarket brown sauce. So I took a deep breath, and poured it over all of the food on my plate. When I sat down, there was an embarrassed silence, and their whole family looked at me in horror. Then someone said: "I see you like porridge, Oliver." I was terribly embarrassed,' he said, and then burst into a prolonged fit of giggles.

On another occasion, our private secretaries and I all laughed out loud as Oliver told the story of buying a very expensive fur coat for his wife, after he had left the Downing Street Policy Unit in the 1980s and secured a highly paid job in an investment bank. 'It was a lovely coat. Cost thousands, even in those days. Well, one day I attended a marvellous dinner for Mrs Thatcher in a palatial house in London. My wife wore her beautiful fur coat. Mrs Thatcher turned up in a fur coat too – but in a rather cheaper sort of Marks & Spencer version. Anyway, it was a wonderful evening, but when we came to leave, we discovered that Mrs Thatcher had walked off by mistake with my wife's very expensive coat, leaving her own frankly rather less glamorous version on the coat rack. She was obviously one of the UK's greatest ever Prime Ministers and the truth is that I didn't have the nerve to ask for it back. My wife, as you may imagine, was rather angry. We saw it a few more times over the years at other social events, all in the company of the Great Lady, but I never had the guts to pinch it back.' Other people in the small cafeteria wondered what aspect of coalition policy was making the five of us laugh so loudly.

We may have got on well, but we did not agree on everything. We did, however, feel able to be very open and honest with each other, so that we didn't waste time on ideas from either party that the other was never going to agree. 'I'm sorry,' Oliver would sometimes say, 'the Prime Minister has looked at this and he is totally opposed. We won't move him.'

'We think your idea on this is completely crazy, and there is no way Nick will sign it off,' I occasionally had to spell out. Having big disagreements was much easier if you just set out clearly and openly your party's position. Our job also included unblocking policy problems across the coalition. On around half the occasions we might succeed, but sometimes we couldn't. On these occasions the PM and DPM would resolve the differences at one of their regular bilaterals. These meetings were often very successful and a lot got resolved through them that had been held up at a lower level in the government. This speaks well of the relationship between PM and DPM, and the generally mature and adult tone they set from the top downwards.

On the mid-term review, there were quite a few Conservative policy ideas that we didn't think much of. One proposal was to hive off the Highways Agency and then charge for the use of its roads – with the revenues being re-invested in new road building and maintenance. Leaving aside the challenging politics of road charging, it was soon clear to us that the detail had not remotely been thought through – for example, the impact on the use of other, nearby, non-charged roads. The Prime Minister told us that he 'loved' the idea, while his own Conservative-run Transport Department quietly lobbied us to kill it. 'We've got enough problems with HS2, without this crazy idea,' they told us.

We were equally dubious about another Conservative proposal: to allow people living in council houses to own their properties for free, in exchange for never claiming housing benefit again. 'I love this one,' said David Cameron. 'This is really radical. Just the sort of thing we should be doing.'

I said to Oliver Letwin that I could not see the policy basis for giving people who just happened to have gained access to social housing huge cash windfalls – in some cases running into hundreds of thousands of pounds. Eventually the Prime Minister's 'favourite radical idea' died a death.

The policy problems were not all on the Conservative side. We Liberal Democrats developed our own policy of 'Earn or Learn' to ensure that all 18–21-year-olds were in work, education or training. I supported the idea and worked on the policy detail. Nick Clegg proposed it to David Cameron. Vince Cable even rushed off and made a speech about it. But the Treasury wasn't convinced that the proposed compulsory options for young people were value for money. Nick then worried that the Conservatives would turn the whole idea into part of their 'welfare cuts agenda'. And Vince hadn't really worked out the implications for his department before making the speech.

Oliver Letwin laughed out loud when I told him that we were no longer going to support our own idea. And when we told David Cameron, he relished our discomfort, mischievously saying: 'Oh, I really liked this idea. I think we should press ahead with it. Can't we sort out the policy glitches? I thought that this was a Liberal Democrat idea, anyway?'

'Earn or Learn' didn't make it into the mid-term review, but it became Conservative policy instead.

There was a more productive outcome on childcare, where both coalition parties wanted a solution that would help parents at a time when cost-of-living concerns were uppermost. We looked at every conceivable policy option, including increasing the number of free childcare hours for the parents of two-, three- and four-year-olds. Eventually, we settled for a tax-free childcare offer, which the Conservatives were particularly keen on.

Nick Clegg took the opportunity of the mid-term review to push two Liberal Democrat priorities. One was the new single-tier pension, which had been designed by Steve Webb. David Cameron took some time to agree to give this reform the green light.

The other priority was to press for the implementation of the Dilnot Report on help with long-term care costs. George Osborne, Danny Alexander and Oliver Letwin were all dubious of the merits of the report – Oliver on the rational grounds that it looked like a public subsidy to well-off citizens, to enable them to pass on their assets, and the Treasury on the basis that it looked like a rather large financial commitment.

Eventually, David Cameron and Nick Clegg decided that we would proceed with the Dilnot proposals, but with a delayed start date. George Osborne suggested that we should pay for this by cutting some of the benefits that went to pensioners, such as attendance allowance and disability living allowance. I pointed out that this would result in many poor pensioners losing current income in order to protect the estates of predominantly richer pensioners. 'This would be rather a bizarre thing to do,' I argued. George Osborne then surprised us by making the case for cutting back on spending on the winter fuel payments, which were received by both rich and poor pensioners alike. Up until now, David Cameron had vetoed any changes in this area, referring back to manifesto commitments that he had made. The Prime Minister again vetoed any change. I suggested instead that the Treasury should freeze the inheritance tax threshold for a number of years, to help pay for the plan – that at least had the logic that it would redistribute largesse so that people unlucky enough to have serious medical problems would secure some financial protection. It seemed sensible to think of the policy as part of the way in which we relieve the taxation of estates. George Osborne initially rejected the idea but later accepted it, raising a few hundred million pounds towards the £800 million per annum cost of the Dilnot plan.

What else was there in the mid-term review? Well, there were a few policies to boost house building, and a new strategy for managing the Highways Agency (with road charging consigned to the dustbin for now). And there was a promise of new legislation to 'extend our freedoms'. Unfortunately, the Prime Minister didn't like most of the proposed extensions to freedom – including improved access to the countryside, which he thought might upset landowners and farmers. The Freedoms Bill therefore eventually died a long, slow, quiet death.

The contents of the mid-term review were largely agreed at a final Quad in late December 2012. Oliver Letwin and I then had to produce a draft of the actual document. I had no idea how much of a perfectionist Oliver would be until we spent a very long evening in his Commons office, going through the draft text line by line. We usefully improved the draft, including removing a rather striking sentence that read: 'The fact that people are living longer than ever before is cause for celebration. It gives us all a chance to work longer.' But after about three hours, I had only managed to move Oliver on to page 4 of a fifty-page document. I confess that a couple of days later, I returned to my constituency and left my adviser, Julian Astle, to finish the process of going through the detailed text with Oliver. It took a marathon ten-and-a-half-hour meeting between the two of them to satisfy both coalition parties. I was relieved to have missed the meeting, but Oliver got his own back, fixing a final conference call on the text for 'teatime on New Year's Day'. At least it wasn't Christmas Day.

The mid-term review – 'The Coalition: Together in the National Interest' – was published in early January. Forty-six pages in length, it was, in truth, a modest evolution of the original coalition agreement, rather than setting great new directions. But this was undoubtedly the right approach – there was still much of our original agreement to be delivered, and it was better to focus on seeing through our ambitious plans on the economy and social reform, rather than going off on some new tangent.

In any case, after a difficult and at times tense year, the review showed that the coalition partners could still come together and establish some common new priorities.

At times in 2012, it had seemed to some informed players that the coalition might not last the course. Indeed, in October 2012, even the Prime Minister asked Michael Gove whether he thought that the Liberal Democrats would stay in coalition for the full five years. The mid-term review helped to bury those doubts.

'If You Lose Eastleigh,
You Must Resign'

FEBRUARY 2013

It was Sunday night, 3 February 2013.

Nick Clegg was working late on his red boxes. It was just before 11 p.m.

The phone on his desk rang, and the Deputy Prime Minister wondered who could be calling so late – perhaps a press officer with news about some story in the Monday papers?

It was, instead, Chris Huhne, the Eastleigh MP who had been forced to resign from the government when the police decided to prosecute him for allegedly getting his former wife, Vicky Pryce, to accept responsibility for a speeding offence which he had himself committed.

Chris Huhne had been fighting the case, and robustly protesting his innocence.

Chris sounded as calm and in control as he always did. He explained that he wanted to update Nick Clegg on his situation.

The former Cabinet minister then explained that his lawyers' assessment was not promising. He made clear that he didn't want to put his family through the full media blaze of a trial and drag his children further into the dispute: 'So, I am going to plead guilty tomorrow, in court. Would it be better for me to stand down as MP immediately, or try to go on to 2015? I want to do the best I can for the party.'

Nick was rather dumbstruck by the news, not least because the former

Energy Secretary had always insisted on his innocence. He was also deeply sad, because although Chris Huhne had been at times a rather ruthless rival, he was also a personal friend. They had been MEPs together, and Chris was the only MP to have attended Nick and Miriam's wedding.

'Chris, I am just incredibly upset for you and your family,' said Nick. 'I cannot imagine how tough it will be.'

But he made clear that he thought the Eastleigh MP had no choice, and would need to stand down, causing an unwelcome by-election.

'OK, I understand,' said Chris. It was a short conversation.

The next day, early, Nick spoke to me on the phone: 'God, it's unbelievable. This is the man who had everything – money, a great family, a successful career, a job in Cabinet, and massive ambition. And now the whole thing has gone – just completely imploded. I don't know whether to be angry with him, or incredibly sad. He has been a friend, but also a rival. And now he is gone from politics for ever. And a by-election in Eastleigh, a marginal seat, under these circumstances is a complete bloody nightmare.'

The next day, Chris Huhne set off to court to enter his guilty verdict. A Lib Dem press officer met him before he left his flat, to offer support and help with the press handling. Chris was clearly under pressure, but also strangely calm. Before he left the house to face the worst day of his life, he turned and said: 'Well. In my life to date I have had three very successful careers – in journalism, in business and in politics. I guess today will mark the beginning of my fourth successful career.' No other member of the Cabinet, perhaps no other politician in Parliament, would have been thick-skinned enough to think in that way at such a time. 'At times he is a complete shit, but he does have balls,' as a fellow Liberal Democrat MP said of him.

Nick Clegg and the Liberal Democrats were now left facing the last thing they needed – a by-election in a held seat, with a modest majority, over the resignation of a Cabinet minister who seemed likely to end up in jail.

If the constituency was lost, Nick Clegg knew that it would be seen as having implications well beyond Eastleigh – it would be taken as a sign that the Liberal Democrat meltdown in local government elections would also be followed by a meltdown in Liberal Democrat parliamentary seats.

It seemed as if things couldn't get any worse – but then they did. The by-election was fixed for Thursday 28 February. The Liberal Democrat Party poured resources in, and were building on top of a strong and well-organised local party, with a strong local government base. At first, everything seemed to be going well. The Conservatives picked a poor candidate and were struggling to hold their own against the UK Independence Party.

In late February there was more unhelpful coverage of the Chris Huhne case, when the judge in the trial of Chris Huhne's former wife, Vicky Pryce, dismissed the jury and ordered a re-trial. The jury could not reach a clear majority decision and – in an extraordinary development – sent the judge a list of questions including such legal gems as: 'Can a juror come to a verdict based on a reason that was not presented in court and has no facts or evidence to support it?' They also asked the judge to define for them the concept of 'reasonable doubt', prompting the grumpy but irrefutable response that 'a reasonable doubt is a doubt which was reasonable'.

Then, more seriously, exactly a week before the day of the by-election, *Channel 4 News* broke a story claiming that the former party chief executive and senior Liberal Democrat peer Lord Rennard had been accused of making unwanted advances towards a number of female party members. With a high-profile by-election test coming up, the story rapidly blew up into a major media storm.

The media quickly moved the Rennard story onto the issue of what Nick Clegg knew or did not know about the allegations, and how the party had dealt with them over a period of years. Initially, a statement had been put out on behalf of Nick Clegg implying that the Liberal Democrat leader knew little about the allegations.

The story had in its early stages seemed to be running in a low-key way. However, it was now alleged by some newspapers that Nick Clegg had known far more than his statement implied. A major political row was brewing. Over the weekend before the by-election, when he was supposed to be relaxing on a rare family holiday in Spain, Nick Clegg spent hours on the phone with his senior political and media advisers, trying to piece together what had happened many years before. There had been allegations that Nick Clegg had been made aware of, but these were of a general nature, and they had largely been handled by other senior Liberal Democrats – including the Chief Whip, and Danny Alexander, the then chief of staff.

What was supposed to be a brief, relaxing break turned into something of a nightmare. Half the weekend was spent fielding phone calls, checking facts from many years beforehand, and drafting and redrafting press lines.

On Sunday evening, Nick Clegg and his family got into two cars and prepared for the journey to Santander Airport, to fly back to the UK. It was pouring with rain when they left the family home, but this soon turned to thick snow, which settled fast. One of the vehicles lost grip on the ice and spun out of control. No one was hurt, but it was a frightening experience.

But there was no time to rest or recover – even at the airport there were yet more calls about the other storm: the Chris Rennard allegations.

When their plane touched down in England, Nick had to go straight to party headquarters in Westminster for an urgent meeting with his senior advisers, to draft a detailed response to media allegations of a cover-up.

On that night's BBC news, the Rennard story was the lead item – and Nick was now at the centre of the storm.

On Monday 25 February, I was awake as usual at 5.30 a.m. The first email of the day was from Olly Grender, one of the party's most experienced press advisers. She had just finished looking at that day's front pages. The email read simply 'Arggghhhhhhh!' The press coverage of the Rennard story was now highly damaging. It was no longer just about the allegations but about how they had been dealt with and who knew what and when. It was a massive media storm – and at the worst possible time. The only beneficiary of all the press attention was George Osborne, as the focus on the Rennard story blotted out what should have been the truly awful coverage of the UK losing its coveted triple-A government credit rating.

All of a sudden, the Chris Rennard storm had turned what had been looking like a comfortable win for the Liberal Democrats in Eastleigh into what now looked like a very, very, close-run race. And Nick Clegg's many enemies in the media – including those who could not forgive him for promoting the Leveson Inquiry into press standards – scented blood.

All that week the newspaper coverage was dire – awful front-page stories for five days in a row in almost every paper. At the Cabinet meeting on 26 February, Nick looked exhausted and drained of colour.

For two days in a row, the intensity of the crisis and the demands on his time meant that the Deputy Prime Minister was not able to wade through all the contents of his nightly red boxes – unprecedented for a man who often worked until 1 or 2 a.m. to ensure that every last government paper was dealt with.

On Wednesday 27 February, I attended a campaigns meeting with Nick,

Paddy Ashdown, and the core campaigning and political team. Everyone looked exhausted and demoralised. Only Paddy was in robust form, making some unprintable comments about Britain's 'right-wing press'. The first item was obviously the by-election in Eastleigh. 'It now looks too close to call. It could go either way. In fact, it looks like a three-way fight between us, UKIP and the Tories,' was the campaign department's gloomy assessment. I still felt that we would just make it – many of the postal votes had been cast before the recent week of wall-to-wall negative coverage. It was decided that whatever the result, Nick Clegg would visit Eastleigh the day after the election. 'If we win, then I obviously want to be there. If we lose, I need to be seen to be confronting the defeat head-on,' was the Liberal Democrat leader's view.

Privately, Nick felt more under assault than ever before: 'This is just an insane frenzy – I have never seen anything like this. The hysterical demonisation of me by parts of the press is just extraordinary.'

In the middle of the week, Nick Clegg's trusted chief of staff, Jonny Oates, asked to see his boss in private. 'Nick,' he said, 'I hate to see all this happening. It's totally unfair on you – an utter travesty. I don't think that this has been handled well enough on your behalf. As your chief of staff, the buck stops with me. I think perhaps I should resign.'

'Don't be silly,' replied Nick. 'I am not having you be some sort of sacrificial lamb. You are the most loyal, committed and sincere person I have ever worked with. Don't beat yourself up on my behalf.' Later he told friends: 'Jonny is such a great person. He always puts me and the party before his own interests. I would trust my life to him.'

On the evening before the by-election, Nick discussed the situation in detail with his wife, Miriam. He told her that he still expected to win in Eastleigh, but that it would be very close. Either way, he didn't want to give his enemies in the media the scalp they were looking for.

Nick told me later that Miriam had been typically blunt. She said that she agreed that the media must not get their scalp, but she added that she also had a simple view: 'If you lose Eastleigh, you must resign.'

Thursday 28 February finally arrived. The newspaper headlines were still awful – for the fifth day in a row. The Deputy Prime Minister was smoking again and was sleeping badly. Hilary Stephenson, the campaigns director, was saying that the chances of a win were no better than 50/50. But Keith

House, the respected local Liberal Democrat council leader, was still predicting a Liberal Democrat victory.

I spent half the day in the Education Department and then drove down to Eastleigh at 3 p.m. The talk was of a big last-minute surge in UKIP support. Everyone looked nervous. It was hard work getting the last people to go and vote – the constituency had been drowned in election leaflets for six weeks, and some voters had already been telephoned three or four times that same day when we came around knocking at 9 p.m. There were one or two doors slammed in our faces. But on the drive home, I predicted we would win – by a majority of around 1,700.

At 11.30 that night, I was back home in London, and I stayed up to see the by-election results. The early signs were good, and at 1 a.m. I texted Nick to say that it sounded like we were going to win and I wanted to congratulate him. Back, instantly, came the message, 'Yep, sounds like we have done it – and done it well.' There then followed a pithy comment about what the besieged Liberal Democrat leader would like to do to certain parts of the media. It wasn't printable. At home, Nick Clegg celebrated with yet another cigarette and admitted: 'God, it's such a relief that it's over. This has been the most draining period since I became leader.'

The final result came through at around 2 a.m. – we had won, with a majority of 1,771, and the Conservatives had been knocked back into third place by a UKIP surge. It was a fantastic result – not least in the middle of a 'crisis of the two Chrises'.

This was the first successful Liberal by-election defence of a held seat in government since 1922, leaving aside the wartime coalition. And it seemed like a good omen. UKIP had apparently succeeded in draining support away from the Conservatives, whose vote had fallen by a similar percentage to our own. Labour were nowhere to be seen, with their vote share hardly moving from the 2010 result – this was a spectacular failure for them, with their two principal competitor parties now in coalition together.

If we could hold a Liberal Democrat seat like Eastleigh in such unpromising circumstances, perhaps we could still expect to hold many of our existing seats at the next general election? Nick Clegg, celebrating the result on Friday 1 March, concluded that 'we can be a party of government and still win'.

Eastleigh was indeed a stunning success. It also turned out to provide false reassurance.

The Budget: Vetoing
Osborne's Cuts

MARCH 2013

The day after the by-election in Eastleigh, the crisis over Lord Rennard was suddenly no longer front-page news. The media focus was now firmly back on the economy.

On 1 May 2013, the Quad plus Oliver Letwin, Jo Johnson and I had just finished a meeting in the Cabinet Room, called to discuss the contents of the forthcoming Queen's Speech. As the meeting broke up, George Osborne said: 'Oh, by the way, I thought I would remind you all that we have the pleasure later this month of a visit by inspectors from the International Monetary Fund. They are coming to look at our economy and our borrowing – to give us some no doubt painful and public advice about changing course.'

David Cameron said: 'Oh God, are they here again already? We really need to persuade them to be as positive as possible about our economic strategy.' He leaned back in his chair, stretched, and said: 'Our best hope, George, may be to take the inspectors out for a nice dinner, then go on to a nightclub and some bars, get them completely drunk and take some compromising photos!' Everyone laughed.

But in the first six months of 2013, the economy was really no cause for amusement on either side of the coalition. Whatever storms blew up from month to month to challenge the coalition and its leaders, the running sore that was sapping the government's health was the lack of growth.

Even the normally orthodox International Monetary Fund had started to make the case in early 2013 for changes in UK economic policy. And the worries were no longer just about flat-lining. On 25 January, the growth figures for the last quarter of 2012 were published by the Office for National Statistics. These showed that the growth in the third quarter of 2012 appeared to be a flash in the pan. The economy had contracted yet again by 0.3 per cent in the last three months of 2012 – and we had now seen no growth or negative growth for four out of the past five quarters.

So as we entered 2013, the economy was now smaller than in September 2011. A further decline in second-quarter growth, if it were to occur, would see the country experience an almost unprecedented triple-dip recession.

The success of the government depended on the economy turning around. And it became clear, too, that the unity of the Liberal Democrats was now also seriously threatened by the state of the economy. In early January, Nick Clegg and Vince Cable sat down privately to discuss economic policy.

The Deputy Prime Minister asked Vince for his views on the economy. The Business Secretary said that he agreed with our existing Liberal Democrat efforts to review the monetary policy mandate of the Bank of England, avoid further rises in fuel duties, and raise the personal tax allowance. But he made clear that wanted to go a lot further. He said that he had lost faith in the government's economic strategy. 'The economy is flat on its back. Interest rates are incredibly low. There is no reason why we should not be borrowing more and spending it on productive investment. This is not some sort of communist view – even the IMF is saying this now. I think George and Danny are being far too conventional. We could be slowing down the fiscal consolidation, borrowing more and investing it in infrastructure.' Vince said that he knew that I had been working on some interesting ways of increasing investment, and he said he thought this was the right approach. He also said that he didn't yet have detailed plans of his own.

The Business Secretary made clear again that he was deeply worried about his own department's budget – which did not enjoy the protection of areas such as schools and the NHS. He said that he was so worried about the possible impacts of further cuts in his budget that he wasn't sleeping properly at night, and he argued for delaying the next Spending Review until after the election and ending the protection of the schools and NHS budgets.

Nick Clegg was somewhat exasperated. He felt they were going over old ground. And he wasn't willing to remove the key protections from education and the NHS. 'We are committed to protecting schools and the NHS for very good reasons. It is written into the coalition agreement. It is just pointless to think of re-opening that – which I don't want to do anyway.'

On the Business budget, the Liberal Democrat leader said he understood the concerns, but he gently noted that Vince had been claiming ever since May 2010 that his department did not have the scope to make cuts, yet in spite of this it had been pretty successful in doing so.

On capital spending, Nick was very blunt: 'I definitely want to do more and as you know we are looking at creative ways to do so, including with off-balance-sheet guarantees. But the chances of us persuading Cameron and Osborne to just borrow billions and spend it on infrastructure are frankly zero.'

Nick also pointed out that it had proved difficult to find 'shovel-ready' projects on which money could be spent quickly. He stressed that it would take time to identify projects and allocate money, and emphasised that this could easily take a couple of years, and that by then the economy would probably be recovering anyway: 'Let's focus on what we can change – monetary policy, lending guarantees and action to boost consumer spending.'

But the two most prominent Liberal Democrats could not reconcile their differences. And Nick was getting more frustrated than ever with his most senior colleague. 'I am really worried about Vince,' he confided the next day to Danny Alexander and me. 'The solutions he is suggesting are either incredibly vague or politically undeliverable. Does he really want us to go back on another pledge and cut the schools budget? Crazy.'

Nick made clear that he was concerned that one day Vince would just 'blow up and walk out – one day we may wake up to a *Guardian* splash saying he has resigned over economic policy differences'.

The Liberal Democrat leader privately discussed the possibility of a reshuffle in which Danny Alexander would replace Vince Cable as Business Secretary, with me returning as Chief Secretary to the Treasury. His coalition partners were pressing for change too. 'Cameron is trying again to persuade me to move or sack Vince,' Nick Clegg told me in early 2013. 'He and Osborne are driven mad by him. But at the end of the day, and with Chris Huhne gone, Vince is the only other real Liberal Democrat "big beast", who is well known to the party and the public. If Vince resigns or I sack him, the party will be divided and weak. That would destroy us. In previous coalitions our party has ended up divided, and that has been disastrous. I do not see how I can justify that risk.'

Nick was also concerned that his top team now had different positions on some of the key economic policy issues. He confided to Jonny Oates: 'We have got to pull our team together on the economy. Danny is still being very rigid over Treasury orthodoxy, Vince just wants to borrow more without specifying for what, and David is pushing for easing up on the inflation target or going for a fiscal boost now and cuts later, as the economy recovers. We have got to pull in one direction as a team.'

And as a freezing January gave way to February, the bad economic news kept coming. On Friday 22 February, Moody's credit agency had announced that the UK's debt was being downgraded from its prized triple-A rating. Though widely expected, this was a significant blow to the government and to George Osborne, the man Labour were now calling 'the downgraded Chancellor'.

Vince Cable also continued to be a cause for concern. In February, he stated publicly that the Liberal Democrats might support Labour in a Commons debate on the mansion tax. The next month, he was publicly questioning whether there should be a spending round at all for 2015/16, and calling for cuts to the protected budgets. That infuriated me, as protecting the schools budget was an important Liberal Democrat achievement, which helped ensure that our pupil premium could actually make a difference in educating disadvantaged children.

In early March, we heard on the special advisers grapevine that Vince Cable had written an article repudiating coalition economic policy, which he was seeking to place in a newspaper or magazine. Downing Street found out too, and the Chancellor and Prime Minister expressed their concerns to Nick. The Business Secretary was asked not to publish the article, but it eventually appeared anyway, on 7 March, in the *New Statesman*. This was just one day before the start of the Liberal Democrat spring conference, and just two weeks before the date of the Budget.

Vince Cable's actions now looked like open rebellion, and a direct challenge to Nick Clegg's leadership. I was angry about this, but I also actually had sympathy with some of the points that Vince was making. I did think that both the Treasury and the Bank of England were being too cautious about nurturing the recovery. But I felt that this sort of public posturing was the least likely way of changing government policy, and had no chance of delivering the right policy outcomes – indeed, by provoking the Chancellor, it seemed to make these much less likely.

I also understood, as Vince seemed not to, that we were more likely to get a pro-growth policy if we focused on measures that were not seen to involve a direct switch to an Ed Balls-type 'Plan B'. Both George Osborne and David Cameron had made clear privately and publicly that they were willing to consider adding lots of 'pluses' to the coalition's 'Plan A'. What they would not do was concede in any way to the Labour plan to formally slow the pace of deficit reduction. I could see why Vince might be attracted to a public U-turn from a Chancellor whose economic competence he did not respect. But I thought there was no chance of delivering progress through some head-on assault.

I was also very concerned when it turned out that a surprisingly well-crafted motion calling for changes in our economic policy had just been tabled for debate at our spring conference. The motion seemed to bear an uncanny resemblance to the arguments set out in Vince's *New Statesman* article. It later turned out that my suspicions were correct, and that the motion seemed to have been inspired by Lord Oakeshott, Vince's self-appointed political lieutenant, whose ambitions for himself and Vince were well known.

I was very worried that if the motion were debated, it would both split the party and quite possibly be carried, given the present state of the economy. After all, even the orthodox IMF was now calling for action to boost growth.

Nick Clegg was worried too, and deeply irritated. He emailed me at 6 a.m. during the conference to say that he was 'seriously pissed off with Vince's attempt to bounce us into a full-blown change of strategy on the back of a *New Statesman* article and a cobbled-together Emergency Motion'.

If the motion were carried despite the opposition of both Nick and Danny Alexander, this would make their positions very difficult. It could even precipitate a leadership crisis, which was probably what Lord Oakeshott intended. Vince's own strategy was less clear – he always seemed more interested in policy substance than in political manoeuvring, and as something of a loner he had not invested time in building up a team of supporters in the parliamentary party.

Fortunately, Nick Clegg's political advisers came up with a clever way of avoiding an embarrassing split on the economy motion. Emergency Motions at Lib Dem conference have to be selected by a ballot of the members attending conference. Because the economy motion was a big issue, it would require all the time allocated for emergency debates. A motion was also down on the highly controversial issue of secret courts, and as many 'loyalists' as possible voted for it – even though it sharply criticised the position of the party leadership. It topped the ballot and therefore knocked out the planned economy debate. The supporters of the 'rebel' economy motion were furious, and tried to move a motion to suspend standing orders, in order to put the economy debate back on. However, the motion to suspend standing orders required a two-thirds majority, and the rebels did not win by the necessary margin.

We had seen off a very big threat to the coalition and to Nick Clegg. If the economy motion had been debated, there is no certainty it would have been defeated, and the implications of this could have been considerable.

Now that Nick had got his own team in line, he had to go into battle with the Conservatives.

And if Vince Cable wanted to borrow to invest, George Osborne was now planning to do precisely the opposite, and was in fact proposing to cut deeper in order to chase the borrowing targets, which were increasingly off-track.

Nick Clegg had his first meetings on the Budget with George Osborne in early February. Budget Day had already been fixed for Wednesday 20 March. The Deputy Prime Minister made clear that the top Liberal Democrat Budget priority was raising the tax-free personal allowance to £10,000 from April 2014 – a full year earlier than planned in the 2010 coalition talks. George Osborne said he was content to deliver this, and in return he was thinking of cutting employers' or employees' national insurance contributions. He would fund this from a windfall of revenue that he was now expecting because of the reform of pensions. The reform would end 'contracting out,' in which certain employees could pay a reduced rate of national insurance contributions to reflect their reduced entitlement to certain state pension benefits. Overall, this seemed a logical strategy to me, in part to compensate those whose national insurance contributions would otherwise rise. I had, indeed, suggested the idea to George Osborne around a year before.

At the early stages of planning, the strategy had seemed to be for a generally cautious Budget, with a few measures to support growth and offset the squeeze on household budgets. The Chancellor also wanted to cut corporation tax to 20 per cent – the lowest rate in the developed world – and cancel fuel duty rises. Neither of these changes gave our side of the coalition problems, provided they could be paid for.

But at the end of February, there was a growing sense of alarm from the Conservative camp and in the Treasury over the grim state of the economy, and a desire to deliver a more 'crowd-pleasing' Budget. The Conservatives had by now lost the Eastleigh by-election, having been beaten into third place by the UK Independence Party.

At a Budget Quad on 5 March, George Osborne unexpectedly tabled a proposal to cut the basic rate of income tax from 20p to 19p – at an annual cost of some £4.5 billion. 'How on the earth are you going to pay for this?' asked Nick Clegg, rather relishing a change in the usual terms of debate.

The Chancellor explained that he could fund the income tax cut by bringing forward the abolition of the contracted-out rebate. This all seemed rather odd to me – bringing forward a tax increase to fund a tax cut! In addition, Osborne revealed that he thought we would need to cut another £5 billion from departmental budgets to fund all that he planned to deliver in the Budget.

Nick Clegg said: 'Sorry, George. It's not on. I don't want to keep cutting services, and you cannot do this at such short notice without a real impact.'

On 6 March, there was yet another Quad on the Budget. This time, George Osborne pitched again for a 1p cut in the basic rate of tax. 'Look,' said Nick. 'I still don't know how you want to fund this.'

George Osborne sheepishly admitted that he was thinking of cutting the NHS Budget to fund the tax cut. Both Danny and Nick expressed their concerns about this.

David Cameron claimed that cutting the NHS budget would not be a problem. He said that at present the NHS budget was underspent and that the coalition could just 'bank' this £2 billion underspend and then 'protect' the NHS budget at this new, lower, level.

Nick Clegg said that he wasn't persuaded, and he pointed out rather bluntly that both parties had previously promised to protect the real NHS budget, and that what the Conservatives were proposing would look to everyone like a clear breach of that pledge.

Nick Clegg asked my advice on the Conservative proposal after the Quad. My view was clear and strong: 'It is the most idiotic and dangerous proposal I have heard since the coalition was formed. Cutting NHS spending is not just going to be very unpopular and look like a clear breach of a coalition pledge, but by the end of the parliament we are going to need that money in the NHS. The NHS budget settlement is far from generous, when you look at the spending pressures.' 'I agree,' said Nick. 'I'm definitely going to veto it then.'

On Sunday 10 March, I was at the Liberal Democrat spring conference in Brighton. Before Nick Clegg's speech, I met up with Danny Alexander to get the latest position on the Budget.

Danny said to me: 'Can we talk somewhere private?' We found a quiet room. Danny said: 'Look, we have just got the figures from the Office for Budget Responsibility on the borrowing forecasts and the growth numbers. It's all much worse than we expected. And it's worse than the forecast we had just a week ago. Borrowing is barely projected to fall. Indeed, it now looks as if it could be higher next year than this year – a complete disaster. And we are no longer projected as meeting our key objective of having debt as a share of the economy falling by 2015/16. We may also miss the target in 2016/17.

'I have spoken to George, and he has decided to dump all his plans for unfunded tax cuts, such as the income tax cut, and I have made clear too that we will not accept the cuts to NHS spending. He wants to look at cutting public spending next year to keep borrowing falling, which may mean going back on promises to allow departments to carry forward underspends from this year to next year. It won't be popular.

'Worse still, the Tories are now saying that they want to make massive further cuts to public spending in order to continue to meet the falling debt target by 2016/17. There is beginning to be a sense of panic among some people in the Treasury, because we have gone on having to revise up borrowing, and revise down growth, in every single Budget and Autumn Statement since late 2010.'

I said: 'Big extra cuts would be crazy, given the current economic circumstances. It would be economic madness, and it would be politically suicidal. We should just move the debt target back one year, as we did last year.'

Danny said he agreed with me, but that things were looking so bad that we might need to consider further caps on public sector pay or even further big tax rises.

Meanwhile, Vince Cable was still threatening not to accept the further cuts to his Business budget, which were likely to be needed to meet existing plans.

'Make sure Vince can live with his settlement,' Nick told Danny Alexander. 'I am not having Vince given an excuse to walk out of the government, for the sake of a few hundred million pounds. Vince may no longer want to be a contributor to this government, but I am not giving him any alibis to leave.'

On Monday 11 March, the day Chris Huhne was sentenced for perverting the course of justice, there was another, crucial, Quad on the Budget. It was one of the most important meetings of the parliament.

George Osborne had managed to massage the spending and borrowing figures in order to project a microscopically small decline in borrowing of just £100 million between 2011/12 and 2012/13. But the key issue for the Quad was that George Osborne was now proposing that the government should make massive further cuts of £13 billion to public spending in 2016/17 in order to meet the second fiscal rule: debt falling as a share of GDP.

The Chancellor even brought along the Treasury's top civil servant, Nick Macpherson, to try to persuade Nick Clegg to agree to these further huge cuts – a highly unusual and perhaps unprecedented development in the history of the Quad.

Last year, I had suggested moving the debt target back by two years, but the Treasury had insisted on only a one-year change. Now we confronted the same issue again.

After the meeting, Nick Clegg gathered his advisers and told us what had happened.

He said that George Osborne had looked very concerned and had stated that missing the debt target for a second year in a row was going to be very damaging to the government's economic credibility.

The Chancellor then shocked Nick Clegg by suggesting new cuts of £13 billion in public spending in 2016/17 – the amount needed to meet the Treasury rule of debt falling as a share of GDP. George claimed that the 'Treasury view' was that these further cuts were needed. He then handed out a sheet of paper that summarised the key statistics.

But Nick Clegg wasn't budging. He told the Chancellor: 'George, this is insane. There is no way I am agreeing to axe another £13 billion or whatever your figure is. That would hammer both public services and the economy. I am not prepared to chase the borrowing targets like this.' The Deputy Prime Minister pointed out that what was being proposed was the complete opposite of the advice being given by the IMF and others. He warned that further big spending cuts could tip the economy over into a new recession: 'We need to stick with Plan A and not panic. We need to hold our nerve. We need to show flexibility and patience. I will absolutely not sign up to this.'

When Nick came back to his office he said: 'That was the toughest Quad yet and one of the most important. They put huge pressure on us, not least by wheeling in Nick Macpherson. But I'm not budging.'

Ten days later, on Wednesday 20 March, the Cabinet met at 8 a.m. to hear a briefing from George Osborne on his fourth Budget. Gone was the plan to cut the NHS budget and gone too was the plan to axe a massive £13 billion from public spending to chase the fiscal rules. Both had been successfully vetoed by Nick Clegg and Danny Alexander – two of their best decisions of the parliament.

Included instead was a £10,000 tax allowance by April 2014, a 1 per cent cut to corporation tax, and frozen fuel duty. Also included was a new allowance to slash employers' national insurance contributions for small businesses.

The overall economic numbers were pretty awful, but this was no surprise. And there were no unexpected sources of revenue in the shape of unpopular tax rises.

About ten members of the Cabinet indicated that they wanted to speak. Most congratulated the Chancellor. Philip Hammond put it rather well when he said that George Osborne should be applauded for 'finding a few old bones and cans of soup in the back of the kitchen cupboard and turning them into a rather impressive dish'.

Only Vince Cable sounded a critical note. He said that it was going to be very difficult to deliver departmental spending cuts in 2015/16, and he said that the Chancellor should be borrowing more to spend on capital investment. He warned of the economy getting stuck in a 'downward vortex', and suggested that 'Treasury orthodoxy is damaging us'. Sir George Young, the Chief Whip, frowned and shook his head as Vince Cable spoke.

Vince's was a lonely voice, and the effect of his intervention was somewhat blunted when he said at the end: 'Of course, I have these concerns but I will be as supportive as I can be in public.'

George Osborne delivered his Budget in the House of Commons in the early afternoon. Liberal Democrat MPs waved their order papers eagerly at the news that our £10,000 tax allowance – which David Cameron had claimed in 2010 was unaffordable – was now to be delivered.

Meanwhile, the Chancellor boasted of his consistency in the face of the economic headwinds: 'There are those who want to cut much more than we are planning to – and chase the debt target. I said in December that I thought with the current weak conditions across Europe that would be a mistake. We've got a plan to cut our structural deficit. And our country's credibility comes from delivering that plan and not altering it with every forecast.'

George Osborne did not point out that the architect of that consistent approach was actually Nick Clegg, who had vetoed George Osborne's own bid to 'chase the debt target'.

The Budget was relatively well received, but the key was what would now happen to the economy. Nobody could be sure. The IMF, Vince Cable and large parts of the City of London were forecasting continued anaemic growth. The Treasury was crossing its fingers for a recovery.

But, almost unnoticed, economic headwinds were now abating. Inflation had peaked at over 5 per cent, but it had now fallen back to around 2 per cent. And the severe crisis of confidence in the Eurozone economies was now also unwinding, after the European Central Bank's new President, Mario Draghi, had promised in July 2012 to do 'whatever it takes' to save the euro.

No one knew it yet, but out in the real economy beyond Westminster, consumers were starting to carefully spend again. Unemployment was falling. Construction activity and manufacturing were gradually picking up.

When the Budget was delivered at the end of March 2013, the economy had actually been growing again for three months. Recession was over. There was to be no triple dip. And the economy would grow again for every quarter until the end of the parliament. The economic and political tectonic plates were slowly moving, but no one yet knew it – certainly not those IMF inspectors, who were scheduled to make their inspection visit in just a few weeks' time.

TRICKSY BELLE OF
MARSHAM STREET

2011–14

To Nick Clegg, she was the 'Ice Queen'. Eric Pickles referred to her disparagingly as 'Tricksy Belle of Marsham Street'. Her relations with Michael Gove were, shall we say, distant. And the Liberal Democrat Justice Minister, Lord McNally, told me that she and Chris Grayling, the Justice Secretary, fought like 'two scorpions in a bottle'.

She was, and indeed still is, the Home Secretary, Theresa May.

May's relations with the Liberal Democrats were rather mixed. Danny Alexander and I had a sneaking admiration for her, as did Nick Clegg. And no one could argue that, on the whole, she wasn't on top of her job.

But she was not naturally a Secretary of State who liked to share the limelight with her junior ministers. Three Liberal Democrats served in the Home Office during the government. She was admired by Lynne Featherstone, she frustrated Jeremy Browne and she drove Norman Baker mad. On this last, it should be said that the feeling was mutual – when a Cabinet reshuffle placed Norman Baker in the Home Office in October 2013, the next day's Cabinet meeting started a most unusual five minutes late, because the Home Secretary was in the Prime Minister's office complaining about her new minister. 'How could you agree to Nick putting this man into my department? Norman Baker, for goodness sake!'

But it wasn't only Liberal Democrats she fell out with. If anything, her relations with Conservative colleagues were rather worse. She would frequently clash with George Osborne over immigration. She rarely got on anything but badly with Michael Gove. She and David Cameron seemed to view each other with mutual suspicion and reserve.

I first met Theresa May on the formation of the government in May 2010. As the new Chief Secretary, I was carrying out the first Spending Review to identify around £6 billion of cuts.

It was just days into the new government. I was sitting in my Treasury Office, overlooking St James's Park – me in one armchair and the Home Secretary in the other, with no officials present.

The truth, I fear, was that at this stage of the government neither of us knew much about the Home Office budget. My job was to know just that little bit more than my 'victim', and to be rather stubborn.

I was struck that Theresa May was the most senior Cabinet minister to come to see me, and she was the last to settle. She looked nervous, and glanced down frequently at her notes.

I felt that she was surprised to find herself as Home Secretary, and I was surprised to find her there too. In such a tough political post I did not, frankly, expect her to last more than a couple of years. I felt in those early days that perhaps she didn't expect great longevity either.

But she has proved herself a far more politically successful Home Secretary than anyone ever expected, and she has on the whole managed to avoid the public relations disasters that have ended the careers of some of her predecessors. Part of her success is surely that she has been very focused on her job, and she has not – usually – allowed herself to be distracted by other considerations.

Theresa May clearly stood apart from the 'inner circle' of the Conservative team. She was not 'one of the boys', and wasn't treated as such. Indeed, there was a distinct frostiness between the Home Secretary on the one hand and David Cameron, George Osborne, Michael Gove and their inner circle on the other, which I never once saw melt away. Some of the most robust clashes at the Cabinet were not between Liberal Democrats and Conservatives, but between Theresa May and George Osborne over her department's rigid attitude to economic immigration, and it was clear that there was no love lost between the two.

The Home Office, of course, turned out to be a key area of contention between the coalition parties.

But this was never universally the case. At the beginning of the government, there was a shared agenda of rolling back some of the Labour government's 'nanny state' proposals, such as identity cards.

And on some of the liberalising agenda, Theresa May proved to be a firm ally of Lib Dem minister Lynne Featherstone: she backed Lynne's bold move to extend marriage rights to same-sex couples and she also gave Lynne support in tackling female genital mutilation.

Theresa May could also be more pragmatic and measured on some of the extremism agenda than David Cameron and Michael Gove wanted to be, and there was often an unflashy but steely common sense about the measures she tried to push forward.

But in many other areas, the Home Office was a coalition battleground, and Theresa May ran her department as a Conservative fiefdom and not as a coalition-friendly space. So the Home Secretary would let Lynne Featherstone advance agreed agendas, but on the whole Lynne was kept out of the areas she was not directly responsible for. Jeremy Browne also found the Home Secretary difficult to get along with, and all the more so after working with the open, generous and cooperative William Hague.

More serious than the Home Secretary's autocratic running of her department were the points of difference on Home Office policy. The biggest divisions came on issues where civil liberties came into conflict with the measures the police and security services wanted to take to protect citizens from crime and particularly from the threat of terrorism.

Ken Clarke, a previous Conservative Home Secretary, had always tried to balance security and civil rights. 'Nick,' he once said, 'I advise you not to take too many briefings with MI5 and MI6. They always try to frighten you to death and get you to agree to something that soon looks like a police state. We have to get the balance right.'

But for the Home Office, Home Secretary and Prime Minister, there was now not much sense of any 'balance'.

With heightened risks of terrorist atrocities, the Home Office wanted to equip the security services with every possible power of surveillance.

Nick Clegg and senior Liberal Democrats could see the importance, too, of targeted surveillance. In the old days, someone who was a serious risk to the public could have their phone tapped and their mail intercepted. But these old routes of communication were dying away, to be replaced by texts, emails, social media and other methods.

The security services wanted everything and everyone to be under surveillance. They wanted the widest possible net, to allow them to increase their chances of preventing terrorist attacks and catching criminals.

But a liberal party was always going to want to balance privacy and security – not least in an environment where private, stored data might end up being leaked or inappropriately accessed. Nick Clegg questioned whether we really wanted to give the security services unlimited powers to collect and store personal data. And he also had to satisfy a party membership that cared deeply about civil liberties and was already upset about Liberal Democrats agreeing to so-called secret courts, where intelligence information that was crucial to a trial but which it was too dangerous to release in open court could be used without being properly open to scrutiny. Surely, it was said, the right of defence in a trial was a basic human right that could not be compromised?

In 2012, Theresa May and the Home Office pulled together a major piece of draft legislation called the Communications Data Bill. It was quickly nicknamed the 'Snooper's Charter'. Some of it seemed sensible and necessary to catch serious criminals. But it took a very 'big net' approach. Nick Clegg insisted on carefully scrutinising it before agreeing anything.

In April 2012, Nick Clegg met the Home Secretary to discuss the proposed Bill. It was a difficult meeting. 'You know, I've grown to rather like Theresa May,' Nick told me afterwards. 'She is a bit of an Ice Maiden, and has no small talk whatsoever – none. I have quite difficult meetings with her. Cameron once said, "She's exactly like that with me too!" She is instinctively secretive and very rigid, but you can be tough with her and she'll go away and think it all through again. But I had to tell her that the existing Bill wouldn't get through the Commons, let alone the Lords. There would be Conservatives like David Davis totally opposed to it, as well as our people. I've told her she has to go away and look at it all again.'

But in spite of the warning, the Home Office proposed very few changes to the Bill. By the end of 2012, Nick Clegg let it be known in the media that he would not therefore let the legislation go ahead in its existing form. The reaction from the Home Office was immediate and unpleasant: a briefing to various newspapers saying that 'Nick Clegg is the friend and protector of paedophiles and terrorists'. It was hardly calculated to win over the Deputy Prime Minister. The relationship between the Home Office and the Deputy Prime Minister's office became acrimonious, and David Cameron seemed unable to get his Home Secretary to be more flexible. Eventually, in mid-December, Nick Clegg and Theresa May got together for what turned out to be a stormy bilateral meeting. 'I think she was a bit shell-shocked by what I said,' admitted the Deputy Prime Minister. Afterwards, Nick Clegg received a more conciliatory letter from the Home Secretary.

Eventually, it was agreed to assemble a Joint Committee of Parliament to carefully consider the Bill and any necessary safeguards. But this was just a row postponed, not resolved.

By the following spring, matters had come to a head again. This time, Nick Clegg had decided that he could not justify supporting the Bill, however upset the Home Secretary was going to be. At a Quad dinner in early April, he warned David Cameron: 'If you think gay marriage has been bad for your party and your supporters then Comms Data is gay marriage on stilts for me.'

In mid-April, the Deputy Prime Minister spoke to David Cameron on the phone to say that he had carefully considered all the arguments and wasn't convinced that the Bill should proceed. 'It was classic Cameron,' Nick Clegg told me later. 'Petulant. He got quite narky. At the end he said that Theresa May was threatening to bring in the head of MI5 to the Cabinet to speak in favour of the Bill. I just told him that wasn't acceptable.'

A day later, Nick Clegg sent out a letter to Theresa May, making clear that he would not authorise the Communications Data Bill to proceed. Relations were now so bad that the two of them sat next to each other in three hours of meetings and didn't exchange a single word.

Eventually, the Prime Minister and Deputy Prime Minister met to 'thrash things out'.

'I'm expecting a real gunfight at the OK Corral,' said Nick Clegg before the meeting. But, face to face, the two leaders talked the whole issue through more calmly.

Cameron explained that he was unhappy, but understood his coalition partner's concerns. But he then said that he wanted something 'in return' for dropping the Bill: tough new 'anti-union' legislation. 'I need some red meat for my backbenchers, given how awful the local election results are going to be.'

Nick Clegg wasn't keen. But he decided to play for time: 'I'll get David

Laws to look at it.' I did look at it; a frosty meeting with Francis Maude followed. I made clear that we didn't accept that there was a strong case for change, and I took the proposals no further. I felt no great obligation to sign up to divisive policies, not least as Francis Maude had been part of the Conservative team that had consistently blocked all reform of party political funding.

A year or so later, in June 2014, when a ruling by the European Court of Justice did threaten to stop the security services from tracking potential terrorists, both sides of the coalition came together constructively to pass emergency legislation. This helped prevent a serious risk to UK security, and involved some excellent work led by the calm, thoughtful and forensic Tim Colbourne, Nick Clegg's deputy chief of staff.

Striking the right balance between the privacy of the individual and the legitimate need for the security services to stop evil people committing appalling crimes will remain a difficult challenge for governments across the free world.

Eventually, we saw that even the Home Office had some limits beyond which they would not go in pursuing a rigid 'law and order' agenda. In January 2014, it was discovered that a Bill that tried to tackle 'anti-social behaviour' was drawn so widely that its provisions were considered likely to end up covering the activities of carol singers, who faced the prospect of being rushed into police custody halfway through their renditions of 'Silent Night'. This proved too much even for Theresa May, and the Bill was quietly amended.

SPENDING CUTS
AND DR CABLE

2013

It was late January 2013 and still very cold. Someone had had the wonderful idea of relocating that week's Cabinet meeting to Leeds City Museum, in order to highlight the government's support for the High-Speed Rail 2 project to the north.

I arrived at King's Cross Station in the early morning, from where the entire Cabinet was due to travel up to Leeds on the same train. I couldn't see where our train was due to leave from, but eventually a helpful assistant guided us to 'Platform Zero', and we were shown to the carriage – standard class of course – that was reserved for Cabinet ministers and the senior civil servants travelling with us.

It was rather like going on a school sports trip, and with no pre-assigned seats you could choose where you sat. Little 'gangs' of like-minded ministers sat together in small groups, while some ministers preferred their own company. The Prime Minister's closest allies and those who wanted to ingratiate themselves sat together, and of course there was always one boy who arrived late, threatening to keep everyone else waiting – on this occasion it was Michael Gove.

I sat in a compartment of eight seats, along with Oliver Letwin, Danny Alexander and the Transport Secretary Patrick McLoughlin. 'I hope the cost of this is all worth it,' one of us said, grumpily. 'Oh,' said Oliver Letwin cheerily, 'it is very good value for money. My return ticket cost only £39.50.'

'Well, mine is £155 return,' I said. 'Yes,' said Patrick McLoughlin, 'for some reason I paid a bit more too – £160.' Danny Alexander's ears pricked up. 'I hope the Transport Department isn't wasting money, Patrick? I might need to look at that in the Spending Review.'

'What did the cost-conscious Treasury pay then?' I asked. Danny fished around for a while in his pocket, eventually producing a ticket. 'Ah,' he said. 'A bit embarrassing, actually. Mine is £260!'

I'm not sure that having the Cabinet meet in Leeds was very productive. Patrick McLoughlin had to make an afternoon statement in the House of Commons, so he was only able to attend for twenty minutes and then had to go back to London.

Nick Clegg, though, had managed to secure a slot to discuss starting the next Tour de France in Yorkshire – a useful boost to the local economy, which the Deputy Prime Minister eventually delivered, in the face of Treasury obstructionism.

The room in the Leeds City Museum assigned for our meeting was so cavernous that the sound of people's voices just disappeared off into space. All I could hear for much of the Cabinet was the Northern Ireland Secretary, Theresa Villiers, sitting next to me muttering: 'I can't hear a thing he's saying!'

One benefit of hours stuck together on a train, however, was the chance for Cabinet ministers to talk. Danny Alexander, in particular, seemed to spend much of the time meeting Conservative ministers to discuss their budget settlements in the upcoming Spending Review, which would fix government spending for 2015/16.

It was quite a sight to see, one by one, the hard men of the Tory right trooping down the carriage, sitting down next to Danny and making their case for a bit more money here, or a little more flexibility there. A few years ago I would never have imagined I would see a Liberal Democrat Chief Secretary to the Treasury taking such responsibility, wielding such power, and doing so with such effectiveness.

Snippets of the conversation drifted over the seats towards me: 'Yes, Philip, I do understand the pressures on the navy, but I am definitely not going to accept that. We've got to bring it in on budget. And I'm not convinced that your officials are really being open with you about those procurement savings I mentioned ... Look, Eric, I want to be helpful on this. It's a priority for me and for George, but not if it's going to break the overall spending totals. And I'm not convinced you've squeezed out all the efficiency savings yet. You need to go back and look at this again.'

I sat just in earshot of Danny, reading my own papers, but with one ear to the conversations going on. I was rather proud of Danny, my successor as Chief Secretary. When he had taken over from me in May 2010, many people in the media doubted that this young and relatively inexperienced man could cut it as Chief Secretary, but Danny had undoubtedly grown into the role. 'His appetite for work and his grasp of the detail is awe-inspiring,' Nick Clegg had said privately to me.

Of course, Danny could also be frustrating for many Liberal Democrats. He was the 'money man' and the person who often had to say 'no' to more public spending. There were also times when people, including Nick, felt that he might have gone a bit native at the Treasury.

I had made the case to Nick in May 2010 for us to take on the Chief Secretary job because I felt that we needed someone in the Treasury to represent the Lib Dem case at the heart of government – not just because deficit reduction was important in itself. In any case, the Treasury civil servants must have been delighted by the seriousness and effectiveness with which Danny did his job. They will also have been delighted that two of the four Quad members were from the Treasury.

In the first couple of years of the parliament, Danny's role in the Treasury could create both upsides and downsides. Having someone to bat for the Lib Dems on issues such as the pupil premium and pensions reform was vital. But there were tensions over the 2012 Budget, and Danny could at times be a tough and unbending presence, even in private meetings with Nick, me and Nick's closest advisers.

By 2013, Danny had been in position for two and a half years. He was on his way to being one of the most effective and long-serving holders of the post of Chief Secretary. He was confident about his position now, and familiar with his job. And in many ways, the 2013 Spending Review showed the Liberal Democrat Chief Secretary at his most confident and effective.

By the time Budget 2013 was over, the Treasury had a good idea of the spending cuts it needed to impose on departments to meet overall public spending plans in 2015/16 – the last year of the parliament, and the last year for which the coalition would set out detailed plans.

The Treasury sent out its cuts targets to departments in April, and the outcome of the Spending Review was expected in late June. It was clear from the beginning that in some departments the difficulty in securing agreement would be greater than in others.

One particular flashpoint, as ever, was the unprotected Business Department. In opposition, Vince Cable had proposed closing down the Business Department in its entirety. But in government, he proved to be a strong champion of his department's interests. And for Nick Clegg and Danny Alexander, dealing with Vince in the spending round was intimately connected with dealing with him over the wider issue of the government's economic strategy, of which he was still very critical.

In late April, after the Budget, the crucial first-quarter GDP numbers showed that the UK had avoided a triple-dip recession, with modest growth of 0.3 per cent. This was a huge relief to the government and was to prove an economic turning point. But at this time it was still too early to conclude that we were out of the woods.

Nick Clegg now discussed both the economy and the Spending Review with Vince Cable. The next day he reported his frustrations to his advisers: 'Oh God. I had a classic blast of Vince yesterday. He's still unhappy about the economic strategy. He thinks growth will remain very weak. He wants to borrow more for investment, and he's saying he just won't make the cuts to his budget that the Treasury wants.'

At a Quad dinner in the same month, David Cameron and George Osborne also raised their concerns about the Business Secretary. George Osborne suggested that Vince's recent critical article in the *New Statesman* strongly hinted that he was preparing to resign from the government.

David Cameron was blunter. He told Nick Clegg that in his view Vince's real ambition was to be Chancellor of the Exchequer in a Lib–Lab coalition; he once more suggested that the Liberal Democrat leader should sack his senior colleague and he pointed out that in his view if the Business Secretary went on criticising the coalition's economic strategy, the Liberal Democrats would get no credit for the recovery when it was finally confirmed.

But Nick was insistent – he wasn't going to sack Vince Cable and cause division in the party. He made clear that he wanted to keep Vince Cable on board. And he pointed out that the economic issues the Business Secretary was raising were serious ones – however frustrating it could be that these were expressed publicly. The Liberal Democrat leader did, however, wonder out loud if Vince himself would want to stay in his existing role for the whole parliament.

David Cameron's ears pricked up, and he smiled broadly. If the Deputy Prime Minister ever wanted to move Vince Cable to another job, the Prime Minister would be up for it. Nick Clegg did not rise to the bait.

David Cameron and George Osborne were not the only politicians arguing that Vince should be moved. In the Liberal Democrats, Paddy Ashdown was making the same case to Nick: 'He is a problem for us. We just cannot have public confusion over what our economic message is as a party. This needs to be resolved soon, or it is a real risk both to party unity and to your position, Nick. Just let me know if you want to do this – remember that I am a trained assassin!'

But Nick was clear in his own mind that he would not dismiss Vince. He was determined to avoid civil war in the party. His main worry was that Vince might suddenly and unexpectedly resign. That would be very damaging. The Liberal Democrat leader was clear that if Vince did resign it would be better if this was over the narrow issue of his department's budget, rather than over the government's entire economic strategy.

In any case, Nick believed that the key moment could come at the 2013 Liberal Democrat autumn party conference. 'If we agree our economic strategy there,' he told Danny Alexander and me, 'we are fine and I have passed the moment of maximum risk to my leadership. But if the economy goes wrong again, or if I lose on the economic strategy in the autumn, I may be out and Vince would be in by acclamation.'

Vince Cable wasn't the only minister who was concerned about the Spending Review. A triumvirate of senior Cabinet ministers were dubbed the NUM – the National Union of Ministers – by some newspapers. These were Philip Hammond at Defence, Vince Cable at Business and Theresa May at the Home Office. All were willing to be very awkward in order to protect their departments.

A complicating factor was that George Osborne and some of the more right-wing members of the Cabinet were keen to re-open the issue of welfare savings. They wanted to position the Conservative Party as the party more able to protect defence and the police because of its willingness to cut more out of the welfare budget.

George Osborne raised the issue of welfare cuts with Nick Clegg again in late May, but Nick was fairly dismissive. However, on Sunday 26 May I was working through my red box when I came across a letter from the Work and Pensions Secretary, Iain Duncan Smith, to the Leader of the House of Commons. The letter asked for a Welfare Reform Bill to be part of the government's final year of legislation.

With some amazement, I read of the contents of proposed Bill, none of which had any cross-government clearance. This was clearly the Conservatives trying a fast one, with a wide range of proposals including removing housing benefit support for young people and capping child benefit to the first two children. Nick Clegg was furious when I warned him of it: 'Ridiculous behaviour by IDS,' he said. 'I had a bilateral with him last week and he didn't even raise this.' We quickly went back through the Treasury and firmly quashed the proposals.

The Spending Review also caused some stresses and strains within the Department for Education, in spite of the fact that a large part of our budget was protected.

Michael Gove was never at his most comfortable in dealing with the Treasury or with spending issues.

In late April, the department received its letter from the Treasury with its savings target for the spending round. This amounted to a target of cutting around £2.5 billion off our total spending on all programmes.

I was surprised that the figure was so large, although of course the Treasury never expects to settle for its opening request. There now needed to be a process of negotiation.

I could not see how we could save more than about £1.5 billion without undermining the real protection of the schools budget – which I was not prepared to contemplate – or else either cutting back on our early years investment or risking the financial stability of the colleges sector.

I spoke to Danny Alexander along these lines, and felt that he was both sympathetic and pragmatic.

On the Conservative side of the Department for Education, the story was less clear cut. Michael Gove started off by saying that we were one of the most successful departments and that we should resist agreeing to any large-scale cuts. Then he started talking about removing the real protection of the schools budget, which I was not prepared to agree. It was difficult to tell if this was a negotiating tactic with the Treasury or whether Michael really felt that cutting the schools budget a bit might be better than the alternatives. The problem was that we really didn't sit down and agree a joint negotiating position.

In late May, I decided to have a detailed session with departmental officials to see if we could identify the savings we needed to get to settle with the Treasury without axing any key priorities. At the last minute, Michael Gove said he wanted to join the meeting, but only as an observer. 'I promise', he said, 'that I will literally say nothing.' This seemed a bit odd.

We relocated the meeting from my modestly sized office to Michael's rather large room. There were about eighteen or twenty officials in the room, covering all the policy areas. Michael sat in the centre of the table, with me on his right. I then took the officials line by line through every aspect of departmental spending, probing for cuts.

Michael was true to his word. He said nothing. But on occasions, he couldn't help letting his views be known. When I came to discuss whether we could make big savings to the school transport budget, Michael nudged me, and without saying anything, he put his hands together into a 'praying' posture. I had no idea what he meant, and he signalled that his lips were 'zipped'. I looked around desperately at the officials for help. 'I think the Secretary of State is saying, Minister, that we need to be mindful of the impact on church schools.'

When I suggested we might trim back on funding for the new 'sports premium', Michael nudged me again, shook his head, and pointed up into the sky.

'Is it something to do with God, again?' I asked. He shook his head.

Someone eventually guessed that the Education Secretary meant that the Prime Minister wouldn't tolerate cuts to his pet scheme to fund more sports advisers. Michael smiled and put his thumbs up. It was a useful if rather odd session.

When the meeting was over, Michael said to me rather worryingly that he had had a recent conversation with the Prime Minister, who was suggesting freezing the schools budget in cash terms. This would move away completely from our coalition pledges to protect the real schools budget and ensure that the pupil premium was genuinely extra money. It was precisely what the Conservatives had suggested in May 2010, and what the Liberal Democrats had then rejected. 'There is no way that Nick Clegg or I can agree that,' I said. 'Yes,' said Michael Gove thoughtfully. 'But it does save £650 million and the Prime Minister and George may get very tough about it.' 'Fine,' I said. 'But it's something that our party won't accept.'

As the Spending Review discussions rolled forward, we were still a long way from agreeing either with the Treasury or within the DfE. We had originally offered the Treasury savings of just £1.25 billion, just half the £2.5 billion they had requested. The offer was instantly rejected.

I considered that we could probably settle with Danny at around the £1.7 billion level, but finding the extra savings stretched the relationship between Michael and me almost to breaking point.

Michael was particularly targeting big savings from the money given to local authorities for running education services. There is no constructive question in education which for Michael Gove leads to the answer 'local authorities', and he wanted as much saved from this £1 billion Education Services Grant (ESG) budget as possible. Michael also wanted to go on subsidising many academy schools by giving them far more money for these 'education overheads' than local authorities and local authority schools would receive.

My view was that we could make savings on the ESG budget, but these had to be deliverable and should not undermine important school and local authority functions. And if we had to make cuts affecting local authority schools I also thought we should make savings in the same areas for academies, particularly where these were already excessively funded compared with other schools.

We might have found an agreement, were it not for Michael's odd manner of negotiating. Most people negotiate by starting apart, and then moving their offers closer together. Michael had an original and alternative way of negotiating, which I had never encountered before.

He started by asking for 20 per cent savings on the ESG. I offered 10 per cent – quite a large amount. He then said he really needed 25 per cent. This seemed odd. But after much agonising and debate, and in order to get an agreement, I said I could go to 14 per cent, but no further. The next draft letter from Michael to the Treasury, which I was shown to approve, proposed a mammoth cut of 55 per cent of the entire budget! 'Is there a decimal point missing?' I asked my private secretary. 'Should it say

5.5 per cent?' She looked rather embarrassed. 'No. I've checked. The Secretary of State wants to propose a 55 per cent cut.'

'In that case I'm not discussing this any further, and my existing 14 per cent offer is off the table. This is bloody ridiculous. I cannot negotiate like this,' I said.

We were supposed to draft a letter to the Treasury that we could both agree with, but this looked impossible. In mid-June, the Conservatives drafted a letter that proposed cutting the schools budget in real terms. I refused to agree it. Then I was sent a draft letter suggesting bigger cuts in welfare instead. I wouldn't agree that. The Secretary of State then proposed cutting back on Nick Clegg's flagship scheme to extend early years education to disadvantaged two-year-olds. I said I wouldn't agree that either. Then I received a draft letter proposing a whole series of painful cuts that I was only willing to contemplate if absolutely necessary and if we both agreed to them, but the letter presented them all as my suggestions – clearly a letter that would be deeply unhelpful if leaked. I was by now very angry, and made clear that I was therefore inclined just to send my own letter to the Treasury. This would be the most chaotic and risky position for the department, as the Treasury would then be presented with two different letters and two different sets of cuts to choose from. It might mean total education cuts being even larger, as the Treasury took proposals from both lists.

Eventually it was clear that we were at a stalemate. The Treasury was also fed up with waiting for our proposal. On the morning of Monday 17 June, Michael Gove and I were both called over to the Treasury to meet with the Chancellor and Chief Secretary.

George Osborne looked a bit tired and was clearly somewhat irritated at the divisions between me and Michael. 'Look,' he said. 'Where are we on the DfE Budget? I'm keen to settle on this soon, and if you don't agree a figure with us quickly it will only be you and Vince Cable left who haven't agreed – and that's not a place you want to be.'

George asked us both what our priorities were. Michael said protecting the academies budget, and then he mentioned schools protection. I said schools protection, and the early years.

'Can't we cut the two-year-old funding back?' the Chancellor asked.

'No,' I replied. 'Nick's 100 per cent opposed to that. I cannot agree any cuts in that area. If you want to raise it with him, you'll need to do so in the

Quad.' George sighed, but then said: 'Let's try to sort this out. If you can find £2 billion of savings, I will settle for that, and not require £2.5 billion.'

'OK,' I said. 'But I've got to be blunt. Based on our conversations over the last few weeks, Michael and I are never going to agree another £750 million savings on top of what we have already offered. But if you exclude the early years money from cuts, we might be able to get to £1.7 billion.'

Other Chancellors might have been angry or impatient by now. But George Osborne is a political realist and a highly pragmatic and transactional politician. 'OK,' he sighed again. 'I can agree to that. But you and Michael have now got to get together constructively and find the savings.'

That concession from George Osborne was crucial, and it reduced the savings total that we needed to a deliverable figure. After we returned to the DfE, we had one more major meeting to try to agree a savings package that both Michael and I could accept. Michael made one more attempt to cut the grant to local authorities by a bigger amount – 31 per cent, instead of his previous, massive, bid of 55 per cent. I made clear that I wouldn't go a penny above cuts of 20 per cent, and only if the academies budget also made equivalent savings. By the end of Tuesday 18 June we had finally agreed a common position and could settle with the Treasury.

By each furiously guarding our own bottom-line positions, we had secured a good final settlement for the department – including continued real protection of the schools budget. But it had been hard work, and had put some pressure on our working relationship. Indeed, I was left thinking that if Michael had been on the Conservative negotiating team in 2010, we would probably never have formed the coalition government – he is a very, very difficult negotiator who fights for every inch of territory. George Osborne is a shrewd pragmatist who understands his own bottom-line position and that of the 'other side', and quickly cuts to the chase.

There was only one further loose end to be tied up on the Spending Review, as far as the Department for Education was concerned. The Treasury wanted to publish a document explaining how all areas of the public sector were making efficiency savings. They wanted a figure to use for the schools system as well. A number of DfE civil servants came to see me about this, having prepared a long and rather inconclusive paper. The difficulty is that as schools were autonomous units, the department had no idea what efficiency savings they were making and had no basis to make any calculations. But officials still pressed me for a number to include.

'What sort of number do you want, though?' I asked in desperation.

'Minister, you can put in any number that you want,' I was told.

'But we've no real basis to pick a number out of the air, have we?' I replied. Eventually, exasperated, I jokingly said, 'How about £87.2 million, then?' Disturbingly, the civil servants started writing the number down. One of them said, 'Yes, we can put in a number like that.'

'But that wouldn't be the truth, would it?' I replied.

'Minister,' was the reply, 'it *would* be the truth. It just wouldn't be the *whole* truth.'

I was more successful in securing a very small saving in Education Department administration costs, but only after I managed to overcome spirited resistance. I had told my private secretary to stop people wasting money on replacing the potted plants in my ministerial office. This caused a mini-revolution. 'I'm sorry, but there is no way we can take away the current, dead, potted plant, without replacing it,' my private secretary was told. 'You see, it's here – on the floor plan. There has to be a potted plant, and we don't have the power to alter the departmental floor plan.' I considered that I did. The dead plant was not replaced.

I was less successful in delivering small efficiency savings in the Cabinet Office, however, where every week a man arrived early in the morning to wind up the clock on my mantelpiece.

Across government, other departments were also settling their cuts with the Treasury – with less noise and argument than had been feared.

Only one department was still causing the Treasury and Nick Clegg real concern: the Business Department and its leader Vince Cable.

In early June, Vince Cable let it be known privately that he would resign if he didn't get a satisfactory settlement on the Business Department budget. On 11 June he had a blunt conversation with Danny Alexander in which he warned: 'If you try to cut my budget too far, I might just walk out of the coalition and I would have a ready-made career for myself as a back-bench critic of the government's whole economic strategy. I have publishers approaching me who would love me to write a book criticising the whole economic policy of the government.'

Nick Clegg and Vince Cable eventually sat down for a private bilateral on the issue. The Liberal Democrat leader was annoyed, as he felt Vince was using his misgivings over wider economic policy to secure a good deal on his departmental budget.

Vince replied that he did consider that the 'deal' with the Treasury was that he had to accept economic policies that he didn't like, but in return the Treasury ensured his budget was looked after.

The tensions over Vince Cable and the Business budget continued for the next two weeks. By the weekend of 22 June, there were even rumours that he might deliver on his threat to resign.

On Saturday 22 June, George Osborne phoned Nick Clegg to try to pin down the final parts of the Spending Review. He said that he was fed up with the Business Secretary making his concerns known through the media: 'The Prime Minister and I have now drawn a line with Vince. We have gone as far as we can to accommodate him. We are not making any further concessions.'

On our regular Saturday evening conference call with Nick, one of his economic advisers reported concerns that Vince Cable was 'right on the edge'.

My suspicion was that Vince was bluffing and that he would settle pretty soon. But nothing was certain, and on Saturday evening it proved impossible to get hold of Vince to fix up a call with Nick.

Finally, a call was fixed for Sunday morning. Nick came out of a Mass with his family to talk to Vince.

'I'm happy with my settlement now,' said the Business Secretary, to Nick Clegg's huge relief.

There was now only one final issue to clear up. George Osborne was pushing for yet another package of welfare cuts. A carefully negotiated package was agreed over the weekend of 22 and 23 June, with direct conversations between Nick Clegg and George Osborne. Nick also insisted on agreeing all the communications for the welfare savings. On a conference call he told us: 'I have said to Osborne that if there are any headlines about "beating up scroungers" then the whole agreement is off. I don't want this coming across as vindictive.'

By Monday, the Spending Review was complete – all agreed, and no resignations. Nick Clegg was pleased, and relieved, that it was all over: 'Danny and George have done great work over the Spending Review – and I have told them both so. Danny in particular has been at his very best – tough,

The Liberal Democrat coalition negotiating team of (*left to right*) Chris Huhne MP, Andrew Stunell MP, Danny Alexander MP, Lord Wallace and David Laws MP arrive at the Cabinet Office in Whitehall, May 2010. © GETTY IMAGES

The full coalition Cabinet, in the 10 Downing Street garden, after its first meeting, May 2010.
© GETTY IMAGES

The *Sun*'s cartoonist sums up the state of the public finances facing the incoming Treasury team of George Osborne and David Laws, May 2010. © ANDY DAVEY/*THE SUN*

The outgoing Labour Treasury minister, Liam Byrne, left David Laws a letter joking, 'I am afraid there is no money.' The public did not see the joke, and the letter became a potent political symbol that was used extensively by David Cameron in the 2015 general election campaign. © PRESS ASSOCIATION

ABOVE Chancellor George Osborne and Chief Secretary David Laws in the Treasury courtyard in May 2010, unveiling the first £6 billion of spending cuts, at a press conference. The Liberal Democrats insisted on adding schools to the other budgets that would be specially protected – the NHS and overseas aid.
© PRESS ASSOCIATION

LEFT Universities minister David Willetts talking to David Laws in Downing Street, as the new Lord Chancellor and Justice Secretary, veteran Conservative MP Ken Clarke, leaves No. 10, May 2010. © PIQTURED

David Laws having breakfast at Mulberry School for Girls in London, on the day after his return to government as Minister of State for Schools and the Cabinet Office, September 2012.
© PRESS ASSOCIATION

A 'Coalicious moment': Education Secretary Michael Gove and Schools minister David Laws arrive together at No. 10 for the first Cabinet meeting following the September 2012 reshuffle.
© PRESS ASSOCIATION

The Laughing Cabinet: The Queen attends Cabinet for the first time in her reign, and manages to lighten the mood in her coalition team, December 2012. © GETTY IMAGES

David Laws (*far left*) worked closely and harmoniously with Conservative Cabinet Office minister Oliver Letwin (*second left*). © GETTY IMAGES

Harmony in the Education Department didn't last long – the Liberal Democrats and Conservatives soon clashed over issues such as qualified teachers, spending on free schools and free school meals, and even the independence of the Schools Inspectorate, Ofsted.

Nick Clegg and his wife, Miriam, visiting a school. The Liberal Democrat policy of free school meals for infant children caused coalition tensions but was a huge delivery success.

William Hague and David Laws face each other across the Cabinet table in late 2014, during talks on 'English votes for English laws'.
© GETTY IMAGES

ABOVE A final team photograph for Liberal Democrats MPs, in the House of Commons Chamber, in March 2015. After the general election, only eight Liberal Democrat MPs were re-elected. © JAMES GOURLEY

'The A-Team' – David Laws and his brilliant and dedicated Yeovil constituency office team of (*left to right*) Claire Margetts, Sue Weeks, Sarah Frapple and Sadye McLean, May 2015. © CHRIS WEEKS

LEFT Nick Clegg – the ecstasy and the agony. The first photograph is of Nick Clegg and his wife, Miriam, arriving to vote at their local polling station in Sheffield in May 2010, at the height of 'Cleggmania'. The second is of an anguished Nick and Miriam arriving at the election count in Sheffield in May 2015 – having already been informed of the scale of Liberal Democrat losses. © GETTY IMAGES

BELOW Nick Clegg with his advisers and political allies in France, June 2015. (*Left to right*) Tim Colbourne, Stephen Lotinga, Tim Snowball, Phil Reilly, Matthew Hanney, Myrddin Edwards, Zena Elmahrouki, James McGrory, Polly Mackenzie, Nick Clegg, Sean Kemp, Lena Pietsch, Danny Alexander, James Holt, David Laws. © JONNY OATES

hard-working, and stubborn as a mule. He has done a great job. The coalition seems to rise extremely well to the challenges of doing the really big things in government. It is often the little things that seem to trip us up.'

On Wednesday 26 June, the Cabinet met at 8.15 a.m. for a briefing from the Chancellor on the outcome of the Spending Review. It was all pretty much as expected. The NHS, schools and overseas aid protected. A modest welfare package to titillate the Tory right, and cuts of between 5 per cent and 10 per cent to unprotected budgets. Somewhat bizarrely, George Osborne also revealed that he would announce a small allocation of money to improve facilities for people visiting the site of the Battle of Waterloo, to coincide with the 200th anniversary of the battle in 2015.

There was a brief, and positive, discussion of the Spending Review, which finished with an intervention from Michael Gove: 'May I say how delighted I am with the extra money to improve the site of the Battle of Waterloo? It is very important that we should take time to celebrate the victory of a strong and purposeful coalition in the face of attempts to restore a bankrupt former regime!' The Cabinet roared with laughter, and George Osborne quickly scribbled down the joke for use later in the House of Commons.

EDUCATION WARS

2013–14

I t was June 2014. It was a rare occasion, the only one of the parliament, when I was obliged to attend one of the meetings of the COBRA emergency committee, which meets in the Cabinet Office to consider serious national security issues – in a room designated as Cabinet Office Briefing Room A, giving the committee its name. On this occasion, Nick Clegg was not able to be present for what turned out to be an important discussion on a potential major new terrorist threat to the UK and other nations.

I took my place close to the top of the table, a couple of places along from where the Prime Minister was due to sit. Already gathered were the heads of the Secret Intelligence Services, along with senior military, police and civil service representatives. On the walls were clocks tracking the time in different parts of the globe. The whole scene looked as if it might have been lifted straight from a James Bond movie. Or is it, perhaps, supposed to be the other way round?

Two minutes before the meeting was due to start, George Osborne came in and sat down on my immediate left. Turning to me, he said, 'Ah, David! How are the Education Wars?'

Until that moment, I hadn't realised quite how prominent some of the disputes within the Department for Education over the last year had become. Now I recognised that there had been so many big rows in education, both publicly and in private, that what had once seemed likely to be the most

'Coalicious' of departments had now become arguably the most fractious. How had this occurred?

It would be wrong to see the period from June 2013 to July 2014 as one long set of rows and disputes in the Department for Education.

In fact, Michael Gove and I agreed on much, and we were delivering together a bold reform agenda.

I was in charge of work to reform the school accountability framework – a dull-sounding but vitally important area of policy. With support from Michael, we significantly raised the bar for how success should be measured at the end of primary school – so that in future, children would be properly prepared to succeed in their GCSEs. We also reformed secondary school accountability – moving away from the discredited 'five A*–C GCSE' measure, which had incentivised schools only to focus on getting their borderline D-grade students to achieve a C grade.

Instead, pupils would, in future, be strongly motivated to study eight GCSEs, and at least five of these had to be selected from the core academic subjects. A new 'Attainment 8' measure would assess average grades in the eight key GCSEs, while a new 'Progress 8' measure would measure school performance not simply by attainment – an easy bar to clear for schools in affluent areas – but by the progress made by pupils. This fairer accountability measure would also give head teachers more incentive to serve in schools with a challenging catchment area.

Michael Gove and I also both supported Ofsted – the Schools Inspectorate – in removing the 'satisfactory' grade from the school inspection system and replacing it with a 'requires improvement' category. This was designed to place more pressure on mediocre schools, so that it was not only the small proportion of totally inadequate schools and colleges that would feel the pressure to improve.

To reinforce the higher expectations for school attainment, to make sure we intervened as early as possible, and to close the dramatic performance gap between the outcomes of poor children and other pupils, I decided to significantly increase the pupil premium in primary schools, so that this reached the level of over £1,300 per child per year, a very large amount. And later in the parliament I ensured that the school pupil premium would be complemented by a new early years pupil premium. I worked closely with Sir Michael Wilshaw, the Chief Inspector of Schools, to ensure that while schools were free to spend the pupil premium as they wished, they would be fully held to account for doing so, and for narrowing the attainment gap.

I also kept a close eye on the delivery of what was known in government as the 'two-year-old offer' – the extension of fifteen hours' free early years education to the most disadvantaged 40 per cent of two-year-olds.

As well as the work on the pupil premium and on school accountability, I led the work to develop a national fair funding formula for schools – again, with the full support of Michael Gove. Michael also gave me strong backing for my work to redesign the system of school capital funding, and I spent considerable time checking that local authorities were preparing properly for a massive rise in pupil numbers.

Both Michael and I wanted to do more to encourage the strongest schools to work with weaker performers, and we both ensured that our senior officials, along with excellent advisers such as Tom Shinner and Chris Paterson, helped to develop proposals to get high-quality school leaders to parts of the country where there were large numbers of failing schools.

Meanwhile, Michael and his excellent, no-nonsense, new Parliamentary Under Secretary, Lord Nash, worked to press on with the academies and free schools programmes, designed to improve the quality of schools, particularly in poorer areas.

And Michael and Liz Truss pushed forward controversial proposals on A-levels and AS-levels, which I generally supported, not least because I was concerned that the last four years of school had become a cramming factory of endless national exams, retakes and mock preparation, which increasingly left precious little time for students to actually learn anything new.

But in a department that both coalition parties gave such strong priority to, there were plenty of areas of disagreement, too.

I remained concerned that Michael Gove was too fixated on increasing academy numbers at the expense of improving the quality of school governance and leadership. With a limited number of high-quality academy providers, the department only really had a school improvement strategy (forced academisation) for the very worst schools. Both David Cameron and I were concerned about mediocre and coasting schools. There were simply not enough high-quality academy sponsors to tackle these thousands of extra schools.

So I wanted to put more pressure on local authorities to improve governance and leadership in their schools, and I wanted more pragmatic and practical measures to strengthen weaker schools – either through partnership with strong schools or by replacing weak leadership.

Michael Gove had rejected my proposal for a 'contestable middle tier' of local authorities and academy chains to hold all schools properly to account. Both the Chief Inspector, Sir Michael Wilshaw, and I wanted to hold local authorities and chains properly to account by inspecting them and challenging the worst ones to improve. Michael did not support this approach. He didn't believe in a middle tier and didn't think local authorities had much to contribute. In any case, while Ofsted already had the power to inspect local authorities, it did not have this power for academy chains. Nor would Michael give Ofsted this power. This was something the Secretary of State and I disagreed on.

There were other areas of disagreement, too.

Michael Gove said he believed in school autonomy, but when it came to curriculum matters, he could be very prescriptive. I largely left Michael to fight over the history curriculum with Nick Clegg. At the time, I had enough on my hands. But I did feel that on the English Literature curriculum Michael was going far too far in trying to dictate precisely which books each student would have to read. I was particularly struck when it turned out that the respectable combination of five books of literature that I had studied at school – Chaucer's *Canterbury Tales*, Shakespeare's *Othello*, F. Scott Fitzgerald's *The Great Gatsby*, some poems of Seamus Heaney, and Stoppard's *Professional Foul* – would now be disallowed from GCSE English Literature. This was because the list did not include a nineteenth-century English novel.

I sent my protest to Michael Gove's office, but received back a diplomatic but decisive put-down, via the Secretary of State's private secretary:

'I'm sorry if we haven't explained the Secretary of State's position properly, and the reason for his specificity,' the note began, ominously.

> The Secretary of State insists on this prescription because the nineteenth century represents the most important period for the novel as a cultural form. This was the century in which the novel became the dominant form of Western literature. A student of English literature who hasn't studied a nineteenth-century novel is like a student of maths who hasn't studied multiplication.

I decided to cut my losses.

I was a little more successful on the content of the English Language curriculum, where Michael Gove was not only seeking to replace a reference to 'standard English' with 'the Queen's English', but was also suggesting that fifteen-year-old students should learn about 'synecdoche' and 'pathetic fallacy'. One of our advisers quietly suggested that Michael Gove 'must be determined to serve up more material for the sketch writers'.

In the 2013 Spending Review, as I record above, Michael Gove and I had our most serious disagreements to date, as each of us battled to protect our own departmental priorities. Ultimately, the cost of our mutual stubbornness was borne by Her Majesty's Treasury.

The coalition cracks that proved harder to paper over were those between Michael Gove's team and Nick Clegg.

In late 2012, Michael Gove and Dom Cummings were battling to get coalition agreement for a controversial announcement on A-levels and AS-levels. Dom Cummings had originally tried to avoid this going through the Home Affairs Committee, on which I sat and which Nick Clegg chaired. When the Deputy Prime Minister insisted on this, it wasn't well received by those around Michael Gove.

Then, on Sunday 2 December, the *Mail on Sunday* – a favourite vehicle of Michael Gove's team – carried a story claiming that the Prime Minister and Deputy Prime Minister had intervened to protect a DfE grant for a Book Trust project. It was claimed that the DfE wanted the grant opened up to competition, but that this had been blocked, following a representation involving Nick Clegg's wife, Miriam, who was said to have raised the matter with her husband after being approached at an event. The story was wilfully misleading – the decision on the grant having come directly from 10 Downing Street – but on the day of the media coverage the DfE refused to put out any press release rebutting it. Nick Clegg's wife, Miriam, was deeply hurt. Nick was furious. The following week, there were further Sunday newspaper stories in prospect that related directly to Miriam.

On Friday 7 December, Nick was due to speak at a fundraising dinner at the home of Yeovil Town Football Club, in my constituency. Just before the dinner, an angry Miriam rang – at the end of her tether over more press mischief making. At the end of the call, Nick spoke briefly to me: 'Miriam is really questioning whether it's all worthwhile, when my job puts her and the children in the line of fire in this way.'

Nick could forgive briefing against him on policy differences. But he felt strongly that he could not allow his wife to become part of the political football game. The Book Trust incident might seem a small thing to most people. But it was something the Deputy Prime Minister could never forgive or forget. And he blamed it firmly on those close to the Education Secretary.

There was a more substantive policy row that soured relations between Michael Gove and Nick Clegg, too – on the seemingly obscure issue of childcare ratios.

In the September 2012 reshuffle, a young, new, female minister arrived at the Department for Education. She was given control of the childcare and early years portfolio. Her name was Liz Truss. She was a former Liberal Democrat activist, who had moved a motion proposing abolishing the British monarchy at the 1994 Liberal Democrat conference. Now she was a Conservative, and she was ambitious and keen to shake things up.

Liz Truss argued that English childcare ratios – the number of staff needed to take care of young children – were too restrictive. She thought that fewer adults were needed to care for children, and that changing the ratios could cut costs and free up money to improve quality. There was something in this argument, but perhaps rather less than Liz believed.

Liz was not, however, someone with great self-doubt. She had strong views and little time for dissent – there was something of the young Margaret Thatcher in her, I once told her, to her obvious pleasure. Civil servants found her tricky to work with, and on one or two occasions when they presented international evidence to help inform her policies, she asked them to set aside the evidence that did not fit her own vision.

Nick Clegg liked Liz, and wanted to help with her proposed reforms. But childcare and early years development was a big priority for him. And Liz's policy proposals infuriated large parts of the early years sector, which considered that the ratio change would endanger young children and reduce quality. It was a complex debate in which some of the proposed changes seemed sensible and some plain daft.

Nick's political advisers were reasonably sympathetic to Liz, but his civil service advisers were more sceptical. They proposed blocking the changes completely, or at least substantially amending them.

Eventually, Nick asked to see Liz in his rooms in the Cabinet Office to seek to resolve matters. Liz hoped for a green light, but she was held on amber.

'Liz,' said the DPM, 'some of this is fine, but some just goes much too far – particularly the change in ratios for really young children. I'd like you to look at these bits again, and come back to me with some new proposals.' It was time for Liz Truss to bend a little. But she wouldn't. In the face of the Deputy Prime Minister's resistance, the junior parliamentary under secretary – the lowest of all ministerial ranks – said nothing. Her head fell. She looked grimly down at the Deputy Prime Minister's long, wooden, polished desk. She then went away, spoke to the PM's office and Michael Gove's office, and sent out a cross-government letter to the Home Affairs Committee (chairman, N. Clegg) asking permission to proceed with her proposals without any amendment. And, on top of that, someone then leaked the row to the *Newsnight* programme that very night. Further political briefing around this was poisonous in the extreme: 'Clegg couldn't be trusted on tuition fees, and he cannot be trusted on this.'

Nick Clegg was very angry. He regarded the Conservative response as a 'nasty, personal attack on my integrity'. He let it be known that he would not be bullied into removing his policy block. Michael Gove, in turn, was also upset – six months of work by his minister seemed to be going up in smoke. A couple of days after the row blew up, on Sunday 12 May, Michael Gove appeared on the *Marr* programme and suggested that Nick was only blocking the childcare ratios as he was worried about a leadership challenge from Vince Cable, and was playing to the gallery of Liberal Democrat party members. It wasn't remotely accurate. But it was serious mischief making. As far as the Deputy Prime Minister was concerned, the childcare ratio proposals were now dead.

The relationship between Michael Gove and Nick Clegg never really recovered from the Book Trust leak and the ratios row.

But in the DfE, while there were robust disagreements, the relationships generally remained good. Lord Nash worked away seriously and with great professionalism on the free schools and academies programme. Edward Timpson kept his head down and got on with the hard work of improving life chances for children taken into care, and Matt Hancock worked intensively on post-16 education.

Michael Gove and I had our disagreements, but the DfE was still an enjoyable and challenging place in which to work.

And there was something fun about working with Michael that made it possible (mostly) to forget the rows.

In January 2013, a head teacher wrote to the Secretary of State suggesting an innovative way of saving her special needs teacher from school budget cuts. Could Mr Gove kindly lend her his supposedly rare breed of dog (she wrongly believed he was called 'Boris') to 'impregnate my bitch'. She had apparently calculated the resulting rare puppies would be enough to close the immediate funding hole in the school budget. It was the most imaginative proposal for protecting frontline services from cuts that I saw in government. And somehow it could only happen to Michael Gove.

And what could one make of a Secretary of State who in June 2013 sent out a long letter to Education Department staff, advising them on how to write good letters?

> Dear Pamela,
> Thank you for your letter of the 17th asking me, on behalf of your colleagues, how I should like letters to be drafted. Letters should be concise, precise and polite. Concision is itself a form of politeness. Ministers, and taxpayers, lead busy lives. Making points briefly saves everyone time. Of course, on occasion, some factual detail, such as the inadvisability of ending a sentence with a preposition or the folly of using 'impact' as a verb or even the ugliness of 'behaviours' as a usage when 'behaviour' covers a variety of human activity, might require a longer sentence…

The letter, which soon leaked, ended with 'Gove's Golden Rules' – ten rules for producing a good letter. Which other minister would spend time crafting such a work? Probably none. Certainly no one who could write with such elegance and with understated humour.

And at times you could only stand back and laugh at the Secretary of State's determined resistance to modern fads and old-fashioned special pleading. In April 2013, I was copied in on his feedback on the responses received by the department to our consultation on proposed changes to the national curriculum.

Against a section summarising consultees' requests for more money to implement changes, he had written: 'The story of vested interests throughout the ages.'

Against a paragraph on the English curriculum, reflecting a 'desire amongst some respondents for a reference to media and multimodal text to be included', he had written the word 'Rubbish', underlined four times.

Under Geography, a request for coverage of climate change was met with the single refrain 'Ignore'.

Under foreign languages, some poor soul had made the case for a 'multilingual "carousel" approach'. 'Absolutely not!', underlined five times, was the succinct response.

On maths, the main concern expressed by respondents was that the new curriculum might be too challenging. 'Hardly.'

On art and design, the ministerial feedback on the responses simply read 'Very depressing!'

More on animal welfare in the primary curriculum? 'No.'

With Michael Gove, you always knew where you were.

And so did everyone else. At Cabinet in September, the Education Secretary reported back on that year's national examination results: 'I am pleased to tell you all that entries to physics, maths and chemistry are up. But it is with great personal sadness that I have to report to Cabinet a 10 per cent decline in entries to … media studies.' Cue general hilarity.

But he could also be a generous and thoughtful boss.

On a beautiful summer's evening in early July 2013, the 'Coalition 2.0' group of MPs and advisers from both sides of the government met, as ever, at the offices of Marshall Wace, at the Adelphi Building, just north of the river Thames.

Paul Marshall, our thoughtful and generous host, who shared our commitment to extending educational opportunities to all children, had arranged a very enjoyable gathering. We sat outside eating, drinking and discussing politics on a warm evening, against the backdrop of beautiful views both up and down the historic river behind us.

I hadn't got any good books for reading on my summer holidays, I complained. Michael Gove suggested something on American politics. I was sceptical. But he sang the praises of a great biography of Lyndon Johnson by Robert Caro. I noted the title down on a piece of paper.

The next day, I arrived at the Department for Education to find a brand-new copy of the first volume of the Caro biography – *The Path to Power* – placed in the centre of my desk, with a card from Michael Gove, expressing his good wishes. It was a thoughtful gesture and it turned out to be an excellent choice.

But when we returned from the summer, it was to a stormier period of relations in the Department for Education.

The Milton Keynes Showdown

JUNE 2013

The Spending Review was finally out of the way, and on Thursday 27 June the Liberal Democrat parliamentary party had planned another of its joyous 'away days' at a hotel near London.

This time we were meeting in Milton Keynes at 1 p.m. I therefore left Westminster at 1.30.

By around 3 p.m., I had arrived at a rather bland hotel and conference centre just on the edge of town. In fairness, it wasn't quite as horrible as some of the places we had been to over the years, but it was soulless and dull.

After finding my room and making a few 'urgent' phone calls, I made my way – slowly – to the conference room in which all of the Liberal Democrat MPs were meeting. After a few minutes, I concluded that I had still managed to arrive a couple of hours too early. I tried to slip out of the back, but was intercepted by the Liberal Democrat Chief Whip, Alistair Carmichael. 'I'm glad you could make it David – eventually,' said Alistair. 'I'm going to need you back in the room for the next session, on the economy, because it's quite important.'

The economy session started with an update on the economic outlook from Chris Saunders, Nick Clegg's highly able and respected economic adviser. There was a lot about how indebted the country still was.

Nick then spoke, to give his own overview of the economic policy debate. I knew that he wanted to settle the party's position on this subject once and for all at our autumn party conference. He felt that we had only just avoided a divisive economic debate at the spring conference, on somebody else's motion. This time Nick wanted to put his own motion down, and he wanted to secure the support of the party and all the MPs – including Vince Cable.

A few days before the away day, Nick had spoken to Vince about the idea and asked him to consider either introducing or summing up the debate at conference. Vince seemed content with the substance of the motion, though he promised to look at the precise wording in more detail.

But after a second conversation about the plans, Vince's position changed. He argued that the motion wasn't strong enough on the need for the government to borrow more for investment spending, to create an economic boost. He asked to be able to put his case to the parliamentary party before conference.

So what was now happening in Milton Keynes over coffee and biscuits was that the two most senior Liberal Democrats were setting out two alternative economic strategies and asking for the backing of MPs.

Nick Clegg explained: 'I'm keen to try to settle our party's position on economic policy, and I intend to do this by putting down a policy motion and debating it at conference this September. I am particularly keen to do this because it seems to me that the economy is turning round, and if it is then I want us to get the credit for that, which we cannot do if some of us are seen to be questioning whether the strategy is right or not.

'Now, there is a very dry old Treasury view that we should just stick to the fiscal rules, be very orthodox and we shouldn't borrow more for investment. Then there is Vince's view, and I will ask Vince to say something himself in a moment, but basically this is that we should be more flexible on the fiscal rules and borrow more to invest. My view, which is what will go into the policy motion, is that we should stick with our fiscal rules, stick with Plan A, but look at how we can do more to support investment in housing and whether we can do more to give local authorities greater freedom to fund investment in areas such as housing and transport. I think this approach is right economically, but I also think it is right politically. Politics do matter. If we talk about borrowing more, that just sounds like Labour, and it undermines the political narrative of the government. And in any case, the truth is that we have been economically flexible as a coalition government, and Danny and I have ensured that when the economy has been slower than expected, instead of chasing the borrowing targets we have as a government just accepted that they will take longer to deliver. Anyway, I'm going to let Vince have his say too.'

Then Vince Cable stood up, looking a little nervous but also determined. 'Thanks, Nick,' he said. 'I do appreciate the chance to set out my views on this, and I would underline that there is a lot on the economy that I agree with Nick on, and I accept that Nick and Danny have been doing a good job to ensure that Osborne doesn't just chase after the fiscal targets when growth is so slow. But I don't accept the Tory narrative that all of the borrowing is due to Labour overspending, and we ought to acknowledge the worldwide recession too. I have to say bluntly that I think the government's fiscal plans are too tight and we ought to be able to borrow more to invest in productive capital investment. That's where I differ from both Danny and, I think, from Nick.'

Frankly, there was some economic sense in some of what Vince was saying. The Treasury could be highly orthodox and unimaginative. But if Vince's proposals had some economic merit, they made very little political sense. Why should we worry about defending Labour's economic record when they were now spending their time attacking us? And where was Vince's plan to boost investment spending in a way that would be remotely acceptable to David Cameron and George Osborne? Both Nick Clegg and Danny Alexander were talking about finding ways to stimulate investment, and some of them sounded a good deal closer to Vince's position than either side wanted to admit. Finally, the economy now finally appeared to be recovering. Wasn't this a time for Liberal Democrat unity?

After Vince had spoken, the debate was opened up to all the MPs present. Around half the parliamentary party spoke. MP after MP spoke in favour of Nick Clegg's position and against Vince Cable's. Some MPs attacked the economics of Vince's position. Many attacked the idea of moving off the coalition economic narrative to a position that sounded like Labour's narrative.

Nick had been told that Vince had been hosting dinners for backbench MPs to win them over, something that sounded quite unlike Vince. And if the dinners had taken place, they had not been a success.

Some of the interventions were quite brutal. Duncan Hames, the Chippenham MP, said: 'We all remember Clare Short and her time in government, with Blair. She opposed most of his policies, but instead of resigning she stayed in the government, throwing stones and being an opposition within. When she eventually resigned and left the government, she had no credibility left.'

I winced. This seemed to me to be far too close to the bone – indeed, it seemed like a provocation to resign.

By the end, of the MPs who spoke, virtually all had strongly supported Nick's position. Vince looked unhappy and uncomfortable.

Eventually, after the last contribution, Nick summed up the debate decisively in favour of his own position, which was hardly in doubt. There was a round of loud applause and table thumping, which Vince understandably did not join. The discussion finished at around 7 p.m., and people broke up for drinks before dinner.

I met up with Nick in the bar: 'Well,' he said. 'I am hugely relieved that it's all over. Now we have a clear position, which everyone needs to unite behind, and Vince cannot be in any doubt about the view of the parliamentary party. We now need to get Vince on side and get him to unite behind this position at the conference. But I am a bit worried that people were too tough and personal with him in there. And actually I meant to sum up in a more constructive and less partisan way. I need Vince on side, not feeling marginalised and disgruntled.'

The next day I was up at 5.15 a.m. to work on my red boxes. I stayed at the away day until about 11 a.m., and then decided to drive back to Yeovil. Paddy Ashdown asked for a lift home, so we set off in the car together.

On the way back down to Somerset, Paddy told me some hilarious stories about his time in the Secret Intelligence Service. Indeed, the stories were so funny that I wondered whether some might have been a little embellished. One involved three MI6-trained ducks, which were apparently drugged, and were then to be used to assist in befriending a female communist operative. The first duck is given too many drugs and dies. The second is eaten by a fox in the middle of its mission. The third does its job successfully. If half of Paddy's stories were true, then there is a great MI6 sitcom series waiting to be written.

Paddy had strong views about other issues. He wanted Vince moved from the Business Department, and felt that we were missing a great opportunity to improve our party's relationship with business. But there was advice for Nick Clegg too: 'Look, the economy is now turning up and I think the prospects for the party could turn up too. We need Nick to be more associated with the economic turnaround. But first we need to get the public to have a more positive image of Nick. Nick needs to look more confident and less defensive. Impressions count. I think it may be a good idea if he wears glasses, and looks a bit more statesmanlike. And he has to get his body language right too. I saw him recently on television and he was adopting what I call the "balls protection mode" – a strange pose with his hands across his groin. That's no good. You need openness. Confidence. Legs open, you know.'

'OK,' I said. 'I'll tell him about the economic policy stuff. Can I leave the half-mooned glasses and the balls protection stuff to you?'

'Absolutely!' said Paddy. He meant it, too.

At Chequers with the
Coalition Cabinet

July 2013

At a Quad dinner in early April 2013, David Cameron had signalled to Nick Clegg that he expected a hung parliament in 2015, and a second coalition between the Conservatives and the Liberal Democrats. The Prime Minister privately guessed that the general election might produce 290 Conservative MPs, 280 for Labour, and 40 Liberal Democrats. He commented that this meant a second coalition was still 'doable'.

With the economy now improving and the battles over political reform out of the way, the relations between the coalition partners were relatively stable in mid-2013.

As we passed the middle of July, thoughts at Westminster turned to the long summer recess, and suddenly for the first time in months the business of government became social as well as professional. I found that my diary included dinner with Nick Clegg on 10 July, another dinner with Michael Gove and his wife, Sarah, on 16 July, and then on 18 July the whole Cabinet was set to decamp to Chequers for an 'end of term' discussion and no doubt for some rare 'coalition bonding'.

I met Nick Clegg for dinner at Il Convivio restaurant, off Ebury Street, on Wednesday 10 July.

'I must tell you', Nick said over our starter, 'about a very odd conversation with Paddy Ashdown.'

'Oh yes?' I said, swigging some wine.

'Yes,' said Nick. 'He came over to see me at the weekend, and went through a lot of key campaign issues. Then he suddenly sounded very, very serious. He said, "I have something important and extremely difficult to say to you." To be honest, I thought it must be a party sex scandal or something. I was just bracing myself for really bad news when he said: "It's about your weight. I need to tell you that you are too fat at the moment. It's not good for your image. As chair of the general election campaign, it's my duty to tell you to exercise more and eat less. And another thing: have you considered wearing glasses? It could be very good for your image." Then he said something about how I needed to open my legs more when I am on television. I told Miriam and she couldn't stop laughing!'

'Extraordinary!' I said. Nick chuckled: 'I do love Paddy. He is the most loyal, most decent, most extraordinary person that I have ever known. He is also such a drama queen at times!'

'I'm not sure that "drama queen" is a description that he would recognise or appreciate,' I said.

Whatever his weight problems, Nick looked pretty relaxed that evening, as we discussed the political challenges of the year ahead: 'I fully intend to lead the party into the next general election now,' he said. 'I feel I've put the fees issue behind me, as much as we can ever do, and I am really enjoying the work I am doing in government. If we lose power at the next election, my assumption is that I will stand down as leader. If not, I would want to go on as leader. But the pressure of my job really falls on Miriam and the kids – and ultimately when I step down needs to be a lot about what is right for them and not just for me.

'If we lose power in 2015, I assume Tim Farron will probably be chosen as the new leader. If we stay in power, then I think we might need a new leader in 2018. I know Danny will want to stand, but he has a lot of work to do to win over the party after the tough stuff he has needed to do as Chief Secretary.'

We then moved on to consider the next government reshuffle, due in the autumn.

Nick started with Vince Cable: 'Vince has been quite frustrating over economic policy and strategy, though I do understand where he's coming from. I am still hoping that he will propose our motion on the economy at the autumn conference, which would ensure party unity. He seems willing to do that, following the away-day debate.'

We both agreed that Vince should probably stay as Business Secretary until the end of the parliament, and that it would certainly be very damaging to party unity if he resigned or was forced to return to the backbenches.

Nick then asked what I wanted to do. I said: 'Look, I absolutely love the role that you have given me in the Education Department and in the Cabinet Office. But one day I would like to return to the Treasury as Chief Secretary – that is unfinished business for me.'

Nick said: 'The way I see it in the Cabinet is as follows. Mike Moore is doing a good job at the Scottish Office, but I am tempted to move him out and give Alistair Carmichael a crack at it. We may need someone more combative than Mike now that the referendum is close. Danny would really like a move to Business, which he'd be brilliant at. But I just don't think I can move Vince. It's possible that I could move Danny to Climate Change, move Ed Davey into your role, and move you back to Chief Secretary at some point. I need to think about that. I also need to mull the timing – this September might be too soon. Cameron wants to do two more reshuffles – one in the autumn and one next July. We talked it over recently. I'm afraid it looks like Cameron is going to axe Ken Clarke altogether this time – he just thinks he's past his time in government.'

I asked what else Nick wanted to achieve from the upcoming reshuffle. He said that he had taken a decision to move Jeremy Browne out of the government – he thought he was 'not getting his hands dirty enough' at the Home Office. 'I'm inclined to move Norman Baker to the Home Office,' said Nick. 'Theresa May really needs marking more closely, and Norman is the man for the job.' I laughed. 'Yes,' said Nick, 'he will drive Theresa May mad and be a complete pain in the backside – but that's what we really need at the Home Office, and Norman is bloody persistent.'

He also said that he wanted to bring in the veteran Lib Dem MP Simon Hughes. 'I like Simon hugely and I think he really deserves the chance to serve as a minister.' Nick also spoke about promotions for Stephen Williams and Don Foster, and said he was thinking of bringing back Nick Harvey, who had been sacked in the 2012 reshuffle.

As we finished the meal, at around 11 p.m., Nick turned to the issue of his relations with the two Conservative members of the Quad – George Osborne and David Cameron. 'The more the government goes on, the more time I have for George Osborne and the more I see the contrasts with Cameron. Cameron does have a lot of emotional common sense, and good abilities as a political leader. But I really don't know what he stands for, other than keeping the Conservative Party in power. He is something of a quicksilver politician. He ducks and weaves to get good press coverage, but he travels very lightly in terms of core beliefs and ideology. With George, he knows where he stands. He's liberal on many social issues, and surprisingly pro-immigration for a Conservative. But he's incredibly right-wing on welfare and I've never seen much evidence that he really cares about the poor and disadvantaged. However, you can deal with him sensibly, and you know that there is a core of belief there to engage with.'

The last formal social event of the summer, before Parliament went into recess, was the Cabinet away day at Chequers, scheduled for 18 July. There were due to be joint coalition presentations from Oliver Letwin and Danny Alexander, on implementation issues, and from Jo Johnson and me on the 'forward agenda'.

Nick Clegg was rather sceptical about the whole event. 'I can tell you why Cameron is so attracted to this away day,' he said, a few days before the event. 'For him, it will all be about spin! It will all be spun as the coalition "rolling up its sleeves" and last week he tried to persuade me to put out some very anti-Labour lines from the meeting, which I don't want to do. I don't want us to be seen to be siding with the Tory Party against Labour. So, don't waste too much time preparing for the presentations. It will just all be spun out in a few lines about the global race and the coalition working together.'

I met Jo Johnson the day before the away day, to at least make sure that we had a sensible presentation to fill our allotted time. We focused on what the government should be delivering in its last two years in office, and we went through the prepared slides. Jo had brought along a rather odd slide in which it appeared that the government was not just going to try to take the credit for a successful Olympic Games (just about credible) but also for winning Wimbledon. He even suggested that we might mention the impending birth of a royal baby. I added that perhaps we might also claim the credit for the unseasonably warm summer weather. I hadn't quite sized up Jo Johnson yet, and it was difficult to know whether to take him very seriously or not. Anyway, we dropped all these points from the presentation. Even the royal baby.

Thursday 18 July was the last day of Parliament before the summer recess. At 8.15 a.m., Julian Astle and I left by car to attend the Cabinet away day. Chequers is a short drive down the M40, near the Buckinghamshire village of Great Missenden. We could tell that we were getting closer to the house, because on the verges were an endless row of poster boards, all displaying their opposition to the High-Speed 2 line, no doubt for the benefit of any passing Prime Minister.

It was an absolutely beautiful, clear, English summer's day, with temperatures touching 30 degrees centigrade. The traffic was lighter than expected, and we stopped in a village near Chequers and had a coffee so we didn't arrive absurdly early.

We eventually reached Chequers at about 10.45 a.m., for an 11.00 a.m. start. There were already some ministers standing around chatting in the drawing room – George Osborne, Michael Gove and Chris Grayling.

The Chancellor and I talked about the economy, including the better recent news on growth. George said he was rather cautious about calling an end to recession: 'The numbers are better but I don't want to get carried away, not least given the state of the Eurozone.' He was very positive about Mark Carney, the new Governor of the Bank of England, and obviously thought he was going to be a breath of fresh air at the Bank.

The general mood, as ministers gradually arrived, was a positive one. The coalition was entering the summer recess in a pretty healthy state. The economy was clearly improving at last, with unemployment falling fast and consumer confidence rising. The polls were improving for the Conservatives and, rather slightly, for us. And to cap it all the weather was good and the country was feeling cheerful after we'd won the Wimbledon men's final for the first time in seventy years or so.

As I'd guessed, the serious business didn't actually start until 11.30 a.m. At that point we were all ushered upstairs to the huge room overlooking the gardens, which has at its centre a near replica of the 10 Downing Street Cabinet table.

Upstairs I met Ken Clarke, who was as ever in good form: 'Ah, at last, a Liberal!' he said, on spotting me. 'I wondered where you all were. I was getting rather worried that none of you were showing up. Don't know why I'm here myself. I can't believe David's fixed a meeting like this for a day when England is playing Australia at the cricket. That's where I should be. Crazy.' And he walked off to get some coffee.

The meeting started with a slightly dull discussion about policy implementation from Oliver Letwin and Danny Alexander.

We then went into the 'political' part of the Cabinet, and civil servants left the room. We started with a polling presentation, which basically showed that Labour's economic narrative wasn't convincing people and that the coalition was preferred on economic policy – a crucial conclusion.

Then Jo Johnson and I delivered a presentation on policy challenges for the rest of the parliament. I kicked off by reminding people that but for George Osborne we would now be just eight months from the start of a general election campaign. In the coalition talks in May 2010, we had all been about to sign up to a four-year fixed-term Parliament when George had suddenly suggested five years 'on the off-chance that the economic recovery takes a bit longer to come through'.

It would be interesting to consider the consequences of that sudden decision to extend the parliament by one more year. As Labour's support was on a declining trend from 2012 onwards, it is tempting to conclude that this last-minute intervention from the Chancellor may have been critical in securing a Conservative majority in 2015.

In my presentation, I emphasised a few points: firstly, that the coalition had to go on governing and delivering right to the end of its term (eager nodding from David Cameron at this), and secondly, that we needed to watch out for any deterioration in the NHS towards the end of the parliament, given the relatively tight NHS budget settlement (by historic standards).

Then Jo and I set out the four overarching themes: stronger economy; easing the squeeze on living standards; a fairer Britain with more rights and responsibilities; and finally more action on opportunity to help people to get on in life.

There was a rather disappointing quality of debate, although a lot of agreement that we needed to do more on housing supply.

Michael Gove said he wanted to raise some questions on existing government policies, and then he embarked on something of an amusing rant, which left some of his colleagues looking angry, some amused and some – like the Prime Minister – a little baffled:

'I have some questions, Prime Minister, for the Cabinet. Do we not need to think more about what we are all doing? Why are we bothering with the Troubled Families unit? What does it cost and will it ever achieve anything?

Some time ago the Home Secretary set up a 'Gangs Task Force'. How is that going? How many gangs have closed down as a consequence of its work? What about cross-government work? How much is going on? What has it ever achieved? Why don't we just stop it? Why do ministers bother going on the *Today* programme? Isn't it a complete waste of time? Why do interviewers on the *Today* programme ask stupid questions about where the money is coming from to pay for government initiatives? Why don't we just say that it all comes from the Treasury? What about party conferences? What do they ever achieve? Why don't we just stop them?' On and on the Education Secretary went, treading on multiple toes.

Theresa May starred icily down at her papers. She had, as Michael had suggested, set up the Gang Task Force and was often, unsuccessfully, seeking to engage him in cross-departmental work.

The Prime Minister looked amused but also a little irritated and decided not to rise to Michael's bait. 'Well, Michael, some very interesting and wide-ranging points for us to consider there. I'm sure we'd all like to give the *Today* programme a miss! But I think it's time for lunch. We've had a very good discussion, and I will ask our press teams to get together to brief out some of the good stuff about the coalition "working all the way to the wire" and so on.'

We then all went downstairs for lunch. There was an indoor buffet, with rather good white wine and rather average chicken. It was interesting to see who mixed with whom – some of the more liberal Conservatives being more inclined to sit with Liberal Democrats than with their rather more right-wing Conservative colleagues. I chatted with the intelligent, civilised, thoughtful, liberally minded David Willetts, who just a few days before had been tipped for the axe in the upcoming reshuffle.

After lunch, we all set off back to our constituencies for the long summer recess. It seemed that there was nothing on the horizon to disturb a peaceful summer. But there was.

SYRIA

AUGUST–SEPTEMBER 2013

The possible implications of the deteriorating situation in Syria first came to my notice in the spring of 2013.

Most serious foreign policy and defence issues were left to be discussed by the National Security Council, of which I was not a member.

But in April 2013, we had a substantive ministerial discussion about Syria, led by the Foreign Secretary, William Hague. It was clear from the Foreign Secretary's overview that the situation in the country was deteriorating and that the Assad regime was using its heavy weapons to try to defeat the rebel forces. These latter were generally seen to be the 'good guys', but they were clearly struggling to make progress against the Assad forces, and the breakdown of order in the country was also allowing the space for more 'bad guys' to enter the country and occupy significant parts of it.

William Hague was clearly making the case for a more activist UK role, a view David Cameron seemed to share. Michael Gove, too, was making the case for UK military assets to be used against the Assad regime.

But the view of senior ministers wasn't by any means unanimously in favour of action. The Defence Secretary, Philip Hammond, warned of the size and power of the Syrian air force. 'This is no Libya,' he said. Patrick McLoughlin, the Transport Secretary, was also incredibly cautious and sceptical. He warned about the limited appetite of the UK public to be involved in 'every single war around the world'. Patrick's view was that the British public were 'battle weary' and unenthusiastic about foreign ventures.

However, the Prime Minister's summing up of the discussion left no doubt about his own views. He warned that the situation in Syria was getting worse and that there was stronger and stronger evidence that the Syrian regime was using chemical weapons against its own people. David Cameron was clear that in his view the UK should play a role in helping to tip the military balance sufficiently to make political negotiations possible. The government, he concluded, would be judged by history on its response and would shortly face some 'difficult choices'. Cameron then said that decisions would need to be brought back to the National Security Cabinet and to the Cabinet itself. It seemed clear that the Prime Minister was preparing us all for the prospect of military action.

I didn't hear any more about the issue of Syria that spring or summer. And on 7 August I left home in London at 2 a.m. for my annual holiday – once again in the south of France. It was always the happiest and most relaxed time of the year. Almost three weeks of sun, wine, good food and reading lay ahead.

Over the summer I read Winston Churchill's masterful volumes of *The World Crisis*, and then moved on to the Caro biography of Lyndon Johnson that Michael Gove had kindly given me as a present in July.

The news from the UK seemed on the whole to be good – a lot of 'silly season' stories about a leadership crisis for Ed Miliband, combined with better news on the economy. We seemed to have reached a turning point on growth, and some of the most respected UK economists were now revising their growth forecasts up. 'Thank goodness we resisted Osborne's crazy plan to lop another £13 billion off public spending,' said Nick Clegg on one call to me. 'It would have been completely unnecessary, and once it had happened it would have been difficult to reverse.'

Apart from a few calls to consider policy options for our conference in September, it was a quiet and restful break. On Sunday 25 August came the saddest day of the year, when I closed the shutters of the house, blocking out the powerful, bright rays of sunshine, and made the long drive back to London. The traffic approaching London was dreadful, and I made a mental note to rant at our Liberal Democrat Transport Minister, Norman Baker, who was always telling me that we didn't need any new road capacity.

The news was now dominated by Syria, and by suggestions that the Syrian government was using chemical weapons against its own population. It was clear to me that while a case was building for military action, we would need to be incredibly careful – the Syrian armed forces were very strong, there were multiple groups operating in the country, and defining success could be very difficult.

Nick Clegg had also enjoyed a relaxing holiday that August – three whole weeks in Spain to recover from what had been a non-stop period of activity, eighteen hours per day, pretty much seven days per week.

He had a restful holiday until Saturday 24 August, when David Cameron called him from his own family holiday in Cornwall. Nick was relaxing outside, on a hot and sunny Spanish afternoon.

The call was short and direct. After apologising for disturbing his holiday, the Prime Minister came straight to the point. He had been called by President Obama, who was deeply concerned about Syria – where there was now clear evidence that the Assad regime was deploying chemical weapons against rebel fighters. Both the Prime Minister and the President had concluded that the evidence was convincing, and that it needed a response – both civilians and rebel fighters could be in the firing line if the use of chemical weapons was allowed to continue.

The Prime Minister was clear about his purpose in calling. He wanted to know whether Nick Clegg and the Liberal Democrats would support an Obama-led mission to strike back against the Syrian regime. There would be no boots on the ground. It would be: 'Very targeted. Very surgical. Obama making the case, with all his credibility.'

David Cameron emphasised that he considered the case for action to be very strong. He was also clear that he needed Nick Clegg's agreement.

Nick Clegg thought quickly but also carefully – he knew that this was a critically important decision. He made clear that while he needed more information and evidence, his intuitive response was that the proposed intervention was doable – particularly if President Obama would publicly make the case for action. But the Liberal Democrat leader was clear that he would not support boots on the ground. The UK should not get embroiled in a civil war. And he emphasised that any action must be multilateral. He also insisted on seeing the Foreign Office advice. He guessed that they would recommend a United Nations resolution.

David Cameron was pleased with the Deputy Prime Minister's response, and agreed that both party leaders needed more time to make final decisions.

He said he felt strongly that action was justified and that President Assad could not be allowed to use chemical weapons against his own people with no response at all.

Later that afternoon, Ed Llewellyn, the Prime Minister's chief of staff, phoned Nick, who emphasised again the need to keep the United Nations on side and asked for this point to be reinforced with David Cameron.

Ed Llewellyn said that he understood Nick Clegg's point, but he wasn't sure the US administration saw things in the same way. He also warned that the US administration was now talking about an airstrike within just days. That suggested that UN consultation wasn't presently part of the strategy.

'Well, it really is important,' said Nick Clegg. 'And I think we must be seen to be acting responsibly with international backing.' Nick Clegg spoke to David Cameron again and emphasised personally the need for UN consultation, and that night the Prime Minister sent a message to President Obama, expressing UK support but also highlighting the importance to the UK of involving the UN – particularly to the Liberal Democrat side of the coalition.

Nick Clegg spoke to key party allies later in the day to check the wider party appetite for action. He also spoke almost non-stop with David Cameron, and the two coalition leaders were working hand in glove.

'I cannot remember a time in the last year when Cameron and I have been so aligned,' Nick told me. 'Cameron is at his most impressive over big international challenges such as this. We share the same instincts that we cannot allow chemical weapons to be used in this way. We have both been challenging the security services and the Ministry of Defence over their strategy. Philip Hammond even wanted to try to get the USA to increase their number of targets. My only complaint is that Cameron has been a bit slow to get the importance of the UN route. I think he saw it initially as some sort of sop to the Liberal Democrats. But now he can see it is important to his own side too. The UK tabled a Chapter 7 Resolution in New York at the UN, and the US went nuts. But they need to understand that after Iraq, people expect these things to be done properly.'

On Tuesday 27 August I received an urgent text from the Liberal Democrat Whips' Office in the House of Commons, saying that Parliament was being recalled on Thursday to discuss the situation in Syria. It was obvious that the UK government would be seeking Parliament's agreement for a targeted military strike against the Syrian regime.

That same afternoon, I called in to see Nick Clegg in his rooms at the Cabinet Office. Nick asked officials to leave and said that he wanted to talk to me about the situation in Syria.

'I want to give you an update on where we are,' he told me. 'Obama was extremely reluctant to get involved in Syria, but the recent chemical weapons attacks have forced his hand. David Cameron and I both agree that targeted action should be taken, but this could be quite a difficult issue with our party – not least with memories of Iraq. I have made clear that we need to go to the UN first, but the blunt truth is that Russia will veto any motion because they regard the Syrian regime as their allies. However, even if we don't get Russia on side, my view is we have to act. Otherwise Assad will go on using these appalling weapons. The strikes would be very, very limited – cruise missiles fired from submarines or other surface vessels. Most of the work would be done by the US, with a bit of help from the UK. Some other European nations are desperate to take part – but I don't think the French have any cruise missiles, so the Americans are desperately trying to find something "useful" they could do.'

Nick said that he had already spoken to people in the party. Paddy Ashdown was fully supportive. Shirley Williams and Simon Hughes were constructive and helpful. Menzies Campbell was very clear about UN approval, and Nick felt that he had some doubts. Charles Kennedy was rather cautious and said that he would need to think about it a bit more.

Nick also said that he had spoken to Tim Farron, who seemed to want to be helpful, but who had made a rather unrealistic suggestion that President Assad should be put in front of the International Criminal Court. Nick had to point out that Assad might not be willing to leave Syria to take up our offer.

Nick then said: 'My main worry is people in our party who saw us stand up against action in Iraq and will somehow say that this is similar and that we are doing the wrong thing. We have to persuade people on an emotional level. I think Obama coming out clearly and credibly for this may well change people's minds. I've spoken to [Vice-President] Biden today to emphasise the importance of the UN route and securing multilateral support, and he seems to get it. Anyway, once we get the OK from Parliament and have pursued the UN route as far as we can go, we should expect the strikes pretty quickly – maybe even this weekend. We are looking at eighteen sites being targeted by cruise missiles in a two-hour burst of action.'

I said that the sooner we could get the strikes over, the better, in every sense. We certainly didn't want resistance to build up in our party and dominate our conference, which was due in just a few weeks' time – and, most importantly, a swift strike would send a clear message to Assad.

Nick concluded by saying that we couldn't take our own MPs for granted. 'Even Ed Davey is pretty wobbly and sceptical about this, and so far I cannot seem to get hold of Vince Cable, who is away in France and out of contact.'

'By the way,' said Nick, before we parted. 'There is another person who is being incredibly difficult over this: Miliband. I spoke to him earlier on today. I am worried about how difficult Miliband could be. It feels like he is pretty nervous and indecisive, and he may find his own people pretty split. But I cannot believe he is going to play politics over this, when Obama is leading and when chemical weapons have clearly been used. If he plays politics, the right-wing press will tear him to pieces and he will be seen to be weak and unfit to be Prime Minister.'

I was supposed to be in my constituency for the whole of the following day, but I came back early for another meeting with Nick on Syria. We were supposed to meet Nick in his Cabinet Office room at 6 p.m., but when we arrived we were told that he was still meeting with the Prime Minister.

Nick finally arrived back at 6.30 p.m, leaving just thirty minutes before he was due to speak to Vice-President Biden again at 7 p.m.

Present were Shirley Williams, Tim Farron, Menzies Campbell, Ed Davey, Simon Hughes, Lord Wallace, Lord Newby and senior advisers.

Nick had only been back from his long holiday for about forty-eight hours, but when he came in he looked frayed and tired. 'Sorry to keep you all,' he said. 'I've been in meetings with Cameron and Miliband all day. It's interesting that big, controversial stuff like this always brings Cameron and me together. He's been very impressive over the last few days. Osborne is, as ever, being rather tactical, and I am afraid Ed Miliband is totally unreliable. I am fast losing respect for him. Every time there is a big decision – Alternative Vote, Lords, Syria – Miliband has the chance to act big, but he always, always, acts small. I really think that if there is a hung parliament after the next general election, and there is a possibility of a Lib–Lab coalition, Miliband's weakness would be a real problem in working together.

'Cameron and I have tried all day to get Miliband on board but every time we move our position to meet his demands, he just moves further away from us. We made six concessions and after each one he just moved again. We've even showed him the Attorney General's advice, and we've agreed on a second vote before military action, and still he won't agree to the motion we want to put down. So I have come to the view that Miliband is just determined to oppose this. Either he cannot unite his party, or he has one eye on public scepticism in the polls.'

Nick then led us all through the events of the past few days, and filled in all the background. He said he was very confident that chemical weapons had been used, though it was more difficult to establish the nature of the command chain from Assad down to the commanders on the front line. Nick emphasised how different the situation was from Iraq, and that Obama was supporting this action even though he had always been incredibly cautious about intervention. Nick said that they were now going to give UN inspectors time to confirm the use of chemical weapons, and that once they had reported there would be a second vote before any military action. This all sounded rather elongated to me, but it did emphasise the trouble being taken to keep Miliband on board and to make a strong case internationally.

Nick said: 'Look, the US haven't welcomed the UN route and there is always a risk that they just lose patience and go ahead anyway, probably with France. But it would be a very bad signal if the US, France and all the nations of the Arab League were united on this, but Britain just sat on the sidelines. The UK would then be in the company of people like Russia, China and Iran.'

The Deputy Prime Minister explained that the strikes would be carefully targeted and he thought they would be a success in stopping future use of chemical weapons: 'The sad fact is that Assad is winning the conventional campaign, so why would he go on using chemical weapons if he knows that will have consequences?'

All in all, I thought that Nick made a strong, passionate and convincing case.

While Nick spoke, Tim Farron looked quizzical and unconvinced, and Menzies Campbell also looked sceptical.

Shirley Williams was the first to speak, and she was strong and supportive, as was Simon Hughes. Tim Farron then spoke, with his odd proposal to take Assad to the International Criminal Court. Tim is regarded as on the left of the Liberal Democrats, but he was invariably thoughtful and constructive, even about some difficult coalition issues. However, on this occasion he wasn't convincing. He suggested that Nick might ring President Putin and get him to lean on Assad, and I could see Nick looking impatient and exasperated. I felt the same way. Tim then said that he had emailed his constituents and 400 had replied, of whom only four wanted military action. I wasn't convinced that you can run the country through some self-selecting focus group.

Menzies Campbell then chipped in, but was rather equivocal. He drew some unconvincing parallels with Iraq. Ed Davey was also a bit on the fence: he started off supportive, but raised so many difficulties that it was clear that he had major doubts.

I hadn't been intending to speak, but decided to do so, to give Nick strong support. I said the case he was making was the right one, and we needed to convince people that this was not Iraq Mark II and would not involve UK troops on the ground. I also said that we should get on with it. The longer we waited, the less powerful the signal we were sending to Assad.

The meeting finished at 7 p.m. for the Biden call. Nick asked Menzies Campbell to stay on for a chat at the end. The split view in our group indicated that the Lib Dem parliamentary party meeting the next day would be a real debate, where Nick could not take support for granted.

Before I left I said to Nick: 'By the way, you keep on saying that Syria is not the same as Iraq.'

'Yes?' said Nick. 'Well,' I continued, 'in that case you need to stop referring to Assad as "Saddam". You did it four times in that meeting.'

'Oh God!' said Nick. 'Sorry. I am totally knackered again!'

The next day was the crunch day. Parliament had been recalled. There would now be a debate and a vote.

In the morning, David Cameron and Nick Clegg spoke on the phone. The Prime Minister warned that his whips had been 'doing the numbers'. If Labour voted against, which now looked likely, David Cameron said that a defeat was quite possible. He guessed that both coalition parties would have rebels who would vote against the motion. William Hague was apparently suggesting that the government might just withdraw its motion and have a 'take note' debate instead.

Nick was dubious. He said that the government would look ridiculous if it recalled Parliament just for a 'take note' motion. He and David Cameron decided to press on with their plan.

Later that morning, Nick spoke again to Ed Miliband. He underlined his view that the case for action was incredibly strong: 'We cannot just stand by and see chemical weapons used. This is totally different from Iraq. You really need to make a choice.'

Ed Miliband replied by saying that he had already made his choice – Labour would be voting against the coalition motion. The Labour leader explained that he could not get his MPs to support the action, and in any case he felt there needed to be 'a much more UN-based route'.

The signs were looking ominous. Public opinion was clearly against action. And the press were lukewarm at best in their support.

Cabinet met at 9.45 a.m. to consider the issue before the debate was due to start at 2.30 p.m. When I arrived in the lobby outside the Cabinet Room, Danny Alexander was talking to George Osborne. Danny had flown back from Afghanistan just that morning.

The meeting started promptly as ever, and David Cameron set out the case for action clearly and effectively – with complete support from Nick Clegg. Nick said that he hoped to have the support of 'a number of colleagues in his own party'. 'Blimey,' said Cameron. 'I hope that it's more than "a number", because we will need those votes!'

The Prime Minister said that we needed to keep the meeting short because we all had a lot of work to do to convince our own MPs before the debate.

About half the Cabinet spoke in support of the position set out by the PM and DPM.

Towards the end of the meeting, there were three clear voices of dissent. One not particularly senior member of the Cabinet made clear that she was completely opposed to military action. She spoke nervously and not particularly well, but she said there were lots of risks and that the public was not supportive. David Cameron said nothing but looked quietly angry. I made a mental note that I did not expect her to survive the next reshuffle. I turned out to be wrong. Two more senior members, both Conservative, were much less direct, but also made clear that they were sceptics.

The Attorney General summed up the legal advice and made clear that action would be legal. We also had confidential reports from the security services, which made clear that the basis for action was sound.

David Cameron didn't attempt to sum up and could not claim unanimous support – which must have irritated him. The Cabinet ended and the Prime Minister and his team rushed off to start calling backbench MPs.

At 12 noon I then went over to Committee Room 11 in the House of Commons for a special meeting of our parliamentary party to discuss this afternoon's key debate.

Nick Clegg kicked off the discussion with a very powerful and forceful argument for targeted military strikes. There was then a very prolonged debate, in which over half of our MPs spoke.

Martin Horwood, our foreign affairs spokesman, surprised me by supporting action. Also supportive were Stephen Gilbert, Duncan Hames, Simon Hughes, Bob Smith (just about), Mike Moore, Ed Davey and me.

Menzies Campbell was just about on side, but only just, and Vince was as lukewarm as you could get without tilting over into complete opposition – he said something about the government needing to publish its legal advice, and said that 'on balance' he was supportive.

Some normally quite loyal MPs, such as Tom Brake, Paul Burstow, Lynne Featherstone and Malcolm Bruce, were really pretty sceptical, and then there were a large number who were opposed, including some ministers. MPs had been called back from their holidays with little notice. Nick Clegg realised that the government had left very little time to persuade both MPs and the public over the strength of the case for action.

Jeremy Browne said he thought that military action was no more than a 'spectacular gesture', which would kill some innocent people and which wouldn't work. Julian Huppert made clear that he would vote against the motion. Tim Farron said that action might well make matters worse. Sarah Teather said that 'violence wouldn't help to deal with violence', and Mike Thornton also seemed to be opposed.

The meeting had gone on for about an hour and a half, and not only was it rather depressing but I had to attend a meeting at the Department for Education. I was just about to get up and leave, when Lorely Burt – sitting immediately to my right – was called. I decided to stay put for her comments, as leaving might have seemed rude.

Lorely started speaking and said: 'I am really rather uncomfortable about what is being proposed. I have never voted against the party on a really important issue before, but on this I think I am going to have to.' Having said this, she was then overcome with emotion, and for a while she could not continue. Jo Swinson, to my left, handed Lorely a tissue to wipe her eyes, and I gave her a squeeze on the arm and a wink as I got up to leave the room at the end of her intervention. Lorely is a lovely person, and not one of those serial rebels who relish parading their opposition to every hard choice. But if people like this were inclined to vote against the government, I realised for the first time that there was a real chance that we might lose the vote.

The debate began at 2.30 p.m., and David Cameron was fine but not great. Most of the interventions from Conservative backbenchers were critical of government policy – another ominous sign. Ed Miliband replied for the opposition and it was soon clear even to his own side that what he was setting out was a tactical position, to unite his own party and exploit government divisions, rather than setting out a principled strategy.

I listened carefully to Miliband's deeply unimpressive contribution and came to the same conclusion that Nick Clegg had done over the past few days – that Ed Miliband simply didn't have the leadership qualities to make a great party leader, let alone a great Prime Minister. Even if he wins this debate, I concluded, he may well be the bigger long-term loser from all this.

I went back to the House of Commons to hear a low-key and unconvincing final opposition speech from Douglas Alexander, and then Nick Clegg was due to sum up for the government. He started reasonably well, but lost the House by refusing to answer a minor but difficult question about the use of British bases.

The debate ended and the House of Commons was packed with MPs ready to vote. The Labour amendment, requiring more time and introducing less clarity, was easily defeated by 332 votes to 220. But then we turned to the critical vote, on the government's own motion. Given the majority on the first vote, I thought that we were going to win, and I walked into our Whips' Office to chat to some of the other MPs and party staff.

After a few minutes, Ben Williams – the Lib Dem Chief Whip's senior official – shouted for the rest of us to be quiet, as the result of the vote was imminent. Then he said, 'Oh God, we've lost.' He could already see that the tellers for the 'Nos' had lined up in front of the Speaker on the winning side.

The Speaker confirmed the result: 'The Ayes to the right, 272. The Noes to the left 285. I think the Noes have it. The Noes have it. Unlock.' Thirty-one Tory MPs had voted against their party. Another thirty abstained.

And only thirty of our fifty-seven MPs had voted with Nick Clegg, while nine had voted with Labour and seventeen had abstained.

There was uproar in the House of Commons. This was the moment for Ed Miliband to be principled and statesmanlike, but he wasn't. If he had been seriously committed to the contents of his own party's motion, he would now have tried to secure a consensus for action on a slower timetable – instead he crowed about the coalition's defeat.

David Cameron responded to the defeat swiftly and decisively. He accepted that we had lost the vote and said that UK armed forces would not now be taking part in any military action against Syria.

It was, in truth, a huge blow to the Prime Minister – the first time a government had lost a vote on an issue of war for over 200 years. Nick Clegg was also deeply disappointed: 'It's dismal. Isolation and grubby opportunism in equal measure,' he commented to me later that night.

Paddy Ashdown was disappointed by the vote but also said – rather over-dramatically, I thought – that David Cameron was now a 'broken-backed Prime Minister' who might have to resign.

Nick Clegg had a different view: 'Yes, it's damaged Cameron and the UK. It's the legacy of Iraq, where people no longer take things on trust. But Cameron has acted with extraordinary agility to just accept defeat and move on. He has an animal-like sense of when he's weak and how to defend himself. And he has actually been very impressive over Syria. In spite of the defeat, its drawn us together again after a long period of bruising coalition disputes. On this issue, we have been completely aligned.'

A couple of days later, Nick Clegg and David Cameron reviewed the rubble of their policy on Syria. The Prime Minister apologised for not getting all his MPs to support him and also said that he had perhaps relied too much on President Obama coming out publicly and forcefully for action. In David Cameron's opinion, that might have persuaded a lot of the people who worried that this was 'all something too much like Iraq'.

Meanwhile, Ed Miliband had secured a short-term victory that some shrewd observers thought might turn into a longer-term defeat. His sceptical position had been on the side of public opinion. But what the public saw was not a strong, principled leader standing up for what he believed in, but a man who was not in control of his party, and who had ducked and weaved over a matter literally of life and death. In a devastating commentary in the

Times newspaper a few days after the vote, under the headline 'Ed Miliband is no leader. He is a vulture', David Aaronovitch wrote:

> The Syria vote crystallised his failings ... and though you can just about see how in a bad year Ed Miliband could become Prime Minister, what I cannot any longer pretend ... is that he would be a good one. I think he would be a disaster. Strangely, I think both the country and his party already know it.

TRADING POLICIES

SEPTEMBER 2013

M y private secretary in the Cabinet Office knocked on the door of my room and came in.

'Minister,' he said. 'We've had the speeches back from No. 10. You may want to look at them.'

'What are these?' I said, looking at the pile of A4 papers now placed on the desk in front of me.

'These are the speeches that Liberal Democrat ministers are planning to give at your party conference. They have to be sent to the key Conservatives in No. 10 and No. 11 to approve. Even though they are to some extent party political, they still need to be seen if the speakers are government ministers – not least if they plan to make policy announcements. And you will need to personally see and approve all the Conservative Cabinet ministers' speeches before their conference too.'

'What an amazing thing coalition is,' I said. 'Did they have any comments on our ministers' speeches?'

'Not really, Minister. But the Business Secretary's speech is quite political. It's caused a few waves in No. 10 and 11.'

I looked at the first few pages of Vince Cable's speech, while my private secretary observed: 'It talks about the "hated Tories", the "nasty party". Oh, and there's a bit here about how the Tories' friends and donors were all behind the "greed and recklessness of the early twenty-first century" and how the Conservatives are now the "Tea Party Tories".'

'I see,' I said, struggling to hold back a laugh. 'Have the Conservatives objected to the speech, then?'

'Not formally, but you might want to see this, Minister.' Scrawled on the top page of the draft of Vince Cable's speech that had been returned by the Conservatives in the Treasury were two words: 'Nauseating rubbish!'

The run-up to the party conference season was always an interesting time.

Both parties wanted to use their week in the media spotlight to showcase their contributions to the government, and both parties wanted to be able to make newsworthy and popular announcements. These should either appeal to the public or to the party faithful, or possibly both. And with the whole political media gathered in the conference venue for almost an entire week, the party view was that you either fed the media or they ate you.

So each year we would draw up a list of our favoured policy proposals and the Conservatives would draw up theirs, and we would then sit down and decide where we were willing to agree on new policies. Ministers would gather together the announcements they wanted to bid for, these would then be filtered by Oliver Letwin and by me, and eventually the Quad would reach a final agreement on who got to announce what.

This year, our first serious meeting with the Conservatives – Oliver Letwin and Jo Johnson – was on 1 August, in Oliver's office in 9 Downing Street.

We both had a single sheet of paper on our policy 'asks', and at the beginning of the meeting we cautiously traded papers.

'Who should go first, then?' said Oliver. 'You,' I said, not wanting to show our hand too early.

First on the Conservative list, and displaying at least a sense of humour, was 'Earn or Learn' – the policy we Liberal Democrats had first proposed as part of the mid-term review and then got cold feet about. Next was ending unconditional housing benefit for the under-25s. Then there was docking child benefit for mothers whose children played truant; better access to GP services; the sale of vacant social housing; single-unit pricing for utilities; ending automatic early release of prisoners; tougher deportation rules; a bland-sounding manifesto to improve town centres; part-time season tickets for rail; a cap on rail fare increases; and a dull-as-ditchwater proposal for a tourism promotion campaign.

It was a mixture of the usual right-wing Tory populist-sounding policies, a few worthy mainstream ideas (usually only half thought out) and some very boring and uncontroversial items.

'OK,' I said. 'Some of this is fine. Some is just dull. Some gives us problems.'

'Which ones?' said Oliver.

'Well, obviously removing housing benefit for young people,' I said. 'We've blocked that before, haven't we? And what's all this right-wing populist claptrap about ending early release?'

'Oh, don't worry about that,' said Oliver. 'It sounds illiberal, but in practice it won't make much difference. The prison parole boards could still make the decisions. It just would no longer be automatic. But it will give us some red meat to throw to our troops. What about your list, then?'

'OK. Well, we have extending the living wage to government employees, and new pay reporting requirements for large companies. We have tackling the abuse of zero-hours contracts and tackling corporate corruption. We have action on tax avoidance; a new school building programme; a rail fares package, including a lower cap on rail fare increases; a more generous housing borrowing cap for local authorities; and – and I know you are going to love this one, Oliver – a levy on the use of plastic bags.'

'Well, it doesn't sound too bad a list,' said Oliver. 'But we are not mad keen on the plastic bag tax – I happen to know that George will absolutely hate it.'

Over the next few weeks we had a series of further meetings with Oliver Letwin and Jo Johnson, to prepare for a couple of Quads to agree the contested areas of policy.

Our negotiations with the Conservatives were given a small boost on 2 September when Jo Johnson left a confidential file on my office table at the end of a negotiating session. This was entitled 'Conservative Conference Policy Plan 2013'. This revealed the Conservative position on all of the disputed policy areas, as well as various prospective Conservative policy announcements for their 2015 manifesto.

We could not resist a quick flick through the file, and then we put it back where he had left it. A red-faced and sheepish-looking Jo Johnson popped back to my office later to collect the papers, while I was out. My staff loyally feigned surprise.

Over the next couple of weeks, a swathe of new policy asks was added to both party lists, while some policies were withdrawn by both sides.

Our first meeting to discuss the conference policy announcements took place in 10 Downing Street on 4 September. George Osborne was in good form, and clearly felt that the lost vote on Syria had done the government no long-term harm. David Cameron was, unusually, ten minutes late. He was looking a little overweight after the holiday season, and a little tired too. We had a brief discussion about that day's Prime Minister's Questions. 'Miliband was absolutely useless,' said the Prime Minister. 'Yet more confirmation that Labour got the wrong brother.'

We agreed a lot of the smaller policy asks of both parties, and then cut to the more contentious issues.

I said that we could not agree to a proposal to allow all cars in town centres to park on double yellow lines for fifteen minutes without penalty. 'Oh, I don't agree with that completely ridiculous idea either,' said the Prime Minister. At this, Jo Johnson blushed and David Cameron added, 'Oh, yes, that was your crazy idea, wasn't it, Jo?'

The Conservatives agreed with a Steve Webb proposal to allow people to buy extra years of state pension by paying in more voluntary national insurance contributions – George Osborne could see that this might actually raise him some money in the short term.

On the plastic bag levy, the Prime Minister said: 'I think we need to be cautious about this for cost of living reasons. Also, it could be pretty unpopular.'

Nick Clegg pointed out that a similar levy had already been successfully implemented in Wales, and in any case since supermarkets already had to fund the 'free' plastic bags there was no reason to think that the policy would add to costs. 'And on popularity,' he said, 'you will be interested, David, to know that this policy is supported by the *Daily Mail*.'

'Since when did the Liberal Democrats start caring about the *Daily Mail*?' laughed George Osborne. 'Anyway, I would need to look at our polling on this.' We mentioned that our own polling showed that the policy was very popular.

On zero-hours contracts, neither David Cameron nor George Osborne really wanted to take any action. But eventually we managed to get them to agree to a consultation on banning exclusivity clauses. I had previously decided to lean on the Tories by warning them that we did not think we would be able to stop our MPs voting with Labour on this issue if it was debated on the floor of the House of Commons. And the Conservatives hated nothing more than the idea of us uniting with Labour and defeating them in Parliament on an issue that would be popular with the public.

On the living wage, David Cameron and George Osborne were immovable. 'I really don't like this policy,' said the Chancellor. 'It will damage jobs.'

But we did agree that Vince Cable could ask the Low Pay Commission for advice on a larger than expected rise in the national minimum wage, and we also agreed to look at increasing the apprenticeship rate of the minimum wage to the under-18 rate.

We didn't get through the full list of policy issues, but we had made a good start.

A week later, on Wednesday 11 September, we were back in Downing Street for the last Quad before party conference season.

That morning there was extensive media coverage of a deeply gloomy speech on the economy by Vince Cable. It implied that George Osborne was complacent about the economy and was stimulating a risky housing bubble.

When we arrived at the Cabinet Room, George Osborne was already there. 'Very helpful speech from Vince last night,' he muttered. 'His behaviour is amazing. He sent his speech over to us to be approved yesterday. We quickly sent back some comments. But he had already briefed out the original version.'

The Prime Minister then came in. 'You talking about the Cable speech? That man must be the last economic pessimist left in the country. It's amazing. The thing with Vince that I always say is that he's a brilliant economic forecaster – he's managed to predict eight of the last three recessions!'

The Prime Minister then kicked off the meeting with his usual style of negotiating with us: 'Look, Nick, I'm grateful for all the work that Oliver, Jo and David have done on this. It's very helpful. On the Conservative stuff, let me be clear with you. Most of our stuff isn't that exciting for me. What is important for us are the new proposals on Workfare, on cutting benefits and on toughening up the immigration appeals system.

'Nick, on your side, you've got a lot of good stuff, including the levy on plastic bags, which is real front-page stuff.

'If you are getting your big stuff, I want my big stuff, including a benefits cut for people who will gain from the extra Workfare support.'

Nick Clegg explained that we were not keen on benefit cuts for vulnerable people. 'Some will be trying to get jobs but may have mental health and other problems. Do we want to penalise those people? Anyway, I spoke to IDS a few days ago – your own Secretary of State on this – and he wasn't supportive of a benefits cut.'

The Prime Minister was dismissive of IDS's view. Both Nick and I dug in over the Conservative plan for a 10 per cent benefit cut. We said we would consider tougher conditionality rules on jobless benefits, but not a 10 per cent cut.

George Osborne then pushed back against our proposal for plastic bag levy. But eventually, and with a more sympathetic PM who clearly didn't want to upset the *Daily Mail*, we secured an agreement, while delaying the introduction of the new levy to autumn 2015 – after the general election.

Nick rejected any further undermining of immigration appeals but agreed the proposal on ending automatic early release. George Osborne joked that he thought this policy had been announced at ten previous Conservative Party conferences.

Eventually we came to the proposals that Vince Cable wanted. The Conservatives grumpily agreed a consultation on zero-hours contracts, but they could not be shifted on the living wage or on the new measures that Vince wanted in order to boost corporate transparency and tackle corporate fraud.

'How can you oppose this stuff on tackling fraud and boosting corporate transparency?' asked Danny Alexander.

'Not popular with business,' mumbled the Prime Minister.

'Not popular with our supporters,' smiled George Osborne.

'Your donors, you mean,' said Nick Clegg.

'OK. I think we're finished,' said David Cameron. 'Nick, you happy?'

'Oh, by the way, Nick, we also agree that George and I will announce the marriage tax break, and you will announce your "cost of living booster".'

'Yes, Nick, and you owe me some more detail on that, please. I need to sign off the costings,' said George Osborne.

'Fine,' said Nick. 'David will get that over to you later on today.'

This last big piece of the jigsaw, unusually not discussed even at the Quad meetings, had been discussed privately by Nick Clegg and David Cameron for the past few weeks.

Earlier in the year, David Cameron made clear to Nick Clegg that he wanted to proceed with his plan – flagged up in the coalition agreement but never supported by the Liberal Democrats – to reintroduce some sort of economic reward for marriage into the tax system. With the subject of gay marriage having upset traditional Conservative supporters, David Cameron was more eager than ever to make progress on this policy. 'I want to announce this at my autumn conference,' Cameron had told Clegg a few months before.

'OK,' said Nick. 'Well, you know my party doesn't support this, and we agreed in the coalition talks that our MPs would simply abstain on it. However, if you are going to spend hundreds of millions of pounds on this, and if you expect me to allow this to become a priority for money, then basically I want an equivalent sum to spend on a policy issue that is important to me.'

'OK,' said David Cameron. 'But I think we agree that both of these policies should be about easing the squeeze on living standards and helping hard-pressed families. George and I don't really just want to spend more on public services without helping people in the pocket.'

Over the period from June onwards, until early September, I led on work to identify what this 'cost of living booster' might be.

We knew we could allocate around the amount that the Conservatives planned to spend on the marriage tax cut – £600–700 million per year.

I drew up a list of five main options: raising the personal income tax allowance further; more investment in childcare; a reduction in fuel duty; extending free school meals to all children in primary schools; and introducing a discount for public transport for 16–21-year-olds who were accessing education, training or work.

We quickly eliminated the first three options. Raising the tax allowance was a policy that we already pressed for in every Budget and Autumn Statement, and we felt that we were likely to deliver this anyway. We were already boosting childcare, with the new tax-free childcare package and Nick Clegg's extension of free childcare to disadvantaged two-year-olds. Cutting fuel duty was expensive, we didn't have the cash to make much difference, and it wouldn't be a very environmentally friendly message.

Nick particularly liked the idea of a discount card giving young people free or heavily subsidised transport on buses and possibly rail. I was also keen because as Schools Minister I was receiving almost daily representations from parents who pointed out the unfairness of support for school transport ending at age sixteen, when the education leaving age had risen to eighteen. This was also a major pressure on many household budgets, and our Transport Minister, Norman Baker, was very keen on the policy as a way of encouraging more use of public transport.

We spent many weeks looking in detail at the policy, and for a while it was the favourite to win Nick's backing. But the more you looked at the details, the more complex the whole thing became, and the more difficult it was to design the right scheme. A large discount or free travel would be too expensive and possibly have very large 'deadweight cost'. But a small discount might not help some young people in areas where there were already discount schemes. And there were all sorts of other practical issues that were tough to fix.

And so it was that one policy emerged as the favourite, and that was the policy of free school meals for children of infant age.

Michael Gove had apparently been in a bar in Marrakesh earlier in the parliament, when he happened to meet John Vincent and Henry Dimbleby. The two men owned a developing chain of restaurants and they expressed strong views about the importance of improving school food.

Michael liked the idea of securing his own successors to Jamie Oliver, who had worked with the previous government to improve school meals. He asked the two men to take on a project to look at all aspects of school food.

The School Food Plan was written by Vincent and Dimbleby, and published in July 2013. Usually, departments like to subtly control such 'independent' reviews, but the two men were clear that they were going to be nobody's patsies. They insisted on writing their own report – in a distinctively non-civil servant style. They also argued, to the horror of Michael Gove's advisers, that school meal standards should be applied to all schools – academies as well as local authority schools.

As well as this recommendation, a later draft of their plan included a quite expensive proposal to extend free school meals to all primary school pupils. Michael Gove's advisers thought the idea was far too expensive, but they also apparently calculated that keeping it in the document might help distract attention from what they considered to be a more controversial proposal to legislate to require all academies to meet school food standards.

So when the School Food Plan was finally published, it included this key recommendation – on the basis of its effect not just on healthy eating, but on attainment. In some schools, there were children who came to school hungry and were unable to focus properly on learning.

Although I had always been considered a rather right-wing Liberal Democrat, I had long been a believer in extending the entitlement to free school meals.

I had first raised the possibility of extending free school meal entitlements with Michael Gove back in February 2013. To my surprise, he said he also favoured the idea – provided we could extract the money from the Treasury.

There were a number of reasons I favoured this policy.

Firstly, I wanted to end the injustice that meant that disadvantaged young people between the ages of sixteen and eighteen who left school to go to college lost their entitlement to free meals simply because of the institution they had chosen to study in. This seemed to be scandalously unjust, and no government had ever sought to defend the anomaly. But nor was any government willing to right this wrong. We could now do that.

Secondly, I had long believed that it made sense for the state to accept the responsibility to feed children properly while they were in the state's care. Of course some parents could afford these meals, but these same parents could also afford to pay for education or healthcare. The point is that where there is an expectation that a service is needed universally, there can be a good case for delivering it in that way. It seemed to me sensible to provide free meals to all children, and I was impressed by the potential gains in terms of healthy eating, more focus in the classroom and more chance to sit down and socialise at the dinner table – sadly a disappearing opportunity in too many households.

I also believed that providing free meals would help to remove a big disincentive to work for many families. Free meal entitlement was currently on the basis of very low income – which really meant being out of work. If you went back into employment, you instantly lost your family's free meal entitlement, and if you had two or three children that could be enough to make work a money-losing proposition.

So it seemed to me that there were multiple potential gains. And of course while this would cost money, countries like Finland had long managed to combine free school meals with finding the resources to run one of the best education systems in the world.

The problem initially was that the policy was just too expensive. We calculated that free meals for all primary school children would cost some £1.2 billion in England alone, with another £40 million or so to fix the injustice of students denied free meals in colleges.

This high cost seemed to rule the policy out. But I met one day with one of the best officials in the Department for Education, Susan Acland-Hood, and asked her to bring me options for spending a smaller amount of money. Susan came back with a series of options, of which the best by far was the idea of rolling the policy out first to children of infant age – for almost precisely the amount of money we had available.

After months of research and deliberation, we finally took the decision to proceed with infant free school meals at a meeting in Nick Clegg's office on Tuesday 3 September.

Nick said: 'OK. We will keep this under wraps until our conference, and make a big splash there. I will have to tell Cameron and George, but that's it. If we tell the Conservatives, this will just leak and the Tories will try to claim all the credit for it.'

'I see the need for secrecy,' I said, 'but I am going to need to do some further planning on the details in my department, and in fairness I just cannot spring this on Michael Gove, without warning, in a policy area within his own department. That would cause real problems.'

'OK,' said Nick. 'Well, I will leave you to brief Michael. But tell him not to let his swivel-eyed special advisers know about it – they would definitely leak it and try to damage us. If we are to tell people in the DfE, it must just be Michael and a few top officials.'

Over the next four days I worked with just a couple of senior officials at the Department for Education to re-check the costings, get these approved by the Treasury, and make sure that we had thought through the major delivery challenges.

Then, on 9 September, a week before our announcement was due to be made, I asked to see Michael Gove – alone – in my office in the House of Commons. We met just after Oral Questions. I told Michael about the agreement and the plans to announce it in a week's time. I also asked him to keep the issue under wraps – and not even tell his trusted special advisers, Dom Cummings and Henry de Zoete.

Michael looked pretty happy when I gave him the news. 'Good,' he said. 'I support this. I know not everyone in government will agree with the policy, but I do. And I am happy with you working in private with officials on this over the next week. And – yes – I promise to tell no one, not even Dom!'

Michael kept his word, and to my amazement the big announcement didn't leak out – indeed, it caught the media by surprise and received very positive coverage when it was revealed over a week later, on Tuesday 17 September.

It was a good beginning, but the early Conservative support for the policy didn't last, and within weeks it contributed to a serious and wider breakdown of coalition relationships within the hitherto 'Coalicious' department.

A Close Shave in Glasgow

September 2013

As our party conference in Glasgow approached, it became clear that securing policy agreements with the Conservative Party would be the easy part.

Somehow, our party policy-making process had conspired to serve up within a few short days some crucial debates on some of the key, flagship, policy issues.

These would be decided, as ever in the Liberal Democrats, by a vote of conference delegates on the floor of the conference hall.

There were to be debates on the future of our nuclear deterrent, on the future of nuclear power, on our policy on tuition fees, on whether to commit ourselves to raising the top rate of income tax and on our entire economic strategy. If these debates went the 'wrong way' from a party leadership perspective, we could go into the conference season as a centrist, liberal party and come out somewhere to the left of Ed Miliband. So there was much to prepare for, and many people to be persuaded and cajoled.

But the biggest debate of them all seemed likely to be the debate on our whole economic strategy.

Nick Clegg's motion on the economy had been chosen to be debated, but already there were some amendments to his motion from the so-called Social Liberal Forum, a grouping on the left of the party. In reality, these amendments were rather badly drawn up and unclear. But one thing was clear – the media and the party would clearly see this as a vote in favour of or against the economic strategy of the coalition government. It would be a crucial moment.

In early September, Nick Clegg met with Vince Cable to discuss the party conference and the variety of motions relating to economic policy. Somewhat reluctantly, Vince said that he would back the Clegg motion, and possibly even speak in favour of it.

My own view was that Vince would find it difficult to stay on message in the economy debate, and I advised that we should ask him to focus on the tax and tuition fees debates, and simply support the economy motion without speaking to it.

The economic data continued to be more positive, and it looked like the economy had returned to healthy growth. This included the construction, services and manufacturing sectors and not just the housing market.

But the closer we got to the conference, the less likely it seemed that the unity would be maintained. Indeed, just days before conference, Vince made a speech that included a direct attack on coalition economic policy, and which seemed designed to undermine the coalition narrative about stronger growth. Nick Clegg was as irritated as George Osborne.

Our conference started in Glasgow on Saturday 14 September. When we arrived, the city was actually warmer and sunnier than London, and I felt in a fairly confident state of mind. We had a lot of positive policy announcements and I expected us to win all the key policy debates.

Only on Sunday evening did the conference threaten to seriously unravel. A story broke that Vince didn't support the leadership's position on the economy, and that he would boycott the debate on Monday morning and refuse to back the key motion. This had all the makings of a major car crash.

Late in the evening I spoke to Nick to find out what was going on. 'Having told me he would back the motion, Vince is now refusing to. It just beggars belief. I just cannot deal with him any more on this. He just seems to be addicted to gloom. It is essential that we win the vote on the economy tomorrow. If we don't, we have a split party, and frankly if I lose the debate I may well need to resign as leader this evening. If I win the debate and Vince refuses to support us, I may have to sack him. We cannot have two different positions on economic policy.'

The long-rumbling row over economic strategy was finally coming to a head. I felt that the relationship between Vince Cable on the one hand and

Danny Alexander and Nick Clegg on the other was in danger of breaking down completely. Indeed, by morning it effectively had.

'Shall I speak to Vince and see if I can get him back on side? He is usually reasonable when it comes to the crunch,' I said.

'You can try to,' said Nick. 'But I am not holding my breath. Vince seems incapable of placing his own views below those of a clearly agreed and collective decision of the parliamentary party.'

The next morning I set my alarm for 5.15 a.m., and I rang Vince's special adviser, Emily Walch, at 6.30 a.m.

Emily was very concerned at the divisions on economic policy and said that there was now a complete breakdown of relations. 'Vince is quite upset about the recent media leaks about his humiliation at the away day, and he thinks there should be more of an attempt to get some sort of compromise position with the Social Liberal Forum,' she said.

I replied: 'Look, you know how much I like Vince, and I have had some sympathy with his arguments about boosting investment spending. But we now have a settled position, and having a bloody great row at conference in front of the media is insane and damaging and can only end in disaster. And I think Vince is being rather naive about the SLF motion. We all know they are trying to change coalition policy, and some of them, including Matthew Oakeshott, want to destabilise Nick – that was what the motion at spring conference was about. I want to see Vince this morning to try to persuade him to toe the line and support the motion. And frankly this is the worst possible time for a party row on the economy – when it is clear the economy is now recovering.'

'OK,' said Emily. 'I'll fix for you to see Vince. But I am not optimistic of changing his mind. Do you mind coming to his room? The media are following Vince around and they detect a big bust-up.'

Eventually I fixed to see Vince at 8.45 a.m., less than two hours before the debate.

Before meeting him, I spoke to Jonny Oates. 'I am glad you are talking to him, and we should try for unity, but my view is that we are going to win this debate anyway,' said Jonny. 'I have some sympathy over Vince's views but he is behaving ridiculously.'

The traffic from the city centre to the conference centre was bad, and by the time I turned up Vince had gone to a meeting of the parliamentary party, fixed for 9 a.m. in the conference centre. When I arrived, Vince and his advisers were already there. We slipped out of the room where MPs were gathering and into a next-door conference room, which was completely empty. We sat down on some chairs at the edge of a big conference table, and Vince looked pretty agitated and uncomfortable.

'Thanks for meeting, Vince,' I said.

'Look, I know what you are going to say,' Vince cut in. 'I do understand that this has now been blown up into a vote of confidence in the leader, and I don't want that. I think this has all been mishandled, and there could have been a compromise with the SLF.'

'I know how you feel,' I said, 'and I agree that the briefing about the row on policy at the away day was very silly and unhelpful. But we cannot have a split on economic policy between you and Nick. And this will look crazy at a time when the economy is recovering. And it would damage the party. We cannot have any sense that there is a split at the top of our party on economic policy.'

'OK,' said Vince. 'Well, I have now decided that I am going to attend the debate. I won't speak in it, but I will support the motion. I just hope we can manage this better in future. The SLF amendments are actually considerably tamer than anything I would want to say.'

'Well, it is very helpful that you are doing that,' I said.

Vince then went next door to the parliamentary party and delivered the same message – allowing our media team to brief out that he was now supporting the motion and would attend the debate.

The debate went ahead and Nick Clegg's motion passed. The journalists attending the conference were all hugely disappointed by the outbreak of agreement. They had rightly scented a huge row which could only have led to the departure of either Vince Cable or Nick Clegg.

At lunchtime, I met the *Guardian* journalists Patrick Wintour and Nick Watt. 'We're writing that Vince bottled it and blinked, and that basically this is the end of "Vincemania",' they told me.

Two days later I spoke to Danny Alexander, just before Nick Clegg's conference speech.

'Vince's position on the economy is becoming a bit of a joke and completely undermining the party's economic narrative,' he said. 'I think Nick should move Vince out of the Business Department and put me in.'

All of the other important party debates – on tax, defence, nuclear weapons and nuclear power – went the party leadership's way, and Nick's leader's speech was a success too. All in all, it was one of the most successful Liberal Democrat conferences for many years. But we came close – too close – to losing either our leader or one of our greatest political heavyweights. It was a very close shave.

IMMIGRATION: CAPS, CHECKS AND SPLITS

2012–15

It was December 2013. In just a few weeks' time, the controls preventing Romanians and Bulgarians from coming to the UK to work were going to be lifted. The Prime Minister was deeply worried that this development would make it even more difficult to cut immigration in the dramatic way promised in the 2010 Conservative Party manifesto. David Cameron wanted more 'tough action' to deter immigrants from coming to the country.

Ministers were meeting in Conference Room A in 70 Whitehall – the centre of the Cabinet Office – to discuss immigration and other issues. Nick Clegg was chairing the meeting. The Environment Secretary, the right-winger Owen Paterson, was explaining how he planned to reduce immigration pressures by abolishing the Agricultural Workers Scheme, which allowed Eastern European workers to come to the UK to do unpopular hard work such as picking crops in the fields.

Someone suggested that while abolishing the scheme might reduce immigration, it could also be very unpopular with farmers – who would no longer find it easy to employ cheap labour for back-breaking outdoor work.

'Oh, but I've thought of that,' said Owen Paterson. 'I think I have the answer. We'll try to get more British pensioners picking some of the fruit and vegetables in the fields instead.' One of the officials taking notes looked up in surprise, clearly thinking that she had heard incorrectly.

She hadn't. And Mr Paterson hadn't finished. 'Of course, getting British pensioners to do this work could lead to an increase in farmers' costs,' he said. 'After all, they may be a bit slower doing the work. I've thought of that too. I think we might arrange to exempt British pensioners from the minimum-wage laws, to allow them to do this work.'

Cabinet colleagues, even the more right-wing Conservatives, listened in stunned silence. The official now realised that she had indeed heard correctly, and tried, unsuccessfully, to stifle a laugh.

'I look forward to you selling that one to the voters, Owen,' I said.

Ken Clarke was less sympathetic: 'I must say I regard all this hysteria about Bulgarians and Romanians as complete rubbish. Total xenophobic tosh,' he said. 'People in this country just don't want to do this kind of work any more. Instead of all this ridiculous rhetoric about 'shooting Bulgarians' and closing down our borders, we ought to welcome these Eastern Europeans who actually are willing to work rather hard, in a way that I'm afraid some of our own people don't actually want to do.'

It might have been thought that immigration would create relatively predictable political fault lines within the coalition government. The Conservatives had in 2010 promised to reduce net migration to 'tens of thousands per year'. Nick Clegg had rubbished this target, not merely because he was liberal in his views and principles, but because he could immediately see that pledges over net migration were undeliverable in a European Union where the inhabitants of most member states could generally travel, without impediment, across borders to secure work.

It is true that most Liberal Democrats were united in wanting to welcome people with skills and talents to our country, certainly from within the European Union.

But on the Conservative side of the coalition, there was a clear split between senior ministers who wanted to cut immigration and take a tough public line on the matter, and those who wanted the UK to be seen to be an open country, which could attract inward investment, talented entrepreneurs and high-spending tourists.

In general, the Cabinet ministers representing the great economic departments of state favoured a more open stance on immigration. This included not only Vince Cable but, more surprisingly, ministers such as George Osborne and Michael Gove – the economic liberals.

The Prime Minister may have been worrying about the tabloid newspapers and the rise of UKIP, but around the Cabinet table most of the discussions about immigration – particularly early on in the parliament – were dominated by Cabinet ministers attacking the Home Secretary, Theresa May, over her department's restrictive immigration and visa rules.

In 2012, George Osborne demanded to know why more was not being done to assist wealthy Chinese businessmen who wanted to bring their cash and investments to the UK. He attacked the Home Secretary over long visa delays and recounted 'horror stories' about unfortunate Chinese billionaires who landed at Heathrow with the equivalent of suitcases of money, only to find themselves strip-searched by burly UK border staff.

At a time when the economy seemed to be flat-lining and growth was the number one priority, the Culture Secretary wanted to know what more could be done to encourage high-spending Asian tourists to come to the UK. Even dry as dust Tory right-winger and Defence Secretary Philip Hammond made the extraordinary suggestion at Cabinet in 2013 that 'Schengen visas' ought to be valid in the UK – giving overseas visitors to the EU an automatic right of entry into the UK. When Ed Davey burst into laughter over this suggestion, David Cameron quickly added, only half-jokingly: 'If that statement by Philip finds itself onto the front page of a newspaper, I'll fire the person responsible – on sight.'

Theresa May did her best to field questions on this subject, but she was not always convincing. I felt that at times she was just inches away from saying to her Conservative colleagues, 'Look, do you want me to cut immigration or not?'

Given the Conservative manifesto pledge to cut immigration, and the national sensitivity of the issue, you might have thought that at least the Home Office would be determined to get on top of the situation.

The immigration system inherited from the previous Labour government was clearly a complete mess. The cross-border flows of people had expanded hugely over the years, and it was now much easier and cheaper for people to get to the UK from far-off lands.

UK immigration systems were poor, and previous governments had abolished many of the entry and exit checks which should allow the authorities to identify people who had overstayed their visas, so that swift and decisive action could be taken.

Even when the Home Office did identify overstayers, there were so many of them in comparison with available border agency resources, and the appeals system was so lengthy, complex and ineffective, that in practice very little action was taken. As a consequence, hundreds of thousands of illegal immigrants were able to stay in the country for large numbers of years.

Even the Prime Minister admitted to having met such people at his advice centres. 'Perhaps', he said in 2013, 'we ought to introduce a route to normalise things for people who have been in the country for so many years that they are never going to leave?' The Liberal Democrat ministers around the table immediately laughed. 'Prime Minister, we tried that line at the last election,' I said. 'The amnesty? It wasn't awfully popular.' David Cameron looked distinctly embarrassed. He seemed to have forgotten that he was one of the people who had previously robustly rubbished the idea.

In 2013, I saw a high-level note on the border and immigration system. It was a pretty devastating indictment of past government failures in this area:

> We inherited both policies and an organisation that were a long way from what was needed – net immigration was barely controlled; service to legitimate customers was poor both at airports and for immigration services; enforcement work was not keeping pace and lacked credibility; the organisation was shambolic (for example ranked worst of 150 central government bodies in the National Officers Process Management Audit); and some of the basics of security at the border had fallen away. Focus and rigour were lacking, both at the strategic level and operationally; we didn't have a picture of the end-to-end system, and basic numbers and reporting could not be relied upon. Historical low productivity, weak operations management, and over-reliance on IT silver bullets had seen control over casework lost, with substantial backlogs in a number of areas.

In my Cabinet Office role, I wanted to ensure that action was taken to improve the operation of the immigration system. My view was that we could not build a consensus for sensible levels of immigration without first restoring public confidence in the system.

I had assumed that sorting out the immigration system would be a priority for the Home Office, too. But when I looked into how much progress was being made, for example on the key coalition commitments to restore entry and exit checks at our borders, I was shocked at how little was going on.

In September 2013, I gathered some of the most senior civil servants in Whitehall together to find out why entry and exit checks had not yet been fully restored.

I naively said to one of the UK's top civil servants, 'My God, how can it all be so bad? Surely this area must be an absolute top priority in the Home Office?'

'Priority, Minister?' was the surprised reply, as if I had made some extraordinary and bizarre suggestion. I glanced around at the other civil servants, who smiled knowingly. And then I was let in on the great secret:

'Minister, immigration has never really been a priority for the Home Office. The Home Office is really only institutionally interested in issues such as crime, disorder and terrorism. Immigration has always been, well, a secondary concern for the Home Office. It is not where reputations have been made, and not where the high-flyers go. Tackling serious crime, Minister – that's a Home Office priority. Avoiding mass prison break-outs, that's pretty important too. A big prison break-out can cost a Home Secretary his job. Terrorism? That's a first rate-priority, along with anything to do with the security services. Immigration? Immigration has always been the poor relation, Minister, the unwelcome and slightly embarrassing aunt sitting alone in the corner, as it were. Most of the top Home Office civil servants don't regard border control as a top priority at all.'

Later, I was told that matters were even more serious than this. One senior civil servant and another very senior minister both told me that the Home Secretary and her top officials were actively opposed to the coalition policy of fully restoring entry and exit checks.

'Let me be blunt,' I was told by one senior civil servant: 'the Home Secretary doesn't want a fully functioning system of entry and exit checks. She thinks it would only highlight the ineffectiveness of the Border Agency and the Home Office and their inability to identify and then eject overstayers. Theresa May is saying that entry and exit checks would be expensive and embarrassing and would distract attention from tackling serious criminals and terrorism.'

This seemed to explain why month after month there was no real action in getting the system of entry and exit checks in place. Nick Clegg and I arranged to see the Home Secretary to apply some pressure. We were told, 'Everything will be fine.' We weren't convinced. Eventually I raised the issue with Oliver Letwin, who was also supportive of delivering on our coalition pledge. He also seemed highly sceptical of whether the Home Office were planning to do anything.

'OK,' I said. 'Look, I don't want to be unpleasant about this. But either Theresa May gets on and delivers entry and exit checks, or this will be a big issue at the next general election, and the Prime Minister and the Home Secretary will need to publicly explain why they have failed to deliver.'

Nick Clegg delivered the same blunt message to David Cameron: deliver on this, or there will be a big row.

Oliver Letwin came back to me a couple of weeks later, to say that the Prime Minister was fully supportive of the policy. He wanted action, even if this eventually highlighted the problem of people overstaying their visas.

And then, very slowly, the Home Office started to get moving on entry and exit checks. In November 2013, Oliver Letwin told me that he had met the Home Secretary and she now appeared to have a workable plan. 'About bloody time,' I replied. 'Ah,' said Oliver Letwin. 'I may have been a little unfair to the Home Office, though. I used to think they weren't fixing the problem of entry and exit checks because they didn't want to. I now realise I may have been wrong. I think it's just that some of their people are completely incompetent!'

We both laughed, Oliver a lot – as he usually did. Entry and exit checks were restored – within days of the May 2015 general election.

Entry and exit checks weren't the only big issue of immigration policy for the coalition government.

There were small one-off disputes, such as on whether Afghan interpreters should be allowed to settle in the UK, in part to protect them from the Taliban after we left the country.

Philip Hammond and David Cameron weren't keen, but Nick Clegg was very insistent, and he was supported by Ken Clarke, who noted, 'There's no way we will resist a serious campaign to let this small group of worthy people come to our country. Remember how we won the campaign on letting the Gurkhas settle here, when we were in opposition? The only people we had on side initially were the Liberals and a single, ageing actress, and we still won.'

In 2013, the Prime Minister and Deputy Prime Minister agreed to introduce an Immigration Bill to try to tackle weaknesses in our system, and to deter migrants from coming to the UK and overstaying their welcome.

Mark Harper, the Conservative Immigration Minister, was to lead on the Bill. I was to vet the contents on behalf of the Liberal Democrat side of the coalition.

A string of meetings followed, taking up much time in my diary. Some were with Mark Harper in my rooms in the Cabinet Office. On one occasion the minister arrived on crutches. 'I broke my leg when I fell off a table in Soho, dancing with my wife at the weekend', announced this sensible-looking and very amiable minister. It seemed unlikely. It was true.

Many of the new policies were easily agreed across the coalition, including action to streamline the ludicrously complex and time-consuming appeals process. Some issues were more complicated.

Many controversial topics were dealt with by the so-called MATBAPS (Migrants Access to Benefits and Public Services) Cabinet Committee. This was eventually chaired by the Prime Minister himself, and included senior Cabinet ministers. Every major department was asked to come forward with policy changes to make it less easy for illegal immigrants to stay in the UK while accessing our benefits and services

In May 2013, we met in the Cabinet Room of 10 Downing Street to discuss a series of thorny policy issues. The Prime Minister was chairing the meeting, and other senior ministers present included Nick Clegg, Vince Cable, Jeremy Hunt, Theresa May, Iain Duncan Smith and Oliver Letwin. I was there with both an Education Department and a Cabinet Office hat on. Before the meeting a civil servant warned me: 'The PM is going to press you on whether there is more we can do to stop migrant children accessing education, and he is also unhappy with Eric Pickles over his proposals on private landlords – which he thinks aren't nearly tough enough.'

David Cameron was definitely in one of his 'action this day, don't give me any reasons why I can't do this stuff' moods. We relatively quickly and satisfactorily agreed proposals on the NHS and on benefits.

We then turned to private landlords. Eric Pickles presented a paper from his Local Government Department, which was cautious and pragmatic.

It suggested targeting resources on 'homes in multiple occupation', which were often used by illegal migrants. The Prime Minister wanted something much bolder – he wanted private landlords to check the immigration papers of every potential tenant and only give them housing if the landlord was confident that they were entitled to be in the UK.

The Prime Minister pushed his case hard. Eric Pickles pushed back hard: 'Prime Minister, can I be blunt with you? I think this is a seriously bad idea. Checking immigration papers is really hard. Many of them, you will be shocked to know, Prime Minister, are frankly forged. What are we asking private landlords to do – act as an arm of the immigration service? I am very dubious. And we could end up in a situation where anyone foreign-looking cannot get into private rented accommodation, because landlords just will not want to take the risk of getting it wrong. It could be very dangerous and divisive.'

I had exactly the same concerns myself, and I had put them to Mark Harper a few days before. 'Mark, I really think checking people's entitlement to be in the UK and work in the UK is very, very difficult for a private individual.'

'No, don't worry,' was the reply. 'It's pretty straightforward.'

But at this meeting, few others took the Prime Minister's side. Nick Clegg and Vince Cable spoke against – in Vince's case, appearing to criticise the whole government focus on immigration.

Conservative ministers were also against the proposal, and one after another they expressed scepticism.

It was clear nevertheless that the PM was determined to get his way. But Eric Pickles, who suddenly seemed to have transformed into what I later described as a 'squidgy liberal', was not giving an inch either. Few ministers were willing to face down the Prime Minister in these meetings, and to go on fighting when he took a clearly different view from them. Eric Pickles was one of them. Only Oliver Letwin spoke in support of the PM, and he didn't look very convinced either.

We were running out of time, and still had a substantive discussion on education issues to fit in.

Suddenly, before even trying to sum up the debate on landlords, the Prime Minister said, 'OK, end of meeting.' He slammed his red briefing file closed, pushed his chair back, stood up and walked out. Everyone else looked baffled. Government meetings never, ever, ended without in some way finishing the agenda. Had the PM really just walked out in a strop? Yes, he had.

As I walked back to the Cabinet Office, Nick Clegg said to me, 'That was pretty petulant of Cameron. He can't stand not getting his own way. Cameron can be great on the big issues when he really engages and takes them seriously – but this is where he is at his worst. He is panicking about UKIP. He wants to look tough. He doesn't think things through. It's all about chasing media headlines.'

The Prime Minister wasn't giving up, though. He instructed Oliver Letwin to get Conservative ministers together and 'get them on side'. By the next meeting of MATBAPS, they were. Liberal Democrat ministers restated our concerns, but our Conservative counterparts were now back on message. The Prime Minister summed up in favour of proceeding with the action to require all private landlords to check immigration status. Nick Clegg said that the Liberal Democrats would need to look again at the detail.

Both Vince Cable and I were still very opposed to the landlords measure. We considered it illiberal, bureaucratic, open to abuse, and likely both to be ineffective and to risk prejudice against anyone 'looking foreign'. It was, in any case, very unlikely that anyone turned down by a landlord would actually be spotted and removed by the Home Office. It seemed more likely that illegal immigrants would either forge papers or go to more dodgy landlords.

The proposal still had to go for clearance via the Home Affairs Committee, chaired by Nick Clegg. Vince Cable and I both insisted on only authorising progress with a very long list of conditions attached, which required further clearance from us. The Prime Minister wasn't pleased. 'Nick, tell your people to take their tanks off my lawn,' he said. 'No,' replied the Deputy Prime Minister. 'Vince and David are just making sure the details of this can really work. That's all I ever promised.'

Over the summer, I took away two huge files of paperwork to read – full to the brim with the consultation responses to the proposal on landlords. It all made bleak reading – confirming my view that we should not be giving approval to a measure that was likely to prove both expensive and ineffective.

I reported back to Nick in September that we should veto this part of the proposed Immigration Bill, or at least insist on a pilot, with nationwide roll-out requiring a further vote and coming only after a general election. Nick agreed with me – while pointing out that the PM wasn't going to be pleased.

To soften him up, I first broke the news to Oliver Letwin, at one of our early morning catch-up meetings. 'He won't be delighted. I think you can expect a "controlled explosion",' was the response. Frankly, I didn't care. When the Conservatives decided they really weren't prepared to support one of our policies, they would just say no. This happened even if the policy was in the coalition agreement – political party funding being a good example.

We also had a few Conservatives encouraging our resistance to some of the more ill-thought-out parts of the Immigration Bill. On 4 September, I had one of my rather enjoyable meetings with Ken Clarke, in his room in the Cabinet Office, overlooking Horse Guards Parade. I noticed that the office looked a little bit bare – not one document or sheet of paper was visible anywhere. It looked as if someone had returned to an office that didn't involve much work, after a very long holiday.

'I'm pleased you Liberals are looking closely at this Immigration Bill,' he began. 'Some of my Conservative colleagues can't be trusted on this subject. They come up with these barking mad, extremist, right-wing views. I'm very much on your side on this. We need to be calm, rational and intelligent. We also need to sort out that Border Agency, which in my experience is a complete shambles – farcical. I am glad you are supporting the reform of the appeals process, though. It's ludicrous – just a way of fat lawyers getting rather fatter. As for this nonsense David is pushing on landlords, it seems to me to be crazy. Eric is clearly opposed. I doubt even Theresa thinks it will work. It's all about UKIP, I fear. But in my experience, immigration is like trying to catch a tiger by the tail – very difficult. And there is a high risk it ends up eating you.'

On Tuesday 24 September, Nick Clegg fixed to talk to David Cameron while he was on his way to Heathrow Airport to travel to the United States. The Deputy Prime Minister had decided to exercise his veto.

Nick later reported the outcome back to me: 'He was furious and very difficult. I just told him it was a stupid policy. I told him that Sayeeda Warsi thought so too. That didn't help! I think he is stressed about his party conference. He probably even knows it's a bad idea.'

After conference, we maintained our veto but allowed a pilot to go ahead.

The Immigration Bill eventually passed, and a lot of it will improve the workings of the system.

But there was an ironic postscript. Mark Harper – 'that nice man Mark Harper' as David Cameron jokingly referred to him, had to resign from the government in February 2014. The reason? His cleaner of seven years turned out not to have permission to be resident in the UK. Perhaps it was not so easy to check immigration papers after all? Anyway, Mark acted speedily and with decency. I was delighted when he returned to the government later in the year. Both Nick Clegg and I had found him to be an excellent colleague and a conscientious minister.

Free Schools, Free Meals
and Matt Sanders's Desk

2013

I was thoroughly enjoying being a minister in both the Cabinet Office and the Education Department, though doing both jobs was certainly stretching. My average working day was still 6.45 a.m. to midnight, and the red boxes arrived, bursting full, every day except Sunday.

Being a minister, below Secretary of State level, could be interesting: you were expected to be more immersed in policy detail than some Secretaries of State had time for, and I found this fun and rewarding.

On the downside, it was necessary to respond regularly to adjournment debates in the House of Commons – sometimes involving only a handful of MPs.

It was evident that I was not the only person who found these debates occasionally irksome. In October 2013, I was due to give the ministerial response to a debate on Snaresbrook Primary School, in the main Chamber of the House of Commons.

The new Deputy Speaker, Eleanor Laing, was presiding in the chair. Halfway through the debate, and very unusually, she sent me a small note, passed down by the whip on the front bench. 'Minister,' it read, 'is there any chance you could cut your speech length in half? I was hoping to finish at 5.40 p.m. so I can catch the 6.10 p.m. train home.' I didn't know whether to be insulted or grateful. But I complied.

In October 2013, David Cameron and Nick Clegg carried out a reshuffle of their ministers, but it was on a modest scale compared with the changes in September 2012 and July 2014.

Mike Moore, the Liberal Democrat MP who was our Secretary of State for Scotland, was removed from his post to make way for the combative Alistair Carmichael. It was a huge disappointment and shock to Mike, with less than a year to go until the Scottish referendum.

Jeremy Browne was also very upset to be sacked, losing his job as Minister of State at the Home Office. I had once again tried to keep Jeremy in post, arguing that he was an able individual and that his forced removal might cause him to question his whole future in the Liberal Democrats. I was right. Jeremy rejected advances from the Conservatives to join them, including an offer from Grant Shapps not to stand a candidate against Jeremy in Taunton if he came out publicly and argued for a Liberal Democrat–Conservative tactical voting alliance of some type against the Labour Party. But Jeremy eventually decided to stand down as MP at the next election – making it almost certain that we would lose his Taunton seat.

In other changes, Don Foster became Liberal Democrat Chief Whip, Norman Baker was sent to the Home Office to keep an eye on Theresa May, Simon Hughes got his opportunity in ministerial office at the Justice Department, and Baroness Susan Kramer was pleasantly shocked to be invited to take over as Minister of State at the Transport Department. Susan proved to be a good minister, though she is sometimes a better speaker than listener. After a few weeks, Nick Clegg's officials had a private message from the office of Patrick McLoughlin, the Transport Secretary: 'Is there anything that Nick can do to get Baroness Kramer to talk less? Our ministerial meetings are taking twice as long since she joined the department. It is seriously impairing the efficiency of the Transport Department.' Nick replied that he thought that this was an issue for the Transport Secretary to resolve.

Nick did consider a much larger reshuffle of his top team. He really wanted Danny Alexander to move to be Business Secretary, and for me to return as Chief Secretary to the Treasury. But Vince Cable didn't want to move from Business, and Danny Alexander did not want to move to Climate Change. So all the other senior positions stayed as they were.

The party conference season had passed relatively peacefully at the Department for Education, and we had been relatively unscathed in the Cabinet reshuffle, with both Michael Gove and I keeping our existing jobs and Liz Truss also staying where she was – to her obvious disappointment.

Nick Clegg and I had wanted to launch a second 'priority school-building programme' to rebuild the schools in the worst condition, but this had been vetoed by Michael, who argued that more work was necessary on the details first.

We had, however, successfully launched the new policies on free school meals at our September conference, and we had also announced tighter guidelines on school uniforms, to seek to stop some schools insisting on excessively expensive clothing that could make it more difficult for children from poorer families to attend some of the best schools.

Michael Gove and Dom Cummings weren't terribly keen on the new uniform guidelines. Indeed, Dom appeared to be concerned that they might interfere with the freedoms of some new free schools and academies – where there was some anecdotal evidence of expensive uniform requirements that sought to mimic private school models. Dom sent me a barbed email setting out what was and wasn't acceptable to his boss, adding: 'There will be no "boater monitoring unit" set up in the Department for Education!'

It was going to be a busy autumn for education policy and delivery, with ongoing work on a national schools fair funding formula, implementation work on the universal free school meals policy, major announcements to be made on school capital expenditure, and a government review on 16–24 education, being led by the Cabinet Secretary, Sir Jeremy Heywood.

In October, Nick Clegg was due to make a speech on education policy, which had been many months in the planning and had been delayed on a number of occasions by events such as Syria.

This speech was designed to focus on school workforce issues – including helping to get more top-quality head teachers to schools in the worst perform-ing parts of the country. We were going to announce a new programme, the details of which we had been working on for many months. As usual, the most difficult issue turned out to be what to name the programme. Nick's office had come up with some ghastly names – 'Titan Heads', 'Super Head Teachers', 'Champion Teachers', 'A-Team Teachers', and – possibly worst of all – 'Rescue Head Teachers'.

I eventually insisted on the initiative being called the 'Talented Leaders Programme', but Nick's football-mad press spokesman, James McGrory, decided to brief out 'Champions League' instead.

Michael Gove was supportive of the new announcement. In a conference call while I was on holiday in France during August, he said: 'I'm delighted to hear about the Deputy Prime Minister's speech. It sounds as if it is going to be rather good!' From 1,000 miles away I thought I could detect a tongue in cheek.

But the speech wasn't only going to set out government policy. It was also going to discuss another area of workforce development, where there was rather less consensus: the issue of whether all teachers in state-funded schools should be fully qualified. Michael Gove had unilaterally removed the requirement for all such teachers to have 'qualified teacher status', by exempting academies and free schools, in an announcement made over a year before.

The Liberal Democrat view was that all teachers should be fully qualified: we were willing to look at how the qualification process should work, but we did not believe that unqualified staff should be able to teach in taxpayer-funded schools. This was a long-standing party policy position, which was popular with the profession and the public, and which Nick had been planning to reassert publicly for many months.

What now conspired to make the issue particularly newsworthy were a number of press stories about failing free schools – including some that had been taking on low-quality, unqualified teachers. The long-planned speech was suddenly going to be more topical and politically combustible than when originally planned.

I was in the south of France over the weekend of 19 and 20 October, on a brief break.

After an unusually second-rate meal out on the Saturday night, I was suddenly inundated with angry text messages from Dom Cummings. He had seen the first editions of the Sunday newspapers, and he didn't sound particularly happy.

Nick Clegg's big education speech was set to be delivered the following week, and his press spokesman, James McGrory, had been charged with briefing out some selected extracts that weekend. James doesn't really do understatement. If you asked him to light a small candle in Shoreditch, you would soon find out that the whole City of London was up in flames.

The newspaper headlines shouted 'Clegg Declares War on Gove'. There followed a breathless account of coalition splits over qualified teacher status, academy freedoms and aspects of free schools policy.

I wasn't delighted. The whole thing looked completely over the top. And we had made a serious mistake by mixing up a government speech which included policy announcements on head teacher supply with political lines designed to set out perfectly legitimate differences in policy between coalition partners.

Michael Gove was furious, as was David Cameron. The next week, the Prime Minister waved the front page of one of the daily newspapers at Nick Clegg, asking, 'What on the earth is this?'

The media, needless to say, generally rowed in behind Michael Gove, and tried to present the whole row as some sort of Liberal Democrat opportunism. It was irritating, because we ended up on the back foot on an issue that we should have been on the front foot on.

In any case, the row was patched up. The speech was delivered. And life moved on.

But it was to be the beginning of a new period of tension at the Education Department, which would last right through until July 2014.

During this time there proved to be three big issues that split the coalition parties: the implementation of free school meals, the prioritising of expenditure between new places and new free schools, and the leadership of Ofsted.

The free school meals policy had been part of the School Food Plan, which Michael Gove had commissioned. And Michael had that said he was a supporter of the policy – though I suspected that it would not have been his top priority for additional money.

Other Conservatives were fundamentally opposed to free school meals – including Dom Cummings, who was still upset that he had not been notified before the policy was announced.

I now spent a huge amount of time seeking to ensure that universal infant free school meals were delivered successfully. Some newspapers, particularly the *Daily Mail*, were very opposed to the plan and it was clear that they would ruthlessly highlight any problems in delivery. We had given ourselves one year to prepare the policy, which was to begin in 16,500 English schools from September 2014.

Before announcing the move at party conference, we had asked a very senior civil servant in the Education Department to complete a note looking at delivery and other challenges. This turned out to be of excellent quality, and meant that we were building on a solid foundation.

But we now considered that there were two further issues that needed addressing to ensure success. The first was that we wanted legislation to place upon all state-funded schools an obligation to deliver the free meals. This was not just about ensuring that schools did what we wanted: it would, crucially, give schools the confidence they needed about policy sustainability, since it was much less likely that a future government would cancel the policy if it had been legislated for.

All that was required was a single, simple, clause in a Bill already going through Parliament. But Dom Cummings and Michael Gove were adamant – they did not want any legislation on this issue, as they did not want to be seen in any way to 'interfere' with the freedoms of academies and free schools. This seemed to me to be an entirely bogus point. Everyone agreed that the duty should apply to all state-funded schools, and so the 'imposition' would be trivial.

For months, the debate rumbled on across government. The advice of lawyers was sought. We considered compromises that might have the same effect – none of which worked. The Permanent Secretary tried to find a solution. So did the Cabinet Secretary. The Chancellor was involved. The Deputy Prime Minister discussed the issue with the Prime Minister on three or four occasions.

Even David Cameron couldn't understand what the problem was: 'I don't know why Michael is being so difficult,' he told Nick Clegg in November. 'If necessary, I will just tell him to do this, but let's see if we can find a solution that everyone is content with first.' We couldn't, and eventually – after four months of arguments – the Prime Minister finally told his Education Secretary in the New Year that there was going to be legislation on the issue. Michael was far from pleased.

And then there was the issue of capital. At the end of 2013, we were due to make a major announcement on school capital allocations. There would be another round of free schools, more money for school maintenance, and a big three-year allocation of money to local authorities for what was called 'basic need' – new school places.

The school population was rising rapidly in size and we urgently needed new school places to accommodate all the extra children. If we got too little money out or if local authorities failed to build places, we could have a crisis in which parents wouldn't be able to get their children into school.

This would blot out entirely any success the government might have on other areas of education reform.

It had not yet become public, but in fact three areas of the country were already, in late 2013, failing to meet their statutory requirement to deliver a place in school for every child who wanted one. But the numbers were small, and most of the children out of school were probably the children of immigrants or asylum seekers, rather than of the vocal middle classes. So only a few of us knew how serious the situation was becoming. We did everything we could to resolve it.

I was therefore very keen to allocate out as much money as possible to local authorities to build extra places, as well as giving them the certainty of a three-year allocation of cash.

Unfortunately, there were pressures elsewhere in the school capital budget. The free schools programme was not managed on a budget-control basis – the department wanted to approve every bid that met its quality and need criteria. As a consequence, spending on free schools was growing fast, and was now hundreds of millions of pounds above the last DfE budget assumptions.

At the beginning of the parliament, spending on free schools was expected to be a few hundred million pounds per year – much less than the amounts that were allocated to local authorities for building much needed new school places and for the maintenance of the 24,000 state-funded schools in England. But by late 2013 and early 2014, the Education Department was estimating that free school spending would rise to around £1.3 billion in 2014/15 and to almost £1.4 billion in 2015/16. In contrast, we were only planning to spend around £1.2 billion per year each on maintaining 24,000 schools and building hundreds of thousands of new places. I began to be very concerned that spending on a few hundred new free schools of yet unproven quality (the Ofsted ratings for new free schools were little different from those of comparable existing schools) was becoming grossly disproportionate when compared to spending on other crucial areas of the capital budget.

Michael Gove now decided that £400 million should be transferred out of the basic need allocations for new places and put in the free school budget line. I opposed this, and wrote a letter making clear my opposition. I pointed out that while free schools did create more school places, most of these were in areas such as London. Cornwall, for example, had had no free school applications at all. That meant that Cornwall would lose some money from its basic need budget but would receive no new school places from the free school programme.

And there was a final big issue on schools capital. While it would be perfectly possible to bring in the new free school meals in schools with inadequate kitchens, it made more sense to improve the schools' ability to produce healthy meals on site. In many parts of the country, school kitchens had been neglected or closed down over the past few decades, so there was now arguably a case for more investment.

My officials calculated that around £200 million was needed across England to bring kitchens up to a good standard. Local authorities already received around £1.2 billion from central government each year for improvement and maintenance of schools. I thought it reasonable that around £50 million of that money could be found, therefore, from local authorities themselves. But I decided to ask Danny Alexander for some extra money as part of the Liberal Democrat 'ask' in the 2013 Autumn Statement. Nick Clegg fully supported this being a priority. I also informed Michael Gove – making clear that this was part of the Liberal Democrat bid for Autumn Statement policies, and was separate from whatever bids he wanted to put in as Education Secretary. I thought he was content for me to make this a Liberal Democrat – rather than DfE – Budget priority.

The Treasury, needless to say, pushed back on our request for £150 million. But Danny Alexander and I had spotted that there was an unallocated sum of school maintenance capital of around £157 million in the departmental budget for 2014/15. Danny suggested that the Treasury would give us an extra £70 million and that we should then use £80 million of this unallocated amount to top up to the £150 million that we needed.

I was satisfied with this. Danny said he would send his officials round to the Education Department to agree the details.

When Dom Cummings and Michael Gove found out what was going on, they hit the roof. They had, without telling me, now asked officials to stop any negotiations on kitchen capital with the Treasury. They had made clear to the Treasury that they didn't want any money at all to improve kitchens. They considered this a Liberal Democrat priority. Their priority was extra money to close the gaping free schools overspend.

The issue came to a head on Tuesday 26 November, a couple of weeks before the Autumn Statement. A team from HM Treasury had set off to meet

Education Department officials at 2.15 p.m., to discuss the final details of what I thought had been agreed. While they were on their way over to the DfE, Michael Gove's office sent a message out saying that he did not wish to support any bid for kitchen capital, and that DfE officials should not communicate in any way with the Treasury over this. It was too late to stop the team from HM Treasury, who had to be met in the lobby of our department, only to be told that their meeting had now had to be cancelled and they couldn't come into the building. They were rather baffled.

Later that day, I phoned Matt Sanders, Nick Clegg's education adviser, to find out what on earth was going on. Matt had two offices – one in the Cabinet Office and the other in the Education Department, where he had for two years shared an office with the Conservative special advisers, including Dom Cummings.

Matt now told me that not only was he irritated and confused by the row over kitchen capital, but he had just received an email from Michael Gove's private office, telling him that his desk in the special advisers' office in the DfE was now needed for other purposes. He was told that his private possessions would be cleared out of the office that day and moved elsewhere within the building. He was rather upset. I was furious. It seemed like a declaration of war.

The next morning, I sent a private email to Nick Clegg, updating him on the row of capital, and informing him of the enforced move of his adviser from his office in the DfE. Nick replied quickly and was clearly very irritated. He then sent a very blunt text to David Cameron, complaining about both issues.

Cameron was preparing for that day's Prime Minister's Questions when the text from the Deputy Prime Minister came through. He angrily asked his staff to get hold of the Education Secretary.

The Downing Street operators – 'Switch' – now tried to connect the angry Prime Minister to his Education Secretary. But Michael Gove wasn't in the building. Instead, the Prime Minister himself conveyed a blunt message: 'What on earth is going on in the DfE? I've got the DPM absolutely incandescent and texting me over school capital and apparently there is also some unnecessary problem over a Lib Dem adviser called Matt Sanders and his desk! Please get Michael to ring me as soon as possible.'

Later in the day, Nick Clegg met up with David Cameron. 'Don't worry.

I've spoken to Michael,' said the PM. 'I've told him to calm things down and also to sort out this ridiculous problem about legislation over free school meals. I really don't want big rows in the coalition over small stuff like this.'

'Yes,' said Nick Clegg, 'we've all wasted far too much time on these small issues. I don't know what is wrong with Michael sometimes.'

The Prime Minister laughed. 'The thing that you've got to remember with Michael is that he is basically a bit of a Maoist – he believes that the world makes progress through a process of creative destruction!'

The Prime Minister and his Education Secretary clearly talked. In the afternoon, Michael Gove and his team seemed decidedly friendlier – though Matt Sanders's desk was still moved. 'Perhaps it's better this way for all of us,' the mild-mannered special adviser suggested to me.

That Friday, the Quad completed their agreements on the Autumn Statement. Danny Alexander telephoned me to say: 'David, I've done a deal with the Chancellor. You get what you want on school kitchens – £70 million more from the Treasury and £80 million more from the unallocated maintenance money in the DfE budget. But, in return, George wants you to lay off the free schools budget – even if that means agreeing the £400 million switch from basic need to free schools that Gove wants. George has also said that he'll phone Gove over the weekend to let him know all this, so that we can put an end to all the rows.'

'OK. I can live with that,' I said, relieved that the long-running dispute was over.

But it wasn't.

Just days later, on 3 December, our press office phoned me to say that Tory special advisers in the Education Department were briefing the media that 'Clegg's free school meals policy is a shambles, and now he wants to take money from basic need – new school places – to bail out a shortfall of money for kitchens'. It was completely untrue – indeed, it was the Conservatives who wanted to take basic need money to fund free schools. I was furious. The Tory adviser was also calling the whole free school meals policy a 'pointless gimmick', even though it was supposedly supported by Michael Gove as well.

The next day, Nick Clegg and I were due to visit a primary school in London to announce the extra money for kitchen capital.

In the morning, hours before the visit, Nick Clegg's office received a message from Michael Gove's office saying: 'No announcement can go ahead which includes the £80 million unallocated monies in our budget.'

This set in train multiple rushed emails and urgent phone calls across Whitehall.

At 10 a.m., a blunt and helpful email was sent out from the Chancellor's office to Michael Gove's. It ended the row: 'I understand your concerns, but this is a Quad agreement and since 50 per cent of the Quad is HMT ministers, that means that ours have agreed to this.'

Nick Clegg was standing in for the Prime Minister at that day's PMQs. Immediately afterwards, he and I left for Walnut Tree Walk Primary School in Lambeth for a brief visit.

While we were there, one of our press officers called me over into a quiet corner. 'You will want to see this.' He showed me the *Guardian*'s online news page – it said that Michael Gove and Nick Clegg were at war over a £200 million hole in the free school meals policy. I was now spitting blood. We were told that it was Dom Cummings himself doing the briefing.

The response from the DPM's own press people was immediate and blunt: 'The DfE advisers are lying, going rogue, being hostile and talking bollocks.' It was not very 'Coalicious'.

When I got back to the DfE, I received a message saying that Michael Gove wanted to see me. I wanted to see him too.

We were supposed to meet at 4.45 p.m., but a vote in the House of Commons had just been called. I went downstairs from my DfE office as quickly as I could – thinking I might need to run over to the House of Commons. But there, parked outside the department, was Michael Gove's black Jaguar.

I opened the door, and climbed in. Michael was sitting on the back seat, looking rather sombre. I later realised that Michael doesn't mind rows. He just hates losing them. And he had lost this one.

As the car pulled away from the kerb, Michael turned to me: 'David, I want to talk to you about free school meals. I am extremely' – and he heavily emphasised the word – '*extremely* angry about the announcement today. I knew nothing about this, and the DPM should have had the courtesy to brief me on it before today.'

In the seat in front of us, I saw our driver prick up his ears, glance in the mirror and turn the radio volume down.

I was determined to give no ground: 'I am sorry if you are unhappy, but we were specifically told that the Chancellor had briefed you over the weekend.'

'The Chancellor did speak to me over the weekend, but not about capital.'

'Well, that's not our fault, is it?' I said. 'He told Danny Alexander he would do. The PM and Chancellor agreed all this at Quad. By the way, we're feeling pretty bruised too. We've been told that it is your special advisers who are trashing the whole free school meals policy in the press today and yesterday. They are briefing directly against a government policy. That is unacceptable.'

The driver seemed to be enjoying the row.

We were now at the Members' Entrance of the House of Commons. The car stopped.

'Anyway,' I said, 'I have just met John Vincent and Henry Dimbleby. They are delighted with both the revenue funding and the capital funding for free school meals.'

Michael said nothing. We headed off to vote – separately. It was the first time we had had a face-to-face row.

Later that evening, another meeting in the Education Department was scheduled to discuss the forthcoming announcements on basic need capital.

I thought the meeting might be cancelled, but it wasn't.

At 6.30 p.m., the meeting was called and I headed for Michael's office, where a few officials and private secretaries were waiting – looking rather sheepish and clearly wondering whether Michael and I were about to have another row.

We walked in to Michael's office, and turned left – away from the long conference table and towards the sofas that were located to the right of his desk. I could not help noticing that the old furniture had been removed, and in its place were some brand-new and super-sized sofas and chairs. We stood there, waiting for Michael to finish off some paperwork at his desk.

There was a chilly atmosphere, and no one wanted to say anything. Eventually, to break the ice, I think, one of the senior officials said: 'I see you have procured some new sofas, Secretary of State?'

Michael glanced up from his desk. 'Yes, Susan, I have,' he said. And then, quick as a flash, 'I've funded them from an underspend in the school maintenance budget.'

I couldn't help laughing.

However much we rowed, we always laughed in the end.

Two weeks later, and in spite of recent tensions, Michael suggested that we should do some sort of duet together at the Education Department Christmas party.

'I thought we could do Morecambe and Wise,' he said. 'Obviously, I would be Eric Morecambe and you would be Ernie Wise. At the end, we could dance off together, using the signature Morecambe and Wise dance.'

'I think I would need to be quite drunk,' I said.

GREEN OR BLUE?

2010–15

D avid Cameron arrived in the Cabinet Room just a few minutes before
the Quad meeting was due to start. He threw down his papers in his
customary place in the middle of the table.

'God,' he said, 'I spent all last night at a business dinner, where they went
on and on and on at me about high energy prices and government policy on
renewables. Eventually, I said to them, "Look, I know you hate the policies.
I get it. And now the guy responsible is in prison. What more can I do?"'

The Conservatives present laughed loudly. The Liberal Democrat members
around the table smiled weakly.

It was now 2013. It had all been so different in 2010, at the start of the
government.

Back in 2010, David Cameron was still trying to re-position his party as
one that cared about the environment and about green issues. Soon after he
was elected as Conservative leader, David Cameron had visited the Arctic
to highlight the risks of global warming and to be photographed 'hugging
a husky'.

The environment had long been an issue of great importance to the Liberal
Democrats, and in the May 2010 coalition talks, the Conservatives – guided
by Oliver Letwin – offered up a long list of environmental policies from
both our party manifestos, to help sell coalition to us. Indeed, there was
more in the original coalition agreement on the environment than on any
other policy issue – nineteen specific policy pledges, compared with only

one on health and five or six on education. The environment section of the coalition talks did not take long and was largely uncontroversial – with the exception of the issue of nuclear power, where there was a carve-out for Liberal Democrat MPs based on the party's opposition to nuclear power (overturned in 2013). This would allow Lib Dem MPs to abstain on any votes on new nuclear power stations.

The issue of the environment and climate change was so important to our party that Nick Clegg requested that the role of Secretary of State for Energy and Climate Change should be occupied by a Liberal Democrat – Chris Huhne. This placed a Lib Dem in an important department in relation to both the economy and the key issue of climate change.

The political problem was that at a time of economic crisis, the environment had dropped way down the list of public priorities. A minority of people cared passionately about green issues, but the majority did not rank them as a concern. And the problem, politically, was that those who cared most passionately about green issues often viewed anything less than policy 'perfection' as a sell-out. It is therefore questionable how much political benefit we received from running this department – most of the public didn't notice, and the green activists who cared could normally never be satisfied with any solutions that would be acceptable to the wider public and to our coalition partners.

In many ways, Chris Huhne was an excellent choice for Climate Change Secretary – economically literate, fantastically bright, politically astute, and capable of ensuring his department punched above its generally low Whitehall weight. Chris was never going to be bullied by the Treasury and nor would he waste time on self-doubt.

With a committed team of Conservative ministers, including Greg Barker and Charles Hendry, Chris set about implementing our ambitious coalition programme of green policies.

Under both Chris Huhne and his successor, Ed Davey, a massive programme of investment in renewable electricity began, which not only supported the economy but also led to a rapid increase in the UK's renewable energy capacity and output.

Ambitious targets were set for reducing carbon emissions, and Ed Davey played a major international role in negotiating a cross-Europe climate change agreement.

Meanwhile the government promoted smart meters, encouraged more energy generation from waste, and sought to tackle emissions from both power stations and vehicles.

Other parts of government were also required to promote the green agenda. In spite of Conservative backbench opposition, the decision was taken to proceed with the high-speed rail network to the north – the so-called HS2. Action was taken by the Environment Department to protect green spaces and the countryside. And Chris Huhne and Ed Davey worked in partnership with Nick Clegg and Vince Cable to establish a 'green investment bank'.

Not everything on the green agenda was a success. Both coalition parties fought early on to claim the credit for a new 'Green Deal' – in which home energy improvements would be paid for over time from savings from lower household energy bills. This was to be one of the government's flagship green policies, and when Ed Davey took over from Chris Huhne in early 2012, George Osborne was quick to tell the new Climate Change Secretary: 'The Green Deal was always my idea. The Conservatives have really pushed this forward.'

The Chancellor was less keen to be linked to the plan when it later proved to be one of the great damp squibs of the government; it was launched, and then rapidly sank. The lead Conservative minister, Greg Barker, had failed to devise a scheme that was attractive to either home owners or to the private rented sector. As a consequence, a large number of Green Deal assessments took place, but almost no Green Deal finance packages. The programme was rightly regarded as a flop – a fine example of a thoroughly good idea that was thoroughly badly designed and delivered.

For the first half of the parliament, the area of environmental policy was not too contentious between the coalition parties. It was clear that the Chancellor had little interest in green issues and was inclined to view the whole agenda as an expensive distraction that could not contribute to economic growth or to Conservative 2015 re-election plans. The Prime Minister retained a greater sympathy for green policies – but with no real engagement. Essentially, David Cameron did not have the subject on his priority list.

Chris Huhne and Ed Davey were therefore free to drive forward their own agenda – with both some support and some challenge from Danny Alexander in the Treasury.

But this Conservative 'benign neglect' of the environment had begun to change to active opposition in late 2012. With higher energy prices and a greater focus on growth, the Conservatives – particularly in the Treasury – now regarded the green agenda with active hostility. Many Conservative MPs also objected to the prospect of onshore wind sites in their constituencies, adding another twist to the new Conservative enviro-scepticism.

In the September 2012 government reshuffle, the highly respected Conservative junior minister in Ed Davey's department, Charles Hendry, was replaced by the unlikely figure of John Hayes, who had little or no interest in green policies. Within weeks, Hayes had made a speech implying that there should be no more development of onshore wind sites: 'Enough is enough!' he proclaimed thunderously. Ed Davey was not amused and was obliged to publicly contradict his own colleague.

In other policy areas, too, there was little Conservative enthusiasm for action. In the Department for Communities and Local Government, Liberal Democrat ministers sought to press the case for high-energy insulation standards. We wanted to phase in so-called zero carbon homes, within a limited time horizon. But house builders lobbied Conservative ministers hard, and the policy had to be negotiated and renegotiated on multiple occasions over a two-year period.

The crunch moment for policy on the environment and climate change came in the autumn of 2013. At the Labour Party conference, Ed Miliband made a surprise, populist, announcement that his party would – when elected – freeze consumer energy prices for two years.

The pledge was opportunistic, ill-conceived and in danger of deterring future investment in energy capacity. The opinion polls immediately showed, however, that it appeared to be extremely popular with the public. The Conservative Party could see that the pledge was foolish and likely to backfire on the Labour leader. 'This is complete socialist twaddle from Ed Miliband, and certain to go wrong,' Oliver Letwin told me. But David Cameron and George Osborne were suddenly not too sure. The public resented higher energy prices and thought the energy companies were profiteering. The polls appeared to indicate that they liked Miliband's idea of a freeze.

Of course, polls can be very misleading. If you ask people whether they would like free food, free beer and free holidays to the Maldives, they are likely to answer yes. If you ask whether they intend to vote for a party promising these things, they may be more sceptical.

The Labour policy was riddled with problems: it risked incentivising the energy firms to ramp up prices in advance of the proposed freeze, and it certainly risked damaging investment in much needed new domestic energy capacity.

But Labour's crowd-pleasing proposal now threw the leadership of the Conservative Party into a complete panic. Instead of sticking with a convincing critique of Labour, the Prime Minister and Chancellor suddenly seemed to be leaping on the low-energy-price bandwagon. In desperation that Ed Miliband might have found a game-changing policy, the Chancellor and Prime Minister decided that the price issue must be sorted out within weeks – in the Autumn Statement. And because the Conservatives did not wish to take on the big energy companies, who seemed in no mood to be bullied, they decided to focus on the green levies that increased consumer prices in order to incentivise more renewable energy generation.

The run-up to the Autumn Statement was fraught. Ed Davey was not willing to allow renewables policy to be undermined, while the Prime Minister and the Chancellor were determined to find a way – any way – of cutting prices.

At Prime Minister's Questions in early October, David Cameron, without agreement across the coalition, suddenly started to hint that the government would look to cut energy prices. Ed Davey hit the roof, complaining strongly to Nick Clegg. Neither had been consulted.

In the afternoon that same day, there was a Quad to discuss the Autumn Statement and energy policy. Nick Clegg was very blunt with the Prime Minister. He told me later: 'I told him that I was really unhappy about his freelancing at PMQs: "This is not the way coalition can operate. You are making a complete mess of dealing with Miliband on the price freeze issue – instead of attacking Miliband's half-baked solutions, you are ending up fighting on Labour's own ground and are turning a fight with Labour into a fight with your coalition partners. All you are doing is pursuing your own party's obsession with green levies. You should be ripping the shit out of this Labour policy because it is an opportunistic con."'

The Deputy Prime Minister made clear to both the Prime Minister and Chancellor his view that the coalition's response to Labour should be far less defensive: 'If you want to have a response to Labour on the cost of living, let's increase the tax threshold or write people a cheque, or scrap the Treasury's idiotic carbon price floor. You are both making a total mess of this.'

David Cameron and George Osborne both looked sheepish. They knew that Miliband's policy was incoherent nonsense, but they did not have the confidence to say so. David Cameron was on the defensive, telling Nick that he was probably right. He also revealed that their election strategist, Lynton Crosby, had been telling them that his polling on the proposed freeze showed that the public didn't really believe the policy made any sense. George Osborne said little. It was clear that he still had his eye on reducing the costs of green policies.

Nick thought that he had made his point strongly with the Prime Minister, but a week later Cameron was again on the back foot over energy prices at Prime Minister's Questions. This time he went further, and suggested specifically that the government was looking at rolling back green levies.

Ed Davey was now incandescent. After Prime Minister's Questions, David Cameron tried to ring Nick Clegg to explain what he had said. 'Tell him I'm not available,' was the reply.

Later in the afternoon, there was another Quad on the Autumn Statement. There was another big row. Energy policy was not the only issue, but it was the trigger.

Nick Clegg confronted the Prime Minister and asked him why he was 'making up policy' like this: 'You cannot behave like this. There are three options: the coalition ends, or we will just start voting as we like on things – with Labour if necessary – or you need to treat us with some respect.' He made clear that if the Prime Minister and Chancellor wanted to keep open the option of a second coalition with the Liberal Democrats, then they needed to be more respectful of their coalition partner's views.

George Osborne sat fuming, and insisted that he was still determined to reduce the cost of green levies and blunt the Miliband attack.

Danny Alexander told me later that Nick was very firm on not giving up on the green agenda. He said: 'I'm sorry, but I am not going along with your narrative of blaming all this on green policies and green levies. You know that what has driven most of the price rise here is the global price of energy. Why aren't you saying that, then? This has got to change. I am sorry – I have no intention of being a prisoner in my own government.'

In the days that followed this row, what happened was what usually happened after big bust-ups in the coalition – things got fixed.

A carefully balanced compromise was put together, with a one-and-a-half-hour discussion on energy issues at the Quad on 7 November. The agreement involved a set of measures to reduce energy prices by a small amount, in order to spike the Miliband guns. But as a price for Liberal Democrat support, the Treasury had to agree to directly fund some of the environmental programmes, rather than these being paid for by energy bill levies.

After weeks of the Miliband price freeze being a big issue in the media, the coverage of it now died away.

And one year on, just before the general election, energy prices were falling – removing any further political resonance from the issue.

However, the tension between the two coalition parties on green issues rumbled on until the end of the parliament. David Cameron had long ago given up on this agenda, and instead he had left the policy area to the control of his Chancellor, who had always regarded the environment as a distraction from bigger issues and a potential anchor on growth.

'Energy and environmental policy has in many ways now become the biggest source of disagreement in the coalition,' Nick Clegg reflected in late 2013. 'I have spent more time arguing about the details of this with Cameron and Osborne than any other issue.'

The Chancellor wanted instead to focus attention on the recovering economy – and he wanted to unite the coalition parties against Labour on the big issues in economic policy.

The Economy Bounces Back

2013

It was a few days after the 2013 Autumn Statement, and all of the world leaders and former leaders were gathered in a vast stadium in South Africa, for a special celebration of the life of Nelson Mandela.

It was shambolically organised. The acoustics were bad. No one could hear a word of what was being said. And it was raining.

But they were all there – Obama. Clinton too. And George Bush Jr.

There was a good turnout from the UK. As well as Nick Clegg, John Major was there. Cameron, obviously. Blair, looking taut and suntanned. Gordon Brown, over in a corner, looking grumpy, with his wife occasionally having to apologise for his behaviour.

Only George Bush seemed cheerful – the life and soul of the event. As Nick Clegg watched a speech by Raul Castro on the television screen in the VIP room, George Bush swept up next to him and glanced dismissively at the speaker: 'Jesus. Y'know, that guy Raul Castro is a total prick,' he said. And then he walked off.

The death of Nelson Mandela, announced just hours after the Autumn Statement, understandably eclipsed what was otherwise a fairly good-news economic announcement – perhaps the best for the coalition government since the general election.

But it didn't change the fundamental picture: that the economy was now bouncing back at last.

At the end of October 2013, we had had the first release of the UK growth numbers for the third quarter of the year. These showed growth of 0.8 per cent for the previous three months – an annualised growth rate of a healthy 3.2 per cent.

At the same time, the first meetings of the Quad took place, to consider the contents of the upcoming Autumn Statement. David Cameron and George Osborne were fixated on trying to find some mechanism to cut energy bills, to 'shoot Miliband's fox'.

Nick Clegg, Danny Alexander and I were concerned that the Conservatives were trying to unpick the government's environmental agenda, and we made the case for a further rise in the personal tax allowance instead. This would take us above the figure of £10,000 for the personal allowance, which was the pledge we Liberal Democrats had made in May 2010.

The early estimates from the Office for Budget Responsibility indicated that they would be revising down their estimates of the future size of the Budget deficit – possibly by quite a large amount.

But George Osborne now wanted to discuss with us what the coalition's future fiscal strategy should be – what needed to happen to government borrowing to get national debt back to 'safe' levels.

The Treasury was commissioned to produce a variety of deficit scenarios and Budget rules. The Chancellor began to suggest that the best 'rule' was that the country should aim for future Budget surpluses in order to reduce debt. He proposed that this should be the new fiscal rule, and that we should no longer have a rule allowing the government to borrow money for investment spending.

Given the size of the deficits that the UK had been running since 2008, there was a clear case for getting the UK Budget back into annual surpluses for a period. But I was worried nonetheless. If we sought to get the Budget too quickly back into surplus, we could end up with very steep cuts to public spending, which could damage public services and undermine the government's ability to advance a progressive, pro-opportunity agenda. It was also clear that the ever-political George Osborne saw the fiscal debate as an opportunity to put Labour on the back foot politically in the run-up to the general election.

George wanted to paint Labour as the party of economic profligacy and borrowing. He wanted us on side in this political mission. He also assumed that the Liberal Democrats would favour a mix of fiscal consolidation that would involve higher taxes but also fewer welfare cuts than in his own scenario. Again, he was content for that relative political positioning of the Conservative Party.

I wasn't keen to leap into George's political trap, and nor did I see any economic literacy in permanently ruling out any government borrowing for 'real' capital spending, for example, on large transport projects. That seemed to lack any economic justification.

More than anything, as the author of the next Liberal Democrat manifesto, I was determined that we would not make commitments on borrowing or spending that we could not or should not keep. So I was determined to agree nothing that I considered undeliverable.

Danny Alexander, on the other hand, was much keener on the idea of running a completely balanced Budget. He wanted a new fiscal rule of 'only spending what we raise'. Vince Cable was at completely the other end of the spectrum. He did not want aggressive targets to cut borrowing, and he believed that borrowing for all investment spending was a good thing.

So started a long debate on fiscal policy within the most senior levels of the Liberal Democrat Party that was not concluded until the early weeks of January – 2015.

Anyway, we prevented anything extreme on fiscal policy going into the Autumn Statement from George Osborne, and managed to sort out solutions to the other policy pinch points.

The Cabinet met at 8 a.m. on Thursday 5 December to hear about the contents of the Budget. It was to be a neutral Budget, but George could barely disguise his pleasure at its contents. He would be announcing the biggest upward revision to growth forecasts for around fifteen years, and a huge cumulative downward revision to future borrowing figures. There was a brief discussion at the end of the Chancellor's 45-minute presentation. Only Vince Cable sounded rather gloomy.

The economy was now clearly coming back to life, just in time for the last year of the parliament.

As the year ended, the leaders of the two coalition parties were thinking the same thing: will the economic upturn lead to an upturn in our political fortunes too?

It would not be long before we found out.

2014

THE FINAL YEAR:
'IF I WALK ON WATER'

2014

Nick Clegg ended 2013 at a celebrity media party in the heart of London. As he mingled with the stars of British broadcasting and the arts before the main event started, he suddenly turned round and was confronted by the distinct looks and voice of the veteran comedian Dame Edna Everage.

'Darling! Possum!' Dame Edna shouted. 'How wonderful to see you! Keep up all your brilliant work. I'm a fan, you know! I'm one of yours.' Then she rather ruined the effect by leaning forward and saying in hushed, conspiratorial, tones, 'Yes, darling. It's SO difficult being a Conservative these days!'

I spent a quiet Christmas and New Year in France, getting some rest before what would be the last full year of the coalition government.

Nick Clegg was with his family in Spain, and also had a quiet Christmas break.

On New Year's Day, I texted Nick to wish him all the best for 2014. The current polls had us on just 10 or 11 per cent. 'Here's to 22 per cent by this time next year,' I texted, jokingly. 'I'd settle for 18 per cent,' Nick replied.

The last six months of 2013 had actually been pretty successful for Nick Clegg and for the coalition. The economic recovery had finally arrived, and the dispute with Vince Cable over government economic strategy was over. We had achieved a successful autumn conference, with the right outcome on all the key issues for our manifesto. The pupil premium was beginning to deliver better outcomes for children from disadvantaged backgrounds. Pensions reform was moving ahead. We had announced the delivery of the £10,000 personal tax allowance – our highest-profile manifesto pledge. The new offer to disadvantaged two-year-olds was being rolled out. Same-sex marriage had been legislated for, and the rows over political reform were behind us. And even on tuition fees, the early evidence was of higher university participation, including amongst children from more disadvantaged families. We also had just announced a popular new policy to deliver free school meals for infant-school pupils.

But in many ways, this list of policy successes highlighted our political problem. We were doing the right things. We were having a huge impact in government. We were stopping the Conservatives from doing many illiberal and regressive things. So why were we getting absolutely no credit for it at all from the polls and the electorate?

Over Christmas and the New Year, Nick Clegg spoke to a number of close friends: 'It's very frustrating at the moment. I feel that we've hardly put a foot wrong in government in the last six months. But it just doesn't seem to make any difference at all. I'm so proud of what we are achieving. I am excited by the difference we are making in government. And yet, it all seems to make bugger-all difference. Nothing moves the dial with the public. I sometimes think that even if I went out and walked on water, people still wouldn't be impressed – they would just ask whether I was incapable of swimming.'

The Liberal Democrat leader decided that there could only be one of two conclusions – either he was no longer an effective vehicle for promoting his party, because of the damage done by tuition fees and the economic austerity. Or perhaps most of the time the public don't pay much attention to politics, and only re-evaluate their views at big moments such as at general elections. 'That's what I have got to hope, I guess.'

Meanwhile, Nick felt increasingly frustrated at having to work with David Cameron and the Conservative Party: 'This is such a different beast from the Tory Party we went into coalition with,' he told me in early 2013. 'Cameron has come within an inch of losing control of his party on immigration and on the European Union. And, now, being in coalition with the Conservative Party feels like being stuck in a cage with a huge, mad gorilla.'

Nevertheless, it was important to secure a clear agreement on the legislation that the coalition would take forward in our last year in government. Oliver Letwin and I worked on this jointly for some months. We decided, under guidance from David Cameron and Nick Clegg, that we didn't want any legislation that would be controversial with the public or that would split the coalition. But we also wanted a serious legislative programme that would show that the government was determined to go on delivering for its full five-year term of office.

David Cameron was already clearly obsessed and nervous about Labour's claim that we were going to witness a 'zombie parliament' with nothing going on. Rarely did a Cabinet meeting pass without the Prime Minister telling us all that: 'We really must nail this Labour nonsense about a zombie parliament. We must show that it isn't true and that we are not worried by it.' It became something of a running joke amongst some of us in Cabinet and we used to swap smiles when we heard the Prime Minister make the same point over and over again.

After what seemed like months of preparation, the senior members of the government finally met on 29 January to discuss the work Oliver and I had done on what was called the 'fourth session legislative programme' – the final Queen's Speech and parliamentary programme.

The Prime Minister seemed more relaxed than he usually did on these occasions, and we soon agreed a string of uncontentious Bills.

But when it came to all Vince Cable's proposals on tightening the enforcement rules for 'dodgy' company directors, the Prime Minister and Chancellor were strongly opposed to taking any action.

'I don't see why this is controversial,' said Nick Clegg. 'Anyway, what I won't accept from your own list is all this stuff to undermine workers' rights. And I really don't understand why you are pushing back again on doing anything on exclusivity clauses on zero-hours contracts. That seems a no-brainer to me and I thought we agreed that last September at one of these meetings?'

'I only agreed a consultation,' said George Osborne.

After a long discussion where it was clear that neither side was going to give way, George Osborne suddenly said: 'Look, we've got to make some progress on all this other stuff. Why don't we agree a truce? You give up on bashing company directors, and we'll give up on bashing the workers.'

We eventually secured the Prime Minister's agreement to proceed with another Pensions Bill, to take forward the latest stage of Steve Webb's ambitious pensions reform programme.

But when it came to two Liberal Democrat-proposed Bills, the Prime Minister could not be budged. The first was on legislating to put in place a binding target of spending 0.7 per cent of GNP on overseas aid. The second was on a recall Bill for parliamentarians found guilty of serious wrongdoing.

'Look,' said David Cameron, 'I just can't get the 0.7 per cent thing past my backbenchers. It would be even worse than gay marriage. It would unite all the people who hate spending money on foreigners with all the people who have a Treasury mindset and don't believe in passing laws for these matters. 0.7 per cent is just un-doable for me. And on recall, well, we could do something. But you can never satisfy people on these things. However tough we are, someone will want to outflank us. It's not a great thing for this stage of the parliament.'

Next we dealt with a 'Bill' sponsored by Oliver Letwin, which turned out to consist of just one side of A4 paper. It was called the 'Social Action, Responsibility and Heroism Bill'. Our adviser, Julian Astle, had dubbed it 'Oliver Letwin's Incompetent Heroes Bill', because Oliver had once explained to us that it would protect from legal action a person who had, for example, dived into a lake to save a drowning woman but landed on her head and seriously injured her. In other words, it was to protect 'have-a-go heroes'. Oliver circulated his Bill for us to look at, and there followed a couple of minutes of laughter, Oliver-baiting and teasing, from both sides of the coalition.

Within no time we had agreed fourteen or fifteen Bills, and we had a pretty serious legislative programme, with a few modest areas of disagreement.

'OK,' said David Cameron. 'Excellent. I think we're done, Nick?'

'Yes,' said Nick. 'But there is one other issue I want to raise: the child poverty targets.'

The relaxed atmosphere ended, and suddenly the Prime Minister and Chancellor looked on the defensive.

Iain Duncan Smith, Oliver Letwin and I had been working for around a year to review the child poverty targets, which were put into law by the last Labour government.

They were open to criticism because they focused on moving people over a fairly arbitrary income line, and because the key poverty target was heavily focused on relative poverty. This meant that in a recession the poor could get significantly poorer but relative poverty would fall if the rich lost income faster than the poor.

Both sides of the coalition wanted to shift attention to the long-term drivers of poverty, including poor-quality education and unemployment. We wanted to give people real opportunity, and not just more benefits and government dependency.

But Iain, Oliver and I all accepted that ultimately money matters, and we could not simply drop the relative poverty measure. So we had come up with and agreed a suite of three new targets – one focused on educational opportunity, one focused on relative poverty and one based on entrenched disadvantage – including unemployment. We all felt that these new measures got the balance right between income and opportunity.

Unfortunately, George Osborne absolutely refused to include in the new targets any measure of income. 'The Chancellor would rather no child poverty measures than one focused at all on relative income,' his adviser told us. But I was not willing to budge on this – I felt that poverty targets with no income measure would be totally incredible.

I was also concerned that the Chancellor's intransigence on this was a very large clue that he intended to cut welfare in the next parliament in a manner that would rapidly drive up rates of both child and wider poverty.

In the current parliament, the coalition had ensured that poverty rates were static or falling. Indeed, in 2011 the Liberal Democrats insisted on a 5.2 per cent uprating of benefits, to compensate for very high inflation. We also insisted on tax hikes on the top 5 or 10 per cent of earners, so that those with the broadest shoulders bore more of the extra burden of austerity. This was when wage rises were much lower. And in a fairly flat economy, low wage rises help to keep relative poverty rates from rising.

However, I could see that a return to growth would eventually boost wages. If this was accompanied by big cuts in some specific benefits and a generalised freeze in all benefit levels, then the poverty rate in the future could rise steeply, as it did under Mrs Thatcher's governments.

The only way to resolve the impasse was to take the dispute to the Quad. Both David Cameron and George Osborne refused to budge. The Prime Minister said: 'I don't mind education and I don't mind unemployment, but I don't want anything on income.' George Osborne said: 'We've modelled this and it looks like relative poverty could go up over the years ahead. I don't want to tie our targets to a measure which I cannot meet.'

David Cameron suggested: 'Look, let's ask David and Oliver to look at it again,' but it was obvious that we would just need to differ on this, and set out our own party positions. It was incredibly disappointing.

As well as all my work in the Education Department and on the final legislative programme, I had a number of smaller policy problems to help sort out. One was the long-running issue of badger culls in Somerset and Gloucestershire, and whether they should be extended to new areas.

TB in cattle had been a major problem for some years now, particularly in the south-west of England. In 2013, the government had started culls of badgers in two pilot areas. The culls were designed to test whether more than 70 per cent of the badger population in an area could be wiped out. This was the threshold that scientists judged had to be met in order to reduce the incidence of bovine TB. Killing a smaller proportion of the population was considered to risk a worse problem, by encouraging badgers to spread out over a wider area, causing more movement and more disease spread.

The whole process of killing badgers – a protected wild species – was highly controversial with animal rights activists. There was also considerable doubt over whether it would work. However, the powerful farmers lobby saw culling as vitally necessary to halt the spread of TB, and they did not want to risk waiting years for a vaccine to be developed.

The Conservatives in coalition, led by the Secretary of State for the Environment, Food and Rural Affairs, Owen Paterson, were strongly in favour of the pilot culls and of extending them as soon as possible to ten or more further areas.

But the policy was more controversial with Liberal Democrats, who tended to split between the 'something must be done' rural tendency and those who were either strongly against killing wild animals or sceptical of the science.

I had to find a Liberal Democrat position, and I was determined to do so entirely on the basis of what the scientific evidence showed. Over the period from 2013 onwards, I had more meetings than I care to remember on this issue, often with DEFRA officials and with the chief scientific adviser at DEFRA and the chief vet.

I wasn't convinced that the chief scientist was much of a supporter of the culls, though in our meetings he trod rather elegantly the fine line between loyalty to his departmental policy and answering my rather direct questions.

But what could no longer be denied, from late 2013, was that the culls had failed in their own terms. The target of killing 70 per cent of badgers in the pilot areas had not remotely been met, even with huge resources and a massive police presence to deter protestors.

In October 2013, Owen Paterson was widely ridiculed when he complained that in the pilot areas the badgers had 'moved the goalposts' by moving around and trying to avoid the marksmen.

At the end of February 2014, I met again with senior DEFRA officials and with DEFRA's chief scientific adviser, Professor Ian Boyd. DEFRA had previously estimated that 66 per cent of badgers in the Somerset cull had been killed, but only 40 per cent in Gloucestershire. They now changed the figures to around 40 per cent in Somerset and 50 per cent in Gloucestershire.

'So, according to our threshold target of 70 per cent, we could actually have made matters worse rather than better as a result of the cull?' I asked Professor Boyd.

Professor Boyd looked a little uncomfortable, but admitted that was true. He also went on to say that the cull evaluation was going to question the humaneness of the trial. We could not rule out that some badgers had not been killed cleanly, but had crawled away and died a slow and painful death.

The two culls seemed to have cost around £7 million, and I did a quick calculation that this amounted to almost £4,000 per dead badger.

'How on the earth can we justify rolling out the culls to more pilot areas on the basis of these figures?' I asked. 'It's hard to justify continuing with the existing pilots, let alone approving more.' At this, the other DEFRA officials, including a private secretary from Owen Paterson's office, looked highly uncomfortable.

Professor Boyd seemed to me to be sceptical of the whole programme, and he agreed with me that we could not use these culls to justify a nationwide roll-out. He said it was 50/50 whether the existing pilots should continue at all. I could see that the evidence and the Liberal Democrat Party were now on a collision course with DEFRA and Owen Paterson – who seemed to have little regard for what the evidence showed.

I summed up by saying that I needed to look very closely at the final independent report on the badger culls, but on the basis of what I had heard I could not support rolling the culls out to other areas.

Weeks passed, and each week my Cabinet Office team tried to extract a copy of the independent evaluation of the cull from DEFRA. Meanwhile, the Conservatives became increasingly agitated about our unwillingness to approve the cull roll-out to additional areas. Oliver Letwin spoke to me on a number of occasions, including once by telephone from China. And within one 48-hour period in mid-March, David Cameron telephoned Nick Clegg four times to urge us to approve the expansion of the culls. 'This is what the farmers want. We need to just get on with it,' was the Conservative line. 'No. I want David Laws to see the evidence first,' insisted Nick.

Eventually, on 24 March, DEFRA relented. A copy of the independent report on the cull turned up in my red box that evening. It confirmed that against a minimum threshold of 70 per cent, fewer than 40 per cent of badgers had been killed. Between 7 per cent and 25 per cent of these might have taken over five minutes to die. The cull had clearly failed badly even against the standards DEFRA had set for it. The report contained a wide range of excuses for the failure, including the complaint that badgers are 'small, shy, cryptic and nocturnal'. Owen Paterson, who is none of those things, cannot have been surprised when a few days later we vetoed his plan to extend the cull to ten other areas.

GUILTY SECRETS AND
SCRATCHY MEETINGS

FEBRUARY–MARCH 2014

It was March 2014. David Cameron and Nick Clegg had completed one of their regular weekly bilaterals. Their officials had left the room, leaving the two of them alone.

David Cameron was in a reflective mood. He admitted that he couldn't read the outcome of the next election. He said that to him there seemed to be a whole range of outcomes, from a Conservative majority to a Labour majority. But he still concluded that a coalition was 'pretty likely'.

And he suggested to Nick Clegg that if there was another coalition between the Liberal Democrats and the Conservatives, he might need to make some move on the Liberal Democrat policy on a mansion tax. But instead of implementing a mansion tax, which he continued to suggest his party donors would hate, he asked Nick whether an option was just to bring in higher council tax bands for the most expensive properties. 'That would be a lot easier for me.'

Nick acknowledged that he was already exploring a similar idea with Danny Alexander. He indicated privately that his party might decide to change the mansion tax into something looking more like higher council tax bands.

The Prime Minister expressed surprise, and then asked that the policy should not be changed until after the election. 'It would give me something to concede on if we do have another coalition!' He also wanted to hear more about Nick's attitude to the Labour Party.

The two leaders then went on to discuss Europe. David Cameron admitted that the 'rump' of his party wanted out on Europe, and he made clear his view that ultimately he would just have to confront them on this. But he admitted that he was worried that if the Conservatives were in government after 2015, they might have a serious split on the issue of Europe, as the Labour Party had in the 1970s. The PM's view was that if the Conservatives were in opposition after 2015, the whole party would 'go nuts' on Europe, and become even more opposed to it. As for Labour, Cameron expressed the view that Ed Miliband had done the only thing he could in avoiding a referendum: 'A Labour government could never win a referendum on Europe.'

The conversation ended with Cameron urging that the two leaders should 'keep the lines open' for another coalition in 2015.

'Cameron is very funny about all this,' Nick said to me the next day. 'He never tells me that he wants to talk about continuing the coalition, but he clearly thinks about it a lot. He talks to me about it when we are alone. It's his guilty little secret, really.'

Most of February and March was spent discussing not a possible future coalition, but another looming Budget. One of the great rhythms at the top of the coalition was the regular cycle of economic events – the Autumn Statement and the Budget each year, and occasional Spending Reviews. These consumed huge amounts of time, as both parties wanted to promote their own policies and fend off unwelcome contributions from the 'other side'. And unlike much else in the government, almost all the key decisions had to be taken by members of the four-man Quad.

Our own preparations for the March Budget started in early January. In the middle of the month, I sent Nick Clegg a note advocating the extension of the pupil premium from schools into early years education. I also pressed for us to cancel a planned £100 million cut to the early years budget – a large percentage reduction that risked our strategy of tackling disadvantage as early in life as possible.

It was not a strategy that the Conservatives in the DfE wanted to support – with the exception of the Early Years Minister, Liz Truss. Dom Cummings, Michael Gove's adviser, heard about my budget proposal and sent out a rather brusque email within the department, saying: 'All this stuff about early years funding and an early years premium is a lot of rubbish. MG is unlikely to regard this as a priority.' But I was determined not to be put off by a little light Conservative opposition.

By the end of January, Nick Clegg, Danny Alexander and I had agreed to look at a number of priorities for the Budget: a further £500 increase in the tax-free personal allowance, to go beyond our manifesto pledge of £10,000, and an early years pupil premium. I was pushing strongly for this premium, but Danny – with his Treasury hat on – was rather less enthusiastic about it.

In the middle of February, there was a first, rather ill-tempered Quad on the Budget. Nick said he wanted another big rise in the personal allowance. George Osborne said that this would be expensive, and he would require a whole series of Lib Dem concessions in return.

Nick said that he resented having to push for big increases in the personal tax allowance in each Budget, which required conceding Conservative priorities in exchange for this, only to find that the Conservatives then wanted to get all the credit for delivering the higher allowance. 'It's like you're selling me an expensive car that you then want to get in and drive off with,' said Nick Clegg. 'This time it's got to be different.'

This prompted something of a row: 'I don't care about the allowance,' said David Cameron. 'It's not my priority.' 'If you think I am just going to deliver a Lib Dem Budget, you've got another thing coming,' said George Osborne.

'Fine,' said Nick. 'In that case, we will say publicly that we pushed for this, and you declined to support it. You can't keep fighting increases in the allowance in this room and then briefing outside that it's all your great idea.'

The Quad ended on bad terms, but George Osborne later spoke to Danny Alexander and accepted that he would now concede to Nick another big rise in the allowance.

'You have to admire Osborne,' said Nick Clegg. 'As soon as he realises that you have check-mated him on something, he just changes his position. It is all very ruthless and pragmatic. As soon as Cameron and Osborne saw I wasn't going to give an inch on the allowance, they just gave way, and the arrangements have been much easier since then.'

A few days later, the Conservatives were back to their old tricks. In a speech, David Cameron was reported as saying that the Conservatives were now pressing for a higher tax allowance. Danny Alexander was spitting blood about it and Nick Clegg was pretty annoyed too. But my response was, 'Look, let's not be naive. This is politics. The Tories are doing what politicians do. In future, we need to get there first ourselves. It's no use playing by the rules when the other team has torn up the rule book.'

Later at that morning's Cabinet meeting, Nick had more reason to be upset by our coalition colleagues. We had a Cabinet discussion scheduled on the legislative programme for the last year of the parliament, something that had been agreed at the Quad earlier. David Cameron had previously vetoed legislation both on putting into law the 0.7 per cent GNP target on overseas aid, and on the promise to bring forward legislation on the recall of MPs.

Now, without any warning, David Cameron did something that never ever happened in Cabinet – he announced a decision on policy that had not been cleared with Nick Clegg and the Liberal Democrats. 'This is a good list of measures but I have looked again at one issue and I now think that we ought to have a Bill on the recall of MPs who are guilty of some wrong-doing,' he said. We could hardly object, but this was no way to run a coalition.

But the 'ambush' now moved into a second phase. George Osborne intervened to say: 'This is a good list of Bills, but it's a pity there isn't anything in here on having a referendum on the European Union.' When I came to make my contribution, I pointed out that legislation on an EU referendum was the last thing the coalition needed in its final year.

Within five minutes of the Cabinet meeting ending, someone on the Conservative side had briefed the media. The Prime Minister was being credited with taking a populist Recall Bill forward, even though he had been the previous cause of it being held up. And the two brief comments about a Referendum Bill had now been presented as a major Cabinet row, with the Chancellor credited with having made a 'dramatic move to secure an EU referendum' and the Liberal Democrats being blamed for 'stopping the people from having their say'.

Nick Clegg was furious. Later that week there was a Quad dinner in 10 Downing Street. He used the opportunity to make clear that he was not prepared to be bounced again in this way, or briefed against on Cabinet decisions: 'I told Cameron that if he wanted to treat Cabinet like a point-scoring exercise, then fine. We can play at that too. But I warned him that he would not like it.'

David Cameron apologised. He admitted to a U-turn on the recall issue and said that he had wanted to avoid the Liberal Democrats taking the credit for it. But he promised it wouldn't be repeated.

It was turning out to be a pretty scratchy month of coalition relations, but the tensions in government appeared as often within the two parties as between them.

On 5 March, Ken Clarke – the former Justice Secretary and now Minister without Portfolio – asked to see me to discuss a plan by his successor, Chris Grayling, to introduce massive increases in the fees charged to people who attend court to face prosecution. These fees were to be levied on top of any fines that might be imposed by the courts. The idea was to raise some money to help the Ministry of Justice to manage within its budget, and to transfer the costs of the justice system to the criminals; this would also include lots of middle-class people guilty of motoring offences.

But Ken Clarke and I were particularly concerned at the huge costs that might fall on those with very low incomes – costs that might either prove unpayable or, in Ken's view, get in the way of rehabilitation.

Ken Clarke was one of my favourite Conservative ministers, and I would never pass up the chance to meet with him. On this occasion, he was on particularly good form. We met over in his office on the fourth floor of Portcullis House. I was accompanied by two political advisers and one civil servant.

The meeting was only scheduled for fifteen minutes. Three-quarters of an hour later, it was still going on. Ken was in expansive form, and it was rather like seeing a grandparent who has a lot to recall from earlier life, and who doesn't get out very much. And, Ken being Ken, there was no beating around the bush: 'Look, David, I'm glad we can work on this together. We really have got to stop Chris's completely dotty plan to levy these extraordinary charges. The whole idea is utterly crazy. It's so crazy that even Theresa disagrees with it, and that's saying something! Chris just wants some populist line that will give him a headline in the papers about being tough on criminals, but this isn't a sensible idea. We will never actually collect much money except from middle-class motorists, who probably vote Tory and aren't at all the victims who Chris or the *Daily Mail* will be thinking of. And we will make rehabilitation worse, because people will come out of prison with a huge debt burden which they can never hope to pay off. Even Michael Howard and Margaret would never have done something like this!

'Chris seems to think that criminals will suddenly go on the straight and narrow in the hope that their debts will be written off for two years' good behaviour, but I'm afraid that this just shows that he has absolutely no idea how the criminal mind works. Barmy!'

I agreed with the points Ken made, and said I was blocking Chris Grayling's plan and would insist on some big changes to the proposed fee structure, not least for those from low-income backgrounds. Ken said that this was good, though he was still intending to argue against the whole principle of the policy. I was about to get up and leave, but it was quickly clear that Ken had not yet finished with his Conservative colleagues.

'I'm afraid to say that my colleagues in the Conservative Party often come up with ludicrous right-wing policies like this, designed to try to buy off the swing voters and appeal to *The Sun* and the *Mail*. Take Theresa's crazy policy last year that you and I opposed, David, saying that anyone who killed a police officer should be imprisoned for ever, while someone who shot a detective or a traffic warden or a firefighter should get a much lighter sentence. This is lunacy.' I could see Ken's civil servants looking nervously at him at this stage. But he was not ready to finish.

'Of course, Theresa only came up with this daft policy because she had to make a speech at the annual police officers conference, and she was worried about getting booed because of all the police pensions reform stuff. So she invented this ludicrous policy and announced it at the conference, and of course barely anybody noticed. It didn't even get her any headlines in *The Sun*. As a former Home Secretary, I could have given Theresa some good advice, if only she had asked me. The problem with Theresa is she hasn't worked out that the way to avoid being booed at the police conference is that you make your speech in the morning session. In the morning they are always much quieter and they haven't had any booze at lunchtime, so you get a much easier ride. You can deliver your speech, not get booed, leave and avoid having to cook up mad, dangerous and expensive policies.' At this stage, even the civil servants were chuckling. I was laughing very loudly.

I tried to bring the conversation back to court charges. 'Of course, if you and I block some of this, Ken, Chris will say he needs the money to meet Treasury spending targets. He will ask us how else he can get the money.'

That turned out to be a red flag to a bull. 'Well,' said Ken. 'As the last Justice Secretary, I can certainly answer that. All we need to do is to close down some of the hundreds of completely unnecessary magistrates' courts which are spread across the country. It is all terribly wasteful. Of course, many of these are in the constituencies of Conservative colleagues, and no MP ever seems to like losing their local court. My own view is that the public couldn't care less. But I tried this in government and I had a lot of push-back from David [Cameron] of all people – just because some piffling court in Oxfordshire in his constituency was at risk.

'I thought I could still persuade the Prime Minister, who is normally quite rational. But every time I got in to speak to him about this in No. 10, I had a terrible counter-reaction from that strange bloke in shorts and a T-shirt [this turned out to mean the Prime Minister's former policy adviser Steve Hilton] who used to burst in on us and blather on about localism and the big society or some such thing. This is crackers, of course. Most people's idea of localism isn't having a local prison or a local court – schools and hospitals, maybe. Anyway, we really need more sensible advisers in 10 Downing Street, but I'm not holding my breath.'

I was enjoying our meeting but beginning to fear I would never get away. Eventually I stood up to go: 'Thanks, Ken. I have to meet Nick to talk about the Budget discussions in the Quad. I really have to go. Meanwhile, do feel free to come to speak at the next Liberal Democrat conference – I am sure our members would like to hear your views on these issues, even if your own members don't agree with you.'

When I got back to the Cabinet Office, the Budget Quad was still going on. Eventually, Nick Clegg and Danny Alexander arrived to give me an update on where negotiations had got to.

Nick had won his battle to increase the personal allowance by another £500. That was good news. He had also managed to get George Osborne to scrap the planned cut of £100 million in the early years education budget.

Progress on the early years pupil premium was slower. I had Nick fully on side, and Danny was being won over too by my determined daily lobbying. But another blockage had emerged. Michael Gove was now trying to stop the early years pupil premium being agreed, even though it would bring extra money into his department. Nick said: 'Cameron and Osborne admitted that they had raised the early years pupil premium with Michael Gove, who apparently hit the roof. He apparently claimed he knew nothing about it, and it was another thing being cooked up behind his back by the Liberal Democrats.' This annoyed me, because I had made no secret of the fact that this would be a Liberal Democrat Budget 'ask'.

Nick continued: 'It was quite amusing, actually. Cameron and Osborne got in a complete mess over the issue. Firstly, they claimed that Michael hated the idea. Then they changed story and said that he was saying that it was his idea all along. Their latest line is that Michael doesn't want it to be a David Laws/Liberal Democrat announcement. And now George is saying he hasn't got the money.'

I said that this was absurd, and as I was only asking for an initial £100 million per year, this was very small beer in the context of the Budget arithmetic. Indeed, I soon found out that George Osborne was planning to give away hundreds of millions of pounds of revenue with a populist move to cut beer duty.

I was now even more determined to deliver the scheme, and after some excellent and rapid policy work from Ruth Shinoda, a civil servant at the Department for Education, we managed to persuade Nick Clegg to insist on the new early years premium, though now reduced to an initial £50 million. But to keep the Conservatives happy, this was announced jointly by both David Cameron and Nick Clegg. Hardly ideal, but what mattered to me more than anything was the policy substance itself.

The Budget discussions rumbled on for a few more weeks, until Budget Day on 19 March.

Beer duty, whisky duty and cider duty were all to be cut. There was a big Conservative-inspired savers package, with more liberal rules on pension annuities, a boost to ISA allowances and a cut in the tax rate on savings income. There was to be a massive cut in air passenger duty rates, because of some knee-jerk pledge by the Prime Minister at a Commonwealth summit (others suspected that the move might be aimed at pleasing prospective Conservative Party donors with links to countries such as India!)

A late entry for consideration from George Osborne was a strange-sounding proposal to rename national insurance contributions as the 'earnings tax'. Chris Saunders, Nick Clegg's highly experienced and politically astute chief economic adviser and I were both deeply suspicious that this was a Conservative plan to make the idea of national insurance contributions – often associated by the public with funding the NHS and pensions – unpopular, in order to justify cutting the tax. Nick Clegg was originally not planning to object to the plan, but eventually he accepted our view and that of Jonny Oates. Nick and Danny Alexander then vetoed the proposal.

On Wednesday 19 March, the Cabinet met at 8 a.m. to hear the final Budget decisions.

George Osborne was on good form. He briefed us on the better growth and borrowing prospects and then went through the Budget announcements one by one. As well as the major changes that I already knew about, there was a plan to cut bingo duty. This and a cut in beer duty were clearly the Conservative idea of appealing to the working classes! In every Budget we are told that there is no money for anything progressive, and then at the end of the day the Treasury finds money from down the back of the sofa to do whatever daft things the Chancellor wants – in this case, cut beer duty, cut bingo duty and give cheaper flights to foreigners. It was all slightly bizarre.

But on the whole it wasn't a bad Budget, and having battled away for two months by myself, I was particularly pleased to have secured the early years pupil premium. I commended the Chancellor in Cabinet on the overall package of measures, including the higher personal tax allowance. 'This is an excellent package for workers, savers and people who drink a lot,' I said.

Afterwards, I met again with Ken Clarke to talk further about Chris Grayling's 'dotty' plans for court cost recovery. Ken seemed rather less impressed by this Budget than most of his colleagues, but at his age he had probably seen it all before. 'I don't know why we all have to meet so early on these occasions,' he complained. 'Margaret never did it this way. I don't normally do early morning meetings. The only time I get up this early these days is to go bird watching.'

The next day, the Budget coverage for George Osborne was excellent, with most of the newspapers delivering adulatory headlines. The polls showed that Conservative support had been boosted by the package of measures. But down in the small print were the latest Liberal Democrat poll numbers. We were still at the rock-bottom level of 10 per cent. Good news was helping the Conservatives. But it was not assisting us.

And our support in the country was soon to be tested in crucially important national and local elections.

THE WORST WEEK YET

APRIL 2014

It was 2.30 p.m. on Tuesday 1 April. I left the Department for Education and hailed a taxi just outside the main entrance to Westminster Abbey. 'You're David Laws, the Lib Dem Minister, aren't you?' the taxi driver said. 'Where do you want to go, then?'

'The Ministry of Sound,' I said.

The taxi driver looked momentarily confused. 'Do you mean the Department of Culture?'

'No,' I said. 'The nightclub.'

'Oh,' he replied, 'I'm not sure there'll be much action there at 2.30 in the afternoon.'

When we got to the Ministry of Sound, I was ushered through the main entrance, where one or two of Nick Clegg's Special Branch security detail were standing guard. Then we made our way through the main dance floor of the nightclub, which was in semi-darkness.

Eventually, I was shown upstairs to a gallery area where Nick Clegg, Danny Alexander, Paddy Ashdown, Tim Farron and Nick's media and policy team were already having drinks and sandwiches.

This was the fourth practice session for a series of two televised head-to-head debates that were to be held between Nick Clegg and the UKIP leader, Nigel Farage.

I have to confess that I was far from an enthusiast for these debates. European and local elections were scheduled for early May, and my view was that flaunting our party's pro-European views was usually a very sure way to lose votes – not least in our south-west England constituencies, where there was a deep-seated and widely held Euroscepticism.

In advance of every set of European elections there was always a debate in our party about whether to lead on our pro-European agenda or whether to talk about almost anything other than Europe. I was always in the latter camp, along with most of our MPs.

However, our MEPs always argued that we should campaign more actively on Europe, and whenever the elections were over they would tell anyone who would listen just how much better we would have done if only we had talked endlessly about our pro-European values and policies.

On this occasion, Nick Clegg and his closest campaign advisers had decided to put Europe centre stage in the elections. And before I had even heard of the idea, they had agreed with the broadcasters to take part in two head-to-head debates with UKIP leader Nigel Farage.

The idea was originally put to Nick by the Dutch Prime Minister, Mark Rutte – a good friend of Nick's. In the Netherlands, one of the liberal parties – D66 – had triumphed in the previous European elections by taking the pro-European case aggressively to the anti-Europeans. The view was now that UKIP needed confronting head on, and that given the party's low poll ratings, we had little to lose.

I was still very worried. I was concerned that parading our pro-European views might not hurt us in a proportional voting system election for Europe but it could hurt us in our parliamentary constituencies, where under our first past the post system we needed to poll 40 per cent or more in each seat to win.

And I was also worried that while Nick Clegg had proved himself a strong performer in the 2010 general election debates, this would be a different proposition. Nigel Farage was a good performer too, and he would be the 'insurgent' in the debate, with Nick having to defend the European Union as well as making the case against an immediate, populist, referendum on Britain's future in the EU. There was also a big risk that the debates would simply give UKIP more air time and help them in the EU elections.

But no one could criticise Nick for his sheer bravery in taking on UKIP in this way. And at last our Euro MEPs would not be able to blame a bad election outcome on our failure to go 'front-foot' on Europe. So on this occasion we would be able to test – possibly to destruction – the theory that talking a lot about Europe was a good way to win votes.

The Conservatives had, of course, no intention at all of joining in the debates. They were determined to watch from the sidelines. But they did contact Nick's office before the debates to let us know that they had been amassing files of attack material to use against UKIP. They offered to pass some of this to us to use in and around the debates to help undermine UKIP. Nick politely declined. He had no intention of either engaging in 'dirty politics' or being in debt to the Conservatives in this way.

The first election debate had already taken place. This was on Wednesday 26 March, and it was shown on Sky TV and LBC. Nick had performed pretty well, and the general view was that it was a 'score-draw', with Nick 'winning' some of the questions and Farage leading on others. The polls declared Farage the winner, but Nick Clegg's 36 per cent rating wasn't bad when you consider that we were on only 10 per cent or less in the polls. The party and media view was that Nick may not have 'won', but he had done pretty well on a sticky wicket.

But the general opinion of Nick's advisers was that in the second debate he needed to engage more with the voters on an emotional – rather than just a rational – basis. And there was a view that now that Nick had performed well in the first debate, he could do better in the second – and win outright.

In this fourth practice session, Nick's performance was the most confident and accomplished of the rehearsals to date. In the earlier sessions, Tim Farron – who played Nigel Farage – had generally got the better of Nick, and had often got under his skin. But on this occasion Nick seemed energised and uncompromising. He had the odd corny joke, like, 'If I am the leader of the party of "In", Nigel Farage is leader of the party of "Put-in"' – a reference to Farage's recent ill-judged comments about the Russian premier.

But in the debrief session at the end of the debate, all of Nick's advisers were delighted by his performance. 'You were brilliant,' said Paddy Ashdown. 'Much better than before. Passionate. Emotional. Engaging. Amusing. I am confident that you can thrash Farage in the second debate.'

Wednesday 2 April was the day of the second and final debate against Farage. Nick was determined to give 100 per cent – and win. He was feeling confident after the success of the final practice session. And as a former MEP, and a person who cared passionately about Britain's role in Europe, Nick also felt a great responsibility on his shoulders.

I got home early that evening in order to watch the debate on BBC2. Nick started well, and he was certainly in 'punchy' form. But I soon worried that if anything he was a little too hyped up, and there were too many obviously planned and rather lumbering jokes. The 'Put-in' joke that just about worked in front of a room of fervent supporters fell as flat as a pancake in front of a studio audience who seemed much more sympathetic to Farage.

And in the second half of the debate, Farage came into his own, with strong performances on the issues of a referendum and EU migration. Nick's answer to a question about what the EU would look like in ten years' time was notably weak, missing the chance to set out a vision of a reformed Europe.

In sharp contrast to the successful election debates of 2010, Nick was no longer speaking as the fresh-faced new boy. Nigel Farage now had that advantage. Suddenly the Liberal Democrat leader found himself having to defend the status quo, with all its imperfections and necessary compromises. It was a much less easy wicket to bat on.

It was far from a disaster, but as soon as that debate was over it was clear to me that Nick had lost. The polls showed that Farage was considered to have won this debate by a 61 per cent to 30 per cent margin – wider than in the first encounter.

But that was not how Nick saw things. His own feeling immediately afterwards was that he had given it his best shot, and that he had done better than in the first debate. He came off the stage feeling that it had all gone well.

The first sign that this was not the case was when he met his chief of staff, Jonny Oates, outside the studio. 'What did you think?' said Nick. 'Well, it wasn't that great,' said Jonny. Later in the evening, Nick saw Ryan Coetzee and Danny Alexander coming out of the media briefing room, looking gloomy. He was given the polling data, which showed a clear win for Farage.

Politicians usually know when they have done well or badly in major media performances. And if you are unsure, the reaction of those closest to you usually gives you a very clear sign. If you have done well, people lavish praise. If you have done badly, people avert their eyes and say nothing. Sometimes, particularly when you know you have done badly, what you actually need is people to be very complimentary – even though neither side quite believes it.

But on this occasion, Nick received little feedback, or the odd awkward look.

People may think that politicians should all be able to take these setbacks in their stride. Isn't a bad media performance just something to live with? They underestimate how much most politicians need positive feedback about their public performances.

Nick had worked hard on the debates. He had taken the risk of holding them. He cared passionately about Britain's role in the EU, and he wanted to help re-elect as many Lib Dem MEPs as possible.

Those of us who were close to him knew that he would be disappointed, but the personal blow was much more than that.

Later that week, Nick told me: 'This whole thing feels so bad. It's also so personal. It was me up there in that debate. I did my best. I thought it was enough. But it wasn't. I just cannot bail out. But my belief in our ability to recover is waning.'

THE LONELIEST DECISION

MAY 2014

I t was Saturday 19 April 2014. Nick Clegg was home, and getting ready to go to bed, when he received a late-night call. It was Paddy Ashdown, for whom a usual business day stretches from 6 a.m. to at least midnight.

'Nick. It's Paddy here. I've been looking closely at the canvass data for the local elections and the Euros. It's not good, I'm afraid. In the local elections, we are going to lose a lot of councillors and get wiped out in London. The hope is that we can do much better in our strong areas, where we have MPs. But the European elections look grim. The worst-case scenario is that we could lose every single one of our seats. I just need to prepare you for this. After these election results, there is bound to be a bit of a crisis in the party. People will call for your head. We need to be ready for that.'

Nick knew that this tough advice was also good advice. The party poll ratings were awful, and he braced himself for the results.

The local and European elections were both set to take place on the same day – 22 May. On 6 May, Nick Clegg and his core team were at the National Liberal Club for one of our weekly 'breakfast' meetings in one of the gloomy, windowless, basement rooms. As usual, there was foul coffee, packets of dull biscuits, and nothing vaguely resembling breakfast.

Ryan Coetzee, Nick's political strategist, led a brief discussion about the likely election results: he thought we would lose about 300 of the 730 local council seats we were contesting, and be left with anything between three and none of our existing contingent of twelve MEPs. Any way you cut it, it would be very bad news.

On the day of the elections, Nick Clegg was up in Sheffield, canvassing with his local party. In the early afternoon, I was holding an advice centre in Yeovil. When I finished, I got a text message to call Norman Lamb, our North Norfolk MP. Norman said that he had been telephone canvassing all day and that he was getting very negative feedback. He also asked me whether I had heard a rumour that some backbench MPs were circulating a letter of no confidence in Nick Clegg. Norman said the talk was of up to fourteen names.

I phoned Jonny Oates, who was out canvassing in his own area of Kingston upon Thames. 'What letter?' was his response, when I spoke to him. He said that he had not heard of a letter but he had heard that a couple of junior MPs – John Pugh and David Ward – were trying to stir up a revolt. I said that I would be amazed if there were really more than five or six MPs who would sign any letter. Anyway, it clearly needed watching.

In the evening, I returned home to South Petherton. Nick Clegg travelled back to London, where he received the first bad news of the night from Jonny Oates: 'The reports from London are very bad, I'm afraid. It looks like something of a catastrophe is emerging for us in the capital.'

There were some areas of relative success, including in Maidstone and in a few marginal Lib Dem/Conservative constituencies. But mostly it was bad news, with just over 300 council seats lost in total. At a national level, it looked like we were still on track for a hung parliament in May 2015, but the results of this election suggested we were set to do very badly in London, Scotland and almost everywhere where we were fighting Labour.

The Liberal Democrat leader spent all Friday on the phone, mostly to those who had lost their seats and in some cases livelihoods. Most people seemed calm and positive, despite the big losses. Tim Farron, the party president, was very supportive, agreeing that Nick should stay on as leader.

It also helped that the media were not just focused on Liberal Democrat losses – the gains being made by Labour were well below those necessary to win a majority in the general election, and a number of newspapers were leading their coverage with a 'crisis for Ed Miliband' story.

But by that evening there were the first signs of trouble: a 'Lib Dems for Change' website had been set up, and it seemed that leadership change was what those behind it had in mind specifically. With the European election results expected over the weekend, things were now heating up – fast.

On Saturday night and Sunday morning, there were endless calls and emails from Paddy Ashdown, warning of disaster. 'We'll probably do worse than the Greens,' Nick was told.

The Sunday newspapers were alive with stories about the petition calling on Nick Clegg to step down. John Pugh MP was being quoted calling for a discussion on 'Liberal Democrat strategy' after the recess – I assumed that meant that he wanted to depose Nick but had little or no support amongst other MPs.

I spoke to Danny Alexander on the Sunday morning, before he was due to do a media round. He said that Nick was considering calling the parliamentary party back during the following week's recess to discuss the situation – we both agreed that this would be a very bad idea. Our joint view was that there weren't many MPs who were serious about a leadership coup, and the mini-revolt would simply fizzle out.

On Sunday evening, the results started to come in from the European elections – they were little short of catastrophic. We had lost every seat other than one in the south-east of England. Catherine Bearder had been elected by a margin of only a few thousand votes – she was now our sole MEP, the leader of our MEPs, the Chief Whip, and presumably the Lib Dem group note-taker as well. Norman Lamb texted me to say that he thought the results reflected not just our national lack of popularity, but public dislike of our pro-European positions: 'Our complacent, uncritical, pro-EU position has once again turned so many of our supporters away.' In Norman's own seat, UKIP had polled almost three times as many votes as the Liberal Democrats. We had certainly tested to destruction the notion put forward in the past by many of our own MEPs that if only we campaigned more on our pro-EU position, we would secure a much higher vote share.

Nick Clegg, meanwhile, felt shell-shocked. Over the weekend, he had planned to stay as leader, but now as he saw all of his former colleagues in the European Parliament losing their seats, he wondered if he should resign.

He spoke privately to his wife, Miriam. They were staying with their children at Chevening, the country house put at the disposal of William Hague and Nick Clegg, just outside London.

He also spoke at length to friends and advisers – Ryan Coetzee, Jonny

Oates and Paddy Ashdown. 'We think you can still pull this party back. These losses are about being in coalition, and not about you. We cannot just change leader and think that the public are going to suddenly love us,' Nick was told.

Ken Clarke had delivered a similar message at one of his recent booze-fuelled lunches with the Deputy Prime Minister: 'Of course your party has lost votes. This is not about you. The Liberals are no longer getting the protest vote, and you have lost a lot of your left wing supporters too – inevitable if you are in coalition with us.'

On Sunday night, the Liberal Democrat leader slept little. The truth was that Nick was struggling to know what the right thing to do for his party was. Even Paddy Ashdown was now sounding a more qualified note: 'Nick, I will support you whatever decision you decide to make.'

On Monday, Nick Clegg awoke, having made his decision: 'It is the loneliest decision you can ever make,' he told me later. 'But I decided that I just cannot walk away. If I did that, I would regret it for ever – I would be the person who ducked out and left his party in the lurch. If I leave now, there will inevitably be a leadership election – it would be a massive and divisive distraction for our party. I'm staying. I think it's the right thing to do.'

Monday was a bank holiday, and I was at home. At 10.30, I was making some mid-morning toast and working through my red box, when a call came through to me via the Downing Street switchboard.

'Minister, the Deputy Prime Minister on the line.'

Nick sounded very tired, but not as down as I had feared.

'I've been through various ups and downs in the last twenty-four hours,' he said. 'And at one stage I was seriously contemplating resigning. But I've always known five years of coalition would be tough, and I have come to the conclusion that just throwing in the towel now wouldn't be the right thing for the party or the country. I don't relish the next year, and I know that there will be a great deal of personal vilification in the media and elsewhere. But staying and fighting seems the right thing to do. There is, however, an issue over how we should be seen to be listening to the message of the defeat. Paddy Ashdown is saying we should now come out and say that we have listened and we will give the British people a referendum on the EU. What do you think?'

I said that although I was no euro-fanatic, I thought that this would look like panic in the face of defeat, and that it would simply look like we were flip-flopping around. We would also lose the support of those people in the party who thought that our position on Europe had been the right one. And I pointed out that in the event that we were in coalition with Labour after the next election, we would then be committed to a referendum, which I thought a Lib–Lab coalition would be incapable of winning. Finally, we would have given away our greatest negotiating card in the event of coalition talks with the Conservatives. Nick said he agreed with my view. He surprised me by saying that Danny Alexander was, however, also supporting Paddy Ashdown's position.

As Nick returned to London from Westminster, private opinion polls released to the *Guardian* newspaper purported to show that the Liberal Democrats were heading for a wipe-out at the next general election. The polls covered constituencies such as Redcar, Wells, Cambridge and Nick's own seat of Sheffield Hallam. Those who wanted Nick Clegg out had clearly started to mobilise.

As soon as I heard of these polls I felt I knew who was behind them. There was only one person who was both well enough off to commission such polls, and Machiavellian enough to use them: Matthew Oakeshott, a key ally of Vince Cable. But without a leadership candidate, there could be no leadership election. At an early morning meeting of Nick Clegg's closest advisers, we realised we had to ensure that Vince was on side, and we had to flush out Lord Oakeshott as the man who could be donating money to help defend Liberal Democrat seats but who was in fact commissioning opinion polls to undermine the party leader.

Stephen Lotinga, Nick Clegg's communications chief, tracked down Vince Cable. The Business Secretary was in China. He had already put out a helpful statement the previous day, saying that there was 'no leadership issue'. He was now asked to put out a statement strongly supporting Nick Clegg, and distancing himself from Lord Oakeshott. He did exactly that, and an angry and embarrassed Matthew Oakeshott resigned from the party the next day.

I heard this news as I was driving down to my Yeovil constituency on Wednesday 28 May. I was listening to the Radio 4 *World at One* programme, where Sir Menzies Campbell was being interviewed, and he was on rather good form: 'Lord Oakeshott has conceived of himself as something of a kingmaker and has on this occasion gone beyond his competencies in the matter.' It was vintage Menzies Campbell, and I laughed all the way from Salisbury to Yeovil.

The final sign that the rebellion was going nowhere was when former MP Lembit Opik went public to call for the resignation of Nick Clegg. Lembit had been on the wrong side of every leadership battle in living memory. When I heard the news, I texted Nick Clegg to tell him he need worry about his position no longer.

With the attempted coup now as good as over, David Cameron tried to persuade his coalition colleague to sack the Business Secretary.

Nick dismissed the proposition, pointing out that he had no intention of splitting his party.

By now, the rebellion was fizzling out. The week after the European election result was a parliamentary recess, and MPs were too busy in their constituencies, or taking a break abroad, to have time for further plotting.

Wednesday 4 June was the day of the State Opening of Parliament. Liberal Democrat MPs met in the Boothroyd Room in Portcullis House for the first time since the elections. A few hours had been set aside for an extensive discussion of the post-election outlook. Jonny Oates and others were still worried that some MPs might try to challenge Nick's leadership, so 'loyalists' were on a three-line whip to attend the whole meeting.

Nick briefly introduced the discussion, and then Vince Cable signalled that he wanted to speak. 'I want you all to know that I had nothing at all to do with the attempts to change the leadership. Matthew Oakeshott was a very old friend of mine, and I knew he was doing some polling in seats like Twickenham and Wells – but certainly not in Sheffield, in Nick's seat. I feel very let down by Matthew and our friendship is sadly now over as a consequence of this. I am fully supportive of Nick, but I do think that we are failing to turn around a very dire situation, and we need a discussion about our exit strategy from coalition and we need more distinctiveness from the Conservatives.'

Almost every MP spoke. Almost all were strongly supportive of Nick, including party president Tim Farron, who spoke without equivocation. Many criticised the few rebels for putting Liberal Democrat divisions in the spotlight, when the focus could have been on Ed Miliband and Labour's failure to 'cut through'.

Jenny Willott made a slightly odd speech, the focus of which appeared to be that her granny wanted Nick to stay on. David Ward, never a great fan of Nick Clegg (the feeling was mutual) made a supportive, but rather back-handed, contribution in which he said that Nick should stay on as it would be a great pity to get rid of a leader who had 'got so many mistakes to learn from'.

The self-appointed ringleader of rebellion, John Pugh, made a rather nervous, mumbling and lonely little speech, in which he said nothing about Nick Clegg's leadership, but appeared to suggest that he had personally done the party a great service by precipitating a useful debate. It was all rather unconvincing and feeble. He had clearly lost his nerve in the face of overwhelming odds.

The two most striking interventions came from the veteran MP Sir Bob Russell and the young minister Jo Swinson.

Sir Bob had often been a sharp critic of the party leadership in the past, and he was certainly no lover of the Conservatives. But he made the most passionate and loyalist speech of all: 'We need to focus on delivering for our constituents in government, and not on stabbing each other in the back. Times may be tough for our party, but as someone who has been in politics for decades, I can tell you that doing something for the people we represent is a lot better than sitting in your office putting out endless press releases saying how bad the government is.'

Almost the last to speak was Jo Swinson. She was standing at the side of the room, near the exit door, looking after her young baby and trying to ensure that the baby did not cry. Jo was our youngest minister, in the Business Department, and she was paying a high personal price for her commitment to politics – juggling a young family, a constituency in Scotland, and a husband who was also an MP but who represented a constituency in Wiltshire. Nor was it expected that she would survive the forthcoming election in Scotland – the polling in her seat strongly suggested that she would lose.

Jo might so easily have made a whinging and worried speech, but instead she was courageous, passionate and punchy:

'I've listened to the debate. It's clear that people support Nick. I support Nick. I think he's doing a great job. So please can we just get on and unite and fight the other parties and not each other? My seat in Scotland isn't going to be easy to hold, but I am determined to fight it hard. When we went into coalition, we all knew we were taking risks and that it wouldn't be easy. But if I had the same chance again, I would do the same thing again. We are making a difference in government – I know that I am, in the Business Department, with policies like shared parental leave. I will fight my seat hard. But if the price for being in government and delivering the things I believe in is that I lose my seat, then that is a price I am prepared to pay.'

It wasn't the last intervention of the evening, but after it nothing more really needed to be said.

The meeting ended with a passionate summing-up by Nick Clegg, and a long and loud banging of desks in support by most of those present. No alternative leader had come forward, and little support for such an option had emerged. The issue of the Liberal Democrat leadership was now settled for the rest of the parliament.

When we left the room after the two-and-a-half-hour debate, there were no media waiting in the corridor outside. They also sensed that the 'Lib Dem leadership crisis' had blown over.

And in any case, there was a better story to follow that day: two senior Cabinet ministers, Theresa May and Michael Gove, were involved in a huge row over extremism policy, on the very day that the Prime Minister hoped to showcase the carefully agreed policies in the last Queen's Speech of the parliament. And David Cameron was furious.

MICHAEL GOVE:
MAKING WAVES

JANUARY–JULY 2014

I t was the morning of Tuesday 15 July 2014.

The newspapers were full of reshuffle speculation. It looked from initial reports that the reshuffle would amount to a 'massacre of the moderates', as Labour were billing the day. Ken Clarke was finally facing retirement from the Cabinet, along with other 'liberal Tories' such as David Willetts, Dominic Grieve and Andrew Lansley. Dominic Grieve, the Attorney General, had never quite been forgiven by David Cameron for making known privately the possibility of his resignation in late 2012, when David Cameron seemed set on breaching UK law by ignoring a possible European Court judgment on prisoner voting rights. To everyone's immense relief, the court judgment went in the UK's favour, avoiding what could otherwise have been a major political crisis.

In the evening of Monday 14 July, the shape of the reshuffle had started to emerge. Willian Hague was standing down as Foreign Secretary to be replaced by the rather bland bean-counter Philip Hammond. A list of soon-to-be-sacked ministers also emerged.

In my diary on 14 July I recorded: 'All the logic points to Michael Gove staying put as Secretary of State for Education, but I can't help feeling in the back of my mind that he still might be moved. However, I cannot for the life of me see where he could be moved to.'

On the Tuesday morning, I was in at my usual time of 6.45 a.m. I chaired some meetings on education policy and was about to leave my office for another meeting when Jonathan Crisp, one of my private secretaries, came in. 'Minister,' he said. 'We've just heard on the news that Michael Gove has been moved from the Education Department. He's going to be the new Chief Whip. Nicky Morgan is taking over at Education.'

'Chief Whip!' I gasped. 'That must be Cameron's idea of a joke. Michael, in charge of party discipline! I cannot think of anyone less well cut out to do that job.'

Michael Gove's departure from the Education Department took most people by surprise – the media, the Education Department, his colleagues in government and his closest advisers. 'God, the whole thing is so brutal,' one of them said to me later. 'One moment he was there, running the whole show. The next minute he was gone. I went to his office to say goodbye, and I was just told that he wasn't coming back. All the pictures on the wall of his office were down, and all his personal possessions were boxed up and sitting outside the office. The whole place had been stripped of every memory of him within half an hour of the announcement.'

The word soon went around in government that it was all down to the 'Lynton Crosby effect'. Apparently the Tory Party campaign chief had found in his opinion polling that Michael Gove was the most unpopular Cabinet minister. He had told the Prime Minister that he wanted a vote winner – a less divisive figure – at Education. And the Prime Minister, now wholly focused on the election, had said yes.

Over the next few days, the story of the surprising and undoubted demotion gradually came out.

Apparently, at the end of the week before the reshuffle, the Prime Minister asked to see his Education Secretary and close friend. He told him that with the election campaign approaching, he wanted his key ally at the centre of government, closely advising him. The heavy lifting had been done at Education and it was time to move on.

The Education Secretary asked for some time to consider the proposal. He wasn't particularly keen to move, but felt that maybe he could be of help at the centre of government. And, in any case, it is difficult in politics to say no to a leader when they want to move you and especially when they are your friend. Michael Gove could have refused to move. The Prime Minister was in no position to sack him. But that was not the relationship Michael wanted to have with his close ally.

So a day or so later, he said yes. Shortly afterwards, he was phoned by George Osborne, who advised him to stay put in Education. 'It's too late, I have already said yes,' replied the outgoing Secretary of State. Afterwards, he may have regretted the decision – not just because it was presented through the media quite explicitly as a demotion, but also because he actually wanted to stay at Education.

Michael Gove's wife, Sarah Vine, publicly signalled her discontent. Dom Cummings was also still a little 'off message', tweeting: 'For many years I have told MG that Cameron's a lightweight, selfish, clown. He didn't want to believe it. Now he knows I'm right. Thanks Dave!'

The Gove demotion may have been the big shock of the reshuffle, but it was not, perhaps, quite as surprising as it seemed. Over the previous nine months, Michael had seemed to be in conflict with just about everyone, from bitter enemies to former close allies.

One senior civil servant said privately: 'Michael has never seemed to be the same person since the government lost the vote on Syria in September 2013.'

It was hoped that the departure of the Education Secretary's combative adviser, Dom Cummings, in early 2014, might lower the temperature. But by removing any restraining influence on Dom himself, it actually had the opposite effect.

Rows between the Education Secretary and Nick Clegg were not unusual, but their frequency and intensity increased markedly from autumn 2013 onwards.

Rows between Michael Gove and other Conservative ministers were not unknown before September 2013, but afterwards they, too, increased in frequency and ferocity. Now Theresa May, Eric Pickles, William Hague, Philip Hammond, Baroness Warsi and other Conservative ministers found themselves clashing with the Education Secretary at different times.

What was equally unusual was that the previously very close relationship with David Cameron also came under strain. The PM and his good friend fell out over issues as varied as capital funding for free school meals, the introduction of a national fair funding policy for schools, whether we should legislate for free school meals, and how many Etonians it ought to take to make a general election manifesto.

David Cameron hated disagreeing with his Education Secretary, and in the early part of the parliament he had more or less contracted education policy out entirely to his trusted lieutenant. But the Prime Minister now thought that his friend was causing too many rows in government, and was beginning to unnecessarily create enemies of former allies.

In late 2013, the Deputy Prime Minister had asked the Cabinet Secretary, Jeremy Heywood, to conduct a review of policies for 16–24-year-olds. The Cabinet Secretary did his best to reach a consensus, but many of his major proposals were blocked by Michael Gove, who disagreed with several of the review's conclusions.

In early 2014, Ofsted was destabilised. Dominic Cummings, whom David Cameron despised, seemed to be running riot. And coalition relations in the department, which had been so strong back in 2013, were now far worse than in any other department.

November 2013, as I have already recorded, had been a very difficult time in the Education Department, with rows over whether we should legislate to guarantee free school meals, invest more in upgrading school kitchens, and switch money from the budget for new school places to the free schools programme.

In the same month, Michael Gove clashed with Eric Pickles at a meeting of the 'Extremism Task Force', chaired by Theresa May. The Education Secretary had already criticised Theresa May and Baroness Warsi in the meeting, before turning on Eric Pickles and his Local Government Department. Mr Pickles was having none of it, and there was a sharp exchange of views.

Shortly afterwards, Nick Clegg had dinner with David Cameron, George Osborne and Danny Alexander. It was a constructive exchange in which the PM seemed to be trying to pave the way for a second coalition with the Liberal Democrats. But the recent rows with the Education Secretary took up much of the discussion.

Nick Clegg later recounted the conversation to me. David Cameron had replied to the Deputy Prime Minister's complaints by saying: 'Look, I understand your frustration over this, Nick. Michael does seem to have gone a bit nuts recently – it's not just about you, though he does seem to have a particular bee in his bonnet about you right now. To be honest, I am being driven around the bend by Michael right now. We know he isn't very popular in the country, and that your party doesn't mind having fights with him. But it isn't good for the coalition to have all these big spats. Why don't the two of you meet and try to sort it all out?'

In late November, however, it was the Prime Minister who was upset when an unusually serious Michael Gove spoke out at Cabinet to condemn an international agreement on Iran and its nuclear weapons.

And in December, the Prime Minister and Education Secretary clashed again, in private. Michael Gove and I had mutually agreed a new national funding formula, to ensure that all English schools received a fair level of funding for each pupil. For many decades the funding rates had varied across the country, for no obvious or rational reason.

The government had previously pledged to introduce the new funding formula, but now that it had come to the crunch moment, neither David Cameron nor Nick Clegg was very keen to proceed.

David Cameron called the proposal 'Michael's plan to lose me the next election', adding, 'Right plan, wrong time.' The point was that some areas of the country would be getting extra money, but other areas would get nothing and fear future cuts – leaving Labour free to campaign against the proposal in marginal constituencies up and down the country.

I soon realised that the plan was going to be put on ice, and I started working on a more limited proposal to uplift funding in the most deserving areas, in 2015. But Michael Gove wouldn't give up. And he was used to getting his way with the PM.

On Thursday 12 December, the Prime Minister and Education Secretary met in 10 Downing Street to discuss the issue. The meeting took twice as long as expected, and there was soon talk in the Education Department of raised voices and a big row. The Prime Minister put his foot down. Michael Gove was not amused. The national funding formula was now put on hold. Instead, with Michael Gove's support, I introduced an alternative plan for minimum funding levels, which delivered almost £400 million more cash to the underfunded areas.

Towards the end of the month, just before Christmas, Nick Clegg and Michael Gove finally met to see if they could settle their differences. The two men came together in Nick Clegg's office in Dover House. This was one, rare, occasion when private secretaries were not allowed inside the room. The opening atmosphere was strained.

Nick Clegg came straight to the point: 'Listen, Michael, we can be at each other's throats twenty-four hours a day, if you like. I don't mind that – our voters absolutely hate you. I can see that from the polls. In different ways, we have both become Marmite politicians.'

Nick made clear his present disdain for the Education Secretary and his team, adding: 'I believe that it was your adviser who dragged my wife through the mud over Book Trust...'

Michael Gove interrupted: 'I think I know what happened on that. I can assure you that it had absolutely nothing to do with me.'

'I said your adviser,' responded the Lib Dem leader. 'You are responsible for your adviser. How would you feel if my office attacked your wife?'

The Deputy Prime Minister then listed other areas of frustration, including over free schools meals, the Heywood Review of 16–24-year-old provision, and the raid on the basic need budget to fund more free schools. He also said that he thought the Education Secretary should be more pragmatic over the need for a 'middle tier' to hold failing schools to account.

Michael Gove then responded: 'Nick, I am sorry – genuinely sorry – that we have had these issues in the media. You may want to know that Dominic Cummings, my main adviser, is leaving. I hope that will help lower the temperature. And I understand that it is frustrating for you that there are policy areas where we don't see eye to eye – like careers education and the middle tier. But I think I am entitled to be a little bruised as well. When I was abroad in October, you launched a direct attack on my policies, including on free schools. And I am frankly hurt at the way you and your party are demonising me. You are presenting me as some swivel-eyed ideologue, some sort of mad, profit-obsessed privatiser. That isn't fair. On free school meals, we are much closer than you think. I am not just a supporter of this policy, but I think I was one of the first in government to suggest it. It is true that Dom Cummings is not a big fan, but he will be leaving soon.'

The meeting was a long one. At the end of it, it was hoped that better relations might result between the two men and their advisers.

Before Christmas 2013, there had been one final meeting of the year of the Department for Education board of ministers, senior civil servants, non-executive directors and senior advisers.

When I arrived, a little late, it was clear that Michael Gove – who was chairing the meeting – was not in the best of moods. After he had finished speaking, he asked who else wanted to comment.

From the far end of the table, a scruffy, unshaven figure put up his hand to speak – Dom Cummings.

'When I first came to this department in 2011, I said we should sack half the staff. I was told it would be impossible and the department would collapse. Well, we have done it, and who actually has noticed? Now I think we need to go even further. We should sack all the incompetent people. There are far too many white men in their middle fifties in this department who are no good.'

At this moment, a lot of white, mid-fifties men around the table looked down at their papers. But Mr Cummings was not finished.

'They should be sacked and replaced by young women in their twenties and thirties. Oh, and one last thing. We need to stop the stupid initiatives from No. 10 and from Clegg.' I groaned, loudly.

At the end of the meeting, I walked straight out to go back to my office. Dom Cummings followed me into the lift. There was a moment of silence, and then he said: 'How are things?' I replied: 'They'd be fine, if you would only stop briefing against the policies of this department.'

The lift door opened, and I got out. From behind me, I heard: 'If people in the Deputy Prime Minister's Office think I've "gone rogue", they ain't seen nothing yet. I intend to use my forthcoming freedom over the weeks and months ahead.'

It was not a promising end to the year.

And if people from the Prime Minister downwards hoped that the Education Wars of late 2013 would cease in 2014, they were to be disappointed.

Dom Cummings was as good as his word. Outside the department, he used his position to stir the pot even more violently. He might have thought that he was assisting his old boss, but each intervention angered not only Nick Clegg but the Prime Minister himself.

Of course, as usual, Michael and I did manage to work together productively in a number of areas – including on fairer funding for schools, on implementation of an early years pupil premium, and on accountability.

We also continued reforming qualifications to introduce more stretch and challenge. In February 2014, I took home a set of GCSE papers to check if they were as 'dumbed down' as the Education Secretary often claimed. I opened the GCSE Physical Education written paper to read:

Which of the following sports would you be likely to engage in if
you were an introvert?
A. Cheerleader
B. Volleyball
C. Cricket
D. Cross-Country Runner

'Oh God,' I thought. 'We have got work to do.'

But in other policy areas, the clashes brought the two of us into direct
confrontation.

In fairness, it was now not only Liberal Democrats who were under
occasional assault.

In late January 2014, the Education Secretary understandably wanted to
know why the Ministry of Defence was making so little progress in rolling
out army cadet units in state schools. Why, he asked, were most of these
units still funded only in fee-paying schools? When Philip Hammond, the
Defence Secretary, mumbled something about it being important not to
damage the recruitment of officers, the Education Secretary bristled with
anger. And when junior Defence Minister Anna Soubry came to my office
a week later for a meeting on the 'military ethos', she was shocked to find
the Education Secretary himself arriving halfway through and treating her
to a volcanic display of rage about MoD foot dragging: 'I am sorry, Anna.
It is totally unacceptable. How can we justify spending millions subsidising
cadet units in private schools when poorer children have to pay themselves
or can't access it? We have got to do something about this.' Of course, the
Education Secretary was absolutely right. But stories soon spread about heated
exchanges and bruised egos. This was a man unafraid of making waves.

In March, Michael decided to use a *Financial Times* interview to attack the
'extraordinary' number of Old Etonians in and around No. 10 – including
the five Old Etonians responsible for writing the next Conservative Party
manifesto: Oliver Letwin, Ed Llewellyn, Rupert Harrison (the Chancellor's
adviser), Jo Johnson and of course the Prime Minister himself. It was indeed a
striking fact and a powerful point. But it was not one that the Prime Minister
could be expected to appreciate.

The first Liberal Democrat/Conservative education row of 2014 was over
Ofsted, the schools inspectorate. I was the minister in charge of Ofsted and

I thought that its chair, Baroness Sally Morgan, and the Chief Inspector, Sir Michael Wilshaw, were both doing a good job in tough roles. I also believed strongly in Ofsted independence.

In late January 2014, I was told that – without consulting me – Michael Gove had met Sally Morgan and told her that her term as chair would not be renewed. Baroness Morgan, formerly a senior colleague of Tony Blair, was told that the Conservatives wanted to appoint more of 'our people' before the general election. I was very unhappy about this and asked Michael to think again.

At the same time, some Conservatives, including Dom Cummings, were pushing for Sir Michael Wilshaw to be 'reined in', or even dismissed from his post. It was true that Sir Michael had a tendency to involve himself in policy debates that fell outside the narrow remit of the Chief Inspector, and that he wanted to be as critical of failing academies and failing free schools as he and the government were of failing local authority schools. The Chief Inspector was concerned that some Conservatives wanted to prevent him from inspecting 'without fear or favour', as he had pledged to do. Both he and I wanted Ofsted to be empowered to inspect academy chains, just as it could inspect local authorities. Michael Gove was strongly opposed to this move. Ofsted had also recently completed a number of unfavourable inspections of the new free schools. This was also causing some friction.

But as a man of robust views who had turned around a number of tough and failing secondary schools, Sir Michael was not someone to be bullied. He wanted his organisation to be properly independent of ministers. He was also unhappy at the planned removal of Sally Morgan, suspecting that a new Ofsted chair would be a Conservative supporter who would either rein him in or manoeuvre him out.

I was both unhappy at not being consulted on all this and also worried that Ofsted's independence could be compromised.

Soon, the whole issue blew up spectacularly. A think tank with close links to the Conservative Party was about to put out a report that was expected to be critical of Ofsted. Sir Michael Wilshaw also heard through the press that Conservative advisers in the Education Department were briefing against him and his organisation. His reaction was both volcanic and public – and on Sunday 26 January the newspapers were full of stories about splits and rows, with the Chief Inspector saying he was 'displeased, shocked and outraged'.

Rarely, if ever, had there been such a public falling-out between a Chief Inspector and an Education Secretary. The Chief Inspector received some aggressive text messages from the Secretary of State's advisers asking him to be 'on message'. He responded in blunt and uncompromising language.

On Sunday afternoon, a surprised shopper in Selfridges' toy department saw a man who looked very much like the Education Secretary having a blazing row on his mobile phone with someone called 'Sir Michael'. By evening, the encounter was recorded on social media. And yes, it was them.

That night, I spoke to Michael Gove, and pressed him to reconsider moving Baroness Morgan – who was actually a very wise and constructive influence on the Chief Inspector. The Education Secretary promised to 'reflect again, given all that has happened today'.

Meanwhile, ever since Dom Cummings's departure from the department, there had been a poisonous drip-drip-drip of leaks on the free school meals policy. It amounted to a malicious attempt to undermine the policy and to imply that it could not be successfully delivered.

Information was selectively leaked to imply that the policy hadn't been costed properly, or that we had too little capital, or that it hadn't been tested (there had been carefully assessed pilots across England under the previous government) or that there was no policy rationale (it had, in fact, been one of the conclusions of Michael Gove's own School Food Plan), or that the department thought the scheme would fail (it was 'red rated' on the departmental risk list, but then so were free schools and extra school places).

In fact, the policy had been planned thoroughly, it was being delivered effectively, and I was confident that it would be a success. But I was increasingly having to use scarce time dealing with malicious leaks rather than concentrating on a delivery challenge affecting 16,500 schools. I was not amused. Nor could I understand how Michael Gove could be allowing his former adviser to deliberately undermine a policy that he personally professed to support.

A week later, on Friday 31 January, already fed up with the handling of the Ofsted issue, and tired of dealing with snipping and obstructionism over free school meals, I received an email from my private secretary saying that Michael had just publicly announced the removal of Sally Morgan – again, without consulting me. This weekend it was my turn to lose my temper, and do so in direct and public terms.

I awoke on Sunday morning to a series of urgent text messages from Michael Gove. I was so angry I was tempted to ignore them, but eventually I called him back. 'David,' he said, sounding a little stressed but trying to stay calm, 'I am about to go on the *Marr* programme on BBC TV. Scanning today's papers, I notice that there are one or two stories about how unhappy you are with me over Ofsted. I'm just looking at the front pages of the *Sunday Times*, *The Observer*, the *Independent on Sunday*...' There was a pause, in which I reflected that our press officer James McGrory must be pursuing his usual, understated approach. '...The *Sunday Telegraph*, BBC News online, Sky News ... I'm only guessing, but I think I may get asked a question or two about it on *Marr*.'

We had, calmly, a short and frank discussion. Neither of us was going to give an inch.

Later that year, Sally Morgan left Ofsted. Sir Michael Wilshaw stayed. But the relationship between the Education Secretary and his Chief Inspector was never the same again.

Both Ofsted leaders had been amongst Michael Gove's greatest allies in delivering educational reform. It seemed to me madness to alienate allies in this way.

David Cameron was angry too. 'The Prime Minister doesn't understand why Michael Gove is picking this fight. And he doesn't want a row about a Tory donor being appointed at Ofsted,' I was told.

In *The Times* on Monday, there was rare criticism of Michael from Rachel Sylvester: Mr Gove, she said, should stop making enemies of friends and start trying to secure the future of education reform. The *Daily Telegraph* had a cartoon of Michael drifting in a boat in the middle of the sea, having lost both oars.

This was the first time that I had clashed publicly with Michael Gove. On this occasion, there was no 'Clegg' aspect to the story.

But the most serious dispute was yet to come.

The simmering row over free schools meals continued, with ever more ludicrous, misleading and downright vicious briefings from Dom Cummings – aimed not only at the policy but at Nick Clegg personally.

I was particularly angry about inaccurate claims that we had raided the budget for new school places to fund extra support for kitchens. In fact, the Conservatives had insisted on raiding the budget for new school places to fund more free schools. I made clear that I was more than happy for the whole subject to be opened up to a Select Committee inquiry, if that was what the Conservatives wanted. I had a huge job to do to successfully deliver the policy – which I would be personally held to account for. I was not amused to be fighting a rearguard action with Michael's former advisers.

In April the Education Wars broke out again into open and messy public conflict. Knives and food were the triggers.

In April 2014, Chris Grayling, the Justice Secretary, suddenly proposed a new set of higher mandatory minimum sentences. One proposal was for a long prison sentence for anyone caught carrying a knife on more than one occasion.

Many Cabinet members, both Liberal Democrat and Conservative, felt that the proposal was unwise and that sentencing should be left to the judges. Ken Clarke, a former Justice Secretary, strongly held this view, as did Oliver Letwin, privately. The Prime Minister was understood to be rather neutral about the issue – which had nonetheless just become more sensitive after a teacher had been stabbed and killed in a school in Leeds.

As there was no consensus on the issue, it was not put on the agenda of the Home Affairs Committee, chaired by Nick Clegg, for debate. At the end of this meeting, on 30 April, Michael Gove suddenly raised the issue and asked why it was not being debated. Nick Clegg explained that there was no consensus on the issue, and thus it was not down to be debated. He closed the meeting, cutting off Michael's complaint.

Three days later the mini-row was public. Splashed across the front page of the *Daily Mail* was the headline 'Clegg bids to block knife crackdown'. Underneath the headline – in case anyone had missed the point – it said: 'Days after shocking classroom murder of Ann Maguire, Deputy PM and other senior Lib Dems refuse to support tightening the law'. Danny Alexander and I were cited as two Liberal Democrats blocking the proposed change. None of the Conservatives who were opposed were mentioned.

We were all furious – not least at the opportunism of linking the row to the death of a classroom teacher, when there was no evidence that the policy would have made any difference.

Nick Clegg was convinced that Michael Gove or his advisers were guilty of the leak: 'Grayling wouldn't dare.' For a while, we considered asking for a police inquiry into the leak, but we decided against it. The message came back from David Cameron's office that they were also blaming Michael Gove, who would be given a 'bollocking' by the PM.

A few days later, there were more leaked DfE emails designed to discredit the free school meals policy, and more bile from Dom Cummings, making all sorts of allegations about Liberal Democrat 'lies' over the policy. It went further than anything yet seen.

On Friday morning, 9 May, the media contacted us about more allegations from Dom Cummings. I carefully drafted a statement to go out from the Education Department press office, rebutting the allegations. However, Michael Gove's special adviser refused to clear the statement for release – even though its contents had been approved by the department's Permanent Secretary. I was incandescent, and said that either the statement would be put out from me or it would go from the Deputy Prime Minister's office. Eventually the press release went out from me, but not as an official DfE 'line'. No one in the media noticed, but the coalition rows were now becoming seriously destabilising.

I now sent a private email to Michael, the strongest and most direct that I had written. I asked him to get his friend and ally under control and to stop the leaks.

An hour later, Michael Gove called me back. 'Look,' he said. 'I don't know where to begin. Dom seems to be in a place where he thinks he's helping me. He thinks he knows my interests better than I do. In fact, it's now making our relationship difficult. No. 10 are also upset with me. My views on this are not the same as Dom. But I cannot control him, although I will now try again.'

That Saturday evening, I was in the Odeon Cinema in Guildford, watching a rather bad film. My private secretary called me to say that the DfE press office wanted me to urgently agree some lines to put out to respond to a story that the Sunday newspapers were going to carry. This would reveal that the free schools budget was £800 million overspent, and that the budget for school places had been raided for £400 million by the Conservatives to bail free schools out. It was going to be a big story – the front-page splash in at least three Sunday papers. I was asked to clear the lines to take quickly, as the Tory advisers wanted to brief the papers.

I made clear that the lines suggested were inaccurate, and that I wouldn't clear them. Panic ensued. I must confess that I enjoyed getting revenge for

Friday's Tory antics. Eventually the lines had to go out from Conservative advisers and not the department's press officers.

The next day, the story certainly did run big – 'Gove's "lunatic" £400m raid to rescue his free schools vision' announced *The Observer*. The *Telegraph* ran with 'Michael Gove and David Laws at war over free schools'. David Cameron, himself on the *Marr* programme, was distinctly unamused. He wanted to lead a united coalition government, not a squabbling mess.

On Monday 12 May, the story still rumbled on. There were TV cameras outside my London house and outside the Education Department.

That morning Nick Clegg and the Prime Minister spoke.

'Look,' said Nick Clegg, 'I'm not apologising for the row over free schools. I am sick and tired of what Gove and Cummings are doing on free school meals, on knife crime, and in other areas. And I am sick and tired of the vicious personal attacks. It has to end.'

The Prime Minister said that he understood the concerns, adding that this was exactly why his former press boss, Andy Coulson, had vetoed Dom Cummings working for the government in May 2010. David Cameron said that he had only relented because Michael Gove had been under huge pressure because of early mishandling by the department of the scaling back of the 'building schools for the future' programme, and he had argued strongly that he needed his former adviser to sort the problems out. 'I should have said no,' said the Prime Minister. 'Cummings has a Rasputin-like influence on Michael – and it's all for the worse.'

Nick Clegg phoned to update me on the discussion with the Prime Minister. David Cameron had apparently concluded by saying: 'I have already made clear that if there are more leaks I would bring in the police. But now we have to call a truce. We have to get Michael and David Laws working together again. We have to stop the Education Department from becoming a totally dysfunctional department.'

'It would help if Michael would make clear once and for all what he tells me privately – that he supports free school meals,' said Nick Clegg.

'Fine,' said the Prime Minister. 'Let's get a joint article done between David and Michael then. I am going to call Michael now.'

In the Department for Education, there was concern about the huge breakdown in coalition relations. The Permanent Secretary told me that there had never before been an occasion where the department was unable to put press lines out from its own press office. 'You do realise that on Saturday we had to put a line out from the Secretary of State as an individual, and not from the department?' he said. 'Of course I know that,' I said. 'Just like Friday when my lines weren't cleared.'

Later in the morning, Michael and I met. We had a blunt discussion, in private, in which we exchanged grievances. I told the Education Secretary that I wanted him to get his former adviser back under control, whether he was still a civil servant or not: 'I don't expect Nick Clegg and Dom Cummings to end up best friends or to take annual holidays together, but it's totally unacceptable to us that he is behaving like this, and we think we are entitled to ask you to stop this nonsense. I know Dom is personally opposed to this policy. Fine. But he must stop making claims that are patently untrue.' It was clear that the Prime Minister had already spoken to Michael Gove and had instructed him to settle things down. We agreed to do an article for one of the newspapers. After forty minutes, things had calmed back down.

The article was written, after endless amendments and much anguish. We eventually had to go through the short piece word by word. At the end of the discussion, Michael Gove said:

'Good. I should say again that I am a passionate supporter of this policy, although not all the issues of implementation.'

I couldn't let that go. 'What do you mean, problems about implementation? You haven't told me before you have any concerns about implementation?'

Michael looked uncomfortable and then said: 'Well, of course it's the issue of capital, and whether we really have got the right amount of capital.'

I snapped back: 'Look, I really don't understand what the Conservative position is on capital. When it was the Autumn Statement last year, you prevented us from bidding to the Treasury for any capital, but now you seem to be saying we haven't got enough. What is your position – that we have too much capital or too little?'

Michael replied, 'Both! We should have bid for more capital, but we need it in a number of areas.' My mouth dropped open. The two private secretaries next to us shuffled uncomfortably in their chairs.

I felt that there wasn't much more to say, when the Tory lines of attack were clearly so inconsistent.

On Thursday, our article was published in *The Times*, under the somewhat unconvincing headline 'We are not at war over free school lunches'.

When the new school year began in September, the policy was a resounding success. There was enough capital and enough revenue, and the overwhelming majority of schools served a hot meal option. And then the media, and Mr Cummings, lost interest.

So the battle over free school meals faded away.

But Michael Gove's battles with fellow Conservative ministers heated up – including a major clash with Theresa May over extremism policy, which overshadowed the Queen's Speech and led to the forced resignation of the Home Secretary's trusted special adviser.

Meanwhile, the Prime Minister now had to deal with some of the same types of vicious attacks that Nick Clegg had experienced.

In mid-June, a profile of Michael Gove in *The Times* was accompanied by direct attacks by Dom Cummings on Ed Llewellyn, the PM's chief of staff ('a sycophant presiding over a shambolic court'), communications director Craig Oliver ('he's just clueless'), and the Prime Minister himself ('a sphinx without a riddle ... bumbles without the slightest sense of purpose').

These words were not appreciated in Downing Street. The criticism was now damaging the PM himself.

Within days, the instruction went out that Dom Cummings was no longer to be allowed to come into the DfE and his pass was to be cancelled.

When Michael was unexpectedly moved from the department in the July 2014 reshuffle, the cover story was that Lynton Crosby was to blame: his polling apparently showed that the Education Secretary was unpopular with both teachers and parents.

But there was more to the surprise move than this. The Prime Minister was fed up with the endless rows. An Education Secretary who had started in office by carefully creating a 'big tent' of supporters for schools improvement, including reform-minded head teachers, modernising Conservatives, Blairite Labour members and some Liberal Democrats, had now ended up in a very small tent indeed. At times, the inhabitants of the tent seemed to be down to just Dom Cummings, Toby Young and Michael himself.

But even more significant were the chaos and division caused by Dom Cummings, and the real anger this provoked in Downing Street.

'I never realised just how much Downing Street hate him and how much damage he did to me,' the former Education Secretary told friends after his move.

✣

With Nicky Morgan now in the Secretary of State's office, the Education Wars of the previous nine months ended abruptly. Peace broke out in the Education Department, and the new Education Secretary and I worked constructively right through until the end of the parliament. We had some differences of view, but not on crucial issues, and these were well managed by Nicky and by her able, constructive and mild-mannered new adviser, Luke Tryl.

It was a relief not to be battling any more with Michael Gove and Dom Cummings. That last nine months had been pretty frustrating at times.

But I also missed my old colleague, and when I reflected back on what he had stood for in government, I had to accept that in spite of our differences, on many issues his passion and motivation were aligned with my own views, even though his policies weren't always as convergent.

Here was the Secretary of State, for example, who had upset many in the education establishment by sweeping away many low-quality 'vocational' qualifications – but wasn't a strong core curriculum what most disadvantaged children needed, to get on in life?

Here was the man who had irritated the Prime Minister by criticising a Conservative manifesto writing process that was to be led by five male Old Etonians and one male graduate of St Paul's. But didn't he have a point?

Here was an Education Secretary who had battled with the Ministry of Defence to make subsidised cadet forces places available in state schools, and not just in the posher independent schools; who had championed gay marriage; who wrote rude letters to Conservative-controlled education authorities telling them to raise the quality of their state schools; who was carrying out a long-overdue improvement in provision for children in care; who had quietly let it be known that he thought the 2012 reduction in the top rate of tax was premature; and who was believed to have told friends that he thought that inheritance tax should be increased and not reduced.

In a Conservative Party that was too often the defender of the interests of those who benefited from the status quo, here was a truly radical advocate of higher standards for all and greater equality of opportunity. Here was a man who quite genuinely wanted to break Britain's class-ridden society open to 'outsiders'.

Michael Gove had been a generous and charming friend, at times a frustrating and formidable foe, a doughty fighter for educational excellence, and a striking example of a politician capable of setting clear aims and objectives and seeing these through.

Two days after Michael left his Education post, one of my advisers wrote to me that 'Michael has discovered what every politician eventually gets to find out – that all political careers end in failure'.

I wasn't so sure. I expected my former colleague to be a rather indifferent Chief Whip, but I predicted that if the Conservatives were returned to power in 2015, Michael Gove would be back either as Home Secretary or as Justice Secretary – and perhaps eventually as both. I should have backed my hunch with a small flutter at Ladbrokes.

Scotland Takes Centre Stage

2010–14

I t was early 2014. Relations within the coalition were scratchy. I was at a meeting of the Social Justice Cabinet Committee. On the agenda was family stability and relationship breakdown – a theme of particular importance to Iain Duncan Smith, the chair of our committee.

As I listened to the debate, I turned to a slide pack that had been sent to the committee by one of the expert outside groups advising us. It was entitled 'Pathways to Separation'. The first slide said:

> Relationships have been found to usually end in one of three ways:
> a) relatively gently after a protracted period of dwindling intimacy, growing dissatisfaction, and cyclical arguments, during which partners grow apart and live separate lives;
> b) after relationships have sustained incremental damage as a result of couples lurching from one crisis to another; escalating incidents of, for example, domestic violence; and recurring unresolved problems until the final straw is experienced by at least one partner;
> c) suddenly and as an unforeseen event initiated out of the blue by one partner.

For a coalition minister, it all felt rather close to home.

Wednesday 6 August 2014 was for me the happiest day of the year. This was the day that my summer holiday started, and I could drive down to the south of France and enjoy over two relaxing weeks in the sun. I knew that this would be last real rest before a long run-in to the May 2015 general election.

As always seemed to be the case in the summer recess, there was something of a crisis on the foreign policy front. Libya was now a mess. Syria was a disaster. There was a major outbreak of conflict between Israel and Hamas – indeed, Baroness Warsi had resigned from her position at the Foreign Office the previous day over the UK's response to Israeli incursions in Gaza.

Vince Cable, with Nick Clegg's support, was pressing for an arms embargo against Israel, but he was making little progress in the face of implacable opposition from Philip Hammond – now Foreign Secretary – and David Cameron.

I wrote a paper on possible Liberal Democrat 'asks' in the coming Autumn Statement – cutting council tax for lower-banded properties, further increasing the personal income tax allowance, boosting NHS funding, introducing a 'respite bonus' for carers, and making some reforms to the 'spare room subsidy' policy. I also spent a little time in mid-holiday checking our latest state of preparations for the implementation of the free school meals policy at the beginning of the school year in September, but otherwise there was little to disturb my rest or my reading, including of the fourth volume of Robert Caro's biography of Lyndon Johnson.

In late August, the media was dominated by the truly shocking and barbaric beheading of a US journalist in Syria – killed on camera by a black-clothed ISIL militant who it appeared might even be a British citizen.

As August passed and September approached, our focus increasingly shifted to the upcoming referendum on Scottish independence. This prospect had hung over the coalition government ever since its formation in May 2010.

Early in the parliament, David Cameron and George Osborne had been keen to force a quick referendum on the Scottish National Party, so that the UK government and not the Scottish administration called the shots.

But the strong view from the Liberal Democrat side of the government – Nick Clegg, Scottish Secretary Mike Moore, and Danny Alexander – was that the UK government could not dictate the terms and timing. That could only play into the SNP's hands, by suggesting that Scotland could not be trusted to control its own destiny. The polls, however, looked as if the SNP were on course to lose a straight 'in or out of the UK' vote. So the UK government agreed a strategy of forcing a single, simple choice in the referendum. We decided to resist giving the SNP the ability to ask a third question about whether Scottish voters wanted extra powers within the UK.

Mike Moore, the Liberal Democrat Scottish Secretary, was low-key, unflashy and mild-mannered. These might have seemed like weaknesses in a politician. But Mike also proved to be patient, strategic, respected and sure-footed. Inch by inch, he secured all the objectives that the coalition government set itself for the referendum question and timing. And in the slippery world of Scottish politics, he had steadily built up a reputation for himself as trustworthy and reasonable.

The decision was taken early on that the campaign for Scotland to stay in the UK should be cross-party, and led from within Scotland, not by the Westminster party leaders – all of whom were English. The respected Labour politician Alistair Darling was recruited to lead the No campaign, and this seemed like a good choice.

The prospect of Scotland voting Yes was regarded as a potential disaster by the leaders of the three main parties. But even though the break-up of the Union was a real risk, it did not seem to most of us to be a high risk – the pro-independence vote always appeared to be in a clear minority. However, a closer reading of the polls showed that many voters were undecided and would make up their minds quite late in the day, so the risk of a sudden turnaround in the outcome was higher than most people realised.

In the reshuffle in October 2013, Nick Clegg decided to replace Mike Moore as Scottish Secretary. It was a complete surprise to Mike, and a massive blow to him. He was widely seen as being a 'safe pair of hands' and was the only Cabinet minister to lose his job in the reshuffle. Nick Clegg had decided, however, that over the next year the referendum campaign was likely to become far more heated and challenging, and he wanted a Scottish Secretary with a more robust reputation as a 'street fighter'. It was a decision with mixed consequences.

Alistair Carmichael, the new Liberal Democrat Secretary of State for Scotland, had the necessary tough reputation Nick was looking for. However, in November 2013 he faced Deputy First Minister Nicola Sturgeon in a head-to-head TV debate on Scottish independence. It was exactly the type of occasion for which Alistair was selected. Unfortunately, he was the clear loser. One colleague of Alistair's said: 'He made a real mess of the debate, and never entirely regained his confidence.'

As 2014, the year of the referendum, began, the mood at the heart of the coalition government began to darken. The polling figures showed a lead for the No campaign, but a declining lead and one that was too slender for comfort. The cross-party 'Better Together' campaign was also making little headway. It was hugely reliant on the Labour Party, which had reigned supreme in Scotland for many years. However, what soon became apparent was the extent to which the Scottish Labour Party was rotten to its core. Many constituency parties were barely functioning and the campaign activity on the ground in too many areas was risibly slight.

In early 2014, the Quad took a new and important decision: to start to exercise much more influence on the campaign from London. This was doubly sensitive. Firstly, because the No campaign had to be seen to be led by the Scottish people themselves. And secondly, because the Cabinet Secretary, Jeremy Heywood, was determined to resist the civil service being drawn into a political debate – though it was no secret that he was himself strongly in favour of the continuance of the United Kingdom.

Danny Alexander became the new but unofficial head of the No campaign in London. Every day, from March 2014 onwards, he chaired a morning meeting of senior ministers and others to direct the campaign. Everything that ministers did or said about Scotland, every official utterance about the implications of Scottish independence, and all the contingency planning for the last few weeks of the campaign were directed by Danny – with the full backing of Nick Clegg, David Cameron and George Osborne.

In late July, there was a wonderful opportunity for Scottish First Minister Alex Salmond to whip up nationalist feeling in Scotland: the Commonwealth Games were being held in Glasgow. Nick Clegg and Danny Alexander were in Glasgow for the beginning of the Games, and they took the opportunity, while on a bus journey from their hotel to the stadium, to talk to the Labour leader, Ed Miliband, about the Scottish referendum vote. 'Look Ed,' said Nick. 'We are really worried that this referendum could actually be lost. And it seems if anything that it is Labour voters who are moving directly to the SNP. In our view, the three parties need to come up with some proposals to devolve more powers to Scotland in the future. That way, we may be able to win back wavering voters and take more initiative in the debate.'

But Ed Miliband was very cautious about any form of cross-party work-ing on devolved powers. 'I don't want anything at all to do with the Tories, even behind the scenes,' he said. Nick commented afterwards: 'The more I see of Ed Miliband and Labour, the more I despair that he is unable to take risks or act decisively. Labour displays a strange mixture of arrogance but absolutely no confidence in themselves.'

Danny Alexander spent much of that summer in Scotland, supporting the 'Better Together' campaign. On 18 August, on a conference call down a crackly mobile phone line from the Highlands, and just one month before referendum polling day, Danny sounded quietly confident that the No campaign was on track for victory. In Scotland, as in the south of France, there seemed to be few dark clouds in the sky.

By early September, we were all back in London. The situation in Iraq and Syria was still serious, and consideration was being given by both the US and the UK governments to bombing raids in both countries to help defeat the ISIL militants.

The polls in Scotland were also narrowing fast, and the UK government began to worry that any controversial military action in Iraq might be exploited by the SNP in the referendum vote. On 4 September, Nick Clegg told us: 'Cameron is going to discuss all this with Obama. Ideally, we don't want anything before 18 September. We all know how cynical Salmond can be.'

Meanwhile, on the same day, there was very unhelpful coverage in *The Guardian*, claiming that senior government figures were considering extending the current parliament if Scotland voted Yes to independence. The first rule of the Better Together campaign had been breached: we had agreed that we should never accept the premise that independence might happen.

There was a growing sense of panic in the No camp as more polls came out showing that their lead was narrowing fast. Even on the foreign exchange markets, the pound began to wobble – a sure sign that those who have to bet money on the referendum outcome were also getting jittery.

On Saturday 6 September, I spent all day working at home on my red boxes. In the evening, we had our regular Saturday conference call with Nick Clegg at 6 p.m. As usual, 'Switch' contacted each participant in order of rising seniority so that the Deputy Prime Minister was not required to wait for others to join before the conference call could start.

It was a long call, and half of it was on the situation in Scotland. Danny Alexander led the discussion: 'I'm afraid there's a poll coming out in the *Sunday Times* tomorrow which is really going to put the cat amongst the pigeons,' he said. 'The rumour is that it shows the "Yes" to independence campaign in the lead for the first time. I still think this is likely to be a rogue poll, but even our own internal tracker polls are closing – and they now look like its neck and neck.'

'This is terrible news,' said Nick. 'Among all the other things going on, this has to be our top priority. If we don't turn this thing around, we will be on this call in two weeks' time figuring out how we deal with an independent Scotland.'

'I'm trying to clear stuff out of my diary for the next fortnight,' said Danny. 'We've been planning for every contingency in these last two weeks and now I am going to have to put those plans into effect.'

Sure enough, the next day the *Sunday Times* splashed on its shock poll, putting the Yes camp ahead with 51 per cent, against the No camp on 49 per cent. There were now just eleven days left to save the United Kingdom.

On Monday 8 September, we launched our 'pre-manifesto' of Liberal Democrat policies for the general election. It was completely blotted out by the growing panic about Scottish independence.

Danny Alexander now moved into overdrive to help turn things around. 'God,' said Nick Clegg to a close friend that week, 'it is really impressive to see Danny swing into action. He isn't a public face of the campaign, and he can't do the emotional connection stuff, but he is a sheer bloody workhorse – raising money, getting the organisation of the campaign in the right place, and pulling every lever to turn things around.'

And every lever was certainly pulled. The three parties talked together and agreed to offer Scotland new powers – 'devo max' – if the country voted to stay in the UK. Danny Alexander and David Cameron hit the phones to get businesses and celebrities to come off the fence and speak out.

And the three Westminster leaders headed north of the border to speak out. This was seen as a potential risk by the No campaign, who felt that three panicked English leaders could be a liability. There was some frustration, in particular, that Ed Miliband kept making unwanted visits to Scotland. His poll ratings showed that he was very unpopular north of the border. Unknown to Mr Miliband, the Better Together campaign deliberately moved many of his public engagements until late in the day, so that they would be too late to be picked up by the broadcast media.

On Tuesday 9 September, Nick Clegg, Danny Alexander and I met in

Nick's office in Dover House at 8.30 a.m. for our weekly strategy meeting. Danny looked exhausted, but was also energised by the campaign. Nick said that he had agreed with David Cameron that the next day's Prime Minister's Questions would be cancelled and the three leaders would fly to Scotland to 'love bomb' the Scots. Danny reported that the polls were stabilising but were still too close to call.

At Cabinet, there was a short but fruitless discussion about the situation in Scotland. Alistair Carmichael was rather subdued. He was in the dog house after a recent interview in which he had broken the key rule about government ministers not speculating on the result of an independence Yes vote. He had even said he might then resign as Scottish Secretary to join Alex Salmond's negotiating team to better negotiate independence with the UK government.

At the Quad on 9 September, Danny Alexander set out what he wanted to do. 'We've got to mobilise banks, businesses and every economic player we can,' he said. 'We have got to highlight the economic risks. That is the game-changer. And WE have got to do this. Better Together just aren't delivering the goods.'

The next day, various government meetings were cancelled as people were sent off to Scotland, sometimes just to deliver leaflets. Wednesday 10 September turned out to the key day of the campaign – a turning point. After numerous calls from Danny Alexander and David Cameron, big business started to come out publicly to say that in the event of a Yes vote they might move some of their operations and jobs out of Scotland. The warnings led the national media, and there was a real feeling for the first time of the Yes camp being on the back foot. It was 'Salmond's Black Wednesday', as Danny put it.

'Danny's played an absolute blinder on this,' said a relieved Nick Clegg. 'If Scotland votes to stay in the UK, Danny will deserve more credit than anyone. He has almost single-handedly got all these third-party people and businesses to speak out.'

On 11 September, the polls showed a five-point lead against independence – not much, but better. 'Our internal polling is going in the right direction,' said Danny.

Meanwhile the Obama administration was determined to push ahead with airstrikes against the Islamic State militants in Syria and Iraq. Nick Clegg spoke to the US Ambassador, making clear that the UK would not be involved in any military action until the referendum vote was out of the way. 'We are not risking the United Kingdom on this,' he said. I suspected the US administration would hold off their own airstrikes too until after Scotland had voted.

David Cameron remained in a state of near panic, but he focused himself professionally on the job in hand, also working hard to mobilise business support. 'God, Nick,' he said, 'I am so incredibly nervous. I really cannot be the Prime Minister who oversaw the break-up of our United Kingdom.'

By the Sunday before polling day, there were three new polls out. Two put the No camp in the lead and one gave a very narrow lead to the Yes campaign. On our Saturday evening conference call, Danny had said that their own polls gave the No camp a lead of between five and eight percentage points. In my diary, I dared to forecast a 10 per cent final lead – 55 per cent No, 45 per cent Yes.

But no one was taking any chances. And on Sunday 14 September there was the most incredible intervention yet. The Queen was attending a morning church service in Crathie Kirk, near Balmoral. After the service, she chatted with a few bystanders. In the presence of a TV camera, she told a member of the crowd: 'The Scottish people need to think very carefully before the vote next week.' It was an extraordinary intervention from a monarch who has made a career of staying above politics. And for such a dedicated professional, there could never be any doubt that it was calculated. The Queen never makes mistakes.

There was now a clear sense that the No camp were back in the driving seat. On Tuesday 16 September, the three main UK party leaders wrote a joint article for the *Daily Record*, headlined 'The Vow', promising Scotland a massive round of further devolution in the event of a No vote. I was personally dubious that this was really necessary and worried that it would trigger further debate in England about the so-called 'West Lothian' question. Why would it be right for Scottish MPs to be able to vote on the whole range of Westminster Parliament policy issues, if many of these votes now related to England only because of devolution to the Scottish Parliament? It seemed to me to be a very slippery slope indeed, with a real risk that 'logical' rounds of reform would lead slowly and inevitably to a break-up of the whole of the United Kingdom.

On Wednesday 17 September, the day before the referendum vote, I was up at 4 a.m., for the second day in a row. By 8.30 a.m., I was in Glasgow, to help the Better Together campaign in Jo Swinson's parliamentary seat. I was collected from the airport by two Conservative activists and driven to Jo's office in a most un-Liberal Democrat car, a very plush Mercedes with automatically adjusting seats that hugged your backside when you went around a sharp bend. This was cross-party cooperation in action!

Jo's organisers were taking no chances of putting off Scottish voters with an MP from south-west England, and they had me out delivering leaflets for most of the day.

One of the press officers also told me that Vince Cable was up in Scotland. 'That's useful,' I commented.

'Not really,' said the press officer. 'The problem is that some idiot in Vince's office has set up an official visit without clearing it with the Better Together campaign. Unbelievably, they have fixed for Vince to visit the headquarters of the Student Loan Company – which processes the repayment of English tuition fee loans. Given that tuition fees are the biggest Liberal Democrat car-crash issue of the decade, this will be a massive self-inflicted wound. We're trying to get it stopped now.'

Later, I heard that the Better Together campaign had angrily phoned Vince on his way to the airport in London. He had had to stop to take a long and difficult call on the issue, and as a consequence he missed his plane to Scotland, and the planned visit to the Student Loans HQ. When he finally arrived, he was put on a street stall in the middle of Glasgow instead.

I travelled back with Vince from Scotland at the end of the day. We sat having fish and chips in a rather uninspiring cafeteria in Glasgow Airport. To my surprise, Vince said he was still quite worried about his Twickenham parliamentary constituency: 'The Tories are pouring money and activists into my seat, and into Ed Davey's. It's really rather worrying, but we are doing what we can.'

We took off from Glasgow at around 9.30 p.m., and the plane banked sharply and swung back over the city to turn south for the journey back to England. Glasgow occupies a huge area of land, and all we could see below were the lights of the city twinkling up to us from the ground. It was an impressive sight. I could not help wondering whether it was my last sight of Scotland as a part of the United Kingdom, but I felt not. The polls were still very narrowly in favour of a No vote, and most of the voters I had met during the day seemed unexcited by the notion of independence.

Thursday 18 September finally arrived – Referendum Day. 'Switch' set up the usual morning call with Nick Clegg at 7.45 a.m. For once, there was no Danny Alexander on the call. There wasn't much to report except that Andy Murray, the Scottish tennis star, had just tweeted out his support for independence that morning. Fortunately, under UK election law, this could not be covered by the mainstream media.

We had a long discussion about what a devo max solution in Scotland would mean in England. I said that we needed to treat this issue with huge care. An 'English votes for English laws' solution could not only help to further stoke Scottish nationalism, by removing powers from their Westminster MPs, but it would also play into the hands of the Conservative Party, who had the majority of seats in England under our unfair first past the post electoral system. Jonny Oates phoned me after the conference call and said that he shared my concerns. We agreed that we needed to provide some detailed policy options as soon as possible. As soon as the Scottish referendum was over, the debate would swiftly move on to these matters.

I spent the day of the referendum in my own constituency, where there was a council by-election in Central Yeovil. For MPs, all politics comes back to the local, and I wasn't taking any chances in my own backyard.

I was back home by 8.15 p.m., when two large red boxes of work arrived from London. At 11 p.m., my constituency organiser rang through to tell me that we had won the Central Yeovil by-election with a 73 per cent Liberal Democrat vote share. Yeovil secured. Now just Scotland to go!

Throughout the day, I had been exchanging a number of emails with Nick Clegg about where we should go post-referendum in terms of the devolution debate in Scotland and England. My strong view was that if we won the Scottish referendum, we then needed to focus on the value of the United Kingdom and how we kept it together. 'Let's be careful not to set too many hares running,' I said. I was not at all keen to open up debates about English devolution. However, the pledges given by the three UK party leaders in the last week of the campaign were now making this a more difficult position to hold.

Unusually, senior civil servants were also letting it be known that there was significant risk if the coalition started to promote 'English votes for English laws' solutions within hours of a Scottish No vote. They felt that they had acted generously to allow the UK government to use its resources to make the case for the Union. They were now deeply worried that hasty actions after the referendum decision could snatch long-term defeat from the jaws of short-term victory.

Willie Rennie, our Scottish Liberal Democrat leader, also urged caution. In an email on Thursday afternoon he wrote: 'The message of the referendum is not that our Scottish MPs should have less influence. The theme should be that Britain will never be the same again and that power must be decentralised.'

On the afternoon of 18 September, David Cameron phoned to speak to Nick Clegg, who was holding an advice centre in his Sheffield constituency. The Prime Minister said that he was assuming that the referendum would be won and that Scotland would stay in the UK. It was, he said, pointless to plan for the disaster scenario. He then proceeded to say that he thought as soon as the referendum was concluded, people were immediately going to ask, 'What about England?' He said that he intended the very next tomorrow morning to 'lean in to the English issue', and start to talk about what should happen next: 'To me, England is now the missing bit of the jigsaw. And I need to keep my rather restive backbenchers happy.'

Nick Clegg acknowledged that people were already asking about the English question. But he also urged care. He said his view was that decentralisation in England was the solution, not 'fiddling with voting at Westminster'.

'We are going to have to disagree on that,' said David Cameron. 'I think Westminster is the big issue. I would like to set up a commission to look at all this, and consider the solutions.'

Nick Clegg said that he would consent to a commission being established – but only if it looked at the full range of potential solutions and if it reached out to all the parties and to all those with expertise.

'All right,' said David Cameron. 'Well, let's stay in touch. I'll be pressed to say something about all this tomorrow morning, and I guess you will be asked too.'

At 6.15 a.m. the next day, I woke up and immediately switched on the radio.

The first voice I heard was Alex Salmond, the SNP leader, conceding defeat – for once, with a degree of graciousness (it would not last long).

The result was exactly as I had expected a week or so ago: 55 per cent No and 45 per cent Yes. A year ago, that would have been considered a very close finish, but after the nerves of the past few weeks, it seemed like a decisive victory.

Danny Alexander was in the television studios in Scotland, about to be interviewed. He allowed himself a few tears of joy and emotion – off camera. 'I have never cried in a TV studio before,' he told friends later. Emotions were running high on all sides.

At 8 a.m., David Cameron appeared outside the front door of Downing Street. He welcomed the result of the Scottish referendum, and announced that he would now be establishing a Cabinet committee to look at the whole constitutional settlement in the UK, to devolve more powers to the other nation states alongside devolution in Scotland.

I watched the Prime Minister's statement from my home in South Petherton in Somerset. As he spoke, there was a massive thunderstorm above my house, with lightning and pouring rain – a warning of impending doom, I wondered? I couldn't help feeling that David Cameron was now setting in motion the very forces that within a decade would break the United Kingdom apart. 'Always remember', Michael Gove had once said to me, 'that the answer to the West Lothian Question is not to ask it!'

At 8.15 a.m., I joined the morning conference call with Nick Clegg. There was a lot of discussion about the Prime Minister's intervention: 'Cameron's statement is going down very badly in Scotland,' warned Stephen Lotinga, Nick Clegg's director of communications. 'The SNP are briefing that this is a betrayal of the commitments on devo max, because the Tories appear to be making the promises on Scotland contingent on agreeing the proposed changes in England. The Conservatives are also briefing very aggressively that this is a "big trap for the Labour Party" – in other words, if Labour refuse to countenance English votes for English laws, they will upset English voters. But if they go along with this, then Labour may never have a majority again to push through policies that will impact in England on issues like education, health and taxes.'

'This has Osborne's fingerprints all over it. Very, very, short-sighted and tactical,' said Nick Clegg. 'I will have to talk to Cameron about this. Otherwise the referendum victory could sour very quickly.'

Throughout the day, the mood in Scotland did rapidly sour. The SNP could see that David Cameron's move had thrown them a lifeline. Nick Clegg angrily emailed David Cameron: 'It really doesn't make sense for us to turn the politics of grievance in Scotland into the politics of grievance in England.'

Meanwhile, we heard that Alex Salmond was privately predicting that the whole botched handling of the referendum aftermath could help deliver another thirty SNP MPs at the forthcoming general election – many of them at our expense.

Over the weekend, Nick Clegg spoke to David Cameron. It was a tense conversation. Nick Clegg warned that the referendum aftermath was in danger of becoming a complete disaster. He said bluntly that the Prime Minister was in danger of guaranteeing the break-up of the UK, with the only beneficiaries being the SNP.

'Look, Nick,' said David Cameron impatiently, 'I just don't care. We've only got one Conservative MP north of the border. Let Labour sort it out. It's now their problem.'

Nick Clegg and Danny Alexander were both furious. 'I used to disagree with the Conservatives but at least respect them,' Nick Clegg told me a week later. 'But now I have contempt for what they have done. It is all so bloody short-termist and short-sighted.'

Danny Alexander was just as critical. 'Over Scotland, we have seen the very best and very worst of David Cameron,' he said. 'He was focused and quite brilliant during the campaign, and worked hard to get big business and others to speak out. But now it's all tactics, tactics, tactics. Short-term party advantage, instead of thinking of the long-term interests of the United Kingdom.'

The Cabinet committee to resolve this issue met on a number of occasions. Labour were invited to give evidence to it, but declined.

The Liberal Democrats insisted that the Scottish devo max solutions that were promised should be taken forward.

I developed a Liberal Democrat proposal for a form of English votes for English laws in which decisions would be taken by English MPs on the basis of vote share at the most recent general election, rather than being based solely on the number of first past the post English MPs elected. The Conservatives were unwilling to support this proposal, and the two coalition parties set out their own separate proposals in a Command Paper, published before the general election.

In Buckingham Palace and at the top of the civil service there was deep concern about developments following the referendum result: 'Who is thinking about the UK interest in all this?' one very senior civil servant said to me in exasperation.

It remains to be seen whether the September 2014 independence referendum in Scotland will be the last.

LUNCH IS SERVED

2014

When, in 2013, it was announced that Nick Clegg had asked me to chair the team that would produce the 2015 Liberal Democrat general election manifesto, the anti-establishment party magazine *Liberator* carried a large photograph of me on its cover. The headline was 'Laws to write general election manifesto'. Underneath was added: 'But for which party?'

Ever since I had co-edited *The Orange Book* in 2004, my reputation in the Liberal Democrat Party and in the media had been as something of a right-winger. The early spending cuts I oversaw in May 2010 clearly bolstered this sense.

It was certainly true that I was an economic liberal – I believed then and now that free markets, choice and competition are the most effective ways of generating wealth and empowering individuals. I regarded state control as often inefficient and unresponsive to individual demands. And I saw nothing progressive about running up large government debts that would have to be paid off by future generations.

But I was also strongly in favour of both personal and social liberalism. For me, economic competence was not the same as callousness. But to redistribute wealth and opportunity, someone had first to create it.

I was brought up as a Catholic, and I believed strongly in the Christian principle of the equal value of every person, and our responsibility to our fellow human beings. For me, it was the apparent callousness of the 1980s

Conservative governments that I had despised and that had driven me to look elsewhere for my political loyalties.

It is ironic that while I was seen as firmly on the right of my party, when I look back on my time in government and consider where I really made a difference, most of my influential contributions were to rather left-of-centre causes. In 2010, I had insisted that our manifesto include a full £2.5 billion pupil premium, to help educate the most disadvantaged children. In 2014, I had successfully made the case for this premium to be extended into the early years. In 2011, I had fought for benefits and pensions to be uprated by the full 5.2 per cent, when the Conservatives had argued for a large real cut in the incomes of the poorest citizens. The Talented Leaders Programme to help improve schools in challenging areas, the vetoing of the Conservative plan to make landlords operate as immigration officers, the further and faster increase in the personal tax allowance – these were all causes I had championed.

As Schools Minister, I had also made the case to Nick Clegg – supported by two advisers, Matt Sanders and Julian Astle – for extending free school meals to 16–18-year-olds in colleges and to infant-school children.

In some parts of the media, our free school meals plan was inaccurately portrayed as some sort of short-term populist vote winning plan. We certainly expected it to be popular, and in general it was. But we also believed that there was a very strong, rational case for what we were proposing.

I had long been in favour of the notion of offering children a free, healthy hot meal at lunchtime. To me, it seemed just common sense that children required to be in school for up to seven hours should be fed properly.

Some people claimed that it made no sense to provide free meals for families whose parents could afford to pay. I did not accept this logic at all. After all, we provide free education, free healthcare and many other free services to people who could afford to pay. Since almost all children needed a healthy meal at school, I considered that it made sense to provide a universal service.

Pilot studies had also shown that having a hot meal was good for child health (most packed lunches being of poor nutritional quality) and that they had a beneficial impact on attainment, making children more ready to learn and concentrate.

But I saw social as well as educational benefits from the policy. It was simply not true that the only families paying for school meals were those who could easily afford to do so. For many families on low incomes, paying for school meals for two or three children was a major burden. And too many children seemed to lack the social skills of sitting down to have a meal, and even of using a knife and fork properly.

Finally, the existing system of means-tested free school meals was a major deterrent to taking up employment. Most parents moving from benefits into employment would immediately lose their entitlement to free meals. I believed strongly in improving work incentives, and saw this policy as a powerful way of helping those parents who were doing the 'right thing' by moving into work.

Finally, it had long angered me, and many other MPs, that there was an anomaly which meant that while young people aged sixteen to eighteen from low-income families received free meals if they went to a school, they lost this entitlement if they went to a college. This was clearly indefensible and unjust, but no government had been willing to make it a priority to correct this injustice.

Two factors opened up the prospect of better funding of school meals. The first was the School Food Plan. The second factor was the Conservative insistence on allocating around £600 million for a transferable allowance to part-recognise marriage (or, more accurately, stay-at-home married parents), combined with Nick Clegg's canny insistence that he should have an equal amount of money to fund his priorities.

I have already explained how we came to prioritise the free meals policy against other lead options. I have also set out the lengthy and generally painful process by which, in late 2013, we secured cross-government support for proper capital funding and for a clear legal duty to be placed on schools. There was still, however, a significant delivery job to do to ensure the policy was a success. In this I was supported by a small but excellent team of departmental officials, led by Jacquie Spatcher and Marc Cavey, as well as a very experienced advisory team and an external group led by the formidable Linda Cregan and Carrieanne Bishop.

With considerable media focus on delivery of the new policy, and under a constant barrage of negative and misleading briefing, I was determined to take no chances. I knew that if hundreds of schools failed to deliver the policy in September 2014, it would be a gift to our opponents in the media – and that failure would damage both the policy and those responsible: Nick Clegg and me.

All the advice I received was that after some huffing and puffing about the stretching lead-in time, the vast majority of schools would successfully deliver the policy. But I was taking no chances. If Vince Cable was right that Gordon Brown had evolved from 'Stalin to Mr Bean', I now went through something of a transformation myself – from laissez-faire liberal to Stalinist overlord. Nothing would be left to chance.

Each week for almost a year I had at least two long meetings on free school meal delivery. Officials produced massive piles of A3 sheets, carefully documenting progress in 152 local authority areas. I asked that all 16,400 schools that had to deliver the policy should be rated green, amber or red for their state of preparation. A similar rating was given to each local authority. Advisers were available to phone or even visit schools that needed help in preparing for the big increase in school meal capacity, and we speedily allocated the extra capital we had secured to upgrade kitchens. In some parts of the country, particularly where there were Conservative-controlled local authorities, the school meals service had long ago been allowed to fall into decline. Disgracefully, many large schools lacked any proper kitchen facilities.

Everything (bar the minor media frenzy whipped up by Dom Cummings) seemed to be going well. But in late March 2014 I was surprised to be visited by two senior officials in the department, both of whom looked a little sheepish. 'Minister, we've been asked to consider the delivery risks around free schools meals,' they told me. 'Obviously, things are going well in colleges and that won't be a problem. But we have considered what we could do to limit delivery risks for schools. We have been asked to put to you the possibility that instead of having to deliver the new duty by September 2014, we could actually amend the legislation to give schools until January 2015 – a bit more time.'

There are some moments in life and politics when it pays not to delay in giving a decisive reply. 'No,' I snapped back, rather angrily. 'Why are you putting this to me? All the indications are that the policy is going well. If we announced this, it would be a public relations disaster, and more importantly it would cast doubt over the whole policy. We are not going to delay one single day.'

The two officials looked a little embarrassed. 'OK, that's clear, Minister. So you are aware, we'll obviously need to report your decision back to the Secretary of State.'

'Fine,' I replied.

But I was irritated. There seemed no evidence at all that a delay was necessary. But now that I had been offered a slower delivery timetable and had turned it down, I knew that all the responsibility and blame would be firmly on my shoulders if things went wrong.

I considered briefly referring the matter to Nick Clegg – after all, his neck would be on the line too. But what was the point? I knew what his response would be: the same as mine, provided I was confident that we could deliver.

From that day onwards, I was even more determined to deliver a successful policy outcome. I had resigned once from this government, and didn't wish to have to depart again.

Every week, I eagerly awaited my weekend red box for the latest report on school readiness.

In early April, around 1,000 of 16,400 schools were still red-rated – which implied that they might not be able to deliver a hot food option by the new school year in September.

Each week I met officials to review the lists. I approved extra capital grants to individual schools in difficult circumstances. I badgered chief executives in local authorities that were reporting the largest numbers of red-rated schools. I worked my small team of officials relentlessly hard. But they delivered every single thing I asked for, and more than was promised – they were dedicated and magnificent.

By early June, the number of red-rated schools had fallen to around 200, though a significant proportion of schools were still amber-rated.

By the end of July, there were just five red-rated schools in the whole of England, and I was able to report to a mildly sceptical Cabinet that in September we would successfully deliver free, hot, healthy meal options to around 1.5 million more children than were presently entitled – in almost every one of the 16,400 eligible schools. I congratulated our DfE officials and assured the Prime Minister that I would maintain 'Stalinist control' over the programme – altered to 'very close ministerial oversight' when the Cabinet minutes were circulated.

By August, local authorities couldn't find a school in the country that wasn't on track to deliver.

Once some parts of the media realised that the policy was on track to be a success, they lost interest in covering it. Others switched attention to how many of the new meals would be hot. We surveyed that too – it amounted to around 99 per cent.

And on the first days of the school year, to ensure we were absolutely on top of what was going on around the country, volunteers in the Education Department phoned every school in England – finding fewer than ten schools that were not already delivering.

Later in the year, the take-up statistics were released, demonstrating that 1.3 million more children were now eating free, healthy, school meals, with 750,000 of these having switched from less healthy packed lunches – and with participation of around 85 per cent nationally and 90 per cent in parts of inner London. Meanwhile, we had ended the ludicrous injustice that had previously left poor students at college without the free meals granted to similar students in schools.

Six months before, I had been hearing from Dom Cummings and others that we would struggle to deliver the policy. It was now top of the Education Department's delivery list, with a green rating and a mark of 10/10. Free schools and academies, by contrast, were both red-rated for risk.

But it was the views of parents, children and teachers that mattered most to me and to Nick Clegg.

One head teacher in south London told me: 'I had a parent who cried with delight when she heard about this policy. She just misses entitlement to free school meals now, because she is in a very low-paid job. This is going to make a big difference.'

In my own constituency of Yeovil, the middle-class chair of governors in one of the schools I visited told me quietly: 'The school is now producing really great meals, and I can now have both my children have the hot meals every single day. Previously, with two children, I could only really afford for them to have school meals twice a week.'

Sometimes our national media is inclined to think that 'middle class' means earning £60,000 or £70,000. Outside London and a few parts of the south-east, middle income is a lot less than this and many people in work struggle to make ends meet. Feeding children properly in school is good social policy and good economic policy too – helping to make work pay for those in low- and middle-income employment. I was and am very proud of our achievement in delivering this policy – and am grateful to the excellent team of officials and partner organisations who made this possible.

Carpet Bombing in the West Country

2014

Nick Clegg was sitting in his office in Whitehall in October 2014 with Ryan Coetzee, his leading strategist. 'I have been looking at the polling from Scotland, and I'm afraid it's pretty bad, Nick.

'We've just had the polling from Danny Alexander's seat and it's awful. I'm afraid that I have to tell you that Danny is so far behind that he cannot now be saved. He's toast.

'But it's not just Danny, of course. The polling in all our Scottish seats is terrible. The problem is that the SNP are now polling well over 55 per cent across Scotland. We've seen nothing like it before. It looks as if they are going to clean up in Scotland. Even Charles Kennedy is well behind and could lose. I fear that unless we can do something, we will lose ten of our eleven seats in Scotland. Only Alistair Carmichael would be left.'

With the Scottish referendum now out of the way, we were firmly focused on the next major electoral test: the general election itself.

Indeed, within government, both parties were now assessing everything on how it would impact on votes in May 2015.

At the Department for Education, I was trying to agree with my Conservative colleagues a major announcement on a new Royal College of Teaching, and action to improve teacher training and teacher qualifications. I had been working on the package for almost a year.

In September, I asked officials why it was taking so long for Conservative ministers and advisers to make a decision on whether they supported my proposals. After an embarrassed silence, one of the officials said: 'Minister, we believe that the policy paper is sitting in the in-tray of a Mr Lynton Crosby. The Secretary of State is content, but we have been told that nothing can go ahead until Mr Crosby has approved it.'

Two weeks later, the message came back that Lynton Crosby was not happy for us to launch anything at all relating to teacher qualifications. 'All Michael Gove's stuff about allowing schools to hire unqualified teachers polls really badly. I don't want us to go anywhere near this issue' was apparently his view.

As well as assessing the state of the campaign in Scotland, our party was carrying out detailed polling in all our other seats, and each week the general election team would meet in Nick's Clegg's office to review progress and to report back decisions about which seats were being prioritised and which were being ruthlessly axed from our target list. Present at these meetings were Paddy Ashdown, chair of the general election campaign; Olly Grender, his experienced and knowledgeable deputy; Ryan Coetzee, Nick's political strategist; chief executive Tim Gordon; and campaigns boss Hilary Stephenson, along with Nick, Danny Alexander, me and senior political advisers.

These meetings became increasingly gloomy, as we had to acknowledge that many presently held seats had to be written off.

On 13 October, it was concluded that Berwick-upon-Tweed, held by Sir Alan Beith since the 1970s, was unwinnable – along with Somerton and Frome, the Lib Dem seat immediately adjacent to my own. Concerns were also expressed about Vince Cable's Twickenham seat.

In November, most worryingly, we discussed evidence that the Tories had added a swathe of Liberal Democrat seats that we had previously considered safe to their target list. This included places such as Bath, Colchester, Kingston upon Thames, Thornbury and Yate, and even my own Yeovil constituency, with its 13,036 majority.

I later discovered that the Conservative whips were trying to get me regularly appointed as a 'Duty Minister' on a Friday – obliged to stay in London all day to cover any business in the House of Commons – to stop me getting back to Yeovil to campaign in my constituency. I did my best, generally with great success, to subvert their strategy.

I had noted a massive increase in Conservative electoral activity since around September. A switch seemed to have been suddenly flicked, and every week when I returned home from Westminster on a Friday, I found that another expensive Conservative leaflet had been delivered to every home in the area – clearly at the cost of thousands of pounds per week. We just could not match this level of spending.

Hilary Stephenson reported the same high levels of Conservative activity across much of the country. 'They seem to be carpet bombing the West Country with literature,' Ryan Coetzee added.

In the light of this, I welcomed Ryan's ruthless tendency to cut out of our plans those seats that we were well behind in. But Ryan often seemed to face opposition from people including Hilary Stephenson to his plan to prioritise. Hilary was even reticent to chop out Simon Wright's South Norwich seat, where the polling suggested we could trail behind in fourth place.

Nick Clegg was still hoping that we could target over forty seats in the general election, but this looked to most of us very optimistic. 'I have not yet made the mental leap to thirty seats or fewer,' he admitted in October. Party president Tim Farron told Nick: 'We will be lucky to get twenty-eight seats.' Nick's political adviser, Matthew Hanney, was still betting on forty-two or forty-three. My thinking was leaning to somewhere between twenty-five and thirty.

Nick was now having to spend more time in his own Sheffield Hallam seat, where Labour were now the main opposition.

As well as preparing for the election battle to come, I was spending a lot of time on the Liberal Democrat general election manifesto.

I had also been chosen by Nick to be a member of what came to be known as the 'Matthew Group'. This was the small team of MPs and peers put together to prepare for possible coalition talks after a 2015 general election. The chair of this team was Danny Alexander, and the other members were me, Lynne Featherstone, Steve Webb and Baroness Sal Brinton (later replaced by Baroness Kate Parminter, after Sal was elected party president). Our work was supported by Matthew Hanney, after whom the group was named.

On 22 September, this negotiating team travelled down together by train to Bath, for a day of discussion and background work. On arrival, we were met by the Liberal Democrat peer Lord Strasburger, who had kindly agreed for us to use his house for the day. It was a magnificent new-build property, set at the top of a hill with beautiful views into the valley below. The rooms were all enormous, with massive glass windows from floor to ceiling, and 180-degree views. We covered a huge range of subjects, including all sorts of machinery of government issues, and which departments we might want to be in if there was another coalition. We also received a hugely detailed paper from our colleagues in the House of Lords: it all boiled down to the essential point that our peers wanted more power, more jobs, more money and more special advisers.

On 22 October, I had dinner with Nick Clegg in a Spanish restaurant near his home in Putney. I wanted a chance to talk more directly and candidly about how he saw the challenges post-May 2015.

I reached the restaurant at around 9 p.m., and asked for the table under the codename I had been given. Nick's restaurant tables were, for security reasons, never booked in his own name.

It was a modest restaurant, effectively a tapas bar. The staff seemed friendly, and I had the impression that they were expecting Nick and knew who he was. We had a very relaxed dinner for a couple of hours. We started by agreeing that Labour were in a complete mess. Their economic policy wasn't credible and nor was Ed Miliband plausible as a Prime Minister in waiting – a deadly combination of negatives. At the recent Labour Party conference, Ed Miliband had delivered his speech without a written script. Disastrously, he had forgotten to mention the need to reduce the UK's Budget deficit, even though this was referenced in the speech text as distributed by the Labour press office. Labour's press team even admitted that their leader had simply 'forgotten to mention the deficit'. There could hardly have been a greater gift to Labour's opponents – a high-profile incident in which the credibility of both Labour's leader and its fiscal policy were simultaneously in the spotlight.

But if Labour were an unappetising prospect as a coalition partner, Nick Clegg was no more enthusiastic about the Conservatives. 'I now think it would be a significant blow for the country if the Tories get in next time,' he told me. 'Cameron is completely captured by his right wing. The Conservatives would be a real risk to our country's interests. Privately, I am not even sure we could do another coalition with the Tories. An EU referendum on their terms isn't in the country's interests and could be hugely damaging to our economy. The Conservatives are increasingly a right-wing party with a leader who spends too much time chasing his party's tail. I've lost respect for the Conservatives, and I am worried about them pursuing a very right-wing agenda post-May 2015 which would increase social divisions and damage our public services.'

I was surprised by how negative Nick seemed to be towards a second Conservative coalition. I made clear that I shared his concerns but added: 'We have to remember, though, that our opportunities may be limited. The public will almost certainly choose any coalition partner for us. And if the Tories are the largest party, they will probably get their EU referendum anyway. At least in government we could help shape the negotiation and the UK government priorities. But my view is that if the Conservatives decided not to campaign to keep the UK in the European Union, then at that stage any coalition would have to end and the Conservatives would be on their own. David Cameron would not want that.'

'You may be right, David,' Nick replied. 'But I am not sure that whatever we negotiated on Europe with the Tories would stick. I think that Cameron just panders too readily to his own party on the EU, so we couldn't rely on him not to move the goalposts on any renegotiation.'

'It seems to me like this,' said Nick. 'Labour are far less impressive than the Tories and far more tribal. But in values terms and policy terms it would probably be quite easy to do a deal with them. The Tories would be easier to deal with on a personal level, and of course we know them by now quite well. But our positions on Europe can't be easily reconciled, and I worry about what they want to do on public services and on welfare.'

'Anyway,' he concluded, 'if we are in coalition next time, I want us to take the Education Department – and I think you should probably go there, David.'

We then had a brief discussion about the Liberal Democrat electoral prospects. 'It looks pretty bad for Danny,' Nick said. 'We've even discussed whether he should leave the Cabinet and just campaign full time in Scotland until the election, but we agreed that the optics of this are just too bad for the party.'

'What about Sheffield?' I asked. 'It's tough,' said Nick. 'We are working really hard there, but Labour will pour people in at election time. I'm taking nothing for granted. It's not impossible that I could lose. I really don't want to become the Chris Patten or Michael Portillo of election night 2015. That would be ghastly.'

The NHS: A Winter Crisis?

2014–15

'You need to know that the NHS almost completely collapsed over Christmas. We came very close to preventable deaths in unsafe hospitals, and the Health Secretary having to resign. We had to throw the kitchen sink in to support the worst hospitals, and get people moving through Accident and Emergency. Of course, the NHS has had hundreds of millions to prepare for winter pressures. God knows what they have done with it.' Oliver Letwin, speaking in the first week of January 2015, gave me his blunt assessment of the huge pressures on the NHS which in late 2014 caused A&E waits to soar, targets to be missed, and some hospitals to effectively close their doors to all but the most serious emergency cases.

The coalition's plan for the NHS was supposed to be stability, with protected real funding. That was what David Cameron, Nick Clegg and George Osborne thought they were signing up to.

But the massive upheaval of the Lansley reforms had unsettled the NHS in 2010 and 2011. Jeremy Hunt – 'the Stalinist with the good bedside manner', as David Cameron once jokingly referred to his Health Secretary – was supposed to be calming things back down and keeping the NHS off the front pages. Lynton Crosby didn't want any 'barnacles on the boat' that might distract from the core Conservative message about economic competence. And both Nick Clegg and David Cameron knew that if anything could throw a last-minute lifeline to a beleaguered Labour leader, it would be an NHS crisis.

But though David Cameron and his Chancellor willed the ends, they weren't very enthusiastic about providing the means – the money. Indeed, in 2012 and 2013, the Chancellor and Prime Minister had even considered cutting NHS spending – once to fund a tax cut and on another occasion to help offset upward pressures on government borrowing from slower than expected growth. Both proposed cuts to the NHS budget had been vetoed by Nick Clegg.

Jeremy Hunt had taken over the running of the Health Department from Andrew Lansley in the autumn of 2012. After the Lansley Bill had stirred up a hornets' nest of opposition, the new Secretary of State had been given a very simple direction by the Prime Minister: 'Keep the NHS out of the news. Stop Labour from making it an election issue. Focus on better patient care, and don't carry out any more misguided reorganisations.'

The budget of the NHS had, then, been protected in real terms by the coalition government. David Cameron and George Osborne seemed to assume that this real protection was very generous, given the generalised public sector austerity. That was not my view or the view of many NHS experts. Over time, the NHS budget has needed to rise by about 3 per cent each year above inflation, to keep up with higher wages, more expensive medical technologies and the pressures from an ageing population.

Labour had spent so much more on the NHS in its last few years in office that NHS finances were very strong in 2010, when the coalition came to power. There was, therefore, a lot of scope to make efficiency savings and to run down large cash reserves, but it was obvious to me that at some stage these easy options would come to an end. At that point, we would need either more money for the NHS or we would see NHS service standards start to decline.

At Cabinet in mid-June 2014, I warned about signs of deteriorating NHS performance. I said that at some stage this government or its successor would need to move back to an NHS budget that was increasing again in real terms. I pointed out that the unacceptable alternative was to allow NHS standards to decline.

This was an unwelcome message in 10 Downing Street and in the Treasury, though one that Nick Clegg quickly embraced. His own view was that we needed to put more money into the NHS – perhaps in the Autumn Statement, which was what I was pushing for. Nick was worried, however, that a full-blown public row with the Conservatives on the NHS would only help the

Labour Party – indeed, this seemed almost the only issue that might help induce a Labour recovery.

Our own Health Minister, the excellent and well-respected Norman Lamb, and I spoke frequently. Norman's view was that the NHS needed another £1–2 billion in 2015, and soon, if the slide in standards was to be halted. Accident and Emergency waiting figures and other indicators of NHS performance were all moving in the wrong direction – and this was before the winter months arrived.

At this stage, Danny Alexander, as Chief Secretary to the Treasury, was yet to be persuaded by the case that the NHS needed more money, and he argued that the Department of Health wasn't managing its existing resources effectively.

In mid-July 2014, Jeremy Hunt received a particularly blunt letter signed by both George Osborne and Danny, telling him to do more to keep within his department's spending limits for the current year and the year ahead. The two Treasury ministers set out a series of demands, and made clear that they were taking the highly unusual decision of removing budget autonomy from the department and from its Secretary of State.

The very next day, the Chancellor and Chief Secretary received an equally blunt and robust response from Jeremy Hunt, rebutting the Treasury's criticisms and pointing out that the NHS was now carrying out 850,000 more operations, 1.2 million more A&E visits, 3.6 million more diagnostic tests and 6.3 million more outpatient appointments than in 2010. The Secretary of State was rejecting plans to limit his budget flexibility, and threatening to call in the Prime Minister to adjudicate between the two departments.

The response from the Treasury was swift and unhelpful: they spelled out that there would be no more money for the NHS that year or the next. The message was repeated in a meeting with the Prime Minister in early August, when Jeremy Hunt's request for extra cash was rejected by both the Chancellor and the Prime Minister.

I could not be sure how well run the NHS finances were, but I was clear whose side of the argument I was on. I wrote to Nick Clegg warning that in my view the NHS was heading over the edge of a cliff, and would need more money, whatever the Treasury was saying. Norman Lamb and I started to talk more frequently, so as to cooperate and work jointly to persuade Nick.

Nick took the same view as Norman and me – that we had to avoid a serious deterioration in NHS standards. In a conference call during the

August holidays, with Danny Alexander helpfully absent on this occasion, he said: 'If we get the NHS wrong, this is the one thing that could hand Labour the election on a plate. I've talked to Cameron on this and we have agreed to hold a Quad on the NHS on 10 September, to see if we can get to the bottom of things. In the meantime, Cameron has told Jeremy Hunt to scrape together extra money for the front line, by cutting other budgets like capital spending – but it's all small beer and much of it makes little sense.'

The planned 10 September Quad had to be moved because of the panic over the independence referendum in Scotland. But on the same day I held my own NHS stock-take with officials in the Cabinet Office and it was clear that key NHS performance standards were declining further.

At Labour's conference in late September, Ed Miliband picked up the threat to NHS finances, with a pledge to put money from a new mansion tax into health spending. But the pledge received limited coverage, as the US administration chose this day to begin bombing strikes on Islamic State fighters in Syria.

Meanwhile, Norman Lamb and Nick Clegg worked on a significant NHS announcement for our own party conference: a big new investment in mental health services. Norman had made this subject a major priority when he took over as Health Minister in 2012 – his own family's experience of mental health issues made him realise both how neglected the service had been in the past, and just how many people were affected by mental health conditions.

Nick Clegg was also a passionate advocate of better mental health provision and, against the advice of some, he and his political adviser Ryan Coetzee decided to make the announcement on new mental health waiting time standards the centrepiece of Nick's autumn 2014 conference speech.

On 25 September, I met with Nick Clegg and Danny Alexander to discuss the NHS. We agreed that at the conference we would also announce a new Liberal Democrat commitment to extra NHS investment in the next parliament, alongside the mental health waiting times package. Nick also agreed that we should push for more money in the Autumn Statement for immediate investment in the health service. Meanwhile, the Deputy Prime Minister told me: 'I talked to Cameron about the NHS this morning, and even he is beginning to soften a bit. I think he is worried about the NHS deteriorating and also he doesn't want the Tories to be painted as the block on more money.' This was good news.

At the party conference in early October, Nick Clegg made his important announcement, highlighting mental health as a major policy priority for the Liberal Democrats. He announced an additional £120 million investment in mental health, along with the first ever national waiting time standards for mental health access – the aim being to put mental health services on an equal footing with physical health services.

It was highly unusual for politicians to highlight mental health services in this way – they had usually been something of a Cinderella issue that was considered to relate to only a small number of people. The truth was that mental health problems directly and indirectly affected millions of people across the country. The work that Nick and Norman Lamb had completed was helping to bring the issue out of the policy and political shadows, and it was warmly welcomed by the mental health charities and by the wider public and commentators.

What made more of an impact on the Deputy Prime Minister was the response from those who actually relied on mental health services. In January 2015, Nick Clegg made a private visit to Liverpool to talk to some very vulnerable patients. 'It was emotionally draining,' he told us later, 'but very inspiring. The tales I heard were heart-rending. But people were saying that we are helping to end the taboo and start a real debate about treating mental health with the same priority as physical health. It's seeing things like this – and the impact of the pupil premium – that really inspires me to do this job.'

It wasn't long before the issue also caught David Cameron's eye. It was increasingly clear what the Conservative political strategy was in relation to the Liberal Democrats. Where the Lib Dems held views that were generally unpopular with a majority of the public, the Conservatives wanted to highlight these issues with high-profile policy spats.

But where we were pushing policy solutions which were popular with the public, on mental health or the personal tax allowance, the Conservatives moved quickly to try to associate themselves with those issues too.

At the first Cabinet meeting after our party conference, David Cameron went out of his way to mention Nick Clegg's mental health announcement: 'This is, of course, an announcement made by Nick at the Liberal Democrat conference, but it must be seen as a coalition priority and it has the full support of both coalition parties.'

Norman Lamb, Nick Clegg and I were convinced that the Conservatives would ultimately fall into line on wider NHS funding too. If they could see that the Liberal Democrats were going to publicly advocate extra spending on the NHS, they would soon lose their reticence and try to align themselves with our position as swiftly as possible.

By mid-October, concerns about the NHS were rising. Jeremy Hunt warned that A&E services were now 'extremely fragile' and might not be able to cope with a bad winter. Simon Stephens, the chief executive of the NHS, was apparently now also working on a report of his own to estimate what funding the health service would need in the next parliament.

At Cabinet on 21 October I gave another warning on the state of the NHS and the need for more money. I said that the strategy of maintaining the budget in real terms had run out of road. We could either put in more cash or accept a notable decline in NHS standards. Jeremy Hunt looked rather pleased with me, but the Prime Minister looked distinctly grumpy. When I finished speaking he said, 'Well, we can all agree with that.'

Norman Lamb, our Health Minister, was by now also pressing for extra NHS funding – and he was doing so openly, with the full support of Nick Clegg.

On 23 October, Simon Stevens made the case publicly that the NHS needed around £8 billion more over the next five years. It seemed to many in the Tory Party and in the media to be a large sum of money. But this was not the original amount estimated.

Simon Stevens had been working on his financial projections for the health service for some weeks. He and his staff had been making best- and worst-case forecasts of the demand for NHS services, as well as best- and worst-case scenarios for efficiency savings. Eventually, based on credible efficiency savings, Simon and his team had actually arrived at an estimate that the NHS would need around £15–16 billion extra per year by the end of the next parliament. This was a large sum, but according to the figures prepared for the NHS chief executive this was around the amount needed just to maintain service quality.

But when this number was shared with advisers and others in 10 Downing Street there was immediately a sharp counter-reaction. 'You have got to be joking,' was the view from No. 10. The Prime Minister's advisers made clear that there was no way the government and the Chancellor were going to sign up to a commitment of this size. Simon Stevens was told that if he used the £15–16 billion figure, this would look impossible and excessive.

'You need to increase your estimates of efficiency savings and get the extra money needed down to a more deliverable sum,' was the message back from the centre of government.

After much consideration, the figures were re-worked with higher efficiency assumptions and the £15–16 billion estimate was suddenly reduced to £8 billion.

When the 'Five-Year Forward View' was published by the NHS in October 2014, the clues to the dispute between the NHS and No. 10 were clear.

The report estimated a huge £30 billion annual gap by 2020/21 between the money needed to maintain the NHS and a continuation of a static real budget for the service (assuming no efficiency savings).

The report estimated that if the same long-run efficiency saving of 0.8 per cent per year was maintained, the funding gap would fall from £30 billion to £21 billion.

But in recent years, with tight pay controls and after Labour's funding bonanza, this efficiency saving had risen to between 1.5 per cent and 2.0 per cent per year. If the recent doubling of annual efficiency savings could be continued, the funding gap would fall to £16 billion. The NHS report admitted that this would 'represent a strong performance – compared with the NHS's own past, compared with the wider UK economy, and with other countries' health systems'.

Instead of using either the long-run NHS efficiency figure or this recent better NHS productivity performance, the £8 billion figure used in public assumed an efficiency saving of almost three times the long-run NHS average. This was in spite of the report admitting that NHS pay could not continue to be held down without creating staff shortages. Norman Lamb, our Health Minister in the government, was concerned about whether the £8 billion was really enough. But once the £8 billion figure was in the public domain, it was effectively impossible to ask for more and be taken seriously. Indeed, at that stage it was unclear whether any political party would be willing to sign up to even the £8 billion figure.

Norman Lamb used the Stephens Report to publicly make the case for more NHS funding for the coming financial year. And he also ensured that a pledge to deliver 'at least' the £8 billion was included in our Liberal Democrat general election manifesto.

The Conservative resistance to extra NHS spending seemed to be weakening too, with David Cameron and George Osborne recognising that they might need to put more money into the health service to avoid both a healthcare crisis and a political disaster.

Nick Clegg discussed the issue further with George Osborne in a private meeting about the Autumn Statement in late October. The Chancellor was irritated by Norman Lamb's public call for higher NHS spending, and said he assumed that this should count as a Liberal Democrat bid for the Autumn Statement.

Nick Clegg made clear that he wasn't going to allow the Conservatives to score extra NHS spending as a Liberal Democrat ask and then take all the credit for the announcement. He was used to the Chancellor arguing for having his own Conservative priorities in Budgets, to 'balance' Lib Dems priorities – and then seeing him try to claim the credit for both sets of measures.

It was clear that health was not a particular Treasury priority but nor were the Conservatives going to let the Liberal Democrats walk off with all the credit for boosting the very popular NHS. Nick Clegg, Norman Lamb and I agreed that the NHS needed at least another £1.5 billion in 2015/16 to help stabilise its position. Meanwhile, Jeremy Hunt was making almost identical demands of his Treasury colleagues.

By early November, we had even persuaded our own ultra-prudent Chief Secretary, Danny Alexander, that the NHS needed extra money. The central plan seemed to be an extra £1.5 billion for the following year – £1 billion from the Treasury and £0.5 billion scrapped together from the Department of Health budget. This was now a 'bottom line' Lib Dem priority for our Autumn Statement negotiations, though we did not want to trade it with the Conservatives for spending of their own on some other Conservative priority.

On 11 November, we decided to up the stakes before the final decisions on the Autumn Statement were taken. Norman Lamb went on the media and made a stark call for an extra £1.5 billion – for 2015/16. He implied that the NHS would 'crash' without the extra funding. Jeremy Hunt was upset by Norman's very public intervention, and sent him a sharply worded message, saying that in his view the two NHS ministers needed to unite against the Treasury rather than going public with their own party positions. Both Norman and I took the view that the more public the issue was, the more pressure would fall on both the Treasury and the Conservative leadership.

The Autumn Statement was now fixed for 3 December. On 20 November, I met up with Nick Clegg, who had just finished a Quad. 'Cameron and Osborne were pretty furious about Norman Lamb's intervention on the NHS. But I think we've now got them where we wanted, and I am not going to allow the Treasury to try to salami-slice down the extra we need for the NHS – in my view it has to be at least £1.5 billion. But Osborne really has got a bloody cheek. He said yet again that he considers the extra NHS money to be a "Lib Dem ask" and then five minutes later he was saying he wanted to announce the good news on the *Marr* programme on the Sunday before the Autumn Statement!'

The NHS eventually got its extra money and during the election campaign most parties signed up to the £8 billion extra, over the period to 2020. What was not known, however, was that the £8 billion figure was already too low – massaged down by an embarrassed Downing Street.

Even if the NHS gets its £8 billion extra in the 2015–20 parliament, this is unlikely to be enough to avoid a marked decline in standards of patient care. We now need a proper long-term study of NHS funding pressures, without interference and distortion from 10 Downing Street and the Treasury, and with credible costings and efficiency forecasts, instead of statistics that have been fixed to address pre-election political sensitivities.

Meanwhile, the issue of NHS funding was not the only pinch point between the parties as the Autumn Statement loomed.

YELLOW JACKETS AND RED LINES

OCTOBER–DECEMBER 2014

Cabinet finished on time, as ever, at 11 a.m. on 21 October 2014. Nick Clegg left the Cabinet Room and turned to head back to his office in Dover House, home of the Scottish Office.

George Osborne asked the Deputy Prime Minister if he had time for a quick word, and the two men slipped into one of the small offices located off the lobby outside the Cabinet Room.

George wanted to talk about the 'English votes issue'. He complained that the new Cabinet committee set up after the Scottish referendum to consider devolution issues in England and elsewhere wasn't making much progress, in spite of holding a number of meetings.

The Chancellor said that the Conservatives had tabled their own proposals on 'English votes for English laws', and they were now waiting for me to come back with the Liberal Democrat position.

'George was as transactional and blunt as ever,' Nick Clegg told me later. 'He complained that you had told Oliver Letwin that you are going to come back with something about linking "English votes" with PR. He said: "Obviously, we can't buy into that. I don't understand why your people aren't playing ball with us on this. The opportunity is basically to gang up against Labour and really put them on the spot on this, by having one united coalition position."'

Nick was equally blunt in his response. He told the Chancellor: 'I'm not sure you really get it on this. We do have a different position from you.

We think the solution is about much more devolution within England. And we don't think you can build an English votes solution in Westminster on the first past the post system. It could lead to grossly unfair results, and could even risk stoking resentment that could break up the UK.'

The Liberal Democrat leader also spelled out that the Chancellor should not just assume the Liberal Democrats would be siding with the Conservatives over the issue: 'We've moved a long way from those golden days of co-operation in May 2010. In those days, you and David were leaders of a Tory Party which had a genuinely modernising and positive outlook. That's all now changed. Your party has lurched so far to the right that it's going to make cooperation between us incredibly difficult in the future.'

George Osborne looked rather shocked. He said he was concerned to hear that Nick Clegg felt that way, and he suggested that the two men should meet soon for a longer discussion. Within a few hours, George Osborne's office had phoned Nick Clegg's to arrange a private meeting to discuss the matter further. 'They are obviously worried they are going to need us after the election,' Nick Clegg concluded.

The Chancellor and Deputy Prime Minister met a week later in Nick Clegg's Dover House office. They had lunch at Nick Clegg's conference table.

George Osborne said he was worried about their recent discussion, and hoped that they could still cooperate in their mutual interest over the months ahead.

Nick Clegg was quick to test the Chancellor's seriousness. He said that he wanted his own home city of Sheffield to be properly included in the government's plan for a 'Northern Powerhouse'. At present the Chancellor seemed to be focusing on investing only in Manchester, near his constituency, and Leeds.

'George is hilarious,' said Nick later. 'He immediately suggested including Sheffield and just dropping Leeds – of course he wanted to look after his own backyard in Manchester. I pointed out that I was arguing to include Sheffield, not to dump on Leeds.'

The two men then went on to discuss in detail the announcements on tax, spending and welfare made at the recent Conservative Party conference.

'I told George that he was making a massive mistake,' said Nick. 'George, you are saying you can balance the books just through welfare savings and spending cuts, while actually cutting taxes for the better off. That strikes me as being incredibly unjust and unfair. You also said that meeting the fiscal rules requires £25 billion more of fiscal tightening. We think you are wrong. Danny tells me that our target means at least £33 billion more of tightening.'

The Chancellor's extraordinary response was: '£25 billion and £33 billion are pretty similar. We can just fudge that a bit.'

Nick Clegg replied that a response of that kind would pretty soon undermine the Chancellor's reputation for fiscal prudence.

The conversation then moved on to the Autumn Statement. George Osborne confirmed that he and Danny Alexander were planning a major infrastructure announcement, including money for new transport schemes. 'David Laws will be pleased,' said Nick. 'He is driving me nuts by mentioning the A303 to Somerset in every damned meeting.' Nick also signalled that he wanted to prioritise extra support for mental health, a higher tax allowance, and the money needed to avoid an NHS crisis. 'All doable,' replied the Chancellor.

'He then said he had a private proposal of his own,' Nick Clegg told me later that day. 'He wants to do a big throw of the dice on inheritance tax – massively lifting the inheritance tax allowance so he can basically say that he has taken the whole of middle-income Britain out of paying it. He says it will cost around £1 billion or £1.5 billion. Of course, this will only really help the top 10 per cent or 20 per cent. However, he is offering a sweetener to try to tempt us. He said that in return for a green light on inheritance tax, he would find the money to deal with the most painful aspects of the bedroom tax, although he had the cheek to say that this would have to be funded by other welfare savings. I said that I was a bit sceptical, but that I would discuss it with you and Danny and then go back to him.'

The meeting ended with Nick Clegg pointing out to the Chancellor that the political benefits for the Liberal Democrats of agreeing major changes in the Autumn Statement and following Budget weren't obvious: 'In every Budget, you end up getting the credit for all the good things, and we never get noticed. I think the Liberal Democrats get basically zero benefit from these fiscal events, and bluntly I don't see why I should help you to help the Conservatives.'

Unsurprisingly, George Osborne didn't agree. He said that he thought that the coming Autumn Statement should be 'a really big fiscal event', but accepted that the 2015 Budget would probably need to be a more modest affair. He finished by saying: 'We need to go on working together. The election is clearly going to be very close. We may need each other.'

At 5.30, Nick called me in to see him, along with his senior political and economic advisers. He recounted to us the discussion he had just held with the Chancellor.

We discussed the infrastructure investments and I made the point that with so many Lib Dem seats in south-west England, it was vital that a Liberal Democrat was the person to announce the plans to convert to dual carriageway the important A303 West Country trunk road. 'But the Tories aren't mugs,' I said. 'There is going to be a massive political fight to claim the credit for all this.'

Then Nick raised the proposition that George Osborne had made to him – trading a huge cut in inheritance tax for measures to reduce the impact of the unpopular bedroom tax.

'Should we seriously consider this?' said Nick.

One by one, we offered our views on the proposed trade. Everyone who spoke was 100 per cent opposed.

'It's a rotten deal,' I said. 'It will be the highlight of the Budget and will boost the Tories, while a small U-turn on the bedroom tax would hardly be noticed. Inheritance tax would be as toxic with many of our supporters as the cut in the 50p rate, and it would look like we were going back on all our recent talk about ensuring those on the highest incomes make a fair contribution to deficit reduction. And anyway George is suggesting that we would have to pay for the bedroom tax changes by cutting more from other areas of welfare, so it isn't much of a concession. The Tories are so damned predictable. They have spent the whole parliament in every Budget trying to give to the very richest and take from the very poorest. At least they are consistent.'

Chris Saunders said: 'It would look like we were conceding a big, new thing to the Tories in exchange for us correcting a mistake we made earlier in the parliament.'

Jonny Oates added: 'We need to kill this stone dead as soon as possible. We should tell Osborne "no" immediately, so that he doesn't come to the first Autumn Statement Quad next week thinking this is going to happen.'

'OK,' said Nick. 'I think we have a pretty clear conclusion on that. I will tell George that we are not interested in his trade and we are not going to back a big inheritance tax cut.'

At the Autumn Statement Quad on 5 November, Nick Clegg spelled out the Liberal Democrat position: 'I've seen the latest numbers from the Office for Budget Responsibility on borrowing, and they are still pretty bad. We need a prudent package, and I'm not interested in agreeing a cut in inheritance tax – this would just look like us signing up to more breaks for the rich while the poor get clobbered.'

Nick told us afterwards: 'It took the wind out of their sails. They realised we don't need an Autumn Statement so they have no influence over us.'

On 7 November, we had fixed for Nick Clegg to make a visit to Somerset, to highlight our efforts to dual the A303 road. We had kept this from the Conservatives in Westminster, as both sides of the coalition were now desperately trying to take all the credit for the coming infrastructure investment strategy, which was due to be announced formally by Danny Alexander in the week of the Autumn Statement. The Conservatives in London did their best to insist that I should stay in Westminster to cover some minor debate, but I managed to extricate myself from this with some difficulty.

Thus it was that on a mild autumn morning I found myself standing next to Nick Clegg in front of a Little Chef at the roundabout that joins the A303 with the A358 in Somerset. We both had to do a lot of pointing at the road for the sake of the television cameras. We were not yet allowed to say that the government was committed to dualling the A303, but we came as close as we could to making the commitment. 'If this is not in the Autumn Statement,' said Nick Clegg, 'I will come to Somerset and lay the tarmac myself.' I was pleased with the press coverage – and we had for once beaten George Osborne to the draw. His visit to the south-west came a few days later.

By Monday, I was hugely relieved that we had managed to get Nick down to Somerset on the previous Friday, because David Cameron was at the Confederation of British Industry conference, and his speech was all about infrastructure investment, with lots of nods and winks about the A303 and other roads. With the election not far off, neither coalition party wanted to concede one inch of good news to the other.

On Wednesday 19 November, there was another Quad scheduled on the Autumn Statement. By now, George Osborne had visited the A303 in Somerset, as well as a variety of other construction and infrastructure sites across the country. Over the past couple of years, his media advisers had sought to change his public image, insisting he should rarely if ever be seen on TV without a high-visibility yellow jacket and a hard hat.

'Hi, George,' said Nick Clegg, as the Quad meeting was about to start. 'I saw you on TV last night on a building site somewhere. It is true that you now go to bed in a hi-vis jacket these days?'

Following our decision to block his plan to cut inheritance tax, George Osborne was now focused on a plan to reform stamp duty, which was charged on property purchases, in a way that led to big leaps in the tax burden at various property price points. He was proposing to smooth the increase in the tax burden, to avoid the big upward steps. This was already Liberal Democrat policy, so we found it easy to agree. Other elements of the Autumn Statement were coming together – including a boost to NHS funding, though both George Osborne and David Cameron were irritated by our public attempts to raise this issue. 'I'll deliver on the NHS if you and Norman Lamb will stop going on about it in public,' said George Osborne.

With the Autumn Statement due on 3 December, attention now turned to how the 'spoils' would be divided up between the two parties.

The Chancellor was due on the BBC's *Andrew Marr* programme on Sunday 30 November, where he wanted to announce the extra money for the NHS. Monday 1 December was set to be 'Roads Day', with ministers fanning out across the country to highlight new road building. Tuesday was to be 'Infrastructure Day', with a statement from Danny Alexander in the House of Commons. And Wednesday would be Autumn Statement Day itself, when changes such as a £100 increase in the personal allowance and the stamp duty changes would be announced. It was agreed that on the Friday after Autumn Statement Day, Nick Clegg would announce the new Sheffield deal from his own constituency in the city.

I was very worried that the Tories would run off with all the biggest prizes, not least because the major infrastructure announcements were those relating to roads. I was worried that we were being fobbed off with a Danny Alexander statement that would actually be of very little value to our party.

As a consequence of my nervousness about the deals we were cutting nationally, I spoke to the ITV regional news reporters in the south-west, who were able to lead the regional news with a well-briefed package about the A303 on Friday 28 November, with an extensive interview with me.

We were less successful on the NHS announcement. In spite of a promise by the Treasury to keep all of their Sunday coverage 'high-level' on the health service, without giving away the numbers, the Sunday papers were all predictably briefed about 'another £2 billion for the NHS'. Nick Clegg was not amused. He asked the Chancellor: 'Is that what you mean about a shared communications plan? I keep quiet on the tax allowance plan, while you do the NHS investment plan as well?'

George's reply was unapologetic: 'Ridiculous. You demanded the money for the NHS. You can't complain when I deliver it. Anyway, you get to announce the extra money for mental health on Monday.'

By 'Roads Day' neither coalition party was willing to give the other a free run at any of the good-news announcements, many of which were in battleground constituencies.

So instead of having a coalition plan to send individual ministers to particular areas, it turned into a free-for-all. Our strategy was that of the dawn raid. Vince Cable flew up to the north-east on Sunday and stayed overnight in order to announce the A1 upgrade on Monday in the early morning, from Alan Beith's constituency. Nick Clegg was doing the same at Stonehenge, to highlight the A303 upgrade. But as it was almost mid-winter, it was still pitch black when the morning news bulletins covered these visits. Later, David Cameron made an identical visit to Stonehenge, and also turned up at the A1, with Sir Alan Beith hovering behind him as he was interviewed by television cameras. Nick Clegg dubbed the day 'The Battle of the Hi-Vis Jackets'.

Nick was still irritated by the leaking of the NHS budget plans, and with an election approaching, he was also nervous of being pictured seated next to George Osborne for the Autumn Statement. On Monday, he told George that he planned to visit Cornwall on Wednesday, and would not attend the Autumn Statement in the House of Commons.

On Tuesday, the newspapers were full of the announcements of the roads investment. A number had photographs of Stonehenge – one with Nick Clegg visiting in the morning, and another with David Cameron there in the afternoon.

At the end of Cabinet on Tuesday, the Prime Minister gave us a brief update on a conference he had attended about the future of Afghanistan. 'It's very interesting there,' he said. 'There is actually a coalition in Afghanistan now. And the leader of the smaller party is effectively the Deputy Prime Minister, but without that title. I understand he's going to be in the UK quite soon. Perhaps you and I could meet him together, Nick, and tell him a bit about how coalition government works?'

'What a great idea,' cut in George Osborne, 'perhaps the two of you could take him down to Stonehenge for the day. You could even be there at the same time!' There was a round of laughter and the meeting ended.

Wednesday 3 December was Autumn Statement Day, and the Cabinet met again at its earlier time of 8 a.m.

The fiscal forecasts from the Office for Budget Responsibility were not quite as bad as expected, but the official government plans relied upon a massive squeeze in government spending for the whole of the next parliament, with no contribution at all from increased taxation.

A smaller number of people than usual spoke in Cabinet, but this included Nick Clegg, Danny Alexander and me. David Cameron looked mildly irritated when, after welcoming most of the Budget, I said that its biggest problem was the lack of credibility of future economic forecasts. I pointed out that the spending plans were unlikely to be deliverable or politically acceptable, so that the borrowing forecasts were only credible if there was a willingness to consider some contribution from taxation. That was the official Liberal Democrat position.

Unfortunately, Vince Cable then decided to set out his own position. He made some similar points to me, but then managed to criticise our party's own economic strategy by saying that even the Lib Dem plans would require us to 'close down' large parts of the police and armed forces.

Nick Clegg and the rest of the Liberal Democrat ministers were pretty frustrated by Vince's contribution. When you are on 7 or 8 per cent in the opinion polls, you cannot afford even the smallest division on your central economic strategy – and certainly not in front of a room full of Conservative ministers. After Cabinet, Nick Clegg said to me: 'I do rather despair of Vince at times. I think he is still unhappy that I am making Danny rather than him our Treasury spokesman at the election. But no other decision would make sense. How could Danny do this job for almost five years and lose it in the last few months?'

Nick then went on to complain that Vince had unilaterally written to the Office for Budget Responsibility, asking the OBR to distinguish between Liberal Democrat and Conservative economic plans in the economic projections they release alongside the Autumn Statement. He pointed out that this was directly cutting across Danny's role.

The Autumn Statement was reasonably well received on the day, but it began to unravel somewhat for the Conservatives in the days after. The independent Institute for Fiscal Studies calculated that future public spending plans in the statement implied that spending on public services as a share of GDP would fall to the lowest level since the 1930s. This reinforced the case I had made at Cabinet on the need for tax to make some contribution to future reductions in borrowing.

Polling data soon showed that a majority of the public thought that George Osborne and the Conservatives were 'going too far, and imposing cuts that [would] endanger important public services'.

This row would rumble on over the next few months, but before the end of the week a more immediate dispute had broken out in the coalition.

Nick Clegg had an assurance from George Osborne that he could launch the Sheffield deal of infrastructure and business investment up in his constituency on Friday 5 December. But on 4 December, Nick was suddenly told that George Osborne was no longer willing to approve the vast majority of what had already been agreed. The launch had to be postponed, even though it was now widely expected.

The row soon became deeply acrimonious. For a week following 5 December, the Deputy Prime Minister and Chancellor swapped increasingly angry messages by text. The Chancellor was not just being difficult – he was refusing to meet up or call.

On 11 December, Nick Clegg demanded to speak to the Prime Minister. It was one of the angriest conversations of the five-year coalition: 'George has crossed the reddest of red lines – not only is he breaking promises but he is screwing me over in my own bloody constituency.'

Eventually, after much work, Nick Clegg secured the Sheffield deal, and it was announced in 2015.

But the row over it lasted for almost two months and led to a complete breakdown in the relationship between the Deputy Prime Minister and Chancellor.

As the year ended, Nick Clegg told me: 'If I lose in Sheffield, the only thing anyone will remember about me is that and tuition fees. I cannot forgive Osborne for undermining me in this way in my own seat.'

It was not a harmonious end to the last year of the parliament.

2015

'Anything for Power'

January–February 2015

Christmas and New Year were the last real opportunity for rest before the election campaign began in earnest. Nick Clegg and his family spent time in Spain, and I was in France for a week. The weather was warm enough to sit outside on the seafront on New Year's Day – a final, glorious luxury before the battle to come.

But the break was short-lived, and we were soon back in England, to be confronted with icy weather and even bleaker opinion polls.

A note from Ryan Coetzee, Nick Clegg's chief election strategist, in January, neatly summed up the current political outlook:

> Bluntly and simply: Labour is midway through a slow-motion implosion because they lack credibility on the economy, lack a credible candidate for No. 10 and lack a consistent and credible message. They will shed many seats to the SNP and win fewer seats off the Tories than expected, thanks to the Greens and their own ineffectiveness. In contrast, the Tories are in a much stronger position, their UKIP problem notwithstanding, because they have a credible candidate for PM with a credible pitch – only the Tories can be trusted to finish the job on the economy. Given all this, the biggest risk we face is a significant shift of voters towards the Tories as Election Day approaches.

We had always assumed that coalition would be politically tough for the smaller coalition partner. But we had also dared to hope that towards the end of the parliament our poll ratings would start to recover, as the economic recovery took hold and people fairly reassessed our achievements.

But if there was going to be one of those famous 'late surges' in Liberal Democrat voting, it was going to be very late indeed. An *Observer* poll on 1 February put our support at a mere 5 per cent.

In January, the latest figures on university entrance in England had been published. In spite of the higher tuition fees, student numbers were up to record levels, and more young people from disadvantaged backgrounds were accessing university, too. The carefully designed, progressive fee repayment system, combined with generous maintenance grants for students from poorer homes, was clearly working. But the media weren't interested. They had written their script on tuition fees four years before.

Worse still, we had always assumed that while our national poll rating might be low, we would dramatically outperform in our own held seats. The by-election victory in Eastleigh, in the face of furious political headwinds, seemed to confirm that view. But now the individual seat assessments seemed to be far less promising.

It was clear that in many held seats we were so far behind that we had no chance of winning. The general election campaign chair, Paddy Ashdown, along with Ryan Coetzee, had to deliver the tough message to many MPs that their funding support from party HQ was now being cut off. In no part of the country did the outlook seem particularly optimistic. In the south-west, the Conservatives now seemed to be targeting every one of our seats – including the traditionally safe seats such as Yeovil, Bath and Thornbury and Yate.

In London, every one of our seats was under pressure – including those with big majorities. Lynne Featherstone and veteran MP Simon Hughes were under attack from Labour, while in south-west London two of our Cabinet ministers – Vince Cable and Ed Davey – were on the back foot in the face of strong Conservative campaigns.

But if the outlook in London and in the south-west was unpromising, it was even bleaker in Scotland, where the Scottish National Party was still regularly recording poll support of between 55 and 60 per cent. In early February 2015, Lord Ashcroft released one of his constituency polls for Scotland. This showed that we were on track to lose all our Scottish seats, with the exception of Alistair Carmichael's Orkney and Shetland constituency, which had a massive Liberal Democrat majority. The poll also showed that Danny Alexander was almost 30 per cent behind in his seat.

Despite these electoral pressures, Danny continued to do his work in the Treasury and for the party with great dedication, efficiency and commitment.

Nick Clegg's own constituency of Sheffield Hallam had never been taken for granted by the party, and a huge effort was made in each set of local government elections during the parliament to hold our local council seats. This was largely successful – in spite of big councillor losses elsewhere in Sheffield, the local government base in Sheffield Hallam remained strong.

Sheffield Hallam was not, in fact, traditionally a Labour area: it included quite affluent areas and had once returned Conservative MPs. But the Labour vote had surged during the coalition period, and the Tory vote had collapsed. So it was always assumed that Labour would make a major effort to win the seat and claim a high-profile scalp.

Most of our own polling had put Nick Clegg marginally ahead in his seat throughout 2014, and the levels of campaigning activity were high – weekly data showed more Liberal Democrat canvassing in the seat than in almost every other constituency in the country.

But early in the New Year a poll for the seat was released by Lord Ashcroft putting Nick Clegg behind Labour for the first time. Newspaper stories now reported that Labour were 'gunning for' Nick in his own constituency.

Officially, the party dismissed the bleak poll findings. But, privately, Nick Clegg was unsettled.

Each week now George Osborne kept popping up with new proposals to spend money around the country – one week it was on coastal towns, the next it was infrastructure projects, the next it was regional economic plans. In each case, we were given almost no time to object to what looked very much like pork-barrel politics.

During the February half-term recess, Nick had to spend much of his time working hard in his own constituency, firming up his own vote and bolstering his campaign. In the same week, David Cameron visited almost thirty Conservative target seats.

As the party leaders and media prepared for the forthcoming election, the issue of the election debates now moved to centre stage.

David Cameron and his advisers had hugely regretted agreeing to the election debates of 2010, after Nick Clegg dominated the first debate, giving a huge boost to the Liberal Democrat campaign. Many Tory MPs believed that this had cost them the election, and they blamed their leader for the blunder.

Even though the national poll figures were very close between Labour and the Conservatives, what these same figures showed was much more encouraging for the Conservatives – who had a massive lead on the credibility of their leader and on their economic policies and perceived economic competence.

David Cameron didn't want to admit it publicly, but he was now determined to avoid the election debates at any cost. In particular, he wanted to avoid what looked like the most likely debate formula – which would include the Conservatives, Labour, the Liberal Democrats and UKIP.

The chosen Conservative means of torpedoing the debates included insisting that if UKIP were included, then the Greens should be too, along with the SNP. As the Conservatives knew, the case for including the Greens and SNP was far weaker than for UKIP, who were now running third in the national opinion polls. David Cameron and his team also knew that neither Labour nor the Liberal Democrats would want the Greens and SNP in the debates.

In early January, Nick Clegg raised the issue of the election debates with David Cameron. He emphasised that having had the first real, televised debates in the May 2010 general election, it was not now sensible or acceptable for any political leader to try to end them. He asked the Prime Minister to agree a sensible debate format, so that the broadcasters could conclude their plans.

But the Prime Minister wasn't budging. 'It's clear that he really doesn't want to do the debates, whatever the cost,' Nick Clegg told me later that day. 'He just looked at me and said: "You must be kidding. Have you seen Ed Miliband's poll ratings recently? The guy is like a boxer who is on the floor. Why on earth should I give him a chance to get back up? I have no interest in letting these election debates go ahead."'

Nick Clegg tried another approach: warning that if the Conservative leader was seen to be running away from the debates, he might suffer a public backlash. But the PM wouldn't budge. He responded that he wasn't bothered if people accused him of 'chickening out'. He pointed out that Nick Clegg had taken on Nigel Farage in the debates on Europe in 2014 and had come off worst. David Cameron was clear that it wasn't possible for government parties to safely take on the 'anti-politics movement' in election debates: 'One powerful line from the Greens or UKIP could sink you or me. The debates can only help Farage, Miliband and the others. I have to be hardnosed about this. I will get a bit of criticism, but I can live with that.'

In the middle of January, the broadcasters decided to capitulate to the Conservative demands over the election debates: they would now include not only UKIP, but the Greens, the Scottish Nationalists and the Welsh Nationalists. The whole thing was becoming absurd – a seven-way debate. The inclusion of the SNP posed a particular risk to those parties with a lot of Scottish seats – Labour and the Liberal Democrats.

'I still think the Conservatives will try to wriggle out of this,' Nick Clegg told me. 'Cameron is apparently now saying that the Democratic Unionist Party must also be included. Next it will be the Cornish Nationalists and then the Yogic Flyers Party.'

Nick Clegg was right. The Prime Minister was not yet ready to accede to the election debates. In early February, David Cameron said that he wanted a 'quiet word' with Nick Clegg at the end of one of their regular bilaterals.

The Prime Minister again set out his view that the election debates were only of help to parties such as UKIP, the Greens and the SNP. He said he wanted to offer the Liberal Democrat leader a deal. The Conservatives would take the blame for pulling the plug on the election debates if Nick Clegg then followed up and also said the debates were a waste of time. Various other blandishments were offered, but Nick Clegg made clear that the debates should go ahead. 'I told him: "It's both ugly and impressive to see what you people will do to stay in power."' David Cameron shrugged: 'Yep. Yep. You're right, Nick. We'll do whatever it takes to stay in power.'

'I Want a Budget'

FEBRUARY–MARCH 2015

O f all the events that defined the cycles of the coalition, the regular Budgets, Autumn Statements and Spending Reviews must take centre stage.
For months beforehand, each party would work out its own objectives
or 'asks'. Then, for almost two months, advisers in the Treasury, Downing
Street and the Deputy Prime Minister's Office would meet to discuss the
options and thrash out the details. Alongside this work, the Quad would
meet on multiple occasions to consider what was and was not acceptable to
each side of the coalition.

When the final package was agreed, it was always the product of both
coalition parties, and every item in every Budget or Autumn Statement had
to be signed off by both sides. Sometimes, the Chancellor would play a
little fast and loose with the actual wording of his statement to Parliament,
only sharing it with Nick Clegg and Danny Alexander a few hours before
its delivery in the House of Commons. But, on the whole, the economic
statements were models of coalition working.

The only problem, from a Liberal Democrat perspective, was that however
great was the Liberal Democrat contribution to each economic statement, these
were always delivered in the House of Commons by George Osborne, the
Conservative Chancellor. So when things went well, the Conservatives tended
to reap all the political benefits. Indeed, towards the end of the parliament,
Nick Clegg's able and influential economic adviser Chris Saunders had only
half-jokingly suggested that 'the only Budget that was any good for the Liberal

Democrat political interest was the Omnishambles Budget – because it hurt the Tories so much'. This was also the economic statement when the Liberal Democrat team had been most ruthless in controlling the media coverage of the Budget, seizing the initiative on the personal tax allowance rise.

Nick Clegg, Danny Alexander and I had therefore decided in early 2014 that the last major economic statement of the parliament should be the 2014 Autumn Statement. We did not want to hand to the Conservatives the political opportunity of some huge populist Budget giveaway in March 2015, just days before the general election campaign was due to start. This strategy was strongly endorsed by Jonny Oates and by other senior advisers.

There were others who worried about a profligate Budget, too. With the process of deficit reduction barely halfway complete, neither the official Treasury nor senior civil servants wanted to see a 'giveaway' Budget. Indeed, early in 2015, Danny Alexander was approached by Nick Macpherson, the cerebral Permanent Secretary to the Treasury, who showed the Chief Secretary some newspaper cuttings from Denis Healey's last Budget in 1979, just before the general election. The Permanent Secretary pointed out approvingly that Denis Healey's last Budget had basically been devoid of content, even though it appeared just before a fiercely contested election. Jeremy Heywood, the Cabinet Secretary, was also known to be concerned that there should not be an imprudent giveaway that the country could not afford.

But there was one person who definitely didn't want a quiet Budget: the Chancellor of the Exchequer.

In mid-January, George asked for a meeting with Nick Clegg. They met in the Deputy Prime Minister's Office in Dover House, adjoining the Cabinet Office. It was their first meeting since the huge row over the Sheffield deal just after the Autumn Statement, and the atmosphere was still frosty.

George Osborne looked a little nervous, and he opened the discussion by saying that he had heard that both Nick and Danny Alexander were going to prevent him from delivering a 'proper' Budget. He argued that this would be a huge missed opportunity for both coalition parties, and that the Budget was an opportunity for both parties to deliver on their priorities and put Labour on the back foot. The Chancellor also indicated that he would be willing to allow Danny Alexander to set out the Liberal Democrat economic strategy in some manner in the House of Commons, provided he got his own 'moment in the sun'.

Nick Clegg was very sceptical, telling the Chancellor that while the proposition was 'seductive', he wasn't buying it. He made clear that he wasn't going to give the Conservatives a free ride in their final Budget – not least after their treatment of him and the Liberal Democrats over issues from the AV referendum to the row over the Sheffield deal.

George Osborne wasn't giving up. He again underlined his offer to allow Danny Alexander an opportunity on the day after the Budget to present a Liberal Democrat statement to the House of Commons. He pointed out that this had never happened before. He also sought to emphasise how much common ground he thought there was between his views and those of the Deputy Prime Minister.

But Nick Clegg wasn't impressed, pointing out that he thought the two men had very different views on social mobility, education, welfare policy and Europe. He also pointed out that the Conservatives were not facing an existential challenge to their existence in the election.

George Osborne disagreed. He said that he and David Cameron had their necks on the line too, and that if they lost the coming election they were finished as leaders of their party. The Chancellor also noted that if Nick Clegg lost his seat it would at least be better for him than the fate that awaited losing Conservatives leaders: staying on in Parliament on the back benches for five years in limbo.

'I hear what you say,' said Nick Clegg. 'But the answer is the same. No great giveaway Budget. We just need a steady-as-she-goes statement, with minimum content.'

The Liberal Democrat team met again in Nick Clegg's office on 3 February for a further discussion on the Budget. We agreed that there would be no great Liberal Democrat 'asks' for the Budget Statement, and instead we discussed a few small items. I wanted another £100 million to invest in the early years pupil premium, which we had introduced a year ago. Both Nick Clegg and I wanted some additional investment in children's mental health services. Jonny Oates wanted action on green policy – perhaps to promote recycling – and other people discussed local infrastructure schemes. All in all, it was pretty small beer. And, for the only time in the parliament, we decided not to press for an increase in the personal tax allowance. Jonny suggested that if there were any 'spare money' to go around, we should use it to reduce the deficit; he had finally become a fiscal hawk.

Meanwhile, the Chancellor was continuing to press for a bigger Budget. In the first Budget Quad, in early February, George Osborne said that he wanted a 'showpiece' tax cut, which should cost around £800 million – the same as the previous year's fuel duty cut. He did not yet reveal what this might be.

In late February, the first concrete proposition arrived from the Chancellor about what he wanted in the Budget. We should have guessed – it was a George Osborne proposition through and through, totally political and designed largely to wrong-foot Labour.

As Danny Alexander ran through George's wish list in a meeting with Nick and me, we could only raise our eyes to heaven and laugh.

The Chancellor was firstly proposing a small rise in the tax-free allowance, by £100–£200. He knew we could hardly oppose this. Then he proposed to cancel an upcoming fuel duty increase; he knew that Danny, as a Highland MP, would be strongly sympathetic to this. The Chancellor also wanted a package of tax cuts for savers, along with lower taxes on beer, cider and spirits. On top of this, he was proposing a bigger than expected rise in the minimum wage: a rise to £7, above the £6.70 being proposed by the independent Low Pay Commission, and clearly designed to wrong-foot Labour.

And there was more: doubling the free hours of childcare for all three- and four-year-olds in working families (to outflank Labour's pledge), and cutting hospital car parking charges (a popular UKIP policy). On top of this, the Chancellor was promising to add in more money for mental health services, to meet Nick Clegg's requirement. There was also a half-baked populist idea to cut value added tax on children at hotels and holiday parks.

'It's very clever. Very George,' I said. 'He's trying to shoot everybody's foxes – ours included.'

'Yes,' said Danny. 'And he is even proposing to steal some of our and Labour's policies to pay for it all – another squeeze on pensions tax relief and higher taxes on the banks. George is particularly attracted to cutting tax relief on pensions, because Labour wants to use this money to reduce tuition fees. So George wants to leave a big hole in their Budget plans. It's all about politics for him. He wants to steal everybody else's policies.'

'We need to respond very carefully to this,' said Nick Clegg. 'George is no fool. He is inviting us either to go along with this much bigger Budget proposition or to risk opposing some of these very populist measures. If we come out against things like a higher tax-free allowance or a cut in fuel duty, you can be certain that it will be leaked against us.'

We had a long discussion about how to respond to the 'Fox-Shooting Budget'.

We agreed that we would support the increase in the personal allowance, and that we would be mad to stand in the way of the freeze in unpopular fuel taxes. Nick and I were also minded to allow the increase in the minimum wage to go through, though this was later aborted, after Vince Cable made clear that he was unwilling for us to overrule the Low Pay Commission (though he did so himself on the issue of the apprenticeship rate of the minimum wage).

We ourselves had advocated the extra money for mental health, but we would raise all the obvious practical issues about cutting hospital car parking charges.

On childcare, we agreed only to support extra money if it was to deliver our policy of universal provision of fifteen hours' free childcare for two-year-olds. We would oppose a package of tax cuts for savers, costing around £800 million, which was most likely in any case only to benefit a rich minority of people – since most of the population either had no savings or had savings in tax-free ISAs. This package of tax cuts for savers was designed by George Osborne to be the centrepiece of his Budget.

Over the next few weeks, the debate about the Budget contents went back and forth between the coalition partners. Both Jonny Oates and I feared that what started off as being a clear strategy to agree a minimalist Budget could end up giving too much to the Conservative Chancellor to announce. We were also both worried that Danny Alexander might be tempted into being more cooperative with the Chancellor because of their close working relationship, combined with George Osborne's offer of a 'Lib Dem Budget Statement' for Danny Alexander on the day after the Budget proper. Neither Jonny nor I regarded this as a big prize, and we thought it would look odd and be totally eclipsed by coverage of the previous day's 'real' Budget.

Jonny and I began to get more nervous in early March, when even the Treasury began to admit that the savings proposal – completely abolishing the tax on savings income – would be likely to cost not merely the original estimate of £800 million, but £1.4 billion, or probably a lot more once interest rates started to rise again.

We suggested that this policy should be blocked, due to its high cost at a time when we were having to make painful cuts to public services and to the incomes of the very poorest people.

Even George Osborne admitted that his cut in savings tax wasn't very well targeted. 'It will only really be of help to stupid, affluent and lazy people, who can't be bothered to put their savings away into tax-efficient vehicles! But it will still be very popular – we have polled it.'

On 8 March, Danny Alexander and Nick Clegg spoke to George Osborne on the phone about the Budget.

Nick Clegg wanted as much money as possible to be spent on increasing the tax allowance, and not on abolishing all taxation on savings, which would particularly help those with the largest amounts of wealth.

George Osborne responded badly, arguing that he was delivering Liberal Democrat policy on the tax allowance, mental health services, pensions tax relief and a new banking tax. Now it was the Chancellor who was threatening to veto all these policies unless he was allowed some priorities of his own.

There was another interesting Conservative decision at this time: George Osborne had got cold feet about his widely criticised Autumn Statement plans on public spending. These were interpreted by the respected Institute for Fiscal Studies as 'cutting the state back to levels not seen since the 1930s'. This was polling badly with the voters, and the Conservatives now asked to be able to revise upwards these public spending plans.

On Monday 9 March, there was a crucial Quad to discuss the Budget. At this stage, there could either be agreement or the whole Budget could fall. Jonny Oates and I were minded to be difficult. We thought that the package for savers was badly targeted and was only likely to help the Conservatives by proving a huge hit with the right-leaning media.

Nick Clegg and Danny Alexander had spent five years working with David Cameron and George Osborne, and they believed in trying to find compromise and common ground. They did not want to end the parliament with a massive political row, and lose policies such as extra money for mental health and for the uplift in the tax-free allowance.

On Tuesday 10 March, we met in Nick Clegg's room for feedback on this crucial Budget Quad. I thought Nick looked a little sheepish as he outlined what had been agreed. Jonny Oates, meanwhile, sat silently, looking miserable.

A grand bargain had been completed in the Quad for the last time in the parliament. A higher personal allowance, more money for mental health and an upward revision to future public spending had all been agreed. Fuel duty would be frozen and alcohol duties would be cut. All this was fine by me.

But Nick and Danny had also agreed to a significant package for savers – not the complete abolition of savings tax, but a less expensive tax-free savings allowance. Neither Jonny nor I were happy with that.

The Quad members had also agreed a significant childcare package, doubling the free childcare allowance from fifteen to thirty hours each week, but only for working families. I was doubly unhappy with this – firstly, because our own priority had been to make the existing free fifteen hours' childcare for more disadvantaged two-year-olds a universal entitlement and, secondly, because the policy was likely to widen inequalities.

I did not find out until later, but Jonny Oates had already privately expressed his concern to Nick Clegg at how much we had given away to the Tories. The Liberal Democrat leader agonised about his decision. 'Have I done the right thing, or have I let the Tories walk off with it all? Have I given the Tories a trampoline into the election? Jonny is arguing that it is all a disaster, but I think his intense distrust of the Tories is obscuring things. Eventually, I was just not prepared to blow the whole thing up, particularly when 85 per cent of it is good Liberal Democrat stuff. And, after all, we ensured that the savings package would not be focused on the rich.'

Over the next few days, I carefully mulled the policy on childcare that had been signed off. We still had one week before Budget Day, and I was very unhappy with what we had agreed to.

Our own strategy on the early years and on childcare focused on two policy priorities. The first was to increase the early years education support made available to children from the poorest families. Educational disadvantage began in the earliest years and became more entrenched in school. To create a fairer society, we needed to intervene earlier. This was why we had introduced an early years pupil premium a year before, to target extra support for the education of the poorest three- and four-year-olds. I had wanted this increased in this final Budget – but it wasn't.

Our second priority was to improve childcare support in the very earliest years, before pre-school, by extending the free fifteen hours for the most disadvantaged two-year-olds to all two-year-olds.

Instead, what the Conservatives had insisted upon was a very expensive policy of doubling of the free hours to all three- and four-year-olds – but only to those in families where both parents were in work. As a childcare policy, this made some sense. As an early years development policy, it made no sense whatsoever. From now on, if this policy was passed, children from poor, out-of-work families would have to leave their nursery or playgroup at midday, while children from a household of two investment bankers could stay on until teatime every day. It was a typical Conservative policy – with absolutely no regard to the interests of those from the lowest-income backgrounds. Effectively, it amounted to a negative early years premium.

I quietly seethed about the policy for the next few days, and communicated my concerns to Nick and Danny.

Nick spoke to David Cameron and suggested making the two-year-old offer universal, instead of doubling the hours for three- and four-year-olds.

David Cameron seemed pretty relaxed about the idea. But later in the day it turned out that George Osborne wasn't prepared to budge on the policy. And the message came back from David Cameron: 'We can't do two-year-olds. Dacre [the editor of the *Daily Mail*] would go mad. He doesn't think that mothers of young children should go out to work.'

Nick Clegg was frustrated. 'The thing to understand about Osborne and Cameron', he said to me, 'is that they don't really care about this type of stuff – they have no strong views and are just led by whatever the latest polling says.'

I pointed out that this was a good reason to insist on our policy.

On Thursday 12 March, I sent Nick Clegg another email pressing him to go back to the Conservatives to push for a change in policy on the childcare issue. Nick said that he thought a change was now not possible, and that he felt I was overstating how bad the policy was. 'This is still going to be very helpful for many parents,' he pointed out. 'Do we really want to be seen to be stopping this, and could we explain simply why we were doing so?'

The issue came to a head on the morning of Friday 13 March. I had been brooding on the problem all week. I was no doubt also tired. We were all campaigning hard in our constituencies, while also trying to deal with increasingly fractious relations with the Conservatives in Westminster.

I drove from my house in Somerset to my constituency office in Yeovil, arriving at 7 a.m. When I arrived at the office, I immediately emailed Nick Clegg: 'This Conservative policy is idiotic and immoral and runs directly counter to everything we believe in and have worked for for the last five years.' I made clear that if the Conservatives insisted on going ahead with the policy, I would have to step down from my position. I accepted that resigning from the government a few weeks before it ended would look odd, and might even be damaging to the party. So I suggested that instead I should quietly step down as the Liberal Democrat Education spokesman.

I felt very strongly about the issue, but it was of course a very unreasonable threat to make. We were all exhausted, and were on the point of the greatest electoral test of the party for fifty years. Standing down would be damaging, and it would be disproportionate to do it now, after Nick and I had worked together so closely for so long.

Nick was extremely patient and tolerant. But he also knew that I was serious. 'David is one of the most remarkably stubborn people I have ever met in my life,' he had observed to a friend during another running dispute three months earlier.

Now, the Deputy Prime Minister asked Danny Alexander to go back to George Osborne to insist on changing the policy to match our needs, or dropping it altogether. The message came back from an equally stubborn Chancellor: 'I'm not moving on this.' Nick Clegg and Danny Alexander therefore exercised their veto and the expensive policy was dropped from the Budget just hours before the 'Red Book' was due to go to the printers.

THE DYING DAYS OF SPRING

MARCH 2015

Imade my way along the Upper Ministerial Corridor in the Palace of Westminster to meet Ed Davey for a discussion about the general election manifesto.

The Secretary of State for Energy was sitting in his office in almost complete darkness, with the room lit up only by a single small table lamp.

'I think you may be taking this energy saving thing too far,' I said, as I sat down in one of the room's green leather chairs.

'It's bloody annoying actually,' said Ed. 'I've been without any power now for about two weeks here – I keep reporting it, but they've done nothing.'

'"Energy Secretary condemned to sit in darkness" – it would make a great diary story,' I said.

'Don't you bloody dare!' replied Ed.

I spent a large part of the last year of government overseeing the writing of our general election manifesto.

Most of the policy issues were relatively straightforward, and the few areas of dispute have already faded quickly into obscurity.

But there was one substantive issue that did take a long time to resolve – a debate that rumbled on at the most senior levels of our party for at least the last eighteen months of the parliament. This was the crucial issue of the party's future fiscal policy – the commitments we would enter into on taxation, spending and government borrowing.

Some of Nick Clegg's team regarded these issues as primarily political and presentational – how close did we want to be to the other two parties, and what did opinion polls show that the public wanted?

But I regarded the pledges we were to make for the future in these areas as absolutely crucial issues of substance. If there was to be a second coalition of some type, then the commitments we made on tax, spending and future government borrowing were really important.

And I wanted continuity between what we said before the general election and what we did afterwards. We didn't want another tuition fees disaster, where we fought the general election on one basis and then acted differently in government.

What made matters difficult was that there were three of us in the senior Liberal Democrat team around Nick Clegg who all had strong and differing views on fiscal policy.

Danny Alexander, as Chief Secretary and eventually also as the Liberal Democrat shadow Chancellor in the 2015 general election, felt that this was primarily a matter for him to lead on. His views were relatively close to those of the official Treasury and of the Conservatives. He wanted to balance the government's budget so that what we raised in tax matched what the government spent. This would broadly align us with the Conservatives and George Osborne. Danny was pretty gung-ho about future cuts in public spending, but he did not wish to go quite as far as the Conservatives on welfare cuts – so he was willing for our future plans to raise more in taxation than the Conservatives.

Vince Cable had a totally different position. He regarded the timing of deficit reduction as being of less importance, and he was willing to take more time to bring the budget back towards balance. Crucially, Vince was also opposed to aiming for a fully balanced budget. He thought it was fine to reduce borrowing to the point where it was no longer funding current spending. But he was content to borrow a large amount of money to fund the government's capital spending. Vince wanted much smaller cuts in government spending, because he thought the planned cuts would already do serious damage to public services. He was therefore in favour of a much higher contribution to future fiscal consolidation from tax rises. So far under the coalition, around 80 per cent of the reduction in borrowing had been from spending cuts and only 20 per cent from tax. Vince wanted the ratio to be 50:50 in the next parliament.

My position was somewhere between that of Danny Alexander and that of Vince Cable. I was opposed to our committing to balance the budget completely in the next parliament. I thought this would either mean unacceptably large cuts to public services and welfare, or it would drive us to propose very large increases in taxation, which would be difficult to sell to the public. I was concerned that we should start to reduce the share of government debt to the overall size of the economy, but I thought it was economically foolish to fund real long-term investment spending from current receipts. I was therefore in favour of a new fiscal rule that would allow borrowing but only for real investment spending, such as on roads and railways, and not for painting bridges or repairing buildings.

As well as Nick Clegg, who was frequently forced to intervene in the long-running Lib Dem disputes over this issue, there was a fourth person involved in these arguments: one George Osborne.

From 2013 onwards, George Osborne was continually trying to get Danny and Nick to sign up to his vision of a balanced budget in the next parliament, with big spending cuts. The Chancellor wanted to align the Liberal Democrats and Conservatives on this key issue – both to put Labour on the spot, and potentially to pave the way for a second coalition, with the economic strategy being based on Conservative plans. Osborne knew that even if we signed up to his balanced budget plan, we would probably not sign up to the scale of welfare cuts that he wanted to deliver. This did not bother him – it would then mean that we could only square the circle by arguing for more tax increases.

George Osborne wanted to fight the 2015 general election on the basis of simple political dividing lines. The Conservatives and the Liberal Democrats would be the parties of fiscal prudence and balanced budgets. Labour would be the party of borrowing, profligacy and debt. Meanwhile, the Conservatives would be for pruning spending and slashing wasteful welfare. The Liberal Democrats would be committed to cutting less but raising more in taxes.

The arguments over this issue rumbled on for well over eighteen months – within the Liberal Democrats and between coalition partners.

In 2014, Danny Alexander wanted to make a speech advocating a fully balanced Budget, with no borrowing allowed even for infrastructure investment. But eventually, after resistance from me and from Jonny Oates, Nick Clegg overruled him.

We agreed instead to my proposal to balance the current budget and allow limited borrowing but only for a carefully defined category of 'real' investment spending.

In May 2014, the Chancellor tried to slip into the draft of the Queen's Speech a reference to 'restoring the public finances to surplus'. It was my job to agree the final draft of the 'Gracious Speech' with Oliver Letwin, before the words were locked down and written on sheepskin, with enough time for the ink to dry before Her Majesty had to deliver it.

Wednesday 28 May 2014 was the last possible day for agreeing the wording of the 'Gracious Speech', and I was in my constituency, as it was a parliamentary recess. I was supposed to be re-opening a new post office at the Co-op on Stiby Road in Yeovil, but I had to keep a small but enthusiastic crowd waiting while I sat in a rather dingy back office on my mobile phone to Oliver Letwin, trying to tweak the final text.

'Oh, by the way,' said Oliver, trying to sound indifferent but failing completely (Oliver is too nice to be a successful schemer). 'George is keen to put back in the wording on aiming to run budget surpluses. It's only a rather minor thing, and apparently it's already government policy.'

I made clear that it wasn't a small change, and I wasn't agreeing it.

'Oh dear,' said Oliver. 'Well, I may have misunderstood. I will check back with the Treasury.'

Half an hour later, I was at South Petherton Hospital and my mobile phone rang.

It was Oliver Letwin again. 'I've spoken to George and he's really rather keen to have this minor stuff on surpluses in. Apparently it's all in the last Autumn Statement anyway.'

'Well,' I said, 'I don't agree that it's minor at all. But why don't we just say that we will stick to the existing fiscal mandate if George wants to claim that this is nothing new?'

There was silence at the other end of the phone. 'Ah, mmmm,' said Oliver. 'Well, we were only hoping to clarify things. If you are willing to move on this, I may even be able to make some more policy concessions on some of the other things your party wants in the Queen's Speech.'

Now I was very suspicious indeed. Policy concessions in exchange for a 'minor' change in wording? I could see that the Conservatives intended to brief out a commitment to running surpluses as the central political message of the Queen's Speech, to put Labour on the spot and to lock us in to Tory fiscal policy.

'No. I really won't change this,' I said. Oliver accepted defeat with good grace.

George Osborne kept trying to secure our agreement to a balanced budget or budget surplus – he wanted to trap Labour into voting against a new 'Charter for Budget Responsibility' that he and Danny Alexander had agreed to publish at the time of the Autumn Statement in December 2014. But Vince Cable and I insisted on the charter being more flexible than the Chancellor wanted, and Labour eventually voted for it too – spotting this ill-disguised elephant trap a mile away.

That left one final big dispute to be resolved before our manifesto was agreed: what would our own plans be for borrowing in the next parliament?

Danny Alexander wanted big cuts in spending in order to meet the fiscal rules by 2017. He was then content for spending to grow again in line with economic growth. But his plan would have involved massive cuts of up to £38 billion, which I regarded as undeliverable at any acceptable political and social cost. The plans I wished to approve would still have meant big cuts, but of a reduced magnitude – more like £25 billion. I also argued that it would be crazy to slash spending aggressively for two years and then grow it rapidly the year after. Surely it would make sense to have both gentler cuts and then a gentler rise in spending?

To those in our communications team, keen to agree the outline of our manifesto proposals, the row seemed esoteric and frustrating. But we were not arguing about some trivial intellectual disagreement – we would have to negotiate on the basis of these plans if we were to end up in coalition again.

By Christmas, Nick Clegg was rather frustrated by the ongoing dispute between his two closest parliamentary allies. Over the holiday, he confided to friends: 'Everything seems to be stuck on the policy side. David Laws and Danny Alexander seemed to be locked in disagreement over the precise details of our fiscal offer. Danny is being far too orthodox – and risks locking us into massive cuts. David is being dogged but getting fixated on the details. And to cap it all, Vince Cable has also been phoning me up, complaining about the trajectory of cuts and savings in 2017/18.'

In early January 2015, the simmering dispute came to a head with some tense meetings in Nick Clegg's office. Neither Danny nor I would give way. Eventually, on 7 January, Nick Clegg said: 'The two of you are my closest political allies. I don't want to adjudicate between you but I will do unless you come up with an agreement very soon that we can all stick to.'

By 14 January, we had finally done a deal. Danny and I both compromised, and I felt that we now had a sensible position. We had agreed £30 billion of savings by 2017/18 – between my figure of £25 billion and Danny's implied proposal of £38 billion. And instead of steep cuts followed by steep rises in spending, there would now be a more reasonable profile.

Comparing our figures with the Conservatives, the big difference was that George Osborne would be aiming to cut £12 billion from welfare by 2017/18 – which seemed impossible to us without unacceptable cuts that would drive up poverty. We proposed just £4 billion of welfare cuts, with £8 billion coming from rises in taxation that would be focused on those on high incomes.[2]

Nick Clegg was relieved. 'Thank God there is finally some white smoke on this one,' he said.

But if relations were thawing in the Liberal Democrat team, there was still a lot to sort out between us and the Conservatives – including in the Department for Education.

In the period between January and March 2015 there were five or six policy disputes in the Department for Education. These were usually not between Nicky Morgan and me – indeed, we were getting along very well together. The tensions were, instead, with the Treasury and with 10 Downing Street.

The first big dispute was on a major set of announcements that we were due to make on school capital allocations – an area on which I led in the Education Department.

We were due to announce extra money for new school places, for school maintenance, for more free schools and for a second 'priority school building programme' (PSBP) – £2 billion of investment to rebuild the schools that were in the worst condition in the country.

I was particularly committed to the £2 billion rebuilding programme, and we had been talking about this in government for almost two years. Some of the schools in question were in a terrible state, with classrooms that were unfit to teach in.

The problem was that the free schools programme had now grown, and it was literally out of control – the Conservatives were determined that it

---

2   After winning the election, George Osborne announced a final package that was closer to our proposal than his own party's.

should not be budget limited, so it was influenced only by how many 'good bids' for new schools were approved.

I supported free schools, where these were run by good providers in areas where extra places were needed. But I did not think that the free schools programme needed to be so large, and I was very concerned about its impact on the rest of the capital programme.

There was a gap of hundreds of millions of pounds between what we wanted to fund and the money we had. I was willing to shave some money here and there from our capital programme, but I was not willing to cut a single penny from tackling the worst condition schools in England in order to bolster a free schools programme that was grossly inflated.

The issue could not be resolved in the Department for Education, so it went up to the Treasury. The Chancellor refused to provide extra money, and instead countered by arguing for cuts of £250 million to the priority school building programme. I was furious, and I provided Danny Alexander with the ammunition to fire: pen portraits of some of the worst condition schools in England that would be lost to the programme if it were cut in this way.

The many schools affected would include the Baverstock Academy in Birmingham, Brinsworth Comprehensive School in Rotherham, Somers Heath Primary School in Thurrock, St John Fisher Catholic Comprehensive School in Chatham and Aylesford and Leventhorpe Business and Enterprise Academy in Hertford and Stortford.

The descriptions I sent across to Danny gave a good sense of just how bad some of the buildings were. Of one school whose rebuilding the Conservatives wanted cancelled, the report said:

> The structural engineer has reported the building as nearing the end of its lifespan. This means the concrete in the building would begin to deteriorate, resulting in a number of health and safety risks such as falling masonry and window casements ... It is only a matter of time before the property becomes unstable ... Several classrooms are undersized and suffer extremes of temperature with summer temperatures reaching 40 centigrade ... in the winter staff and students keep their coats on.

I was not willing to leave schools like this out of the programme.

George Osborne refused to budge. Everyone waited for me to concede some small cuts to the PSBP, assuming this was inevitable. Instead I sent the message back: 'The minister would rather announce no capital programme at all for schools until after the election than cut anything from the priority school building programme.' Danny Alexander also helpfully made clear that with no agreement on this programme, the extra free schools could not go ahead either. Within days, George Osborne had given way, and I had my £2 billion capital programme. I was delighted – with the support of Nick Clegg and Danny Alexander we had ensured that sixty or seventy of the schools in the worst condition in England would be rebuilt after all. It had been a well worthwhile row.

I was particularly unimpressed a few days later when I discovered that the Prime Minister now wanted to personally launch the programme – which the Conservatives had tried so hard to scale back. There was another row. Nick Clegg launched the programme instead.

This was just one of the many disputes in these last weeks of government. When the School Teachers' Review Body recommended pay rises for senior teachers of up to 2 per cent, the Chancellor wanted it vetoed. Danny and I threatened to make the coalition dispute public, and the Chancellor quickly gave way.

Another dispute on schools capital with the Chancellor was also resolved in my favour after Danny again threatened to hold up the free schools announcement.

I was also very concerned when 10 Downing Street tried to torpedo the publication of an important review into managing dangerous asbestos in school buildings. I was furious that an issue of pupil safety was being treated in this way, and I was determined that my review and its conclusions would see the light of day. After I had sat on approval of various Conservative policies that were awaiting Home Affairs Committee clearance, Oliver Letwin phoned me up to offer to unblock the asbestos review if I would unblock something the Conservatives wanted. The asbestos review got published.

Downing Street also wanted to block the publication of new tables showing the performance of academy chains and local authorities. This was an excellent piece of work that had been ongoing in the department for over a year, and it was exactly the sort of accountability we needed to address underperformance in the worst chains and local authorities. It was finally released after I refused to sign off on publication of the government's overdue response to a report on academies.

There was one final education issue that I was concerned about. The department had some time ago received an application for the 'expansion' of a grammar school in Kent – the Weald of Kent School.

This 'expansion' was around ten miles away from the existing grammar school, and it looked remarkably like an entirely new school, rather than an expansion. If it was a new school, it was illegal under education law. The department had to make a judgement on this issue, and I insisted on being closely involved. I was suspicious that the Conservatives might feel obliged to approve the grammar school for political reasons, as it was being backed by local MP and Tory Cabinet minister Michael Fallon. UKIP were also the main political opposition to the Conservatives in Kent, and they were arguing for more grammar schools – and making political hay out of the issue.

Eventually, the advice came back from officials in the Department for Education. I had made sure that the officials would deliver objective legal advice and not just what they thought ministers might want to hear. After careful consideration, my own conclusion was that on balance the plan looked more like a new school and not an expansion. If so, it should not be approved.

I spoke to Oliver Letwin the very next day, in my breakfast catch-up meeting with him in the cafeteria in 10 Downing Street. 'I consider that the proposal is likely to be a new school under the existing law, and not an expansion. If that is correct, it's illegal. I know this one will be difficult for you lot. But it seems to me there are three options. Firstly, we can rule it out now. I would be quite content with that. Secondly, you could take more time to make a decision, delaying it until after the election. I can live with that too. Finally, you might want to ignore the advice and go ahead and approve the grammar school. But I won't agree that, and if you do this, it is bound to become public and there will be a huge row.'

'I get the message,' said Oliver Letwin. 'I will relay it to the Prime Minister.' The issue remained buried until after the election, when the new Conservative government approved the 'expansion' plan.

It wasn't just in the area of education where there were disputes to be settled. The Conservatives were blocking some of our policies, so we blocked quite a few of theirs. In coalition, new policy required sign-off from the Home Affairs Committee – chaired by Nick Clegg. Cabinet ministers had to 'write around' for permission to go ahead with new policies. Until every member of the committee had agreed the policy, it could not be launched. I generally served as the Liberal Democrat 'sweeper' who blocked the policies that we didn't agree with or who sometimes chose to hold up Conservative policies when they were being unreasonably difficult about ours. I usually only blocked the occasional policy, but by the middle of March I was holding up ten separate policy announcements: two from the Transport Department, two from the Treasury, two from the Home Office, two from the Local Government Department and two from the Department for Culture, Media and Sport. I had decided that if the Conservatives wanted to be difficult, we could be awkward too.

And in some areas there were genuine and significant disagreements. I spent a large amount of time blocking illiberal and half-baked policies from the Department for Communities and Local Government, run by Eric Pickles. The department was now trying to secure agreement just before the election to some new, very right-wing, policies that made it almost impossible for the traveller community to find sites to stay on. Concerns were raised with me by a very passionate and persistent constituent, who pointed out that almost every organisation or individual who had replied to the government consultation had opposed the new 'Pickles plan'. Indeed, the police were particularly critical – arguing that the new measures were so unreasonable that they were bound to worsen the problem of illegal encampments. I refused to give clearance to this proposal until I had tested it – possibly to destruction. I was pretty sure, however, that if I did block the proposal this action would immediately be leaked to the newspapers, in a nasty right-wing populist context. So I had to be sure to get the decision right.

Now, finally, our manifesto was fixed. The final education disputes were settled – almost wholly to my satisfaction. And the Budget was more or less agreed.

It had been a busy final few months, but suddenly the end of the coalition government loomed into sight.

An icy January gave way to a better February, and finally to the first pleasant days of March. I no longer needed to canvass in a warm and waterproof jacket, and at last there was a distinct feel of the countryside coming back to life.

But for those of us in the coalition, there was a strange juxtaposition of an environment coming back to life and a government fading away. Winter was on the way out. But we in government were now in the dying days of spring.

Beer and Crisps at No. 10

MARCH 2015

M arch 2015 was a month of 'lasts'. The last Education Questions, on the floor of the House of Commons. The last meeting of Cabinet committees. The last ministerial meeting in the Department for Education. The last Budget. The last meeting of our parliamentary party. The last Select Committee appearance. The last bilateral with Oliver Letwin. The last speech in Parliament. The last Cabinet. The last Deputy Prime Minister's Questions. The last Commons vote. The last meeting in Nick Clegg's office. The last walk along the Cabinet Office corridor, through the connecting door into Downing Street, along the red carpet and down that famous staircase with photos of all the past Prime Ministers. The last kipper in the Downing Street cafeteria, served by the wonderful Alison. The last Cabinet committee clearances. The last departmental submission received and actioned. The last letters signed. The last goodbye to staff and colleagues.

It could have been a time of great sadness, but it wasn't. There wasn't time for that.

It could have been a time of massive coalition rows and public bust-ups, as the constraints of coalition gave way to the open warfare of election campaigns. But it wasn't like that either. The coalition started with pretty good relations between the parties, and it ended that way too.

That doesn't mean that there wasn't the odd row, as I have already recorded. And, of course, Nick Clegg and Michael Gove crossed swords with each other until the very end. The Conservatives had been trying to get the Liberal

Democrat MP for Taunton, Jeremy Browne, to defect to them. Instead, following a breakdown in relations with Nick Clegg, Jeremy had decided to stand down from Parliament. But he didn't go quietly, giving a number of unhelpful newspaper interviews.

At the Cabinet on 3 March, we discussed Latin America. We had finished the discussion and were about to move on to the next item, when Michael Gove intervened: 'Prime Minister, I feel that the whole Cabinet will want to record its thanks to Jeremy Browne – the Honourable Member for Taunton – who did such brilliant work in Latin America as a Foreign Office minister.'

Conservative ministers laughed, glancing round at a distinctly nonplussed Nick Clegg.

'I'll second that,' said George Osborne. 'Jeremy Browne is certainly a master of diplomacy, isn't he, Nick!'

It was all quite good-natured ribbing. After Cabinet, Nick Clegg and David Cameron exchanged brief words over the discussion. 'Michael was on good form today, wasn't he?' Nick Clegg said, in jest.

David Cameron laughed. 'The thing that you have to remember about Michael is that he is at times quite genuinely mad!'

I was now spending only half the week in Westminster, and the other half canvassing in my constituency, and it was the same with most MPs. The election starting gun might not yet have been fired, but the race was most certainly on. This was the most exhausting phase of the parliament. I felt I was doing six jobs simultaneously: local MP, Education Minister, Cabinet Office minister, chair of the general election manifesto, election campaigner and organiser, and – of course – member of our coalition negotiating team. It was rewarding but also exhausting. And I was already counting down the days to 8 May 2015, when the whole election campaign would finally be out of the way.

In the Quad meeting in early March, there were the first signs that the Conservatives were planning to put the threat of the SNP at the heart of their campaign. With Labour now widely predicted to lose a swathe of seats in Scotland, it was becoming increasingly likely that they would be unable to govern alone. Yet if Labour needed Scottish Nationalist votes, this could be very damaging, and leave English voters exposed to the potential demands of nationalist MPs.

David Cameron showed Nick Clegg a copy of a giant Conservative election poster of the SNP leader, Alex Salmond, with Ed Miliband in his pocket.

The poster was going up in Oxford Circus. Nick warned against sowing division in the UK, but David Cameron was dismissive, saying that Scotland was now Labour's problem.

'I am worried about how the Tories are stirring up the Scottish issue in England,' Nick said to us later. 'It's very damaging, immature and short-sighted. And if they handle Scotland like this, just think what a mess they will make of Europe.'

On Saturday 7 March, I had to stay in London for the final meeting of the Federal Policy Committee, to approve our general election manifesto. Nick Clegg was there, given the importance of the occasion, and at my request Danny Alexander had also come all the way down from Scotland, for just a two-hour discussion of our economic plans. He might easily have made an excuse not to be there, given how shaky his constituency was looking. But – quite typically – he was doing his duty to the party and to the government right to the bitter end.

After a long meeting, we finally agreed a manifesto with a number of clear but very carefully costed pledges: finishing the job on deficit reduction, but doing it fairly and with a proper balance between welfare cuts and tax rises; investing more in improving education and the NHS, including more action to improve mental health services; increasing the tax-free personal allowance to £12,500 per year; and tackling environmental problems and climate change.

It all went more smoothly than expected, after a masterly performance by Nick Clegg's policy adviser, Polly Mackenzie, who carefully led members of the FPC through each complex policy issue.

By 8 March, George Osborne had already started to leak out some of the Budget details – notably the planned increase in the personal tax allowance. We could hardly complain. He just happened to get in first.

At the penultimate bilateral meeting between Nick Clegg and David Cameron, the Conservative leader said he thought the election was looking close, and would probably result in a hung parliament. He indicated that the two leaders might soon have to negotiate another coalition. Nick Clegg tried to change the subject, and pointed out that he didn't think the two parties could bridge their differences on Europe. David Cameron reassured him that he believed the referendum was definitely winnable.

On Wednesday 11 March, Nick was due to have lunch with Charles Kennedy at the National Liberal Club, to get some final advice from the former leader before the election campaign began. Nick turned up on time, but there was no sign of Charles. 'I had a tomato juice by myself and then I left,' Nick Clegg told his office later. 'I am worried about Charles. He is such a great asset to the party, and is such an astute politician.'

The next day, Charles Kennedy was on *Question Time*, but his performance was unimpressive, and it looked like a mistake for him to have been allowed on the programme.

On Friday 13 March, Nick Clegg attended a service at St Paul's Cathedral to mark the end of the thirteen-year UK engagement in Afghanistan. Both David Cameron and Ed Miliband also attended.

Ed Miliband wanted to talk about the election debates; Nick Clegg was determined to change the subject. Instead, he asked the Labour leader about his position on the SNP, and expressed surprise that he hadn't already ruled out a deal with them yet. Ed Miliband nodded knowingly, but said little.

'I find Miliband difficult to read,' said Nick later. 'Cameron just blurts everything out, and is totally open. There is something very cautious, almost secretive, about Miliband.'

The weekend of 13–15 March was the final Liberal Democrat Party conference of the parliament, in Liverpool. The weather was unseasonably cold and rainy.

Danny Alexander gave a keynote address on the economy, in which he suddenly produced a yellow box from behind the speakers' rostrum – which he held up, as if he were the Chancellor of the Exchequer, about to deliver a Budget. I wasn't terribly keen on this gimmick, though it seemed to attract the attention of the press photographers.

The speech was solid and workmanlike, but the message on fiscal prudence was rather ruined when the Chief Secretary announced: 'I am committing to balancing the budget by 2010.' An alert member of the audience shouted out, 'I think you mean 2017?' Danny paused for one brief moment, and glanced up. 'Well spotted, that man,' he replied. It wasn't ideal.

The next day, Norman Lamb was obliged to deliver a more difficult speech – a Sunday newspaper had splashed with a private story, revealing in detail his son's mental health problems. It was very difficult for Norman and his wife, Mary, but both were brave and resilient. Norman received a standing ovation of support – both for his personal circumstances and for his excellent work in government on mental health.

On Sunday 15 March, Nick Clegg was due to give his leader's speech. We all knew that it could be his last, if we were not back in government after the election.

By tradition, the leader's speech is always preceded at the Liberal Democrat conference by a fundraising appeal. This can be entertaining, and on other occasions it can be a very damp squib indeed. This year there was rather too much, for my liking, about 'legacies'. Moments before the Deputy Prime Minister arrived on stage for his last keynote speech of the parliament, the party treasurer was telling people who might be planning to die in the near future that they should consider leaving some of their money to the Liberal Democrats. You wouldn't call it a warm-up act.

In spite of this, Nick's speech was a strong performance – passionate, and setting out clearly both what we had achieved in government and what more we might deliver given another opportunity.

At the end of the speech, Nick waved to his cheering and resilient party from the conference platform as he received the customary standing ovation. Then he waved again, embraced his wife, Miriam, walked past me and disappeared into the crowd, with his security guards following behind.

On the evening of Tuesday 17 March, we had the last meeting of the parliamentary party before the general election. Afterwards, Nick hosted a drinks party, and in the early evening Liberal Democrat MPs met in the House of Commons Chamber, after the end of business, for a final photograph of all fifty-six of us.

Most Liberal Democrat MPs were there, but we found ourselves waiting, as ever, for Simon Hughes, who had a reputation for always being late (and sometimes even a little long winded). Norman Baker, our MP for Lewes, had once worked for Simon Hughes as a parliamentary researcher. 'Simon was great,' he said, 'but his time-keeping was terrible. Once, he even turned up twenty-three hours late for a meeting in the Whips' Office – a record.'

Everyone, however, was very fond of Simon – 'the Peter Pan of politics', as Nick Clegg once affectionately called him – and he received a large cheer when he eventually arrived.

We had one group photograph taken in front of the Speaker's Chair, and another with all of the MPs seated behind Nick Clegg as he stood at the government dispatch box, waving his arm dismissively at an imaginary opposition. It was a cheerful, end-of-term occasion, but as I sat on the green benches I could not help wonder how many of us would be back after the next election – and in my mind I could not remove an image of this same photograph with all of the MPs who lost their seats erased from the picture. It was not a happy thought.

The next day, 18 March, was Budget Day. In one of the newspapers was a leak of George Osborne's flagship policy of cutting tax on savings income. On the 7.40 a.m. conference call with Nick Clegg, the Deputy Prime Minister reported that George Osborne had 'gone bonkers' after seeing the front page of *The Independent*, which had splashed on the story. Jonny Oates replied: 'Well, the leaks aren't from us, so it's no use Osborne complaining.'

Cabinet met at 8 a.m. to hear the Budget contents. The TV cameras were there to take some photographs, before the substantive discussion began. With the media in the room, George Osborne could only speak in generalities: 'This is going to be a good Budget, and it's the product of excellent and very close coalition cooperation,' he said. Then the photographers left the room. 'You can say what you really think now, George,' joked the Prime Minister.

The Chancellor went through the Budget details. Borrowing lower than expected. Debt about to fall as a share of GDP. Labour's foxes shot on public spending. A higher tax allowance. Frozen fuel duty. Cuts in alcohol duty. Extra money for mental health. A package for savers.

There was a brief discussion, and for once even Vince Cable wasn't too gloomy.

I mentioned that in May 2010 George Osborne had told the Liberal Democrats that a £10,000 personal allowance was unaffordable. 'I congratulate the Chancellor for proving himself wrong in every Budget and Autumn Statement since,' I said. But I also highlighted my view that the public spending plans were likely to prove undeliverable without a significant deterioration in public services and a big rise in poverty. David Cameron and George Osborne looked a little grumpy about this critical note. Cabinet meetings on the Budget were supposed to be 'slap on the back' occasions.

I watched the Budget later from my office in the Department for Education. George was in confident form, with many jokes – some of them rather contrived. A recent magazine photoshoot had embarrassed the Labour leader, Ed Miliband, by revealing that his London house appeared to contain not one but two kitchens. George Osborne explained how the government was determined to improve mobile phone signals – 'so that in the unlikely event that a person had two fridges in two quite separate kitchens, they would be able to control both simultaneously with a single mobile phone'. The government benches roared with approval. Even some Labour MPs enjoyed the joke.

The Chancellor's statement ended with a very good line about a 'comeback Budget for a comeback country'. It was on message, but it was also clear what subconscious narrative the Chancellor wanted to communicate – and it was reflected back to him on the front page of the next day's *Times* newspaper, with its picture of George Osborne and its banner headline: 'The Comeback King'. Even *The Independent* ran with: 'Osborne throws the kitchen sink at Miliband'. The days of the 'Omnishambles Budget' were well behind George Osborne now.

Meanwhile, the day after the Budget – Thursday 19 March – Danny Alexander presented his own 'Budget' to a near empty House of Commons, with a yellow Budget box, jeering MPs and an angry Speaker. It wasn't great.

Over the weekend, Nick Clegg felt tired and unwell – not an ideal start for a general election campaign. But he had been working non-stop every day, without a break, since the beginning of the year. On Sunday, he spent the whole day in bed. Then, to make matters worse, he ripped the muscles in his back while exercising on Monday morning. It was the last full week of coalition government, and on Monday morning the Deputy Prime Minister arrived at his office in Whitehall in a filthy mood feeling like death warmed up.

But business had to go on, and Monday 23 March was the occasion of the last bilateral with the Prime Minister, in Cameron's small office adjoining the Cabinet Room.

It might have been the last meeting, but there were still a range of middle-rank issues on the agenda: some Home Office disputes, a discussion of the Dissolution Honours List, and the sensitive issue of financial support for the children of asylum seekers.

But it was obvious to Nick Clegg that the Prime Minister had bigger things on his mind, with just over six weeks until the general election.

And then the meeting was over. No champagne. No fireworks. But no rows or poison either – not a bad achievement for two leaders of very different political parties after five years in power together.

When he got back to his office, Nick Clegg reflected on his last formal meeting with David Cameron: 'Well, that's it then. It's obvious that his mind is turning to another coalition, and he said to me that we should keep our options open for 8 May. I think by now, after five years, I know Cameron pretty well – his strengths and his weaknesses. Despite everything, I find him good fun and easy to work with. And he is often at his best when really under pressure. He has a fast, quicksilver mind. But he has his flaws too. I've become disenchanted by his carelessness over issues such as Scotland and the Union. His judgements on policy are swift and not always very well thought through. But my God, he has a classic nose for political survival. He ducks and he weaves. He always believes that he can get himself out of a tight corner. One day, he won't.'

That same day, I wrote a final 'leak-proof' letter to the Home Affairs Committee, refusing my permission to Eric Pickles to go ahead with his populist assault on travellers. I emphasised the view of the Association of Chief Police Officers – that the proposals were likely to increase the number of illegal encampments. I knew there would be a row. But I was comfortable, with the police on my side.

By now, there had been a lot of 'lasts' in March, but Tuesday 24 March felt like a pretty big day in the history of the coalition – it was the day of the last Cabinet meeting.

I was at my desk in the Cabinet Office at my regular time of 6.45 a.m., before making my way to the Downing Street cafeteria for some burnt bacon.

At 9.30 a.m., all the Liberal Democrat Cabinet ministers met in Nick Clegg's office in Dover House so that we could go over to Cabinet together. Most of us were there – Danny Alexander, Ed Davey, Alistair Carmichael, Jo Swinson (who could at times attend Cabinet as Equalities Minister), Don Foster (our Chief Whip), and Simon Wight, Nick Clegg's parliamentary private secretary.

We walked through the Cabinet Office corridors and down the main staircase and came out by the bike racks, where Downing Street meets the back wall of the Cabinet Office. There we waited for Nick Clegg and for Vince Cable – who was wearing his trademark hat.

We then trooped up Downing Street together and paused for a final photograph outside the famous front door of No. 10.

We were right on time for the Cabinet, and most Conservative ministers were already seated at the famous table, which was covered from end to end with beer bottles and plastic containers full of crisps. We had been warned by Nick Clegg about this the previous day: David Cameron had asked a local brewery in his constituency to produce a 'Co-ale-ition' beer, to be presented to each member of the Cabinet. On the back of the label was a photograph of the full Cabinet and underneath this was the caption: 'An unconventional pairing, this experimental beer has astonished doubters and exceeded expectations. Time for some creative thinking with this carefully crafted beer; hints of oak and zesty lemon deliver a truly distinctive refreshing flavour that lasts the distance.' The sell-by date, I noted, was 2016.

Not to be outdone, Nick Clegg also had a present for the Cabinet members – a container of Henderson's Yorkshire Sauce crisps, named 'Coalition Crunch'.

It was a nice gesture from both party leaders at this final Cabinet. A photographer dashed around the table to record the occasion – and who knows what future historians will think when they see the table covered in beer bottles.

David Cameron then started the meeting. He reflected on all that had happened and much that had been achieved since 2010. He seemed a little nervous and even a little emotional. He didn't say much about the contribution of his Liberal Democrat colleagues.

Nick Clegg responded, speaking confidently and proudly, but with no hint of emotion. He was generous and gracious about his time working with the Conservatives in government – prompting a further, brief, contribution from David Cameron who also commented on how productive the coalition of two separate parties had been.

And then George Osborne gave an update on the economy. Being George Osborne, there had to be a joke: 'Colleagues will be interested to know that the latest inflation number for the UK has just been released. Inflation is now 0.0 per cent. So there you have it – Labour has been campaigning for two years on the cost of living and now it has all come to precisely nothing.' There was a loud round of laughter – perhaps rather more than the joke merited.

We then had three discussions: one on mental health policy, led by Nick Clegg and Jeremy Hunt, a second on implementation achievements, led by Oliver Letwin and Danny Alexander, and a third on the situation in Syria and Iraq.

I decided to make a few comments in the debate on implementation achievements. I never believed in speaking for the sake of it at Cabinet, but this was the last chance to contribute, and having been in at both the end of the government and at its beginning I wanted to say something.

'Oliver and Danny's presentation reminds us how much we have achieved since May 2010. This government was formed to address the country's economic problems, and on that agenda we really have succeeded in turning the corner. But our record is not just about the economy. We should be particularly proud of the reforms which we have made in areas such as education and pensions, and of social reforms such as equal marriage, which have done much to challenge prejudice and discrimination in our society. We should also be proud to have honoured our commitment to the poorest people in the world, even in a time of austerity.

'This is the first real coalition in UK history. I think we should also give credit to the Prime Minister for the fantastic way that he has led this government since 2010.' At this point, a number of Conservative ministers looked surprised and perked up, and David Cameron glanced down the table at me.

'Yes,' I continued. 'The Prime Minister should be commended for leading the coalition so brilliantly, and for proving to the whole country how effective coalition governments can be and how much better they are than weak single-party governments. He has paved the way for many more coalitions in the future.' My final words were drowned out by both laughter and jeers.

The Prime Minister himself laughed and shrugged his shoulders. 'I suppose I will have to take praise, wherever it comes from.'

We than had a brief discussion about foreign policy and the Prime Minister closed the meeting. It felt a little bit of an anti-climax, but this was no time for tears or tantrums, and ministers picked up their papers, balanced their crisps and beer on their Cabinet folders and left the room for the last time in the parliament.

As they got up from the Cabinet table, George Osborne turned to Nick Clegg and whispered, 'I think we'll both be back here together after the election.'

Outside the Cabinet Room, in the lobby, attendants kindly gave out small bags so that we could put our beer and crisps in them, and avoid the sight of the full Cabinet parading down Downing Street as if we were off to a bargain basement student party.

I usually made my way back to my room in the Cabinet Office through the connecting door between No. 10 and the Cabinet Office building – through the sliding doors with the sign that says 'No cats beyond this point'. On this occasion, it seemed more appropriate to leave through the front door.

Meanwhile, out in the Downing Street garden, special advisers gathered together for a final team photograph with the Prime Minister and Deputy Prime Minister. It all felt a bit like the beginning of the coalition in May 2010, when the Cabinet was photographed together out in the Downing Street garden on a warm, spring day.

Nick Clegg and David Cameron talked briefly as they walked down the garden to have their photographs taken together. The Prime Minister doubted that his party would win an absolute majority in the coming election. His mind was clearly turning to the possibility of a second coalition.

When he got back to his office, Nick Clegg felt more positive than for some weeks. 'I'm proud of what we have done in government. We are basically leaving the country in good order. I somehow didn't feel emotional at Cabinet today, but I know that we've done the right things for the country. We've delivered a five-year coalition – something that many people said was impossible. God knows if we'll be rewarded by the electorate, but I think we deserve to be.

'I'm not going to miss most of the Tories, but there are some that I really like and might stay in touch with – Osborne, funnily enough, in spite of our rows. David Cameron, I guess – after all, we've been through quite a lot together. Oliver Letwin, with his decency and his wonderful professorial quality. Ken Clarke. Definitely Ken Clarke – he is truly brilliant.

'But what I will really miss is the officials and advisers who I have worked with – they are a great bunch.

'Anyway, I am really looking forward to the election campaign. We have something important to say, and now I just want to get out there and say it.' He would not have long to wait.

THE BIG FOUR

2010–15

I t was 2014, and Francis Maude, the Minister for the Cabinet Office, was threatening a 'fundamental review' of the civil service – both its size and its political independence. He wanted to know, for a start, why the amount of office space occupied by the average civil servant had barely fallen over the previous few years. Civil servants frowned and quietly noted that Mr Maude still happily operated from the largest office in all Whitehall – a room so famously vast that it could have happily accommodated a game of five-a-side football for forty-somethings. Young children had been known to get lost in smaller spaces.

In any case, the top civil servants didn't much like what they were hearing. I suddenly discovered that a series of unexpected meetings with senior civil servants were inserted into my diary, in which I was warned, not too subtly, about the risks of reform. And when I met Francis Maude to discuss the matter – without civil servants – I was within hours delicately asked by my private office for a 'read-out'.

The risks of 'hasty' reform were quietly but firmly set out for me. If large redundancy payments for top-tier civil servants were scrapped, how would we ever get rid of the poorest performers? If more political appointments were introduced, how would the famed civil service independence be safeguarded? And, in a meeting that would have graced the pages of a *Yes Minister* script, what would be the unintended consequences for politicians if there was further dramatic cutting back of civil service numbers?

'Minister, if some departments are cut further they will effectively become unsustainable. People are then surely going to ask whether we actually need all the departments we've got. Do we need both an Environment Department and a Climate Change Department? Do we need Departments for Wales, Scotland and Northern Ireland, when we have devolved governments? Should we not merge the Culture Department into the Business Department? Do we need both Justice and the Home Office? And if we did all this, wouldn't we need, Minister, well ... fewer ministers? Far fewer ministers? Fewer Cabinet ministers too? Perhaps fourteen or fifteen around the Cabinet table, instead of thirty? And perhaps fifty in total, not almost a hundred, as there are now?' Sir Humphrey would have been proud.

I am probably being a little unfair. Politicisation of the civil service was a real risk and would have been damaging – and we Liberal Democrats were determined not to allow that. Meanwhile, the Prime Minister was – probably rightly – distinctly uninterested in those 'machinery of government' questions that had often excited, and distracted, his predecessors. Nor would either coalition leader have been much attracted by the political practicalities of shrinking a Cabinet of around thirty members to one of fourteen or fifteen.

So it was that as I sat in the last Cabinet meeting and glanced around the crowded table, I could still see the thirty or so faces who made up both the formal Cabinet and those who 'attended' Cabinet – a distinction with little practical effect.

Most of these people had big and important jobs, with many decisions to take every day – though, in reality, a Cabinet of thirty is too large to have substantive discussions in and it is questionable whether we really do need all of the departments that we currently have.

While many of these people, however, do important jobs, it is not always clear that they individually make a massive difference to the government's overall direction. Replace most ministers, and put in someone else, and the impact this makes in individual departments is often modest, let alone to the direction of the government itself.

In any government, only a few people really matter – by which I mean really make a big difference to broad policy directions. I now want to consider who these people were in coalition and seek to make a fair and balanced assessment of their contributions – which are spread liberally throughout this account.

The 'Big Four' who really counted were the members of the Quad: David Cameron, Nick Clegg, George Osborne, and Danny Alexander – in that order.

Other important members of the government – Oliver Letwin, Theresa May, Michael Gove and Vince Cable – I have described elsewhere in sufficient and compact detail to allow the reader to make a judgement of their own.

What assessment, then, did I make of these four key individuals, after five years in government?

The Prime Minister, David Cameron, is sometimes described in this account in unfavourable terms. It is true that he could often be petulant and impatient when he did not get his own way. But it would be unfair to judge a Prime Minister against such a standard. On issues of huge importance, such as Europe or English votes, he sometimes seemed willing to take massive risks with the national interest to pursue party advantage or manage party divisions. He once told Nick Clegg: 'The problem you have is your MPs like you but your activists hate you. My problem is the other way round.' It wasn't entirely true, but this was a Prime Minister who had to take seriously a large band of Conservative MPs who never quite trusted him.

It is also true that David Cameron was more prone than he should have been to pursuing short-term fixes or gimmicks, on issues from immigration to housing, without thinking through serious and long-term solutions to complex problems.

But any fair judgement of David Cameron needs to be a good deal more nuanced than this. He had brought his party back from irrelevance, and seized the opportunity to create a stable coalition government when many of his colleagues would have baulked at the risks involved. From a Conservative Party perspective, he was clearly very successful – winning the AV referendum, keeping Scotland within the United Kingdom, and delivering a second term of majority Conservative government.

David Cameron was also an excellent coalition Prime Minister. He understood that to survive, not least in times of austerity, coalitions had to be real partnerships where the smaller party was included in all the key decisions. He established, or allowed to be established, the Quad, which gave the Liberal Democrats two of the four places in the real 'inner Cabinet'. And where this didn't fix things, he would meet Nick Clegg in their weekly bilaterals, which would most often end with a swathe of difficult decisions being resolved maturely between the two men.

David Cameron was never a deeply ideological politician, and while this sometimes meant that his policy instincts lacked a reliable compass, it also meant that he was temperamentally suited to being a leader of a two-party government where the Prime Minister had to both act as a party leader and be capable of being seen to act beyond party.

David Cameron was once said to have claimed that he wanted to be Prime Minister because he 'would be good at it'. In many ways he was. Work was efficiently dispatched and decisions were quickly taken. Meetings started on time and the best-briefed person in them was usually – not always, but usually – the Prime Minister. David Cameron liked efficiency and focus at all times – and he expected this from all his ministers. These days, senior politicians are watched extraordinarily closely by the media, their colleagues and the public. Every blemish is magnified a thousand times. But being Prime Minister is not an easy job, and I think it fair to record that David Cameron's confident self-assessment was an accurate one.

The Prime Minister was often at his worst on the small issues and the issues that upset the right wing of his party and the media. He was at his best on the really big, non-political issues – on Syria, on Northern Ireland, and in dealing with crises.

I remember in 2014 hearing the Prime Minister sum up impressively at Cabinet on a couple of particularly difficult and delicate international issues. 'This is a man who looks at home as Prime Minister,' I wrote in my diary that night. 'Can I see Ed Miliband beating him? No. Cameron does not look or feel like a one-term Prime Minister.'

It seems likely that when David Cameron stands down he will be regarded by historians as a good Prime Minister but not as a great one. There was once 'Thatcherism'. I think people knew what 'Blairite' and 'Brownite' meant too. There is no Cameron equivalent.

'David's a lovely person – but I have no idea at all what he stands for,' Ken Clarke once admitted to coalition colleagues about his party leader.

David Cameron changed the Conservative Party because he wanted it to win elections. But in power, the commitments to social justice, green policies, civil liberties, European pragmatism and political reform seemed to be quickly jettisoned.

To be a great Prime Minister, you need to have a great mission, and you need to focus relentlessly on this and see it through.

The Prime Minister will also, of course, ultimately be judged on the biggest gamble of his premiership: the referendum on Europe. This commitment was given by Cameron for reasons of party management and electoral tactics. But if the PM now secures the outcome he wishes, and the UK stays in the EU, he will confirm another self-judgement – of his ability to duck and weave his way out of a difficult position. However, as Nick Clegg noted after his final meeting with the Prime Minister: 'He always believes that he can get himself out of a tight corner. One day, he won't.' If David Cameron gambles on Europe and loses, this will for ever define and deface his legacy.

Nick Clegg was by undoubtedly the second most powerful member of the coalition government – more influential than the Chancellor. I do not pretend to be impartial about the former Liberal Democrat leader; we are close allies and friends.

But if David Cameron was and is a natural Conservative, his coalition partner and Deputy Prime Minister, Nick Clegg, definitely wasn't. Of course, Nick was similar in age, education and background. But he is a natural, reforming, internationalist liberal, who wanted to shake up British politics, liberalise British society and open up access to opportunities for every child from every background.

David Cameron and Nick Clegg may have had similar upbringings but their values and characters were distinctly different.

At a Cabinet in 2012 where we spent just ten minutes discussing the Eurozone crisis and then forty-five minutes discussing in immense detail the operation of the British honours system, the Deputy Prime Minister expressed his exasperation at the country's obsession with such a 'feudal' system. 'I shall take no lessons on the wickedness of the establishment from the Lord President of the Privy Council,' quipped George Osborne, but Nick Clegg's commitment to reform was more than skin deep.

'It's interesting', confessed Nick to allies after two years as Deputy Prime Minister, 'that the more I do this job the more, not less, pro-reform I become. I just hate the way our country operates – the unhealthy love–hate relationship between the press and politicians, the establishment, the Lords, an outdated Parliament, the lack of local freedoms and accountability.' Political reform, civil liberties, educational opportunity, internationalism – no one close to Nick Clegg ever doubted what made him tick.

Of course, the Deputy Prime Minister had made one big mistake in government. This was to have misjudged the political price of walking away from the pledge on tuition fees – as I explained earlier in this account. It is only fair to record that all those senior colleagues who might have influenced that decision in government – Vince Cable, Danny Alexander, Chris Huhne and myself – also made the same mistake, and fully share the responsibility.

David Cameron also broke some important Conservative election pledges – on inheritance tax, for example. But in other areas he grimly stuck to policy commitments that he knew made little sense, because he saw the risk of political damage from one of those feared 'split-screen moments', as he called them. And so, by the end of the parliament, millionaires and elderly Cabinet ministers continued to receive their winter heating payments. It was bad policy, but perhaps better politics.

The Conservative leader also had a sharp nose for political survival, and a ruthlessness to go with it.

It took Nick Clegg longer in government to find that brutalist streak within himself, and as he himself admitted, he may have tried too hard early in the parliament to show that coalition could work, when he might have done better simply to veto controversial policies such as the NHS reforms.

But from 2012, after the AV referendum, the Deputy Prime Minister showed that he was more than capable of acting toughly – vetoing Conservative policies on the Snooper's Charter, boundary reform, nursery ratios, fire-at-will employment laws, NHS cuts and the 2013 Tory plan to slash £13 billion extra from public spending totals, to mention just a few. In truth, Nick Clegg never relished the unpleasant rows and stand-offs that these decisions caused. But he learned the lessons of 2010 and 2011, and perhaps we should not regret it when one of our senior politicians instinctively prefers constructive engagement to brutal, partisan calculation.

Inevitably, an appraisal of Nick Clegg is now coloured, heavily coloured, by a knowledge of how the election turned out in May 2015.

But a fair assessment of Nick Clegg's contribution should weigh much more than this.

Here was a man who led his party to its highest vote share in the history of the Liberal Democrats; who helped create a stable government which lasted for the full five-year parliament; who kept his party united throughout that entire period; who juggled massive responsibilities in government with limited resources; who actively exercised huge power on behalf of his party every single day of the government; who blocked some of the most extreme and illiberal measures proposed by the Conservative Party; and who helped keep Britain in the United Kingdom while avoiding the distraction of prolonged debates about our role in Europe. Under his leadership, the Liberal Democrat Party reformed the personal tax system; put Britain's finances firmly back on course to balance; targeted more money at the poorest pupils in schools; radically reformed the pensions system; took the first steps to put mental health services on a par with physical health services; moved the Royal Mail out from under the dead hand of state control; and legislated for equal marriage. By 2015, most of the Liberal Democrat manifesto priorities of 2010 had been delivered and those which were not had either been rejected by the people (AV) or by Conservative MPs (Lords reform). By May 2015, Mr Clegg could hardly be said to have delivered his party political success. But he certainly delivered the country much of what he had promised in 2010.

George Osborne might have stood as Conservative leader in 2005, but he had the self-knowledge and good sense to know that his friend David Cameron had more chance of success than he did. Self-knowledge and good sense are not always in excess supply in politics.

The Chancellor was one of the key figures in forming the coalition and in sustaining it for five years. George Osborne is a politician's politician. He is intrigued by politics and is one of those rare individuals who follows the subtleties not only of his own party but of others. He generally understood in 2010 and throughout the coalition what his coalition partners needed and wanted, and he was good at cutting to the bottom line and doing deals. As the parliament advanced, Nick Clegg's appreciation of George Osborne's skills grew, and the two Quad members often took to resolving matters between themselves directly – presenting their conclusions as a done deal to David Cameron.

George Osborne is much more consistently liberal – with a small 'l' – than David Cameron. While the Prime Minister would often judge a policy by its seaworthiness in the *Daily Mail*, the Chancellor was more inclined to return to liberal first principles, sometimes even seeking to out-liberal his coalition partners. In 2014 when Nick Clegg was arguing, alongside David Cameron, for tighter regulation of betting shops, the Chancellor responded: 'As a liberal,

I'm not in favour of excessive regulation. And anyway, you may think that if you close a betting shop you will get something nice, like a muesli shop, but you won't. You'll probably just get an empty shop.'

On immigration, the Chancellor could always be found arguing in Cabinet for studiously liberal policies – fewer controls for entrepreneurs and high-value investors, care in dealing with genuine foreign students, and enthusiasm for letting in high-spending Chinese tourists.

On Europe, while George Osborne's views are Eurosceptic in the most limited sense, here was a man who was hardly enthusiastic about a European referendum and who really wanted the whole issue to just go away.

But if George Osborne is small-'l' liberal on many issues, he is no Liberal Democrat. On civil liberties, his instincts are broadly Conservative. On foreign policy, he is neo-Conservative. And while he wanted the coalition with the Liberal Democrats to succeed, his interest was in power for himself and his own party and not in some starry-eyed permanent pact. I never doubted that George was a fully paid-up political carnivore, and that ultimately he wanted our votes and our voters, not a coalition for its own sake. When he offered us the prospect of a 'coupon election', it wasn't as an act of charity. And when it came to the general election, he visited the seats of Liberal Democrat ministers, including me, to seek to defeat us. Of course, I would have done the same to him, if I had thought we could win his seat.

Finally, while George Osborne could come across on television and radio as sometimes distant and even sneering, in private he was self-deprecating, relaxed and amusing. In company with George Osborne you were always only one sentence away from a rather good joke – usually at someone else's expense. But the Chancellor could often laugh at himself too – as he had to in June 2013, for example, when President Obama kept referring to him as 'Geoffrey' at a major international summit in Wales. The Prime Minister and his deputy teased 'Geoffrey' about this for some weeks afterwards.

After the Omnishambles Budget, the Chancellor made a big effort to change his public image. Out went the City backdrops and the long periods of submarine-style inactivity. In came a new hairstyle and yellow high-visibility jackets – by 2015 there could barely be a bricklayer in England who hadn't personally been assisted in his work by the Chancellor of the Exchequer.

There was, in spite of all George Osborne's small-'l' liberalism, one major area of disagreement between the Liberal Democrats and the Chancellor.

George might be socially liberal – in favour of gay marriage, for example – but he wasn't really a great champion of social mobility or social justice. Of course, he bought into Michael Gove's school reforms, but there was never any sense of why. And he saw the social security budget as a giant cash-cow for the Treasury to milk, and not as something that was really necessary to help poor and vulnerable people who might need the support of the state through no fault of their own.

Maybe that will change if the Chancellor eventually moves next door to 10 Downing Street. Maybe, like his political hero, Johnson – Lyndon, not Boris – the Chancellor will broaden his political appeal over time and develop new causes. He needs to for his own sake and the country's.

And will he stand for Prime Minister next time? Almost certainly. It made sense not to when there was a more viable friend ready to take the job. But I cannot see George Osborne deferring to Theresa May, Philip Hammond or that great entertainer and opportunist Boris Johnson.

We have now arrived at the fourth and final member of the Quad, Danny Alexander – Luke Skywalker to my Obi-Wan Kenobi, if you recall Michael Gove's comparison.

In a youthful government, Danny Alexander was in 2010 one of the youngest and least experienced Cabinet members. He made some mistakes, in my view, including over the timing of the 50p tax cut, over the NHS Bill, and obviously on tuition fees (along with his senior colleagues, including me). He could also be a little too orthodox at times and there were one or two occasions when his lectures on fiscal prudence might have been shortened a mite.

But in all other respects, he was an outstanding minister and Liberal Democrat. And what he lacked in age, he made up for in maturity. He was a fully paid-up, adult member of the coalition government – which he played a key role in sustaining from beginning to end.

His appetite for work was voracious. His commitment to make the coalition government work for the people of our country was almost matchless. Of course he made some mistakes, but he was required to take numerous decisions every day of the week, for every year of the government – and the vast majority of these he got right. He was also sure-footed politically, and one of the least likely people to cause political problems or embarrassment.

Danny Alexander was one of the longest-serving and most powerful Chief Secretaries in the history of the role, and I would be very surprised if he wasn't also one of the best. And though he never neglected his responsibilities to improve the public finances, he also worked hard to turn Liberal Democrat policies into practice – whether the pupil premium, the higher tax allowance, or policies on the NHS or the environment. In almost three years as Schools Minister, I do not recall any occasion when he failed to give me full support on delivering what I wanted – yes, even when it required a cheque to be written.

Finally, if his economic contribution to the government wasn't enough, he was also one of those who worked hardest and to most effect to keep Scotland in the United Kingdom. That is not a bad legacy.

Saying

Goodbye

MARCH 2015

'Confidential Economic Briefing for the Prime Minister and Deputy Prime Minister', was the title of the ten-page briefing paper that I found in my red box one weekend in mid-2014.

Thinking I might be about to see some fascinating unpublished insights into the most up-to-date state of our economy, I quickly flicked over a couple of pages to a section on 'Key Statistics'.

'Asda Semi-Skimmed Milk – 49p,' I read.

Then:

800 gram Hovis medium wholemeal loaf – £1.35p.

Heinz Baked Beans – 68p.

Mars Bar – 54p.

Average price of pint of beer in London – £3.60p [Sheffield – £2.70p].

The list continued on and on, finishing with:

Latest No. 1 Hit Single: 'I will never let you down' by the Kosovo-born British singer-songwriter Rita Ora.

Top Five Films: *Bad Neighbours, The Amazing Spiderman 2, The Other Woman, Rio 2, Pompeii.*

Politicians may not always know the top rate of capital gains tax, but they don't want to be accused of being 'posh boys who don't know the price of milk'.

And in the weeks and months ahead, all of the top British politicians, particularly the party leaders, could expect to come under quite unprecedented levels of policy and personal scrutiny. The general election campaign was imminent.

Wednesday 25 March was the last 'real' day in government. After this, I would be back in my constituency, and the civil service would only contact ministers for input on very urgent matters. We would be in 'purdah', when government is essentially handed over from politicians to civil servants on a 'care and maintenance' basis.

I was up at 5.30 a.m. and into the Cabinet Office for 6.30. At 7.45 I went down to the No. 10 cafeteria to collect breakfast for the last time.

Later in the morning, I left for Drapers' Hall in the City of London. Nick Clegg and I were due to award pupil premium prizes to the schools in England that had been the most effective in improving educational outcomes for children from disadvantaged backgrounds. It was a wonderfully happy and positive occasion. Neither Nick Clegg nor I could imagine doing anything more enjoyable on our last 'real' day in government.

The pupil premium was a policy that Nick Clegg first wrote about before coming into Parliament, and which I helped to flesh out as Education spokesman in opposition between 2007 and 2010. It was a policy I was very passionate about, and I had been prepared to resign if a fully funded pupil premium had not been included in our 2010 general election manifesto. So neither Nick nor I could be more proud to see the policy being delivered in real schools and making a big difference to real pupils. This was what being in government was all about.

Neither of us could stay to join the head teachers for their slap-up meal, but instead we slipped away after the main ceremony was complete and returned to Westminster.

Meanwhile in the House of Commons, David Cameron was wrong-footing Ed Miliband by ruling out an increase in value added tax, in the last Prime Minister's Questions of the parliament.

In the afternoon, I went over to the House of Commons to vote for the last time in the parliament – in a 'deferred division'. As I placed my ballot paper before the House of Commons clerk and left the 'No' Division Lobby, I did not realise that I had cast my last ever vote as an MP, after fourteen years.

I went back to the Department for Education, and held my last meetings with policy teams. We said our thanks and goodbyes, and I tried not to get emotional. I had enjoyed every minute of my time in the department and had thoroughly enjoyed working with dedicated and talented officials, including in my private office.

There was a mini-flood of last-minute letters to sign and submissions to authorise. And then my private secretary, Lydia Bradley, came in with a rather rude and belligerent letter from Eric Pickles, ranting about my failure to clear his new proposals on traveller sites, and threatening to make public the dispute. I enjoyed signing a blunt letter back to him, making clear that I wasn't budging and that I was disappointed that he was not taking more seriously the police concerns expressed. Oliver Letwin later told me that he was pleased I had vetoed the proposals. 'Oh good, I always thought that was rather daft,' he admitted, with typical off-message Letwin candour.

There were some short speeches by ministers in the atrium of the Education Department, thanking officials for their hard work, and then I went back upstairs to say goodbye to my brilliant private office team of Lydia Bradley, Sam Cook, Georgina Manley, Ursula Ritz, Wilhelmina Blankson, Matt Sanders and Chris Paterson.

Afterwards, I walked back over to Parliament for more drinks and good-byes. I met up with my Cabinet Office staff, Natalie Perera, Jonathan Crisp, Julian Astle and Katie Harrison, in Oliver Letwin's office in the Lower Ministerial Corridor. In true coalition style, Oliver and I held a joint event with our two teams.

Julian Astle asked Oliver about an article in that day's *Spectator* magazine, which suggested that the Prime Minister and senior Conservatives were preparing for and looking forward to a second coalition with the Liberal Democrats. 'Is this true, Oliver, and are you the one doing all the work?' Oliver Letwin did his very best not to hear.

I didn't stay long at the drinks, but instead went down the corridor to my own office. I had already cleared my DfE and Cabinet Office rooms of all personal possessions. Now I threw into the dustbin the last items from my House of Commons office. I expected to return to Parliament after the election, but perhaps not to government. And in any case, I had a horrible memory of meeting the former Liberal Democrat MP Susan Kramer in Parliament a few days after the May 2010 election. Susan had lost her seat in Richmond, and as our negotiating team walked through Parliament to get to Nick Clegg's office during the coalition talks, we passed Susan, who was struggling along a corridor with plastic bags full of personal possessions, cleared from her office. It was a very sad sight and I vowed that if I lost my seat I would not need to return to Parliament to collect anything.

I locked the door of my office for the last time, and caught a taxi to a restaurant where I was having a meal with close friends. I may have drunk a little too much, and I wasn't back until midnight.

The next day my alarm went at 4.30 a.m., and by 5.30 I was collecting my car from the second deck of the underground car park at the Palace of Westminster. The policeman at the front entrance of Parliament slowly pushed back the large black gate that bars entry to the palace, and my car slipped out into Parliament Square. Had I known that it was for the last time, I might have taken a final look back. I was now on my way to my constituency of Yeovil. The real election campaign was, at last, under way.

A FINAL SUPPER

APRIL–MAY 2015

It was lucky I wasn't superstitious. Halfway down to Somerset, on the very first day of the campaign, my car engine appeared to be giving up the ghost. I only just got back to Yeovil.

But I remembered that in 2010 it had been even worse – on the first day of that campaign I got a puncture that stopped my car within half a mile of leaving my house.

Now I was back in Somerset, and I would be spending 80 per cent of my time in my constituency until election day. Election campaigns are always part local and part national. But on this occasion, with dire national opinion poll ratings, the party assumed that local work and profile were even more important. At a dinner in the National Liberal Club in late 2014, Charles Kennedy had suggested that 'the national Liberal Democrat ship is sinking. What we need now are fifty-six different life rafts.'

Yeovil was supposed to be one of those well-designed Liberal Democrat life rafts. We had held the seat since 1983, when Paddy Ashdown had wrestled it away from the Conservatives after seventy-two years of Tory control. I had built the majority up to over 13,000 in May 2010 – the largest majority in the history of the seat. I wanted our strength to be great, specifically so that we could survive the bad times as well as the good.

In reality, our local campaign had started some seven months before, in early September. Since then, I had been out knocking on doors in every spare hour – certainly on Fridays and Saturdays, but increasingly on Sundays and

Mondays too. By election day, we had delivered a huge amount of literature and spoken to over half of the 80,000 voters in the constituency. Normally that would be enough to win. But this time wasn't normal.

In 2010, our national poll rating had hovered around 25 per cent. This time it was as low as 7 per cent. We had lost many left-wing voters to the Greens and a few to Labour. Many former Labour voters, who had long ago switched to the Liberal Democrats, were now voting UKIP. They did not like Europe or support immigration. For many of these voters, UKIP offered exactly the policy mix they wanted: left-wing on pensions and the NHS, but right-wing on Europe and immigration.

What was also different this time around was that the Conservatives were clearly throwing huge resources at Liberal Democrat seats in the West Country. For months, there was no sign of a Tory campaign. Then, in September 2014, it was as if a switch somewhere had been turned on, and a massive tidal wave of expensive, postage-paid literature arrived in my seat on an almost weekly basis. We could not easily match that level of spending.

Of course, I was up and down to London regularly to support the national campaign, including the launch of our manifesto, and debates on education. But a lot of my time was spent out on the doorstep.

In the freezing days of January and February it was at times tough to stay out for up to seven hours each day. But most people were friendly and in most areas our support still seemed to be good.

Occasionally you would get a difficult customer, wanting to have a long row with you on a cold day, when you had already been canvassing for six or seven hours. On one occasion in Yeovil, I could feel my hand in my right pocket involuntarily trying to snap a pen, as I tried not to lose my temper with one particularly difficult lady.

On another day, I confronted an unpleasantly aggressive older man on a driveway on the outskirts of Yeovil who had an unusual line of questioning: 'What do you think Queen Victoria would say about our country today? What do you think she would have said about all the Eastern European migrants?' I wasn't sure, though I wanted to say something about German ancestry. But he had already moved on: 'Come on, come on. What about Henry VIII, what would he have thought about all the scum who sit around at the bottom end of town?' Did I have a view on what Shakespeare's opinion might be on the state of the European Union? As I tried to back away down the driveway, he refused to let me go. I had to work hard to remain courteous.

But for the most part, my constituents were fantastic – welcoming, friendly and very tolerant of being disturbed at all times of the day and night.

For most candidates, the local campaigns are something of a blur. Each day passes and the end seems so, so far away. And suddenly the postal votes are out and a great landmark has passed. And then there is a week to go. And then you just count down the days.

I was fortunate enough to be accompanied by a number of brilliant local volunteers. Together we delivered leaflets and knocked on doors for ten hours a day.

Nick Clegg's own campaign really got going after Monday 30 March – the day on which he and David Cameron had to make separate visits to Buckingham Palace to present themselves to the Queen and officially end the parliament.

By now, key members of the Liberal Democrat team talked by conference call every day. On Saturday 28 March we briefly discussed the choreography of Monday's visit to see the Queen. 'We need to do something different,' said Paddy Ashdown. 'We don't want Cameron going in a big chauffeur-driven car first thing in the day, and Nick just following half an hour later in another big, posh car. Nick and the Liberal Democrats need to look different. Couldn't Nick go by Mini or something? Maybe drive himself? Or perhaps he could stroll through St James's Park to Buckingham Palace, chatting to people and feeding the ducks on the way?'

There was silence on the conference call. 'I think that would look weird, not different,' someone finally said. Stephen Lotinga, head of communications, was more diplomatic: 'Paddy, I'm not sure that would work with this notice. Nick's security people would need to plan something like that well in advance.'

Being 'different' after being in government for five years was going to be difficult.

Just as the local campaign is often simply a blur, the national campaign frequently goes that way too. And sometimes the national campaigns, despite all the work that goes into them, make little impact on the actual voters out in the real world beyond Westminster. Usually, only a few things cut through. What would it be this time?

Well, Labour's surprise announcement to tighten up on non-dom tax status wrong-footed the Conservatives for forty-eight hours. The first election debates were seen by millions of people, but with seven party leaders competing for time, there was no real 'cut-through' moment. Nick Clegg did well in the debates – very well – and this was reflected in doorstep comments. But it seemed more to be firming up the existing vote, rather than winning over new voters.

However, one fresh factor did loom large in this election: the Scottish angle.

I was canvassing in the Middle Touches area of Chard, in Somerset, in early March when the first voter said to me: 'I normally vote Liberal Democrat. But I really don't want Miliband getting in and being dependent on the Scottish Nationalists. That would be bad for the economy and it would fleece us English voters. I'm really sorry. I am voting Conservative this time.'

At the time, I was surprised and regarded this as just the random conclusion of a random voter. It was, in fact, a straw in the wind.

Vince Cable hardly helped. On a visit to Scotland, he speculated about the possibility of some sort of Labour–Liberal Democrat–SNP arrangement after the election. Nick Clegg, all of our Scottish MPs and most of our English MPs were furious, and Vince quickly withdrew his comment.

But with the SNP likely to take huge numbers of Labour seats in Scotland, the possibility of an Ed Miliband-led government reliant on SNP votes was a real one. Moderate English voters weren't entirely sure that they liked Ed Miliband or trusted Labour on the economy. They were very sure that they did not want a Labour government that was in coalition with or reliant upon the votes of the SNP.

Ed Miliband – all too late – tried to rule out a deal with the SNP. What he could not and would not rule out was forming a minority government that was dependent on SNP votes. The Conservatives saw the weakness and went in for the kill. Suddenly what seemed like a fringe issue in the national political debate became a central issue of the election.

Nick Clegg quickly ruled out a deal with the SNP too. Indeed, in an interview with the *Financial Times* on 24 April, he went somewhat further and appeared to rule out any deal with Labour if the resulting coalition was reliant on some sort of formal or informal agreement with the SNP.

Within hours, I had the Labour politician and former Cabinet minister Andrew Adonis on the phone. 'What does all this mean?' he asked. I assured him that Nick Clegg was only ruling out a deal with the SNP, and not necessarily a minority coalition government. In fact, the *FT* accurately reported Nick's views.

Some of us weren't keen to get too drawn into this debate. What would happen if this was the outcome of the election, we asked? It would be madness to box ourselves in and hand the keys of Downing Street to a minority Conservative government. And if people were worried about a hung parliament with the SNP holding the balance of power, they were likely to vote Conservative whatever the Liberal Democrats were saying.

But in private emails on the morning the *Financial Times* interview was published, Nick Clegg was very clear what he meant: 'Surely we would not ever enter a coalition where we do not command a majority in Parliament without the say so of the SNP? That would be mad – in office, but not in power etc. In that case, confidence and supply is the only and best option surely?'

To create a competing scare story to encourage voters away from the Conservatives, our national campaign team came up with the idea of 'Bluekip' – the supposed risk that the Conservatives and UKIP would form a government or pact. I wasn't impressed, and nor were some others close to the campaign. 'Bluekip' was a nice sound bite, but not a serious, competing proposition. UKIP were only on track to win one or two seats. That could not compare with the SNP, who now looked on course to clean up across the whole of Scotland. I would have preferred, instead, a more robust campaign warning of the risks of an outright Conservative government.

Nick Clegg, meanwhile, was enjoying the campaign. It was very well resourced and effectively managed by Paddy Ashdown, Olly Grender, Lena Pietsch, Jonny Oates and others – with the pressures and burdens kept away from the party leader so he could focus on 'performing' and not dealing with day-to-day crises.

The seven-way election debate had gone well for the Liberal Democrat leader. He had attacked Labour on its economic mismanagement, but had then turned on David Cameron over the threat to education funding.

With ten days to go before the election, Nick Clegg assessed the campaign with his closest advisers: 'I am really enjoying all this. And knowing that it's the last time helps – I definitely won't be leader in 2020. I am old enough to know now that I have to relish moments like this. I think the message is the right one – strong on the economy, but also for a fairer society.'

The campaign in his own constituency of Sheffield Hallam was now going well. Nick and his team were successful converting Tory voters to the Liberal Democrat cause. Nick Clegg met Ed Miliband at a military commemoration event and the Labour leader signalled that his party was no longer targeting the constituency. 'You do realise that we are not putting any central support into Hallam, don't you?' The Liberal Democrat leader guessed that he was being buttered up in case his support was needed in a hung parliament.

Nick Clegg concluded that the general election was still in the balance, but he was increasingly concerned about the risks of a minority government. If there were coalition talks, he was determined to strike a hard bargain: 'I will be tougher this time. Last time, I may have been a little too reasonable. This time I will be more ruthless.'

In Yeovil, my canvassing campaign rolled on day after day, with little relaxation, although I did attend the occasional Yeovil Town football match. That didn't make me feel any less nervous: Yeovil were heading for a second consecutive relegation after long years of success. When the club chairman whispered to me, 'It looks like we're going down – but it will be a great chance to rebuild again', I hoped that there wasn't going to be a parallel between Yeovil Town football and Liberal Democrat politics.

As we came towards the end of the campaign, the polls were still tight. Some gave a Conservative lead and others a Labour lead. All agreed that there had been no Liberal Democrat 'surge'. On the doorsteps in Somerset, our support still seemed strong. But we were set to have local elections on the same day as the general election – were some voters going to vote for us locally but for the Conservatives nationally?

In Legion Road in Yeovil, in the last days of the campaign, I called on a man who was marked down on our canvass sheets as a Liberal Democrat voter. He seemed a little reticent to say who he was going to vote for this time, but eventually he said: 'Well, I guess what the country really needs is for the government to stay pretty much as it is.' He was a supporter of the coalition – and I explained confidently that I was the 'coalition' candidate in this area, having helped to create the coalition in 2010 and having served as a minister for the past three years. I marked him as a probable supporter and moved on. But there was no 'coalition' option on the ballot paper, and as I walked off around the corner on a warm spring day I wondered if this voter and others were trying to tell me something I wasn't keen to hear – that however much they had liked the coalition, they were swaying towards the Conservatives to avoid the 'nightmare' option of Ed Miliband being propped up by the SNP.

A few days before the election I spoke to my good friend and fellow

Liberal Democrat MP Norman Lamb – a respected Health Minister since September 2012. We swapped stories from each other's seats. Norman was not under attack in his seat from the Conservatives, so he had been able to travel around the country supporting other candidates.

Norman said he was sure that we were going to lose the seat of Norwich South, and he confirmed that Sir Bob Russell was under huge pressure in Colchester – not a good sign. Norman said: 'I'm getting really worried about how many seats we may lose. It feels like an electoral tsunami is descending on us and everybody in the party is just being far too calm. The party is putting up quite a battle, but I cannot help thinking of that film in which a few hundred British troops are facing thousands of spear-wielding Zulus. But are we at Isandlwana or Rorke's Drift? Will it be a complete massacre, or will the small band win out against overwhelming odds?'

In late April, there were one or two direct clashes between the Liberal Democrats and the Conservatives. Danny Alexander highlighted possible Conservative plans to cut £8 billion from child benefit and child tax credits – forcing the Conservatives temporarily onto the defensive, and causing David Cameron to rush to rule out tax credit cuts. George Osborne was upset.

Danny Alexander also went on the record claiming that a senior Conservative had once said in a private meeting to his Liberal Democrat counterparts: 'You look after the workers and we'll look after the bosses.' Danny was furiously cross-questioned on which Conservative had uttered these words. He did not reveal that the person he had in mind was George Osborne, with whom he had worked so closely in the Treasury. When he checked his records, the wording was slightly different. In a Quad discussion over the final legislative session in 2014, George Osborne had suggested that the Conservatives would give up on their proposed legislation to undermine employment rights if we gave up our proposals to deal with corporate fraud: 'You give up on bashing company directors, and we'll give up on bashing the workers.' It amounted to much the same thing.

Late in the campaign, the Conservatives started to talk more openly about targeting the strongest Liberal Democrat constituencies in the south-west. On Sunday 26 April, David Cameron himself visited Norton sub Hamdon in my constituency – the home village of general election campaign boss Paddy Ashdown. It was certainly putting a marker down. But our canvass data still looked OK, and our postal voters seemed to be sticking with us, as far as we could tell.

The following week I was up in London for a day and I called in to party headquarters, just over the road from the Treasury building in Westminster. I passed our campaigns and polling guru, Ryan Coetzee. 'By the way, Ryan,' I asked, 'what does the polling data from my seat look like?'

'It's basically fine,' said Ryan. 'Anyway, we're not really looking at your seat. If we lose Yeovil, we'll only have about ten seats left.' I was a little reassured, but I still felt very uncertain about what the final outcome would be, both locally and nationally.

One likely outcome on election night was for Danny Alexander to lose his seat in the Highlands. He had fought an incredibly hard campaign in an unseasonably cold Scotland. And on the regular election conference call in late April, he confidently predicted that he would hold his seat. Nobody else believed this was possible, because the SNP were just so far ahead in Scotland, and our poll rating was even lower than in England.

I wanted to make sure we had done some clear thinking about how we would act in the event of a hung parliament, and what would happen if Danny lost his seat. Could he still lead the negotiating team? My view was that the optics of someone leading the negotiating team after losing their seat was not good. Jonny Oates shared my view, and thought that Danny should stay on the team but that I should step up to lead the negotiations, on the assumption that I had held my own seat.

We agreed with Nick Clegg that we needed to have a final pre-election meeting to talk through all the likely scenarios – and we fixed this for 8.30 p.m. on Sunday 3 May, at my house in Kennington, in central London. The meeting was to include just Nick Clegg, Danny Alexander, Jonny Oates and me.

That day, I was up at 4.45 a.m., in order to drive up to Liverpool to speak at the National Association of Head Teachers annual conference. The weather was atrocious as our education adviser, Matt Sanders, and I drove up a waterlogged M5 motorway. We almost didn't make it when the car started to 'aquaplane' on one particularly flooded stretch of road, and I came close to losing the steering.

By 6 p.m., I was back in London, where I was attending a final meeting of our main negotiating committee in party headquarters. Present were Lynne Featherstone, Steve Webb, Baroness Kate Parminter and party president Sal Brinton, along with Nick Clegg's senior political adviser, Matthew Hanney, and our top policy adviser, Polly Mackenzie. Danny Alexander joined us about an hour into the meeting, as his flight from Scotland was delayed.

We had a long discussion about issues of both policy and practical planning. We knew that any negotiations were likely to take longer than they had in May 2010, and we decided that although we only expected this to amount to another forty-eight hours, we did not want to give ourselves any artificial deadlines. We also had to plan for a meeting of national party members to vote on any coalition agreement.

We then discovered for the first time from Sal Brinton that the national party had already decided that the emergency conference would be in Liverpool on the Saturday after election week. Assuming negotiations did not start until the Saturday or Sunday, that gave us only six or seven days to tie the whole thing up. Steve Webb and others suggested that the conference might be put back a week. 'I'm sorry, but that's just not possible, Steve,' said Baroness Brinton. 'We've already booked Liverpool, and if we put this back we will have to pay for the hall twice. We just can't afford to do that. Also, many members will be away the following weekend, because there's a holiday coming up, so it wouldn't be very convenient for many people.' Steve Webb and Lynne Featherstone looked a bit unimpressed. I was quietly pleased that we now had some self-imposed deadline. We wanted enough time, but not so long that people thought that we could go on negotiating for ever!

Our meeting broke up at about 8 p.m. I received a text from James saying that Nick Clegg's security advance guard had turned up to check out the house and its access points – and they were suggesting that the Deputy Prime Minister might now arrive earlier, at 8.15 p.m.

As we walked towards the lifts in party HQ, I asked Steve Webb and Lynne Featherstone how their seats were going. Lynne Featherstone seemed a little cautious and pessimistic, but Steve Webb was much more confident – indeed, he said that the next day he was taking a car load of activists from his constituency to help out in nearby Bath. This latter seat was now much more marginal, as our former MP, Don Foster, was stepping down.

Danny and I caught a taxi in Parliament Square to make the five-minute journey to Kennington. I asked how things were going in Scotland. To my surprise, Danny said: 'Better than the media thinks, in my view. On a good night, we could hold five or six of our seats. It's very close in my constituency, and very tough – but we seem to be getting a lot of Conservatives and people who don't want independence to vote for us tactically, to keep the SNP out. I think Charles Kennedy should be OK in his seat. But it has been tough campaigning – the temperature has been in single figures on most days, and we had snow settling in my area one day last week! I think Labour are going to do very badly. I think Douglas Alexander and Jim Murphy will lose their seats. A pity, because it seems that Ed Miliband had decided that Douglas Alexander would lead any coalition talks with us – and I think Douglas is a pretty decent guy.'

I had to admire Danny's resilience. One betting page had him down as 99 per cent certain to lose his seat. But there was no panic, no self-pity, no defeatism and no sign of back-peddling on his national party commitments.

When Danny and I reached the house, James had opened some Chablis and ordered in some very good Indian food from the nearby Kennington Tandoori restaurant. We were soon joined by Jonny Oates, who turned up looking cheery and relaxed.

Nick Clegg arrived on time at 8.30 p.m. He looked rather tired, pale faced – as he often does – and slightly on edge. We sat down at the dining room table and immediately started eating and drinking.

Nick cut straight to what he wanted to say: 'I've obviously been giving all this stuff a lot of thought. Let me be blunt: I just don't presently see the scenario where we are going to be able to go into government. I think we are heading back into opposition, and on that scenario I would expect to stand down and pave the way for a leadership contest later this year. If we could deliver a coalition that had an outright majority, it would I think be quite easy on policy terms alone to do a deal with Labour – provided they signed up to a proper deal on deficit reduction. That I think would on balance be preferable over another coalition with the Conservatives – because of the high risk that a referendum on Europe would end up with our country leaving the European Union. This is a massive issue for me. I don't want to end up in the history books as the guy who led the party into government for seven years, where at the end of our time we then end up leaving Europe. If we leave Europe, that would not only be thoroughly bad for the UK – it would probably be the end of the UK. I don't want that on my conscience.

'Clearly, we don't have the same issue with Labour. But frankly with Labour there is an even bigger practical obstacle – I just cannot see the arithmetic in which we could form a stable, majority government with Labour by ourselves. I think a minority Liberal Democrat–Labour coalition would be massively dependent on the SNP. That would be a disaster for the country and it would do huge damage to our party, and it would totally destroy us in our remaining seats – most of which will be Conservative facing – in 2020. So although we've come here tonight to discuss coalition options, I just think the chances of all this happening are rather remote.'

There was a short pause in the discussion. Neither Danny Alexander nor I – nor the rest of the coalition negotiating team – were quite this sceptical about the chances of a second coalition.

Danny Alexander was the next to speak: 'Nick, can I just come back and challenge you on that? Firstly, you say that if we could form a majority coalition with Labour there should be no objection to that. I agree. But I want to challenge your view about the Conservatives and the EU. And I speak as somebody who is very passionate about the EU and our membership of it,' he said, glancing disapprovingly at me. 'We have to remember that we are fighting this election on the basis that we want to be in government delivering our manifesto. It's going to be difficult after the election to suddenly say we are not interested in creating a stable government or delivering our manifesto, but we want instead to go into opposition. I think that if all the main parties are campaigning for an "In" vote in the European referendum, it can still be won. So I am not in favour of ruling out a coalition with the Tories if the two of us could effectively form a majority government – perhaps with a few DUP MPs tagged on.

'On the SNP issue, I agree with you that this is much more difficult. I'm obviously fighting the SNP in my own seat, and I know how unpleasant they are. But we have to think about this very carefully. What would be the counterfactual if we ended up refusing to go into a minority coalition with Labour? If we said no to Labour, could we end up in a worse situation by putting the Conservatives in power instead, or having a second general election – which would be absolutely devastating for us?'

Jonny Oates agreed with Danny and said that one of our prime objectives needed to be to avoid a second general election any time soon. 'That would wipe us out completely,' he predicted.

I spoke next: 'I basically agree with Danny. It is easy to think of the downsides of the various obvious options, but we have to think about what happens if we refuse coalition, too. If we have to go in with the Conservatives, they will clearly insist on a referendum on the EU – indeed, even if Cameron was willing to dump this policy, his party would not allow him to. That would be a big risk for us: I continue to believe that an EU referendum is basically a coin toss – heads we stay in, tails we leave. A big call. If we do accept an EU referendum and go in with the Conservatives, I think we should insist on three conditions. Firstly, we should deliver most of our manifesto, and the economic and social strategy of the government should look more like the Liberal Democrat manifesto than the Conservative one. Secondly, we should first agree with Cameron what the EU negotiating red lines should be. Finally, we should make clear to the Tories that the coalition would end three months before an EU referendum if the Conservative Party planned to recommend leaving the EU. Neither George nor Cameron would want the coalition to end, so that would be a big incentive for them to lead the campaign to stay in.'

Jonny Oates said: 'Yes, but I would add another condition to that: there should be two Europe Ministers. One Liberal Democrat and one Conservative.'

Nick thought for a while, and then said: 'OK. Let's test this situation with a possible Conservative coalition out a bit further. I still can't see us being in coalition with Labour, because I think that the SNP are going to kill Labour in Scotland, and I cannot see any scenario where we want to be in a government that is dependent on SNP support.'

We then had a long discussion about the chances of winning an EU referendum. Nick said: 'David's right that if we agreed to an EU referendum our price would be control of much more of the economic and social agenda – that, rather than yet another attempt to push through constitutional reform. We could even insist on securing the role of Chancellor of the Exchequer this time.' Danny joked that he would be happy to take on the challenge.

I then said, 'Even if we don't get Chancellor, we should push for it. I would probably also ask for Education and Health. Then I would want us to keep Chief Secretary to the Treasury, DPM, Climate Change, and have a joint Minister for Government Policy in the Cabinet Office.'

Nick said: 'OK, but I still don't know. It's still going to be touch and go with the Tories over Europe, but we should keep our options open. I suppose I just feel a bit of a sense of gloom over us having to do another five years with the Tories in government. Some of their people drive me mad. I also just hate the Tory sense of entitlement – the "right to rule" thing that Cameron, Osborne and all of them have. And I really struggle with their attitude to the poor and disadvantaged – I find their lack of interest or compassion really difficult to understand. Maybe, maybe, you lot are right that this EU issue is just about manageable. But I personally still doubt it.'

'Let's be clear,' I said. 'The EU issue is still a huge risk. No one can guarantee how the public would vote in a referendum. But a minority Conservative government, with no Liberal Democrat influence, is a risk too. And if the Tories form any sort of government, an EU referendum becomes highly likely.'

We then moved on to discuss the Labour options, and the issue of the SNP. We all agreed that the prospect of any sort of reliance – formal or informal – on the SNP was deeply unattractive. 'The media would destroy us, and at the following election we would lose most of our Tory facing seats,' said Nick Clegg again.

But Jonny Oates warned that we had to be very careful what we said about Labour and the SNP after the election results were public: 'Firstly, we mustn't weaken our negotiating position with the Tories by ruling a Labour deal out. Secondly, we need to consider whether we would really want to put the Tories into government rather than Labour. That is a big question. And finally, we just have got to avoid a second election at all costs.'

It was now almost 10 p.m., and we had eaten through a lot of food – though there was still a good deal sitting uneaten. We had also worked through almost three bottles of wine – and that was after Danny had switched to Diet Coke after his first glass.

Nick Clegg then said: 'Danny, I know that you have to leave soon to catch the sleeper up to Scotland. Did you want to say something about the negotiating team?'

Danny leaned forward and folded his arms: 'Yes, look, my view is that I want to stay on the negotiating team whether I lose my seat or not – which I am not expecting to do. However, I don't think I could be the public face of the group if I lost my seat, so I propose that if this happens David should take over chairing the committee and being its public face.' Nick nodded. It was clear that he and Danny had already discussed the matter together.

I said that I would happily take on the role, assuming I held my seat. I said it was good that Danny would remain on the team, but I said that if more than one person lost their seat, it would probably be necessary for the other person to leave our group. We could not be seen to make up our negotiating team with a lot of defeated former MPs. Nick looked a bit surprised at the prospect that anyone else might lose their seat. 'Lynne Featherstone,' said Jonny Oates to Nick. 'Her seat is looking quite tough.'

Nick said: 'Danny, we hope you will hold your seat, of course, but if not, would you want to go to the Lords?' Danny responded quickly: 'Nick, no, I am absolutely clear that I don't want to go there. If I've lost my seat, I don't want to come back to Parliament through some other route. I would just get on with other things.'

Nick then said: 'I need to just come back to my own position. My view, notwithstanding all that we have said, is that it will be very difficult for us to go into coalition if we have fewer than about thirty-five seats. And it would be terribly difficult for me to stay on as leader if we had suffered the loss of more than half of our parliamentary colleagues.'

I interrupted at this point to say: 'The truth, Nick, is that we are likely to have fewer than thirty-five seats and – crucially – that is now what people are expecting. I don't think it's obvious at all that we should opt out of government if we get, say, twenty-six seats. I don't think it will help me in my seat next time if we have given up the ability to deliver most of our manifesto. And frankly, now that we are down to 8 per cent or 9 per cent in the polls, the downside is surely limited, and if we can do a good job and avoid another "tuition fees", we might even increase our support in the next parliament.'

Danny added: 'If we have more than thirty-five seats then we would have no problem doing a coalition. If we have twenty-five to thirty-five seats it's probably OK, but not definitely.'

It was clear that both Danny and I thought that coalition was still a good possibility and should be our aim. Nick was more sceptical about whether it could be delivered. He also looked tired, and was clearly considering his own position if the results were bad.

Nick summed up: 'OK. That's as far as we can go today. I should just make clear, though, that if we are not in government, I will announce immediately that I am standing down as leader. But I think we need a good, long leadership election to really test out all the candidates. It would not be good if someone like Tim Farron was anointed as leader with no debate or scrutiny at all.'

At that precise moment, my mobile phone started to vibrate with a text message coming through. It was a message from Tim Farron to all Liberal Democrat MPs: 'Thinking of you all. Very best wishes for Thursday. Good luck! Tim Farron'.

I read the message out. 'I think the leadership campaign may be starting a little sooner than expected,' I said. Nick raised his eyes to heaven.

Nick finally asked me how many seats I thought we would win. 'A year ago, I thought thirty-five,' I said. 'Now, twenty-six or twenty-seven. The polls in Scotland are part of the reason.' Nick winced. He clearly wanted more than thirty seats.

At that point Danny Alexander rose from the table. 'OK. My cab is here. I need to go.'

It felt like an important moment – our last meeting before a momentous election. We knew that the next time we got together there was a real chance that we would be out of government, Nick would no longer be leader and Danny would no longer be an MP.

Jonny shook Danny's hand, saying, 'Your constituents will be mad if they do not re-elect you, Danny. And if they don't, we should ask for all that money back that has been sprayed around your area – the extra ski lifts and the gold-lined roads!'

Danny and I then said our goodbyes, and finally Danny shook hands with Nick Clegg. The two had been inseparable political allies for over eight years. It was a sad moment. Danny was very resolute, but in truth we all expected him to be one of the 'Portillo moments' of the 2015 election.

Danny left, and then Nick said that he had to get back home as well. As he put his coat on I exchanged a few last words with him, to cheer him up before the battle to come. 'I think you have done a fantastic job in this campaign, and a great job in government. Please don't rush into any decisions about your own future too early on election night. The party will need you and the country may still need you too.'

Nick smiled and nodded a bit. But I felt that he only half absorbed what I had said. Jonny and Nick then left together, and James and I cleared up the plates and had another glass of wine. 'This could turn out to be the "Last Supper" of the core Cleggites,' I said to James.

The Aftermath

MAY 2015

On the day before the general election, I sent Nick Clegg a last message of good wishes, to cheer him up and help to fix a conference call shortly after the exit polls were released.

I received generous good wishes by text from Nicky Morgan, the Conservative Education Secretary, and from the Labour peer Lord Adonis. On election night, both David Cameron and Ed Llewellyn sent chirpy text messages to Nick Clegg at around 9.30 p.m. – they were getting their coalition insurance in early.

The dramatic and unexpected outcome was signalled by the first BBC exit poll, released at 10 p.m.

The Conservatives polled almost 37 per cent of the vote, with Labour on 30 per cent, UKIP on 13 per cent and the Liberal Democrats on just 8 per cent – well down on our 2010 share of 23 per cent.

The Conservatives secured 331 seats, up almost 30 from 2010. Labour were down 24 to just 232 seats. The SNP climbed from 6 seats to 56 seats, on just 4.7 per cent of the UK national vote. The Liberal Democrats fell from 56 seats to just 8. This was the same total as the Democratic Unionist Party.

Over the previous four years, the Liberal Democrats had also lost ten of their eleven MEPs, eleven of their sixteen Scottish Parliament MPs, more than half of their 4,000 councillors, and now very nearly two thirds of 2010's 6.8 million voters. In over half of the UK's parliamentary constituencies the Liberal Democrat candidate lost their deposit, polling less than 5 per cent. It was a brutal political price to pay.

Nick Clegg resigned as Liberal Democrat leader the day after the general election. He received a heartfelt and generous message of good wishes from George Osborne.

He was succeeded in July by Tim Farron, who narrowly beat Norman Lamb in the leadership election.

Ed Miliband also resigned immediately. The Labour Party elected the extreme left-wing MP Jeremy Corbyn to replace him – against all early expectations.

David Cameron formed a new, majority Conservative government, and most senior ministers remained in post. Nicky Morgan stayed at Education, and Michael Gove was promoted to Justice Secretary, where he immediately set about making progressive reforms in a largely consensual manner.

On 1 June, former Liberal Democrat leader Charles Kennedy died of a brain haemorrhage, linked to his alcoholism, at the age of just fifty-five. Having lost his seat, he had privately signalled to Nick Clegg that he would like to be considered for the House of Lords, and he and Sir Menzies Campbell were Nick Clegg's top priorities for a peerage.

Nick Clegg's resignation was announced in central London on 8 May in an emotional speech drafted by Nick and his speech writer, Phil Reilly.

Struggling to compose himself, this is what Nick said:

> I always expected this election to be exceptionally difficult for the Liberal Democrats given the heavy responsibilities we've had to bear in government in the most challenging of circumstances. Clearly the results have been immeasurably more crushing and unkind than I could ever have feared. For that, of course, I must take full responsibility, and therefore I announce that I will be resigning as Leader of the Liberal Democrats. A leadership election will now take place according to the party's rules.
>
> For the last seven years it's been a privilege, an unlimited honour, to lead a party of the most resilient, courageous and remarkable people. The Liberal Democrats are a family, and I will always be extremely proud of the warmth, good grace and good humour which our political family has shown through the ups and downs of recent years. I want to thank every member, every campaigner,

every councillor, every parliamentarian, for the commitment you have shown to our country and to our party.

It is simply heart-breaking to see so many friends and colleagues who have served their constituents so diligently over so many years lose their seats because of forces entirely beyond their control.

In 2011, after a night of disappointing election results for our party in Edinburgh, Alex Cole Hamilton said this: if his defeat was part payment for the ending of child detention, then he accepted it with all of his heart. Those words revealed a selfless dignity which is very rare in politics, but common amongst Liberal Democrats. If our losses today are part payment for every family that is more secure because of a job we helped to create, every person with depression who is treated with the compassion they deserve, every child who does a little better at school, every apprentice with a long and rewarding career to look forward to, every gay couple who know their love is worth no less than anyone else's, and every pensioner with a little more freedom and dignity in retirement, then I hope at least our losses can be endured with a little selfless dignity too.

We will never know how many lives we changed for the better because we had the courage to step up at a time of crisis. But we have done something that cannot be undone, because there can be no doubt that in government we created a Britain that is far stronger, fairer, greener and more liberal than this country was five years ago.

However unforgiving the judgement has been at the ballot box, I believe the history books will judge our party kindly for the service we sought to provide to the nation at a time of great economic difficulty and for the policies and values which we brought to bear in government – opportunity, fairness and liberty – which I believe will stand the test of time.

To have served my country at a time of crisis is an honour that will stay with me for ever. I hope those who are granted the opportunity to serve our country in government now and in the future will recognise the privilege and responsibility that they've been given. It's the greatest thing they'll ever do.

It is, of course, too early to give a considered account of why we have suffered the catastrophic losses we have, and the party will have to reflect on these in the time ahead. One thing seems to me clear: liberalism, here, as well as across Europe, is not faring well against the politics of fear. Years of remorseless economic and social hardship following the crash in 2008 and the grinding insecurities of globalisation have led people to reach out to new certainties: the politics of identity, of nationalism, of us versus them, is now on the rise.

It is clear that in constituency after constituency north of the border, the beguiling appeal of Scottish nationalism has swept all before it, and south of the border a fear about what that means for the United Kingdom has strengthened English conservatism too. This now brings our country to a very perilous point in our history, where grievance and fear combine to drive our different communities apart. I hope that our leaders across the United Kingdom realise the disastrous consequences for our way of life and the integrity of our United Kingdom if they continue to appeal to grievance rather than generosity, and fear rather than hope.

It's not an exaggeration to say that in the absence of strong and statesmanlike leadership, Britain's place in Europe and the world, and the continued existence of the United Kingdom itself, is now in grave jeopardy. The cruellest irony of all is that it is exactly at this time that British liberalism, that fine, noble, tradition that believes we are stronger together and weaker apart, is needed more than ever before.

Fear and grievance have won, liberalism has lost. But it is more precious than ever and we must keep fighting for it. That is both the great challenge and the great cause that my successor will have to face. I will always give my unstinting support for all those who continue to keep the flame of British liberalism alive.

On the morning of the most crushing blow to the Liberal Democrats since our party was founded, it is easy to imagine that there is no road back, but there is – because there is no path to a fairer, greener, freer Britain without British liberalism showing the way. This is a very dark hour for our party but we cannot and will not allow decent liberal values to be extinguished overnight.

Our party will come back, our party will win again. It will take patience, resilience and grit. This is what has built our party before and will rebuild it again.

POSTSCRIPT

THE COALITION –
AN ASSESSMENT

Before concluding this volume, it is worth trying to answer three questions. How successful was the coalition, as a form of government?

What might be a fair balance sheet of the coalition's successes and failures?

What mistakes did the Liberal Democrats make in government, or by going into government, that might explain why the general election result was so disastrous?

DID THE COALITION WORK?

Let us start by evaluating the coalition, as a form of government.

Before the 2010 general election, the Conservative Party and parts of the media warned that a hung parliament, and a coalition, would deliver weak government, with economic and political paralysis. These predictions could not have been more inaccurate.

Coalition talks were completed in swift time. A coalition agreement was published and ministers were appointed. A bold economic strategy to eliminate the Budget deficit was put in place, and radical plans were set out on tax policy, welfare reform, education and social reform.

Arguably, this coalition of two political parties who had been arch enemies was both bolder and more united than many previous single-party governments. And, as Tony Blair and Gordon Brown often reminded us, division is more than possible in single-party governments.

There were a number of reasons why the coalition was so successful. Firstly, the relations between its senior members were very good. David Cameron, Nick Clegg, George Osborne, Danny Alexander, Oliver Letwin and I all got on pretty well. We differed on policy – frequently – but there was in general an absence of the type of personal animosity which could otherwise have undermined the government. It is worth saying that relations below this level in government were also, generally, very good. David Cameron and Nick Clegg deserve more credit than anyone else for establishing and maintaining this friendly atmosphere, which lasted right through to the end of the coalition.

Secondly, this was a coalition government formed from two parties that had both been in opposition prior to 2010. This meant that much of our agenda could be defined against the previous Labour government, which had been in power for a very long thirteen years. We established a strong coalition agreement, with a clear and ambitious policy agenda. And there was a distinct sense of overarching mission – to clear up the economic mess we inherited from the previous administration. The two coalition party leaders had also been elected on a clear mandate to move their parties more towards the centre ground. So under Nick Clegg, the Liberal Democrats had become more liberal and less statist. And under David Cameron, the Conservatives had sought to move away from 'right-wing' priorities to give greater weight to issues such as the green agenda, civil liberties and social justice – though much of this 'compassionate Conservative' agenda did not survive for long once in government.

Thirdly, and crucially, the coalition was established as a true government of equals. The Liberal Democrats might have had far fewer MPs and ministers, but we had significant power. The Deputy Prime Minister was a Liberal Democrat with real clout – including chairmanship of the highly influential Home Affairs Committee. The permission of this committee was necessary for many policy changes in government. The Chief Secretary to the Treasury, the Chancellor's deputy, was in charge of all public spending – and was a Liberal Democrat. When this post was allocated at the beginning of the coalition, it was almost by accident that it came to us. Nick Clegg had been thinking of sending me to be Secretary of State for Transport. Only my own suggestion that we should take the Treasury post led to a last-minute change of heart. Even then, the Chief Secretary job was regarded as one of the more junior roles in government. In reality, it became one of the most powerful posts in a coalition. Our involvement at the heart of the Treasury also helped avoid what could otherwise have been a major split in the coalition on economic policy – a split that would have been very much more likely if Vince Cable, the Business Secretary, had remained as the Liberal Democrats' principal economic spokesman. Fourthly, the coalition evolved, by accident, an 'inner Cabinet' – the Quad – consisting of PM, DPM, Chancellor and Chief Secretary. This informal group turned out to be the ultimate policy arbiters of the government – and it consisted of two Conservatives and two Liberal Democrats. The Quad avoided the Liberal Democrats feeling marginalised or ignored in government, and hence it avoided alienation. The significance of the regular PM/DPM bilaterals has also been understated by political commentators and historians to date: they were another 'fully coalitionised' mechanism for making key decisions in government, and by definition the Liberal Democrats had equal representation. Finally, both parties felt relatively 'comfortable' in coalition, and their self-interest kept them together. For the Liberal Democrats, it was our first taste of real power in living memory. MPs and most party members liked the fact that we had real influence for once, and the party had fully and almost unanimously endorsed the coalition agreement in May 2010. Nobody could argue that they had been bounced or bullied by the party leadership. For the Conservatives – most Conservatives – politics was about being in power. Well, they were in power, and they had a healthy majority thanks to the coalition. Some of the more moderate Conservatives also preferred a coalition with a centre-ground liberal party rather than having to rely for support on the hard-right of their own party. In addition, a break-up of the coalition suited neither party until at least the very end of the term of office. This was because the tough economic environment meant that neither party could be confident of doing well in the event of an early election. So both self-interest and a sense of mission kept the parties in power and the coalition show on the road.

For all these reasons, the coalition must be given very high marks indeed for its resilience and for its success as a form of government. It is, of course, possible to think of various tweaks that could have advanced the operation of a second coalition. But these would be pretty small improvements. The coalition defied the predictions of many, and turned out to be a roaring success as a way of doing government. And many of its policies benefited from the joint input and political perspective of two parties.

DID THE COALITION DELIVER?

How, then, should we evaluate the policy achievements of the coalition government?

Both coalition political parties regarded the economic and social recovery of Britain as their main objective, along with keeping the UK together. Nick Clegg regarded economic and political reform as the 'twin pillars' of the coalition agreement, but it is unlikely that the Conservatives felt the same way about the latter priority.

At the beginning of the parliament, it was hoped that the process of wiping out the Budget deficit could largely be completed by the parliament's end. This proved too optimistic. This was not, fundamentally, because the Treasury underestimated the impact of fiscal contraction. It was because growth was hit when consumer incomes were undermined by a huge rise in global food and energy prices, while business investment and economic confidence were damaged by the severe crisis in the Eurozone.

The coalition was fortunate that that these two problems unwound half-way through the parliament, at a time when the UK fiscal and monetary authorities were showing a lack of imagination over how to respond to the prolonged economic slump. It was also important that in late 2012 and early 2013 Nick Clegg vetoed Conservative plans to cut public spending more sharply in the face of higher borrowing forecasts and the loss of the triple-A credit rating. In fact, coalition fiscal policy was more pragmatic and flexible than the political rhetoric suggested, and – thanks to Nick Clegg and Danny Alexander – the coalition resisted the temptation to tighten fiscal policy in the face of early disappointments on growth.

By mid-2013, the economy was growing again, and by the end of the parliament, borrowing had been reduced by around 50 per cent as a share of the economy – good progress under the circumstances.

The coalition's record on employment growth was also impressive – employment rates moved to record levels, buoyed by a flexible labour market, stronger work incentives (including the higher personal tax allowance) and the recovering economy. Claims for jobseeker's allowance fell dramatically.

The coalition government delivered generally better oversight of financial services, a new industrial policy that commanded broad business support, and a huge reduction in rates of corporation tax. Thanks to the Liberal Democrats, the long-overdue privatisation of Royal Mail took place.

Relative poverty changed little. This was partly a result of Liberal Democrat influence in relation to tax and benefit reforms, but it was also because slow economic growth suppressed wage growth. Neither of these factors is likely to be present in the 2015 parliament.

Pensions reform, led by Steve Webb, was a major success. The new single-tier pension, the triple lock and auto-enrolment will all help to reduce future pensioner poverty, while strengthening incentives to save.

Education policy was also a success. The Liberal Democrats ensured the delivery of a new pupil premium, to help to close the attainment gap between poor children and their peers. Michael Gove led the reform of qualifications, to ensure that more pupils were taking subjects that would be of value in the labour market and in life, and to end incentives for some pupils to take qualifications only to achieve easy 'league table' points. Both coalition parties reformed school accountability in a helpful way, and focused more attention on replacing the leadership and governance of weak schools.

The new tuition fee system, while damaging the Liberal Democrats politically, turned out to be good policy. Universities were therefore better funded, and less reliant on government controls over student numbers. Disadvantaged students attended universities in higher, not lower, numbers.

Energy policy ensured massive investment in renewable energy sources, and in health policy – thanks again to Nick Clegg – there was a new momentum behind improving mental health services, although it will now take some years of sustained investment and reform for big improvements to be seen.

The coalition generally survived without any serious splits on European policy, which must be regarded as a success of sorts.

Though most of the political reform agenda – the Alternative Vote, boundary changes, Lords reform and party funding reform – failed to progress, the UK stayed together. The referendum on Scottish independence was won by those who supported the Union, and some significant steps towards real devolution of power from Westminster were taken. Nevertheless, there is no doubt that Liberal Democrat hopes that political reform would prove the 'second pillar' of the coalition were dashed.

Finally, the coalition delivered some important liberalising and progressive reforms, in spite of opposition from large numbers of Conservative MPs. The passing of the legislation recognising same-sex marriage was a major step forward in equality. The coalition also delivered for the first time the pledge made by the UK in the 1970s to meet the UN target of spending 0.7 per cent of gross national income on overseas aid. This was a notable achievement at a time of austerity in government finances.

It is worth considering what the coalition's policy failures were. As mentioned above, there was very little progress on the constitutional reform agenda, largely because of Conservative obstructionism. However, Britain has now moved to fixed-term parliaments, increasing political and policy certainty and reducing the unfair advantage to the party in power.

Conservative promises to reduce immigration were not met – unsurprisingly, as no significant action could be taken to limit net migration from the rest of the European Union, something Nick Clegg had warned about in the 2010 election debates. This was why the Liberal Democrat leader had wisely refused to write a net annual immigration ceiling into government policy.

While pensions reform was a great success, Universal Credit was delayed and some of its more desirable policy features were undermined. While claims for jobseeker's allowance fell sharply, the number of people out of work due to sickness – those claiming employment and support allowance – remained very high. Supporting people of working age with disabilities and illnesses back into work should be a high priority for the current parliament.

The Lansley reforms to the National Health Service must be counted a failure. The Prime Minister and his Chancellor deserve blame for failing to properly understand and scrutinise them and for allowing them to proceed. The changes caused unnecessary instability and uncertainty at a time when the NHS should have been firmly focused on more efficient delivery, and they led to the departure of a tier of generally better-quality managers. The reforms also broke off many of the levers that had allowed one of the largest organisations in the world to be managed. And they used up the limited public appetite for NHS reform on changes of little value.

WHAT MISTAKES DID THE
LIBERAL DEMOCRATS MAKE?

The purpose of a political party is to deliver its values and policies in government and – by sustaining its political strength – to go on doing that into the future. The Liberal Democrats delivered much in government, as this book describes, but the scale of the defeat in May 2015 will significantly impair the party's influence for many years. What went wrong?

It is tempting to go back and second guess every major policy and political decision of the parliament. Should we have torpedoed the NHS Bill? What impact did the so-called bedroom tax have? Was putting up VAT a mistake? Should we have stuck closer to the Conservatives, or should we have worked harder to differentiate ourselves? Perhaps Nick Clegg should have sat somewhere else at Prime Minister's Questions?

I think it unlikely that any of these important but second-order issues really made much difference to the scale of our election defeat. Within months of going into coalition, Liberal Democrat support collapsed in half, as Lord Rennard predicted it would back in 1998 when he wrote his prescient memorandum to Paddy Ashdown on the electoral consequences of coalitions for small parties. From 23 per cent in the general election, the Liberal Democrats were down to just 11 per cent three months later – and three weeks *before* the Browne Review had published its proposals on tuition fees.

After the tuition fees mess, the party had fallen to around 8 per cent in the polls, where we stagnated for most of the parliament.

Some of us thought that there would be a recovery late in the parliament, but arguably we then lost some further votes to both the Green Party and UKIP in the last year of coalition.

We also hoped, not least after the Eastleigh by-election, that we would as a party out-perform in our strongest areas of support, helping us to hold more seats than our national vote share might imply. But the swing against us was as high in our held seats as in our non-held seats.

Nor were we correct to think that we might out-perform the national swing in seats where we were fighting our Conservative coalition partners, even if we did badly against Labour and the SNP. In fact, our worst region was the south-west of England, where the swing against us averaged 20 per cent. In Scotland, our vote share fell by just 11 per cent.

It seems likely that there were only, therefore, a few issues that were significant enough to have made any difference to our electoral success. A large decline in our vote share was the almost inevitable result of going into power with a right-wing party at a time when many unpopular decisions were required to reduce the Budget deficit.

There seem to me to be six substantive issues to consider, which really might have had a bigger impact on our prospects than the odd policy victory here and there. These are as follows: Should we have gone into coalition at all in 2010? Should we have taken a different role in coalition? Could we have won the Alternative Vote referendum? Should we have stopped the rise in tuition fees? Should Nick Clegg have stepped down as leader before the end of the parliament? Should we have left the coalition prior to May 2015?

I shall leave the most fundamental question to consider last – was the decision to go into coalition in May 2010 the right one?

I have already described how the Liberal Democrats got into such a great mess on tuition fees. We should have dropped this policy commitment well before the 2010 general election, when it was clear that in an environment of austerity, any progressive political party should be targeting available resources on schools and early years education rather than on free university tuition. But having failed to drop this policy before the election, we should simply have vetoed the rise in fees recommended by the Browne Report. The savings would have had to be found from elsewhere. But at least we would not have had this huge political albatross around our necks.

It is difficult to know how much effect on our support there would have been had we vetoed the tuition fees rise. Many voters who cited this in complaint against us may simply have been unhappy that we were in government with the Conservatives, taking tough financial decisions. In government, our support had fallen significantly, before the rise in tuition fees was agreed. Many of the voters we had attracted when Tony Blair and Gordon Brown were in power were from the left politically and had joined us over issues such as the Iraq War. With or without fees, many of these voters did not want the Conservatives anywhere near power. But if we had vetoed the fees rise we would have removed from our critics the greatest policy stick with which they could beat us. So, it may have been worth a percentage point or two in the polls.

The next question is whether we should have taken a different role in coalition. We did secure two important roles: the Deputy Prime Minister post and the Chief Secretary to the Treasury. These are both powerful jobs, but they have one thing in common: they are both 'deputy' jobs – the PM and the Chancellor get the greatest public visibility. Nick Clegg was powerful, and extremely busy, but it is unclear whether the public knew just how much power he and Danny Alexander held – too much of our influence was wielded behind the scenes.

Our other Cabinet posts were not of the front rank. Vince Cable, as Business Secretary, was in an important economic portfolio, but one that always going to play second fiddle to the Chancellor. Vince Cable might have developed the party's links more closely with business, but this did not seem to happen – and many business people felt that Vince was too critical of them.

Climate Change was an important department for a party that believed in the importance of green issues. But it was a small department and lacked much public profile. The Treasury also exercised significant influence over policy.

Our last major Cabinet post was Scottish Secretary. Again, this was a post of limited influence, in an era of Scottish devolution.

From 2012, I returned to government as Minister of State in both the Cabinet Office and the Department for Education. I attended Cabinet, and again wielded considerable influence with little public profile.

In summary, in 2010 we opted to maximise our influence within government, rather than maximising our visibility to the public.

Arguably, we should have negotiated hard for more Cabinet posts, and for more senior posts, in 2010. Although we had only fifty-seven MPs to the Conservatives' 300+, we had polled 23 per cent of the UK vote, versus 36 per cent for the Conservatives. It is unlikely that we would have secured the position of Chancellor, but we perhaps should have insisted on leading at least one big public services department – probably Education. This was a department Nick Clegg intended to secure for the Liberal Democrats had there been a coalition in 2015. Nick might also have demanded a higher-profile job for himself in 2010 than leading for the government on political reform. This was an important area for us, but perhaps could have been managed by another Liberal Democrat minister, leaving the Deputy Prime Minister able to take another role, such as Home Secretary – though this would be to risk serious work overload.

In conclusion, it seems to me that we should have insisted on one or two more high-profile Cabinet roles, including the leadership of a major public services department. But it is difficult to believe that this would have led to a significant improvement in our electoral performance.

The referendum on the Alternative Vote system was a crucial moment in the coalition. We insisted on an AV referendum precisely because we expected our vote share to decline significantly in coalition, and we needed to make the electoral system fairer and to correspond more closely with our overall vote share. We spent a great deal of time thinking about how to secure a referendum. Arguably, we spent too little time considering how a referendum could be won.

Some people have suggested that the AV vote came too soon in the parliament, and should have been delayed until later on. I see absolutely no evidence that this would have led to any more favourable an outcome. The problem was that the other parties would not contemplate a referendum on a simple, proportionate, alternative to first past the post. We therefore had to compromise. But by compromising on AV, we were supporting a system that was complicated and not remotely proportionate. Voters struggled to understand the proposed system and were put off by the idea that the second-placed candidate could end up as the winner.

Many voters also could not understand what problem AV was meant to fix. Had the country not got more or less what it already wanted, with the existing voting system – Gordon Brown out of power, but the Conservatives forced to cooperate with the Liberal Democrats?

Crucially, neither of the other major political parties supported AV. The Conservatives were strongly opposed, while Labour were divided, and had therefore backed away from their 2010 manifesto pledge to introduce the new AV system.

In short, a third party on barely 10 per cent of the vote was left making the argument for change against well-organised opposition, with one major party strongly opposed and the other apparently indifferent. Winning a vote on changing the national electoral system may well require the active support of at least one of the two biggest political parties. Or it probably requires strong leadership from an insurgent campaign by 'outsiders'. On this occasion, the AV campaign had none of these potential assets. That is not to say that we should have dropped the referendum on electoral reform – indeed, at one point in the parliament the Yes vote was ahead in the polls. But, in future, a stronger coalition of support for change needs assembling.

I turn next to the question of whether or not Nick Clegg should have stood down as leader before the 2015 election. It will be clear from my account that this is something that Nick himself gave detailed consideration to from spring 2012 onwards. I am perhaps not well placed to answer this question. Nick Clegg was and is a friend of mine. I greatly admired and liked him, and thought that he was a huge asset to our party and to the country. When he asked for advice on his own future, I replied both as a friend and as a political adviser.

After Chris Huhne was forced to resign, there was only one Liberal Democrat who had the party support and public profile to become leader and to offer an alternative to Nick Clegg. That person was Vince Cable. Vince had been popular with the public, and he both looked and was more obviously different from David Cameron than Nick Clegg was. Given the damage to Nick's 'brand' over trust and tuition fees, it is difficult to believe that Vince taking over as leader could have made matters more difficult for the party.

But it is not obvious that Vince taking over from Nick Clegg would have made much positive difference either – which is corroborated by most of the polls that asked this question. And this was before a new leader was subjected to all of the media and other attacks that had been experienced by Nick Clegg and which came with the territory of being a Liberal Democrat Deputy Prime Minister. After all, on tuition fees, had Vince Cable not been the very Cabinet minister who had designed the policy, voted for it and defended it on the floor of the House of Commons?

And on the big issue that dominated much of the coalition, while Vince was right to warn about some of the pressures facing the economy in 2011–13, he was ultimately wrong-footed when the economy bounced back in 2013.

More seriously, Vince was relatively close to Ed Miliband, and would clearly have preferred a coalition with Labour in 2015 to one with the Conservatives. He talked to Ed Miliband regularly, and even tried to persuade him in 2014 not to pledge to cut tuition fees – without any success. So eager was Vince to consider a Labour coalition that on a visit to Scotland in early 2015, he publicly raised the possibility of some sort of Liberal Democrat–Labour alliance, with implicit or explicit SNP support. That idea was toxic in many of our Conservative-facing seats in England, as well as in all our seats in Scotland. The idea of a Liberal Democrat–Labour–SNP tie-up would have made the Conservatives' job even easier in our key seats in May 2015.

So in my view, changing the leader would have made little or no difference.

What of leaving the coalition early, as Lord Oakeshott occasionally advised? I will not discuss this option at length. I never felt it had much attraction. The public would see the Liberal Democrats as giving up on our responsibilities to govern, and it would have looked unreliable and opportunistic. Bailing out early might even have counted against us if people felt that a hung parliament could not deliver stable government.

So, in conclusion, perhaps the Liberal Democrat support might have been marginally higher if we had vetoed the rise in tuition fees, and taken a more powerful and visible role in government. And certainly we should have thought more deeply about how to secure cross-party support for a change in the voting system.

But it is difficult to conclude that any of this would have been game changing in relation to our 2015 result. The truth is that we took one really big decision and one really big decision only. That was to go into coalition in May 2010, rather than attempting a confidence and supply agreement with the Conservatives, or trying to knit together a multi-coloured coalition with the Labour Party and others. What of that – truly crucial – decision? Was it the right one?

We are now well into the world of counterfactuals, and we can only therefore speculate.

I think we can quickly dismiss the idea of a multi-party 'traffic light' coalition. This was never really a viable alternative, as I explained in my book about the formation of the coalition.[3] Such an arrangement could not have lasted, and seems likely to have led to a second general election and a Conservative outright majority.

Had we established a confidence and supply arrangement with the Conservative Party, this also seems likely to have collapsed within a short period of time – and at a time of maximum advantage to the Conservative Party. Another election would have followed, in which it seems likely that after Labour's thirteen years in power the electorate would have given the Conservatives a chance to govern by themselves. As Chris Huhne predicted at the time, the Liberal Democrats would almost certainly have lost seats – perhaps many of them.

In this scenario, there is no reason to believe that Ed Miliband would not

---

3   22 *Days in May*, David Laws (Biteback Publishing, 2010)

have become Labour leader and nor is there reason to think that the SNP surge would not have happened. So even if we had stayed on the opposition benches, it seems highly likely that the Liberal Democrats would have lost many votes and MPs by 2015.

But we know that smaller parties in coalition often take a disproportionate hit, and it is difficult to believe that if we had stayed on the opposition benches we would have fallen quite so far as eight MPs and 8 per cent of the vote. So there was a price to pay for coalition. Was it worth it?

We could of course have remained on the superficially safe opposition benches, clinging to our political purity and putting out our press releases, angrily denouncing every new tax rise and every spending cut. We had previously showed that we were rather good at this. But political parties need power to put principles into action. Popularity without power is a pretty sterile and uninspiring long-term vision for any political party.

When Nick Clegg faced a botched coup attempt in June 2014, he received overwhelming support from his MPs to stay on. As I recounted earlier in this book, one of the last MPs to speak that night was the youthful MP for East Dunbartonshire, Jo Swinson. She was a junior minister in the Business Department, with a young child. Both she and her MP husband, Duncan Hames, now faced the serious prospect of losing their seats and careers within the year. Jo spoke for many colleagues and Liberal Democrats when she said, calmly but passionately: 'When we went into coalition, we all knew we were taking risks and it would not be easy. But if I had the same chance now, I would do it again. We are making a difference in government. I know that I am in my department ... I will fight my seat hard. But if the price of being in government and delivering the things I believe in is that I lose my seat, well, that is a price I am willing to pay.'

I am repeating here sentences that I cited in an earlier paragraph, but they are worth repeating – they sum up what many of us felt, and still feel, about our time in government.

Of course, we could have stayed out of power in 2010. And, of course, that would probably have been safer for the Liberal Democrats. But political power is worth accumulating only if it can be used constructively. It should not be hoarded as if it is an end in itself. Political parties must be more than press-release factories – they must deliver change.

We Liberal Democrats should never present the decision we took in May

2010 as some sort of great act of self-sacrifice. It was a huge privilege to contribute to the better government of the United Kingdom. Every day in government was an opportunity to make our economy stronger and our society a fairer and more tolerant place. And we knew that we were taking a risk with our party's strength to deliver the policies we believed in.

Between 2010 and 2015, for the first time in decades, the Liberal Democrats did deliver real change. No one can doubt that. And no one can doubt that we achieved far, far more than we would have done had we stayed in opposition. What we cannot yet know is what price we will pay in future influence because of the setbacks we suffered as a consequence, and therefore what the net balance of overall advantage to the Liberal cause will be.

So, to the question of whether the Liberal Democrats were right to go into coalition in 2010, the careful political scientist or serious commentator will at this moment give no clear answer. We will not truly know for some time.

For myself, reflecting back on my time in politics and on the Liberal Democrat achievements in government of which I remain proud, I join with other colleagues in concluding that for me, losing my seat on 7 May was a price I was and am willing to pay.

APPENDIX ONE

KEY LIB DEM ACHIEVEMENTS IN GOVERNMENT, 2010–15

May 2010: The coalition agreement scraps Labour's identity card plans.

May 2010: David Laws announces the first spending cuts to reduce the deficit, while protecting education, the NHS and overseas aid.

June 2010: The coalition confirms the Lib Dem plan to introduce a triple lock to boost future increases in the state pension.

June 2010: Nick Clegg announces plans for a £1 billion Regional Growth Fund, which is later significantly increased in size.

June 2010: The coalition confirms the first step in increasing the personal income tax allowance, by £1,000, to achieve the Liberal Democrat manifesto commitment by 2015.

October 2010: Danny Alexander completes the first major coalition Spending Review.

October 2010: Nick Clegg announces a £2.5 billion pupil premium, in line with the key Liberal Democrat manifesto commitment, while also protecting school spending in real terms.

October 2010: Nick Clegg announces new fifteen-hour early years education entitlement for disadvantaged two-year-olds.

January 2011: The government introduces a £2.5 billion banking levy, in line with the Liberal Democrat manifesto.

January 2011: Nick Clegg announces plans for shared parental leave.

April 2011: The personal income tax allowance rises from £6,475 to £7,475.

April 2011: Liberal Democrat Pensions Minister Steve Webb delivers the new triple lock to uprate the state pension.

September 2011: Royal assent is given to the Fixed Term Parliaments Bill.

September 2011: The pupil premium of £430 per child is introduced.

December 2011: Nick Clegg ensures that pensions and benefits are uprated by the full 5.2 per cent inflation rate, to avoid increases in poverty.

April 2012: The green investment bank is established by Nick Clegg and Vince Cable.

April 2012: 5.2 per cent uprating of benefits and pensions to protect those on low incomes from surging food and energy prices.

May 2012: The Liberal Democrat-inspired Protection of Freedoms Act becomes law.

May 2012: Vince Cable vetoes Conservative plans for 'fire at will' employment laws.

October 2012: Nick Clegg vetoes Conservative plans for £10 billion of welfare cuts.

January 2013: Steve Webb sets out plans for a new universal single-tier pension.

January 2013: Nick Clegg announces a new cap on long-term care costs, as proposed in the Dilnot Report.

March 2013: Nick Clegg vetoes Conservative plans to axe an extra £13 billion from public spending.

April 2013: Nick Clegg vetoes the 'Snoopers's Charter' Bill.

June 2013: Danny Alexander completes the 2014/15 Spending Review.

July 2013: David Laws and Nick Clegg announce that the primary pupil premium will rise to £1,300 in 2014 and the secondary pupil premium to £900 – meeting the Liberal Democrat manifesto pledge to introduce a £2.5 billion annual premium for disadvantaged children.

July 2013: Nick Clegg and David Laws announce higher maths and English standards for primary schools.

July 2013: Legislation for equal marriage, pioneered by Lynne Featherstone, passes into law.

September 2013: Nick Clegg's new entitlement to fifteen hours' free childcare for the 20 per cent most disadvantaged children begins.

September 2013: Nick Clegg announces free school meals for all infant-school pupils in England, and for 16–18-year-olds from low-income backgrounds who are studying in colleges.

September 2013: Nick Clegg announces a new levy on single-use plastic bags, from autumn 2015.

October 2013: Royal Mail is privatised by Vince Cable, while retaining a universal postal service and protecting the post office network.

October 2013: David Laws announces a new accountability regime for secondary schools in England, scrapping the five A*–C target, and moving to an 'Attainment 8' GCSE target, with more focus on pupil progress.

March 2014: The first same-sex marriages take place in England.

March 2014: David Laws announces fairer funding for English schools, with a new minimum funding level.

April 2014: The personal tax allowance rises to £10,000, taking 3 million people out of income tax and delivering the Liberal Democrat general election pledge.

April 2014: Nick Clegg and David Laws announce a new early years pupil premium, going beyond the Lib Dem manifesto pledge on a schools premium.

September 2014: The free two-year-old entitlement to early years education, introduced by Nick Clegg, is extended to the 40 per cent most disadvantaged children.

September 2014: Spending on the pupil premium reaches the manifesto pledge of £2.5 billion per year, with a primary school premium of £1,320 per child and a secondary school premium of £935 per child.

September 2014: Free school meals are introduced successfully in England for all infant-school children and for 16–18-year-olds from low-income families studying in colleges.

September 2014: Scotland remains in the United Kingdom after the referendum vote, with Lib Dems Danny Alexander, Mike Moore and Alistair Carmichael playing key roles in the 'In' campaign.

October 2014: Nick Clegg announces new mental health access standards.

March 2015: Mike Moore's Private Member's Bill legislates to deliver 0.7 per cent of national income for development assistance – the first such legislation in a G7 country.

March 2015: The Budget confirms that the government's deficit has been cut in half as a percentage of gross domestic product.

April 2015: New rights to shared parental leave are introduced by Jo Swinson and Nick Clegg.

April 2015: The personal tax allowance rises to £10,600 – going beyond the Lib Dem manifesto pledge.

April 2015: Comprehensive entry and exit checks are restored at UK borders, after Lib Dem pressure.

APPENDIX TWO

LIB DEM MINISTERS IN GOVERNMENT, 2010–15

Deputy Prime Minister and Lord President of the Council: Nick Clegg MP.

Chief Secretary to the Treasury: David Laws MP (to 29 May 2010); Danny Alexander MP.

Secretary of State for Business, Innovation and Skills: Vince Cable MP.

Secretary of State for Energy and Climate Change: Chris Huhne MP (to February 2012); Ed Davey MP.

Secretary of State for Scotland: Danny Alexander MP (to 29 May 2010); Michael Moore MP (to October 2013); Alistair Carmichael MP.

Minister of State, Cabinet Office: David Laws MP (from September 2012).

Minister of State, Foreign and Commonwealth Office: Jeremy Browne MP (to September 2012).

Minister of State, Ministry of Defence: Nick Harvey MP (to September 2012).

Minister of State, Health and Social Care: Paul Burstow MP (to September 2012); Norman Lamb MP.

Minister of State, Department for Education: Sarah Teather MP (to September 2012); David Laws MP.

Minister of State, Home Office: Jeremy Browne MP (from September 2012 to October 2013); Norman Baker MP (to November 2014); Lynne Featherstone MP.

Minister of State, Ministry of Justice: Lord McNally (to December 2013); Simon Hughes MP.

Minister of State, Department for Work and Pensions: Steve Webb MP.

Minister of State, Department for Environment, Food and Rural Affairs: David Heath MP (from September 2012 to October 2013).

Minister of State, Transport: Baroness Kramer (from October 2013).

Advocate General for Scotland: Lord Wallace of Tankerness.

Parliamentary Under Secretary of State, Department for Business, Innovation and Skills: Ed Davey MP (to February 2012); Norman Lamb MP (to September 2012); Jo Swinson MP.

Parliamentary Under Secretary of State, Department for Transport: Norman Baker MP (to October 2013).

Parliamentary Under Secretary of State, Home Office: Lynne Featherstone MP (to September 2012).

Parliamentary Under Secretary of State for Wales: Baroness Randerson (from September 2012).

Parliamentary Under Secretary of State, Department for Communities and Local Government: Andrew Stunell MP (to September 2012), Don Foster MP (to October 2013); Stephen Williams MP.

Parliamentary Under Secretary of State, Department for International Development: Lynne Featherstone MP (from September 2012 to November 2014); Baroness Northover (from November 2014).

Parliamentary Under Secretary of State for Environment, Food and Rural Affairs: Dan Rogerson MP (from October 2013).

Deputy Chief Whip: Alistair Carmichael MP (to October 2013); Don Foster MP.

Deputy Leader of the House of Commons: David Heath MP (to September 2012); Tom Brake MP.

Assistant Government Whip and Chief Adviser to the DPM: Norman Lamb MP (to February 2012).

Assistant Government Whip: Mark Hunter MP (to October 2014).

Assistant Government Whip: Jenny Willott MP (from February 2012 to November 2014).

Assistant Government Whip: Lorely Burt MP (from November 2014).

Deputy Chief Whip (Lords): Lord Shutt (to May 2012); Lord Newby.

APPENDIX THREE

LIB DEM SPECIAL ADVISERS
IN GOVERNMENT, 2010–15

Jonny Oates, Chief of Staff to the Deputy Prime Minister, 2010–15. (DPM
    Director of Communications and Deputy Director of Government
    Communications, May 2010–August 2010).
Alison Suttie, Deputy Chief of Staff, 2010–11.
Jo Foster, Deputy Chief of Staff, 2011–13.
Tim Colbourne, Deputy Chief of Staff, 2013–15, DPM Senior Policy Adviser,
    2010–13.
Richard Reeves, Director of Strategy, 2010–12.
Ryan Coetzee, Director of Strategy, 2013–14.
Polly Mackenzie, Director of Policy, 2010–11, 2013–15.
Julian Astle, Acting Director of Policy, 2011–12, Policy Adviser 2012–15.
John Foster, Policy Adviser, DH and DWP, 2011–13, Acting Director of
    Policy, 2012–14, Policy Adviser to the Chief Secretary to the Treasury,
    2013–15.
Chris Saunders, Chief Economic and Business Adviser to the DPM, 2010–12,
    2013–15.
Matthew Hanney, Head of Political Office, 2010–12, Constitutional Reform
    and Political Relations Adviser, 2012–15.
Hollie Voyce, Head of Office (Political), 2013–15.
Veena Hudson, Senior Policy Adviser, 2011–14.
Conan D'Arcy, EU and Trade Adviser, 2014–15.
Lena Pietsch, DPM Press Secretary, May–August 2010, DPM Director of
    Communications and Deputy Director of Government Communications,
    2010–13, Director of External Relations, 2013–15.
James McGrory, DPM Press Secretary, August 2010–14, Deputy Director

of Communications and DPM Spokesperson, 2014–15.

Myrddin Edwards, Media Adviser, 2014–15.

Olly Grender, Acting DPM Director of Communications and Deputy Director of Government Communications, 2012.

Emma Gilpin-Jacobs, DPM Director of Communications and Deputy Director of Government Communications, 2013.

Stephen Lotinga, DPM Director of Communications and Deputy Director of Government Communications, 2014–15.

Sean Kemp, DPM Head of Media, 2010–13.

James Holt, DPM Head of Media, 2013–14.

Phil Reilly, DPM Head of Media, January 2014–December 2014, DPM Speechwriter and Media Adviser, 2014–15.

Ruwan Kodikara, DPM Head of Media, 2014–15.

Zena Elmahrouki, DPM Speechwriter and Media Adviser, 2012–14.

Christine Jardine, Scotland Media Adviser, 2012.

Shabnum Mustapha, Scotland Media Adviser, 2012–15.

Matt Sanders, DPM Adviser on DfE, DCMS and Cabinet Office, 2011–15.

Monica Allen, DPM Adviser on FCO, DfID and MoD, 2011–15.

Adam Pritchard, DPM Adviser on DfT, DCLG and DEFRA, 2013–15.

Verity Harding, DPM Adviser on Home Affairs and MoJ, 2011–13.

Alex Dziedzan, DPM Adviser on Home Affairs and MoJ, 2013–15.

Emily Frith, DPM Adviser, DH and DWP, 2013–15.

Ben Williams, Lib Dem Chief Whip's Adviser, 2010–15.

Elizabeth Plummer, Adviser to the Deputy Leader of the Lords, 2010–15.

Will de Peyer, Adviser to the Chief Secretary to the Treasury, 2010–15.

Julia Goldsworthy, Adviser to the Chief Secretary to the Treasury, 2010–13.

Peter Carroll, Adviser to the Chief Secretary to the Treasury, 2013–15.

Emma Coakley, Media Adviser to the Chief Secretary to the Treasury, 2015.

Katie Waring, Adviser to the Business Secretary, 2010–12 and to the Climate Change Secretary 2012–13.

Giles Wilkes, Adviser to the Business Secretary, 2010–13.

Emily Walch, Adviser to the Business Secretary, 2012–15.

Ashley Lumsden, Adviser to the Business Secretary, 2013–15.

Vanessa Pine, Media Adviser, 2015.

Duncan Brack, Adviser to the Climate Change Secretary, 2010–12.

Joel Kenrick, Adviser to the Climate Change Secretary, 2010–12.

Chris Nicholson, Adviser to the Climate Change Secretary, 2012–15.
Paul Hodgson, Adviser to the Climate Change Secretary, 2013–15.
Willie Rennie, Adviser to the Secretary of State for Scotland, 2010.
Euan Roddin, Adviser to the Secretary of State for Scotland, 2010–15.

INDEX